The Victor Book of the Opera

THIRTEENTH EDITION

Revised by Henry W. Simon

PICTURE EDITOR: GERALD FITZGERALD

THE HISTORICAL BACKGROUND AND ACT-BY-ACT SUMMA-
RIES OF 120 OPERATIC MASTERWORKS—AND COMPLETE
LISTINGS OF THE BEST AVAILABLE RECORDINGS, AN OUT-
LINE HISTORY OF OPERA, AND OVER 400 ILLUSTRATIONS OF
THE GREAT COMPOSERS, THE GREAT SINGERS AND THE
GREAT SCENES OF GRAND OPERA IN ALL ITS HISTORIC
SPLENDOR.

SIMON AND SCHUSTER · NEW YORK

PUBLISHED BY SIMON AND SCHUSTER
ROCKEFELLER CENTER, 630 FIFTH AVENUE
NEW YORK, NEW YORK 10020

THIRTEENTH EDITION

FOURTH PRINTING

Synopsis of Alberto Ginastera's Bomarzo *courtesy of Boosey & Hawkes, Inc.*

SBN 671-20054-2

LIBRARY OF CONGRESS CATALOG CARD NUMBER: 68–11017
DESIGNED BY EVE METZ
MANUFACTURED IN THE UNITED STATES OF AMERICA
PRINTED BY THE MURRAY PRINTING CO., FORGE VILLAGE, MASS.
BOUND BY AMERICAN BOOK–STRATFORD PRESS, INC., NEW YORK

Contents

LISTING OF THE OPERAS BY COMPOSER 8
PUBLISHER'S PREFACE 11
AN OUTLINE HISTORY OF OPERA 14

THE OPERAS

The Abduction from the Seraglio (Die Entführung aus dem Serail) 27
Adriana Lecouvreur 30
Alceste 40
Aïda 34
Amahl and the Night Visitors 42
Andrea Chénier 44
Arabella 47
Ariadne auf Naxos 51
The Ballad of Baby Doe 54
The Ballad Singer (La Gioconda) . . . 176
Un Ballo in Maschera (A Masked Ball) . . 263
The Barber of Seville (Il Barbiere di Siviglia) 58
The Bartered Bride (Prodaná Nevešta) . 62
The Bat (Die Fledermaus) 153
Bluebeard's Castle (A Kekszakállú Herceg Vára) 64
La Bohème 66
Bomarzo 71
Boris Godunov 73
Capriccio 79

Carmen 81
The Cavalier of the Rose (Der Rosenkavalier) 373
Cavalleria Rusticana (Rustic Chivalry) . 89
La Cenerentola (Cinderella) 93
The Child and the Sorcerers (L'Enfant et les Sortilèges) 132
Cinderella (La Cenerentola) 93
The Cloak (Il Tabarro) 398
Clowns (Pagliacci) 301
The Consul 96
Les Contes d'Hoffmann (The Tales of Hoffmann) 400
Le Coq d'Or (Zolotoy Pyetushok—The Golden Cockerel) 99
The Coronation of Poppea (L'Incoronazione di Poppea) 196
Così Fan Tutte (So Do They All) . . . 101
The Daughter of the Regiment (La Fille du Régiment) 106
Les Dialogues des Carmélites 109
Dido and Aeneas 114

Contents

Don Carlos 116	Knyaz Igor (Prince Igor) 329
Don Giovanni (Don Juan) 120	Lakmé 206
Don Pasquale 125	Lohengrin 209
Elektra 128	Louise 214
L'Elisir d'Amore (The Elixir of Love) . 130	The Love of Three Oranges (Lyubov K
L'Enfant et les Sortilèges (The Child and	Trem Apelsinam) 217
the Sorcerers) 132	Lucia di Lammermoor 220
Die Entführung aus dem Serail (The Ab-	Lucrezia Borgia 223
duction from the Seraglio) 27	Luisa Miller 226
Ernani 134	Lulu 230
Eugene Onegin (Yevgeny Onyegin) . . 137	Lyubov K Trem Apelsinam (The Love of
Falstaff 139	Three Oranges) 217
La Fanciulla del West (The Girl of the	Macbeth 234
Golden West) 181	Madama Butterfly 237
Faust 143	The Magic Flute (Die Zauberflöte) . . 241
La Favola d'Orfeo (Orfeo) 291	Manon 247
Fidelio 150	Manon Lescaut 251
La Fille du Régiment (The Daughter of	The Marriage of Figaro (Le Nozze di
the Regiment) 106	Figaro) 254
Die Fledermaus (The Bat) 153	Martha 259
Der Fliegende Holländer (The Flying	A Masked Ball (Un Ballo in Maschera) . 263
Dutchman) 156	The Mastersingers (Die Meistersinger) . . 275
La Forza del Destino (The Force of	Medea 266
Destiny) 159	The Medium 269
Four Saints in Three Acts 163	Mefistofele 272
Die Frau ohne Schatten (The Woman with-	Die Meistersinger (The Mastersingers) . . 275
out a Shadow) 165	Mignon 281
Der Freischütz (The Free-Shooter) . . 170	Nabucco (Nabucodonosor—Nebuchad-
Gianni Schicchi 174	nazzar) 284
La Gioconda (The Ballad Singer) . . . 176	Norma 288
The Girl of the Golden West (La Fanciulla	Le Nozze di Figaro (The Marriage of
del West) 181	Figaro) 254
Giulio Cesare (Julius Caesar) 202	Orfeo (La Favola d'Orfeo) 291
The Golden Cockerel (Zolotoy Pyetushok—	Orfeo ed Euridice (Orpheus and Euryd-
Le Coq d'Or) 99	ice) 294
Guillaume Tell (William Tell) 450	Otello 297
Hänsel und Gretel 183	Pagliacci (Clowns) 301
L'Heure Espagnole (The Spanish Hour) . 186	Parsifal 306
Les Huguenots 188	The Pearl Fishers (Les Pêcheurs de
The Human Voice (La Voix Humaine) . 442	Perles) 312
Idomeneo, Rè di Creta (Idomeneus, King of	Pelléas et Mélisande 314
Crete) 191	Peter Grimes 319
The Impresario (Der Schauspieldirektor) . 194	Pique Dame (Pikovaya Dama—Queen of
L'Incoronazione di Poppea (The Coronation	Spades) 323
of Poppea) 196	Porgy and Bess 326
Jenůfa 199	Prince Igor (Knyaz Igor) 329
Julius Caesar (Giulio Cesare) 202	Prodaná Nevěsta (The Bartered Bride) . . 62
A Kékszakállú Herceg Vára (Bluebeard's	I Puritani (The Puritans) 332
Castle) 64	

Contents

Queen of Spades (Pikovaya Dama—Pique Dame) 323

The Rake's Progress 335

Das Rheingold 440

Rigoletto 338

Der Ring des Nibelungen (The Ring of the Nibelungs) 344

    Das Rheingold 346

    Die Walküre (The Valkyrie) . . . 350

    Siegfried 356

    Götterdämmerung (Twilight of the Gods) 360

Romeo and Juliet 367

La Rondine (The Swallow) 370

Rustic Chivalry (Cavalleria Rusticana) . . 89

The Swallow (La Rondine) 370

Der Rosenkavalier (Cavalier of the Rose) . 373

Salome 377

Samson and Delilah 379

Der Schauspieldirektor (The Impresario) . 194

Semiramide 382

La Serva Padrona (The Servant Mistress) 386

Siegfried 456

Simon Boccanegra 388

So Do They All (Così Fan Tutte) . . . 101

La Sonnambula (The Sleepwalker) . . . 392

The Spanish Hour (L'Heure Espagnole) . 186

The Strayed One (La Traviata) . . . 416

Suor Angelica (Sister Angelica) 396

Il Tabarro (The Cloak) 398

The Tales of Hoffmann (Les Contes d'Hoffmann) 400

Tannhäuser 404

Thaïs 409

Tosca 412

La Traviata (The Strayed One) 416

Tristan und Isolde 421

Il Trovatore (The Troubadour) 426

Les Troyens (The Trojans) 430

Turandot 435

Twilight of the Gods (Götterdämmerung) . 360

The Valkyrie (Die Walküre) 350

Vanessa 438

Voina i Mir (War and Peace) 444

La Voix Humaine (The Human Voice) . . 442

War and Peace (Voina i Mir) 444

Werther 448

William Tell (Guillaume Tell) 450

The Woman without a Shadow (Die Frau ohne Schatten) 165

Wozzeck 453

Yevgeny Onyegin (Eugene Onegin) . . . 137

Zolotoy Pyetushok (Le Coq d'Or—The Golden Cockerel) 99

Die Zauberflöte (The Magic Flute) . . . 241

PICTURE CREDITS 457

DISCOGRAPHY 459

INDEX 469

LISTING OF THE OPERAS BY COMPOSER

SAMUEL BARBER (1910–   )
Vanessa 438

BÉLA BARTÓK (1881–1945)
Bluebeard's Castle 64

LUDWIG van BEETHOVEN (1770–1827)
Fidelio 150

VINCENZO BELLINI (1801–1835)
Norma 288
I Puritani 332
La Sonnambula 392

ALBAN BERG (1885–1935)
Lulu 230
Wozzeck 453

HECTOR BERLIOZ (1803–1869)
Les Troyens 430

GEORGES BIZET (1838–1875)
Carmen 81
Les Pêcheurs de Perles 312

ARRIGO BOITO (1842–1918)
Mefistofele 272

ALEXANDER BORODIN (1833–1887)
Prince Igor 329

BENJAMIN BRITTEN (1913–   )
Peter Grimes 319

GUSTAVE CHARPENTIER (1860–1956)
Louise 214

LUIGI CHERUBINI (1760–1842)
Medea 266

FRANCESCO CILÈA (1866–1950)
Adriana Lecouvreur 30

CLAUDE DEBUSSY (1862–1918)
Pelléas et Mélisande 314

LÉO DÉLIBES (1836–1891)
Lakmé 206

GAETANO DONIZETTI (1797–1848)
The Daughter of the Regiment . . . 106
Don Pasquale 125
L'Elisir d'Amore 130
Lucia di Lammermoor 220
Lucrezia Borgia 223

FRIEDRICH von FLOTOW (1812–1883)
Martha 259

GEORGE GERSHWIN (1898–1937)
Porgy and Bess 326

ALBERTO GINASTERA (1916–   )
Bomarzo 71

UMBERTO GIORDANO (1867–1948)
Andrea Chénier 44

CHRISTOPH WILLIBALD von GLUCK
(1714–1787)
Alceste 40
Orfeo ed Euridice 294

CHARLES GOUNOD (1818–1893)
Faust 143
Romeo and Juliet 367

GEORGE FRIDERIC HANDEL (1685–1759)
Julius Caesar 202

ENGELBERT HUMPERDINCK (1854–1921)
Hänsel und Gretel 183

LEOŠ JANÁČEK (1854–1928)
Jenůfa 199

RUGGIERO LEONCAVALLO (1858–1919)
Pagliacci 301

PIETRO MASCAGNI (1863–1945)
Cavalleria Rusticana 89

Listing of the Operas by Composer

JULES MASSENET (1842–1912)
Manon 247
Thaïs 409
Werther 448

GIAN CARLO MENOTTI (1911–   )
Amahl and the Night Visitors 42
The Consul 96
The Medium 269

GIACOMO MEYERBEER (1791–1864)
Les Huguenots 188

CLAUDIO MONTEVERDI (1567–1643)
L'Incoronazione di Poppea 196
Orfeo 291

DOUGLAS MOORE (1893–   )
The Ballad of Baby Doe 54

MODEST MOUSSORGSKY (1839–1881)
Boris Godunov 73

WOLFGANG AMADEUS MOZART (1756–1791)
The Abduction from the Seraglio . . . 27
Così Fan Tutte 101
Don Giovanni 120
Idomeneo, Rè di Creta 191
The Impresario 194
The Magic Flute 241
The Marriage of Figaro 254

JACQUES OFFENBACH (1819–1880)
The Tales of Hoffmann 400

GIOVANNI BATTISTA PERGOLESI (1710–1736)
La Serva Padrona 386

AMILCARE PONCHIELLI (1834–1886)
La Gioconda 176

FRANCIS POULENC (1899–1963)
Dialogues des Carmélites 109
La Voix Humaine 442

SERGE PROKOFIEV (1891–1953)
The Love Of Three Oranges 217
War and Peace 444

GIACOMO PUCCINI (1858–1924)
La Bohème 66

GIACOMO PUCCINI (*cont.*)
Gianni Schicchi 174
The Girl of the Golden West 181
Madama Butterfly 237
Manon Lescaut 251
La Rondine 370
Suor Angelica 396
Il Tabarro 398
Tosca 412
Turandot 435

HENRY PURCELL (1659–1695)
Dido and Aeneas 114

MAURICE RAVEL (1875–1937)
L'Enfant et les Sortilèges 132
L'Heure Espagnole 186

NIKOLAI RIMSKY-KORSAKOV (1844–1908)
Le Coq d'Or 99

GIOACCHINO ROSSINI (1792–1868)
The Barber of Seville 58
La Cenerentola 93
Semiramide 382
William Tell 450

CAMILLE SAINT-SAËNS (1835–1921)
Samson and Delilah 379

BEDŘICH SMETANA (1824–1884)
The Bartered Bride 62

JOHANN STRAUSS, JR. (1825–1899)
Die Fledermaus 153

RICHARD STRAUSS (1864–1949)
Arabella 47
Ariadne auf Naxos 51
Capriccio 79
Die Frau ohne Schatten 165
Der Rosenkavalier 373
Elektra 128
Salome 377

IGOR STRAVINSKY (1882–1971)
The Rake's Progress 335

PETER ILYICH TCHAIKOVSKY (1840–1893)
Eugene Onegin 137
Pique Dame 323

AMBROISE THOMAS (1811–1896)

Mignon 281

VIRGIL THOMSON (1896–   )

Four Saints in Three Acts 163

GIUSEPPE VERDI (1813–1901)

Aïda 34
Un Ballo in Maschera 263
Don Carlos 116
Ernani 134
Falstaff 139
La Forza del Destino 159
Luisa Miller 226
Macbeth 234
Nabucco 284
Otello 297
Rigoletto 338
Simon Boccanegra 388

GIUSEPPE VERDI (*cont.*)

La Traviata 416
Il Trovatore 426

RICHARD WAGNER (1813–1883)

Der Fliegende Holländer 156
Lohengrin 209
Die Meistersinger 275
Parsifal 306
Der Ring Des Nibelungen 344
    Das Rheingold 346
    Die Walküre 350
    Siegfried 356
    Götterdämmerung 360
Tannhäuser 404
Tristan und Isolde 421

CARL MARIA von WEBER (1786–1826)

Der Freischütz 170

Publisher's Preface

THE EVOLUTION OF *THE VICTOR BOOK OF THE OPERA*

IN THE OFFICE of Francis Robinson, Assistant Manager of the Metropolitan Opera Association, may be found copies of each of the twelve editions of *The Victor Book of the Opera* preceding this one. It is probably the only place in the world, outside of the Library of Congress, where the development of this fascinating record of musical history may be studied.

For the series has, for well over half a century, supplied the principal operatic education for hundreds of thousands of Americans. Although there were older, more disinterested opera guides on the market when the first Victor book came out (including those by Streatfield and by Upton, which are still in print), none even approached, in those days, the popularity of the Victor book. Precise figures are unavailable, but it is estimated that well over 700,000 copies have been distributed, and the majority of them in the early years, before the competition of cheap paperback reprints. But even with the plethora of such books on the market today, thousands of older people will testify to their nostalgic affection and respect for the Victor series, with its accurately told stories, its history of each opera, and above all the hundreds of pictures of beloved stars in their favorite roles.

Despite its general reputation for sound scholarship, the series was not conceived primarily as a contribution to musical education but quite unashamedly as a sales promotion project. The title page of the first edition (copyrighted 1912 by the Victor Talking Machine Company, Camden, N.J.) is reproduced at the right.

At the bottom was a reproduction of the familiar white dog sticking his nose into the horn of a primitive phonograph and the legend "His Master's Voice." (RCA Victor still uses this drawing as its colophon.) There were 375 pages 5⅝" x 8" in size, and the price was two dollars, though dealers were encouraged to give one away free with each purchase of a Victor Talking Machine. There were indeed three hundred pictures, many of them postage-stamp size, but the paper was of good quality and the reproductions excellent for those days. The plots of the operas were, except for the works from which there were many recordings, brief, and the descriptions of records, complete with size and price, couched in the more dignified advertising lingo of those days. The operas treated—and there were truly seventy of them—were not chosen on the basis of those most often heard in American opera houses (though all the standard works were, of course, included); instead an attempt was made to include every opera from which anything was recorded in the Victor catalogue.

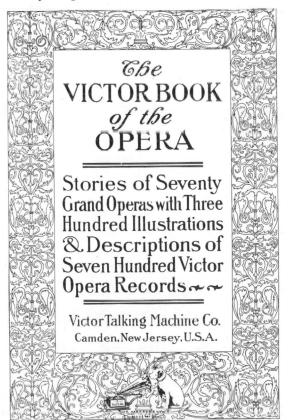

Thus, for example, there was one page devoted to Massenet's *Le Roi de Lahore* (which had had some performances the previous century in New Orleans but did not reach New York till 1924). There was a twelve-line plot summary, a translation of the single aria recorded for Victor by Emilio de Gorgoza ($3; twelve inches), a pitch for the singing, and no pictures. At the other extreme of attention, there was *Faust* (which the 1919 edition assured us "is today sung throughout the world more than any five other operas combined"). *Faust* was allotted twenty-two pages, with four full pages devoted to reproductions of romantic paintings on such subjects as "The Aged Philosopher Wearies of Life," "Marguerite's Surrender," and "The Death of Valentin." The plot and action were rehearsed in considerable detail, punctuated with small photographs of major singers in their respective *Faust* costumes, and listings, with descriptions of recordings. The final trio recordings included one single-side twelve-inch disc by Farrar, Caruso, and Journet which could be had for five dollars contrasted with a ten-inch double-faced disc by Hueget, Lara, and De Luna—with Zaccaria's "Flower Song" on the other side—for only seventy-five cents.

This first edition evidently proved popular with both customers and dealers, for revised editions began to come out almost every other year, growing fatter and fatter. The fourth, for example, in 1917, had grown to 553 pages (still the same small size) with 120 operas, 700 illustrations, and descriptions of 1200 records. Samuel Holland Rous was credited as author, and he concentrated largely on puffing the records. *Carmen*, for example, was introduced with nine lines given to the history of the opera, followed by a sixteen-line biography of Bizet. Then, in two-thirds of a page, the entire story of *Carmen* was synopsized, after which there followed twelve pages of descriptions of arias, duets, etc., and their recordings. The title of the book was also changed for a good business reason. No longer was Camden selling "talking machines"; they were selling "Victrolas" (a registered trademark), and the book accordingly was nominated *The Victrola Book of the Opera*.

Skipping now to the tenth revised edition of 1929 (which reverted to the original name and was reprinted in 1936 and 1939 with further revisions and additions but not called a new edition), we find that, though the book is basically the same in concept, there are distinct improvements. The salesmanship aspect is still there, but confined largely to introductory matter, such as a double-page spread of portraits in mufti of twenty-eight singers labeled "Some of the Great Artists of the World Who Have Made Records for Victor" and a Preface that extols the quality of the then-new "Higher Fidelity Victor Records." So extensive is the Victor catalogue now

that no effort was made to include the story of every single opera from which Victor had recorded as much as a single number. Thus, in 1912 two pages were devoted to *Semiramide* because the book could list a recording of the Overture by Arthur Pryor's Band plus two more recordings of the same number by the Police Band of Mexico City. In 1939, however, the story of *Semiramide* was gone, but the opera still appeared in the Table of Contents, directing the reader to page 531, the page in an appendix of recordings from operas not treated in the body of the book. On the other hand, the new editor and reviser made an attempt to bring into the book accounts of new operas, provided they were in any way represented in the Victor catalogue. Thus, a whole page and a half was given to the then-new *The Emperor Jones* by Louis Gruenberg, with a picture of Lawrence Tibbett as Jones, with the sole excuse of a recording by Tibbett of the spiritual "Standin' in de Need of Prayer" as arranged in that score. That account of the opera, with an even larger picture of Tibbett as Jones, remained in every subsequent edition of the book, after the work itself had long been shelved, apparently with the pious desire to encourage the production of more American operas.

The editor and reviser responsible for such forward-looking innovations (including a larger page size and better picture layouts) was the late erudite and witty Charles O'Connell, then Director of Artists and Classical Repertoire for the copyright holders of the book, now called the RCA Manufacturing Company, Inc., and no longer the Victor Talking Machine Company. Besides the physical improvements in the appearance of the book and the effort to update the Table of Contents, Mr. O'Connell furbished up the writing, contributing a good bit of his own type of eloquence, especially to the accounts of the works of Wagner, in which he was something of a specialist as a conductor.

In 1936 the trade publishers Simon and Schuster took over the wider distribution of the tenth revised edition, and in 1949, when the success of long-playing recordings had revolutionized the Victor catalogue, bringing many complete-opera recordings into the list, a new revision of the text and Table of Contents was undertaken by the two music critics of the New York *World-Telegram*, Louis Biancolli and the late Robert Bagar. Accounts of new operas were added, old ones with few or no recordings dropped; dozens of pictures of current star singers replaced some of the earlier ones (though the most charming of the oldest were retained); a better page size and type face were introduced; the old descriptions of individual records and the quotations of translated texts were omitted along with the inadequate musical quotations; and a discography of all Victor operatic recordings, whether of individual arias or of complete operas, was added at the back of the book. Gone, too, was the puff copy for the Victor Company. It became a handsome trade book, and the price was raised to $3.95. But so rapidly did the opera recording and producing industries grow in those days, that in 1953 the book had to be once more extensively revised, with forty new pictures, and nine new operas (this time from the hand of Bart Winer) added for the twelfth revised edition.

The book was now 654 pages in length, the page size 6″ x 9″, and what with the marked rise in production costs, it had to be priced at $5.95, which, at less than one cent a page for heavily illustrated book on fine paper, was still a bargain. Six printings, 65,000 copies, and eight years later it was found that the plates of the many old and fascinating pictures—some of them retained from the first edition printed 41 years earlier—were in such bad shape that they simply could not be sent through the presses still another time. To have ransacked museums for other old pictures, to have made yet more additions to the text, to have made all the new layouts and plates required, would have meant raising the price still further, probably to $7.50. In the 1950's this price seemed exorbitant, and the book was allowed quietly to go out of print.

But it was not forgotten. Too many Americans had grown up with "The Victor Book"; too many, apparently, had a longing for a reliable and comprehensive opera guide that, with its hundreds of pictures of stars and productions, both current and historical, was more than a reference book, something not only readable but filled with the glamour and nostalgia that grand opera feeds on. One day in 1966 George Marek, Vice President of the RCA Victor Record Division, approached Simon and Schuster to request that this continued demand be met. What RCA Victor wanted, he said, was a new edition keeping the most attractive features of the old ones, bringing up to date the much enlarged repertoire of the world of opera, and opening up the discography to the best of the splendid recordings of complete operas done by Victor's competitors. That is, the publications of other companies were to be listed, complete with casts and order numbers, beside Victor's own; and if Victor had not recorded any given work complete, it was nevertheless to be included along with the listing of whatever companies did have complete recordings. This was a remarkably intelligent and generous approach to take, but Victor regarded the step simply as good business for the entire industry in fulfilling a felt need; and to prove their conviction of the soundness of the proposition, they offered to underwrite a major share of the expense of preparing the new edition.

This proved to be a long and delicate task. For, while every effort was made to keep as

much as possible of the work of previous writers and editors intact in order to preserve the flavor of a book which had by this time become a classic, the repertoire had so much altered—so many operas in the 1949 edition had been all but forgotten, so many older operas were being revived and twentieth-century ones gaining acceptance—that a consensus of what to include and what to drop could be reached uneasily only after hours of conferring with RCA Victor officers and outside experts. The number of operas handled, for reasons of space, could not be increased; yet it was decided that the choice must reflect as well as possible, the entire history of opera and the current activity on the stage and in the studios. The ultimate decisions, which could not possibly please everyone, were left up to the new editor, who wrote all the additional opera summaries (with some kindly offered assistance from Gerald Fitzgerald of *Opera News* and Francis Rizzo, Gian Carlo Menotti's secretary) and rewrote many of the older accounts of operas in the light of more recent scholarship and to give them more prominence on account of their re-entry into stage and studio repertoires.

A brief account of the kinds of operas added in this extensive revision and of those deleted to make room for them will show some interesting trends in the development of operatic taste during the almost twenty years between this edition and the last previous one. Thirty of the 121 titles in the twelfth edition had to go, and most of the excisions were made with regret. After all, they had all once been works of importance—or at least popularity. First went the nine "operas" of Gilbert and Sullivan simply on the ground that they are operettas rather than grand operas and in the repertoire of no major opera company. (On the other hand, another operetta, *Die Fledermaus,* was kept because it *is* in the repertoire of large opera companies and performed by major operatic singers.) Next, the works of Meyerbeer, which had not been represented in decades on American stages, were sacrificed. Only *Les Huguenots* was kept because of Meyerbeer's great importance in the history of opera and with the excuse that this one work had been recently revived in Italy with considerable success and a recording of old vocal highlights is currently available in America. Then there were certain American operas, once apparently promising but now almost forgotten, which had to go —the aforementioned *Emperor Jones,* Deems Taylor's *The King's Henchman* and *Peter Ibbetson,* and others. So we went through the list with a regretful but determined blue pencil.

But the additions, for which many more were nominated than could possibly be included, are perhaps more significant in showing how taste is changing in certain respects. They can be divided into three categories—the pre-nineteenth-century operas that have, especially in the past ten years, elicited many revivals; the numerous nineteenth-century operas, especially of the *bel canto* school, that such artists as Callas and Sutherland have caused to be "rediscovered"; and twentieth-century works that give some indication of becoming a more or less staple part of the repertoire. The earliest operas added were Monteverdi's *Orfeo* and *L'Incoronazione di Poppea* (previously the earliest had been Purcell's *Dido and Aeneas,* and that had been so cavalierly treated that its revived importance made requisite a much more extensive presentation), and two more Mozart operas. Of nineteeth-century works, enough new productions and recordings had come into being to demand the inclusion of Bellini's *I Puritani,* Cherubini's *Medea,* Donizetti's *Lucrezia Borgia,* Verdi's *Luisa Miller* and *Nabucco,* and numerous others. And the twentieth-century demanded inclusion of several Strauss operas that had once been written off but are now being revived. Berg's *Lulu* (*Wozzeck* being retained from the previous edition), Douglas Moore's *The Ballad of Baby Doe,* Benjamin Britten's *Peter Grimes,* Poulenc's *Dialogues des Carmélites* and *La Voix Humaine,* and many more.

Now, these may have been bad guesses. Five years from now any or all of them may again have receded into obscurity. For the fact is that the really popular operas—the *Aïdas, Fausts, Carmens, Lohengrins* that get played year in year out in every country and in almost every language—number somewhere in the thirties and no more. They have all been in every edition of *The Victor Book of the Opera* and of every other opera guide published since the latest of them was produced, that is, *Madama Butterfly* in 1904. But there is constant ferment in taste and intellectual curiosity outside of this hard core of perennial favorites, and we hope that the present selection may reflect that ferment with fair accuracy as it seemed to look in 1968.

This thirteenth edition has been entirely reset with a far larger page size (8½" x 11") than ever before and in double columns to allow for greater fluidity in the use of pictures. Tribute must be paid here to the untiring efforts made by Gerald Fitzgerald in collecting from many corners of the world over a thousand historical and modern illustrations, many of them never published before in this country, and in lending a knowing hand in their final selection.

THE PUBLISHER

AN OUTLINE HISTORY OF OPERA

ITALY

ABOUT THE YEAR 1580 a group of Florentine scholars and musical amateurs began discussing the possibility of adapting music to the drama. They believed that the ancient Athenians had performed their tragedies in a sort of musical declamation. This practice the Florentines endeavored to revive and from their attempts modern opera was born. For opera may be defined as a play in which the actors sing throughout, accompanied by an orchestra.

Avoiding the complex polyphony that was characteristic of the music of the period, the Florentines sought, instead, a style of solo music that would permit the words to be distinct—emotionalized speech rather than sustained song. The instrumental accompaniment was to be merely a support and background. The first application of this style of recitative to an entire play was made by Jacopo Peri and Giulio Caccini, both of whom set music to the text of Ottavio Rinuccini's *Dafne* (1597). In 1600 *Euridice,* another poetic drama by Rinuccini, was set to music by Peri, and again by Caccini.

The next step in the development of the new art was made by Claudio Monteverdi (1567–1643), whose *Orfeo* was produced at Mantua in 1607. Like his Florentine predecessors, Monteverdi emphasized dramatic expression but employed more elaborate musical means. His experiments led him to some of the boldest innovations in musical history. He called

Claudio Monteverdi (1567–1643)

for a larger orchestra than had been previously demanded and made skillful use of it to intensify dramatic mood.

The next important step in the development of opera was taken by Alessandro Scarlatti (1659–1725). He emphasized the musical element of his works, sometimes at the expense of the dramatic, and was the first to make considerable use of the so-called *da capo* aria (Francesco Provenzaie is supposed to have been its inventor). In this form the first portion of an aria is repeated after a second has intervened, hence the Italian name *da capo*, which means "from the beginning." Although satisfying musically, this device is not suitable to all dramatic situations. Yet so great was its musical appeal that it came to be used with increasing frequency. Customarily the singer embellished the repetition with scales, trills, and other types of vocal display of his own devising, whether appropriate to the dramatic situation or not. As such improvisational additions to the score as written by the composer could not well be carried out in duets and other concerted numbers, there were very few of these, and the chorus, too, was used most sparingly. *Opera seria* thus became practically a costumed program of arias sung against scenery—often very elaborate—and telling a story, usually quite preposterous. The cast of characters was chosen from mythology or ancient history, though the events might bear only a superficial resemblance to the ones recorded by ancient poets and historians. The acting was highly formalized, with prescribed gestures and even stances, the leading singer in any scene almost invariably occupying stage front center.

Despite these absurdities—or maybe partly be-

cause of them—the standard of execution in the singing was extremely high, especially among the *castrati*. These were men who, usually around the age of twelve, had been castrated and rigorously trained in vocal technique and in composition as well. By the time they were grown men, they had often attained impressive height and great lungs, and, if contemporary reports are to be believed, were capable of such volume and such control over their very high voices as to be irresistibly moving even to listeners not especially fond of music. With their masculine appearance and feminine voice ranges, they enacted either male or female roles; and this ambisextrous privilege was enjoyed by the women singers as well. If, in the seventeenth or eighteenth century, you were going to hear an opera about Orpheus (and there were dozens composed on this subject), you could never be sure before you saw the program whether Orpheus would be sung by a man or a woman. Although the convention of having men sing female characters disappeared with the *castrati* early in the nineteenth-century, opera audiences today still tolerate women in men's parts. Gluck's Orpheus, originally written for a *castrato*, is today usually cast with a mezzo-soprano, while Richard Strauss, as late as 1911, composed the title

Christoph Willibald von Gluck (1714–87)

15

Gioacchino Rossini (1792–1868)

Gaetano Donizetti (1797–1848)

Vincenzo Bellini (1801–35)

role of *Der Rosenkavalier*, a young lover, for a soprano or a mezzo. Cherubino in Mozart's *Magic Flute* and Siebel in Gounod's *Faust* are two surviving examples of what the Germans call *Hosenrollen* (trouser roles) still seen frequently.

Side by side with the Italian *opera seria* there developed a humorous counterpart, *opera buffa*, short comedies often offered as relief between the acts of an *opera seria*. Its closeness to real life saved this genre from degenerating into the formalism of *opera seria*. In earlier times the dialogue was spoken; later it was set to what was called a *recitativo secco*, or "dry recitative"—a lightly accompanied form of recitative particularly adapted to rapid or humorous dialogue.

Italian opera was infused with a new breath of life at the beginning of the nineteenth century through the work of Gioacchino Antonio Rossini (1792–1868), who wrote both serious and comic operas. In the invention of brilliant vocal melody he showed unrivaled genius. Rossini also gave added prominence to the orchestral accompaniment. His school was continued by Gaetano Donizetti (1797–1848) and Vincenzo Bellini (1801–1835). Both showed marked gifts in composing melody of a serene and limpid beauty.

Their successor Giuseppe Verdi (1813–1901), one of the world's greatest dramatic composers, began his career with such works as *Oberto* (1839) and *Ernani* (1844), written in a style akin to that of Bellini and Donizetti, but already displaying greater vigor and dramatic force. Throughout his long

career Verdi revealed a growing development of dramatic and orchestral power without any accompanying loss of music inspiration. Evident, too, was a growing seriousness of purpose. Verdi's final works are remarkable for their depth of expression, clearness of characterization, freedom of form, and richness of harmony and orchestration. Indeed, many regard *Otello* (1887) and *Falstaff* (1893) as his crowning achievements.

Among Verdi's successors in carrying on the tradition of nineteenth-century romantic opera in Italy was the librettist for his last two operas—Arrigo Boito (1842–1918), whose *Mefistofele* (1868), an adaptation of Goethe's *Faust*, is still often revived and has been recorded by distinguished casts. Boito, like some other of his Italian compatriots and contemporaries, was more or less influenced by German operatic writing—particularly Wagner. These men included Umberto Giordano, whose *Andrea Chénier* (1896) is still part of the standard repertoire, Ermanno Wolf-Ferrari, whose *Secret of Susan* (1909) and *Jewels of the Madonna* (1911) held most operatic stages for a period of about thirty years and then pretty much disappeared. The same fate has overcome Italo Montemezzi's highly romantic *The Love of Three Kings* (1913). On the other hand Amilcare Ponchielli's *La Gioconda* (1876) is now approaching its hundredth anniversary in the repertoire with almost undiminished popularity.

Ponchielli was one of the principal teachers of the greatest genius in Italian opera since Verdi—Gia-

Umberto Giordano (1867—1948)

Pietro Mascagni (1863–1945)

Ruggiero Leoncavallo (1858–1919)

Giuseppe Verdi (1813–1901)   *Amilcare Ponchielli (1834–86)*   *Giacomo Puccini (1858–1924)*

como Puccini (1858–1924). A gifted melodist, endowed with an uncanny flair for dramatic effect, Puccini had a distinct style of his own but never hesitated to adapt the most foreign of ideas if they could be made to serve his musical purposes—whether it was Oriental scales and themes or some of the harmonic ideas of the latest echo from Paris. In the opera at least, *Il Tabarro,* he wrote a little masterpiece of *verismo,* that school of brutal realism in stories of modern lower-class people, the most successful examples of which were the first—Pietro Mascagni's *Cavalleria Rusticana* (1890) and Ruggiero Leoncavallo's *Pagliacci* (1892). But since the death of Puccini no Italian operas seem to have entered the repertoire that captures all stages.

FRANCE

IN FRANCE opera had its rise in the ballet—elaborate spectacles performed for the entertainment of the seventeenth-century court. This may account for the interest in scenic effect that has characterized much French opera. When in 1645 an Italian opera troupe appeared in Paris for the first time, it gave fresh impetus to the musical phase of court performances. Jean Baptiste Lully (1632–1687), the first important composer of French opera, reflects the conventional life of the court for which he wrote; yet in his effort to make the words distinct and in the prominence which he gives to the visual elements of staging and pantomime, he set the pattern for the French opera of the future. Without altering the basic style, his successor, Jean Philippe Rameau (1683–1764), enriched it with a more varied harmony and greater orchestral prominence.

Meanwhile, a new form, *opéra comique,* was slowly evolving from the crude plays with interspersed songs which had long been popular with the French masses. Among the early writers of *opéras comiques* André Ernest Modeste Grétry (1741–1813), is outstanding. His works are notable for the vivacity and sparkle which enliven his formal eighteenth-century style.

Conventional Italian *opera seria* grew in favor in France during the eighteenth century, so that in the course of time two schools of thought arose—one preaching greater freedom and the importance of the dramatic and poetic side of opera, the other maintaining the superiority of *opera seria* with all its fixed formulas. The proponents of the former school found a powerful spokesman and standard-bearer in Christoph Willibald Gluck (1714–1787). Conscious of the inadequacy of the prevailing style, which he had used in many operas, Gluck attempted something of a reform in several of his later works. In this he met with little success, for Vienna, the scene of his first efforts, had wholly succumbed to the Italian school. Gluck then moved to Paris as a city that might prove more responsive to his theories.

Briefly stated, Gluck's thesis was that the music must always perfectly express the drama it accompanies. Nothing extraneous should be introduced for mere display, either vocal or orchestral. In his greater works Gluck attains an unprecedented dramatic force and expressive appeal.

Gluck's success, however, did not go unchallenged. His opponents brought to Paris the Italian Niccolò Piccinni, a composer of stereotyped *opera seria.* A sharp and acrimonious rivalry developed; indeed, so bitter was this "War of the Gluckists and Piccinnists" that it soon threatened to go beyond the purely verbal and aesthetic. The principles of Gluck finally triumphed, and even the embattled Piccinni was soon adopting his rival's manner, though with little success. Piccinni's music is today largely forgotten, but Gluck's *Alceste* and *Orfeo ed Euridice* are known to every music lover.

With the triumph of Gluck, Paris became for a time the center of European opera. During the next century a number of gifted operatic composers made it the scene of their greatest activity. Though many were of foreign birth, they soon adapted their native characteristics to the needs of French taste and style. Gasparo Spontini (1774–1851), whose *La Vestale* was a spectacular success, created a fashion for subjects of a heroic nature unfolded amid lavish

Giacomo Meyerbeer (1791–1864)

Georges Bizet (1838–75)

Charles Gounod (1818–93)

scenic and orchestral color. In this he was followed by Jacques Halévy (1799–1862), composer of *La Juive,* and Giacomo Meyerbeer (1791–1864), among whose best-known works are *L'Africaine, Les Huguenots,* and *Le Prophète.* A genius of vast theatrical resource, Meyerbeer ranks among the greatest operatic innovators. Because of their gorgeous settings, large dramatic conceptions, and taxing demands for brilliant singing and acting, Meyerbeer's best works are truly "grand opera" in the most picturesque sense of the term. Admittedly, they are often marred by trivialities, pompousness, and an inability to exploit musical ideas to their fullest in artistic expression. But both his success with audiences and his influence on other opera composers (including Verdi and Wagner) were enormous, and one of these years we may see a revival of interest in his operas outside of France, where they have never left the stage.

The heroic grand-opera style was in time replaced by one of a simpler and more direct human appeal, as exemplified in Charles Gounod's *Faust* (1859) and Georges Bizet's *Carmen* (1875), two of the enduring pillars of the world repertory. In both, the dramatic use made of accompanied recitative between the more formal vocal numbers again reveals the recurring French emphasis on the text. One of the most famous and prolific of later French composers was Jules Massenet (1842–1912). His style is marked by a suave melodiousness and refinement rather than by dramatic vigor. Gustave Charpentier, in his *Louise* (1900), presented a study of modern sociological problems and a picture of contemporary life. Written by a man of pronounced socialist sympathies, *Louise* has been called the first "proletarian opera." By the manner in which he makes the music cling inseparable to the mood and cadence of the text, Claude Debussy, in *Pelléas et Mélisande* (1902), again reverted to the principle of the original Florentine founders of opera.

Since *Pelléas et Mélisande* no major French opera has survived long in the international repertoire, although such effective one-acters as Maurice Ravel's

Jules Massenet (1842–1912)   *Gustave Charpentier (1860–1956)*

L'Heure Espagnole (1911) and full-length works like François Poulenc's *Dialogues des Carmélites* (1956) receive occasional performances, at the San Francisco and New York City Operas.

Claude Debussy (1862–1918)

GERMANY

IN GERMANY we find the beginnings of opera dominated by Italian traditions. During the seventeenth and eighteenth centuries the court of every kingdom and principality maintained its own Italian or Italianized opera theater. During this period, however, there also emerged in the folk theaters a native product, the *Singspiel* (song play)—a light, often farcical or burlesque play in which spoken dialogue was interspersed with singing. Significantly, the characters were of humbler and less remote origin than those of court opera.

The first of the great German composers to write operas of lasting worth was Wolfgang Amadeus Mozart (1756–1791). Important as Mozart's work in the symphony, concerto, and string quartet was, his contribution to opera was perhaps even more significant. Two of his greatest works, *Le Nozze di Figaro* (1786) and *Don Giovanni* (1787) are written to Italian texts, with "dry recitatives." They are, in fact, magnificent descendants of the Italian *opera buffa*. On the other hand, *Die Zauberflöte* (1791) and *Die Entführung aus dem Serail* (1782) are set to German texts with spoken dialogue. Both these works show traces of the national style in their music and the influence of the *Singspiel* in the nature of their plots. Mozart ranks with the greatest of opera composers because of his unerring powers of characterization, his uncanny ability to express every shade of emotion, and his inexhaustible melodic invention.

If Mozart had learned much from his Italian and French predecessors, Ludwig van Beethoven (1770–1827) in turn learned much from Mozart and made significant advances of his own. For his one opera *Fidelio*, shows the same profound originality and expressive individual power that mark his symphonic compositions. A consummate skill in using the or-

Maurice Ravel (1875–1937)

Francis Poulenc (1899–1963)

Wolfgang Amadeus Mozart (1756–91)

Ludwig van Beethoven (1770–1827)

Carl Maria von Weber (1786–1826) *Richard Wagner (1813–83)* *Richard Strauss (1864–1949)*

chestra to evoke atmosphere and depict the emotional turmoil of the characters is a striking feature of this sublime score. As in the *Singspiel*, spoken dialogue is used between the musical numbers.

Already foreshadowed in the work of Mozart and Beethoven, the Romantic movement reached its operatic peak in the music of Carl Maria von Weber (1786–1826). The interest in the beauties of nature, the fascination for the terrors of the supernatural, the fanatic love of the exotic, whether European or Oriental, and the widespread enthusiasm for national folklore—all characteristic of the Romantic movement in general—now found expression in the operas of this musical Romantic. *Der Freischütz*, notable for its typically German folk story, characteristically national melodies, and ingenious tone painting in harmony and orchestration, is Weber's acknowledged masterpiece.

With the stupendous achievement of Richard Wagner (1813–1883), opera recalls once more the aims and ideals of the early Florentine group. For Wagner the quintessence of opera was drama. Music became increasingly a means of heightening the dramatic action and intensifying the illusion of life. Word and note were now indissolubly bound in a single unity of expression, and in this tremendous fabric Wagner's orchestra became a new instrument

of massive power. No longer a mere accompaniment, it was now a running commentary on the events and emotions of the story unfolding on the stage; it caught every shifting nuance of feeling, it evoked memories and associations through a wondrous scheme of *Leitmotiven*, or leading themes. The orchestra was now alive to every suggestion of past happenings and every hint of the future, and throughout this complex web of tone one caught ominous strains of prophecy, often giving the entire score something of the tension and fatalism of Greek tragedy. Though Wagner had learned a great deal from Beethoven and Weber, his real forerunner in artistic outlook was Gluck, who had similarly stressed the pre-eminence of expression and drama in opera. This goal Wagner reached only after many years of groping, years during which his manner and style were partly imitative, as in *Rienzi*. And to the very end, he experimented with new devices of orchestral form and color, achieving what many regard as his most masterly synthesis of ideal and inspiration in *Parsifal*.

A faithful disciple of Wagner's was Engelbert Humperdinck (1854–1921), whose complete assimilation of the master's idiom is especially evident in the orchestral scoring of *Hänsel und Gretel*. This delightful fairy opera, of course, boasts a folksy

Engelbert Humperdinck (1854–1921) *Alban Berg (1885–1935)*

spirit of childlike fantasy which owes nothing to Wagner.

It was Richard Strauss (1864–1949), however, who dominated the whole scene of post-Wagnerian opera in Germany. Like Wagner, Strauss amplified and enriched the voice of the orchestra, creating, moreover, a whole emotional and pictorial language of his own. Strauss showed a phenomenal versatility of style, from the barbaric splendor and realism of *Salome* (1905) and *Elektra* (1909) to the delicious humor and nostalgia of *Der Rosenkavalier* (1911) and the wit and passion of *Ariadne auf Naxos.*

Of the many German operas in the more difficult modern idiom the one that has gained acceptance

most widely in both Germany and outside is Alban Berg's tragedy of a simple soldier, *Wozzeck* (1925). Leading German composers, from Hindemith (1895–1963) and Arnold Schoenberg (1874–1951) to Gottfried von Einem (1918–   ) and Hans Werner Henze (1926–   ) continue to receive performances in Germany. Karl Orff (1895–   ), who composes in a more easily accessible idiom, might be cited as an exception; but the one stage work that has really won world-wide popularity, the *Carmina Burana* (1936), though sometimes staged, was intended to be sung as a cantata, tells no story, and is really not an opera at all.

Henry Purcell (1659–95)

George Frideric Handel (1685–1759)

ENGLAND

IN ENGLAND opera has been largly dominated by foreign influences. The native-born Henry Purcell (1659–1695) showed a remarkable ability in his incidental music to various masques and plays, and especially in his one real opera, *Dido and Aeneas.* This work, produced in 1689 at a "boarding school for young gentlewomen," London, was subsequently given in concert versions, often quite mutilated, until its 1895 revival as a complete opera for the Purcell bicentenary. Later it obtained performances in both operatic and concert versions, a goodly number of which were of amateur sponsorship. It has been said, and with more reason than at once appears, that had Purcell not died prematurely, the history of opera in England might well have taken a different course.

With the death of Purcell English music, and with it opera, fell into a two-century period of stagnation. George Frideric Handel arrived in London, in 1710, and an era of opera in Italian, which had begun just previously, flourished in England, as elsewhere in Europe, excepting, perhaps, France, where the vernacular for operatic texts had strong supporters. Handel's *Rinaldo,* improvised within two weeks of his arrival, was a great success. More and more works for the lyric theater came from his pen, and he enjoyed, because of these, as well as compositions in other forms, a huge vogue.

Handel's stage music is not strictly of Italian derivation, since it combines elements from several schools. With the increasing popularity of works in the classical Italian tradition by Hasse and Porpora,

Bedřich Smetana (1824–84) *Alexander Borodin (1834–87)* *Modest Moussorgsky (1839–81)*

Handel's operatic works, for all their estimable qualities, presently suffered a decline.

Handel's stage works were in the *opera seria* style, and because of their striking dramaturgic absurdities suffered severe ridicule, along with other such works, at the hands of Joseph Addison and other London wits. When in 1732 the satirical *Beggar's Opera*, with text by John Gay and popular music compiled by Johann Pepusch (like Handel, a transplanted German), became a fashionable hit, the fortunes of *opera seria* in England had already begun to decline, and not too long afterwards Handel turned his dramatic genius to composing oratorios, the field of his greatest attainment.

The Beggar's Opera was not an opera in the sense we have been using it at all, but rather a "ballad opera," a series of tunes in the public domain chosen and arranged by a musician to fit a book of dialogue and lyrics written by a "man of letters." Many were performed both in England and her American colonies, but they were much more akin to what later developed into musical comedy and operetta than to the subject of this book and this history. The British talent for the lighter forms of music combined with elegant satire saw its finest flowering in the succeeding century with the operettas of W. S. Gilbert and Sir Arthur Sullivan, and the most viable operas the British produced were works of two Irishmen, Michael Balfe and Vincent Wallace, whose *Bohemian Girl* and *Maritana*, respectively, both produced in the 1840's, were extremely popular for almost a century. Both were tuneful, sentimental works and not of sufficient musical caliber to be respected on the European continent. There was little serious opera composed in England in the nineteenth century.

The twentieth, however, has seen a renaissance of interest in operatic composition. Gustave Holst, Ralph Vaughan Williams, Sir William Walton, and a number of others have all composed able and viable operas during the past half century, some of which have had occasional performances in countries outside of England. But the most successful of all the British opera composers has been Benjamin Britten. Highly prolific in other musical forms as well, he has composed a number of operas that have been widely performed and well received, and one of which, *Peter Grimes* (1945), shows the vitality that may gain it a place in standard repertory.

RUSSIA

IN RUSSIA the first definite break away from the Italian tradition was made by Mikhail Ivanovich Glinka (1804–1857). In his patriotic *A Life for the Tsar* and the legendary *Russlan and Ludmilla* he paved the way for Russian nationalism in music. His style is lyrical and obviously influenced by Italian forms, but the Russian flavor of his melody and harmony is unmistakable. His successor Alexander Sergeivich Dargomijsky (1813–1869) is notable for his use of the declamatory style. The famous nationalist group of "The Five" (Balakirev, Rimsky-Korsakov, Moussorgsky, Borodin, and Cui), while heatedly disclaiming adherence to Wagnerian theories, yet seem to show something of the influence of his work. However, their major operas possess originality and a distinctly Russian quality. Certainly in Moussorgsky's *Boris Godunov* and *Khovantchina*, Borodin's *Prince Igor*, and Rimsky's *Le Coq d'Or* and *Sadko*, we have some of the most significant contributions to the modern operatic stage, irregularly as these works may be now scheduled for performance. And there is no question as to Tchaikovsky's gifts as an operatic composer, bearing in mind his *Eugene Onegin* and *Pique-Dame*.

In more recent times Russia claims two notable composers of opera, the discerning and precise Serge Prokofiev and the vigorous Dmitri Shostakovich, although neither has made the lyric theater his special

Peter Ilyich Tchaikovsky (1840–93) *Nikolai Rimsky-Korsakov (1844–1908)* *Serge Prokofiev (1891–1953)*

field. Prokofiev's *The Love of Three Oranges* has been justly appreciated for its musical subtlety, and his *War and Peace* has earned the unqualified approval of at least its Russian listeners. Shostakovich's *Lady Macbeth of Mzensk* is a forceful, blatantly ironic opera, which has had an unhappy career in Russia, first winning and soon losing the Soviet hierarchy's favor. More recently, in a revised version called *Katerina Ismailova* after its heroine, has started on a freshly successful career both at home and abroad.

UNITED STATES

OPERA IN THE UNITED STATES has been given more or less with regularity since the eighteenth century, antedating, in fact, the formation of the Union. During the nineteenth century the popularity of opera was increased by the establishment of permanent opera houses: in New Orleans, the Théâtre d'Orléans (later destroyed by fire); New York, Academy of Music and Metropolitan Opera House; Chicago, Chicago Auditorium—all these in addition to other theaters in various cities which have not functioned continuously as opera houses. There have also been traveling companies, not excluding the postseason tours of the Metropolitan Opera Company and the Chicago Civic Opera Company (latterly discontinued), besides a host of brief operatic seasons, festivals, and single performances in major localities.

But while America consumes an enormous number of repertory grand operas, and many Americans have composed many operas intended for international success, none has succeeded well in this peculiarly European enterprise. For some reason or other, American operas have been successful and made a real contribution to musical culture only when they have been produced as musical shows, usually for Broadway. The Metropolitan Opera has produced works, all of them of more than passing competence, by Frederick Converse (*The Pipe of Desire,* in 1910, the first American work ever performed there), by Reginald De Koven, by Howard Hanson, by Bernard Rogers, by Gian Carlo Menotti, by Samuel Barber, and others. Few have lasted in the repertoire for more than a season or two; very few ever received performances on any other stage.

But when Menotti (whose background and culture are as much Italian as American) produced other operas than the ones he wrote for the Metropolitan and produced them for a run in other theaters, he was very successful, especially with *The Medium* (1946) and *The Consul* (1950), and subsequently these two entered the repertoire of the New York City Opera. Neither of these musical plays, however, would be appropriate for a truly grand opera stage. Nor would

Benjamin Britten (1913–   ) *Samuel Barber (1910–   )* *Gian Carlo Menotti (1911–   )*

George Gershwin (1898–1937)

Douglas Moore (1893–   )

Virgil Thomson's *Four Saints in Three Acts* (1934), which was first acted in a small theater in Hartford, Connecticut, later produced on Broadway as well as in a theater in Paris; nor would what is perhaps the most viable of all American "operas"—George Gershwin's *Porgy and Bess* (1935), which has traveled all over the world. Even those American operas which have had the most acceptance by the smaller repertory companies—like Carlisle Floyd's *Susannah* (1965) and Douglas Moore's *The Ballad of Baby Doe*

(1956)—lean rather toward the musical show than toward the tradition of grand opera. And none of them, of course, has had the success of or been so typical of American culture as the true musical shows of Rodgers and Hammerstein or Lerner and Loewe, some of whose works are, in many respects, closer to opera than to the old-fashioned musical comedy or operetta. Perhaps the true American opera will still find its greatest development in the medium of television or of the motion picture.

Virgil Thomson (1896–   )

Alberto Ginastera (1916–   )

The Operas

The Abduction from the Seraglio

DIE ENTFÜHRUNG AUS DEM SERAIL

CHARACTERS

Pasha Selim	*Speaking part*	Pedrillo, *his servant*	Tenor
Constanza, *beloved of Belmonte*	*Soprano*	Osmin, *overseer of the Pasha's*	
Blonda, *her maid and beloved of*		*country place*	Bass
Pedrillo	*Soprano*	A mute	Mute
Belmonte, *a Spanish nobleman*	*Tenor*		

Janissaries, Slaves, Guards

The action takes place in Turkey in the sixteenth century.

COMIC OPERA in three acts. Music by Wolfgang Amadeus Mozart. Libretto in German by Gottlieb Stephanie, actually an altered version of the text by Christoph Friedrich Bretzner for Johann André's opera *Belmont und Constanze oder Die Entführung aus dem Serail* (Berlin, May 25, 1781). First performance, Burgtheater, Vienna, July 16, 1782. First performance in the United States, German Opera House, Brooklyn, N.Y., February 16, 1860. Metropolitan première, November 29, 1946, in an English translation by Ruth and Thomas Martin, with a cast including Eleanor Steber as Constanza, Pierrette Alarie as Blonda, Charles Kullman as Belmonte, Dezso Ernster as Osmin, Hugh Thompson as Selim, John Carter as Pedrillo, and Ludwig Burgstaller as the Mute; the conductor was Emil Cooper. Yet, despite the Metropolitan's initial neglect, for 165 years it has achieved the distinction of being the earliest German opera to be frequently performed on the world's operatic stages today. It is now a staple of the New York City Opera.

This *Singspiel* was Mozart's first great success and written at one of the rosier times in his short and seldom rosy career. Though far from being financially secure, he married Constanze Weber a few weeks after the première of this work, whose heroine's first name is the same as the bride's. The music, while varied in style, seems to reflect the happiness of its composer, and its colorful gaiety is emphasized by the use of "Turkish" effects, which were very popular at the time.

ACT I

Belmonte, a young Spanish nobleman, is eager to get a glimpse of Constanza, his beloved, who has been kidnaped, together with her maid Blonda, and brought to the seraglio of the Pasha Selim. Pedrillo, Belmonte's servant, as it happened, was with the girls when they were spirited away, so that he, too, is in the Pasha's toils, although he has managed, by artful maneuvering, to become the gardener at the Pasha's country place.

Osmin, the Pasha's overseer, testily refuses to give Belmonte much satisfaction, since he suspects him of being in league with Pedrillo, who has become a particular hate of his. Belmonte and Pedrillo, however, chance to meet, and they are overjoyed. The servant discloses that Constanza is unharmed, though, he says, it is the Pasha's plan to make her his favorite, much as she is repelled by the idea.

Mozart conducting his Abduction *in Berlin, 1789*

Belmonte tells Pedrillo that he has a ship lying outside the harbor and that everything is in readiness for an escape.

In the meantime, the Pasha and Constanza are seen, as Belmonte hides himself. While the Pasha, left alone, is walking in the garden, Pedrillo approaches him with the suggestion that a certain gentleman whom he knows would make a very good architect for His Excellency, and the Pasha promises to give this person an audition on the morrow. The Pasha departs, and Osmin joins Belmonte and Pedrillo in a lively trio which ends with the pair's slipping by him to get into the palace.

ACT II

After discouraging Osmin's ludicrous love-making, Blonda is joined by the distracted Constanza, whom she tries to console. As Blonda leaves, the Pasha enters, protesting his love for this new girl. In rebuttal Constanza sings the beautiful and brilliant aria *"Martern aller Arten"* ("Tortures unabating"), in which she says that no amount of torture or agony can make her love him. With that she exits, leaving the Pasha deeply troubled. Blonda appears, and she is a little disappointed in finding both Constanza and the Pasha gone. Can they have come to some *rapprochement*, she wonders. As she thinks of such things, the ubiquitous Pedrillo bustles in, telling her of Belmonte's arrival and the plans they have laid to abduct the naturally willing ladies, and also that she is to inform Constanza of all this. Left alone, Blonda muses on the new state of things and expresses her pleasure in the joyous aria *"Welche Wonne, welche Lust"* ("What delight, what joy").

As soon as she leaves the stage, Pedrillo comes in, later joined by Osmin. The two engage in a comical scene, in which the overseer is given copious drafts of wine to drink, with the logical consequence of his becoming tipsy and, therefore, manageable. Pedrillo, developing superhuman strength, takes this mammoth on his back and drags him off, soon returning alone, to make the fourth in a quartet with Constanza, Belmonte, and Blonda, which is one of the score's high points.

ACT III

At night, in an open area before the palace, Pedrillo is seen making arrangements for the escape and, after a few moments, is joined by Belmonte, whom he urges to sing a serenade, for Pedrillo has been singing to Blonda for so long, of nights, that it would create suspicion if no song were sung that evening. Belmonte obliges him by delivering the lengthy aria *"Ich baue ganz auf deine Stärke"* ("I dedicate my all").

The singing awakens Constanza. She looks out; and when Belmonte sees her, he ascends a ladder, and in a few moments both are seen making their escape through the palace door. Pedrillo, left behind,

Salzburg: Kurt Böhme (Osmin), Murray Dickie (Pedrillo)

The Metropolitan Opera's 1946 production, featuring Eleanor Steber as Constanza and Hugh Thompson as Pasha Selim

delivers his signal serenade and, presently, runs up the ladder to Blonda's room. However, the voices have shaken a mute from out of his sleep, and he immediately awakens Osmin. The latter, though still under the influence of the wine, realizes what is happening when he sees the ladder before Blonda's house. In his clumsy manner he climbs to the window, arriving there just as Blonda and Pedrillo come to it from inside. The lovers, however, flee through the door, only to be brought back in company with Belmonte and Constanza under guard.

In the final scene, which takes place in a hall of Selim's palace, the Pasha censures Constanza for her apparent perfidy, although she assures him that Bel-

monte is the man to whom she has long been betrothed. Belmonte, at this point, declares that his father will be glad to pay any ransom for their freedom. And when the Pasha discovers that Belmonte's father is Lostados, a Commandant of Oran and his greatest enemy, he gloats with a particularly malignant pleasure. However, he relents, admonishing Belmonte to tell his father that he, Selim, releases the son of Lostados willingly, finding the greater satisfaction in returning good for evil. The joy of Constanza and Belmonte is increased when both Blonda and Pedrillo are also freed, over the stormy protests of Osmin. The opera closes with the ensemble singing a song of praise to the Pasha.

29

Adriana Lecouvreur

CHARACTERS

Adriana Lecouvreur, *an actress*	*Soprano*	Mlle. Dangeville, *actress of the*	
Maurizio, *Count of Saxony*	*Tenor*	*Comédie Française*	*Mezzo-soprano*
Michonnet, *stage director*	*Baritone*	Poisson, *actor of the Comédie*	
Princesse de Bouillon	*Mezzo-soprano*	*Française*	*Tenor*
Prince de Bouillon	*Bass*	Quinault, *actor of the Comédie*	
Abbé de Chazeuil	*Tenor*	*Française*	*Bass*
Mlle. Jouvenot, *actress of the*		Major domo	*Tenor*
Comédie Française	*Soprano*		

Actors, Actresses, Servants, Guests

The action takes place in and near Paris in 1730.

OPERA in four acts. Music by Francesco Cilèa. Libretto in Italian by Arturo Colautti based on the play of the same name by Eugène Scribe and Ernest Legouvé, which in turn was based on certain events in the life of the great French actress Adrienne Lecouvreur (1692–1730). Première at the Teatro Lirico, Milan, November 6, 1902, with Angelica Pandolfini as Adriana, Enrico Caruso as Maurizio, and Giuseppe de Luca as Michonnet. First performance in the United States at the French Opera House in New Orleans, January 5, 1907. First performance at the Metropolitan Opera House, November 18, 1907, with the beautiful Lina Cavalieri in the title role, Caruso as Maurizio, and Antonio Scotti as Michonnet. Revived there for Renata Tebaldi in the season of 1962–63 and again for the opening night of the 1968–69 season.

The subject of this opera, a one-time laundress and the daughter of a drunken hatter named Couvreur, was probably the greatest French actress of her day, in both comedy and tragedy. The triangle love story of the opera, involving the Princesse de Bouillon and Maurice, the Count of Saxony, is well documented. Maurice was actually the greatest

and last love of Adrienne's life, and the Princess apparently did actually try to poison her, though with lozenges, not with flowers. The lozenges were tested on a dog with fatal results. But some months later, while acting a tragic role, the actress collapsed. Five days after that she died. Maurice, as in the opera, was at her deathbed. There were also a priest, who refused her the final rites, and Voltaire, one of her many earlier lovers. Voltaire said she died of indigestion, but no one really knows.

Francesco Cilèa, a gentle and well-liked man, composed a number of operas in the *verismo* style of the turn-of-the-century Italian composers, such men as Puccini, Giordano, and Mascagni. *L'Arlesiana,* based on the same play for which Bizet had composed his popular incidental music, and *Adriana Lecouvreur* are still frequently performed in Italy, but only the latter has had much success in other countries. It is a singer's opera, the name role being a particularly good vehicle for a fine singing actress. The orchestration, however rich in some passages, never overshadows the voice, and the melodic lines often rise to a sweep and passion that can be enormously effective. Leitmotivs are used throughout, though in a less subtle and more obvious way than in the operas of Puccini and other verists, and of course they are not developed symphonically as with Wagner.

ACT I

SCENE: *Backstage at the Comédie Française*. At a performance of Racine's *Bajazet* half a dozen actors and actresses, about to go on, are hectoring the stage director Michonnet for help with costumes and props. He gets things under control with his aria *"Michonnet su!"* The Prince de Bouillon wanders in, accompanied by his ever-present shadow, the gay Abbé de Chazueil, and asks after his current mistress, the actress La Duclos, who is not there and, in fact, never appears in the opera despite the rather important part she plays in the story. Everyone becomes quiet when Adriana Lecouvreur comes out of her dressing room, still rehearsing some lines she is about to deliver on stage. When her colleagues start admiring her, she modestly responds with her aria *"Io son l'umile ancella del genio creator"* ("I am the humble handmaid of creative genius").

With the act beginning, Adriana and Michonnet are left alone, and he is about to declare his long-lived love and propose marriage when she confides in him her own love for one Maurizio, whom she believes to be an officer in the service of the Count of Saxony but who really is the Count himself. Michonnet, crestfallen, leaves and Maurizio appears, having gained entrance surreptitiously by climbing a ladder. He addresses her passionately as *"La dolcissima effigie,"* and she responds by saying that she will be playing only for him tonight. Before she leaves to make her stage entrance, she pins a small bouquet of violets in his buttonhole. They have made an assignation for that night, and Maurizio returns to his box.

The Prince now returns with his ever-obliging Abbé, who has come across a letter apparently from La Duclos making an assignation in the Prince's own villa near Paris—but it is to be with Maurizio, not with the Prince. Actually, this letter is from the Princesse de Bouillon, but as the Prince does not know this and as he is a bit tired of his mistress anyway, he gaily plans a surprise party for the lovers, inviting four of the actors to join him and the Abbé in the fun. A delightful sextet develops (*"Un gaio festina"*).

And now Adriana is acting her big scene in the play. Michonnet watches from the wings and comments, heartbrokenly, on her wonderful art. Maurizio comes in, for he has received the Princess' note and must break his engagement with Adriana. As a prop letter is missing for her recitation, he manages to send her a note, which she gets on stage, and her

Renata Tebaldi (Adriana), Franco Corelli (Maurizio)

deep disappointment lends an especially poignant note to the delivery of her tragic speech. As she returns backstage, she receives the excited acclaim of her colleagues—and then agrees to join the Prince's surprise party after the play.

ACT II

SCENE: *Reception hall of the Prince's villa*. The Princesse de Bouillon is agitatedly awaiting Maurizio and sings a long soliloquy on the agonies of love. Presently the Count arrives, and the Princess suggests that the violets he is wearing may have something to do with his tardiness. To quiet her suspicions (for she fears anyway that he loves her no longer), he says that the flowers were intended for her, and makes her a present of them. The somewhat uncomfortable dialogue is interrupted by sounds of the arrival of the Prince and his party, and Maurizio just manages to hide the Princess in a dark room off the hall. The Prince greets Maurizio good-humoredly. He is not at all angry, and he even hints that perhaps the Count may take La Duclos off his hands. Maurizio at once perceives the Prince's misconception and, determining to save the Princess if

The historical Adrienne Lecouvreur, painted by Greuze

he can, plays up to it. In this venture he gets an unexpected ally. Adriana arrives and is introduced to the Count of Saxony, for the first time learning of her lover's real rank. When the Prince's party goes off to see about supper, Maurizio, declaring his love once more, tells Adriana, quite truthfully, that the woman he was meeting was not Duclos but someone of much higher rank who was helping him politically and whom she must help him to save now. But he does not reveal the Princess' name.

And so, for the sake of her lover, Adriana goes into the dark room and gives the Princess a key to the garden whereby she can make her escape. Neither woman can recognize the other, but both admit their love for Maurizio and know they have a dangerous rival. Before the acts ends, Michonnet (who has also tried to find out who is in the dark room) gives Adriana a bracelet he has found on the floor.

ACT III

SCENE: *A sumptuous hall in the Prince de Bouillon's palace.* Several months have passed, during which Maurizio has been in Latvia on political and military missions, and only vague rumors about him have reached Paris. As the act opens, the Abbé is directing preparations for a gala social occasion to be offered his guests by the Prince. The Princess wanders in, still wondering about the identity of her rival for the love of Maurizio, and the Abbé pays her empty little compliments in a charming, rather old-fashioned love song. When the guests begin to arrive, Adriana among them, the Princess at once believes that she recognizes the distinctive voice that had spoken to her in the dark room at the villa. She announces, falsely, that news has come of Maurizio's being hurt in a duel, and Adriana's reaction, which is to faint momentarily, convinces the Princess she is right. Maurizio himself enters a moment later, perfectly healthy, and narrates, in answer to requests, his remarkable triumphs against the Russians (*"Il russo Mencikoff"*).

Now a small ballet company, which the Prince has provided for entertainment, presents the old story of *The Judgment of Paris,* and at its end the leading man presents the apple not to Venus but to the Princess. In her triumph, the Princess begins to bait Adriana, who responds by displaying the bracelet Michonnet had found at the villa. This hint of the power she holds over her rival does not endear Adriana to the Princess. To cover up, the Princess suggests that the actress perform a scene from *Ariadne Abandonée* but instead she delivers a speech from Racine's *Phèdre,* which concerns an adulterous wife. While Maurizio is carrying on an open (but silent) flirtation with the Princess, Adriana begins reciting—to the accompaniment of the orchestra—in the melodramatic, old-fashioned sing-song of French classical tragedy. Then, toward the close, she bursts into her singing voice, steps up to the Princess, and—still in the lines of Racine and the character of Phèdre—violently insults her. (The real Adriana Lecouvreur did something very much like this to the real Princesse de Bouillon, but it happened at the Comédie Française.) Everyone tries to cover up this breach of etiquette; the Princess, under her breath, vows vengeance; and the Prince politely escorts the actress from the room.

ACT IV

SCENE: *Adriana's drawing room.* It is weeks later, and Adriana has not returned to the stage but lies in bed most of the time sick for love of the absent Maurizio. It is her birthday, and old Michonnet has come to call. The maid tells him the state of things, and Michonnet sends off a note to Maurizio asking him to come at once. Hearing of Michonnet's presence, Adriana joins him, and the two exchange not very happy views on unrequited love. Presently a quartet of her colleagues at the Comédie Française call to ask her to return to the stage and to bring her birthday gifts, the most charming of which is a

32

madrigal they sing for her, *"Una volta c'èra un principe"* (*"Once upon a time there was a prince"*). But the present that moves her most is a set of diamonds from Michonnet which have sentimental value for her because of an association with Maurizio.

Finally there comes a mysterious gift, a box with a card from Maurizio. Inside she finds the violets she had given him at the theater, now all withered and dead. She is deeply hurt, for she believes they are a symbol of what Maurizio now thinks of their love. She expresses her grief in the famous aria *Poveri Fiori."* She does not, of course, know that Maurizio had given them to the Princess, who had forged the card and sent them as an act of revenge. Nor does she know how terrible that revenge is. For the flowers have been poisoned, and when she tries to smell them, she suddenly grows weak, and Michonnet hastily sends away the other visitors. A few moments later Maurizio arrives in response to Michonnet's message, and for a brief while the lovers are ecstatically reunited. But the poison continues to do its work; Adriana dies with Maurizio and Michonnet by her side.

Act III ballet, The Judgment of Paris, *as choreographed for the Metropolitan Opera in 1963 by Alexandra Danilova*

Aïda

CHARACTERS

Aïda, *an Ethiopian princess*	*Soprano*	Amonasro, *King of Ethiopia*	*Baritone*
The King of Egypt	*Bass*	Ramfis, *high priest*	*Bass*
Amneris, *his daughter*	*Mezzo-soprano*	A Messenger	*Tenor*
Rhadames, *captain of the guard*	*Tenor*	A Priestess	*Soprano*

Priests, Priestesses, Captains, Soldiers, Officials, Ethiopian Slaves and Prisoners, Egyptians, etc.

The action takes place at Memphis and Thebes during the epoch of the Pharaohs.

OPERA IN four acts. Music by Giuseppe Verdi. Libretto in Italian by Antonio Ghislanzoni, aided by the composer, from the French of Camille du Locle, after a prose sketch by the Egyptologist Mariette Bey. First produced, Opera, Cairo, Egypt, December 24, 1871. First United States performance, Academy of Music, New York, November 26, 1873. First Metropoliton Opera performance November 12, 1886, in German, Anton Seidl conducting. *Aïda* has been performed there more often than any other opera—533 times through the 1967–68 season.

Ismail Pasha, Khedive of Egypt, approached Verdi through intermediaries, in 1869, suggesting that he compose an opera for the new Cairo theater, to celebrate the opening of the Suez Canal. Not only did Verdi refuse the commission, but he successfully resisted, for a time, the arguments presented by his friend, Camille du Locle, who may or may not have been the Khedive's choice for librettist. The Suez Canal was duly opened in 1869 and, too, the new theater in Cairo, but *Rigoletto* not *Aïda* was the work to signalize the event.

Du Locle, a persistent individual, whose blandishments had thus far proved unavailing, finally sent Verdi a four-page sketch of an opera plot based on an Egyptian subject (allegedly authentic), which the distinguished Egyptologist Mariette Bey had done. On seeing it, Verdi could scarcely hold his excitement, and from the rough draft a scenario was contrived by du Locle and himself. So, with contrac-

tual arrangements completed, Ghislanzoni chosen to versify the scenario in Italian, and January 1871 picked as the date for the première in Cairo, the composer set to work on his music.

In this manner, piece by piece and with much detailed correspondence between composer and librettist (which serves to prove Verdi's important contribution to the libretto), grew the story of the Egyptian hero who spurns the hand of a princess for the love of a slave—the captive daughter of a hostile sovereign—wherein jealousy and patriotism unite to bring destruction to the lovers.

As so often in his career, international affairs and politics interfered with the first performance of Verdi's *Aïda*. This time it was the Franco-Prussian War. Costumes and scenery, which had been designed under the expert eye of Mariette Bey, remained in beleaguered Paris until the close of the war, thus necessitating a postponement. But the opera was at last given its première, and from all accounts it was a triumph. Among the chief singers were Pozzoni (Aïda), Grossi (Amneris), Mongini (Rhadames), Steller (Amonasro), and Medini (Ramfis). When *Aïda* was first given at La Scala, Milan, February 8, 1872, Verdi was recalled thirty-two times amid a tumult of applause, and was given an ivory baton and a diamond star with the name *Aïda* in rubies and *Verdi* in other precious stones.

Musically, *Aïda* is of enormous interest in that it is the first work in Verdi's "mature" style, that is to say, a style revealing a new harmonic sense, sudden and surprising modulations, a greater richness of orchestral scoring. Verdi was accused by some of having imitated Wagner, which, of course he did not do, although he would have been totally insensitive to the advances made by the German composer had he not profited by some of them, while, in the main, adhering to the Italian tradition. He composed no numbers for exhibiting the technical skill of singers in florid runs and trills, but wrote instead music that is always appropriate to the action of the drama, yet music that is always melodious and congenial to the voice. The orchestra is not treated in the complex symphonic style of Wagner, but it is more colorful than that previously known in Italian opera, still without ever submerging the singers. In keeping with his subject, Verdi created effects in his music that are plausibly Oriental, although *Aïda* is as Italian an opera, from first note to the last, as he ever wrote. Realizing that presenting the life of ancient Egypt called for much pageantry, he wrote rousing choruses for crowds of people and also rather exotic dances to enhance the Oriental aspects of the whole. The characterizations are all skillfully drawn—Rhadames, bold and romantic; Amneris, in varying moods, imperious and angry and jealous, or in terror; Aïda, simple and loving; Amonasro, crafty; Ramfis, stern and pompous; characters that are revealed in music as well as in words. All these features combine to make *Aïda* the absorbing music drama it truly is, and they help explain its enduring popularity.

ACT I

SCENE 1: *A hall in the palace (through the great gate at the rear may be seen the pyramids and the temples of Memphis).* After a calm prelude based on a brief theme that recurs several times during the opera, since it typifies the gentle Aïda, the curtain rises, revealing a hall in the palace of the King (or Pharaoh) of Egypt. The high priest of Isis, Ramfis, is telling Rhadames that the enemy Ethiopians are reported to be on the outskirts of Thebes and the Valley of the Nile. In reply to Rhadames' questions, he adds significantly that the goddess Isis has appointed a certain brave young warrior leader of the army that will be sent against the invaders. Left alone, Rhadames ponders over this news, occasional fanfares of trumpets creating a martial atmosphere. He dreams of himself as the "brave young warrior" and of the glory that would be his to return at the head of his victorious forces, in the recitative beginning "*Se quel guerriero io fossi*" ("If I were that warrior"). Then he dwells with pleasure on thoughts of Aïda, as the music changes from the warlike to the ardent and loving, with Rhadames now wholly

committed to his womanly ideal in the famous aria "*Celeste Aïda*" ("Heavenly Aïda").

Rhadames' ecstasy is interrupted by the entrance of Amneris. She does not know—nor does anyone else at court—that her slave Aïda is the daughter of the Ethiopian king, Amonasro. Curious about Rhadames and his love musings, she questions him guardedly, secretly hoping that she is the object of his passion. When Rhadames, merely to cover his confusion, answers that he was dreaming of heading the Egyptian armies in the coming campaign, Aïda appears, and, by the glance that flashes between the other two, Amneris learns where Rhadames' heart lies. The Egyptian princess, cautious and wily, takes Aïda aside with a show of friendship, asking her the reason for her anxious demeanor. Aïda says simply that she has been disturbed by the news of the war between her country and Egypt. Rhadames, meanwhile, suspects that Amneris has guessed the true state of things, and the varied emotions of these three personages are expressed in a dramatic trio.

The King enters with his entourage and a messenger arrives with the tidings that the Ethiopians

Aïda (Birgit Nilsson) and Rhadames (Carlo Bergonzi)

are approaching the city under their king, Amonasro. *"Mio padre!"* (*"My father!"*) Aïda exclaims in an aside. The King nominates Rhadames leader of the army, and Amneris presents him with a banner. Then, having been charged by the King to defend the Nile, the Egyptians depart.

Emotionally transported by the sentiments, Aïda cries with the others, *"Ritorna vincitor"* ("Return victorious"). But presently alone, she suddenly realizes the significance of her words. And in an aria that begins with the phrase she has just shouted, she expresses her dismay, praying for death.

SCENE 2: *The Temple of Vulcan.* Through the long rows of massive Egyptian pillars in the dim Temple of Vulcan, we see in the distance a great altar, illuminated by a soft light from above. Statues of deities abound, and from golden tripods rises the smoke of burning incense. Ramfis stands at the altar, dominating this ceremony of prayer and dedication while, outside, priestesses sing an eerie incantation. The deeper voices of the priests join in, and soon Ramfis and the whole assemblage invoke blessings on the expedition. A stately sacred dance is performed by the priestesses, while Rhadames enters and receives the consecrated veil, sword and armor. The music rises to a climax, as all turn to the altar. Rhadames exhorts the god Ptah to protect Egypt.

ACT II

SCENE 1: *A hall in the apartments of Amneris.* Amneris is surrounded by slave girls who are singing a song in praise of her beloved. She occasionally cries ecstatically, *"Vieni, amor mio"* ("Come, my love"). Then she falls back indolently on the couch, while Moorish slave boys dance for her.

Aïda approaches, and Amneris bids her other slaves depart. Left alone with the Ethiopian princess, she slowly gains her confidence. Then, studying her closely for any possible telltale sign, she leads Aïda to believe that Rhadames has been slain in battle. The spurious words are electrical, and Aïda gives a great cry of pain. And now that Amneris knows the truth about the love between Aïda and Rhadames, she announces that Rhadames lives and that she "the daughter of the Pharaohs," is Aïda's rival.

Aïda is helpless. She implores mercy and makes no attempt, now, to conceal her love, but Amneris promises her only death for her temerity. The sound of festival music outside, announcing the return of the victorious Egyptians, suggests a further idea of revenge. Aïda, Amneris says, shall witness Rhadames' triumphal procession and his obeisances to Amneris, as she sits beside her father, the King.

SCENE 2: *Outside the city walls.* A great throne has been erected at the city gates to welcome the conquering army. The King and his court, the priests, and the people are all there assembled. A majestic hymn, *"Gloria all' Egitto, ad Iside"* ("Glory to Egypt and to Isis"), is intoned. The Egyptian troops enter, preceded by musicians who play on long brazen trumpets. Then follow dancing girls who wave aloft welcoming palms. Dancers perform a colorful ballet to music that mounts in excitement.

The song of praise is resumed, and still other troops enter. The soldiers carry war banners, while slaves bear sacred vessels and effigies of the gods. Rhadames appears in a horse-drawn chariot. He descends at the height of the jubilation, and the King steps down from his throne and embraces him, declaring, "Savior of the country, I salute thee!" Rhadames kneels before Amneris as she places the crown of victory on his head, and the King swears by his crown that Rhadames shall have any wish he desires. Rhadames, however, asks first that the prisoners be brought in. Thereupon the captives enter, and among them is Amonasro, who is unrecognized in his plain officer's garb. Aïda knows, though, and she rushes to him, unable to restrain herself. He cautions her not to reveal his rank, and, summoned by the King, he acknowledges his daughter, admitting the enormous defeat and, lying in a convincing manner, describes how the "King of the Ethiopians" pierced by wounds, died at his feet. Amonasro begs pityingly that the prisoners be freed. The populace joins in the plea in a surge of compassion. Last, Rhadames, reminding the King of his promise, asks for the life and liberty of his captives. The priests, led by Ramfis, object, but the King overrules them, though with the stipulation—at their insistence—that all be liberated save Amonasro and Aïda, who shall be kept as hostages. The King declares that Rhadames shall have his daughter's hand in marriage as reward for the victory.

The finale of this act involves a number of different sentiments expressed in musical threads that are beautifully interwoven in a great pattern: Amonasro swears to avenge himself; Amneris is exultant; Aïda reflects tearfully on the futility of her life; Rhadames spurns the throne of Egypt as not being "worth the heart of Aïda"; the King and the priests and the populace join in singing the glory of Egypt and Isis, and all these form a powerful dramatic and musical climax to the scene.

ACT III

SCENE: *The banks of the Nile: moonlight (the Temple of Isis can be seen behind the palm trees).* The mysterious mood of this scene is evoked by the soft,

ACT II Triumphal Scene of Aïda, *as staged in 1963 by the Metropolitan Opera, with Katherine Dunham choreography*

widely spaced staccatos of the strings, followed by a wistful melody in the oboe. Sounds of voices, softly chanting a hymn, can be heard from within the temple. Soon Amneris and the high priest alight from a boat and proceed to the temple, there to invoke blessings of the gods on the union between the princess and Rhadames. As they disappear, Aïda enters for her secret tryst with Rhadames. She sings of vague fears, wondering if this is to be their last farewell. Should that be so, she says, the waters of the Nile shall be her grave and give her, perhaps, peace and oblivion. Soon her thoughts go to her childhood, to those carefree days in her beloved homeland, and with a deep longing for it all she sings, *"O patria mia"* ("O my native land").

Aïda's reverie is interrupted by her father, who declares forthwith that Rhadames' love for her may yet provide their means of escape and also a victory over these "infamous Egyptians." She recoils at the thought, but after being denounced as a "slave of the Pharaohs" and the sole cause of the miseries visited on the Ethiopians, she tearfully consents. Rhadames, at this point, is approaching, and Amonasro—with a last warning to his daughter—runs off to hide among the palms. Rhadames enters and embraces Aïda, singing, *"Pur ti riveggo, mia*

dolce Aïda" ("I see you again, my sweet Aïda"). But urged by her father's injunction to work on Rhadames' love, she asks that he prove his devotion by fleeing with her. Rhadames resists her for a time, but the enchantment of the night, the allurement of her presence, and the desperate prospect of marriage to Amneris all weaken his resolve.

Under the bewitching influence of Aïda, Rhadames goes as far as to paint a glowing picture of life for them in some foreign land—maybe Ethiopia. And while he is in that blissful state, Aïda strategically puts the question, "By what road shall we avoid the Egyptian hosts?" He lets slip the information that the army will not take to a certain path until the morrow, even disclosing the name of the place. Here Amonasro appears out of the dark, and, with a fierce joy, repeats Rhadames' words, besides revealing his own identity: "King of the Ethiopians."

Rhadames is horrified, and he agitatedly speaks of the dishonor he has brought upon himself. It is pointed out to him with subtle casuistry by Amonasro that he is guiltless; it is fate that has betrayed him. He is assured that happiness awaits them all in Ethiopia. Moreover, he dare not stay, but must make good his escape with Aïda.

Amneris, coming from the temple, has overheard.

Elisabeth Rethberg, a Metropolitan Aïda from 1922 until 1942

Mad with jealousy, she rushes out and denounces the three, her wrath blazing forth with especial virulence against Rhadames. Amonasro and Aïda escape, but Rhadames, filled with remorse, remains behind to yield himself to the priests.

ACT IV

SCENE 1: *A room in the palace.* Amneris is desperate; Rhadames is to be tried as a traitor. "Could he only love me," she exclaims, "I would save him!"

She decides to try, and the accused man is brought in. Exerting all her powers, she tries to persuade him to promise never to see Aïda again. He refuses, declaring that death is a blessing if it is for Aïda's sake. The love of Amneris is transformed into hate, and she calls on the gods for revenge.

Guards conduct Rhadames to the judgment room, while Amneris is left to suffer alone as she hears the punishment she has herself brought about pronounced on the man she loves. As she turns, she sees Ramfis and the priests solemnly entering the judgment hall, and she cries, "Behold the fatal ministers of death—do not let me behold those white-robed phantoms!" Her lamentation, the stern voices of Ramfis and his priests conducting the trial in the room below, combine to produce a doubly tragic sense of foreboding. Amneris, in torture, covers her face with her hands; but she cannot shut out the terrible voices of Rhadames' accusers. Through it all, he remains silent. Finally, the voice of Ramfis pronounces the sentence—death by burial alive beneath the temple of the god whom Rhadames has offended. The priests re-enter and again file impassively across the room, before the despairing eyes of Amneris. In a paroxysm of mingled wrath and anguish she denounces them, saying, " 'Tis they who offend heaven with their cruelty." But the priests answer, "He is a traitor, he shall die!"

SCENE 2: *The Interior of the Temple of Vulcan (above, the temple proper, where the chanting*

Louise Homer, in her 1900 Metropolitan Opera début role, Amneris

Leontyne Price as Aïda, in the La Scala staging

priests intone their endless litanies; below, under the very statue of Osiris, the deity of the nether world, is the tomb where Rhadames has been condemned to die). The hero believes himself alone, and his reflections are embodied in the incomparable music of the aria *"La fatal pietra sovra me si chiuse"* ("The fatal stone upon me now is closing").

His thoughts soon turn from his own miserable fate to Aïda, and he prays that happiness may be hers. He is startled by the thought that in the shadow of the tomb he sees Aïda. He is not mistaken, it is she! She says that she has come to share death with him. Her father slain, his troops scattered, she has crept to earth like a stricken animal, her heart foreseeing the sentence to be passed upon Rhadames. Overwhelmed by the thought of her enormous sacrifice, Rhadames tries in vain to move away the heavy stone sealing the tomb. He sings, *"Morir! si pura e bella!"* ("To die! so pure and lovely"), and Aïda repeats the melody, singing of the "ecstasy of an immortal love."

Meanwhile, the priests above in the temple are going through their mysterious rites, solemnly chanting, "O mighty Phtha."

Together the lovers resign all hopes on earth and unite in a great duet, singing, *"O terra, addio"* ("Farewell, O earth"). The melody is in broad, calm phrases, suggestive of the limitless sweep of

Robert Merrill, a current Metropolitan Amonasro

infinity, and peaceful as eternity. It is sung in unison—even the close blending of the voices being a symbol of the absorption of the lovers into an unending union free from all things earthly. Amneris, repentant and disconsolate, enters the temple above to weep and pray over the tomb of her beloved. Below, in the oppressive darkness of the tomb the lovers, clasped in one final embrace, repeat their farewell to earth and its sorrows.

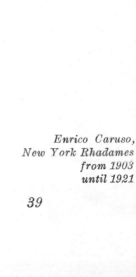

Mario Del Monaco as Rhadames at the San Francisco Opera

Enrico Caruso, New York Rhadames from 1903 until 1921

Alceste

CHARACTERS

Admetos, *King of Pharae*	Tenor	Apollo, *the Greek sun-god*	Tenor
Alceste, *his wife*	*Soprano*	Apollo's high priest	*Baritone*
Evander, *a messenger*	*Tenor*		

Priests, Priestesses, Attendants, and the People of Pharae

The action takes place in Pharae in ancient Thessaly.

OPERA IN THREE ACTS, sometimes in two. Music by Christoph Willibald von Gluck. Libretto in Italian by Raniero de' Calzabigi, after Euripides. First produced in Vienna on December 26, 1767. Despite criticism from a portion of the public on account of the soberness of the music, the lack of brilliant coloratura, it was a success. Nine years later, however, when Gluck had revised the work extensively, even altering some of the characters and plot, it

Nicolai Gedda (Admetos), Eileen Farrell (Alceste)

failed in Paris. Gluck wrote philosophically: "*Alceste* can only displease when it is new. It has not yet had time. I say that it will please in two hundred years." It did not take that long. Pauline Viardot proved a sensation in the leading role when Paris revived the opera in 1861, and all Europe took it to heart. America, however, did not stage it professionally before January 24, 1941, when the Metropolitan Opera Company produced it with Marjorie Lawrence in the title role. It was also the opera chosen by Kirsten Flagstad in 1952 for her last Metropolitan appearance. The score is customarily a compromise between the original version for Vienna, which was in Italian, and the original Paris version, which was in French.

In 1769, two years after the original Viennese production, the score was published, prefaced by a dedicatory epistle to the Grand Duke of Tuscany, later Emperor Leopold II. This proved an epoch-making document. Librettist and composer made a strong plea for naturalness, simplicity, and directness in operatic writing. The statement was an attack, too, on the decorative excesses of Italian opera. Gluck had begun his famous reform of opera. A new fusion of action and music had come about.

The issues raised by *Alceste* plunged Gluck into an artistic war with Niccolò Piccinni, standard-bearer of the conventional Italian style. The famous clash of the Gluckists and Piccinnists was allegedly touched off by Marie Antoinette in a search for new thrills. Soon all Paris had taken sides in this battle.

The tragic breadth of *Alceste* may be readily sensed in the Overture. The action of the opera is eloquently foretold in the alternating themes of fate and pleading, in the dark colors of the orchestra, in the poignant phrases of noble feeling.

ACT I

SCENE 1: *A courtyard of the palace of Admetus.* The citizens of Thessaly pray to the gods to save their king, who is mortally ill. After Evander, a herald, tells them that no power on earth can save Admetus, the queen, Alceste, arrives with her two children to add her lamentations to those of her subjects. Hoping for the intercession of the god Apollo, she tells the people to follow her into the temple.

SCENE 2: *The Temple of Apollo.* The High Priest bids the god recall that Admetus once sheltered him, then Alceste tries to appease the god's fury with offerings. In answer, an oracle proclaims that the king can be spared if a friend agrees to take his place in death. In fear, the mourners flee the temple, leaving Alceste alone. Seeing there is no one else to make the sacrifice, she pledges to forfeit her own life, invoking the gods in the celebrated aria *"Divinités du Styx."*

ACT II

SCENE: *A hall in the palace.* Admetus and his court rejoice in his sudden recovery. The king asks Alceste the name of the friend who has offered his life for him, and Alceste in tears finally confesses that it is she herself. Admetus refuses the sacrifice, but Alceste, firm in her resolve, bids her loving subjects a touching farewell.

ACT III

SCENE 1: *The gates of Hell.* Alceste fearfully seeks death. Admetus follows his wife, begging to die too, but it is too late. As Alceste steps into the fold of the ghosts of hell, Apollo suddenly appears, saying that by virtue of their great love, the power of death has been stayed.

SCENE 2: *The realm of Apollo.* The royal couple is hailed by the people with songs and dances, a celebration of life's victory over death.

Act II of the Metropolitan Opera première in 1941, with René Maison as the king and Marjorie Lawrence as his wife

Amahl and the Night Visitors

CHARACTERS

Amahl, *a crippled 12-year-old*   *Boy Soprano*

His Mother   *Mezzo-soprano*

Kaspar   *Tenor*

Melchior   } *the Three Kings*   *Baritone*

Balthazar   *Bass*

Page   *Baritone*

Shepherds and Villagers

The action takes place Christmas Eve, on the road to Bethlehem, in the year of the birth of Christ.

OPERA IN ONE ACT. Music and libretto by Gian Carlo Menotti. Commissioned by the National Broadcasting Company, it was the first opera written expressly for television (Menotti had previously written radio's first opera, *The Old Maid and the Thief*). The first performance, by the NBC-TV Opera Theater in New York, was appropriately given on Christmas Eve, December 24, 1951. Menotti directed his own work, with a cast consisting of Chet Allen as Amahl, Rosemary Kuhlmann as his mother, Andrew McKinley, David Aiken, and Leon Lishner as the Three Kings, and Francis Monachino as the Page. Its first stage performance was on February 21, 1952, when the opera department of Indiana University presented it in Bloomington. It has had hundreds of school and college performances, and millions hear and love it each year when, on Christmas Eve, the National Broadcasting Company's network televises it.

SCENE: *Amahl's cottage on a winter night, the sky brilliant star-filled.* Amahl, his crutch beside him, plays his pipe outside the cottage as his mother goes about her household chores within. Reluctantly he leaves off playing and enters the cottage when his mother calls him to come to bed. When she wonders what kept him outdoors so long, he tells her of the miraculous sky with a star as "large as a window."

But she is used to his exaggerations and puts it down to his old habit. His lying is not her immediate worry, for unless they become beggars, she sees no way out of their poverty. Amahl is delighted—what a good beggar he'll make! They go to bed with little hope for the morrow.

In the distant hills the Three Kings and their Page, with a lantern to guide them, wend their way toward Bethlehem. Amahl, on his pallet, listens to the singing, then hobbles on his crutches to the window. The Page leading the procession, the Kings come into view: Melchior bearing a coffer of gold, Balthazar an urn of incense, and Kaspar a chalice of myrrh. Melchior knocks on the cottage door, and Amahl's mother bids him answer it. When he returns with the news that a king is outside, she accuses him of making up stories as usual and sends him on a second trip to the door. After the third trip and the report that there are *three* Kings outside, she settles the matter by going herself. The Kings seek shelter, and though she has little, Amahl's mother offers her home with good grace. The Kings sit down on a bench, while the Page spreads a carpet before them on which he places gifts for the Holy Child. When his mother goes for firewood, Amahl questions the Kings on their authenticity, then discovers a jeweled box, which the slightly deaf and childlike Kaspar opens, revealing its contents:

The three kings receive the gift of Amahl's crutch in the NBC–TV Opera Theater world première, first seen in 1951

jewels and beads—and licorice. Amahl's mother returns and sends him to their neighbors for food for the Kings. She eyes the rich gifts laid on the floor of her rude cottage and is told that they are gifts for the Child, but she can think only of her own child, hungry and cold.

The call of the shepherds is heard, and, led by Amahl, they timidly enter the cottage to lay their gifts before the Kings. As entertainment they offer a dance, for which Balthazar thanks them, then bids them good night. As his mother prepares to sleep on the floor, Amahl asks Kaspar if among his magic stones he has one that can cure a cripple. But deaf Kaspar doesn't understand the boy, and Amahl, in defeat, lies down upon his pallet. The Kings fall asleep on the bench, leaning against each other, with the Page at their feet.

Amahl's mother, unable to sleep, cannot resist an impulse to steal some of the gold—there is so much —for her boy's sake. But before she can safely return to her bed, the Page awakens, catches her stealing, and grabs her. Amahl goes to his mother's rescue, beating the Page in a vain attempt to release her, whereupon Kaspar signals the Page to let her go. She may keep the gold, Melchior says, for the Child they seek needs no gold: His kingdom will be built on love. As they prepare to leave, for it is growing lighter outside, Amahl's mother begs them to take back the gold—all her life she has waited for such a king and if she were not so poor she, too, would send a gift. But Amahl has nothing to offer save his crutch, and before his mother can stop him, he takes a step toward the Kings, proffering his gift. Amazed at his ability to walk unaided, the Kings

decide that it must be a miracle from the Holy Child. Amahl, overjoyed, dances about until he overdoes it and stumbles, but nothing can down his good spirits. The Kings and the Page touch the blessed child before departing, and Amahl begs his mother to allow him to accompany them and present his gift himself. When she gives in, he straps his crutch to his back, bids her good-by, and joins the Kings at the end of their procession. Taking out his pipe, he plays a tune and walks happily on, while his mother, standing in the doorway of the cottage, waves him good-by.

Chet Allen (Amahl) and Rosemary Kuhlmann (the mother)

Andrea Chénier

CHARACTERS

Andrea Chénier, *poet*	*Tenor*	Incredible, *a spy*	*Tenor*
Carlo Gérard, *a revolutionary*		Fouquier-Tinville, *public prosecutor*	
leader	*Baritone*	*of the Revolution*	*Bass*
Countess di Coigny	*Mezzo-soprano*	Roucher, *Chénier's friend*	*Baritone*
Maddalena, *her daughter*	*Soprano*	Fléville, *a writer*	*Baritone*
Bersi, *her maid*	*Mezzo-soprano*	Schmidt, *a jailer*	*Bass*
Madelon, *an old woman*	*Contralto*	Dumas, *Tribunal president*	*Baritone*
Mathieu, *a revolutionary*	*Bass*	Major domo of the Countess	*Bass*
The Abbé	*Tenor*		

Guests, Servants, Peasants, Soldiers, Revolutionaries, Judges, Prisoners

The action of Andrea Chénier *occurs in Paris before, during, and after the French Revolution.*

La Scala: Mario Del Monaco (Andrea Chénier), Maria Callas (Maddalena)

OPERA IN FOUR ACTS by Umberto Giordano. Libretto in Italian by Luigi Illica. First produced at La Scala, Milan, March 28, 1896. First American performance at the New York Academy of Music, November 13, 1896. First performance at the Metropolitan Opera House, March 7, 1921, with a cast headed by Claudia Muzio and Beniamino Gigli.

Giordano, flourishing during the Italian period of *verismo* (a form of naturalism), called his opera a *dramma di ambiente storico* (drama with historical setting). André de Chénier (1762–1794), a gifted poet of French-Greek descent who combined classic breadth and Romantic fervor in his work, was executed in the years of terror and intrigue following the French Revolution. Before going to his death he wrote a last poem in prison. Illica, with a librettist's license, naturally romanticized the poet's career, making shrewd use of Chénier's prison poem, and creating a drama of personal conflict that ends in a typical operatic situation: the lovers are reunited in death at the guillotine. Dramatic arias, fervid declamation, and the unusual setting of a revolutionary upheaval have combined to make *Andrea Chénier* Giordano's best-known opera. None of his other subsequent operas, among them *Fedora, Madame Sans-Gêne,* and *La Cena delle Beffe,* has rivaled it in popular appeal.

44

Act I of the 1953 Metropolitan Opera revival: Fléville (George Cehanovsky) introduces the shepherd's pastoral

ACT I

SCENE: *The ballroom of the château di Coigny.* Preparations are being made for a ball. Gérard, a servant, bitter at the sight of his aged and ailing father, bewails the lot of the poor and denounces the wasteful rich. Impatiently he awaits the outbreak of revolution in France, partly because he is secretly in love with the Countess' daughter Maddalena, who herself longs for freedom—freedom from a life of dull aristocratic routine. When the guests have finally gathered, a court pastoral with idealized shepherds and shepherdesses is enacted. Music suggesting the countryside is sung, and a ballet pantomime is staged in the stately style of an eighteenth-century idyl. Among the guests is the poet-patriot Andrea Chénier, famous for his gifts of poetic improvisation. The Countess urges Chénier to improvise on some theme of his own choosing. Chénier at first refuses, but yields when Maddalena coquettishly cajoles him, even venturing a suggestion: "Let Chénier improvise on the subject of love." The poet begins, but soon he reverts to the grave theme of oppression. The song—"*Un dì all' azzuro spazio*" ("Once o'er the azure fields")—becomes an impromptu tirade against tyranny and a burning plea for the relief of the poor. Bitterly, Chénier flails the pride and apathy of the rich, the wrongs inflicted on the subject classes.

A chorus of indignation greets the fiery idealism of Chénier's *Improviso.* Only Maddalena, drawn by the poet's zeal, is stirred by this new creed. To bring back the festive mood, the Countess commands the musicians to play dance music. Suddenly a clamor is heard outside the ballroom. The door flies open, and a band of ragged men and women burst in, led by Gérard. The intruders are ejected, and Chénier follows them.

ACT II

SCENE: *The Café Hottot in Paris.* The Revolution an accomplished fact, Chénier has now come under suspicion for opposing Robespierre. Spies have been ordered to watch him, and Roucher has come to warn his friend to flee before it is too late. Bersi, Maddalena's maid, has meanwhile been conversing at a nearby table with a spy. There is an ominous moment as a death cart rolls by on its way to the guillotine. Bersi has handed Chénier a letter from a mysterious unknown, pleading for help and a rendezvous. Chénier refuses to heed his friend's warning and awaits the stranger. The lady, of course, is Maddalena. They declare their love for each other and prepare to flee together. Word, however, has reached Gérard, now a revolutionary functionary, of the rendezvous. Gérard bursts in on the love scene and attempts to seize the girl. As the rivals draw swords, Roucher hurries Maddalena away. Gérard is wounded and nobly exhorts Chénier to save himself and Maddalena from their enemies. When Gérard's friends arrive, they demand the name of the assailant. Gérard pretends not to have recognized him.

ACT III

SCENE: *The revolutionary tribunal.* Recovered from his wound, Gérard now appears before a revolutionary tribunal with a fervent plea for money for France. A collection is taken up, and jewels are contributed by the women. Madelon, an old woman, steps forward and volunteers her grandson to the defense of France against her enemies. Amid the mounting mood of patriotism the crowd sings, *"La Carmagnole."* A spy enters to report Chénier's arrest to Gérard, who thus has a chance to dispose of a rival and win Maddalena for himself. Yet, as he prepares the official denunciation of Chénier, Gérard hesitates. He recalls the poet's stirring verses, his espousal of the cause of the poor, his flaming nobility. This man an "enemy of his country"? (*"Nemico della patria"*), he asks himself sardonically. Can he sacrifice a friend to satisfy his passion for Maddalena? Gérard broods over the problem in music throbbing with the conflict of honor and desire. Almost cynically the orchestra chants a fragment of *"La Marseillaise."* Finally Gérard yields and signs the fatal document. At this moment Maddalena appears. She learns of Chénier's arrest and in a touching aria—*"La mamma morta"*—she tells of her mother's death and offers herself to Gérard in exchange for Chénier's freedom.

The girl's entreaties having won Gérard over, he vows to help the man she loves. As the trial proceeds, the crowd grows increasingly excited over the charges made against Chénier. There are loud cries of "Death to the traitor!" and against this surging wrath, the poet's own defense is of no avail. Even Gérard's eloquent plea that the charges are false proves futile. Gérard embraces the doomed poet, who is dragged away to the crowd's cries of *"À la lanterne!"* ("To the scaffold!").

ACT IV

SCENE: *The prison of Saint-Lazare.* It is midnight in the gloomy cell. Chénier, awaiting execution, is writing his last poem, *"Come un bel dì di Maggio"* ("As some soft day in May"). As he sings, the poet's firm belief in truth and beauty seems to mock the prison walls. Roucher listens attentively to his friend's farewell verses. Maddalena and Gérard now appear. Preferring death with her lover to life without him, she has bribed the jailer to substitute her name for that of another woman. Exultantly the lovers depart when summoned for the death cart.

Act III courtroom scene at the Metropolitan Opera with Andrea Chénier (Franco Corelli) defending the meaning of his poetry

Arabella

CHARACTERS

Count Waldner, *a retired officer*	Bass	Matteo, *an army officer*	*Tenor*
Countess Adelaide Waldner, *his wife*	*Mezzo-soprano*	Count Elemer, *suitor of Arabella*	*Tenor*
Arabella, *their elder daughter*	*Soprano*	Count Dominik, *suitor of Arabella*	*Baritone*
Zdenka, *their younger daughter*	*Soprano*	Count Lamoral, *suitor of Arabella*	*Bass*
Mandryka, *a landowner from Slavonia*	*Baritone*	The "Fiakermilli," *a cabaret entertainer*	*Soprano*
		A Fortuneteller	*Soprano*

Servants, Three Gamblers, Guests, etc.

The action takes place in Vienna in 1860.

OPERA IN THREE ACTS. Music by Richard Strauss. Libretto in German by Hugo von Hofmannsthal. First performance, Dresden Opera House, July 1, 1933, with Viorica Ursuleac, Alfred Jerger and Margit Bokor, Clemens Krauss conducting. First American performance, given in an English translation by John Gutman, Metropolitan Opera House, New York, February 10, 1955, with Eleanor Steber, George London, and Hilde Gueden, Rudolf Kempe conducting.

Arabella was the last opera for which the libretto was supplied by the distinguished playwright-poet Hugo von Hofmannsthal. After many composer-demanded revisions—especially in Act I—the librettist sent Strauss what turned out to be the final version. FIRST ACT EXCELLENT. HEARTFELT THANKS AND CONGRATULATIONS, wired the composer from Garmisch to Vienna. But von Hofmannsthal never saw the wire. It lay on his desk on the morning of the funeral of his son, who had committed suicide two days before. As the poet bent over to reach for his hat, he suffered a stroke from which he died within a few hours without recovering consciousness. Although Strauss in truth was not completely satisfied with every detail of what von Hofmannsthal had sent him, he made no emendations, in honor of the friend who had worked so well with him on *Elektra, Der Rosenkavalier, Ariadne auf Naxos, Die Frau ohne Schatten* and other operas.

The nature of the work stems from a suggestion of Strauss's that the two men collaborate once more on a comedy more or less in the vein of the highly successful *Der Rosenkavalier.* The story itself is based on a tale written by von Hofmannsthal some years earlier entitled "Lucidor," although the finished libretto is very different from the tale. The comparison with *Der Rosenkavalier* is inescapable. Both stories take place in Vienna (though approximately a hundred years apart); both center around the engagements and marriages among titled folk, however vulgar some of them may be shown to be; both involve secondary plots depending on mistaken identity due to the presence of a girl dressed up as a boy; both make much of Viennese waltz time—and so forth. But the differences are even greater, the chief of them being that in 1929 to 1932 (the period during which Strauss worked on the score) the composer, while just as skillful as he had been thirty years earlier, was less fresh, less inspired. There is much that is fresh and fine in *Arabella* but also much that strikes most critics as second and even third-drawer Strauss—that is, competent but rou-

Lisa Della Casa in title role of Strauss's Arabella

tine. It was successful at its première and even more successful later in the year, when the great Lotte Lehmann sang the leading role in Vienna. Today it still is often given in Germany; but it took over twenty years to reach America and then, despite a splendid production in English, failed to catch on. Three subsequent revivals at the Metropolitan starring Lisa Della Casa have fared far better.

ACT I

SCENE: *The drawing room of Count Waldner's hotel suite in Vienna.* Countess Adelaide Waldner is having one of her weekly sessions with a gifted fortuneteller, who not only plays on her client's easily aroused emotions when discussing the family's problems, but does some uncannily accurate predicting. We learn during the course of the session (carried on mostly in recitative) that the Count has lost so much money that he can scarcely pay his bills, that he is even at this moment losing at cards, that the family is now in Vienna hoping that the beautiful elder daughter will make a rich marriage very quickly, and that a younger daughter, Zdenka, is disguised as a boy, and accordingly called Zdenko, for their present impecuniosity does not permit the support and outfitting of two nubile daughters. Zdenka is, indeed, in the room, quietly moaning over the ever-increasing pile of bills and, with polite lies, putting off dunners who present still more. Finally, the fortuneteller sees in the cards not only a wealthy "fiancé" ("Count Elemer, certainly," says Adelaide) but also one who will interfere—the proverbial tall, dark, and handsome stranger. So excited is the Countess that she rises and asks the fortuneteller to continue in her own room.

Matteo, a lieutenant in the Italian army and one of Arabella's four suitors, now calls and, finding his love "out for a walk," complains of her cold behavior to him even though, it is true, he did have a warm letter from her a few days ago. Before he leaves, he has threatened suicide if he cannot win the girl. Zdenka is appalled, for she is secretly in love with Matteo, and it was she herself who had forged the letter from Arabella. She is perfectly willing to sacrifice herself for the man she loves, even to the extent of remaining a boy forever.

When Arabella returns from her walk, there is a long and beautiful duet between the two sisters, who are genuinely devoted to each other and utterly frank, excepting where it concerns Zdenka's feelings for Matteo. Arabella admits that she is attracted by many men but that she always knows very quickly that each is not "the right man." That is how she feels about all these suitors—Matteo and the Counts Elemer, Dominik, and Lamoral. Maybe it will be different if she meets that tall stranger she saw looking at her in the street. Anyway, she must make up her mind tonight, when she is to be at the coachmen's ball, a great event that marks the end of the carnival season. Maybe Elemer . . . But Zdenka urges that it should be Matteo, or he will commit suicide. Arabella begins to understand her sister, but their confidences are ended by the arrival of Count Elemer in a jovial mood, for he and the other Counts have drawn lots, and it is his privilege to invite her for a sleigh ride now and to accompany her to the coachmen's ball tonight. Flirtatiously, Arabella tells him that Zdenka must come along on the ride and that they will shortly be ready. Before she leaves to dress, she notices from the window the "earnest-eyed" stranger standing outside.

Not long after, the tall, dark, earnest-eyed stranger is announced by a servant as "Mandryka," whom Waldner takes to be an elderly ex-fellow-in-arms to whom he had written suggesting that he needed help. But the stranger turns out to be the nephew of the recently deceased wealthy Slavonian and his only heir. Waldner had enclosed a picture of Arabella, and the present Mandryka fell so desperately in love with it that he sold off a whole forest (only a small portion, however, of his extensive holdings) to raise the money for an expensive trip to Vienna in the hope of winning the girl. Here, he says, taking out his wallet and offering it to Waldner, is that forest. Won't the Count help himself? Waldner gets not only one but two thousand-gulden notes and assures Mandryka that Arabella is not engaged, and wouldn't he like to meet his wife and daughter right now? Horrified, the formal gentleman from the country says he would much prefer to be invited to call this afternoon or evening at the ladies' convenience.

Zdenka thinks her father out of his mind with worries when she finds him waltzing out of the room with two bank notes in his hand; and when Matteo returns to ask whether Arabella has not left a note for him, she assures him that he will have it that evening at the coachmen's ball. When he has left, and while Zdenka is dressing, Arabella muses on her various suitors, wonders about the stranger, and finishes her aria brilliantly anticipating becoming the queen of the coachmen's ball. The two sisters leave for their coach ride as the curtain descends.

ACT II

SCENE: *A large public ballroom.* At the foot of the grand staircase Mandryka is finally introduced to Arabella by her father, and for both of them it is a stunning moment. But left together they soon find their tongues; and—between interruptions as she waves off the three Counts who ask her to dance—he tells her of his brief first marriage, of how he wishes her to rule his domain on the Danube with him; while she, beginning rather flirtatiously by asking how such a serious gentleman can come to such a ball and how he happened to see a picture of her in faraway Slavonia, ends up by acknowledging her love for him and promising to live and to die with him. He tells her, too, that on the night of a betrothal in Slavonia, a girl would offer her beloved one glass of clear water to acknowledge her giving herself to him. But now, says Arabella, she must be allowed one hour for dancing and saying good-by to her girlhood.

The waltz music strikes up, dancers come in from every side, and a pretty professional entertainer, the darling of the coachmen, known as the "Fiakermilli," presents a bouquet to Arabella. In a brilliant coloratura aria she announces that Arabella has been elected queen of the ball, and Arabella joins the waltzers. In a complicated scene, in which much goes on at once, Mandryka shares his good news first with the Countess and then with Count Waldner; Matteo again complains to Zdenka about Arabella's neglect of him; Waldner goes back to his gambling; and Mandryka orders tables to be brought in, champagne for everybody, and all the flowers in Vienna to be bought for Arabella to dance on.

While preparations are being made, Arabella bids a final good-by to each of her three Counts—first to Dominik, with whom she has been dancing and who walks away sadly; then to Elemer, who takes his medicine with less grace and suspects it is the stranger who has displaced him; and finally to Lamoral, whom she has always regarded as a mere boy and who is happy to receive a farewell kiss from Arabella—his first and last—and also a farewell

waltz. Matteo, in a suicidal mood, is now stopped by Zdenka, who assures him that Arabella, though apparently not noticing him, has been thinking of him all the time. To prove this she produces an envelope with a key in it—the key, she says, to Arabella's room, or rather the one next to it. She delivers this with the message that Matteo is to be there in a quarter of an hour, and then she who sends the key shall do everything he could want to make him happy. Zdenka is, of course, dissembling, for the key is to her own room; but Mandryka, who overhears the conversation, can scarcely believe his ears. Could there be another Arabella at the dance? Yet Arabella seems already to have left; and when the Fiakermilli asks him not to keep the girl entirely to himself, he bursts into a fury; and when his servant delivers him a tender note from Arabella wishing him a good night, he scornfully reads it aloud, noting that it must have been written in haste as it is signed only with a small "a." Now he whoops it up, drinking champagne, singing a drinking song with the Fiakermilli, jumping on the table, and—shouting now—asks the going Viennese rates for a key to the room of a countess. This sobers everyone, and Arabella's parents finally prevail on Mandryka to walk to the hotel to find the missing girl. "An honor," says Mandryka sarcastically—and drunkenly invites the rest to have a good time.

ACT III

SCENE: *The lobby of Waldner's hotel.* After a fairly long prelude (the only act to have one), Matteo is

George London as Arabella's wealthy suitor, Mandryka

seen *en déshabille* on the balcony, but he disappears when the entrance bell rings. It is Arabella, who comes in alone from the ball, as if in a dream of happiness, and she sings of her joyful future. Matteo, returning fully clothed, is astounded to see her there, for he is still under the impression that he has been making love to her upstairs. For her part, she cannot understand his protestations that he has, only minutes before, promised to leave her alone hereafter and all he now wishes is to see her eyes once more, which he had been unable to do in the dark. Before the truth can emerge, the elder Waldners (accompanied by three card playing cronies of the Count's) and Mandryka (accompanied by servants) arrive, and Mandryka at once recognizes Matteo as "that damned fellow with the key." His conclusions are reasonable enough, especially when Matteo gallantly, but without conviction, denies any wrongdoing. The ineffectual Waldner calls for his pistols (they have been sold); Arabella in vain tries to reassure Mandryka; Mandryka, with scorn, offers the happy couple financial help, and orders his servants to find a couple of sabers to duel with Matteo. With everyone at complete loggerheads, Zdenka, now in negligee and with her hair streaming behind her, rushes down the stairs and begs her father's forgiveness. By this time other hotel guests have come out from their rooms, wondering what is going on, while the three gamblers say, "Oho! Oho!" (the only lines they have in the whole opera). But everyone else realizes the truth of the situation; and as Zdenka miserably protests that she was planning to drown herself, Arabella takes her in her arms and comforts

Hilde Gueden as the boy Zdenko, really the girl Zdenka

her. The reactions of everyone are quite in character. The young lieutenant decides that it must have been Zdenka whom he loved all along and proposes marriage. Waldner and his wife are delighted; he blesses the couple and then invites his cronies into another room to continue gambling. Mandryka offers the young couple financial assistance but is heartbroken, for he is convinced that his lack of faith has cost him Arabella. As for the curious guests—their curiosity has been satisfied, and they retire.

Left alone at last, Arabella offers Mandryka a glass of clear water that she has ordered. It is a symbol that they are engaged, and after he has drunk it, he smashes it. Ecstatically, they fall into each other's arms; Arabella then rushes upstairs as Mandryka looks longingly after her.

Act III of Arabella, *the hotel, as given at the Royal Opera House, London, with Lisa Della Casa and Dietrich Fischer-Dieskau (r.)*

Ariadne auf Naxos

CHARACTERS IN THE PROLOGUE

The Major-Domo	*Speaking role*	The Dancing Master	*Tenor*
Music Master	*Baritone*	The Wigmaker	*Bass*
The Composer	*Soprano*	A Lackey	*Bass*
The Tenor (*Bacchus in the opera*)	*Tenor*	The Prima Donna (*Ariadne in the Opera*)	*Soprano*
An Officer	*Tenor*	Zerbinetta	*Soprano*

CHARACTERS IN THE OPERA

Ariadne		*Soprano*	Arlecchino	*Baritone*
Bacchus		*Tenor*	Zerbinetta	*Soprano*
Naiad		*Soprano*	Scaramuccio	*Tenor*
Dryad	*Nymphs*	*Contralto*	Truffaldino	*Bass*
Echo		*Soprano*	Brighella	*Tenor*

The action takes place in Vienna in the eighteenth century.

OPERA IN PROLOGUE and one act. Music by Richard Strauss. Libretto in German by Hugo von Hofmannsthal. Première of original version at Stuttgart, October 25, 1912, with Maria Jeritza in the title role and the composer conducting. First performance of revised version at Vienna, October 4, 1916. In this performance, also starring Jeritza, Lotte Lehmann substituted for a better-known soprano in the role of the Composer and became famous virtually overnight. Later in her career Lehmann often appeared as Ariadne. First American performance at the Academy of Music in Philadelphia, November 1, 1928. In this performance, by the Civic Opera Company, the roles of the Wigmaker and Harlequin were taken, before he became a motion picture star and one of America's leading recitalists, by Nelson Eddy. First performance by the Metropolitan Opera, December 29, 1962.

When the rehearsals of *Der Rosenkavalier* were not going very well, the great stage director Max Reinhardt stepped in imaginatively and was accorded credit for rescuing what turned out to be the greatest success Strauss and Hofmannsthal ever had. As a thank-offering, the composer and librettist then prepared for Reinhardt a greatly cut version of Molière's *Le Bourgeois Gentilhomme*, complete with incidental music and a one-act opera, *Ariadne auf Naxos*, that was supposed to be the entertainment given in the play by Monsieur Jourdain. In this form it was a *succès d'estime* at its première and in a number of productions in various cities of Europe. But the combination of eighteenth-century French comedy with an opera half classical, half *commedia dell' arte* in plot and almost all post-Wagnerian in music never seemed to jell entirely satisfactorily and was very expensive to put on. So a few years later Molière was jettisoned and the librettist and composer supplied a fresh and charming prologue and somewhat simplified the original score of the opera. This is the version always given today, even though Sir Thomas Beecham, who introduced the original to London, characteristically maintained that the improvements were not improvements at all.

The incidental music for *Le Bourgeois Gentil-*

Theodor Uppman (Harlequin), Gianna d'Angelo (Zerbinetta)

homme, for which no place could be found in the revised version, is often played as a suite—one written for thirty-nine virtuosi.

PROLOGUE

SCENE: *Large room in the home of a wealthy Viennese with part of a stage visible at the rear.* When the curtain rises after the Prelude, we see many participants preparing for an entertainment to be given in the evening for the guests of the owner of the house. The wealthy man's pompous Major-Domo enters almost at once and condescendingly confirms the Music Master's impression that the opera commissioned for the occasion will be followed by clowns performing comedy in the outmoded *commedia dell' arte* manner, and he adds, when the Music Master protests, that both performances must be over by nine o'clock, for that is when the fireworks are scheduled. The Music Master cannot bear to inform his protégé, the young Composer, of such desecration, but he is temporarily saved from the embarrassment because the Composer has other things on his mind. He wishes to rehearse once more with the fiddles (but they're playing for the diners, he is told by a supercilious lackey); he thinks of a fine new melody and writes it down (but when he tries to give it to the Tenor, he finds him in an argument with the Wigmaker); he wishes to consult with the Prima Donna (but finds her engaged with her hairdresser). Then he catches sight of Zerbinetta *en déshabillé,* the leader of the comedy troupe, and is at once attracted. But the Music Master lowers his spirits once more by telling him of the insult to his art that is being planned—only to hear still worse. For the Major-Domo enters once more and announces that the plays are not to follow each other after all. No—

his master has given instructions that they are to be done simultaneously. Everyone is struck with consternation. How is this to be done? That, says the Major-Domo, is up to the talented performers—and he huffs out.

The Dancing Master, however, sees no real difficulties. His comedy troupe can improvise their parts. All they need to know is the plot—which the Music Master gives Zerbinetta, who relays it to the rest of the troupe. All that will be necessary is to have the Composer cut out a few arias so as to meet the nine o'clock time limit. The Composer's despair is considerably alleviated by the attentions of Zerbinetta, who, with a few words of wisdom—mostly about herself and how she is a much more serious person than she appears on the surface—completely wins the Composer's heart.

But it is time now for the show to begin. The Music Master summons everyone; the Composer sings an inspired hymn to music. And it is only when he sees the vulgar company of comedians preparing to ruin his opera that despair descends on him again. He runs off—and the curtain comes down.

THE OPERA

SCENE: *A desert island with a grotto; the sea in the background.* After the Overture—largely an orchestral version of the lament of Ariadne, which is to follow—we see Ariadne lying in the grotto, watched over by three so-called elementary beings—Naiad, Dryad, and Echo. Ariadne, as in the Greek myth, has been deserted by Theseus on the island. In her lament she longs for death, and it is the function of the comedians, according to the compromise worked out in the Prologue, to try—in vain—to cheer her. In the middle of Ariadne's monologue Arlecchino tries first with an encouraging little song. At the end

Sena Jurinac as the Composer in Ariadne's *Prologue*

Ariadne (Leonie Rysanek) is revived by Bacchus (Jess Thomas) in the finale, as seen at the Metropolitan Opera

of the lament, the whole company of comedians tries, with a quintet led by Zerbinetta, during which they all dance. Ariadne does not even notice them.

Then Zerbinetta tries going it alone and sings the showpiece of the opera, doubtless the most elaborate and difficult coloratura piece ever written. In it she preaches her philosophy of love. That is, quite contrary to Ariadne's belief in being faithful unto death, that even while a girl is in love with one man, she feels an attraction for the inevitable next. However much impressed the audience may be, Ariadne is not. She retires to her grotto in the middle of the aria. So a second song-and-dance act is staged by the comedians, who this time act out a little drama illustrative of Zerbinetta's pyrotechnical sermon. She flirts with one after the other of the four men, finally disappearing with Arlecchino and leaving the other three to search for her.

With the stage empty, the three Dryads enter in great excitement, for they have seen a god approach-ing from the waters. It is Bacchus, and Echo tells how he has recently escaped from the snares of Circe. Off stage, Bacchus' voice is heard calling, and Ariadne comes from her grotto. When Bacchus enters, for a moment she thinks he is Theseus come back, but then thinks she recognizes him as the god of death. Ecstatically she welcomes the release that she has longed for. As for Bacchus, he falls immediately in love with Ariadne and sings passionately to her. In this long, essentially Wagnerian, duet she finally succumbs to him. The lovers and the island seem to disappear, but Zerbinetta sticks her head out of the wings to sum it all up as it looks to her:

> *Once a new god comes along,*
> *We are conquered—and dumb.*

And as if to verify her last word (*slumm*), the opera closes with the now invisible Bacchus singing ecstatically without a word coming from Ariadne.

The Ballad of Baby Doe

CHARACTERS

Mrs. Elizabeth (Baby) Doe, *the heroine* — Soprano

Horace A. W. Tabor, *the hero* — Baritone

Augusta Tabor, *wife of Horace* — Mezzo-soprano

Samantha, *her maid* — Mezzo-soprano

Mama McCourt, *Baby Doe's mother* — Contralto

Father Chapelle, *a priest* — Tenor

Chester A. Arthur, President of the U. S. — Tenor

William Jennings Bryan, *Democratic candidate* — Bass

Silver Dollar, *Tabor's grown-up daughter* — Mezzo-soprano

Miners and Miners' Wives, Servants at Various Establishments, Guests at Various Parties, Cronies of Tabor, Augusta, and Baby, etc.

The action takes place from 1880 to 1899 in Colorado, Washington, D.C., and California.

OPERA IN TWO ACTS. Music by Douglas Moore. Libretto in English by John Latouche. Commissioned in honor of the Columbia University bicentennial (1954) by the Koussevitzky Foundation of the Library of Congress. Première July 7, 1956, at Central City, Colorado, by the Central City Opera Association. Entered the repertoire of the New York City Opera Company, April 3, 1958. On February 10, 1957, the opera was nationally televised by the CBS network, and since then it has had independent productions by more than a dozen opera companies across the country, including the Santa Fe Opera, which took its production to Berlin and Belgrade on a 1961 tour.

The opera exhibits far greater historical fidelity than do most historical librettos, in following the last twenty years of the career of Horace A. W. Tabor, who died in 1899, and of his second wife Elizabeth, who froze to death in 1935, the lone occupant of the long-deserted Matchless Mine. Her cabin there is still a minor tourist attraction.

The local color of the very colorful turn-of-the-century West is projected not merely through scenery and costumes but through the rhythms and idiom of both the words and the music. The rhythm of the waltz underlies many of the more sentimental moments, and folk-dance rhythms are employed as well. Most of the libretto is written in prose, and Professor Moore (he was head of Columbia University's music department when he composed the score) has shown great skill in projecting the various kinds of speech rhythms characteristic of the time and place, whether that speech be women's gossip, men playing poker, a wife nagging a husband, political oratory, or even serious discussion of commerce. It must have been quite a challenge to set a line like "England, France and Germany are all erecting retaliation barriers so that they discriminate against American raw products." Yet Professor Moore set it for a male quartet with as much ease— and in canon form, too—as he did the final conventional quatrain with its silver-threads-among-the-gold sentiment:

> *As our earthly eyes grow dim,*
> *Still the old song will be sung.*
> *I shall change along with him*
> *So that both are very young.*

ACT I

SCENE 1: *Outside the Tabor Opera House in Lead-ville, Colorado, 1880.* A drunk is thrown out in the street from a saloon, and before being shoved off by the bouncer and some of the girls from the saloon, he boasts that Horace Tabor wants to buy his Matchless Mine. Tabor, who is mayor of Leadville and a tough old man in his fifties, emerges from the opera house with four cronies. They have left the performance because a string quartet is playing, and in the high-spirited chorus and dance that follow, it is made clear that Tabor, who owns most of the town, is a hail-fellow-well-met and that he has built the opera house only because his wife Augusta, who runs him as he runs the town, has demanded some culture for the place. She, along with some other ladies, put an end to the carousing, Augusta delivering a lecture to Horace on proper behavior at such an occasion. The other men, equally under the thumbs of their wives, return to the concert to hear Adelina Patti sing, but Tabor lingers behind.

Now the romantic interest enters, and the music is in waltz time to the end of the scene. Baby Doe has just arrived in town from Central City, and she quietly asks Tabor for directions to the Clarendon Hotel. He is immediately smitten by her prettiness and gives her the directions politely, along with his name and a welcome to town. Then, when Augusta summons him, he goes back into the opera house.

SCENE 2: *Outside the Clarendon Hotel that evening.* The Tabors and their friends, returning from the concert, sing a little chorus about the charms of the music ("Like as if the muses had've all de-scended"). All then go home, excepting Tabor, who sits before the hotel, which is where he lives, for a last cigar. Two girls pass making unpleasant remarks about Baby Doe, which is how Tabor learns her name. Through an open second-floor window he then sees Baby Doe playing the piano elegantly as she sings a sentimental ballad. He applauds, she comes to the window, and he sings to her in a way that makes it quite clear he is deeply smitten. She thrusts out her hand for him to kiss, but when Augusta calls, he obediently retires.

SCENE 3: *The Tabors' living room in the hotel.* Some weeks later, cleaning up Horace's desk, Augusta finds first a check made out to purchase the Matchless Mine, which dismays her, and then a pair of white gloves, which pleases her till her maid shows her a gift card with sentimental verses addressed to Baby Doe. This makes her truly angry, but when Tabor comes in, she attacks him first on his recklessness in buying yet another silver mine. He defends himself vigorously in an aria telling of his readiness to take chances, when following Augusta's advice would have kept them poor. But when Augusta brings out the evidence of the gloves, Tabor tactlessly and foolishly contrasts the youth and attractions of his new-found love with the middle-aged severity of his wife. Now driven to a cold fury, Augusta dons a hat and shawl and departs on her announced mission—to "drive that woman out of town."

SCENE 4: *The lobby of the hotel.* Apparently Augusta has done an effective job. Baby Doe comes

First scene of the New York City Opera production of Baby Doe, with Walter Cassel as silver king Horace Tabor

Tabor's wife, Augusta, as played by Frances Bible

down the stairs with all her luggage, asks the bellhop to find out when the next train for Denver leaves, and sits down to write her mother a letter. As she writes, she sings the contents, which tell her mother that everything is over between herself and her husband Harvey Doe but that she must leave Leadville, where she has come since parting with him, because though she has ·found the right lover, he is married, and it would be wrong for her to interfere. Augusta finds her at the writing table and begins to tell her firmly she had better give up Horace. Much to her surprise, Baby Doe quite agrees, says that she is about to leave, and then sings an aria saying what a wonderful and unusual man Horace is. Unwisely, Augusta corrects her. Horace, she says, is a baby who needs a good managing type of woman like herself to look after him. Then, with polite goodbys, she leaves. Baby has been shocked by what she sees is in store for the man she thinks deserves much better. She tears up her letter, throws herself into Tabor's arms when he comes in, and vows she will never leave him. The scene ends with a love duet and the couple climbing the stairs together.

SCENE 5: *A room in Augusta's house in Denver.* Tabor has left his wife and is now keeping Baby Doe in a hotel. A group of Augusta's friends try to persuade her to tell the story to the newspapers and thus create a scandal that will frustrate Tabor's political ambitions. She steadily refuses until they tell her of the rumor that Tabor is secretly divorcing her in another county where he has a judge under his control. Then Augusta swears vengeance.

SCENE 6: *A large reception hall at the Willard Hotel in Washington, D.C., 1883.* Tabor has divorced

Augusta, been appointed U.S. Senator to fill a vacancy, and become something of a useful figure in the Republican party. He has just been married to Baby Doe, and Mrs. McCourt, the bride's mother, is proudly and fussily presiding over the wedding reception, at which there is a lot of political talk before the newlyweds arrive. There is also gossip about the prevalence of males at the reception: numerous wives have refused to attend because of Baby Doe's reputation. However, when Tabor and Baby arrive, the party takes on much more life, with Tabor acting the hail-fellow-well-met politician and plying his guests with drinks. The subject of bimetallism comes up once more, and Baby charms everyone by giving, in an aria, a completely feminine and personal argument in favor of the unpopular silver. Thereupon Horace orders in his wedding gift to his bride, which turns out to be the set of jewels Queen Isabella pawned to finance the discovery of America—or so the jeweler had told Tabor. Enchanted, Mrs. McCourt tells Father Chapelle, who had officiated at the wedding, that she wishes Harvey Doe could be there. And who is Harvey Doe? Why, Baby's first husband, whom Lizzie had divorced. The priest is appalled: he had never heard that Baby Doe was a divorcée. Others are shocked, too, and the party is about to break up disastrously when it is saved by the entrance of President Chester Arthur. He proposes a toast, and everyone drinks the health of the bride and groom.

ACT II

SCENE 1: *Balcony off the ballroom of the Windsor Hotel, Denver, 1893.* The Governor of Colorado is giving a ball in honor of Horace Tabor, and a quartet of Augusta's old friends are angrily discussing his second wife's pretensions and character. Their husbands can't quite agree, and when Mrs. McCourt and Baby come out, the ladies turn their backs on them and take their reluctant husbands off. Baby, in another aria, explains to her mother that this sort of reception bothers her not a bit. Those women are simply jealous, and in the ten years now of her married life to Horace, her love for and appreciation of that sterling character have always deepened.

Quite unexpectedly Augusta is announced, and Mama McCourt rushes off to find Horace. But Augusta has come in friendship. She tells Baby how much she admires her dangerous ability to give love wholeheartedly, unquestioningly, as she herself had never been able to do. But her real reason for coming has been to warn Baby that Horace is overstretched financially and he must be convinced to stop backing silver before he is completely ruined. Horace arrives and starts to berate Augusta for coming at all, but the older woman is defended by the younger. Augusta then leaves and Baby hints at what she has learned. Horace admits to some setbacks but promises that silver will come back. Does she believe him, will she gamble with him? For answer, Baby Doe removes her necklace and tells Horace to "place my bet on silver along with yours." The scene closes as she promises him, no matter what happens, always to hang on to the Matchless Mine.

SCENE 2: *A gambling table.* Four cronies of Tabor's are playing poker (all that is seen on the stage is the table and the men seated around it), deriding Tabor's ambition to be elected governor, and commenting on how he has asked some of them for help in backing silver. When Tabor joins them, he is cordially greeted, but when he shows symbolically, by pushing out large stacks of chips, how he is backing his Matchless Mine by selling hotels, shops, and railway stock and asks them to come in, too, they give excuses. And when he brings up the subject of William Jennings Bryan, the great prophet of silver and perenniel Democratic candidate for the presidency, they turn on him. Republicans can't back a Democrat, they say—and they leave him alone. The scene ends with a soliloquy by Tabor vigorously expressing his contempt for such cowards.

SCENE 3: *A pro-Bryan political rally outside the Matchless Mine, 1896.* The crowd is already gathered, among them Baby Doe with Tabor's two little girls, the elder of whom prattles away about Daddy's being an even greater man than Bryan. Tabor addresses the crowd, which responds strongly, making reference to Bryan's famous "Cross of Gold" speech. Then Bryan comes on the platform and is greeted with tumultuous cheers. He delivers a typical campaign speech, with religious and moralistic overtones, and in the midst of it takes up the younger Tabor child in his arms when she presents him with a bouquet of roses. The speech ended, the crowd forms a procession and sings a victory march.

SCENE 4: *A room in Augusta's home in California.* Through the window Augusta hears the newsboys shouting the headlines of Bryan's defeat in a landslide by McKinley. She is visibly shaken, when Mama McCourt is announced. Baby's mother has come to plead with Augusta to give some financial help to Tabor, who is now ruined. Augusta refuses, gently but firmly, and Mama leaves, muttering about its being Tabor's own dollars that are being withheld. Then, in a long soliloquy, Augusta recalls her old love for her former husband and she deeply

Baby Doe Tabor (Beverly Sills) at her wedding to Horace

regrets that now it is impossible for her to go back to him once more, bringing help.

SCENE 5: *The stage of the Tabor Grand Opera House, Leadville, 1899.* A poorly dressed and much older Tabor stands on the stage and is about to be turned out by the doorman, when he identifies himself. A pompous political figure appears in a spotlight, seen only by Tabor, and presents him with a complimentary gold watch. Tabor speaks to him, and the doorman, thinking him mad, goes off to fetch assistance. Then the figure of a woman appears in the spotlight, whom Tabor takes to be his mother and who scolds him as she might have done when he was a boy. But as he approaches her, she throws back her bonnet, and it turns out to be the young Augusta, in the days of their courtship. Their wooing commences, and then they are joined by friends of hers and by miners, and the whole history of Horace's rise is recalled. But Augusta, now older once more, warns that he will die and be forgotten; and we get a look into the future when the figure of a prostitute between two customers sings a vulgar ragtime tune. The prostitute turns out to be Tabor's younger daughter, who was christened "Silver Dollar." Desperately, Horace cries, "Ain't there something, someone . . . that I can hold on to?" It is then that the figures disappear and the real Baby Doe comes on, summoned by the doorman. She has come to take him home, and as she sings comfortingly to him, he sinks to the floor, and she puts her cloak over him. During her final aria, as she sings of her unending love, she changes into an old woman. The stage of the theater is transformed into a bright view of the Matchless Mine, before which she sings the final ecstatic stanzas as snow slowly begins to fall.

The Barber of Seville

IL BARBIERE DI SIVIGLIA

CHARACTERS

Count Almaviva	*Tenor*	Basilio, *a music teacher*	*Bass*
Bartolo, *a physician*	*Bass*	Figaro, *a barber*	*Baritone*
Rosina, *his ward* *Mezzo-soprano or Soprano*		Berta, *a maid*	*Mezzo-soprano*
Fiorello, *the Count's servant*	*Baritone*		

The action takes place at Seville during the seventeenth century.

COMIC OPERA in two acts. Music by Gioacchino Rossini. Libretto in Italian by Cesare Sterbini, after Beaumarchais' comedy. Première at the Teatro Argentina, Rome, February 20, 1816; first New York performance (in English), Park Theater, May 3, 1819; New York première, in Italian, given during Manuel García's initial American season, Park Theater, November 29, 1825. First Metropolitan Opera performance, November 23, 1883.

The Barber of Seville was a failure at its first performance, the reasons ascribed to that being many and varied. Chief of these, however, was that Rossini had dared to compose an opera on a subject that had been successfully treated by the esteemed Paisiello ten years before Rossini was born. It is because of this, in fact, that *The Barber* was first produced under the title *Almaviva, ossia L'inutile Precauzione* (*Almaviva,* or *The Useless Precaution*). Another reason for the failure was the singing by García (as Almaviva) of a serenade of his own composing, which, as he tuned his guitar on the stage, earned gales of laughter. On the second night Rossini's charming serenade *"Ecco ridente"* replaced it, and the public received this and the whole opera with respect and enthusiasm.

The story is told of Rossini's imperturbable calm as his work, on opening night, was experiencing hisses, catcalls, and sneering shouts. He sat quietly at the piano, apparently unconcerned by it all, and when the performance was ended, he went home and to bed, where a singer, come to console him, found him fast asleep!

THE OPERA is preceded by a gay and sprightly overture, although it is not the one heard at the première. It is supposed that the overture used then was an original one based on Spanish themes. The Overture heard in our time stems from a previous opera of Rossini's, *Elisabetta, Regina d'Inghilterra,* and it had served also as curtain raiser for Rossini's *L'Equivoco Stravagante* and *Aureliano in Palmira.*

ACT I

SCENE 1: *A street in Seville.* The young and handsome Count Almaviva is deeply in love with Rosina, the ward of the mean and suspicious old Dr. Bartolo. In the gray light of dawn he comes with a band of musicians to serenade his beloved. The musicians play a ditty for her; then the Count himself sings to the accompaniment of their guitars, *"Ecco ridente in cielo"* ("Dawn with her rosy mantle").

He pays his musicians, evidently generously, for they are moved to express their gratitude with such enthusiasm that surely they must waken the sleeping Rosina, and he has considerable trouble ridding himself of them. He seems inclined to linger near his loved one's house, even though she does not come out to thank him for the charming song; and as someone else seems to be coming down the street toward the house, making a great deal of noise for such an early hour, Almaviva conceals himself to see who this might be. The newcomer is none other than Figaro, the barber of Seville. But besides being a barber, he is a sort of jack-of-all-trades, a so-called factotum, whose profession gives him entry to the homes of people of all stations; and thus he is a convenient instrument for the execution of the intrigues of young lovers as well as of old rogues. He displays his loquacious character and the happy life he leads, in the brilliant and exceedingly rapid aria *"Largo al factotum"* ("Room for the factotum").

The Count recognizes the barber, whom he has known before (as who in Seville has not?), and enlists him, with the promise of money, in the project of a meeting with Rosina, whom he has learned to love only from afar. Figaro is sure he can arrange it, but at that moment Rosina appears on the balcony, drops a note for her unknown serenader to pick up, and then is quickly ordered back by Dr. Bartolo. The Count is in rapture to find that the note is extremely cordial and asks the name of her unknown serenader. On the insistence of Figaro, he sings her a second serenade, *"Se il mio nome"* ("If my name you would know"), telling her he is called Lindoro and that he loves her. His reason for not revealing his real name, as he tells Figaro, is that he does not wish her to be influenced by the glamour of his rank.

The two plotters hide for a moment as Dr. Bartolo comes from his house. He gives strict orders to the servant that no one is to be admitted except the music master Basilio. The doctor hopes, with Basilio's aid, to arrange to marry Rosina this day, appreciating, as he does, the girl's dowry as much as the girl. After he disappears down the street, the Count and Figaro finish their plan. Troops are coming to the city, and Almaviva, disguised as a dragoon, must arrange to be billeted on the unwilling Bartolo. The scene ends with a jolly duet as the lover expresses his delight over the prospect of success while the barber expresses his over the prospect of being paid.

SCENE 2: *A room in Bartolo's house.* Rosina, reading a note from her Lindoro, is, naturally enough, rather agitated, and gives vent to her feelings in the delightful and brilliant coloratura aria *"Una voce poco fa"* ("A little voice I hear"). Almost every resource known to the coloratura singer's art must be called upon to render this glittering number.

When the highly spirited Rosina has run from the room, the guardian, Bartolo, enters with Basilio the music master, who is also a not inconsiderable master of intrigue himself. Bartolo is telling the music master that he wishes to marry Rosina himself— news doubtless already well known to Basilio, who informs him that the noble Almaviva has been haunting the neighborhood, and both immediately conclude that he is the mysterious serenader. Basilio suggests that they start some disgraceful rumor that will make Rosina reject the Count. He explains, in the broadly humorous aria *"La Calunnia"* ("Slander's Whisper"), that a calumny begins like a tempest howling through dreary forest caverns, until, its

Act I, Scene 2: Don Basilio (Cesare Siepi) advises Dr. Bartolo (Fernando Corena) to slander Count Almaviva

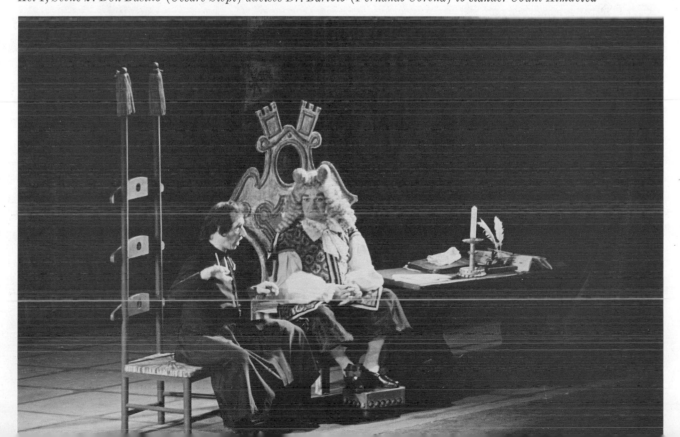

Giuseppe de Luca as Figaro

full fury gathered, it falls, a terrific lightning flash, on its helpless victim.

Rosina returns accompanied by Figaro, who tells her that her guardian plans to marry her himself. Laughing at the idea, she coyly inquires about the young man she has seen from the balcony. Figaro admits he is an excellent youth. Rosina is impatient to see him, and Figaro assures her that her lover awaits only a line from her, then he will come. She gives the letter—which she had already written.

When Figaro has left with the letter, Bartolo enters in hopes of finding out about the serenader of that morning. He suspects that Figaro may be carrying messages between his ward and this stranger. The girl's blushes and the ink marks on her fingers betray her; she answers that she has used the ink as a salve for a small cut. He calls attention to a freshly trimmed quill pen and a missing sheet of paper; she replies that she used the paper to wrap up some sweets for a girl friend and the pen to design a flower for her embroidery. The old man's rage and the girl's impertinent answers are characterized in the music of this scene, one of whose features is the aria *"A un dottor della mia sorte"* ("To a doctor of my standing"), in which Dr. Bartolo cautions his young ward to forgo matching wits with a doctor of his rank.

A loud knocking is heard at the door—the Count, in his soldier's guise, pretending to be drunk. The old doctor, suspicious of the disguise, indignantly resists the order for the quartering of soldiers and pretends to go off to hunt for a license he has that grants him exemption from such imposition. This gives the lovers a brief moment to exchange words, and Almaviva manages to slip a note to Rosina. There is a grand to-do of sly intrigue amid much excitement in a quintet involving Rosina, Berta, Bartolo, Almaviva, and Figaro. Soon soldiers summoned by Bartolo arrive, and they arrest this peace-disturbing intruder, but immediately release him when he secretly reveals his identity to the astonished officer.

ACT II

SCENE: *A room in Bartolo's house.* Though the soldier scheme has fallen through, Figaro soon invents another. As the curtain rises, we find the old doctor wondering if the drunken soldier may not be an emissary of Count Almaviva. He is interrupted by a stranger, none other than the Count himself pretending to be a Don Alonso, a music teacher. He explains that Don Basilio is ill, and that he has come in his place to give Rosina her music lesson. He makes his entrance in a greeting that is musically superb for its oiliness and polite sarcasm, *"Pace e gioia"* ("Peace and joy").

To allay the suspicions that begin to arise in Bartolo's mind, the Count, in a bold stroke, produces

Tito Schipa as the amorous young Count Almaviva

Salvatore Baccaloni as Bartolo

the note written by Rosina to her charming Lindoro. Asserting that he found it at the inn where Count Almaviva is staying, he offers to make Rosina believe she is the Count's dupe. The idea pleases Bartolo; in producing such a bit of slander, this strange music master has proved himself a worthy pupil of Don Basilio! Rosina enters for her lesson. (Rossini wrote at this place a song for mezzo-soprano, the original Rosina voice. But when Rosina became a coloratura soprano, it was not used. The artist singing the role of Rosina sometimes interpolates an air of her own choosing, a privilege which singers of the past once exercised to the point of extreme anachronism.)

Figaro arrives, declaring, in spite of Bartolo's remonstrance, that this is the day he must shave him. When Bartolo gives him his keys to go fetch some linen, Figaro steals the key to the balcony, saving it for future use. Don Basilio, the real music teacher, appears, and the Count, reminding Bartolo of their scheme to deceive Rosina, points out that the matrimonial agent-music teacher must be disposed of. Dr. Bartolo immediately asks the startled Basilio how he comes to be walking about in a fever. When the Count slips a purse in his hand, the wondering Basilio is convinced that they all want him to behave as if he were ill and diplomatically takes hasty leave. The lovers plot their elopment while Figaro detains Bartolo at shaving with generous splashes of soap in his eyes. Finally, the suspicious Bartolo approaches the preoccupied lovers and discovers that he is again being duped. The three conspirators laugh at him and run out, followed by the doctor, purple with rage.

Bartolo, driven to play his last card, shows Rosina the note, saying that her supposedly devoted Lin-

doro is conspiring to give her up to Count Almaviva. Justly infuriated, Rosina offers to marry Bartolo at once, reveals the plan to elope, and bids him have Lindoro and Figaro arrested when they arrive. As soon as he has gone to bring the police and the marriage broker, the Count and Figaro enter by means of the stolen key. Rosina greets them with a storm of reproaches, accusing Lindoro of pretending to love her in order to sacrifice her to the vile Count Almaviva. The Count, delighted that Rosina, unaware of his identity, should prefer a true though poor lover to a scheming nobleman, now reveals himself, and the lovers are soon embracing amid a shower of blessings from Figaro.

They are interrupted by Don Basilio, who has returned in the office of notary and marriage broker, to unite Rosina and Bartolo, but with the aid of a pistol he is persuaded to marry Rosina to the Count instead. When Dr. Bartolo arrives a few minutes later with the police, it is too late, for the marriage contract has been signed, and Rosina is the wife of the distinguished Count Almaviva. The doctor decides to accept his hard luck philosophically, while the irrepressible Figaro bestows on all present his garrulous good wishes.

Amelita Galli-Curci as Dr. Bartolo's ward, Rosina

The Bartered Bride
PRODANÁ NEVĚSTA

CHARACTERS

Kruschina, *a peasant*	*Baritone*	Hans, *Micha's son by a first marriage*	*Tenor*
Kathinka, *his wife*	*Soprano*	Kezal, *a marriage broker*	*Bass*
Marie, *their daughter*	*Soprano*	Springer, *manager of a theatrical*	
Micha, *a landowner*	*Bass*	*troupe*	*Bass*
Agnes, *his wife*	*Mezzo-soprano*	Esmeralda, *a dancer*	*Soprano*
Wenzel, *their son*	*Tenor*	Muff, *a comedian*	*Tenor*

Comedians, Circus Performers, Villagers

The action takes place in Bohemia in the nineteenth century.

Emmy Destinn as the Bartered Bride

COMIC OPERA in three acts. Music by Bedrich Smetana. Libretto in Czech by Karel Sabina. First performance, National Theater, Prague, May 30, 1866. First United States performance, Metropolitan Opera House, New York, February 19, 1909, in a German translation by Max Kalbeck, with the title *Die Verkaufte Braut;* Gustav Mahler conducted.

A spirited, amusing opera that teems with comical situations, *The Bartered Bride* established Smetana as the first "national" composer of Bohemia (later Czechoslovakia). And it is said he was practically driven to that high office by a chance remark of the noted Viennese conductor Johann Franz von Herbeck's to the effect that Czechs "were simply reproductive artists," a challenge which Smetana met willingly and, as he proved, successfully. The work is strongly folk in feeling, possessing a brilliant score with a flow of rich melody from overture to finale.

Originally *The Bartered Bride* was in two acts, consisting of twenty musical parts connected with spoken dialogue. Smetana divided his first act into two; he augmented his score with an aria for the heroine, a male chorus, and a dance number; and later he converted the spoken dialogue into recitative

—with all of which he brought the opera to the form we know today.

An OVERTURE bristling with good humor and pretty melody precedes the opera. It is an excellent piece which, oddly enough, was played in this country some twenty years before the opera's arrival here. Its themes are all heard again in the finale of Act II.

ACT I

SCENE: *A public square before an inn.* Hans and Marie sit rather disconsolately at a table, discussing the obstacles in the path of their love. For today, on the anniversary of the consecration of the village church, Marie must accept a suitor of her parents' choice. Hans, suddenly emboldened, assures her that she will marry no one but him. He departs, on hearing approaching footsteps, and soon the marriage broker Kezal, together with Marie's parents, enters. They talk with her about a prospective suitor, Wenzel, a rather silly rustic, whom she will hear none of, insisting that she loves Hans. Be all that as it may, her father writes out a promise to Micha that, no matter what happens, Marie will marry Micha's son.

ACT II

SCENE: *Inside the inn.* Young Hans and Kezal are tilting convivial glasses. There is an argument, in which Hans, romantic that he is, expounds on the joys of love, whereas his companion, a very practical man, insists that love is nothing at all without money. A moment later Marie and Wenzel have an interview. He, a bit simple-mindedly, listens as she explains that she loves another man; also that she knows of a girl he could really care for. Wenzel, quite affected by her interest, agrees to give up the idea of marrying Marie.

In the meantime, Kezal, a little distracted by the headstrong Marie, attempts to bribe Hans. At first the latter will hear none of it, but, as a crafty idea strikes him, he finally agrees only on condition that Marie shall marry no other man but Micha's son. He makes this very clear, and Kezal, overwhelmed by his success, draws up a contract, which Hans signs. They go to Marie's parents, who are also happy now that all seems to have been so easily arranged.

ACT III

SCENE: *A public square before an inn (as in Act I).* A traveling troupe of circus performers puts on a show. Among them is the tightrope dancer Esme-

Gottlob Frick (Kezal), Pilar Lorengar (Marie) and Fritz Wunderlich (Hans) in West Berlin production

ralda, and she seems most desirable to Wenzel. He dons a bear costume and goes through several tricks at the instigation of the troupe's manager, who just picks out anyone at all, since his regular man is intoxicated. Wenzel's parents come along and, finding him in the middle of this droll performance, try to bring him to Marie. But well briefed, as he had been by the young woman, and fearing her just a little bit, he refuses to marry her. Nevertheless, his parents finally persuade him, and they head for Marie's house.

There Kezal informs Marie, rather gloatingly, that Hans has relinquished all claims on her—for money, of course. She disbelieves him, but he shows her the proof, the contract signed by Hans, calling for a consideration of three hundred crowns. After some moments of confusion for Marie, Hans, the son of Micha by an earlier marriage, is found acceptable not only to Marie, as he always was, but also to her parents. All ends very happily for them, but Kezal, who has lost his three hundred crowns, is a much sadder man.

Bluebeard's Castle

A KEKSZAKÁLLÚ HERCEG VÁRA

CHARACTERS

Bluebeard   *Bass*   Judith, *his recent bride*   *Soprano*

The action takes place "once upon a time," in Bluebeard's castle.

OPERA IN ONE ACT. Music by Béla Bartók. Text in Hungarian by Béla Balázs. Première, May 24, 1918, Royal Opera House, Budapest. American première (in concert form), Dallas Symphony Orchestra, January 8, 1946. First performance staged in the U.S., the New York City Opera, October 2, 1952.

Bartók's only opera was written in 1911, when the composer was thirty years old. The libretto was intended by Balázs for Zoltán Kodály, who, for obscure reasons, chose not to set it. Bartók's score, when submitted for consideration by the Royal Opera in 1912, was rejected as unplayable, but six years later the theater changed its mind. Performances abroad (initially in Germany) followed the première, but shortly afterward the librettist found himself in political disfavor, and Bartók, refusing to allow his collaborator's name to be suppressed, saw the opera withdrawn from further performance. It was not until after World War II that the work received international recognition as an important operatic landmark, and since that time it has been widely produced, to ever-increasing acclaim.

The Bluebeard legend, an ancient one, was recounted in the version by which it is best known today by Perrault, in his late-seventeenth-century collection of fairy tales. Balázs' libretto transforms the familiar plot into symbolist drama. Like Maeterlinck before him (whose own treatment of the same material, *Ariane et Barbe-Bleue,* was set virtually

verbatim by Paul Dukas in his 1907 opera, and no doubt served as a model for the Hungarian poet's work), Balázs fitted the tale with a wholly unexpected denouement. The last of the forbidden doors is opened to reveal that all of Bluebeard's former wives are still alive.

If Balázs followed in the Belgian's footsteps, Bartók, for his part, seems to have been influenced by the Debussy of *Pelléas et Mélisande.* There are several obvious parallels between the two operas: an allegorical and relatively static plot, an atmosphere of unrelieved somberness, the fluid and expressive use of large orchestral forces as the primary means of dramatizing the "action," and a vocal line evolved from a scrupulous sensitivity to the text—although here Bartók was responding not only to the characteristic inflections of his native speech but also to the traditionally quasi-recitativo form of Magyar folk song.

SCENE: *The great hall of Bluebeard's castle.* Bluebeard and Judith are seen standing in the bright sunlight of the castle's open doorway. As he slowly descends the stairs into the great hall, Bluebeard turns to his bride: "Judith, are you still beside me?" The warning bell is ringing loudly, he tells her; her father and brother, already armed, are preparing to rush to her rescue. To his repeated question Judith reassures him of her love. She hesitates a moment at the threshold, but only because her wedding dress has become caught. She has willingly left home and family behind, she tells her husband, and she does not falter now in her love. As they descend the steps together, the castle door swings shut behind them.

The huge hall is plunged into almost total darkness. Barely visible are seven huge doors. Judith, awed by the castle's gloom, learns that sunlight can never enter the windowless place. The walls are damp, as if the very stones were weeping. Noticing the doors, she asks Bluebeard why he keeps them locked. "So that no one may see what lies behind them," he replies. But Judith insists that they be opened, each and every one, and that light and air be made to drive away the castle's impenetrable gloom. "Open, open, open!" she cries, pounding on the first door. There is a warning rush of wind, half moan, half sigh; but Judith interprets this as the walls' encouragement to her in her task of liberation, and begs Bluebeard to yield up his keys.

Judith takes the key and unlocks the first door. A bright red light cuts through the darkness, revealing Bluebeard's torture chamber. Judith exults that the light of day has begun to dispel the darkness, but Bluebeard points out that the bright glow is merely light reflected in a pool of blood.

Judith demands all the other keys. Warning her that they are both endangered by her curiosity, he gives up a second key. When the second door is opened, Bluebeard's armory stands revealed. Judith notices with awe that all of the weapons are bloodstained, but still unfrightened by what she has seen, she asks that the remaining doors be unlocked.

In a golden stream of light, Judith sees Bluebeard's treasury. Bluebeard then offers her all his gold and jewels, but Judith is dismayed to find that they are smeared with blood.

The fourth door opens to reveal Bluebeard's secret garden, bathed in a blue-green light. But the very flowers are steeped in blood. To her question, "Who has bled upon your garden?" Bluebeard remains silent, bidding her only to unlock the fifth door.

A brilliant light floods the hall. Beyond the fifth door, a window looks out onto the countryside. Judith is lost in admiration for the size and splendor of her husband's realm. He now offers her this and all his other possessions, bidding her be happy with these and the love he bears her. But seeing that the sky is darkened by blood-red clouds, Judith asks that the two remaining doors be opened. Bluebeard gives her another key, saying that it will be the last. As Judith opens the sixth door, the light in the hall grows dim once more.

Before her lie the still, gray waters of a gloomy lake. "Tears, all tears," her husband sadly tells her. Shuddering at this scene of desolation, Judith seeks comfort in Bluebeard's loving embrace. The last

Sadler's Wells, London: Victoria Elliott, David Ward

door, he tells her, shall remain locked forever; Judith's love brings light and life enough for him. But even as he kisses her, Judith's thoughts turn once again to the remaining mystery. Who before her shared his love, she wonders. Were his former wives lovelier than she? When he replies evasively, she demands the final key.

Judith falls back amazed from the newly opened doorway. Bathed in a bluish light, Bluebeard's wives, three in number, crowned and dressed in queenly splendor, advance solemnly toward Bluebeard, who kneels before them. "Alive," breathes Judith, "they are all alive." But Bluebeard no longer hears her. In an ecstatic apostrophe to his wives, he says that he found the first of them in the morning, the second at midday, and the third at evening time. At these words Judith laments that her own beauty cannot compare with theirs; but Bluebeard, praising her, who came to him by night, above the others, arrays her in a starry mantle and crown of diamonds. Weighted down by the garments and the jewels, Judith slowly follows the other wives into the seventh chamber, and the doors swing to behind them. Bluebeard, ever doomed to solitude beyond the reach of human love, stands alone as darkness once more engulfs the hall.

La Bohème

CHARACTERS

Rodolfo, *a poet*	*Tenor*	Alcindoro, *a state councilor*	*Bass*
Marcello, *a painter*	*Baritone*	Mimi, *a maker of artificial flowers*	*Soprano*
Colline, *a philosopher*	*Bass*	Musetta, *a grisette*	*Soprano*
Schaunard, *a musician*	*Baritone*	Parpignol, *a toy vendor*	*Tenor*
Benoit, *a landlord*	*Bass*	A Custom-House Sergeant	*Bass*

Students, Working Girls, Citizens, Shopkeepers, Street Vendors, Soldiers,
Restaurant Waiters, Boys, Girls, etc.

The action takes place in Paris in the 1830's.

OPERA IN FOUR ACTS. Music by Giacomo Puccini. Libretto in Italian by Giuseppe Giacosa and Luigi Illica. Based on episodes from Henri Murger's *Scènes de la Vie de Bohème*. First produced at the Teatro Reggio, Turin, February 1, 1896, under the direction of Arturo Toscanini. First performance in the United States at Los Angeles, October 14, 1897. First performance at the Metropolitan Opera House on December 26, 1900.

La Bohème aroused quick public response, thanks to its heart-warming melodies and absorbing drama. Many early critics, however, objected strongly to its story, its music, even its romantic freedom. Turinese writers bemoaned what they called a decline in Puccini's powers; some dubbed the new work a mere potboiler, others dismissed it as an *operina* or operetta, and here in New York the *Tribune* critic flailed the new work as "foul in subject and fulminant and futile in its music." In due course, however, even the critics were won over by the bubbling verve and intense fervor of the music. Today most operagoers would rank *La Bohème* among their ten favorite operas.

Much of Puccini's early life went into this fervid tale of struggling young artists. Puccini remembered those frugal conservatory days in Milan when a sumptuous banquet in his dingy garret consisted of "soup, cheese, and half a liter of wine," when wood and coal had to be smuggled past a watchful landlady for a bit of forbidden home cooking. The landlady is said to have wept over the thought of her indigent young boarder who preferred music to food. Years later when Puccini dwelt at Torre del Lago, he became the center of an artistic coterie that met in a nearby villa. The group of painters, poets, and composers discussed art, played cards, joined in harmless pranks on the neighbors. At times Puccini would dash in excitedly with fresh manuscript. He would rush to the piano, and the Club Bohème of Torre del Lago would be the first to shed tears over little Mimi's pathetic fate. Through Puccini's opera, which they watched take shape with eager interest, the friends all fell in love with the ailing attic waif. In *La Bohème* Puccini wondrously transmutes those bleak early years in a Milanese attic and the gay camaraderie of the Club Bohème into a nostalgic picture of the Latin Quarter of Paris in the fourth decade of the nineteenth century.

ACT I

SCENE: *In the attic.* The cold, bleak garret dwelling of the inseparable quartet—Rodolfo, poet; Marcello,

John McCormack as Rodolfo

painter; Colline, philosopher; Schaunard, musician —is certainly large enough to accommodate such a family. The sparse furniture makes it seem doubly spacious. For the fireplace—devoid of fire—the few chairs, the table, the small cupboard, the few books, the artist's easel, appear like miniatures in this immense attic. Marcello, busily painting at his never-finished canvas *The Passage of the Red Sea*, stops to blow on his hands to keep them from freezing. Rodolfo the poet gazes through the window over the snow-capped roofs of Paris. Marcello breaks the silence by remarking that he feels as though the Red Sea were flowing down his back, and Rodolfo answers the jest with another. When Marcello seizes a chair to break it up for firewood, Rodolfo halts him, offering to sacrifice the manuscript of one of his plays instead. The doomed play now goes into the flames, act by act, and as it burns, the friends feast their eyes on the blaze, but gain scant warmth from it. The acts burn quickly, and Colline, who now enters stamping with cold, declares that since brevity is the soul of wit, this drama was truly sparkling.

Accompanied by errand boys, the musician Schaunard bursts in cheerfully, bringing wood for the fire, food and wine for the table, and money— plenty of it, from the way he flashes it. To his enraptured companions he relates how an eccentric English milord has been paying him liberally for playing the piano to his parrot. The festivities are cut short by the arrival of the landlord Benoit, who begins to demand his long overdue rent, then is mollified by the sight of money on the table. As he joins the comrades in several rounds of drinks, he grows jovial and talkative. The young men feign shock when the tipsy landlord begins to boast of his affairs with women in disreputable resorts, protesting that they cannot tolerate such talk in their home; and he a married man, too! The gay quartet seize the landlord and push him out of the room, *sans* rent money.

Rodolfo remains behind to work as his companions go off to the Café Momus to celebrate. He promises to join them in five minutes. He now makes several fruitless attempts to continue an article, and a timid knock at the door finally interrupts his efforts. Rodolfo opens, and a young girl enters shyly. While explaining that she is a neighbor seeking a light for her candle, she is suddenly overcome by a fit of coughing. Rodolfo rushes to her side to support her as she begins to faint and drops her candle and key. He gives her some water and a sip of wine and then, recovering the candle, lights it, and, after accompanying her to the door, returns to his work. A moment later Mimi re-enters. She has suddenly remembered the key and pauses at the threshold to remind Rodolfo of its loss. Her candle blows out, and Rodolfo offers his, but that, too, soon goes out in the

Alma Gluck as Mimi

draft. Left in the dark, they grope together along the floor for the lost key. Rodolfo finds it and quietly pockets it. Slowly he makes his way toward his visitor, as if still searching for the key, and sees to it that their hands meet in the dark. Taken unawares, the girl gives a little outcry and rises to her feet. "Your tiny hand is frozen" (*"Che gelida manina"*), says Rodolfo tenderly; "let me warm it for you."

Rodolfo assists the girl to a chair, and as he assures her it is useless to hunt for the key in the dark, he begins to tell her about himself. "What am I?" he chants; "I am a poet!" Not exactly a man of wealth, he continues, but one rich in dreams and visions. In a wondrous sweep of romantic melody he declares she has come to replace these vanished dreams of his, and now he dwells passionately on her eyes, eyes that have robbed him of his choicest poetic jewels. As the aria ends, Rodolfo asks his visitor to tell him about herself.

Simply, modestly, the girl replies, "My name is Mimi" (*"Mi chiamano Mimi"*), and in an aria of touching romantic sentiment she confides that she makes artificial flowers for a living. Meanwhile she yearns for the real blossoms of spring, the sweet flowers that speak of love.

Rodolfo is entranced by the simple charm and frail beauty of his visitor and sympathizes with her longing for a richer life. The enchanted mood is broken by the voices of Marcello, Colline, and Schaunard calling Rodolfo from the street below. As Rodolfo opens the window to answer, the moonlight pours into the room and falls on Mimi. Rodolfo, beside himself with rapture, bursts out with a warm tribute to her beauty, and soon the two of them unite their voices in impassioned song: *"O soave fanciulla"* (*"O lovely maiden"*). Mimi coquettishly asks Rodolfo to take her with him to the Café Momus, where he is to rejoin his friends. They link arms and go out the door, and as they go down the stairs, their voices are heard blending in the last fading strains of their ecstatic duet.

ACT II

SCENE: *A students' café in the Latin Quarter.* It is Christmas Eve. A busy crowd is swarming over the public square on which the Café Momus stands. Street vendors are crying their wares, and students and working girls cross the scene, calling to one another. Patrons of the café are shouting their orders to waiters, who bustle about frantically. The scene unfolds in a joyful surge of music, blending bits of choral singing, snatches of recitative, and a lively orchestral accompaniment. Rodolfo and Mimi, walking among the crowd arm in arm, stop at a milliner's, where the poet buys her a new hat. Then the lovers go to the sidewalk table already occupied by Colline, Marcello, and Schaunard.

Parpignol, a toy vendor, bustles through the crowd with his lantern-covered pushcart, trailing a band of squealing and squabbling children, who pester their mothers for money to buy toys. As the children riot around him, Parpignol flings his arms about in despair and withdraws with his cart. Meanwhile the Bohemians have been ordering lavishly, when suddenly there is a cry from the women in the crowd: "Look, look, it's Musetta with some stammering old dotard!" Musetta, pretty and coquettish, appears with the wealthy Alcindoro, who follows her slavishly about. Musetta and Marcello had been lovers, had quarreled and parted. Noticing Marcello with his friends, the girl occupies a nearby table and tries to draw his attention. Marcello at first feigns indifference, and when Mimi inquires about the attractive newcomer, Marcello replies bitterly, "Her first name is Musetta, her second name is Temptation!" Musetta now sings her famous waltz *"Quando me'n vo,"* in which she tells how people eye her appreciatively as she passes along the street.

The melody floats lightly and airily along, a perfect expression of Musetta's lighthearted nature. Presently the voices of the other characters join in— Alcindoro trying to stop her; Mimi and Rodolfo blithely exchanging avowals of love; Marcello beginning to feel a revived interest in Musetta; Colline and Schaunard commenting cynically on the girl's behavior. Their varied feelings combine with Musetta's lilting gaiety in an enchanting fusion of voices. Musetta now pretends her shoe hurts, that she can no longer stand, and Alcindoro hurries off to the nearest shoemaker. The moment he disappears from sight, she rushes to Marcello. The reunited lovers kiss, and Musetta takes a chair at Marcello's table. The elaborate supper ordered by Alcindoro is served to the Bohemians along with their own. As distant sounds of music are heard, the crowd runs excitedly across the square to meet the approaching band. Amid the confusion the waiter brings in the bill, the amount of which staggers the Bohemians. Schaunard elaborately searches for his purse. Meanwhile as the band comes nearer and nearer, the people along the street grow more and more excited. Musetta rescues her friends from their plight by instructing the waiter to add the two bills together and present them to Alcindoro when he returns. A huge crowd now rushes in to watch as the patrol, headed by a drum major, marches into view. Musetta, lacking a shoe, hobbles about, till Marcello and Colline lift her to their shoulders and carry her off triumphantly to the rousing cheers of the crowd. Panting heavily, Alcindoro runs in with a new pair of shoes for Musetta, and as he slumps dejectedly into a chair he receives the collective bill.

Act II of the Metropolitan Opera National Company staging: the bohemians at the Café Momus on Christmas Eve

ACT III

SCENE: *A gate to the city of Paris (the Barrière d'Enfer)*. A bleak, wintry dawn at one of the toll gates to the city. At one side of the snow-blanketed square stands a tavern, over the entrance of which, as a signboard, hangs Marcello's picture of the Red Sea. From within the tavern come sounds of revelry. Outside the gate a motley crowd of scavengers, dairy women, truckmen, and farmers have gathered, demanding to be let through. One of the customs officers warming themselves at a brazier saunters over to the gate and admits the crowd. From the tavern comes the sound of Musetta's voice. Peasant women pass through the gate, declaring their dairy products to the officials. From a side street leading out of the Latin Quarter comes Mimi, shivering with cold. A violent fit of coughing seizes her as she asks one of the officers where she can find Marcello. The officer points to the tavern, and Mimi sends a woman in to call him. Marcello, rushing to her side, greets her warmly with a cry of "Mimi!" "Yes, it is I; I was hoping to find you here," she replies weakly. Marcello tells her that he and Musetta now live at the tavern; he has found sign-painting more profitable than art, and Musetta gives music lessons. Mimi tells Marcello she needs his help desperately, for Rodolfo has grown insanely jealous and the constant bickering has made life unbearable.

When Rodolfo comes from the tavern to call Marcello, Mimi slips behind some trees to avoid being seen. Now Mimi overhears Rodolfo complaining to Marcello about their quarreling. Just as he announces his decision to give her up, Mimi reveals her presence by another coughing fit, and Rodolfo rushes to embrace her, his love returning at the sight of her pale, fragile beauty. But she breaks away, and sings a touching little farewell song, in which she says she bears him no ill will, that she will now return to her little dwelling, that she will be grateful if he will wrap up her few things and send them to her.

Meanwhile Marcello has re-entered the tavern and caught Musetta in the act of flirting. This brings on a quarrel, which the couple continue in the street. As Mimi and Rodolfo bid each other good-by—"*Addio, dolce svegliare alla matina*" ("Farewell, a sweet awakening in the morning")—their friends almost reach the point of blows in their quarrel. The music vividly mirrors the difference in temperament of the two women—Mimi, sad, gentle, ailing; Musetta, bold and belligerent—as well as the different response of the two men. "Viper!" "Toad!" Marcello and Musetta shout to each other as they part. "Ah, that our winter night might last forever," laments Mimi. Their resolve to part weakens in the new mood of tenderness, and as they leave the scene Rodolfo sings, "*Ci lascieremo alla stagion dei fior*" ("We'll say good-by when the flowers are in bloom").

ACT IV

SCENE: *In the attic (as in Act I).* Rodolfo and Marcello, having again broken off with their mistresses, are back in their garret, living lonely, melancholy lives. Rodolfo is at his table, pretending to write, while Marcello is at his easel, also pretending. They are obviously thinking of something else—of their happy times with Mimi and Musetta. When Rodolfo tells Marcello that he passed Musetta on the street looking happy and prosperous, the painter feigns lack of interest. In friendly revenge, he tells Rodolfo he has seen Mimi riding in a sumptuous carriage, looking like a duchess. Rodolfo tries, unsuccessfully, to conceal his emotions, but a renewed attempt to work proves futile. While Rodolfo's back is turned, Marcello takes a bunch of ribbons from his pocket and kisses them. There is no doubt whose ribbons they are. Rodolfo, throwing down his pen, muses on his past happiness. "O Mimi, you left and never returned" (*"O Mimi, tu più"*), he sings; "O beautiful bygone days; O vanished youth." Marcello joins in, wondering why his brush, instead of obeying his will, paints the eyes and lips of Musetta.

Their mood brightens momentarily as Colline and Schaunard enter with a scant supply of food. With mock solemnity the friends apply themselves to the meager repast as if it were a great feast. When a dance is proposed, Rodolfo and Marcello begin a quadrille, which is quickly cut short by Colline and Schaunard, who engage in a fierce mock duel with fire tongs and poker. The dancers encircle the duelists, and just as the festive mood reaches its height, Musetta bursts in. She brings sad news: Mimi, who is with her, is desperately ill. The friends help Mimi into the room and place her tenderly on Rodolfo's bed. Again Rodolfo and Mimi are in each other's arms as past quarrels are forgotten. When Musetta asks the men to give Mimi some food, they confess gloomily there is none in the house, not even coffee. Mimi asks for a muff and Rodolfo begins rubbing her hands, which are stiff with cold. Musetta gives her earrings to Marcello, telling him to sell them to buy medicine and summon a doctor. Then, remembering Mimi's request, she goes to get her own muff. Spurred by Musetta's example, Colline resolves to sell his beloved overcoat to make some purchases for Mimi. In a pathetic song he bids farewell to the coat, and departs with Schaunard to find a buyer. Rodolfo and Mimi are now alone. Faintly her voice is heard: "Have they gone? I pretended to be sleeping so that I could be with you. There is so much to say."

The lovers unite their voices in a duet of poignant beauty as they recall the days spent together, of the first time they met, of how she told him her name was Mimi. Reminiscent strains of melody are spun by the orchestra as the couple dwell on their attic romance. Mimi wants to know if Rodolfo still thinks her beautiful. "Like dawn itself!" he exclaims ardently. Suddenly Mimi, coughing and choking, sinks back in a faint. Rodolfo cries out in alarm, as Schaunard enters and asks excitedly what has happened. Mimi, reviving, smiles wanly and assures them everything is all right. Musetta and Marcello enter quietly, bringing a muff and some medicine. Mimi eagerly seizes the muff, which Musetta insists Rodolfo has purchased for her. Growing weaker and weaker, Mimi at last falls asleep—or, so it seems. Marcello heats the medicine; the other men whisper together, and Musetta begins to pray. Rodolfo has fresh hope, now that Mimi is sleeping so peacefully. Schaunard tiptoes over to the bed. Mimi is not asleep—she is dead! Shaken, he whispers the news to Marcello. Rodolfo, having covered the window to keep out the light, notes the sudden change in his friends at the other end of the room. As he realizes the truth, the orchestra pounds out fortissimo chords full of tragic impact. Musetta kneels at the foot of the bed, Schaunard sinks into a chair, Colline stands rooted to one spot, dazed, while Marcello turns away to hide his grief. Rodolfo rushes across the room, flings himself on Mimi's bed, lifts her up, and sobs brokenly, "Mimi! . . . Mimi! . . ."

Rodolfo (Richard Tucker) and Marcello (Robert Merrill) in the garret, Act IV of the Metropolitan Opera's Bohème

Bomarzo

CHARACTERS

Pier Francesco Orsini, Duke of Bomarzo	*Tenor*	Nicolas Orsini, *his nephew*	*Tenor*
		Julia Farnese, *his wife*	*Soprano*
Gian Corrado Orsini, *his father*	*Bass*	Diana Orsini, *his grandmother*	*Contralto*
Maerbale, *his brother*	*Baritone*	Pantasilea, *a courtesan*	*Mezzo-soprano*
Girolamo, *his brother*	*Baritone*	Silvio de Narni, *an astrologer*	*Baritone*

A shepherd boy, Abul, a messenger, prelates, courtiers, servants, astrologers

The action takes place in Bomarzo, Florence and Rome during the sixteenth century.

OPERA IN TWO ACTS (fifteen scenes). Music by Alberto Ginastera. Libretto in Spanish by Manuel Mujica Láinez, after his own novel of the same title, published in Argentina in 1962. Première by the Washington (D.C.) Opera Society on May 19, 1967; introduced into the repertory of the New York City Opera Company on March 14, 1968. Both performances conducted by Julius Rudel, with Salvador Novoa in the title role, Claramae Turner as Diana Orsini, Isabel Penagos as Julia Farnese, Joanna Simon as Pantasilea and Richard Torigi as the astrologer Silvio de Narni; settings by Ming Cho Lee, costumes by José Varona and stage direction by Tito Capobianco.

On commission from the Coolidge Foundation, Argentina's foremost contemporary composer undertook to expand an earlier work—a cantata based on the novel that had fascinated him for several years. He concluded by writing entirely new music for the stage version. Ginastera's imagination was captured by the character of Pier Francesco Orsini, Duke of Bomarzo, whom the author Mujica Láinez had conceived after visiting the fantastic gardens of Bomarzo near Viterbo in Italy, peopled with gargantuan stone carvings of monstrous allegorical figures. In Mujica Láinez's Gothic tale, the Duke is a weak, selfish, tormented and rather sinister figure—an anti-hero, whom Ginastera found appropriate to treatment in modern times because "Bomarzo is looking for immortality. Like a Sartre character, he is looking for a *raison d'être*. All existentialist characters are involved with this sort of problem. These are vital, excited, accelerated times; one's work has to reflect this, as some of our films do."

Because of the psychological violence of some of its scenes, notably an erotic ballet in which Bomarzo's fantasies and frustrations unfold around him, the projected Argentine première at the Teatro Colón, Buenos Aires, was banned by the government, giving the work a publicity of shock that belies its subtlety and aristocratic musical style. Ginastera, born in Buenos Aires on April 11, 1916, started out writing in a national vein in his earlier works, but his operas *Don Rodrigo* (1964) and *Bomarzo* show a highly international style in which twelve-tone procedures are combined with archaisms (plainsong and medieval modes), improvised passages and experimentation (quarter-tones, tone clusters). In his vocal writing, Ginastera has been widely acclaimed for his ability to create expressive, plastic melody within the twelve-tone framework. His formal organization of scenes according to musical structures, like Berg's in *Wozzeck*, is very tight but is not meant to be noticed by the listener.

New York City Opera: Bomarzo (Salvador Novoa) flees the embrace of the courtesan Pantasilea (Joanna Simon)

ACT I

As the hunchback Duke of Bomarzo lies dying in his garden of monsters, his secret past unfolds before him. He relives a scene from his childhood in which his two brothers ridicule him and force him into women's clothes. His father thrusts him into a secret room where he sees a skeleton which pursues him, dancing, until he faints. Later, his astrologer predicts endless life for him; when a magic spell is invoked, the foreboding peacock scream is heard for the first time. In the exotic mirrored room of Pantasilea, a courtesan, Pier Francesco sees his crippled image reflected and offers Pantasilea his sapphire necklace to release him. In Scene V we hear his grandmother reassuring him of his future. On a rock nearby, his oldest brother Girolamo slips and falls to his death, calling for help, but the grandmother refuses to allow Pier Francesco to go to his brother. Pier Francesco succeeds to the Dukedom upon the death of his father. At the ceremony he meets Julia Farnese, and in this same scene he is approached by a hooded stranger who seems to be the ghost of his father. After the ceremony the Duke, alone on the terrace, identifies himself with the enigmatic hump-backed rocks in his garden; the figures of Julia, Pantasilea, and Abul appear, each dancing with him and each trying to take possession of him. In Scene VIII we see him returning from a battle. He stands before the newly completed portrait of himself as a handsome Roman prince, but next to it sees his true self reflected in a mirror. Terrified, he shatters the mirror.

ACT II

The Duke is concealed in the Farnese palace where he jealously watches Julia and his brother Maerbale. When wine is served, he rushes in to hand Julia the glass; it spills over her dress and the dark stain becomes a prophetic sign. In the following scene the wedding of the Duke and Julia has taken place and the guests have departed. As the Duke conducts his bride through their chambers, the face of the devil appears to him in one of the works of art. The dream of the Duke on his wedding night is depicted in a frenzied dance involving the forms of future Bomarzo monsters and painted figures from the Etruscan graves. The Duke flees his bridal chamber and seeks refuge in the ancestral gallery, where he embraces the statue of the Minotaur, finding solace in its dreadful image. Scene XIII takes place several years later: the Duke, convinced that Julia and Maerbale have been deceiving him, succeeds with the help of the astrologer in having his brother killed by the slave. Maerbale's son Nicolas is a witness. In the astrologer's laboratory the figures of the ancient alchemists come to life and dance as the astrologer prepares the potion for Bomarzo's immortality. Nicolas, again, is watching in the shadows. In the final scene, Bomarzo drinks from the chalice and knows that Nicolas has poisoned him. He appeals in vain to his beloved rocks to save him from death. A shepherd boy, singing, approaches the lifeless body of the Duke, and bending down, kisses him.

Bomarzo (Salvador Novoa), grandmother (Claramae Turner)

Boris Godunov

CHARACTERS

Boris Godunov, *Tsar of Russia*	Bass	Varlaam and Missail, *vagabond*	
Xenia, *his daughter*	Soprano	monks	*Bass and Tenor*
Feodor, *his son*	Mezzo-soprano	Tchelkalov, *Secretary of the*	
Marina, *daughter of the*		Duma	Baritone
Voyevode of Sandomir	Mezzo-soprano	Innkeeper's Wife	Mezzo-soprano
Prince Shuisky	Tenor	Police Official	Bass
Gregory, *a novice, afterwards the*		Rangoni, *a Jesuit monk*	Baritone
Pretender Dmitri	Tenor	A Nurse	Mezzo-soprano
Pimenn, *a monk and chronicler*	Bass	An Idiot	Tenor

Two Jesuits, Chorus of Boyars and People, etc.

The action takes place in Russia and Poland, 1598–1605.

OPERA IN PROLOGUE and four acts (sometimes in three). Music by Modest Moussorgsky. Libretto in Russian after Pushkin and Karamzin, by the composer. First uncut performance on February 8, 1874, at the Maryinsky Theater (Imperial Opera House), St. Petersburg. First performance in the United States (in Italian), March 19, 1913, at the Metropolitan Opera House, New York, with Arturo Toscanini conducting and a cast headed by Adamo Didur (Boris), Louise Homer (Marina), and Paul Althouse (Dmitri). On December 9, 1921, Feodor Chaliapin, singing in Russian while the rest of the cast used Italian, presented his overpowering portrayal of Boris for the first time at the Metropolitan. Among the distinguished bassos since Chaliapin who have given outstanding portrayals of the hapless Tsar are Ezio Pinza (in Italian), Alexander Kipnis (in Russian), George London (in English as well as in Russian), Boris Christoff and Nicolai Ghiaurov (both in Russian).

Boris Godunov is the acknowledged masterpiece of a strange, erratic genius whom many regard as the greatest name in Russian music. Poor, sickly, ad-dicted to drink and drugs, and compelled to work at distasteful tasks, Moussorgsky somehow managed to leave the world a legacy of beauty and power. Undisciplined in many ways, Moussorgsky left much of his work incomplete and amorphous. Yet, he was a man of emphatic principles in art and adhered to an unwavering ideal of truth and sincerity. Despite the pressure of tradition and politics, he pursued his path toward a new naturalism and honesty in music. In *Boris Godunov* he chose a theme frowned upon by the authorities and employed a style flouted by the academicians. In making the Russian people the true protagonist of *Boris Godunov*, Moussorgsky expounded a democratic creed, and in using a technique of realism he alienated the champions of a strict classicism. Thus, *Boris Godunov* is not only the greatest of "national" music dramas but also the fiery manifesto of a new operatic order.

Boris Godunov at first seems nothing but a sequence of episodes, a historical panel drawn from a tangled epoch in Russian history. Actually there is remarkable unity. The continuity is deep and psychological, linking the destiny of a man and a nation

Bolshoi Theater production of the Coronation Scene, with the American bass-baritone George London as Tsar Boris

in a wondrous polyphony of ideas. Moussorgsky ruled out irrelevancies. For standard contrivances like set arias and vocal display one must look elsewhere. The melodic line is governed not by accepted form and pattern, but by the expressive needs of the moment, the mood and emotional crisis of a situation. Since the people dominate the drama the choral outbursts are prominent and powerful. And the orchestra here, as in Wagner, becomes an integral part of the fabric, heightening atmosphere, accenting feeling, setting a scene pictorially and emotionally. What makes *Boris Godunov* national becomes equally apparent in the shape of the melodies, the occasional use of folk motives, the modal devices of Russian liturgy. A Russian folk song weaves through the massive web of the "Coronation Scene," and for local color Moussorgsky even resorts to authentic Polish dance rhythms in the scenes set in Poland. Nor does Moussorgsky overlook the effect of recurring themes in his delineative scheme.

There are at least half a dozen versions of the score, no two of which are exactly alike in the scenes included or the order of those scenes. Moussorgsky himself made two, adding the Polish scene in the second because the first had been criticized for its lack of love interest. After Moussorgsky's death, his friend Rimsky-Korsakov made two more versions, bringing glitter, smoothness, and high professionalism to the orchestration. (It is the second of Rimsky's versions that has been most frequently per-

formed, and accordingly we follow that version in the account given of the story.) Then, in the 1940's, Dmitri Shostakovich, in an act of piety, restored most of Rimsky's orchestration, and Karol Rathaus and John Gutman prepared still another—a compromise based mostly on Moussorgsky's second version—for the Metropolitan Opera Company's revival in English in 1953.

It should be noted that scholars have recently acquitted the historic Boris Godunov of the murder which motivates the central tragedy of the opera. Moussorgsky, like the poet Pushkin and the historian Karamzin, accepted Boris' guilt as an undisputed fact.

PROLOGUE

Dmitri, younger brother and only heir of Tsar Feodor, has been assassinated at the instigation of Boris Godunov, one of the Tsar's privy councilors. When Feodor himself died, Boris cleverly masked his royal ambitions by retiring to the Novodievich monastery near Moscow. Secretly, however, he has given instructions to herd the people into the square before the monastery and force them to demonstrate in favor of himself as their next Tsar.

SCENE 1: *A public square before the Novodievich Monastery near Moscow.* After a brief orchestral

74

prelude built on a recognizably Russian theme, the curtain rises. A crowd, goaded by police officers, is kneeling before the monastery, imploring Boris to accept the crown. "Why do you abandon us? Have mercy upon us, O Father!" they chant in a ringing appeal. Tchelkalov, secretary of the Duma, emerging from the monastery, silences the populace by announcing gravely that Boris remains unyielding. He urges them to beseech God to intercede for the good of Russia. With the glow of the setting sun falling across the square, a band of chanting pilgrims is heard in the distance. As the pilgrims approach and begin to distribute amulets, they, too, lift their voices in entreaty, urging more and more prayer. Then they withdraw, and with them their song "Great Is Your Glory" dies away in distant whispers.

Scene 2: *The Great Square between the Cathedral of the Assumption and that of the Archangels in Moscow.* The curtain rises on a brilliant scene, rich and picturesque in color, sound, and movement. Giant bells are pealing. In the background, gleaming brightly, are the cathedral domes. The square is thronged with festively garbed people. Gay-colored banners flutter among them. Against this picture the wealthy boyars begin their stately procession toward the Cathedral of the Assumption, and, rising in their midst, is the stately figure of Boris, the new Tsar. From the portico of the cathedral Prince Shuisky shouts, "Long live Tsar Boris!" and the people take up the cry in a burst of acclamation, "Glory to Tsar Boris!" In an eloquent address, Boris assures the

people that though he will always have their cause and Russia's at heart, he is yielding to their will with great sadness. Doubts and fears for Russia and himself weigh upon his mind, he confesses, and now, invoking the aid of God, he asks the people to join with him in a prayer.

ACT I

Scene 1: *A cell in the Monastery of the Miracles at Chudovo.* Pimenn, an old monk and chronicler, is bent over his monastic tome inscribing the dire events of recent years. Gregory, a novice, asleep on a cot, suddenly wakes from a nightmare. Pimenn counsels prayer to the novice, and as he goes on to narrate the murder of Dmitri, the novice listens breathlessly. When he learns that the slain boy was his own age, a sudden thought crosses his mind. Pimenn leaves, and Gregory utters his thought: He will spread the report that Dmitri still lives! Thus, Gregory, the false Dmitri, will become Tsar of Russia, avenge the boy's death, and outwit the assassin usurping the throne.

Scene 2: *An inn at the Lithuanian border.* Spurred by his mad ambition, Gregory has fled the monastery. With two companions he arrives before an inn at the Lithuanian border. Varlaam and Missail, clad in monkish robes, enter first, startling the innkeeper's wife, who has been singing a tender, folklike melody. Gregory, a farm boy's clothes replacing his monastic garb, follows the friars into the inn.

Metropolitan Opera: as Gregory (Nicolai Gedda) listens in corner, Varlaam (Fernando Corena) sings about Ivan

Three artists celebrated for Boris: *Fyodor Chaliapin (Boris), Kerstin Thorborg (Marina), Boris Christoff (Boris)*

The others explain that they met Gregory on the road and that he is anxious to cross the border into Lithuania. Bottle in hand, Varlaam, a boisterous and worldly soul, now sings a lively drinking song, a song rich in earthy humor and grim realism, with a sweeping *élan* that is peculiarly Russian. With fiendish glee it tells of the great Ivan the Terrible and how he once smashed a rebellion of the Tartars of Kazan by exploding mines in their midst. His song completed, Varlaam falls into a drunken sleep. Gregory's plan is to cross the frontier and, if his luck holds, to raise an army in Poland. But government officials, apprised of his flight, have warned the border patrol. Soldiers now enter the inn and eye the odd trio with suspicion. Gregory reads out the description of the fugitive from the semi-literate officer's warrant, but he rephrases the wording to describe Varlaam. In the confusion following Varlaam's slowly spelled-out reading of the warrant, Gregory makes his getaway through a window.

ACT II

SCENE 1: *The Tsar's apartment in the Kremlin.* Boris' children, Feodor and Xenia, are together with their old nurse. Xenia is grieving over the death of her fiancé. To distract her, the nurse first sings a simple children's song, and then begins a game with handclapping obbligatos, in which Feodor, raising his head from a huge map of Russia he is studying, joins. The game stops abruptly as Boris enters. Observing the map which Feodor had been poring over, he affirms proudly that some day this knowledge will be of use to him. When the children have left, his face darkens as he muses on the future, and he delivers a magnificent monologue in which he reveals the great stress he is under. The greatest power is now his, yet he never knows peace of mind. Six long years he has been Tsar, and still the same

haunting memory obsesses him. He cannot escape the vision of the murdered Dmitri; day and night it plagues him. There is a frenzied rise of horror as Boris implores God to have mercy on him.

When the monologue ends, Prince Shuisky is admitted into the chamber and brings more bad news. A wild rumor is circulating that the slain Dmitri is still alive and open rebellion is brewing among the people. Shuisky tells the shaken Tsar that the Poles will back the Pretender, that he must mobilize his forces at once. Iago-like in his treachery, Shuisky now plays on Boris' superstitious nature. Possibly a miracle has come to pass, he suggests. Perhaps this is no false Dmitri, but the real one, the Dmitri whose body, he now remembers, showed no signs of decay several days after his death. Boris is frantic with a ghastly sense of certainty. Might not a murdered child rise from his grave to avenge the evildoer? When Shuisky departs, Boris falls back in his chair, shattered by an agony of remorse and terror. At this point the orchestra sets up a sinister throb, as of the ominous march of fate, measured in a relentless clocklike beat. Tortured by the burning memory of his deed, Boris shrinks back in horror as Dmitri's apparition seems to loom before his deluded senses. Boris is at the peak of his wild seizure, his conscience searing him like a brand. Exhausted and broken, he sinks to his knees, praying, "God have mercy on the guilty soul of Boris!"

ACT III

SCENE 1: *Marina's room in the castle of the Voyevode.* Marina's ladies-in-waiting sing her songs about love, but she tells them that she prefers tales of adventure and derring-do. Left alone, she sings, in the rhythm of the Polish mazurka, an aria which informs us that she hopes to realize her royal ambitions through Dmitri—for by this time Gregory has

76

already begun to raise an army in support of his claim to the throne, and he is a guest at her father's castle. The sinister figure of the Jesuit monk Rangoni glides into the apartment, and he sternly lectures the beautiful Polish aristocrat. It is her duty, he says, to convert all Russia to the true church of Rome once she has become Tsarina. Marina is terrified, yet determined.

SCENE 2: *The garden of a Polish palace.* As Gregory waits for Marina among the deep shadows of her palace garden, the festive sounds of a banquet reach him from inside the palace. The guests stream out into the garden, and the orchestra strikes up a courtly but vivacious polonaise. As the ranks form and the stately, swaying patterns of the polonaise take shape, the guests sing, "Forward against Moscow . . . to victory!" The dance ends, and as the music fades away, the guests re-enter the palace. Marina rushes to Dmitri and begins gently to taunt him for his lack of ambition, skillfully playing on his love for her, and in a great flourish Dmitri finally succumbs. He will himself lead the attack against Moscow; he will seize the throne from the usurper Boris; he will make Marina his queen! With its seductive mazurka rhythm, the music of this duet is a unique blend of romantic fervor and national color.

ACT IV

SCENE 1: *Outside a monastery.* Outside a monastery door, peasants debate the claims of the pretender. A group of urchins run in, chasing a Simpleton. When Boris and his retinue pass, distributing alms, the Simpleton asks the Tsar to kill the boys the way he once killed Dmitri. Boris shudders but protects the fool.

SCENE 2: *In the palace of the Kremlin.* The Duma is discussing measures to be taken against the Pretender Dmitri and the rebellious peasantry. Shuisky tells the assembled nobles of the secret agony of Tsar Boris which he has witnessed, but this only adds to their confusion, for Shuisky's insinuation is clear to all. The excited talk is cut short by the sudden entrance of Boris. There is a deathlike silence, as the self-tortured Tsar, muttering incoherent denials of guilt, stalks through the hall to the throne. As he seats himself, he momentarily regains a majestic calm. Shuisky begs Boris to grant audience to an aged monk who waits outside. In a forlorn hope that this man of God may bring peace to his tormented soul, Boris assents. Pimenn, the old monastic chronicler, enters and tells a strange story. In the dead of night an old shepherd who had long been blind had come to the monastery to report a marvelous experience: a childlike voice had counseled him in a dream

to kneel in prayer at the tomb of the slain Dmitri. This the shepherd had done, and a miracle had happened! He had been cured of his blindness! Boris listens with growing horror and finally gives a wild shriek of terror and collapses.

When Boris regains his strength, he asks to be left alone with his son. And to Feodor he addresses a farewell full of agony and pathos, rising at times to poignant tenderness. "Farewell, my son," he sings; it would be wiser for Feodor not to inquire how his father had gained the throne; let him rule justly and fearlessly, and defend their faith. With fatherly solicitude Boris asks him to watch over their beloved Xenia, and with his hands resting on the boy's head, he prays God for forgiveness.

The solemn tolling of bells is heard as the voices of the people outside the palace rise in prayer for the soul of their sovereign. Russian choral music reaches its summit here. Against it surges the growing terror and agony of the haunted Tsar, reaching a climax of stupendous power. Boris, growing ever weaker, cries out, "Lord, grant Thy mercy . . . forgive this my deed . . . O death!" Priests join the nobles in a funereal procession through the hall. Boris rises in a final access of majesty, exclaiming, "Wait! I am still your Tsar!" Then, clutching at his heart, he sinks into a chair, writhing in a power-

Nicolai Gedda as Gregory, the false Dmitri (Act IV)

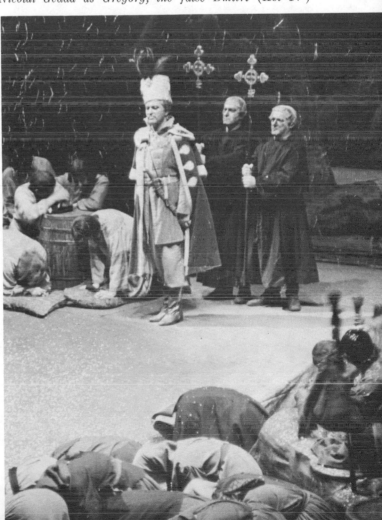

ful death agony. The words "God, have mercy!" come from his trembling lips; then summoning up his remaining strength, he points to his son and cries, "Behold your new Tsar!" One last spasm of a giant anguish, a cry of "Mercy!" and death at last brings him peace as the nobles stand by murmuring, heads bowed as if in prayer.

SCENE 3: *In the Forest of Kromy.* Peasants and vagabonds drag in a boyar who has fallen into their hands. He is bound and gagged, and the crowd gathers around him in the clearing and begins to heap taunts and insults upon him. As they raise their voices in unison, their actions become clear; they are cursing Tsar Boris, the boyars who support him, and all they stand for. "Glory to this great boyar and to his Tsar Boris!" they chant in mock hallelujah. A village fool approaches, followed by a troop of jeering children. The Simpleton seats himself on a rock, and, swaying idiotically, sings a plaintive song which is soon lost in the shrill mockery of the children, "Hail to our great fool!" A fresh note of rebellion is added as Varlaam and Missail are heard some distance off, voicing a chantlike tirade at the cruel Boris. This provokes the crowd to more excited utterance, and we hear a stupendous chorus attesting loyalty to Dmitri and a thirst for revenge. "Death for the regicide!" the cry rings out. Two luckless Jesuits, wandering in at this point, join in hymning Dmitri, this time in Latin, *"Domine, salvum fac Regem Demetrium Moscoviae, Regem omnis Russiae!"* ("God save Dmitri, King of Moscow! King of all Russia!") Neither the people nor the friars, however, seek interference from Rome. The two Jesuits are seized, bound, and led off to be hanged. Martial music is heard as troops file past the clearing, and the crowd sets up a fervid cheer. Dmitri—the false Dmitri—appears. "Glory unto our lawful Tsar!" the peasants shout. As he rides by, the Pretender promises them protection from oppression. In jubilant spirits, the crowd follows him into the forest. It is now snowing. The idiot, alone in the gathering dusk, observes a red glow in the distance, an indication that the rebels have already begun their work. Simply, yet with profound tragic import, he mourns the grievous state of Russia's people and the great calamities still to come:

The foe will come and blood will flow;
Let thy tears flow, poor, starving people!

Act IV, Scene 1: Shuisky (Paul Franke) mounts throne as Feodor weeps over body of his father, Boris (George London)

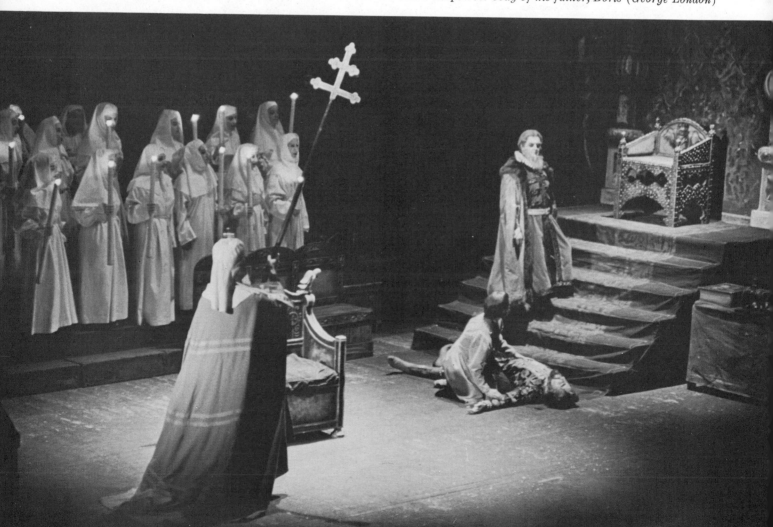

Capriccio

CHARACTERS

The Countess Madeleine	*Soprano*	Clairon, *an actress*	*Contralto*
The Count, *her brother*	*Baritone*	La Roche, *a theater director*	*Bass*
Olivier, *a poet*	*Baritone*	Monsieur Taupe, *a tenor*	*Tenor*
Flamand, *a composer*	*Tenor*	Two Italian Singers	*Soprano, Tenor*

Musicians, Servants, a Dancer

The action takes place near Paris about 1775.

OPERA IN ONE ACT. Music by Richard Strauss. Libretto by Clemens Krauss and the composer. First performance at Munich, October 28, 1942, with the librettist conducting. The first American performance was given by the Julliard School of Music, New York, on April 6, 1954. The San Francisco Opera Association mounted the first professional performance in the United States on October 25, 1963, with Elisabeth Schwarzkopf as the Countess.

The theme of this work—which is more important in opera, the words or the music?—is one that has been discussed (and often decided, though not always the same way) ever since opera began. Richard Strauss and the conductor Clemens Krauss discussed it at length during their preparation of the première of *Arabella* in 1933. Six years later conductor and composer began collaborating on the libretto for an entire opera to be devoted, inconclusively, to further discussion of the question. One act may not seem to be too much to devote to this important question in aesthetics, but if the act is almost two and a half hours long, it does seem a bit much even with a lady-or-the-tiger ending to the gentle love interest. It was the last opera Strauss composed.

SCENE: *A parlor in a rococo castle overlooking a park.*

At about the time and near the very city where Gluck was trying to reform opera by making the

Elisabeth Schwarzkopf as Madeleine: San Francisco Opera

Erté's production of Capriccio *for the Opéra-Comique in Paris, with Elisabeth Schwarzkopf as the Countess*

music serve the words instead of vice versa, a charming Countess named only Madeleine is holding a salon on that very subject. Each of the guests (the members of the cast listed above) has a direct professional interest in the subject excepting the Count. His interest is more indirect—entirely through his regard for the actress Clairon. As the discussion progresses, it also becomes evident that the two professionals most directly concerned, the composer and the poet, are rivals for the affections of the Countess, who is very fond of both of them. In addition, they are friends, and one has set music to the sonnet of the other.

Before the guests leave, it is decided that Olivier shall write the libretto and Flamand the music of an opera, and that all those present shall be characters and portray themselves. And it is also understood that Madeleine will decide between the rivals the next morning.

Left alone, Madeleine has one of those long soliloquies, complete with mirror, that Strauss loved to provide his leading ladies. She wonders which art—which artist—she should accept: she sings over the sonnet, partly to her own harp accompaniment; she looks into the mirror and asks for wisdom (but gets no answer); and finally, when the major-domo tells her that supper is served, she goes out quite light-heartedly, her mind still not made up.

Carmen

CHARACTERS

Don José, *a brigadier*	*Tenor*	Micaëla, *a peasant girl*	*Soprano*
Escamillo, *a toreador*	*Baritone*	Frasquita ⎱	*Soprano*
Zuniga, *a captain*	*Bass*	Mercédès ⎰ *gypsies*	*Mezzo-soprano*
Morales, *a brigadier*	*Baritone*	Carmen, *a cigarette girl and a*	*Soprano or*
Dancaire ⎱ *smugglers*	*Baritone*	*gypsy*	*Mezzo-soprano*
Remendado ⎰	*Tenor*		

An Innkeeper, Guide, Officer, Dragoons, Cigarette Girls, Gypsies, Smugglers

The action takes place in and about Seville in the 1820's.

OPERA IN FOUR ACTS. Music by Georges Bizet. Libretto in French by Henri Meilhac and Ludovic Halévy, based on the novel of Prosper Merimée. World première at the Opéra Comique, Paris, March 3, 1875. First American performance, Academy of Music, New York, October 23, 1878 (in Italian). In English it was given at Haverly's Fifth Avenue Theater, March 2, 1881. The opera entered the repertory of the Metropolitan on January 9, 1884, in Italian; Zelia Trebelli sang the title role.

Bizet died on June 3, 1875, the night of the opera's twenty-third performance in ninety days at the Opéra-Comique; yet it has been suggested that heartbreak over its failure brought about his untimely demise. This theory is further refuted by the fact that in the same season fifty performances were given the work. Actually, although the ultrarefined sensibilities of the Parisian critics of the 1870's were somewhat stunned by the opera's rather stark realism for those days, the public, for its part, found the piece interesting and even exciting. By the time eleven years had passed, *Carmen* boasted its five hundredth showing at the Opéra-Comique, on October 23, 1891; its thousandth performance took place there thirteen years later, on December 23, 1904, and its twenty-five hundredth performance occurred in June 1947.

On the basis of *Carmen*, Bizet has come to be ranked among the greatest of operatic composers. Though successful in winning the famous Prix de Rome at the Paris Conservatory, where he studied, he cannot be said to have had a financially profitable career. He was always hard pressed for funds, and, like Wagner, he was once compelled to waste valuable time in making cornet arrangements of popular tunes. Nevertheless, his talents won recognition among fellow musicians, including Liszt, who, it seems, was always able to recognize genius.

In *Carmen* Bizet found a perfect subject for displaying his masterly ability in portraying local color musically—an ability that he had also revealed in *Les Pêcheurs de Perles,* and the glowing incidental music to Daudet's drama, *L'Arlésienne.* Yet in *Carmen,* despite his talent for local color, he never pauses to paint pretty though unessential tone pictures. Through all the lively scenes and the gay, reckless melodies that constitute a suitable and well-nigh indispensable background for the plot, one feels a sense of foreboding, of impending disaster, that grows in intensity until the final curtain. Only a master of musical dramatics would be able to create with his sure, deft touches this steady crescendo of emotion.

Carmen is, moreover, one of the few operas that

Jeannette Pilou (Micaëla) and Nicolai Gedda (Don José)

win nearly universal approval. The man in the street whistles and loves its melodies; the operagoer is thrilled by its swiftly moving scenes and tensely emotional music; the opera star is enthusiastic over its possibilities for singing and acting; the musician admires its well-conceived and masterfully handled musical numbers, its thorough musicianship and excellently wrought orchestration.

This ardent drama, skillfully evolved from Prosper Merimée's story, is portrayed with felicity and distinction in Bizet's music—music in which every scene, every character, is clearly reflected. The "Fate" motive which sounds so ominously just before the brilliant scene of the first act is echoed again and again through the score, changing its form in a dozen ways. In the card scene it flickers through and through, like an angry tongue of flame in a bank of smoke. At the end, when the tragedy is done, it blazes forth luridly. Of this so-called "Fate" motive a story of supposed Oriental origin is told: When, according to Mohammedan tradition, Satan was cast from Paradise, he remembered only one strain of the music he had heard there. This, known as "Asbein," or the "Devil's Strain," Bizet used with fine symbolic as well as perfect musical fitness.

The Prelude brings before us, with a sudden stir of gay commotion, a vivid picture of the colorful

crowd that we will see pouring into the ring at Seville, in the last act. Magnificent, dark Spanish beauties with their lace mantillas and heavily embroidered silken garments, their escorts in gala attire even more brilliant, the excitement of the bullfight that is about to take place. This high-spirited music is interrupted, for a time, by the proud, steady beat of the world-famous "Toreador Song," gorgeous in its orchestral version. For a moment the orchestra sounds the "Fate" motive, ominously—then the curtain rises on

ACT I

SCENE: *A square in Seville.* It is the noon hour and the square is filled with townspeople, girls who work in the adjoining cigarette factory, and soldiers from the nearby guardhouse. Through this scene of activity comes a simple peasant girl. She tells the soldiers she is hunting for a corporal named José. He will not be there till the time the guard changes, they say; then, beginning to flirt, they ask her to remain till José comes. She runs away like a timid animal that has been frightened.

An intriguing little march tune is heard, played by fifes and trumpets, at first distant, then growing nearer. It is the change of guard that arrives, preceded by a troop of street urchins imitating the step of the dragoons who follow armed with their lances. Captain Zuniga and Corporal José are among them. The urchins and grownups watch with excited admiration the military ceremony of changing guard.

When that is over, some of the soldiers gather

Franco Corelli as Don José, his operatic début role

around Don José and jokingly tell him of the fair-haired girl who asked for him. "Micaëla," he explains, then adds, "I love her." Indeed, there are some beauties among the girls who have been watching the guard change, but José has not given them one glance. Now he sits astride a chair, preoccupied in trying to join the links of a small chain that has broken.

The bell of the cigarette factory strikes the hour for recess, and the cigarette girls wedge through the crowd toward the factory gates, loitering on the way to make eyes at the soldiers and young men who lounge around the square. The languorous calm of the noon hour and the coquettish charm of these Spanish girls are beautifully pictured in the music.

Suddenly there is a stir among the people, the "Fate" motive is heard in the orchestra, and a shout goes up, "Carmen!" A girl darts through the way that the crowd makes for her. "Love you?" she calls insolently to the men who swarm around her with their attention. "Perhaps tomorrow, but not now!" Then, to the swaying, insinuating rhythm of a habañera, she begins to sing, an enticing gleam in her eyes.

While singing, she glances often at José, and many times dances so near that she almost touches him; moreover, by insinuating inflections of her voice she seeks to win his attention. Apparently unaware of her presence, perhaps fortified against her attractions by thoughts of Micaëla, the handsome soldier is occupied busily, almost obstinately, with the broken chain.

"But if I love you, beware!" she sings, and tearing a blood-red flower from her bodice, she throws it boldly at him. He springs to his feet,

Regina Resnik as Carmen

Geraldine Farrar (Carmen) and Enrico Caruso (Don José)

seemingly about to rush madly at her. Instead he meets the look in her eyes and stands petrified on the spot. Carmen, with a cold, jeering laugh and a toss of the head, runs into the factory, followed by the other cigarette girls.

José stoops hesitatingly, as if against his will, and picks up the flower lying at his feet. He presses it to his nostrils, inhaling its mysterious perfume in a long, enchanted breath. Then, as if unconscious, he thrusts the flower under his blouse, over his heart.

At this very instant Micaëla returns and runs to José with exclamations of joy. She brings news from home, and money from his mother's savings. His mother has also sent him a kiss. This, too, Micaëla delivers, but most shyly and modestly. She cannot remain long, but her coming brings a welcome change of thought. José exclaims to himself, "Who knows of what a demon I was nearly a prey!" Alarmed at hearing this, Micaëla asks what the peril may be. He replies that it is nothing, and they sing a nostalgic duet.

When Micaëla has gone, he takes Carmen's flower from under his blouse and is about to throw it away. Just then there are screams of terror in the cigarette factory, and a minute later the square is crowded with frightened girls, soldiers, and townspeople. From the agitated exclamations of the cigarette girls

Act I of Carmen *as designed by Nicola Benois for La Scala*

it is learned that Carmen has quarreled with one of them and stabbed her with a knife. The soldiers drive away the crowd, and Carmen is brought out and questioned. She answers insolently with a gay "Tra la la la" in a most contemptuous manner.

The officer loses patience at her conduct, orders her hands tied behind her back, and enters the guardhouse to write a warrant.

José is left alone to guard Carmen. Pacing back and forth across the square, he seems to be avoiding her. "Where is the flower I threw at you?" she coquettishly asks. Then she begins softly to sing the song known as the "*Seguidilla*," in which she tells him they will meet at the tavern of Lillas Pastia, near the wall of Seville.

"Keep still!" interrupts José, but Carmen continues unabashed, and the tormented dragoon knows that she is making the vulgarest of love to him, for purposes of her own; yet he cannot resist her beauty and her song. She murmurs to him insinuatingly, and turns, holding toward him her bound wrists. He loosens the knot quickly, but leaves the rope so that it still appears to be tied.

A minute later the captain comes from the guardhouse with a warrant for Carmen; following him are the soldiers; and the crowd, drawn by curiosity, fills the square. The captain orders José to take Carmen to prison. She is placed between two dragoons, and under the command of José the party starts. As they reach some steps at the back of the square, Carmen quickly frees her hands, pushes aside the soldiers, and, before they realize what has happened, dashes away, amid the gleeful shouts of the onlookers.

ACT II

SCENE: *The tavern of Lillas Pastia.* The second act is preceded by a brief orchestral introduction, the steady-rhythmed music of the dragoons of Alcalá. At the inn of Lillas Pastia, gypsy smugglers from the mountains, joined by some officers and soldiers, have been having a feast. Now, the table in confusion, some of them sit back to smoke, others play the guitar, while a few begin to dance. Carmen sits watching the dancers, heedless of the attentions of Zuniga; then suddenly, she rises and begins a song of gypsy life, whose measures increase speed, as Frasquita and Mercédès join in; and, finally, with the ballet doing a gypsy dance, the scene takes on a roistering, swirling abandon.

The energetic, forward-moving rhythm, the piquant lilt of the melody, the surprising colors of the harmony, and the delicacy of the orchestration are made more vivid by the impetuous clashing of the gypsies' tambourines. Carmen joins the dance, which grows faster and more impulsive.

It is about time for the inn to close, and while all are hurriedly preparing to leave, one of the officers conveys to Carmen the valuable information that the handsome young corporal, who has been under arrest since the time he allowed her to escape, has just been released from prison.

Suddenly, from outside come shouts, "Long live the toreador! Hail Escamillo!" The famous bullfighter, victor of the ring at Granada, enters and, joining in their toast, sings a fiery tale of the bullring, a glowing description of quick action, reckless daring, bloodshed, shouts of a great crowd—and love, the "Toreador Song." The melody, a rousing delineation of all this, also reveals to us, more forcibly than words, Escamillo's character, brave to the point of recklessness, self-confident, and boastful. Escamillo's manner impresses Carmen greatly, but her heart is still set on José.

The toreador departs, followed by the excited, cheering crowd. Zuniga tries to induce Carmen to go with him, but she refuses. He says he'll come back later. It is growing late, and the innkeeper again begins to close up, and Carmen remains with her gypsy girl friends Frasquita and Mercédès. Two of the smugglers approach them. They need the help of the girls in seducing the coast guard into forgetting duty. In a rollicking quintet they spontaneously express their amusement at the idea.

The men are anxious for the girls to start at once, but Carmen wishes to wait; she confesses she expects José, and, as luck would have it, his voice is heard in the distance, singing a military air, the theme of the interlude before this act. The gypsies peer through the shutter and admire his appearance, suggesting that Carmen persuade him to join their band. Enthusiastic over this idea, she hurries them from the room just before José enters.

She welcomes him with joy, then at once makes him jealous by telling him that Morales and the officers made her dance for them. But now she will dance for José alone.

She begins to dance, to an odd little tune of her own composing and the clicking of her own casta-

nets. José is absorbed in her motions. From the distance a bugle call signals "retreat," summoning all soldiers back to quarters. José stops the dance; he must go. Carmen laughs at the idea and resumes her dance. The sound of the bugle call draws nearer, passes by, and fades away in the distance, mingling with the melody of Carmen's song. Again, with an effort José tears himself away from the fascination of her actions. "You don't understand," he cries, "I have to go back to quarters."

"What a fool I am!" exclaims Carmen sarcastically. "I wear myself all out trying to entertain this gentleman . . . I thought he loved me . . . the bugle calls, and he runs off!" Then in a sudden fury she hurls his cap and saber at him and shouts, "There! go, my boy, directly to the barracks!"

Greatly hurt and humiliated, José seizes her by the arm, declaring, "You *must* hear me, Carmen!" He takes from his uniform the flower she gave him that fateful day in the square at Seville. To a hauntingly lovely melody that grows by degrees to an impassioned climax, he tells her how he kept this flower with him during his dreary life in prison, as he sings, *"La fleur que tu m'avais jetée"* ("This flower you threw to me").

Carmen seems to be touched, but she is more determined than ever that José shall go off with her to the freedom of the gypsies' life, the adventures, dangers, and escapes, the long nights under the free winds and the stars. José is nearly won, but, then starts up with a sudden realization: "A deserter of my flag . . . be shamed, dishonored!" He rushes

Olive Fremstad, Carmen at the turn of the century

Marcel Journet as Escamillo

toward the door and answers her "Good-by" with "Farewell forever!"

At this very instant there is a knocking at the door, and a second later Zuniga bursts in. He stops suddenly as he sees José, and says coldly to Carmen, "Your choice isn't so good . . . you don't do yourself justice to take a mere soldier when you might have his officer!" He brusquely orders José to go. The soldier, naturally, refuses; the officer strikes him, and José, mad with rage, draws his saber. Carmen, to prevent bloodshed, screams to her companions for help. Officer and soldier are overpowered and separated. Some of the gypsies lead Zuniga away under close guard. For José the life of a law-abiding subject and loyal dragoon is done. Guilty of insubordination and of an attempt upon the life of a superior, he can only join the gypsies, become a deserter and an outcast—and the lover of Carmen. The act closes with a brilliant chorus in praise of the free life.

ACT III

SCENE: *A mountain pass.* An interlude of lyric beauty precedes the third act. A pastoral melody, simple, but most exquisitely graceful, is first heard in the liquid tones of the flute and then taken up in imitation by other instruments; meanwhile the harp adds color and motion to the background. The tranquil purity of this interlude is a relief from the emotional strain of the preceding act. This piece stems from the incidental music Bizet composed for the play *L'Arlésienne.*

The smugglers are gathering at their meeting place, a wild, desolate spot in the heart of the mountains. First one smuggler appears on a lofty pinnacle of rock in the distance, then several, finally the entire band, scrambling down over the barren rocks toward their camp. Their gradual arrival and stealthy movements are vividly pictured in music.

Carmen and José are among them. José is not happy in this mode of life. Just now he is obsessed by thoughts of his mother; she still believes he is an honest man.

"If you don't like our way of living here, why don't you go?" Carmen asks sarcastically.

"And leave you! Carmen! If you say that again . . ." he mutters and places his hand menacingly on his dagger.

Carmen merely shrugs her shoulders and calmly replies, "You may kill me, what does it matter? I will die as fate dictates." José sulks away, and Carmen watches Frasquita and Mercédès, who are telling their fortunes with cards. These girls are having a gay time, for the cards predict love, wealth, and happiness. She seizes a pack of cards and coolly begins to tell her own fortune. In silence she shuffles and draws: "Spades!—death!" she exclaims darkly, under her breath. She recoils as from some unseen hand that threatens her. From the orchestra is heard the terrifying "Fate" theme. "First I, then he!" she adds, indicating José, then continues to shuffle the cards, while she sings the "Card Song."

Her spirit of bravado does not desert her, however, and when the leader of the band of smugglers announces that it is a favorable time to attempt the mountain pass with their contraband goods, she is all activity in helping prepare for the departure. After José has been stationed behind some rocks to watch for any surprise attack, the smugglers set out

Act III: Carmen (Risë Stevens) reads her fortune in the cards, in 1952 Metropolitan Opera sets by Rolf Gérard

Act IV: The crowd gathers by the bullring in Seville, in the 1967 Metropolitan Opera sets by Jacques Dupont

through the pass, singing joyfully at their anticipated conquest of the guard.

A guide comes from behind a cliff toward the
camp, then quickly withdraws. It is Micaëla whom
he has directed to this haunt of desperate characters.
She comes seeking José and she sings a tuneful air,
praying for heaven's protection, *"Je dis que rien ne
m'épouvante"* ("I say that I am not fainthearted").

A shot rings out, and in terror she hides among
the rocks. José has fired at a stranger coming up the
pass. He might indeed have fired again, but the
carefree manner in which the man waves his hat and
exclaims, "An inch lower and it would have been all
over with me!" causes José to put down his gun and
go to meet him. It is Escamillo. In a moment the
men recognize each other as rivals. Daggers flash,
soldier and bullfighter struggle together. Escamillo
falls, José's dagger at his throat. But the smugglers
have returned, attracted by the sound of the shot.
Like a flash, Carmen is between the two men and
seizes José's arm. Escamillo rises, gallantly thanks
Carmen for having saved his life, then with his usual
bravado invites them all to the bullfight at Seville,
and calmly takes his leave. José again rushes after
the toreador, but is restrained by the gypsies. Just
then Micaëla is discovered and brought in. She begs
José to return to his mother. Carmen interrupts and
tauntingly says that he should go, this life is not for
him. He turns to her excitedly, replying, "You tell
me to go with her, so that you may run after your
new lover."

The gypsies also advise him to leave, but he is
firm. Then Micaëla pleads: "One last word, José,
your mother is dying!" Now repentant and alarmed,
José will go. He turns back for a moment, however,
and calls darkly to Carmen, "Be happy . . . I'm
going . . . but we'll meet again."

As José leaves with Micaëla, the toreador is heard
in the distance, singing his boastful song.

ACT IV

SCENE: *A square in Seville.* A third intermezzo
indicates the changed scenes of the opera—a rapid,
impetuous dance, tones of plaintive longing mingled
with impassioned gypsy-like phrases grow to a
tumultuous climax, then die away with a pleading
phrase in the oboe and a few runs and chords by
other woodwind instruments—a mood of vague foreboding.

A brilliantly dressed crowd is waiting in the
square before the bullring in Seville for the procession into the arena. Street hawkers with oranges,
fans, cigarettes, and wines are vigorously shouting
their wares. Soldiers, citizens, peasants, aristocrats,
bullring loafers, black-haired, black-eyed women,
Spanish beauties with towering combs, floating
mantillas, and embroidered silken shawls; all these,
a many-colored throng, move excitedly about the
scene. From the orchestra rings out the bright, vivacious theme of the Prelude to the opera. The procession is approaching, and the crowd cheers and applauds the divisions of the parade that go by and
enter the arena. "The *alguacil*, the *chulos*, the *ban-
derilleros*, all in green and spangles, waving their
crimson cloths! The picadors with their lances! Now,
Escamillo! Hail! Bravo! Escamillo!"

A thunderous shout goes up as the toreador enters,

Carmen on his arm. She is stunningly brilliant in her Spanish dress, and appears to be radiantly happy. Escamillo now takes leave of her, saying that if she loves him she soon will have reason to be proud. Completely won, Carmen vows that her heart could hold no other love.

A blare of trumpets and a march in the orchestra announce the entry of the alcalde. During this, two of Carmen's gypsy friends approach. They warn her to leave the place. José has been seen in the crowd, they say, and he appears to be desperate. Carmen calmly replies that she is not afraid; she will stay, wait for him, talk to him.

When the alcalde has entered the arena, the entire crowd follows, the brilliant music of the procession dies out in the distance, and Carmen is left face to face with Don José. She looks at him fearlessly and says, "I was told that you were here, warned." José is haggard and wan; from his sunken eyes glows a dangerous light. "Carmen," he begs hoarsely, "come, let's go far from here, begin life again. I adore you!" "It's useless for you to keep repeating that you love me," she answers impatiently, "I don't love you any longer." "But I, I love you, I worship you!" he pleads and threatens at the same time. "What's the use, superfluous words!" is her indifferent answer. "Well," he urges, "if I can win your love, I'll be a smuggler, anything you wish, all—but don't leave me, don't forget our past, how we loved each other!"

Her freezing answer is, "Carmen never will yield! Free was she born, free shall she die!"

A sudden fanfare is heard from the arena; there are loud shouts of "Hurrah! Hail to the toreador!" At the shout of victory Carmen lets escape a little cry of pride and joy. During this Don José has had his gaze fixed on her. She starts to run toward the entrance. Insane with jealousy, he stops her.

In a sinister tone he mutters, "This man they are shouting for, he's your new lover!"

She defies him with, "Let me pass."

"On my soul! you'll never pass! Carmen, come with me!"

"Leave me, Don José."

"You're going to meet him . . . you love him?"

"Yes, I love him! Even before death, I'd repeat, I love him."

Again there is a fanfare of trumpets and a shout of "Viva, toreador!"

Carmen again tries to enter the arena. José stops her violently. His voice bitter with despair and jealousy, he again threatens: "And so I've sold my soul so that you can go to his arms and laugh at me!" The "Fate" theme sounds turbulently in the orchestra. From the arena is heard another fanfare, then the song of the crowd acclaiming Escamillo victor. With a defiant cry, Carmen throws away José's ring and darts toward the entrance of the amphitheater; there José overtakes her. A dagger flashes . . . Carmen falls. The crowd comes pouring from the arena, singing praises of the toreador. Don José declares himself guilty and, bending over the lifeless form, cries out heartbrokenly, "Carmen . . . my adored Carmen."

Carmen (Grace Bumbry) in her final moments with Don José (Nicolai Gedda) as given at the Metropolitan Opera

Cavalleria Rusticana

RUSTIC CHIVALRY

CHARACTERS

Santuzza, *a village girl*	Soprano	Alfio, *a teamster*	Baritone
Lola, *wife of Alfio*	Mezzo-soprano	Mamma Lucia, *mother of Turiddu*	Contralto
Turiddu, *a young soldier*	Tenor		

Peasants and Villagers

The action takes place in a Sicilian village on an Easter day in the latter part of the nineteenth century.

OPERA IN ONE ACT. Music by Pietro Mascagni. Libretto in Italian by Giovanni Targioni-Tozzetti and Guido Menasci, based on a short story by Giovanni Verga. World première at the Teatro Costanzi, Rome, May 17, 1890. American première at the Grand Opera House, Philadelphia, September 9, 1891. A few weeks later Rudolph Aronson and Oscar Hammerstein raced to produce the New York première first, Aronson winning with a matinee dress rehearsal at the Casino Theater on October 1, and Hammerstein claiming a technical victory with a regular performance that night at the Lenox Lyceum. The Metropolitan Opera Company first produced the spectacular novelty the following December 30. Emma Eames was Santuzza and Fernando Valero Turiddu. The performance was in Italian, unlike the Aronson and Hammerstein versions, which were in English. Eames, though vocally superb, was regarded as temperamentally unsuited for the part of the volcanic Sicilian heroine. It was Emma Calvé who brought fire and power to the role at her Metropolitan debut on November 29, 1893. A still more sensational performance was that directed by Arturo Toscanini on December 17, 1908, when the cast consisted of Emmy Destinn, Maria Gay, Marie Mattfeld, Enrico Caruso, and Pasquale Amato.

Mascagni was an impoverished music teacher, living at times on a meager plate of macaroni a day, till his one-act masterpiece brought him fame and fortune. The son of a Leghorn baker, he had been obliged to study music secretly as a boy, as his father intended him for a career in law. The timely intervention of a sympathetic uncle and the sponsorship of a wealthy titled amateur settled the issue. Pietro went to the Milan Conservatory. There, however, the routine of study plagued him. The encouragement of Amilcare Ponchielli proved futile, and soon the boy ran away from school. After some arduous years with a traveling opera company, he married and settled down in Cerignola. Marriage only added to his financial woes, and his income from teaching and odd conducting jobs in town was scant. One day in 1889 the music publisher Sonzogno offered a prize for a one-act opera. Mascagni promptly set to work, having discovered an excellent libretto in the realistic tale of Verga, standard-bearer of the Italian school of *verismo*. Utterly dissatisfied with the score, Mascagni put it aside. Luckily his wife, whose faith in the opera was stronger than her husband's, stole off secretly to the post office one afternoon and mailed it. The little opera won first prize.

When it was produced at the Teatro Costanzi in Rome, its success was immediate. The audience was wild with excitement, clamoring for the young unknown who had suddenly moved to the forefront of

Emma Calvé as Santuzza, her Metropolitan début role, 1893

First Santuzza and Turiddu: Gemma Bellincioni, Roberto Stagno

Italy's new composers. The composer's fame was made. Medals were struck in his honor, the city of Cerignola greeted him with torchlight processions on his return; and Mascagni relates in his memoirs that the entrance to his home was so jammed with cheering townspeople that it was necessary to haul him up to the first-story balcony on a knotted bedsheet. Later the King bestowed the Order of the Crown of Italy upon him—an honor that had not come to Giuseppe Verdi till late in life. A whole new chapter in naturalistic opera writing opened with *Cavalleria Rusticana,* and people warmed to it instantly wherever it was played. Its rich Latin melody, its dramatic impact, its pulsing passion combined to establish it securely in the repertories of the world. The compactness and unity of the story were ideal for a one-act opera, and even as a stage play, Eleanora Duse showed how this simple, passionate conflict in the lives of Sicilian peasants could become a drama of poignant power.

PRELUDE

An orchestral prelude introduces us to the drama of stormy passions we are to witness. The music evokes a folkish background of warm color, and ominous phrases are heard hinting at Santuzza's fateful jealousy and the tragedy it will bring. But soon the music grows romantic in mood; from it blossoms the beautiful "Siciliana" of Turiddu, "O

Lola, bianca come fior di spino," a serenade with guitar-like accompaniment heard from behind the curtain. It is an avowal of undying love to Alfio's wife, Turiddu's former sweetheart. "White as a flower," Turiddu calls Lola, swearing that if he were to die and go to heaven, he would refuse to enter if she were not there too.

SCENE: *Easter morning in the deserted square of a Sicilian village.* On one side stands a church, on the other a wineshop and the dwelling of Mamma Lucia. Church bells are ringing, and in the distance voices are heard singing, as peasants gather for the Easter Mass. The orchestra gives out a bright and joyous melody in typical folk vein, expressing the carefree holiday mood of the people as they stream into the square. The women are singing of Eastertime, of tender love. The men join in, hymning the charms of women and their industrious ways. Some of the villagers enter the church; others form little groups, and then walk off in different directions. As their voices fade away in the distance, Santuzza appears. She approaches Mamma Lucia's dwelling and calls out to her. "What is it?" asks the old woman. "Where is Turiddu?" the girl asks anxiously, repeating her query over and over. Mamma Lucia evades answering: "Do not ask me. I do not know. I want no trouble!" Santuzza now pleads with her with mounting ardor, "Tell me, for God's sake, where is Turiddu hiding himself?" Mamma Lucia replies finally that Turiddu has gone to Francofonte to buy wine. "That's not so," Santuzza cries. "Last night he was seen in the village." The mother's suspicions are aroused, for she has not seen her son. When she invites Santuzza to enter the house with her, the girl shamefacedly reminds Lucia that she cannot enter, that she is an outcast, excommunicated (*"Non posso entrare in casa vostra. Sono scomunicata"*). The moral law of the Sicilian village forbids her entering Mamma Lucia's home. "What of my son?" the mother asks, alarmed.

Before Santuzza can reply, the cracking of whips and the jingling of bells are heard. Alfio the village carrier is approaching, and as he reaches the square, he sings a lively song in praise of the teamster's career, adding some words of eulogy for his beautiful and loving wife Lola, who is home, waiting for him. A crowd follows him and joins in his song. Alfio asks Mamma Lucia if she can sell him some of her fine wine. "Not just now," she replies. "Turiddu has gone to buy a fresh supply of it." Astonished, Alfio exclaims, "But Turiddu is here in town! I saw him myself this very morning. He was standing not far from my cottage." Mamma Lucia is about to express surprise, when Santuzza checks her and Alfio departs. From inside the church now comes the voices of a choir singing the *"Regina Coeli"* ("Queen of Heaven"). The crowd outside joins in with "Hallelujahs." The peasants then kneel in prayer and sing the Resurrection hymn *"Innegiamo, il Signor non è morto,"* led by the voice of Santuzza.

The people now enter the church, and Lucia and Santuzza are again alone. The mother asks Santuzza why she motioned her to keep silent when Alfio spoke of seeing Turiddu in the village. Santuzza now gives us the needed background to the drama developing among them. She reminds Mamma Lucia that her son was once engaged to Lola, that while he was away serving in the army, Lola forgot him and married Alfio. Then Turiddu returned. Crushed when he learned the truth, he proceeded to console himself with Santuzza, whose reputation he ruined. Now Lola, weary of Alfio, has enticed Turiddu back and is jealous of Santuzza. Mamma Lucia now learns from the distraught girl that during Alfio's frequent absences Lola and Turiddu have been together. This is all divulged, with mounting passion and pathos, in Santuzza's great aria *"Voi lo sapete"* ("Well you know, good mother"), which reaches a pitch of frenzied despair at the point where the girl reveals that Lola and Turiddu love one another again.

Shaken by Santuzza's anguished confession, Mamma Lucia heeds her plea to go into the church to pray for her. As she does so, Turiddu enters the square, also on his way to church. Surprised at seeing Santuzza outside of church on Easter day, he tries to avoid talking to her, but she insists on speaking to him. She upbraids him for lying that he has been to Francofonte. He was seen near Lola's house by her husband, she shrieks; he still loves her! Turiddu denies it, and Santuzza is suddenly frightened when he hints that his life will be in danger if Alfio learns the truth about his visits to Lola. Raising his voice, Turiddu cries that he will not be the slave of Santuzza's wild jealousy. "Strike me, insult me," she sobs in mingled love and desperation; "I forgive you, but my suffering is too much for me!"

Lola's voice is now heard in the distance, singing a lighthearted song about a radiant flower, the mood of which suggests the coquette. As Lola enters she grasps the situation at a glance, and the two women exchange words bristling with irony and innuendo.

The Easter morning procession enters the church as Santuzza (Zinka Milanov) kneels in prayer, at the Metropolitan Opera

Turiddu (Daniele Barioni) toasts Lola (r., Rosalind Elias) and his fellow villagers, as staged at the Metropolitan Opera

Turiddu is left almost speechless with confusion. With a shrug, the flirtatious Lola enters the church, beckoning her lover to follow. But Santuzza detains him, pleading vehemently, "Do not leave me, Turiddu!" "Why do you follow me around?" retorts Turiddu. "Why do you spy on me at the church door?" Turiddu's anger mounts as the girl's desperate frenzy grows, and finally, as Santuzza shouts, "Betrayer," he flings her roughly to the ground. As he strides defiantly into the church, Santuzza hurls a furious curse after him: "May this Easter bring you bad luck!" and falls, sobbing frantically.

When she looks up again, Alfio is approaching. "God himself has sent you!" she exclaims to him. "At what part of the Mass are they?" he asks calmly. "It is rather late," Santuzza replies, adding significantly, "Lola went with Turiddu." Alfio, in surprise, asks, "What did you say?" and Santuzza blurts out the whole story that while he earns an honest living his wife is betraying him with Turiddu, Turiddu who is rightfully hers, Santuzza's. Alfio's voice rises in wrath, as he listens dumfounded. "If you are lying, I'll rip your heart open!" he threatens. But he is convinced and, after a pause, thanks Santuzza and vows to have his revenge that very day. Leaving Santuzza dazed and fearful of the tragedy her jealousy is bringing on, Alfio stalks off, uttering cries of *"Vendetta!"*

Santuzza leaves, and the square is deserted for a few moments. It is time for a pause in this seething frenzy of dramatic outcries and clashes. A calm, devotional mood rises from the orchestra now, as the *"Regina Coeli,"* earlier sung by the choir, returns to remind us it is Easter, a day of peace and piety. In contrast, there follows a haunting melody, tense with religious fervor, but suggesting, too, the hot, searing passions of the previous scenes. This orchestral episode is the famous *"Intermezzo,"* a concert piece popular the world over.

As the strains of the *"Intermezzo"* soar to a climax and finally die away, people begin to emerge from the church. A crowd is now assembled outside Mamma Lucia's wineshop. Turiddu is in high spirits, for Lola is with him and Santuzza is nowhere about to plague him. Turiddu invites his friends to partake of his mother's wine. Glasses are filled, and he leads them in singing an infectious drinking song, in which the sparkling magic of wine is hymned in jubilant tones. As Alfio enters, all greet him cordially. Turiddu offers him a glass, but Alfio gruffly refuses it. "Your wine would become poison in my stomach!" he snarls at Turiddu. Turiddu retorts, "At your pleasure," and empties the glass on the ground. Lola is frightened, and several women confer hastily, approach Lola, whisper to her, and take her away with them. The two men exchange a few sharp words, and then give a challenge in the Sicilian village fashion of the time: the men embrace and Turiddu bites Alfio's ear in token of acceptance.

After Alfio leaves for the place appointed for the duel, Turiddu calls out to his mother. With mounting alarm, the mother listens to him as he begins an aria pulsing with tragic import and filial love, *"Mamma, quel vino è generoso."* He is going away, he says, and may not return. "If I should not come back, be a mother to Santuzza, the girl I vowed to marry," he pleads. To quiet her fears he assures her that it is only the wine that makes him talk this way. Then he kisses her and rushes off with a farewell sob. Mamma Lucia follows him for a few steps, shouting his name in despair. Santuzza enters and throws her arms about her. The square now begins to fill again. A nervous expectancy is in the air. The taut excitement grows as a murmur of voices is heard in the distance. Then the cry of a single woman rises shrilly: "They've murdered Turiddu!" Terrified women rush into the square. Santuzza gives an anguished shriek and collapses. Women rush to Mamma Lucia's side as she, too, reels and faints. The stupefied crowd looks on in horror.

La Cenerentola

CINDERELLA

CHARACTERS

Don Ramiro, *Prince of Salerno*	*Tenor*	Clorinda, *his daughter*	*Soprano*
Dandini, *his valet*	*Baritone*	Tisbe, *another daughter*	*Mezzo-soprano*
Alidoro, *the Prince's philosopher*	*Bass*	La Cenerentola, *his stepdaughter*	
Don Magnifico, *Baron of Monte Fiascone*	*Bass*		*Mezzo-soprano*

Courtiers and Servants

The action takes place in Salerno at no specified time,
but the costumes are usually late eighteenth century.

OPERA IN TWO ACTS. Music by Gioacchino Antonio Rossini. Libretto in Italian by Jacopo Ferretti based on an earlier French libretto, *Cendrillon*, prepared by C. G. Etienne for two other composers. First performance at the Teatro Valle in Rome, January 25, 1817. First American performance at the Park Theater, New York, June 27, 1826, with the name role sung by Maria Garcia, then seventeen, who was to become the leading soprano of her day under her married name of Maria Malibran.

On Christmas Day 1816 the librettist started feeding Rossini the words of the opera and the première occurred precisely one month later. Not only had the book been written and the music orchestrated, but the parts had been copied and learned and sufficient rehearsals taken place to assure—a failure. But like *The Barber of Seville* (which, according to the composer, took him under two weeks to write), *La Cenerentola* became a great success after its first bad reception. It never quite equaled the popularity of *The Barber,* and today it is nowhere nearly so often mounted as the most popular of all Rossini operas, or as it was a hundred years ago. The reason does not lie with any inferiority of the music. Many critics even prefer the score of *La Cenerentola* to what is usually regarded as his masterpiece—maybe because *The Barber* has become too familiar. Its effectiveness relies, even more than *The Barber,* on brilliant coloratura singing—a commodity in much shorter supply today than in Rossini's time. Yet, whenever a brilliant coloratura mezzo-soprano takes on the leading role, the opera can be—and usually is—revived with enormous gratification to the public, which seems to make a fresh discovery each decade. It has happened thus with Conchita Supervía in the 1930's and Giulietta Simionato in the '40's (in Europe) and more recently, in America, with Frances Bible.

As for the story, children should be warned not to expect any fairy godmother, pumpkin coaches or other magic familiar from the old tale of Charles Perrault. This is a more mundane and sophisticated version with a "philosopher" replacing the fairy and not a wand or a pumpkin—or even a coach—on stage.

OVERTURE

The Overture is one of Rossini's best and thoroughly typical, complete with crescendos, dancy tunes, sweetly melodic ones, and a perky piccolo.

Cinderella (Sylvia Friederich) with Magnifico (Arnold Voketaitis) and stepsisters (Mary Beth Piel, Ellen Berse)

Rossini borrowed it from his earlier opera *La Gazzetta* and, in turn, borrowed a portion of the Overture for one of the finales in *La Cenerentola*. He may be forgiven this self-borrowing, a common practice of his (as well as assigning two unimportant arias to the pen of a composer named Agolini) if we recall that he composed the opera in twenty-four days.

ACT I

SCENE 1: *A room in the home of Don Magnifico.* La Cenerentola (whom we will hereafter call by her familiar translated name, Cinderella) is making coffee for her two spoiled stepsisters, Clorinda and Tisbe. As she works, she sings a simple ballad with a prophetic significance. It is about a king who sought a wife and chose the kindest and most innocent of three candidates. Disguised as a beggar, Alidoro, Prince Ramiro's philosopher, enters the house, is sympathetically treated by Cinderella but curtly dismissed by her two stepsisters, who denounce the heroine for having wasted refreshments on a beggar.

An invitation is delivered by Prince Ramiro's servants to a ball, for the Prince is looking for a bride on the command of his dying father. Both ugly sisters feel sure that they will be able to win the sovereign with their charms, and they listen rather impatiently to their father, still in nightcap and dressing gown, tell of an absurd dream from which the girls' chattering has awakened him. The patter aria (in the style of *The Barber's* familiar "*Largo al factotum*") tells how he, in the shape of a very wealthy ass with wings, flew to the top of a belfry. His pre-Freudian interpretation is that this clearly

means his daughters will make him the grandfather of kings.

After the two sisters have gone off to prepare themselves for the ball, another man in disguise visits the house. This actually is the Prince, but since he is making a private search for a bride who shall love him for himself and not for his rank, he is disguised as his valet, one Dandini. Cinderella, confused by having to greet a handsome young man alone, drops a tray of dishes, and the natural consequence (in a fairy tale) is that the two young people fall in love at first sight. There is a tender love duet, but neither discovers who the other really is. The duet is ended by Cinderella's being summoned to help her sisters; and while the Prince muses on the attractions of his newly found love, Dandini, disguised as the Prince and attended by his followers, comes in—and Alidoro slips in as well.

The stage is now set for one of Rossini's great finales. The two sisters and their father make up to the disguised Dandini, who, amused and disgusted, encourages them but whispers aside to his Prince what horrible creatures they all are; the Prince tells Dandini to be more discreet; the father and his two girls insist that his third daughter is dead and Cinderella a mere servant; Alidoro lets Cinderella know that he will help her to the ball though she has been refused permission; and the chorus just comments.

SCENE 1: *A room in the palace of the Prince.* Guests are gathering for the dinner to precede the ball, with Dandini still acting the part of the Prince. Clorinda and Tisbe try to make up to him, and he flees to an antechamber where, in a funny duet, he tells his master how dreadful both of them are. They follow, nevertheless, and Dandini informs them that if he marries one, the other must take his valet. This they find very unacceptable indeed. Then Alidoro brings in the masked but obviously beautiful and beautifully gowned Cinderella. Everyone agrees that this is the woman the Prince ought to choose—that is, everyone but Tisbe and Clorinda, who think the unknown looks too much like Cinderella for the Prince to be attracted. As for the Prince, he does not recognize the lady either but finds her voice strangely affecting. Don Magnifico, who is acting as chief butler for the occasion, fussily demands that everyone now go to the banquet hall and, with nothing resolved, there is a second—and particularly effective—finale, based on the music of a part of the overture.

ACT II

SCENE 1: *At the Prince's palace.* The two sisters quarrel about which one of them is to marry the Prince, and when they have left the stage, Dandini (still disguised as the Prince) proposes marriage to Cinderella, for he has fallen in love with her. But Cinderella refuses the great honor for, she admits, she has fallen in love with her suitor's valet. This the real Prince overhears and, realizing that she is really his unknown inamorata, proposes on his own behalf. Cinderella accepts, but only with the proviso that he must first find out who she really is—and she gives him one of two matching bracelets she is wearing so that he may be able to trace her. To close the scene, there is an amusing duet between Don Magnifico and Dandini, in which the valet finally reveals his identity to the fiercely ambitious and disappointed father.

SCENE 2: *At Don Magnifico's home.* Cinderella once more sings her ballad of the prince who married the best of three, and her two stepsisters find fault with her for looking so much like the masked lady at the ball. Outside a storm is brewing (set in motion by the philosopher-scientist Alidoro and set to some of Rossini's best storm music), and the Prince and Dandini, in their proper attire, come in to escape it. Cinderella hides her face, but Ramiro, seeing the matching bracelet on her arm, steps forward and claims her as his bride. Her relatives are shocked and angry, but the Prince refuses to have anything more to do with them.

SCENE 3: *The throne room of the Prince's palace.* Don Magnifico has come to beg forgiveness before the entire court, but the Prince remains adamant against the whole trio of in-laws. The good, kind Cinderella, however, wins over her Prince by singing, *"Nacqui all' affano"* ("Born to sorrow"), a brilliant and a very difficult rondo, which is the best-known number in the opera. Everyone then rejoices and lives happily ever after.

Giulietta Simionato as Cinderella in the outdoor staging of the final scene of Cenerentola *at La Scala designed by Pierluigi Pizzi*

The Consul

CHARACTERS

John Sorel	*Baritone*	Foreign Woman	*Soprano*
Magda, *his wife*	*Soprano*	Anna Gomez	*Soprano*
The Mother	*Contralto*	Vera Boronel	*Contralto*
Secret Police Agent	*Bass*	Magician	*Tenor*
Secretary	*Mezzo-soprano*	Voice on the Record	*Soprano*
Mr. Kofner	*Bass-baritone*		

The action takes place "somewhere in Europe" soon after World War II.

MUSICAL DRAMA in three acts. Music and libretto in English by Gian Carlo Menotti. Written for the Broadway theater rather than the opera house, and produced by Chandler Cowles and Efrem Zimbalist, Jr., it had its world première in Philadelphia, at the Shubert Theater, on March 1, 1950. After a two-week tryout there, it opened on Broadway at the Ethel Barrymore Theater, on March 15, where it ran for 269 consecutive performances. The original cast consisted of Cornell MacNeil as John Sorel, Patricia Neway as Magda, Marie Powers as the Mother, Leon Lishner as the secret police agent, Gloria Lane as the Secretary, George Jongeyans as Mr. Kofner, Maria Marlo as the Foreign Woman, Maria Andreassi as Anna Gomez, Lydia Summers as Vera Boronel, Andrew McKinley as the Magician, Francis Monachino as Assan, and Mabel Mercer as the voice on the record; Menotti staged his own work.

After winning the New York Drama Critics' Circle Award as the best musical play of the year as well as the Pulitzer Prize for music, *The Consul* was produced successfully in European cities—Milan, London, Paris, and Vienna. Not only was it effective as music; its drama of a woman trying to escape to a free world was particularly pertinent to peoples living under the threat of an ever-encroaching police state. On October 8, 1952, *The Consul* joined the repertory of the New York City Opera Company with Patricia Neway in the role she created.

ACT I

SCENE 1: *The Sorel home—a grubby apartment above the street, in a large city—early in the morning.* Through the open window comes the sound of a French record played in a café below. John Sorel stumbles into the apartment, wounded, calling his wife. Magda and his mother rush in and dress his wounded leg. He had been at a secret meeting when the police, tipped off by someone, had raided their quarters and they had to run for their lives.

His mother scornfully asks him why he doesn't bring home bread for his hungry child instead of fear and blood, but John and Magda know that bread is a small price to pay for freedom. They hear sounds in the hall, and the women hide John on a roof leading from the alcove of their flat and put away his things and clean the bloodstains he trailed along the floor.

The Secret Agent and two plainclothesmen come in and make a thorough search of the apartment, John's mother wondering if there will ever be an end to such things. The Secret Agent questions Magda about John, and she claims that she has not seen him for two weeks. When he asks her for the names of John's friends, enemies of the state, and she pretends ignorance, he warns her that there are ways of making people talk, and leaves. When the police are gone, Magda and the mother help John back in. He is convinced now that he must cross the frontier that night. Go to the consulate, he tells Magda, say who you are and ask for help; but on no condition must she ever get in touch with their friends. As for news of him, when a child throws a stone against the window, see Assan the glass cutter, and he'll bring word of anything. John leans over the cradle to kiss his baby son, then bids Magda farewell ("Now, o lips say goodbye").

SCENE 2: *The waiting room of the consulate, later the same day.* Elderly Mr. Kofner and the Foreign Woman wait patiently for the Secretary to finish typing. Again they are put through the consular red tape of documents to be procured. Following John's instructions, Magda has come to ask for help. But when she tries to give her name and tell her story, she discovers to her dismay that her name is a number, her story a case, and the Consul is too busy to see her. She must fill out papers and come back next week. The waiting room meanwhile has filled with three others—Anna Gomez, Vera Boronel, and the Magician, who performs tricks to help pass the time—time so precious to all of them. The act ends with the five visa applicants joining in a quintet, "In endless waiting rooms."

ACT II

SCENE 1: *The Sorel home, a month later.* The French Song is again sounding through the window when Magda comes home after another fruitless day spent waiting at the consulate. She and John's mother have had no word of him, and the baby is sick. The grandmother plays with the apathetic baby, then sings him a lullaby ("I shall find for you shells and stars"), while the weary and distraught Magda lies down. Even in sleep she can get no rest, for she has a nightmare in which John returns, with the consulate Secretary accompanying him as Death. Waking with fright, and fearing her baby will die and she will never see John again, she gains a moment of hope when a stone comes crashing through the window. She telephones Assan, according to the plan, and he will come to fix the window-pane. There is a knock at the door, and the Secret Police Agent enters to bargain with Magda—if she gives him the names of John's friends, she will be allowed to join her husband. Magda orders him out, but before he leaves, Assan arrives. His suspicions aroused, the Secret Police Agent waits until Assan begins working on the pane before he leaves. At last Magda can question Assan, and learns that John is hiding out in the mountains, waiting for her to cross

the border first. Assan gone, she realizes that John's mother has been unusually quiet—the baby is dead.

SCENE 2: *The consulate, a few days later.* The same persons are waiting. Anna Gomez is handed a form and told to come back ("Oh, yes," she answers, "tomorrow and the day after tomorrow"). Magda again tries to see the Consul, but has to take her place in line. The Magician, who can perform every trick but the supposedly small one of procuring a visa, proves his right to the title of artist by making a watch disappear. Further to impress the aloof Secretary, he hypnotizes all those in the waiting room and convinces them that they are at a ball, dancing with their loved ones. The weird dance frightens the Secretary, and she demands that he stop them, whereupon he wakes them up.

After awaiting her turn to speak to the Secretary, Magda learns that there is no news for her and, besides, there are other documents to be got. But the secret police are after her, Magda says; can she not see the Consul? Finally, in desperation at the Secretary's evasions, she screams out, "Liar!" She won-

Act I: Marie Powers (the mother), Patricia Neway (Magda)

Magda (Patricia Neway), in despair, hurls away endless forms

that it is useless, the Consul will not see her, Magda will not go home. Vera Boronel comes in and learns that there is good news for her. Happily she signs document after document handed her by the Secretary. Assan enters, looking for Magda. He tells her that John is returning, for he has heard of the deaths of his baby and his mother. John must not come back, he warns her, or all his friends' lives will be in danger—Magda must stop him. Magda knows a way. She writes a note to John and asks Assan to send it to him; it will convince him not to return. As the bubbling Vera receives the last of her papers, Magda gets up stiffly from the bench, spilling her many forms on the floor, and leaves. Vera discovers Magda's pocketbook, but Magda has already gone. The Secretary says that Magda can get it the next day, when she comes back as always.

Alone, the Secretary is haunted by the faces of those always waiting—she has had to maintain her impersonality to hold on to herself. As she prepares to leave for the night, John Sorel enters, looking for Magda. The Secretary tries to send him home, but he cannot go, for the secret police are outside. She tells him of the back way out and hands him his wife's pocketbook, but before he can escape, the secret police rush in. Though they cannot arrest him in the consulate, he knows there is no way out and leaves in their custody. The Secretary, who has never seen a case become a story, promises John she will see the Consul about their case in the morning and will let Magda know what has happened to him. She picks up the telephone to make the call.

SCENE 2: *The Sorel home, after Magda's return from the consulate.* The Secretary's telephone call is still sounding as the curtain rises but stops before Magda enters, moving like a sleepwalker and repeating to herself, "I never meant to do this." With John's coat she closes the crack at the window and, with her own, the crack at the door, then takes a chair before the stove and sits down. She opens the gas jets, pulls a shawl over her head, and bends over the fumes. As she goes under, the room takes on an eerie quality, and she has a series of visions—the figures of the waiting room and John and his mother tell her that "Death's frontiers are open. All aboard!" But Magda is terrified when they do a macabre waltz—a dance of death—and rush at her. John's mother asks her to join the dance, but Magda clings to life. She knows she is dreaming, and she wants to wake. The visions end with John and his mother bidding good-by and the Magician putting her back to sleep over the gas jets. The room returns to normal, and Magda is gasping over the hiss of the gas jets. The telephone begins to ring. Magda hears it, stretches out her hand feebly, but it is too late. She falls limp as the phone continues to ring.

ders if there actually is a consul—if hope really lies behind that door leading to his office ("To this we've come: that men withhold the world from men"). And the Secretary's answer is to hand her a paper to be filled out requesting an appointment with the Consul. Papers, always more papers; she is Magda Sorel—occupation: waiting. Finally moved by Magda's despair, the Secretary goes to see if the Consul will see her. She returns with the good news that he will see her as soon as the man now in his office leaves. Through the pane of his doorway Magda sees two figures shaking hands in good-by, and as the visitor comes out, she rushes to go in. But the visitor is none other than the Secret Police Agent, and Magda faints.

ACT III

SCENE 1: *The consulate, several days later.* Magda is alone, waiting. Though the Secretary advises her

Le Coq d'Or

ZOLOTOY PYETUSHOK — THE GOLDEN COCKEREL

CHARACTERS

King Dodon	*Bass*	Amelfa, *the royal housekeeper*	*Contralto*
Prince Guidon } *his sons*	*Tenor*	The Astrologer	*Tenor*
Prince Aphron }	*Baritone*	The Queen of Shemakha	*Soprano*
General Polkan	*Bass*	The Golden Cockerel	*Soprano*

The action takes place in a mythical land.

OPERA IN three acts. Music by Nikolai Rimsky-Korsakov. Libretto in Russian by Vladimir Bielsky, after the poem by Pushkin. First performance given at Zimin's Private Theater, Moscow, October 7, 1909. American première, Metropolitan Opera House, March 6, 1918, in French, when it was produced as an opera-pantomime in the stage version devised by Mikhail Fokine for Diaghilev's Ballet Russe. In this version the members of the ballet enacted the movements of the personages of the drama on the center of the stage, while singers, in academic cap and gown, were ranged in jury boxes on either side. A revival at the Metropolitan on February 4, 1937, was in the work's purely operatic form, the singers enacting their own roles. In the cast were Ezio Pinza as King Dodon and Lily Pons as the Queen.

This, the last and most popular of Rimsky-Korsakov's operas, was at first banned from the stage by the Russian censor, owing to a particular element of satire in the story which, it has since been assumed, was aimed at Russia's conduct of the war against Japan. By the time it was finally staged, the composer was dead.

At the height of his powers when he composed this work, Rimsky-Korsakov surmounted many unusual difficulties in his musical treatment of the libretto. Learned professor and author of erudite musical treatises and contrapuntal pieces, the composer, by the beauty of his melody, the opulence and daring of his harmony, and the brilliance and originality of his orchestration successfully met the challenges like the superb craftsman he truly was, in a score both acid and humorous and thoroughly in the spirit of the fantastic tale.

PROLOGUE

A muted trumpet intones a characteristic motivo of the "Cockerel." Then bizarre melodies and harmonies are heard from the orchestra, and an ancient Astrologer appears before the curtain. He tells us that through his magic he will show us a fable of olden times; he suddenly disappears, and the curtain rises.

Dodon (Norman Treigle), Amelfa (Muriel Greenspon)

ACT I

SCENE: *The council chamber of King Dodon.* King Dodon sits in council of state; he is harassed by many cares, for warlike neighbors insist on attacking his country. He would much prefer peace, for he is lazy and gluttonous and would not have his feasting disturbed. His sons, the Princes Guidon and Aphron, propose various absurd plans of attack, but the wise old General Polkan disagrees with their suggestions, and soon the assembly is in an uproar. Now the Astrologer enters and offers Dodon a Golden Cockerel which will always give warning when danger is near. The ruler is delighted and says that he will give the Astrologer as a reward anything that he may desire, whereupon the Astrologer remarks, with a certain cynicism, that treasures and honors bring only worry, but he accepts the monarch's word with thanks. Reassured by the gift, Dodon is put to bed in great state. His regal dreams are interrupted by the Cockerel sounding the alarm; the enemy is invading the country, and Dodon sends his two sons, each in command of half an army. Again his slumbers are disturbed by a signal of danger. The King, accompanied by Polkan, sets out in command of an even greater army.

ACT II

SCENE: *A narrow mountain gorge.* By the faint moonlight a desolate mountain gorge is seen. Dodon arrives with his troops. He finds the bodies of his sons and their men slain—they have been fighting one another. He sheds a few formal tears. Day begins to break over the mountain, and, as the mist rises, a brilliantly decorated tent is perceived nearby, apparently the enemy's. Dodon and his men prepare to attack. A cannon is brought up, but just as it is ready to be fired, the folds of the tent tremble, and the soldiers run away. The sun is now rising from behind the mountains, and there appears from the tent the beautiful Queen of Shemakha. Raising her arms as in prayer, she salutes the sun with a song—an exotic melody, colored with extraordinary chromatics and strange modulations, known as the "Hymn to the Sun."

Dazed and fascinated by her beauty and her singing, Dodon falls in love with her. She in turn ridicules the old monarch, luring him on to sing and dance, much to the amusement of her courtiers, for his voice is broken and his step doddering. Finally, summoning his courage, he makes his awkward proposal. She seems to hesitate and then yields, only on condition that General Polkan shall be executed.

ACT III

SCENE: *A street in Dodon's capital.* Dodon and the new Queen are welcomed back to the capital in the most extravagant splendor. The bride is already bored by her quavering husband. The Astrologer appears and demands as his reward—the Queen! Dodon begs him to accept, instead, riches or power. The Astrologer is firm; Dodon becomes angry and strikes him with his scepter. The Astrologer drops dead. There is a sudden thunderstorm, the scene grows dark, and the Golden Cockerel is heard crowing. The bird flies at Dodon, pecks him on the head, and the old ruler falls lifeless. The Queen is heard laughing, and when daylight returns she has vanished. The people sing a weird lament. Who now will be their King?

EPILOGUE

As the curtain falls, the Astrologer again appears and, reminding us that this is merely a fairy tale, says—quite enigmatically—that in Dodon's kingdom only the Astrologer himself and the Queen are real people.

Act II as performed during the 1930's at the Metropolitan Opera, with Lily Pons as the Queen, Ezio Pinza as Dodon

Così Fan Tutte

SO DO THEY ALL

CHARACTERS

Fiordiligi, *a wealthy beauty from Ferrara* — Soprano	Guglielmo, *an officer engaged to Fiordiligi* — Baritone
Dorabella, *her sister* — Soprano or Mezzo-soprano	Ferrando, *an officer engaged to Dorabella* — Tenor
Despina, *their maid* — Soprano	Don Alfonso, *a cynical bachelor* — Bass

Soldiers, Servants, Musicians, etc.

The action takes place in Naples late in the eighteenth century.

OPERA IN TWO ACTS. Music by Wolfgang Amadeus Mozart. Libretto in Italian by Lorenzo da Ponte. First performance at the Burgtheater, Vienna, January 26, 1790. American première at the Metropolitan Opera House, March 24, 1922. Now usually given there in the English translation by Ruth and Thomas P. Martin.

The unsubstantiated story goes that the plot is based on some real-life intrigue in the court of the Emperor Joseph II. Be that as it may, the work was commissioned by the Emperor after a particularly successful revival of *Le Nozze di Figaro*, written by the same composer and librettist. Although many critics agree that the score is just as fine as—and perhaps even more subtle than—*Le Nozze* and *Don Giovanni*, it has never been nearly so popular as those two great masterpieces. The fault has generally been laid to the libretto. Some have found it too trivial for a whole evening's entertainment, and the nineteenth century considered it downright immoral. Many tinkerers tried to make it more acceptable, and it has been staged probably under more different titles than any opera in history. Some examples: *Who Won the Bet?*, *The Girls' Revenge*, *The Guerrillas* (all in Germany); *Flight from the Convent* (Denmark); *The Chinese Laborer* (France

—and what could that have been like?); and *Love's Labor's Lost* (also France), in which the well-known team of operatic adapters, Barbier and Carré, who adapted *Romeo and Juliet* and *Faust* for Gounod, completely discarded the da Ponte comedy and fitted the music, as best they could, to Shakespeare's. The original subtitle was *The School for Lovers*. The Metropolitan announces its English performances as *Women are Like That*, and a literal English translation of the title would land one in modern American slang: *All Females Make Like That*. Today, of course, no one would dream of tampering with either the text or the music. It is played as a stylized eighteenth-century comedy, and as the beautiful and subtle score is better and better understood, it is also appreciated that below the glitter and nonsense of the action there is much more than whipped-cream comedy.

OVERTURE

The Overture to *Così Fan Tutte* contains only one motive from the opera, that which is sung by Don Alfonso and the two young men toward the close of Act II to the words "*Così fan tutte.*" After a short, slow introduction, there appears a gay, bubbling sequence, typical of Mozart in his lightest moments,

John Brownlee as Alfonso at the Metropolitan Opera

interspersed with rapid exchanges between leading instruments. When this has been developed to a certain extent, the *"Così fan tutte"* motive returns, and presently the Overture comes to a close.

ACT I

SCENE 1: *A café.* Ferrando, Guglielmo, and Don Alfonso are sitting together at a table, having a general discussion about the constancy of women. Ferrando, very much in love with Dorabella, gets quite personal about it, mentioning the great trust he reposes in his own young lady, Dorabella, whose loyalty is the equal of her beauty. Not to be outdone, Guglielmo rushes to Fiordiligi's defense, and, for a moment, it begins to look as if the conversation will turn into a free-for-all. Don Alfonso, an aging bachelor, calm and very cynical, takes all of this zeal in stride, quite poised and assured in his knowledge of the world and its ways, a knowledge obtained, doubtless, from a lifetime of experience. He insists all women can be unfaithful.

At any rate, the discussion soon comes to the point where a wager is made—the stake, one hundred sequins, and the terms, Ferrando's and Guglielmo's complete agreement to do everything Don Alfonso prescribes for the next twenty-four hours. But, he cautions, nothing of this must be communicated to their "Penelopes," as he ironically refers to the young women. So certain are Ferrando and Guglielmo of winning that they begin to speculate how they will spend the money, and, finally, all three drink a toast to the wager.

SCENE 2: *A garden overlooking the Bay of Naples.* Dorabella and Fiordiligi, seated in the garden of their house, are gazing with ecstasy on medallions of their lovers. And to music of expressive beauty, contrasting with the kittenish quality of the textual lines, the sisters almost try to outdo one another in praise of their respective heroes.

Thus, as they are carrying on in rhapsodic mood, Don Alfonso appears on the scene. He is quite agitated, the orchestra depicting this to perfection, and after a few seconds of time in which he seems to regain his composure, he tells them that the worst has happened—Ferrando and Guglielmo have been ordered off to the wars. So desolate are they, he continues, that they have not the courage to bid their loves good-by in person, but that if the young women could withstand a painful interview of parting, they might come. He signals at once, and the two officers appear, as if by magic.

The ensuing quintet concluded, there is heard a drum roll, announcing the imminent departure of the officers' ship. A regiment of soldiers marches by, the usual crowd of townspeople dogging its steps, while they sing of the glories of the martial life. There is a tearful farewell between the lovers, during which even Don Alfonso, cynic though he is, does not remain unmoved. The ship leaves, and Don Alfonso joins the ladies in a prayer for a safe voyage. But when they leave, he is again the detractor of womankind, and sings smugly to that effect.

SCENE 3: *An anteroom in Fiordiligi's and Dorabella's house.* Despina, maid to the two sisters, enters with a tray containing cups of chocolate which she has prepared for her mistresses. Before their arrival she launches into a diatribe against domestic service. She is the typical servant-comedienne of broad farce, complaining, rather shrewd, impudent, and, in the long run, loyal.

Fiordiligi and Dorabella come into the anteroom and almost immediately indulge in an exaggerated show of their grief. Dorabella is heard in a recitative, *"Ah! scostati"* ("Ah! begone!"), and an aria, *"Smania implacabili"* ("Implacable wrath"), descriptive of her rebellious mood. Despina, meanwhile, counsels the young women—through purely self-arrogated powers—to do as their heroes are probably doing, that is, have a good time. And in the aria *"In uomini, in soldati"* ("In men, in soldiers") she expresses her contempt for all males and their philandering traits. At this the two ladies bounce up and leave the scene in righteous indignation.

To add to the confusion, Don Alfonso now appears

and bribes Despina to aid him in his scheme. With him are two spurious Albanian noblemen, who, of course, are Ferrando and Guglielmo in more or less comic disguises. The scheme is to supplant the ladies' lovers with these two likely gentlemen, who are not recognized by Despina. So, placing Don Alfonso in a hiding place, Despina summons her mistresses, who, as can be imagined, are horrified at the presence of two men in their house, and at such a time. When Don Alfonso enters, with due formality, he is agreeably surprised at finding these gentlemen, who, he declares, are good friends of his, and he makes much of his joy at seeing them again.

It is the lovers' job to be as ardent as possible, a little matter which, to be sure, is wildly magnified. The ladies at first protest mightily at this improper turn of events, and Fiordiligi sings, in what must naturally be assumed to be a serious vein, a lengthy protestation of her faithfulness. This is all contained, however, in a recitative followed by the well-known burlesque aria *"Come scoglio"* ("Like a rock"). Guglielmo's answer to that is *"Non siate ritrosi"* ("Don't be so shy"), a subtle and truly charming piece.

Nevertheless, the girls depart very haughtily, and the two masqueraders practically collapse from laughter, pointing the finger of ridicule at Don Alfonso and the apparent failure of his anti-female theories. He says, pointedly, however, *"E voi ridete"* ("And you laugh"), reminding them that the twenty-four hours of the wager are not yet over. Now Ferrando is given an aria, *"Un' aura amorosa"* ("A breeze of love"), a sentimental song all about the theory that love brings love, and such.

The disguised officers depart, leaving Don Alfonso alone with Despina, and in the ensuing colloquy their little scheme to break down the ladies' resistance is further advanced.

SCENE 4: *The garden of Fiordiligi's and Dorabella's house.* The two young women, in moods of melancholy reflection, sing the duet *"Ah, che tutta"* ("Ah, what a destiny"). Barely have they finished when Ferrando and Guglielmo rush in, each of them

Act I, Scene 3, in the Metropolitan Opera production, with Eleanor Steber, Blanche Thebom as sisters, and Patrice Munsel as Despina

Despina (Lucrezia Bori), Dorabella (Frances Peralta)

holding up, so that all may see, a bottle containing, we are told, a poison of which both have taken a draft. Don Alfonso, following on their heels, and Despina set out for the doctor. In the meantime, the young men go through all sorts of fraudulent contortions, and the ladies, not unsympathetic now, gently minister to the youths.

Don Alfonso returns with the "doctor," who is none other than Despina in a grotesque getup, and, after much mumbo-jumbo with a magnet, she seems to restore them to health. As the officers come to, they renew their amorous tactics, whereupon the sisters again leave in disapproval.

ACT II

SCENE 1: *A room in Fiordiligi's and Dorabella's house.* Still quite indignant, the sisters are briefed by Despina, now as herself again, on the possible attractions offered by the two "Albanian noblemen," and on how, perhaps, the sorrows they bear may now be in some measure compensated in an interesting manner. Alone, the sisters discuss this new and provocative suggestion, discovering that they might find some amusement in the company of these undeniably personable strangers, provided, however, that all is done with care and propriety. So, Dorabella selects the dark one (Guglielmo) for herself, and Fiordiligi, of course, the other. And they come to this important decision in the engaging duet

"Prenderò quel brunettino" ("I'll take the dark one"). After this Don Alfonso enters, and invites them to the garden, where a surprise awaits them.

SCENE 2: *The garden.* Ferrando and Guglielmo, still in their disguises, are on a barge moored to the landing place. There are singers and players, and the two men sing a duet serenade to the ladies. When the latter appear, Ferrando and Guglielmo continue their courtship. There are some conventional remarks, and Guglielmo, left alone with Dorabella, manages to soothe her enough to place around her neck a heart on a chain, which, he says, is a token of his great esteem for her, removing, at the same time, a necklace with a miniature of Ferrando. Ferrando, on the other hand, returns from a short walk among the trees with Fiordiligi not entirely successful with his wooing. Presently, Ferrando and Guglielmo discuss their respective experiences, and, in summation later with Don Alfonso, it is rather agreed that thus far, at least, half the bet has been won by him. The latter, not content with half a wager, would still prove to Guglielmo that Fiordiligi is as vulnerable as the other lady has shown herself to be.

SCENE 3: *A room in the house.* Dorabella receives congratulations from Despina on her sensible behavior. And when Fiordiligi comes in, with an apparent air of displeasure, we learn that she disapproves of her sister's behavior, while, at the same time, envying her a bit. And at this point Dorabella gives her a talk on being practical about things, and when Dorabella leaves, Fiordiligi decides to take a step in the only honorable direction. She orders Despina to fetch the officers' uniforms of Ferrando and Guglielmo (although it is not made clear just how these came to be reposing in the sisters' wardrobe). Her idea is that there is but one way in which she and her sister may retain their honor, and that by both donning the uniforms and joining their men at the front. But Ferrando, still the Albanian, rather unpropitiously enters, and with increasing ardor on his part and proportionally diminishing resistance on Fiordiligi's he succeeds in getting her admission that she loves him in the aria, "Per pietà ben mio" ("Forgive me, my love"). To all of this Guglielmo and Don Alfonso have been witness, and now it is Guglielmo's turn to eat humble pie. At first the young men would seek all sorts of redress for the faithlessness of their sweethearts, but Don Alfonso counsels them, in the song *"Tutti accusan le donne"* ("All blame the women"), that all women would act as they have done, and it is best to marry them, as they had originally planned, for they are no different from others. Besides, he adds, the men love them, don't they? Here Despina appears, saying that the sisters have made up their minds to marry their

Albanian swains, and have, therefore, sent for the notary.

SCENE 4: *A large room in Fiordiligi's and Dorabella's house.* The wedding feast is being prepared, under the watchful direction, of course, of Don Alfonso. The four protagonists enter, and soon a company of townspeople join them, singing a chorus of good wishes. The sisters and the officers, still garbed as Albanian noblemen, thank Despina for her part in making their happiness possible. And when the guests have departed, the two couples drink toasts all around.

In the midst of this ironic jubilation Despina appears, this time in the costume of a notary. With due (and grotesque) courtesy the contract arrangements are agreed upon and signed. Just then a distant drum roll is heard, and Don Alfonso, who has run to the window, anounces that Ferrando's and Guglielmo's regiment has returned from the wars, and, alas, that both young men are with it.

The spurious Albanians are rushed out of the room in the great turmoil that follows. Don Alfonso consoles the terrified and, understandably, very penitent sisters, while the young men hastily redon their original uniforms. As the real Ferrando and Guglielmo now, they return and express surprise at the rather tame response of their sweethearts and also at the presence of a notary. Besides, Ferrando has picked up the marriage contract, which Don Alfonso seems to have dropped, not without purpose.

To add to the sisters' consternation, Don Alfonso now asks the young men to look in the other room, which they do, and after some seconds for a quick change emerge as the Albanians. Guglielmo now gives to Dorabella the miniature of Ferrando, and both men sarcastically shower praise on the "doctor" who saw them safely through a dose of poison.

Now that the sisters know everything, they are completely humiliated. However, it is Don Alfonso who patches up things, with the thought that it was all done for the good of the lovers. The opera ends with a lively finale whose gist is to take things as they come.

Finale: Dorabella (Rosalind Elias), Ferrando (Richard Tucker), Despina (Roberta Peters), Alfonso (Donald Gramm), Guglielmo (Theodor Uppman), Fiordiligi (Leontyne Price)

The Daughter of the Regiment
LA FILLE DU RÉGIMENT

CHARACTERS

Marie, *the "daughter of the regiment"*	*Soprano*	Tonio, *a Tyrolese peasant*	*Tenor*
Sulpice, *master sergeant of French Grenadiers*	*Bass*	The Marquise de Birkenfeld	*Mezzo-soprano*
		Hortensius, *her steward*	*Bass*
		The Duchesse de Krakenthorp	*Mezzo-soprano*

Soldiers, Peasants, Aristocrats, Servants

The action takes place in the Swiss Tyrol about 1815.

Joan Sutherland as Marie in Sandro Sequi's staging of The Daughter of the Regiment *at the Royal Opera House, London*

LIGHT OPERA in two acts. Music by Gaetano Donizetti. Libretto in French by Jules Henri Vernoy de St. Georges and Jean Francois Alfred Bayard. Première at the Opéra-Comique, Paris, February 11, 1840. First American performance at New York, July 19, 1840 with Patti, in Italian. First performance at the Metropolitan Opera House, January 6, 1902 with Sembrich, in French. The first, and much the most popular, of the many light works Donizetti wrote for the French stage, *La Fille* was—and is—a favorite with coloratura sopranos who have fancied themselves in the costume of a nineteenth-century drum majorette. Among the great ones for whom this work has been revived have been Jenny Lind, Henriette Sontag, Adelina Patti, Marcella Sembrich, Luisa Tetrazzini, Frieda Hempel, Lily Pons, Lina Pagliughi, Anna Moffo and Joan Sutherland.

Like *The Bartered Bride*, this work was originally a light opera, or musical comedy, with spoken dialogue, and was supplied with recitatives after its original success so it could be produced at the more staid opera houses whose tradition of "grand" opera insisted that all lines must be sung. In this case, the notes were added for the Italian production at La Scala, Milan, in the year of its French première. Its spirit remains, however, thoroughly in the musical comedy tradition, as does its familiar plot formula: boy-meets-girl, boy-loses-girl, boy-gets-girl. Old-fash-

Jenny Lind, celebrated Marie during the nineteenth century

ioned though it is, its tunes remain enchanting, and one of its numbers, the "*Salut à France*," was a durable favorite with French regimental bands for over a century.

ACT I

SCENE: *A valley in the Swiss Tyrolean Alps.* Off stage the Twenty-first Regiment of French Grenadiers is engaged in battle, while on stage the Tyrolean peasants and the Marquise de Birkenfeld, accompanied by her steward, pray for success. Our heroes are, of course, victorious, and our heroine Marie sings a fine air, with a great coloratura cadenza, expressing her satisfaction with the warriors who have brought her up from childhood. For she was found on the battlefield and raised by the entire regiment—and particularly by old Master Sergeant Sulpice—to be their *vivandière*, a kind of quartermaster in feminine form. Marie wears a military uniform and beats the drum as she then leads the male chorus in a spirited *rataplan* (which is an onomatopoeic word signifying a song accompanied by a drum).

Left by themselves, Marie tells Sulpice of a young peasant who recently rescued her from falling over a precipice and how she has thereupon fallen in love with him. Sulpice is disturbed, for it had always been the plan of the Twenty-first to marry her to the best of the grenadiers. Their dialogue is interrupted by some soldiers dragging in the young man him-

Frieda Hempel, World War I Marie at the Metropolitan Opera

self—Tonio—whom they have caught hanging around the encampment and naturally taken for a spy. Marie soon explains who he really is; Tonio decides to enlist; everyone joins in another rousing military number—"The Song of the Regiment"—and then, after a love duet between the two juveniles, there is another *rataplan*.

The Marquise de Birkenfeld returns to the scene to ask for a safe-conduct, and Sulpice remembers that "Birkenfeld" was the name found on the papers in the clothing of the child Marie when first she was taken into the regiment. The Marquise examines the papers and pronounces Marie her long-lost niece. She insists that the girl must come with her to the Castle of Birkenfeld to be brought up as an aristocrat, and the act closes with everyone despondent because the best of friends must part—and Tonio has enlisted in vain.

ACT II

SCENE: *A hall in the Castle of Birkenfeld.* The Marquise tries conscientiously to instruct Marie in the ladylike arts of drawing-room song and dancing the minuet. Unfortunately for her, she made the kindly error of inviting the old Sergeant Sulpice as a companion for her protégée, and the two are cutting pranks by going from respectable songs into military music, including even a *rataplan*. Yet they know that Marie must learn, for it has been decreed that she is to marry a scion of the noble house of Krakenthorp.

The good old Twenty-first marches by, and Marie, finding that Tonio has been made a captain for gallantry in the field, cannot resist her old love, and they make plans to elope. The kindly Marquise, however, finally admits the truth of Marie's birth. She is not a niece after all, but the Marquise's own illegitimate child. Marie now feels duty-bound to stay with her mother. The Krakenthorp clan and other guests, who have been expected that very day, now arrive, and before long Marie sings for them a spirited aria in praise of her own recent existence as a *vivandière*. The Krakenthorps are all appalled at the prospect of such an alliance, and the good-natured Marquise bows wisely to the inevitable. She herself places Marie's hand in Tonio's.

The opera closes with one more rendition of a fine marchlike chorus from Act I, the "*Salut à France.*"

Marie (Lily Pons) takes song lesson from the Marquise (Irra Petina) at the Metropolitan, during World War II

Les Dialogues des Carmélites

CHARACTERS

Blanche de la Force	*Soprano*	Sister Constance	*Soprano*
Madame de Croissy, *the Prioress*		The Marquis de la Force, *Blanche's*	
	Mezzo-soprano	*father*	*Baritone*
Madame Lidoine, *the new Prioress*	*Soprano*	The Chevalier de la Force, *his son*	*Tenor*
Mother Marie	*Mezzo-soprano*	The Chaplain	*Tenor*

Other Carmelite Nuns, Commissioners, a Jailer, a Doctor, a Servant, an Officer, Crowds

The action takes place in Paris and Compiègne in 1789.

OPERA IN THREE ACTS. Music by Francis Poulenc. Libretto is the play in French prose by Georges Bernanos, with very minor cuts, based on a novelet by Gertrude von Le Fort. The story is based on a historical event. Première at La Scala, Milan, January 26, 1957, in Italian. Première in French June 21, 1957, at the Opéra, Paris. First performance in the U.S. on September 20, 1957, at San Francisco, in English. Televised by the NBC Opera Company, December 8, 1957, in English. It won the opera award that season of the New York Music Critics' Circle. The work has had many stage productions since, both by professional companies and by opera workshops, including one, in 1965, in Pittsburgh, given, appropriately, in the cathedral.

Like Debussy's *Pelléas et Mélisande*, this opera uses as a libretto a play in prose that had already been successful without a musical setting, and like Debussy, Poulenc was remarkably successful in remaining completely faithful to the spirit and the text of the original, sacrificing only a very few lines and no scenes whatever, as Debussy was obliged to do. Poulenc's problem would seem to have been even greater, for Bernanos' play, despite its melodramatic and highly effective ending, has a very thin story line, is devoid of conventional love interest, and is composed—as the title promises—largely of dialogues of a religious nature. The composer resolved this problem with great skill, tact, and taste. There

are, of course, no set arias, but the dialogue and its emotional overtones are heightened by the musical setting of the prose speech. As a result, the few set concerted numbers, largely prayers in Latin, stand out all the more as a realistic and dramatic part of life. This is most striking in the *"Ave Maria"* sung—almost whispered—*a capella* in Act II, when the new Mother Superior has finished her first, slightly embarrassed and very moving address to the nuns. It is, of course, most effective of all in the last scene when, as the crowd sings its own tune, the Carmelite nuns mount the scaffold singing the *"Salve Regina,"* their music growing ever weaker as the thumping of the guillotine is heard off stage.

Poulenc is deservedly famous for the wit and elegance of many of his songs and the delight and high spirits of such compositions as the two-piano concerto and the ballet *Les Biches*. At the same time he achieved high seriousness in much of his choral music, and perhaps nowhere better than in *Dialogues des Carmélites*, which was one of his last completed works.

ACT I

SCENE 1: *The library of the Marquis de la Force.* The Marquis de la Force, during the early days of the French Revolution, is napping in an easy chair

New York City Opera: Death of the old Prioress (Clara-mae Turner)

fears in such an exposure. She is already terribly afraid of the world—so much so that he considers her quite ill. Yet when Blanche comes in a moment later, she speaks lightly and affectionately to her father and brother, saying that she even found her danger rather refreshing. It is only a pose, for she almost faints at this point, and the Chevalier is not fooled by her explanation that the services at the convent were tiring. As she leaves for her own room, he insists she must have candles, for she is so afraid of the dark.

When the Marquis is again alone, he hears a cry of terror, and Blanche, visibly shaken but with an air of determination, comes back to him. She has been frightened by the shadow of a servant lighting the candles; but more than that, she has finally determined to enter the Carmelite order and become a nun. The world is too much with her; she cannot live in it; she will give herself to God. During all this her neurotic fears are evident but her natural dignity and religious convictions overpower them, and she speaks with a calm assurance. Her father puts up only a feeble resistance, and when she throws herself at his feet imploring his pity, he quietly strokes her head.

SCENE 2: *Parlor of the Carmelite convent at Compiègne.* Separated by a grille, Blanche and the old Mother Superior of the Carmelites are having a dialogue about why Blanche is drawn to the Carmelites and what the meaning and purpose of the order is. Blanche, seeking a heroic life, appears to have been drawn to the order because its rules are severe. The Mother Superior explains that while the rules of the order may be severe, the aim is not the achievement of a heroic life thereby. That would be far too easy. The order exists not for mortification of the flesh or the protection of virtue, but for prayer, and God does not test one's strength, but one's weakness. Blanche weeps for joy at these harsh ideas; they make the Carmelite order seem that much more valuable to her, and she tells the tired old Mother Superior what name she has chosen for herself as a nun. It is to be Sister Blanche of the Agony of Christ. The Mother Superior blesses her.

SCENE 3: *A tower room of the convent.* While sorting vegetables, the very youthful Sister Constance chatters away lightly about things that have amused her and is rebuked by the very serious Sister Blanche for talking like that while the Mother Superior is dying. But Constance (a most attractive figure) finds not only life but death, too, amusing. Blanche gently tries to suggest that God may have other ideas, but the affectionate young humor is irrepressible. Lightly (but actually prophetically) she tells Blanche that she has always wished to die

when his son, the Chevalier de la Force, bursts in much disturbed because his sister Blanche has not returned from church services and he has heard that Blanche's carriage was surrounded by an angry mob. For a moment the old Marquis has terrifying memories of twenty years earlier when his own wife, returning from a royal wedding, was similarly attacked, rescued just in time, but returned dreadfully shaken and that night died in giving birth to Blanche. But the Marquis pulls himself together and belittles the danger Blanche may be in. His carriage, he says, is sturdy, his horses sound, and the driver a faithful servant. The Chevalier is not so sanguine. It is the effect on Blanche's sensitive nature that he very young and, in fact, as soon as she saw Blanche, she thought it would be a fine thing to die together with her. Blanche is appalled by the pride implicit in the sentiment and forbids Constance to go on. The young girl is apologetic and bewildered.

SCENE 4: *A small room in the infirmary.* Obviously on her deathbed, the Mother Superior is speaking of the desolation of the process of dying to her trusted old friend Mother Marie. She is worried, too, about Blanche, whom she must soon be leaving, and she entrusts her spiritual care to Mother Marie, for the girl, she fears, lacks strength of character. When Blanche comes to her, she speaks with deep affection but firmly instructs her to stay true to her own sweet and simple nature, never to rebel against it, and to trust her honor not to her own keeping but to God's.

Blanche leaves, and the doctor and Sister Anne enter. Exhausted by her interview with Blanche, the sick old woman asks for drugs and, when they are not given her, becomes delirious. God, she cries, should attend to her, not she to God; then, in a hoarse voice, she says she sees the chapel of the Carmelites bespattered with blood. Finally, when Blanche returns, the Mother Superior recognizes her and wants to speak with her once more. But it is too late. She dies before she can begin.

ACT II

SCENE 1: *The nuns' chapel.* At night, the room lit by only six candles, Sisters Blanche and Constance are completing their watch over the body of the Mother Superior, uttering a requiem prayer in Latin, when the clock strikes and Constance goes to fetch the next pair of sisters. Left alone, Blanche is frightened and goes to the door, leaving the body momentarily unattended. Mother Marie, entering at that moment, first reproves Blanche and then, seeing how frightened she is, comforts her, excusing her from further prayers, and telling her that the morning will be time enough to beg God's pardon.

INTERLUDE: *Before the curtain.* Sisters Blanche and Constance, bringing flowers for the Mother Superior's grave, discuss the ways of God, and the naïve younger girl utters one more strange and prophetic thought. This is that the Mother Superior had such a bad death, a death "much too small for her," that it must mean someone else will find a far easier, more comfortable one. "People die for each other," she says, "or, who knows? even *in place of* each other."

SCENE 2: *The chapter room.* As the curtain rises, the members of the chapter are passing before Madame Lidoine, who has been appointed the new Mother Superior, kissing her hand in token of obedience.

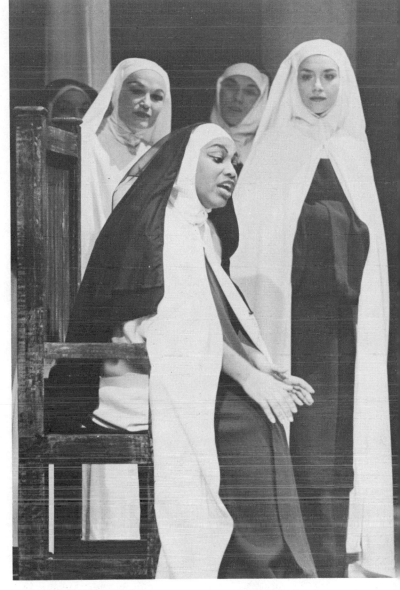

San Francisco Opera: Dorothy Kirsten (Blanche), Leontyne Price (Mme. Lidoine), Sylvia Stahlmann (Constance) in Act II

She makes a simple address stressing the characteristic of humbleness that marks the order, without ambition even for martyrdom, its central duty being that of prayer. After a few more words from Mother Marie, she leads the sisters in singing the beautiful, unaccompanied "*Ave Maria.*"

INTERLUDE: *Before the curtain.* The Mother Superior and Mother Marie learn from Sister Constance that a rider has driven up to the secret side gate, and he turns out to be the Chevalier de la Force asking to speak to his sister. The Mother Superior delegates Mother Marie to listen, unseen, to the interview.

SCENE 3: *The parlor.* As Mother Marie listens on one side, the Chevalier de la Force asks Blanche to come home again, for she is in danger where she is, and she looks haggard from her fear. Blanche, however, will not be moved. She is no longer the Chevalier's "little lamb," and whatever her fears may be, she is now a daughter of Carmel, free and happy, and a companion of her brother in a danger she does not deny but seems to welcome. The Chevalier, confused and made unhappy by her apparent physical weakness and spiritual independence, leaves. Blanche fears that she sinned by acting too proudly, and Mother Marie recognizes this but comforts the younger woman.

SCENE 4: *The sacristy.* The Chaplain of the order has just completed the last Mass he is permitted to celebrate and leads the nuns in the "*Ave verum corpus.*" At its close he reassures the fearful Blanche that he will be safe, for he will discard his vestments, hide near the convent, and come whenever he can. When he has left by a secret door, the nuns comment on the fear that is spreading everywhere with the suppression of religious orders, a fear that is especially gripping Blanche, who regards it as a disease. A moment later the Chaplain returns, having almost been caught by the crowd outside, and he is offered a shelter he is reluctant to accept for the danger it must bring to the order if he is found there. His fears are immediately realized when there are shouts from a crowd outside to open the door. Fearlessly, little Sister Constance opens it, admitting four commissioners, as guards hold back the crowd. One of the commissioners reads an order that all religious establishments must be evacuated and the buildings sold. With great dignity and fortitude, Mother Marie accepts this order, remarking that in times like this the people have need for martyrs. In an aside, another commissioner tells her that he intends no brutality, for he had only recently been a sacristan deeply devoted to the abbott of his monastery, and he offers to lead away the crowd while the nuns make their preparations. When the commissioners have left, Blanche is entrusted with a small figure of Jesus which at Christmastime was always carried around from cell to cell. At once moved and frightened by this mark of trust, Blanche exclaims on the tininess of the Child—and drops the figure, which breaks to pieces. "Now all that remains," she cries, "is the Lamb of God!" Outside, the crowd is heard hoarsely beginning the revolutionary "*Ça ira.*"

ACT III

SCENE 1: *The chapel.* In the chapel of the Carmelites, which has been ravaged by a revolutionary mob, the nuns are assembled under the guidance of Mother Marie, the Mother Superior having been forcibly detained from attending the meeting. Mother Marie asks for a unanimous vote to have the chapter take the vow of martyrdom, and the Chaplain, now in pathetically torn street clothes, takes the individual votes behind a screen. Throughout, Sister Constance keeps a devoted eye on Sister Blanche, who she (along with others) suspects may be too weakened and fearful to vote for such a stern and frightening measure; and when the Chaplain reports the vote, he says there was only one against the vow. However, it was not Blanche but Constance who had thus voted, in sympathy for Blanche; and when she discovers that Blanche's courage had after all not failed, she changes her own vote to make the measure unanimous. Blanche and Constance, as the youngest, take their vows first, but as the others continue in order, Blanche, now unobserved, flees from the chapel.

INTERLUDE: *Before the curtain.* The Carmelites, now in ordinary clothes and carrying their gowns in small bundles, are congratulated by an officer on their obedience to commands; but he also warns them that they must not resume their occupation as nuns or gather together again. The officer then leaves, and Mother Marie reluctantly agrees to abide by the Mother Superior's decision to warn the Chaplain not to say one last Mass, for it is too dangerous. Such going back, thinks Marie, is not in accord with the spirit of the vow of martyrdom they have all taken.

SCENE 2: *The library of the Marquis de la Force.* The once handsome room, like the chapel of the Carmelites, has been ravaged by a mob; its aristocratic owner has been guillotined; and Blanche is living in the house as a servant to some revolutionary masters. A folding bed and a stove have been placed in the room, and Blanche is cooking a stew when Mother Marie bursts in dressed as a civilian. She demands that Blanche come with her to a safer place, but the girl, still fearful, thinks that her present status will make her overlooked. She becomes nervous and upsets the pot of stew, and Mother Marie helps set it right. Blanche cries over this kindness, yet she cannot make herself go with her would-be savior. For a moment she draws herself up and says that she must live up to her adopted name, Sister Blanche of the Agony of Christ. Then Mother Marie gives up—insisting only that Blanche remember an address to go to where she can be safely received. Blanche says she will not come, and the scene ends as she responds to a rasping voice off stage demanding her attention.

SCENE 3: *A prison cell at the Conciergerie.* All the members of the chapter save Blanche and Mother Marie are prisoners in the miserable cell, and the Mother Superior addresses them, telling them to have courage and that she now assumes the vow of martyrdom which they all had taken in her absence. Someone asks where Blanche is, and Sister Constance confidently predicts that she will come to them: she saw it in a dream. Then the jailer enters, accompanied by a drummer, and reads an order of the Revolutionary Tribunal condemning to death the whole chapter for helping enemies of the revolution. The civil name of each of the members is read out, but that of Blanche de la Force is not among them. Once more the Mother Superior addresses them for the last solemn time.

INTERLUDE: *Before a curtain showing a street near the Bastille.* The Chaplain, meeting Mother Marie, tells her that all have been condemned to death and that the execution will be carried out at the latest the next day. Mother Marie decides that she, though not condemned, must join the others to fulfill her vow, but the Chaplain tells her that this is a matter which God must decide, not Mother Marie.

SCENE 4: *The Place de la Revolution.* As the Carmelites descend from the tumbril that has carried them here, the steps of the scaffold may be seen, though not the guillotine itself. A crowd is assembled to watch, and among them is the Chaplain, wearing a cap of liberty and secretly giving absolution and making the sign of the cross as each nun begins the ascent of the scaffold. They sing the *"Salve Regina,"* but their chorus diminishes as the guillotine's thumps are heard off stage. Almost the last to ascend is Sister Constance, and her face beams with an ineffable radiance as she sees Sister Blanche making her way through the crowd. Blanche, too, mounts the steps and sings—but cannot complete—the last four verses of the *"Veni Creator."* The murmuring crowd slowly disperses.

Final scene of Dialogues des Carmélites *as staged at the world première by Margherita Wallmann at La Scala, Milan*

Dido and Aeneas

CHARACTERS

Dido, *Queen of Carthage*	*Mezzo-soprano*	Sorceress	*Contralto*
Belinda, *a lady in waiting*	*Soprano*	Aeneas, *legendary founder of Rome*	*Baritone*
Attendant	*Mezzo-soprano*		

Spirit, First Witch, Second Witch, Courtiers, Sailors

The action takes place in ancient Carthage.

Kirsten Flagstad as Dido, at Mermaid Theater, London

OPERA IN THREE ACTS. Music by Henry Purcell. Libretto in English by Nahum Tate, based on his play *Brutus of Alba*, based in turn on Book IV of Virgil's *Aeneid*. Written for and first produced by the Chelsea School (for girls only) in 1689, probably in December. First American production, in concert form, at Town Hall, New York, by forces from the Metropolitan in Artur Bodanzky's version. First American staged performance, February 18, 1932, by the Juilliard School of Music. Revived September 9, 1951, at the Mermaid Theatre in London, it ran for about a hundred nights. Kirsten Flagstad sang Dido—her last operatic role.

The librettist Nahum Tate was England's Poet Laureate, one of her very worst, as an inspection of the libretto proves. Nevertheless, it sings well. Josiah Priest, who as headmaster of the Chelsea School commissioned the work, was also London's leading ballet master. This may partly account for the large amount of dancing in the opera. And the fact that the school was one for young ladies must account for some of the differences between Tate's plot and Virgil's—for example, Dido's dying of a conventional broken heart rather than by suicide.

There are a number of unique features in the history of this beautiful work. It is the only complete opera written by the composer. It was given a few times in London by professionals (the last time in 1704 as an interlude between the acts of *Measure for Measure*) and then forgotten for over a hundred and fifty years. It is today regarded as unquestionably

114

Dido (Janet Baker) laments her betrayal by Aeneas, in the Glyndebourne Festival production of 1964

the greatest opera ever composed by an Englishman. And perhaps its final aria, "Dido's Lament," is the most moving aria for mezzo-soprano ever composed.

ACT I

SCENE 1: *Dido's throne room.* The tragic Queen of Carthage, surrounded by her ladies-in-waiting, is urged by her faithful attendant Belinda to "shake the cloud from off your brow." In a series of arias, duets, and choruses it becomes clear that the Trojan Prince Aeneas, fleeing the ruins of Troy, has landed in the North African kingdom and that everyone believes it would be wise for Dido to marry him. Aeneas himself enters and presses his suit with the support of the ladies. Dido softens, and the scene ends with a gay "Dance of Triumph."

SCENE 2: *The cave of the Sorceress.* The Sorceress, with her attending witches, plots the ruin of Carthage and of Dido, with choruses of evil laughter. Off stage are heard hunting calls (orchestrated for strings) indicative of the hunt which Dido and Aeneas are now engaged in.

ACT II

SCENE: *A grove.* With the hunt reaching its end, the whole court pauses in a beautiful spot to celebrate. Distant thunder interrupts, and on the urging of Belinda ("Haste, haste to town") everyone leaves the stage. Only Aeneas is stopped by one of the Sorceress' followers disguised as Mercury, the messenger of the gods. "Mercury" commands Aeneas, on the word of Jove, to dally no longer in Carthage but to fulfill his mission, which is to found a new Troy—that is, Rome—on Latin soil. Though he bitterly regrets that this will mean leaving Dido, Aeneas is persuaded of his divine duty.

ACT III

SCENE: *The harbor of Carthage.* Led by one of them, the Trojan sailors sing a lively farewell to their gay doings in Carthage and then dance as they make their final preparations for departure. The Sorceress and her followers also sing and dance in glee as they see their plot taking effect. Witches and sailors finally join in the general high spirits.

With the stage cleared, Dido tells Belinda of her foreboding of evil, and Aeneas confirms her fears. He tries to tell her that the gods are responsible for his desertion; and proudly and scornfully Dido rejects his explanation and rejects him, too, when he promises to defy the gods and stay. A sober chorus, in contrast to the gay opening of the scene, prepares us for the great final aria "When I am laid in earth." The simple descending figure in the bass line is repeated throughout, as Dido utters her movingly, eloquent farewell to life: "Remember me, but ah! forget my fate."

Don Carlos

CHARACTERS

Philip II of Spain	*Bass*	Elizabeth of Valois	*Soprano*
Don Carlos, *his son*	*Tenor*	Princess Eboli, *lady-in-waiting*	
Rodrigo, *Marquis of Posa*	*Baritone*	*to Elizabeth*	*Mezzo-soprano*
Grand Inquisitor	*Bass*	Tebaldo, *Elizabeth's page*	*Mezzo-soprano*
A Friar (Charles V)	*Bass*	A Heavenly Voice	*Soprano*
		Countess of Aremberg	*Mime*

Flemish Ladies, Inquisitors, Gentlemen and Ladies of the Court, Members of the
Populace, Pages, Guards, Familiars of the Holy Office, Soldiers, Magistrates

The action takes place in France and Spain in the sixteenth century.

OPERA IN FIVE ACTS. Music by Giuseppe Verdi. Libretto in French by François Joseph Méry and Camille du Locle, founded on a tragedy by Schiller. First performance at the Opéra, Paris, March 11, 1867. United States première at the Academy of Music, New York, April 12, 1877, in Italian. Also in Italian, *Don Carlos* entered the Metropolitan repertory on December 23, 1920, with Rosa Ponselle, Margarete Matzenauer, Giovanni Martinelli, Giuseppe de Luca, Adamo Didur, and Marie Sundelius in the principal roles. In 1950, after an absence of twenty-seven years, *Don Carlos* returned to inaugurate the managership of Rudolf Bing.

Don Carlos belongs to an intermediate stage of Verdi's career as a composer. Coming after the magnificent successes of *Il Trovatore, La Traviata,* and *The Masked Ball,* it shows Verdi reaching out toward the fuller, richer style with which he was later to become associated in *Aïda.*

Schiller's highly dramatic tragedy inspired Verdi to compose some thrilling operatic music. Moreover, the fact that he was writing for the French lyric theater may have influenced him to follow, somewhat, the example of Meyerbeer in conceiving his work on a grandiose scale.

Sixteen years or so after the world première of *Don Carlos* Verdi, apparently finding its libretto a bit cumbersome, gave his Italian librettist Antonio Ghislanzoni authority to shorten it to four acts, he himself revising the score. Although he considered this abbreviated version musically stronger with the excision of Act I, a third edition reinstated Act I, retaining, however, most of the alterations in the previous revision.

ACT I *(often omitted)*

SCENE: *The forest of Fontainebleau.* Spain and France are technically at war, but Don Carlos, the Infante of Spain, has been affianced to the beautiful Elizabeth of Valois. Secretly, and in the disguise of a Spanish envoy, he has come to France to catch a glimpse of the girl he is supposed to marry. He has this chance as a hunting party rides through the forest of Fontainebleau, and he falls in love with her at once. (The aria in which he sings of this new-found love is, somewhat altered, introduced into the second act when the first act is omitted.) Presently Elizabeth and her page Tebaldo, having lost the rest of the hunting party, pass by once more, and Carlos offers to lead them home. Elizabeth dismisses Tebaldo, and Carlos lights a fire in the growing dusk. She questions him about her Spanish fiancé, and he, assuring her of that gentleman's staunch loyalty, draws a picture of himself from his pocket and says it was confided to him for her by the Infante. Elizabeth immediately recognizes Carlos from his picture, and a love duet follows.

But Tebaldo returns, heralding the approach of the head of the Spanish mission to the court of France. Philip, King of Spain and father of Carlos, has proposed that he himself should marry Elizabeth of Valois. The decision is left up to her, but she is so earnestly pressed, in the interest of peace, to take the King, that she sacrifices her new-found happiness.

ACT II

SCENE 1: *The Monastery of San Giusto in Madrid.* Led by a mysterious friar, the monks sing an impressive prayer before his tomb for the peace of the soul of Charles V, grandfather of Don Carlos and the late Emperor of the Holy Roman Empire.* As Charles had done, Carlos has come here to forget his troubles, and he sings of his love for Elizabeth (that is, if the aria has not already been sung in Act I). He welcomes his close friend Rodrigo, Marquis of Posa, just returned from Flanders, who urges him to

* This is the ''Don Carlos'' who sings the leading baritone role in Verdi's *Ernani* (see p. 134).

Chicago Lyric Opera: Rodrigo (Tito Gobbi), Philip (Nicolai Ghiaurov)

Giovanni Martinelli, the first Don Carlos at the Metropolitan Opera, in 1921

go to that country, now bitterly oppressed by Spanish rule, and bring relief. It may, too, lighten his depression over his love for his stepmother. The two men swear eternal friendship in a ringing succession of major thirds. A procession led by King Philip and his young bride passes through the church, and Carlos is almost overcome by the sight of Elizabeth. But the voice of the mysterious friar leading the chant encourages him, as do the words of Rodrigo. The two young men again swear eternal friendship.

SCENE 2: *A garden outside the monastery.* The ladies of the court are awaiting the Queen; and the Princess Eboli (a historical character who always wore a patch over one eye), with the assistance of Tebaldo, sings a colorful Moorish romance. Shortly after the Queen arrives, Rodrigo comes bearing messages for her from Paris, and he asks her to persuade Philip to give Carlos an interview. She says that she will see Carlos alone first. In the duet between the young lovers that ensues, Carlos first asks Elizabeth to use her influence with Philip to have him sent to Flanders; and then, though he has tried to restrain himself, his love makes him reproach her for having married his father. Though Elizabeth still loves Carlos, she shows herself the stronger of the two by pleading her duty. Carlos, in a fit of emotion, falls at her feet (the historical Carlos having been subject to fits all his life), and when he rises again, tries to take the Queen in his arms. Elizabeth severely reproaches him for his actions, and he rushes away.

When the King comes on the scene, he is furious to find Elizabeth unattended and orders her attendant, the Countess of Aremberg, to return to France. Elizabeth tries to console the distraught woman.

Act III, Scene 2, as staged at the Metropolitan: Elizabeth (Raina Kabaivanska), Don Carlos (Bruno Prevedi) and Philip (Jerome Hines)

When the King and Rodrigo are alone, there is a long and strong duet between them in which the trusted nobleman begs for relief for the Flemish. The King argues that severity rather than freedom brings happiness to a people, and that it is really the Inquisition, in the person of the Grand Inquisitor, that insists on such a policy. The King shows his further trust of Rodrigo by telling him of his misgivings about Elizabeth and Carlos.

ACT III

SCENE 1: *In the palace garden.* Carlos has received an unsigned request for a rendezvous, and thinking it to be from Elizabeth, passionately declares his love to a masked figure who meets him in the dark. It turns out, however, to be Eboli, who is naturally furious when Carlos displays his dismay. She accuses him of loving his stepmother, and she cannot be calmed down even by the excellent diplomat Rodrigo, who intervenes. Rodrigo even threatens to kill the woman, but she continues to vow vengeance and

expose the lovers. She indignantly leaves the two, and the scene closes with Carlos' turning over to Rodrigo some incriminating correspondence from Flanders, with a reiteration of the friendship theme.

SCENE 2: *The great square in Madrid.* The Inquisition is about to burn a group of heretics, who are already bound to stakes at the back of the stage. The people are rejoicing over the prospect when the King enters in a procession. Carlos introduces some representatives from Flanders, who beg for relief for their country. Philip refuses it, and a grand ensemble results with many begging for mercy for the suppliants, but the King and the monks standing firm. Carlos then demands that he be sent as governor to Flanders, and when his father refuses this too, the young man draws his sword in anger. Philip orders him disarmed, and when no one dares touch the Prince, Rodrigo once more saves the situation by asking his friend for the sword and turning it over to the King. For this service, Rodrigo is made a Duke, and attention is now turned to the waiting victims of the Inquisition. The fires are lighted; everyone joins in a chorus of rejoicing, and a voice from heaven proclaims pardon for the souls of the dying.

ACT IV

SCENE 1: *King Philip's room in the palace.* Alone, the King sings his great soliloquy *"Ella giammai m'amò"* ("She never loved me"). The stern and blind old Grand Inquisitor has been summoned, and when he arrives, Philip tells him he has decided either to forgive Don Carlos entirely or to have him executed. Would the Church back him if he decides on the sterner course? The old man rationalizes the proposed death by reminding the King that God had sacrificed his Son's life for the good of the many— and then goes further and demands the life of Rodrigo, a far more dangerous foe to the church. Despite threats, the King refuses, claiming that Rodrigo is the only human being he can trust. The powerful and stormy scene ends with the blind old man led out by a servant and the King feeling more alone than ever.

Elizabeth comes in saying that her jewel box is missing. The King replies that it is on his desk and demands that she open it. When she refuses, he does so himself and finds there a picture of Don Carlos. With dignity, she denies his charge of infidelity, and when he threatens her with death, she faints. The King's call for help brings in Princess Eboli and the ubiquitous Rodrigo, who convince the King of Elizabeth's innocence, and an eloquent quartet ensues in which each character gives voice to his own private sorrow. Left with Elizabeth, and full of remorse, Eboli admits that she had stolen the jewel box and given it to the King. Furthermore, she admits to having been the King's mistress. Elizabeth demands that Eboli either go into exile or enter a convent as a nun. She then sweeps from the room, and Eboli closes the scene with the great contralto aria *"O don fatale,"* in which she curses the gift of beauty she had been given. Knowing Carlos is now in danger, she vows to save him.

SCENE 2: *A prison.* Carlos has already been seized, and Rodrigo comes to bid farewell, for the incriminating correspondence has been found in his possession and he knows his days are numbered. Carlos protests that he will tell the truth, but even as they are talking, a man enters and shoots Rodrigo with an arquebus. With his last breath, Rodrigo tells his friend that the Queen is awaiting him at the Monastery of San Giusto. The King now enters and, much moved by the sight of Rodrigo's body, offers his sword back to his son. But Carlos spurns the man who, he thinks, has had his dearest friend murdered. The noise of a crowd is heard outside and, overrul-

ing his attendants' fears, the King has them admitted. They angrily demand the release of Don Carlos, and it is only through the intervention of the stern old Grand Inquisitor, who conveniently appears, that Philip is saved from a serious insurrection.

ACT V

SCENE: *The Monastery of San Giusto.* As she awaits Carlos, Elizabeth sings sadly of the farewell she must now say to him; and when Carlos joins her (he having escaped during the insurrection with the aid of Eboli), they sing the third of their duets. It is to be truly a farewell, for he has decided that, with the death of Rodrigo, he must go to lead the Flemish. While they are in each other's arms for the first and the last time, the King and the Inquisitor find them. Philip demands the immediate death of his son, but the mysterious monk from the monastery appears; they all think he may be the ghost of Charles V. Carlos is spirited into the tomb of the old Emperor.

Act IV, Scene 1: Queen (Raina Kabaivanska), Princess Eboli (Grace Bumbry)

Don Giovanni

DON JUAN

CHARACTERS

Don Giovanni, *a nobleman*	Baritone (*or Bass*)	
Leporello, *his servant*	Bass	
Don Pedro, *the Commandant*	Bass	
Donna Anna, *his daughter*	Soprano	

Don Ottavio, *Donna Anna's fiancé*	Tenor
Donna Elvira, *a lady of Burgos*	Soprano
Masetto, *a peasant*	Bass (*or Baritone*)
Zerlina, *betrothed to Masetto*	Soprano

Peasants, Musicians, Dancers, Demons

The action takes place at Seville in the seventeenth century.

OPERA IN TWO ACTS. Music by Wolfgang Amadeus Mozart. Libretto in Italian by Lorenzo da Ponte, partly founded on Giovanni Bertati's *Don Giovanni, ossia Il Convitato di Pietra* (*Don Juan, or The Stone Guest*). The complete title of the Mozart-da Ponte opera is really *Il Dissoluto Punito, ossia Il Don Giovanni* (*The Reprobate Punished, or Don Juan*). First performance, National Theater, Prague, October 29, 1787. First American performance given at the Park Theater, New York, May 23, 1826. Metropolitan première took place on November 29, 1883, with a cast including Emmy Fursch-Madi, Christine Nilsson, Marcella Sembrich, Roberto Stagno, Giuseppe Kaschmann, and Giovanni Mirabella.

The Don Juan theme, whose origin has been traced to legends out of Spanish monasteries no longer in existence, was first treated by Tirso de Molina (Gabriel Tellez) in a dramatic play, dating from 1630, which, more or less, is the source for da Ponte's libretto. Other dramatists who have utilized the legend have been Molière, for his comedy *Don Juan, ou Le Festin de Pierre* (*Don Juan, or The Stone Guest*), 1665, and Thomas Shadwell, in his *The Libertine*. The legend has received numerous treatments by many men of literature, and the composers who have turned to it for inspiration number among them, besides Mozart and Gazzaniga (who

did the setting for Bertati's libretto), Gluck, who composed a ballet based on it, and Dargomijsky, who wrote a four-act opera on the theme to a libretto by Alexander Pushkin.

Don Giovanni was at once popular with the general public and beloved and admired by connoisseurs. Widely varied geniuses—to name only a few—have all testified to its greatness: Beethoven (who was horrified by its perversion) and Rossini, Wagner and Gounod.

This *dramma giocoso* began its career as an *opera buffa*, but Mozart was so carried away with the dramatic possibilities of the story that his music makes of it something much greater. For the opening and pen ultimate scenes he composed some of the most remarkable dramatic music ever written. The intermediate scenes, although treated in the spirit of comedy, are invested with music charming and gloriously inventive. Through his melodies, at first seemingly so attractively naïve, Mozart delineates the characters of his drama in a most subtle manner. Where later composers might have required involved harmonies, polyphonic treatment of themes, and elaborate orchestration for a thorough exposition of the dramatic ideas, Mozart uses his incomparable, simple melodies, and attains an equally great effect.

The story is told that at the first rehearsal of this

opera, Mozart, who was directing, was not satisfied with the way in which the actress playing the part of Zerlina gave her cry of terror from behind the scenes. He left the orchestra, and, ordering a repetition of the finale of the first act, concealed himself on the stage behind the wings. There stood Zerlina, awaiting her cue. When it came, Mozart quickly reached from his hiding place and pinched her. She gave a piercing shriek. "That's the way I want it," exclaimed the composer, returning to the orchestra.

It is said that on the eve of the general rehearsal, that is to say, two nights before the première, friends of Mozart reminded him that the overture was still unwritten. The composer pretended to grow nervous about it, and went to his room. About midnight he began work. His wife was at his side and kept him awake with stories and with punch. At seven in the morning when the music copyists came, the work was done.

OVERTURE

The Overture begins with the solemn music of the banquet scene, which takes place at the end of the opera, when the Commandant's statue, accepting

Ezio Pinza as Don Giovanni

Ljuba Welitsch as Donna Anna

Don Giovanni's invitation, visits him during his dinner. This is followed by music of much gayer and brighter quality, perhaps a characterization of the bold, pleasure-seeking Don.

ACT I

SCENE 1: *A courtyard of the Commandant's palace in Seville.* Leporello, wrapped in his cloak, is waiting in a garden outside a house in Seville. He complains that he has rest by neither night nor day, and he adds, "Gaily he within is sporting, while I must keep off all intrusion." The complaining servant quickly conceals himself as his master Don Giovanni comes excitedly from the house, pursued by Donna Anna. The sounds of their voices bring the Commandant, Donna Anna's father, to the scene. A duel soon follows, and the gray-haired Commandant falls dying from a stroke of the agile Don, who at once flees with Leporello. Donna Anna has run for aid, and when she returns she is grief-stricken to find her father dead. With her is her betrothed, Don Ottavio. Noble youth that he is, he endeavors to calm her despair and joins with her in swearing vengeance upon the unknown assailant and murderer.

SCENE 2: *A lonely square outside of Seville.* While fleeing along a desolate road, Don Giovanni and his inevitable Leporello spy a woman approaching who seems to be weeping bitterly. Giovanni says that he will go to console her. "As you've done eighteen hundred others," murmurs Leporello. But on drawing nearer, the Don starts back in surprise. It is Donna Elvira, whom he has deserted even while eloping with her. She berates him for his deceitfulness. Giovanni attempts to explain his sudden disappearance. If she will not believe him, let her hear what Leporello says about it. While the servant holds her attention for a moment, the deceiver quickly slips away. When Donna Elvira turns to Giovanni, he is gone! Leporello tells her to be comforted, singing the celebrated "Catalogue Song," *"Madamina, il catalogo è questo"* ("Dear lady, this is the catalogue"). What comfort Donna Elvira may receive from Leporello's arch enumeration of the Don's philanderings is hard to imagine. This sprightly patter song is a splendid example of Mozart's musical felicity with words.

SCENE 3: *A country spot near Don Giovanni's castle.* In the country, villagers are making merry with singing and dancing, in honor of the forthcoming marriage of Zerlina and Masetto. Don Giovanni joins the gathering and, having cast covetous eyes upon the village bride, orders Leporello to invite all to his castle, then cleverly detains Zerlina.

The maiden is greatly flattered by the Don's gallantry and his offer of marriage. The courtly grace of Giovanni and the hesitant yielding of

Don Giovanni (Cesare Siepi) courts Zerlina (Mirella Freni)

Elisabeth Rethberg (Elvira), Pavel Ludikar (Leporello)

Zerlina are admirably expressed in the duet *"Là ci darem la mano!"* ("Thy little hand, love"). Just as Giovanni seems to have won the girl, Donna Elvira appears, and by her denunciation shows the noble's real character to Zerlina, who at once hurries to her betrothed. Donna Anna and Don Ottavio also come upon the scene. To them, Don Giovanni so far is merely an acquaintance not associated with any of the dark deeds of the former evening. Donna Elvira's accusations, however, begin to raise suspicions, and in Giovanni's parting words Donna Anna recognizes the voice of her father's murderer. She leaves Don Ottavio, who renews, to himself, his vow to avenge her wrongs. He sings of his love for her in the exalted beauty of the aria *"Dalla sua pace!"*

SCENE 4: *The garden of Don Giovanni's castle.* Don Giovanni has ordered a festival at his castle that evening. In the garden, together with other peasants, Masetto and Zerlina are still quarreling over the Don's amorous overtures to her. The youth upbraids the girl for her faithlessness in yielding so easily to Giovanni, and tells her to go away forever. She pleads with him, singing the wistful and lovely aria *"Batti, batti, o bel Masetto"* ("Scold me, dear Masetto"), in which she seeks his forgiveness.

Upon hearing such a plea, Masetto, of course, forgives her. Don Giovanni now approaches, and after an attempt to smooth things over with the jealous husband-to-be, he invites all into the castle. Leporello opens a window for a moment, and we hear the strains of the minuet that is being danced within. As he stands there enjoying the evening air, three masked figures enter the garden, and Leporello invites them to the festivities. When they have accepted, Leporello goes to admit them. The masked characters are none other than Donna Anna, Donna Elvira, and Don Ottavio, who, before entering the palace, pause to pray for heaven's aid in achieving vengeance, their voices joining in the solemn trio "*Protegga, il giusto cielo*" ("May heaven aid our cause").

SCENE 5: *Don Giovanni's castle.* In Don Giovanni's castle the festivities are progressing merrily. The graceful and courtly minuet is danced as two more earthy dances are performed simultaneously in different rhythms.

During the dancing Giovanni has contrived to lead Zerlina to an adjoining room. Suddenly the dance is interrupted by her screams for help, and a moment later the Don comes in, sword in hand and dragging Leporello. But this ruse fails to convince anybody of Giovanni's innocence. Donna Anna, Donna Elvira, and Don Ottavio unmask and confront Giovanni; but he, ignoring their accusations, draws his sword and, forcing a passage through the crowd, escapes.

ACT II

SCENE 1: *Before Donna Elvira's hotel.* At the rise of the curtain, Don Giovanni and Leporello are after still another conquest—Elvira's maid. Leporello complains about his recent treatment by Don Giovanni, and the latter placates him with money. Donna Elvira then comes to the window, and, since she cannot quite forget her love, she is still vowing revenge. The Don changes cloaks with Leporello, and with the help of darkness and this disguise, the

Act II, Scene 5: Surrounded by girl friends, the Don enjoys supper while waiting for his Stone Guest to appear.

servant succeeds in luring away Donna Elvira, who rejoices that her lover has returned. Meanwhile Giovanni serenades the maid in a most ingratiating air, *"Deh, vieni alla finestra"* ("Come to the window"), while accompanying himself on a mandolin.

Masetto approaches, and Giovanni, trying to conceal his identity, assumes the manner of Leporello. Masetto is hunting for Giovanni to kill him, or at least give him a good beating, but the clever Don administers the drubbing to Masetto instead. Thus Zerlina finds her betrothed lying in the street in a sore and battered condition. She asks if he is badly hurt, and he replies that he is wounded not only in body, but in heart. Zerlina prescribes a balm in the engaging aria *"Vedrai, carino"* ("You shall see, dearest").

SCENE 2: *The garden of the Commandant's palace.* Leporello does so well with his ludicrous impersonation of Don Giovanni that he cannot get away from Donna Elvira. Before the house of Donna Anna, however, the pair are confronted by the various persons whom Don Giovanni has wronged; Leporello is forced to reveal himself and flee from their wrath. Don Ottavio, who is present, again affirms his intentions of bringing justice upon Giovanni; he then sings the great aria *"Il mio tesoro intanto"* ("To my beloved"), a difficult piece of florid *bel canto*.

SCENE 3: *Before the statue of the Commandant in the graveyard.* In fleeing from his master's accusers, Leporello chances upon Don Giovanni. It is now long past midnight, and as they grope about in the darkness they come upon a statue erected to the memory of the Commandant. Giovanni orders Leporello to invite it to supper with him at his palace. The statue nods acceptance; Leporello trembles, but his master is undaunted.

SCENE 4: *In the Commandant's palace.* Don Ottavio implores Donna Anna to forget her sorrows, for the villain will soon be apprehended and be punished for his deeds. And he asks her to marry him. But her answer, tender and considerate, is that she cannot while still mourning her father. However, she continues, she does love him and assures him that they will marry in time, as she sings the aria *"Non mi dir"* ("Beloved mine, do not say").

SCENE 5: *A banquet hall in Don Giovanni's castle.* In the castle a banquet is spread. While Giovanni eats, his own private orchestra plays airs from operas of the day. Leporello, looking on rather nervously, comments on the music that is being played. "That's a song I've heard too often!" he says concerning a Mozart number, which is *"Non più andrai"* from *The Marriage of Figaro*.

The musicians take their leave. Donna Elvira unceremoniously enters and, on her knees, entreats Giovanni to change his ways. He is firm—cold in his refusal. She leaves, hopeless. In the corridor she screams; she re-enters the room and runs out through another door. Giovanni orders Leporello to see what it is; the servant comes back crying, "The man in stone!" He refuses to open the door. Giovanni boldly takes a candle, draws his sword, and goes into the corridor. A moment later he backs into the room; there follows him, with slow, heavy footsteps, accompanied by fearsome music, the statue of the Commandant. "You have invited me . . . I am here!" it says. Leporello has sought refuge under the table, but Giovanni coolly orders him to serve the meal.

"Don Giovanni," utters the statue, "I have been your guest; will you be mine?"

"Yes!" replies the Don, still fearless. The statue grasps his hand, to seal the bargain, and the Don is held in its stony grip. Wrenching himself free, Don Giovanni spurns the suggestion of repentance. A fiery pit opens, and the Don disappears in flames, brave to the end.

To impart to the opera a "happy ending," an epilogue is sung before the curtain, in which Donna Anna, Donna Elvira, Zerlina, Don Ottavio, Leporello, and Masetto take part. Leporello tells them of Don Giovanni's fate, after which they all rejoice, for their cause has been righted.

The Statue (Giorgio Tozzi) greets the Don (Cesare Siepi)

Don Pasquale

CHARACTERS

Don Pasquale, *an old bachelor*	*Bass*	Dr. Malatesta, *a physician*	*Baritone*
Ernesto, *his nephew*	*Tenor*	A Notary	*Bass* or *Tenor*
Norina, *a young widow*	*Soprano*		

Valets, Chambermaids, Dressmakers, etc.

The action takes place in Rome early in the nineteenth century.

OPERA IN THREE ACTS. Music by Gaetano Donizetti. Libretto in Italian by the composer and "Michele Accursi" (pseudonym of Giacomo Ruffini, a political exile from Italy, whose real name appears in later editions of the score), based on Angelo Anelli's libretto for Stefano Pavesi's opera *Ser Marc' Antonio*. First performance, Théâtre-Italien, Paris, January 3, 1843, with the so-called great "Puritani Quartet" —Grisi, Mario, Tamburini and Lablache. American première, New York, Park Theater, March 9, 1846, in English. The initial performance in the United States in Italian occurred at the Astor Place Opera House, November 29, 1849. Metropolitan Opera première: January 8, 1899, with Sembrich, Salignac, Scotti and Pini-Corsi. An important revival at the Metropolitan on April 5, 1913, offered Lucrezia Bori, Umberto Macnez, Scotti, and Pini-Corsi in the principal roles, with Arturo Toscanini conducting. With Salvatore Baccaloni as the Don, the opera obtained another auspicious revival at the Metropolitan on December 21, 1940, the other including Bidù Sayão and Nino Martini. Recently Fernando Corena has held a virtual monopoly on the title role.

This delightful work shows Donizetti's excellent gifts for comedy. His music sparkles with verve and good humor, in which respects it matches the gaiety of the libretto itself. When Donizetti composed this comic masterpeice (and most critics say it is the best he ever did), he was forty-five and had already had

well over sixty stage works produced. He was a very fast worker: *Don Pasquale* took him a little over a fortnight to complete.

A gay little overture brings forward a few of the melodies of the opera proper. They serve admirably to set the mood for the work.

ACT I

SCENE 1: *A room in Don Pasquale's house.* Don Pasquale is displeased with his nephew Ernesto, and particularly with the latter's devotion to the charming young widow Norina. Yet Dr. Malatesta, the Don's friend and physician, is in perfect sympathy with the lovers, and promises to aid them. He starts forthwith by singing the praises of a fictitious sister of his to Don Pasquale, who by this time has become completely enamored of the mysterious lady, decides to marry her sight unseen, and thus cut Ernesto entirely out of his will. His enthusiasm is depicted in the song *"Ah! un fuoco insolito"* ("Unwonted fire"). When presently Ernesto appears, he is roundly scolded and given the information about the Don's decision to marry. Ernesto is irate when he discovers that it was his friend Malatesto who contrived the evildoings, and he sings of his despair in the aria *"Sogno soave e casto"* ("Fond dream of love").

Norina (Bidù Sayão), sweetheart of Ernesto, plots a mock marriage to Pasquale with Malatesta (Frank Valentino)

SCENE 2: *In Norina's house.* The next scene reveals Norina, the lady in the case, who is disliked by Don Pasquale and loved by Ernesto. She is discovered in her room, reading a romantic novel, and she laughs merrily, for, as she says in the lively *"So anch' io la virtù magica"* ("I, too, know the magical craft"), the tricks and tears and wiles of accomplishing a man's enslavement are known to her. Norina knows that Malatesta has a plan for deceiving Don Pasquale, and he now tells her of it. It requires that Norina shall masquerade as the sister of Malatesta and so plague the Don that he will sicken of the idea of marriage and probably force Norina to marry his nephew Ernesto, which is, of course, exactly what Norina and Ernesto desire. They rehearse the part Norina is to play when she meets Don Pasquale.

ACT II

SCENE: *Don Pasquale's house.* After a brief prelude, the curtain rises, disclosing Ernesto, who is still bemoaning his sad fate. He soon departs, and Don Pasquale enters, arrayed in his finest. He is awaiting the arrival of his future bride, who appears, heavily veiled, escorted by Malatesta. She is exceedingly shy and coy, and Don Pasquale, of course, has no idea of her true identity. In any case, he is delighted with her and proposes marriage, to which, after some high-pressure salesmanship on the Don's part and a studied restraint on hers, she consents. The Notary is brought in, and Don Pasquale, with much legal verbiage, dictates the terms of the marriage contract and signs it. Just as Norina is also about to sign it, Ernesto is heard without. He enters, recognizes Norina, but by frantic gestures and whisperings is persuaded to remain silent and to act as witness to the marriage contract. As soon as this is done, Norina abandons her affected timidity and turns instantaneously into a vicious termagant. She will have nothing to do with Pasquale and announces her intention to retain Ernesto as usher in her house. The Don objects to this, and Norina ferociously reproves and even threatens him. Then in the presence of Pasquale she summons the household staff and outlines a scheme of living so extravagant that her husband-to-be is choked with rage and declares he will not pay her bills.

ACT III

SCENE: *The same*. Norina, marvelously gowned, is giving orders to a troop of servants, while Pasquale is contemplating the huge pile of unpaid bills his marriage has produced. He attempts forcefully to dissuade Norina from going to the theater and for his pains has his ears soundly boxed by his vigorous lady. As she goes on her way, she drops a letter, which Pasquale discovers to be an appointment for a rendezvous. With jealousy added to his other troubles, he is in complete despair, and the plotters now feel that Pasquale has been sufficiently tortured. Malatesta offers to correct matters if Pasquale will give him carte blanche. This the Don is glad to do, with the condition that Norina leave his house at once. Ernesto comes to serenade Norina, who presently joins him, and while they are talking, Pasquale and Malatesta approach. Ernesto withdraws.

Don Pasquale accuses Norina of secreting a lover in the house. She denies this, and Pasquale's search for the miscreant is fruitless. The solution comes when Pasquale calls Ernesto and promises him a

Cesare Valletti as Pasquale's nephew, Ernesto

liberal allowance if he will marry Norina and get out of his house. This Ernesto is only too glad to do, and presently it is discovered that Dr. Malatesta's spurious sister and Norina were the same person, that the marriage of Don Pasquale was a mock marriage, and that all his misfortune is the result of a mischievous scheme. But the old man is so happy to extricate himself from his troubles that he sends his nephew and the bride away with his blessings.

Act III: Malatesta (Frank Guarrera) and Pasquale (Fernando Corena) plot how the latter will get free of his wife

Elektra

CHARACTERS

Clytemnestra, *widow of Agamemnon*	Elektra ⎱ *her daughters*	Soprano
Mezzo-soprano	Chrysothemis ⎰	Soprano
Aegisthus, *her lover* — Tenor	Tutor of Orestes	Bass
Orestes, *her son* — Baritone		

Servants and Followers

The action takes place in Mycenae some time after the fall of Troy.

OPERA IN ONE ACT. Music by Richard Strauss. Libretto in German by Hugo von Hofmannsthal after Sophocles. This, incidentally, was his first collaboration with Strauss. First performance, Dresden Hofoper, January 25, 1909, with a cast comprising Anna Krull as Elektra; Margarete Siems as Chrysothemis; Ernestine Schumann-Heink as Clytemnestra, and Karl Perron as Orestes. Ernest von Schuch conducted. The work was first given in the United States at the Manhattan Opera House, New York, February 1, 1910, in a French translation by Henri Gauthier Villars, the cast consisting of Mariette Mazarin, Alice Baron, Jeanne Gerville-Réache, Gustave Huberdeau, and Jean Duffault (Aegis-

Jean Madeira as Clytemnestra at the Munich Festival

thus), with Henriquez de la Fuente conducting. Revived at the Metropolitan in the original German, December 3, 1932, with Gertrude Kappel, Göta Ljunberg, Karin Branzell, Friedrich Schorr, and Rudolf Laubenthal. Since then the Metropolitan has seen several notable revivals: with Rosa Pauly in 1938, Astrid Varnay in 1952, Inge Borkh in 1961 and Birgit Nilsson in 1966.

Richard Strauss's score for this work is emotionally powerful; it teems with extraordinary realistic effects, and further displays his remarkable orchestral imagination. It is a quite singable score, in spite of its often violent qualities, and as examples of that there are Elektra's invocation of Agamemnon, some of the music assigned to Clytemnestra, and those passages of tender beauty which follow the scene of recognition between Orestes and Elektra.

SCENE: *Courtyard of the palace.* There is one set, which shows the rear of the palace in Mycenae. Adjacent are the servants' quarters. King Agamemnon, murdered by his wife Clytemnestra and her lover Aegisthus, lies in a visible grave, over which his daughter Elektra mourns his death. Both she and her sister Chrysothemis have been reduced to being servants by their despotic, evil mother, as well as by Aegisthus, who now rules in the slain king's place. Orestes, brother of Elektra, has made good his escape from Mycenae.

In the meantime, Elektra mourns and prays for revenge, invoking her father's spirit and vowing that his children will one day dance in joy upon his grave. Her only concern is how to obtain this revenge, for she herself feels unequal to the task.

Clytemnestra, a sinister figure, appears during one of her daughter's lamentations. The Queen remarks on her inability to sleep, and inquires of Elektra, whom she flatters as being "wise," what blood rituals or sacrifices may be made, that her serenity and untroubled sleep may be restored. The answer to all this is scorn and mockery from Elektra, as she predicts in a scathing attack the dire events that will overtake Clytemnestra and her paramour. Fear-stricken before this avenging figure, the Queen recoils, but when one of her confidantes rushes in to whisper something to her, suddenly Clytemnestra's mood changes to rapture. Mystified, Elektra is soon informed of the reason for the transformation, for Chrysothemis comes to her sister with the tragic, though wrong, information that their brother is dead.

There is a scene in which Elektra tries to persuade her sister to commit the retributive act, but Chrysothemis says that she is incapable of it, and with that she departs.

In the shadow of the gate we see a stranger, and we know it is Orestes, although neither Elektra nor her brother knows the other at first. When recognition finally comes, Elektra again launches into a tirade against her mother and Aegisthus, but she finds in Orestes one who is most eager to avenge Agamemnon, and his sister's ecstasy is unconfined.

Accompanied by his old tutor, Orestes rushes into

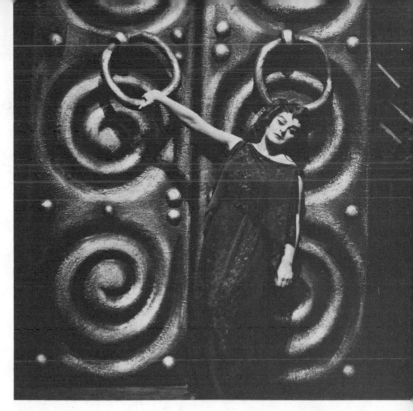

Birgit Nilsson's first Elektra, at Stockholm Festival

the palace, and from the cries within of Clytemnestra we know that she has been struck down. Aegisthus enters the yard through the gate, and Elektra detains him with a mock servility. Soon he makes his way into the palace, where he, too, meets his fate. There is a great rushing about of women, as Elektra embraces her sister and together with her sings a frenetic duet of their liberation. Then Elektra, as she had promised, dances triumphantly on her father's grave until she falls, lifeless.

First Metropolitan Opera production of Elektra *in 1932, with Joseph Urban's décor which was used for over three decades*

L'Elisir d'Amore

THE ELIXIR OF LOVE

CHARACTERS

Adina, *a wealthy and independent young woman* — Soprano

Nemorino, *a young peasant, in love with Adina* — Tenor

Giannetta, *a villager* — Soprano

Belcore, *a sergeant of the village garrison* — Bass

Dr. Dulcamara, *a traveling quack doctor* — Bass

A Landlord, a Notary, Peasants, Soldiers, Villagers

The action takes place in a little Italian village during the nineteenth century.

OPERA IN TWO ACTS. Music by Gaetano Donizetti. Libretto in Italian by Felice Romani, after Scribe's *Le Philtre*. First performance, Teatro della Canobbiana, Milan, May 12, 1832. In the United States it was given first in English at the Park Theater, New York, June 18, 1838, and later in Italian, at Palmo's Opera House, New York, May 22, 1844. This excellent *opera buffa* has obtained numerous performances at the Metropolitan Opera House (the first took place on January 23, 1904), where such celebrated tenors as Enrico Caruso, Beniamino Gigli, and Tito Schipa have appeared as the hero Nemorino. It was at a presentation by the Metropolitan, given in the Brooklyn Academy of Music, December 11, 1920, that Caruso first showed signs of the illness which was later to cause his death.

L'Elisir d'Amore is one of the brightest pieces in the category of comic opera. Donizetti is said to have composed the score in exactly fourteen days. Its clever and amusing plot provided the composer with many opportunities to display his creative facility with subjects of a light and carefree nature. Also, he composed for this work the expressive aria *"Una furtiva lagrima,"* which has been a favorite of tenors ever since.

ACT I

SCENE 1: *The homestead of Adina's farm.* It is a glorious summer's day, and Adina sits surrounded by her friends as, led by Giannetta, they sweetly sing. From a distance the lovesick Nemorino gazes at Adina with rapture and expresses his feelings in the aria *"Quanto è bella"* ("How lovely she is").

A burst of laughter from Adina startles everyone. She reads the legend of Tristan and Isolde, in which the knight wins the lady's affection by means of a wonderful elixir. Nemorino sees no mirth in the tale but sighs wishfully for some of the magical draft.

Martial music is heard, and the dashing Sergeant Belcore appears with a bouquet for Adina. She has but few smiles for him, and Nemorino, somewhat encouraged, renews his suit as soon as Belcore departs. Adina, though respecting this worthy young fellow, finds him rather dull and tells him to go visit his sick uncle, and that his suit is useless.

SCENE 2: *The town's marketplace.* A great commotion is heard among the villagers, and Dulcamara, a quack doctor, makes his appearence, riding in a splendid carriage. He has a whole trunkful of wonderful nostrums whose virtues he extols in the comic aria *"Udite, udite, o rustici"* ("Hear me, good folk"). To Nemorino, the doctor seems heaven-sent, and he immediately petitions him for some love elixir. Although a bit puzzled, the doctor loses no time in producing a bottle of strong wine which he says is the coveted potion. Nemorino gives the doctor his last coin, and, as soon as he sees him depart, drinks the entire bottle.

The elixir being, in reality, nothing but *vin ordinaire*, Nemorino feels exalted and begins to sing and dance, and Adina, coming in, is astonished to see her lovesick swain so merry. Feeling sure that the potion will bring the lady to his feet, he pays no attention to her, which piques her so much that when the sergeant arrives and renews his suit, she consents to wed him in three days. Nemorino laughs loudly at this, which so enrages the lady that she sets the wedding for that very day. This, in turn, sobers Nemorino, who fears that the marriage may take place before the potion works, and he begs for delay, singing his heartfelt plea, *"Adina, credimi."* Adina and the others only laugh at him and begin preparations for the wedding.

ACT II

SCENE: *Interior of the farmhouse.* There is a great wedding-day feast. The notary arrives, and the party goes to an inner room to sign the contract. Dulcamara, however, remains loyal to the table. To him comes Nemorino, whose uncle is dying, and whose sweetheart is marrying another. And the elixir did not work! Dulcamara produces another bottle, but pockets it when Nemorino is unable to pay for it. Belcore appears, and Nemorino desperately confides his misery to him. Belcore suggests that he enlist as a soldier, for which he will receive twenty crowns.

This colloquy takes the form of a wonderfully melodious duet in which the sly sergeant cajoles the hesitating swain with promises of pay and renown. Finally, Nemorino signs the articles, and each sings of what is uppermost on his mind.

Nemorino takes the money, runs in search of the doctor, and drinks the second bottle of love potion. The peasant girls, having heard that the death of Nemorino's uncle has just made him rich, begin to pay him attention. Adina capitulates when she sees her now freshly heartened lover approach, surrounded by sixteen girls. Nemorino is thus convinced that the elixir has worked and, moved to compassion at the sight of Adina's tears, sings the romance *"Una furtiva lagrima"* ("A furtive tear"), a remarkably beautiful melodic inspiration.

Adina soon returns, bringing the soldier's contract, and says that Nemorino must not go away. All misunderstandings are now cleared, and Belcore arrives to find his bride-to-be embracing another. He considers the situation with true soldierly philosophy, saying, "There are other women." As he goes off, the villagers tell Adina and Nemorino of the latter's good fortune. The doctor claims credit for the reconciliation, and the curtain falls as he is relieving the peasants of their wages in return for bottles of his wonderful elixir of love.

Dr. Dulcamara (Fernando Corena) enters via balloon in the Metropolitan Opera staging designed by Robert O'Hearn

L'Enfant et les Sortilèges

THE CHILD AND THE SORCERERS

CHARACTERS

The Child	*Mezzo-soprano*	A Shepherd	*Contralto*
His Mother	*Contralto*	The Armchair	*Basse Chantante*
The Louis XV Chair	*Soprano*	The Grandfather's Clock	*Baritone*
The Chinese Cup	*Mezzo-contralto*	The Teapot	*Tenor*
The Fire		The Little Old Man	
The Princess	*One coloratura soprano*	("*Arithmetic*")	*One tenor*
The Nightingale		The Frog	
The Cat	*Mezzo-soprano*	A Tree	*Bass*
The Dragonfly	*Mezzo-soprano*	The Settle, The Sofa, The	
The Bat	*Soprano*	Ottoman, The Wicker	*Children's Chorus*
The Little Owl	*Soprano*	Chair	
The Squirrel	*Mezzo-soprano*	Numbers	*Children's Chorus*
A Shepherdess	*Soprano*		

Shepherds, Frogs, Animals, Trees

The action takes place in a large old house in Normandy in the first quarter of this century.

OPERA IN ONE ACT. Music by Maurice Ravel. Libretto in French by Colette (Sidonie Gabrielle Gauthier-Villars). First performance at Monte Carlo, March 21, 1925. First American performance at San Francisco, November 19, 1930.

While Ravel was undergoing a frustrating experience as an ineffective soldier in World War I, the novelist Colette sent him the libretto for a ballet. At the time he could do nothing about it, and when the war was over, the ballet had been turned into what the author called a *fantaisie lyrique*—the imaginative and witty libretto of this opera. In 1920, the war over, Ravel got seriously to work on the score, which is a marvelous admixture of one part parody, one part tenderness, one part what musicians call mickymousing (that is, literal representations of the sounds of objects in action), and all parts loveliness. Ravel's total operatic output consisted merely of this brief work and the one-act *L'Heure Espagnole*. Each is perfect in its own way. Of the two, *L'Enfant* has received fewer productions, not because it is in any way inferior, but probably on account of the large cast and the tricky scenic effects required. It was Ravel's hope that it might one day become an animated cartoon, like Walt Disney's *Snow White and the Seven Dwarfs*.

SCENE: *A large room with a fireplace, a squirrel in a cage, wallpaper with shepherds and shepherdesses, etc.* It is afternoon and the Kettle over the fireplace is singing. So is the Cat. The Little Boy is doing his homework, very much irritated by it; and when his mother comes in with his tea and asks how he is getting along, he sticks his tongue out at her. So he is to be left strictly alone until suppertime. Now the boy really loses his temper. He breaks dishes, he pulls the Cat's tail, he upsets the Kettle, he uses the Poker to tear off strips of wallpaper. He even tears pages out of his story book and swings on the pendulum of the Grandfather's Clock.

From this point on we may assume the events to be part of "A Naughty Boy's Dream," for that is the subtitle of the opera. The boy begins to sink into a Chair, which moves away from him, bows to another Chair, and begins a strange dance. Other objects seem to turn on him for his bad behavior. The Clock strikes *ding-ding* excitedly and can't seem to stop; the Cup and Teapot have a double-talk quarrel, partly in Chinese and to the rhythm of a fox trot; the Fire spits at the boy and chases him about the room; the Shepherds and Shepherdesses come down from the torn wallpaper; and even the Princess from the torn book comes to life and then eludes him by sinking through the floor. And a little old Gentleman, together with a lot of Numerals, emerges from an arithmetic book to torment him with ununderstandable problems in arithmetic. It is all impossible but as real as a nightmare.

After more such events (including a hilariously realistic cat duet sung by a bass and a mezzo), the doors and ceiling of the room disappear, and the Child finds himself in a garden, which he loves. But even here he finds enmity, enmity from a Tree whose bark he had cut, from a Bat whose mate he had killed, from a Squirrel whose friend he had put into a cage, from a whole chorus of Frogs. They push and punch him into a corner. But everything changes when he binds up the paw of a wounded Squirrel. They see that there is good in him; they help him to call for his mother; they lead him toward the house. With confidence, the boy calls out, *"Maman!"* He has awakened, and the little opera ends.

Act I, Scene 1, as performed by the University of Indiana in Bloomington

Ernani

CHARACTERS

Don Carlos, *King of Castile*	*Baritone*	Elvira, *betrothed to Don Silva*	*Soprano*
Don Ruy Gomez de Silva, *a grandee*	*Bass*	Giovanna, *her nurse*	*Mezzo-soprano*
Ernani, *a nobleman turned bandit chief*	*Tenor*	Riccardo, *Don Carlos' lieutenant*	*Tenor*
		Iago, *Silva's esquire*	*Baritone*

Attendants, Mountaineers, Bandits, Followers of Don Silva, Followers of the King,
Spanish and German Nobles and Ladies, Electors, and Pages

The action takes place in Aragon, Aix-la-Chapelle, and Saragossa in 1519.

OPERA IN FOUR ACTS. Music by Giuseppe Verdi. Libretto in Italian by Francesco Piave, after Victor Hugo's play *Hernani*. First produced at the Teatro la Fenice, Venice, March 9, 1844. United States *première,* in the original Italian, at the Park Theater, New York, April 15, 1847. First Metropolitan performance on January 28, 1903, with a cast headed by Marcella Sembrich, Emilio de Marchi, Antonio Scotti, and Édouard de Reszke. In the Metropolitan revival of December 8, 1921, Rosa Ponselle and Giovanni Martinelli sang the parts of Elvira and Ernani. More recently these roles have been entrusted to Zinka Milanov and Leontyne Price, and Mario Del Monaco, Franco Corelli and Carlo Bergonzi.

When Victor Hugo's flamboyant *Hernani* was first produced in Paris it was at once seized upon as a fiery manifesto of romanticism. Two schools clashed over it, the Romantics and the classicists. The fervent rhetoric of the play, its unrestrained passions and ringing bombast suited the heightened mood of the day, and Parisians went through the streets chanting or mocking its surging Alexandrines. It was a day when problems of art broke up friendships. True Romantic that he was, Giuseppe Verdi was also swept off his feet by the impetuous rush of Hugo's lines. And the opera shows it, in the high-pitched emotionalism, the melodramatic outcries, the melodic sweep. This is the young Verdi, the Verdi of the first of the four periods of a magnificent development, pouring out inexhaustible melody with youthful abandon and a lordly unconcern for the considered unity and balance that were to come later.

Mario Battastini as Don Carlos in Ernani, *circa 1890*

As with several other operas by Verdi, *Ernani* ran into trouble with the authorities. The rebellious mood of the Italian people made their Austrian rulers doubly vigilant of the stage. The conspiracy in *Ernani* had to be modified. Hotheaded Italians might be incited, the censors contended. Objection was also raised against the undignified use of a hunting horn on the stage, but Verdi's protest prevailed here. Hugo himself was anything but flattered by the opera. When it reached Paris, he fumed against what he regarded as a travesty of his play, even insisting on the characters being transformed into Italians and that the work be given under a different name—*Il Proscritto*. Nevertheless, *Ernani* did for Verdi what the play had done for Hugo: it brought him prestige and recognition outside his own country. And even today listeners throb to the power of the young giant that surges through this vibrant score.

ACT I

SCENE 1: *A mountain retreat in Aragon.* Don Juan of Aragon, a Spanish duke deprived of wealth and placed under a ban by the King, has become the bandit Ernani. In the mountain camp of his band he is meditating gloomily on the approaching marriage of Elvira, the woman he loves, to the elderly grandee Don Ruy Gomez de Silva. Resolved to prevent this loveless union, he asks his followers to pledge their help in abducting the woman whose beauty he now describes in a tender aria, *"Come rugiada."* Ernani and his men depart in the direction of Silva's castle.

SCENE 2: *Elvira's chamber in the castle.* Elvira is alone, brooding over her coming marriage, which she is powerless to prevent. Grief-stricken, she thinks of her long-lost lover Ernani and calls on him to rescue her. With the words *"Ernani, involami"* ("Ernani, fly with me") she begins a coloratura aria of great brilliance that combines vocal display with a touching expression of despair. Don Carlos, King of Castile, who is also enamored of Elvira, enters the room disguised and makes violent love to her. Elvira repulses him, and he is about to drag her off by force when a secret panel opens and Ernani steps forth. Don Carlos recognizes him and exclaims, "You are Ernani, assassin and bandit!" The ensuing quarrel grows bitter and menacing, with Elvira trying to protect Ernani. Suddenly the door flies open, and Silva appears. He is astonished to discover two men fighting over his bride on the eve of their wedding. Wrathfully, he bids his soldiers bring his armor and sword, but his attitude abruptly changes. He has recognized the King and, though secretly enraged,

Rome Opera staging with Mario Del Monaco, Antonietta Stella

now bows in deference. Don Carlos urges Ernani to depart, but Ernani indignantly refuses till Elvira adds her own plea. In the confusion that follows, Ernani escapes.

ACT II

SCENE: *A hall in Don Silva's castle.* Elvira and Silva are about to be married. Ernani has disappeared, and reports have reached Elvira that he is dead. A squire announces that a holy man is outside seeking the hospitality of the nobleman. Silva, believing the pilgrim will bring happiness to the household sheltering him, instructs the squire to let him in. The holy man enters, thus entitling himself to Silva's protection as a guest. This is no pointless formality, for the holy man enters and, as Elvira enters in her bridal attire, he promptly throws off his disguise, revealing himself as Ernani. The bandit chief demands to be turned over to the King, preferring death to life without Elvira. At that moment the King's arrival is announced. Silva, bound to shield his guest, conceals Ernani in a secret passage.

The King enters and orders Silva to surrender the bandit, but Silva haughtily refuses, and the King orders the castle searched. Finding no trace of Ernani, he carries off Elvira as hostage. Silva now summons Ernani from his hiding place, and, taking down two swords, challenges him to a duel. Ernani is compelled to refuse, for his host has just risked his life for him. Silva taunts him, flinging the word "Coward!" at him. Ernani decides to fight, but asks for one last look at Elvira. When Silva tells him the King has carried her off, Ernani berates him: "Fool, the King is our rival! He wants her for himself!" He thereupon proposes that he and Silva join forces against the King, and the grandee consents. Once Elvira is saved, Ernani swears to give himself up, as a pledge of which he gives Silva a hunting horn. Once the horn is blown, Ernani vows by the memory of his father that he will kill himself.

ACT III

SCENE: *A vault in the Aix-la-Chapelle cemetery.* Don Carlos is led to the gloomy catacombs of Aix-la-Chapelle, the tomb of the Emperor Charlemagne, having been informed that the conspirators intend to meet here. The solemn atmosphere of the place induces a mood of reverence in him for his great ancestor. Hiding himself, he overhears the talk of the conspirators. Ernani, joyous at the chance of avenging his father's death, is chosen to assassinate Don Carlos. A sudden booming of cannon announces that Don Carlos has been proclaimed Emperor. As electors and courtiers enter from a secret door, Don Carlos orders the plotters arrested and put to death. When Elvira begs for mercy, he countermands the order and sets them all free, including Ernani. As a further gesture, he unites the long-divided lovers, and all now raise their voices in a magnificent tribute to the new Emperor's magnanimity—"*O sommo Carlo*" ("O noble Carlos")—all except the vengeful Silva, whose sinister mutterings come fitfully through the stirring chorus of praise.

ACT IV

SCENE: *The palace in Aragon.* After their marriage Elvira and Ernani are on the terrace, rapturous in their new-found happiness, when suddenly a horn sounds, the fatal horn that reminds Ernani of his pledge. Silva has neither forgotten nor forgiven! Sinister as death itself, he arrives and solemnly demands fulfillment of the oath. Deaf to Elvira's pleas for her husband's life, Silva offers his enemy the choice of a dagger or a cup of poison. Ernani bids Elvira a touching farewell and then seizes the dagger and drives it into his heart. Elvira faints over his lifeless body, and Silva is left gazing with evil triumph upon his terrible revenge.

Act II: Don Silva (Jerome Hines) confronts Elvira (Leontyne Price) and Ernani (Franco Corelli), at the Metropolitan

Eugene Onegin

YEVGENY ONYEGIN

CHARACTERS

Madame Larina, *a landowner*	*Mezzo-soprano*
Tatiana } *her daughters*	*Soprano*
Olga	*Contralto*
Eugene Onegin, *a young dandy*	*Baritone*

Lensky, *his friend*	*Tenor*
Prince Gremin, *a retired general*	*Bass*
Triquet, *a French tutor*	*Tenor*
Filipievna, *Tatiana's nurse*	*Mezzo-soprano*
Zaretski, *a gentleman*	*Baritone*

Peasants, Party Guests

The action takes place in and near the city of St. Petersburg during the nineteenth century.

OPERA IN THREE ACTS. Music by Peter Ilyich Tchaikovsky. Libretto in Russian by the composer and Konstantin Shilovsky, after the poem of Alexander Pushkin. First produced by the students of the Imperial College of Music at the Little Theater, Moscow, March 29, 1879. Its first public performance occurred in Moscow, April 23, 1881. The opera was introduced to the United States in concert form by the Symphony Society of New York, in English, February 1, 1908. The Metropolitan première took place, in Italian, on March 24, 1920. More recent revivals have been given in English.

Eugene Onegin is the most successful of Tchaikovsky's operas, although none of his stage works is consistently performed in the repertoires of the world's major opera houses, save in Russia. However, Tchaikovsky's music, although not a typical operatic score, since it shows little development of dramatic ideas, is yet sympathetic in its portrayal of the leading characters. These, however, are mirrorings of himself, more or less, defeated, frustrated, utterly subjective personages. The score offers three pieces—Lensky's melancholy aria, Tatiana's "Letter Song," and the Waltz—which have been for many years concert-hall favorites.

Giuseppe de Luca (Eugene Onegin) and Claudia Muzio (Tatiana)

ACT I

SCENE 1: *A garden adjoining Madame Larina's house.* To Madame Larina's home near St. Petersburg come her daughter Olga's fiancé, Lensky, and his friend Eugene Onegin, a Russian gallant, rather bored, and particularly so by rural scenes. Olga's romantic sister, Tatiana, falls in love with Onegin at first sight.

SCENE 2: *Tatiana's room.* Tatiana is sleepless that night. She asks Filipievna to tell her a story, one to soothe her, and the nurse does so, as she relates the story of her own wooing and marriage, a long time ago. In a moment of candor Tatiana reveals her love for Onegin, and she bids the nurse fetch her pen, ink, and paper and then depart. In her youthful ingenuousness she writes to Onegin, expressing all that she had not dared say in his presence, and she asks him to meet her. This is the great Letter Scene, which Tchaikovsky composed before the rest of the score.

SCENE 3: *The garden.* Onegin meets Tatiana, as requested, but spurns her confession of love, saying that he has neither time nor inclination for affairs of the heart. Tatiana runs away in utter dejection, overcome with shame.

ACT II

SCENE 1: *A living room in Madame Larina's house.* A ball is being given in honor of Tatiana's birthday. And here is heard the charming and brilliant Waltz. Onegin, who is present, ignores Tatiana and pays deliberate court to her sister instead. This arouses the jealousy of Lensky who challenges Onegin to a duel.

SCENE 2: *A mill by a wooded stream.* Lensky awaits Onegin at the place appointed. He looks over the desolate winter landscape, and thinking of his youth, which seems so remote, and of death, which seems so near, he sings the piece known as "Lensky's Aria." Presently, his opponent appears, the duel takes place, and Lensky falls as Onegin, realizing his folly, is overwhelmed with remorse.

ACT III

SCENE 1: *Hall in the palace of Princess Gremina (Tatiana), several years later.* Onegin is among the guests at a reception given by Prince Gremin, Tatiana's husband. There he is astonished to find Tatiana the wife of a man of distinction and in high favor with the Tsar. He now realizes that he loves her, resolving to win back her affection.

SCENE 2: *Tatiana's boudoir.* Tatiana enters, bearing a message from Onegin in which he begs to see her. Confused by the turn of events, firm in her resolve to remain true to the man she has married, yet apprehensive concerning her feelings toward Onegin, Tatiana awaits his coming. He enters and, aware that she has been weeping, falls down at her feet. The interview is a most unhappy one, Tatiana reminding him of his cruelty that day in the garden of her mother's home, yet admitting that she has forgiven him. Slowly she says that she still loves him. Together they sing of the happiness that was once so close to them, and the futility of their present plight. Tatiana, recovering, finally bids him on his honor to depart, and leaves him standing silently for a moment. And then, with a final cry of anguish, he departs, as the curtain falls.

Act II, Scene 1: Triquet (Alessio De Paolis) sings for Tatiana (Lucine Amara) and the guests of Madame Larina

Falstaff

CHARACTERS

Sir John Falstaff, *a fat, seedy knight*	*Baritone*	Anne (Nannetta) Ford, *their*	
Bardolph } *his hangers-on*	*Tenor*	*daughter*	*Soprano*
Pistol	*Bass*	Fenton, *suitor to Anne*	*Tenor*
Ford, *a wealthy burgher*	*Baritone*	Dr. Caius, *another suitor*	*Tenor*
Alice Ford, *his wife*	*Soprano*	Meg Page, *a neighbor*	*Mezzo-soprano*
		Dame Quickly, *servant to*	
		Dr. Caius	*Mezzo-soprano*

Servants, Citizens of Windsor

The action takes place in Windsor, England, in the fifteenth century.

OPERA IN THREE ACTS. Music by Giuseppe Verdi. Libretto in Italian by Arrigo Boito, after Shakespeare's *Merry Wives of Windsor* and *King Henry IV*. First performance, Teatro alla Scala, Milan, February 9, 1893. Initial production in the Western hemisphere, Buenos Aires, July 8, 1893. Première in the United States at the Metropolitan, February 4, 1895, with Victor Maurel, who had created the role in Milan as Falstaff. A brilliant revival was given March 20, 1909, under Arturo Toscanini at the same house with Antonio Scotti in the title role. On January 2, 1925, Lawrence Tibbett received such a sensational ovation for his account of the secondary baritone role of Ford (Scotti was still singing Falstaff) that he was soon elevated to primary roles. Another brilliant revival—this one in the season of 1963–64—introduced three great talents to the roster of the Metropolitan—Leonard Bernstein, the conductor, Franco Zeffirelli, the designer and director, and Geraint Evans, the baritone.

It has been said that Verdi's muse was essentially a tragic muse, yet with this work, composed in his eightieth year, he proved to some critics (Rossini, now dead, had been one of them) that he could write with great wit and an almost Mozartian boyishness. His music brightly illuminates the story of "Fat-paunch," as the character emerges out of Boito's libretto, and, further, shows no lessening of the technical skill he had possessed all during his career.

Verdi did not, as formerly, compose ten, but two hours a day, while working on *Falstaff*. Still the opera made good progress. And one evening in November 1890 Boito virtually informed the world of what was going on by proposing a toast to "Fat-paunch."

Fifty-three years had passed since Verdi had composed a comic opera. The earlier one had been *Un Giorno di Regno*, and that, for all the gaiety of some of its music, is scarcely a true comedy, for its very involved libretto stood in the way. But in *Falstaff* the aged composer was dealing with an ingenious and orderly libretto and a richly comic one, besides. Boito, despite the many liberties he had taken with the original story of *The Merry Wives of Windsor*, and the borrowings from *Henry IV*, supplied the composer with a concentrated book, beautifully balanced in every way, and highly literary in quality.

In the music of *Falstaff* Verdi departs from tradi-

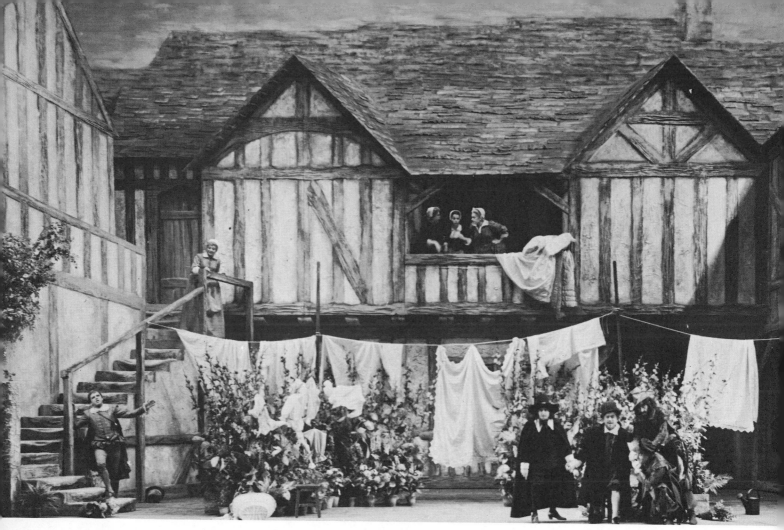

Act I, Scene 2: Franco Zeffirelli staging at the Metropolitan, with Merry Wives above and scheming men below

tions to which he had held so long. Here we do not find, as in *Aïda* or *La Traviata* or even in *Otello*, arias and duets and trios and ensembles packed with drama and emotional excitement. In fact, the music, being a definition of the comedy and the characters, is light and airy and almost as casual as a breeze. At least, it sounds that way, although it required an immense technique to achieve that. For the *Falstaff* music is episodic, fragmentary in essence, which it obviously needed to be, thanks to the mercurial quality of the libretto. However, by an accumulation of such fragments, such bubbly and delicately tinted character and plot identifications—never, as in Wagner, depending on psychological development or thematic extension—the general impression is hardly that of a scattering of clever things, but of a tightly knit, extremely well-ordered score.

What a wonder that Verdi, after composing a long line of tragic operas, should end his career with a comedy! That this work should be, in addition, a masterpiece, taking its rightful place beside Mozart's *Marriage of Figaro*, Wagner's *Die Meistersinger*, and Rossini's *Barber of Seville*, is a tribute to the versatility of his genius.

Of particular interest, in a score that teems with interesting matters, are Falstaff's monologue on honor, the quartet by the women in the garden, Ford's soliloquy, Falstaff's song *"Quand'ero paggio del Duca di Norfolck"* ("When I was the Duke of Norfolk's page"), and the concerted finales of each act.

ACT I

SCENE 1: *A room in the Garter Inn.* The jovial, fat old rogue Falstaff is with his friends Bardolph and Pistol at the Garter Inn, where Sir John quaffs his huge drafts as his friends look on. Dr. Caius rushes in and quarrels with the knight and his two men because, he claims, they picked his pocket during a drinking bout the night before. However, he is soon thrown out, and Falstaff, reflecting on the low state of his financial resources, writes two identical letters —one to Mistress Page, the other to Mistress Ford— by which he hopes to make a profitable liaison with the wives of two rich burghers. When the two rogues refuse to deliver the letters for Falstaff, pleading their "honor," Falstaff delivers the ironical monologue on honor, a paraphrase of the great soliloquy in *Henry IV, Part II*. The scene ends with Falstaff chasing the two men out of the inn with a broom.

SCENE 2: *In Ford's house*. In Ford's home the two women compare the letters and, discovering them to be alike, plan revenge. In this they are joined by the men, Ford, Fenton, and Dr. Caius: even Bardolph and Pistol will help, for they, too, having smarted under Falstaff's gibes, want vengeance and have told Ford of the old knight's designs on Mistress Ford. Fenton is on hand because he is in love with Mistress Ford's daughter, Anne, even though Ford himself plans to have her marry Dr. Caius. Dame Quickly is sent to invite Falstaff to an interview with Mistress Ford, and meanwhile the men arrange to have Ford introduced to Falstaff under an assumed name.

ACT II

SCENE 1: *A room in the Garter Inn*. Bardolph and Pistol hypocritically beg to be taken back into Falstaff's good graces and then bring in Dame Quickly. She delivers her message and, having flattered old Sir John almost to distraction, she leaves and the knight expresses his self-satisfaction in the monologue beginning *"Va, vecchio John"* ("Get along, old John"). Bardolph now introduces Ford as Signor Fontana (in Shakespeare he is called Brook), the latter begging Falstaff, with offers of gold, to intercede for him with Mistress Ford. The knight tells him he has already made a rendezvous with the lady and goes out to dress himself in his best attire, while Ford, in his jealousy, delivers his famous soliloquy on the faithlessness of women. When Falstaff returns, decked out in extraordinary finery, there is a little scene of amusing effect, as Falstaff and Ford (or Fontana) do an Alphonse-and-Gaston act before going out the door, and finally decide to exit together arm in arm.

SCENE 2: *A room in Ford's house*. Dame Quickly reports to the ladies that Falstaff is coming to woo Mistress Ford, but before he can come, Anne has a chance to tell her mother that Ford wants her to accept the repulsive Dr. Caius. The mother is very sympathetic. Falstaff is announced, Mistress Ford takes up her lute, and everyone else hides behind the screen. Scarcely has the fatuous old knight begun his wooing, when Ford is heard coming. Falstaff quickly hides behind the screen. Ford enters with the other men and, hoping to find the rakish knight, begins a search of the house. As soon as the men are out, the women hurriedly conceal Falstaff in a large laundry basket they have thoughtfully provided, pile soiled clothes over him, and fasten down the lid. A moment later Ford returns, having thought of the screen.

Victor Maurel as the fat knight, La Scala première, 1893

Falstaff (Fernando Corena) woos Alice (Ilva Ligabue)

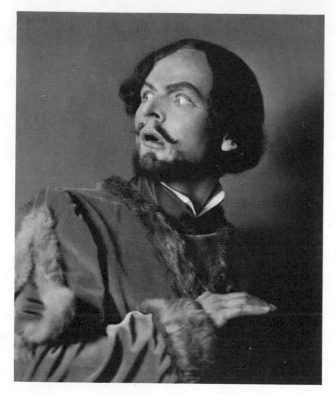

Lawrence Tibbett as Mr. Ford, his first great success

Cloe Elmo, Quickly of the NBC broadcast under Toscanini

Even as he enters, he hears back of it a sound suspiciously like a kiss—Fenton and Anne are having an unrehearsed love scene of their own! Ford rushes out, more enraged than ever. Thereupon his wife has the servants empty the basket into the Thames, which flows below. Ford returns in time to be shown the knight climbing clumsily from the water, laughed at by all who see him.

ACT III

SCENE 1: *Before the inn.* Falstaff is back at the inn, sad and disillusioned. He reviles the wickedness of the world, and as he gulps down his mulled wine, gradually begins to regain his courage and, of course, his ego. This transformation is accompanied by the orchestra in a brilliant passage which, beginning with a pianissimo trill, grows into a fortissimo, indicative of the rebirth of his faith in himself. Dame Quickly appears and, after a rebuff or two, succeeds in restoring the knight's confidence in her. She arranges another meeting between him and Mistress Ford. He is to disguise himself as the Black Huntsman and await the lady by Herne's Oak in Windsor Park at midnight. As the two go into the inn, in order to discuss the plans more privately, the conspirators, who have been eavesdropping shame-

lessly, come forward and go over their plot to give Sir John his final blow. Ford and Dr. Caius take the occasion to hatch another plot—that is, to trick Anne, through a disguise, into marrying the doctor that very night.

SCENE 2: *Herne's Oak in Windsor Park.* It is a moonlit night, and almost everyone is disguised. Falstaff and Mistress Ford meet, and the knight begins his awkward love-making. Immediately eerie sounds are heard; Mistress Ford runs away in mock terror, while Falstaff throws himself face down on the ground, for it is fatal to gaze upon supernatural beings! The whole company enter disguised as fairies. They seem to stumble upon Falstaff accidentally, then give this "impure mortal" a sound thrashing, until he promises to mend his ways. Though Ford has agreed to give Anne in marriage to Dr. Caius, the women, set on helping Fenton's cause, have confused the men in their disguises. Thus, when masks are suddenly removed, Dr. Caius finds that he has been "married" to Bardolph. In the laughter that follows, Ford agrees to bless the union of Fenton and Anne, and all ends happily—save for Falstaff, who, at least, can laugh at the discomfiture of Ford. And the opera ends in a magnificent fugue by voices and orchestra on the theme, first stated by Falstaff, that "all the world's a jest."

Faust

CHARACTERS

Faust	*Tenor*	Siebel, *a youth, in love with*	
Mephistopheles	*Bass*	*Marguerite*	*Mezzo-soprano*
Valentin, *Marguerite's brother*	*Baritone*	Martha, *neighbor of*	
Wagner, *a student*	*Baritone*	*Marguerite*	*Mezzo-soprano*
Marguerite	*Soprano*		

Peasants, Townspeople, Soldiers, Students, Priests, Boys, etc.

The action takes place in Germany in the sixteenth century.

OPERA IN FIVE ACTS. Music by Charles François Gounod. Libretto in French by Jules Barbier and Michel Carré, based on Part I of Goethe's dramatic poem *Faust*. First performance at the Théâtre-Lyrique, Paris, March 19, 1859. American première, in German, in Philadelphia, November 18, 1863. Produced one week later, November 25, at the New York Academy of Music, in Italian. In the original French the opera was first performed in America in New Orleans on November 20, 1866. *Faust* (in Italian) opened the Metropolitan Opera House on October 22, 1883, with Christine Nilsson, Sofia Scalchi, Italo Campanini, Giuseppe del Puente, and Franco Novara. Performances of *Faust* later became so numerous there that the music critic William J. Henderson, with the Bayreuth Festspielhaus in mind, once referred to the Metropolitan as the *Faustspielhaus*.

The origins of the *Faust* legend are buried in historical mists. Ballads, folk tales, and dramas were inspired by Faust's sinister pact with the devil. Variations multiplied, and each poet contributed some fresh touch or new character. Christopher Marlowe's *Dr. Faustus* enshrined a famous vision of Helen of Troy, she of "the face that launched a thousand ships." It was Goethe's poem that achieved the final synthesis of poetry and philosophy. Thereafter Faust became an international obsession. Overtures, symphonies, and tone poems, even an oratorio

and several ballets, sprang from Goethe's masterpiece. Operas based on episodes from it soon became legion. Berlin, Spohr, Boito, Berlioz, and Busoni are among the composers who conceived *Faust* in terms of sung drama. And in 1925, in Soviet Russia, Marxists carried the legend one step further and staged Gounod's *Faust* in satiric modern guise, with the hero an American millionaire living sumptuously in a Berlin hotel.

If Goethe's poem gave universal shape to this winter's tale of the Middle Ages, Gounod's version, which uses the Faust-Marguerite episode as basis, became its musical counterpart in the affections of operagoers the world over. Yet, the opera achieved scant success at its first performance in Paris, and even less in Milan. Soon, however, it caught on and became an international craze, possibly the greatest opera craze in history. In the late 1860's *Faust* was flourishing briskly in England, for a while even threatening to crowd all other operas out of circulation. The opera was a great favorite of Queen Victoria's. Shortly before her death she summoned a group of French singers to Windsor Palace. Though old and weak and sick, she listened happily to her beloved music from *Faust*. Each time a familiar phrase was sung, the Queen's lips parted in a smile of recognition. A veritable furor greeted *Faust* on its arrival in America. In the twenty years preceding

Chicago Lyric Opera's staging of Act II, the Kermesse Scene, with Nicolai Ghiaurov as Mephistopheles

the opening of the Metropolitan Opera House the opera had already built up a huge following here. Thus, the choice of opening opera for the new house was a fairly easy one for its first impresario, Henry Eugene Abbey. And for the title role Abbey brought over Italo Campanini, the great Italian tenor who had earlier proved quite a sensation as Faust in London. The soprano was the Swedish prima donna Christine Nilsson, whose Marguerite had already been acclaimed at the Paris Opéra.

Yet, at the beginning, *Faust* had been anything but a bed of roses for Gounod. In setting the greatest poem in German literature to music he invited the acid gibes of the critics, especially the pompous savants across the Rhine. Then Carvalho, the director of the Théâtre-Lyrique of Paris, insisted on assigning the role of Marguerite to his wife, though Gounod had the soprano Ugalde in mind. Shortly before the première officials objected to the cathedral scene. Finally, the tenor caught a bad cold. Add the lukewarm reception of the opening night, and everyone was ready to agree the production was a fiasco. But soon the power and beauty of Gounod's music, the human drama and spectacle of fantasy and sorcery, worked their charm on the public. Before the season was over, there were fifty-seven performances. For the subsequent London production of *Faust* in English Gounod wrote an additional aria for the celebrated baritone Sir Charles Santley. This

was Valentin's "Even bravest heart may swell." It was felt Sir Charles deserved greater attention than the score already accorded the role of Valentin.

PRELUDE

The brief prelude to *Faust* gives little more than a clue to the drama about to unfold. The mood of portent is sounded in the fateful single note heard from the full orchestra and then a long, slow fugal passage suggests, the medieval scholar's study. The pace quickens to an episode suggesting Faust's anguish of mind, followed by Valentin's beautiful melody *"Avant de quitter ces lieux."* The prelude ends in stately and solemn fashion.

ACT I

SCENE: *Faust's studio.* Faust, an aged philosopher and alchemist of note, is poring over a huge volume that lies open on the table. Half discernible in the flickering light of a lamp are the strange tools of medieval necromancy scattered about the room. Musty parchment rolls are seen on all sides. The expiring lamp is a symbol of the despair and weariness in the heart of this learned man. Life and the pursuit of knowledge have finally disillusioned him, and the universe remains an unsolved riddle. Tired of the struggle to find a meaning in it all, Faust resolves on suicide. He fills a goblet with poison and raises it to his lips. Outside his murky chamber day has been dawning. Faust pauses as a cheerful song of young peasants passing by in the street comes through his window. He goes to the window, and as his rage and envy mount at the sight of humanity, he curses life and calls aloud to Satan for help.

There is an eerie flash of light, and Mephistopheles, in gallant attire, appears. By turns gay, cynical, and ingratiating, he proposes a compact. In return for wealth and power, Faust shall sign away his soul. The philosopher spurns riches and glory and demands the gift of youth instead. Mephistopheles agrees. Youth and love shall be Faust's as long as he pledges his soul. As Faust falters at the awful prospect, the fiend tempts him with a glowing vision of the lovely Marguerite seated at a spinning wheel, her beautiful blond braids falling down her back. In rapture Faust gazes at this picture of youth and loveliness, and as the orchestra weaves a shimmering web of magic, he addresses the vision, *"O merveille"* ("O wonder"). Faust, ready now to pawn his immortal soul, in one determined gesture seizes the proffered potion, raises it in a toast to the vision, and gulps it down.

The evocation vanishes, and Faust undergoes a magic transformation. As the light returns, the gray beard and scholarly garb have disappeared. In place of the bent and wearied philosopher there stands an elegantly clad cavalier, eager for adventure. Mephistopheles promises he shall see Marguerite that very day. There is a spirited duet, and Faust impetuously dashes out of the study, followed by the grinning fiend.

ACT II

SCENE: *The public square of a German town.* A crowd has gathered to celebrate the *kermesse,* or village fair. Students, soldiers, burghers of all ages are milling about in gay confusion. There is drinking, talking, flirting, and quarreling. A lively chorus, differentiating the moods and manners of each group, pictures the colorful scene: soldiers are heard chanting martially; women set up a bantering chatter; old man gossip in facetious falsettos. Toward the end, the groups unite in a chorus of six parts, a magnificent piece of ensemble writing. Among the crowd is Valentin, Marguerite's brother. About to join his country's army, Valentin reveals to his friends how troubled he is about leaving his orphan sister alone. In a beautiful and tender melody (*"Avant de quitter ces lieux"*—"Even bravest heart may swell") he asks heaven to watch over her. Siebel, his young friend, secretly in love with Marguerite, generously assures Valentin that

during his absence he will see that no harm comes to her. The student Wagner, wishing to banish the solemn mood of the moment, mounts a table before an inn and begins to sing a ribald ditty concerning a rat.

Mephistopheles, pushing through the carnival crowd, breaks in on Wagner's song and proposes to sing one of his own. This is *"Le Veau d'Or"* ("The Calf of Gold"), a bold and sinister hymn in praise of Mammon, cynically describing how men are drawn by gold to evil, and ending in a weird dance led by Mephistopheles himself. Vastly entertained, the crowd looks on in amazement as the Evil One proceeds to execute feats of magic. As he tells fortunes and reads palms, the simple peasants are left gaping. In a moment of playful malice Mephistopheles seizes Siebel and swears that whatever flower he touches will wither in his hands. Wagner, enchanted by the newcomer's gifts, proposes a toast. Wine is brought, but Mephistopheles tastes it and hurls it down in disgust. He will give them a finer wine to drink, he says. As he strikes the barrel of Bacchus used as a sign over the inn, wine gushes out copiously. All are permitted to name their favorite vintage and drink at this magic source.

Mephistopheles offers a toast to Marguerite. Valentin, enraged at hearing his sister's name publicly flaunted, draws his sword and lunges at the devil. Mephistopheles instantly traces a magic circle about himself, and as Valentin's blade crosses it, it breaks in half. Valentin, promptly realizing what he is contending with, in approved medieval fashion holds aloft the crosslike hilt of his broken sword. Mephistopheles recoils in terror from the Christian symbol as the soldiers follow Valentin's example in raising their swords hilt-up and join in a noble chant, rich and sonorous in its growing fervor. The solemnity of the moment quickly subsides in the revival of the festive spirit. The crowd now takes up

Marguerite (Victoria de los Angeles) in Garden Scene

Faust *trio: Mephisto (Édouard De Reszke, 1890's), Faust (Edward Johnson, 1920's) Marguerite (Nellie Melba, 1890's)*

a dance, the "Kermesse Waltz," which swirls with lilting exuberance from the orchestra.

In the midst of this merrymaking Marguerite approaches, making her way timidly through the whirl of dancers. Prayer book in hand, she is returning from church. Siebel wishes to join her, but each time he starts toward her, he is blocked by the suave yet ominous figure of Mephistopheles. Meanwhile, Faust has reached her side. Respectfully he offers to escort the "highborn and lovely maid" home. Confused and blushing, Margeurite modestly refuses, pointing out that she is neither highborn nor lovely, and in any case can find her way alone. As she walks on, Faust watches her blissfully. Mephistopheles, having observed the coy rebuff, laughingly suggests to Faust that perhaps his aid will be needed in winning Marguerite. The crowd now resumes the waltz, and the square is again an animated scene of whirling dancers lost in carefree gaiety.

ACT III

SCENE: *The garden before Marguerite's house.* Trees, shrubs, and flower beds surround Marguerite's dainty little cottage. Siebel enters the garden and begins gathering some roses and lilies for the girl he has promised Valentin to watch over. As he sings a sweet melody of love ("*Faites-lui mes aveux*"—"Gentle flow'rs in the dew"), the flowers fade quietly in his grasp. Mephistopheles' dire prophecy has come true! Suddenly a happy thought comes to Siebel. He goes to a nearby font of holy water, dips his hand in, and once more touches the flowers. The fiend's power is now unavailing, and Siebel resumes his delicate air. Presently he disappears among the shrubs, returning with a bouquet

of flowers which he fastens to the door of the cottage. Then he hurries off.

From behind the bushes Faust and Mephistopheles have been observing Siebel. Faust gazes ardently at Marguerite's garden, and as Mephistopheles leaves him with the promise to bring back the treasure to go with these flowers, he begins a tenderly romantic cavatina, addressed to Marguerite's humble cottage, "*Salut, demeure chaste et pure*" ("All hail, thou dwelling"). What true wealth amid such poverty! sings Faust ecstatically. Mephistopheles returns with a casket of jewels which he places near Siebel's bouquet. The intruders scurry for cover as Marguerite suddenly enters the garden. Dreamily, her thoughts on her recent encounter, she seats herself at the spinning wheel and begins to sing, at first wondering softly who the stranger was. Then she turns to a simple song of long ago ("*Le Roi de Thulé*"), quaint and charming, telling of the faithful King of Thule who had had a cup of gold made in memory of the woman he loved. Thoughts of Faust again intrude. The spinning stops, the song is broken off, and Marguerite once more wonders what his name was. Impatient with herself, she resumes the song, then stops her spinning and walks toward the house. The bouquet catches her eye, and she guesses it is from Siebel. Then she starts as her eye catches the casket. Throbbing with expectancy, she opens it and is dazzled by the brilliance within. Jewels! Marguerite begins to try on the sparkling gems, and as she looks at herself in a mirror she bursts out into the famous "Jewel Song" ("*Air des Bijoux*"), an aria sparkling with girlish rapture and coquettish delicacy.

Martha, the old gossip, now enters the garden and gushingly compliments Marguerite on her handsome appearance. Her rapture is cut short by Mephistopheles, who appears and salutes her gallantly.

From him Martha learns of her husband's death, but her grief is brief, for this elegantly sinister stranger has already caught her fancy. Faust offers his arm to Marguerite, and the four now promenade through the garden, which is growing dim in the gathering dusk. The couples pass one another, and at times their voices blend in bright, rich harmonies. Martha grows more and more interested in the red-robed cavalier, as Marguerite is slowly becoming enamored of Faust. As it begins to grow dark, she entreats Faust to leave. He embraces her ardently, but she slips out of his grasp and flees into the shadows of the garden, Faust in pursuit. Meanwhile, Mephistopheles, wearied of Martha's attentions, eludes her, and, safely alone, launches into a solemn "Invocation" (*"Il était temps!"*), in which he calls upon the night and the flowers to conspire with bewitching shadows and soft perfumes in his diabolical designs on Marguerite's soul. The evil incantation ended, he slinks off into the night.

Marguerite and Faust return. Remarking that it is growing late, the girl gently bids farewell, but Faust pleads to remain at his beloved's side. The night's enchantment is beginning its subtle work. Marguerite plucks a flower and removes it petals one by one in an age-old game, finally exclaiming joyously, "He loves me!" "Believe the flower!" Faust cries out, drawing nearer. As he utters the phrase *"D'une joie éternelle"* ("Of joy everlasting"), a wondrous love duet begins with their combined echo of the word *éternelle*. At length Marguerite breaks away from her lover and runs into the house. She pauses at the door to throw him a kiss and promises to meet him the following day.

Mephistopheles again steps into the picture, taunting Faust on his innocence. "Wait till you hear what she tells the stars!" he counsels him. Marguerite opens her casement window, and as Faust listens enchanted she sings her song of rapture to the night, *"Il m'aime"* ("He loves me"). The melody soars in passion, and Marguerite finally cries out, "Ah, hurry back to me, my beloved!" Faust rushes to the open window, and with a strangled cry of "Marguerite!" clasps her to him. The lovers are lost in the deepening night, through which comes the sardonic, triumphant laughter of the fiend.

ACT IV

SCENE 1: *Marguerite's room* (often omitted). Marguerite is alone in her room, busily spinning, and brooding over her betrayal. Outside are voices taunting her. Siebel, ever faithful, approaches her, swearing vengeance on Faust. Marguerite stops him with the declaration that she still loves the man who deserted her, and Siebel assures her of his eternal fealty in the touchingly simple melody *"Si le*

bonheur" ("When all was young"). Then Marguerite reveals that though all spurn her now, at least the church is still open, and there she will go to pray for her child—and for him.

SCENE 2: *Inside the church.* A few women cross the scene and Marguerite follows them and kneels to pray. In reply she hears the mocking voice of Mephistopheles, reminding her of her sins. A choir of demons jeeringly calls out her name. Prayer is useless, says the fiend. And Marguerite's despair grows as the church choir awesomely chants of the Day of Judgment. She faints at the fierce cry of Satan, *"À toi l'enfer!"* ("You are damned!"), and the congregation, coming from the service, is aghast.

SCENE 3: *A square before the church.* At one side of the square is the church, at the other is Marguerite's home. Martial music is heard as the troops return home victorious. Valentin greets Siebel, who, confused, evades his questions about Marguerite. The assembled troops now voice the joy of their homecoming in the famous "Soldiers' Chorus" (*"Gloire immortelle de nos aïeux"*—"Immortal glory of our ancestors"). Ready to die are we, like our brave forebears, they sing, but now it is peace and time to return to loving arms. The jubilant crowd disperses.

Nineteenth-century Garden Scene at Covent Garden, with Adelina Patti and Mario (r.) as the young lovers

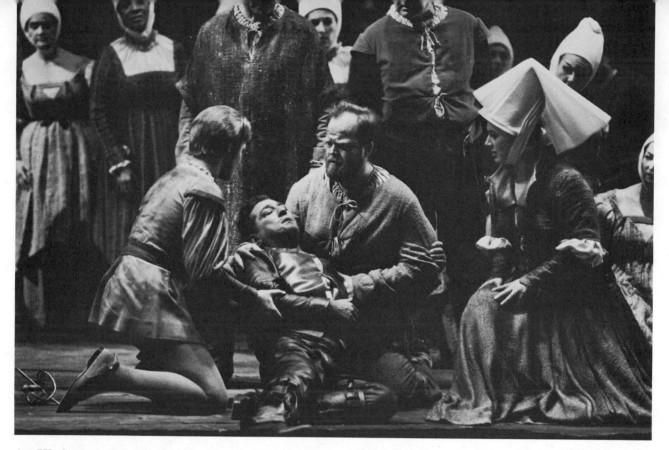

Act IV, Scene 2: Valentin (Robert Merrill) dies, comforted by Siebel (Marcia Baldwin) and Martha (Gladys Kriese)

Valentin, alarmed over Siebel's evasive remarks, rushes into the cottage. A cynical little theme is heard in the orchestra as Mephistopheles approaches, followed by Faust. The fiend is ready to enter, but Faust, torn with grief over his shameful conduct, restrains him. Mocking him, Mephistopheles stations himself below Marguerite's window and, strumming a guitar, sings an insulting serenade (*"Vous qui faites l'endormie"*—*"You who pretend to be slumbering"*), each stanza of which ends in a taunting laugh.

Outraged, Valentin bursts from the house, sword in hand. Mephistopheles retorts scornfully to Valentin's angry charges, and the brother challenges them. Faust reluctantly raises his sword in defense. Mephistopheles applies his black magic, and Valentin falls, mortally wounded, as the murderers flee. The noisy quarrel has drawn townspeople to the square, and they find Valentin writhing on the ground. As he dies, he mournfully tells his friends it is too late now to give him any help. In words of biting harshness he curses his sister for the shame and tragedy her love for Faust has brought them. The crowd pleads with him to relent and show mercy, but it is too late. Valentin dies, and Marguerite falls at her brother's feet, sobbing frenziedly. The people kneel and pray for the peace of his soul.

ACT V

SCENE 1: *The Brocken in the Harz Mountains* (often omitted). In search of further adventure Mephistopheles brings Faust to witness the revels of Walpurgis Night. These were held, according to medieval legend, on the eve of May first on the Brocken, the highest peak of the Harz Mountains, in Germany. On this desolate height, wrapped in ghostly mists, witches and demons hold their unholy orgy. Lightning flashes luridly over the gruesome scene. At a summons from Mephistopheles the shades of the great courtesans of history appear to the strains of sensuous ballet music. Lais, Cleopatra, Helen of Troy, Phryne are evoked in the dazzling vision. Suddenly, amid the wanton revelry there rises the image of Marguerite, crushed as if by the blow of an ax. Faust starts back abashed. He demands that Mephistopheles take him to her side.

SCENE 2: *A prison.* Marguerite, her mind almost shattered, is awaiting death for killing the child she has borne Faust. Mephistopheles and Faust have come to rescue her. They must work fast, for this is the morning of her execution. As Marguerite lies asleep on a straw bed in her dingy cell, Faust orders Mephistopheles to leave, for fear he will add to the poor girl's anguish. Marguerite awakens when Faust calls softly to her. Delirious, she seems at first unaware of his presence. As in a dream she sings quietly of their first meeting, of the night in the garden. Tenderly, dimly, as from afar, the music of the *kermesse* and the garden scenes returns in wistful, nostalgic echoes. Faust frantically urges her to come with him. As Marguerite raves on, her broken mind unable to cope with reality, Faust, in despair, realizes he cannot reach her.

Mephistopheles calls out impatiently that they must hurry. The horses are ready for their escape, he shouts, as the pulsating accompaniment of the orchestra suggests the sounds of trampling and neighing, with the song of the "Calf of Gold" heard in the basses. Marguerite suddenly draws back in fear as her vision clears and she sees Mephistopheles.

She calls out to God for protection, her voice soaring in angelic purity, as she seems to glimpse the joy of heaven and forgiveness. Faust and Mephistopheles struggle vainly against her vision, but Marguerite has found the strength to fight the tempting voices of Faust and his demon friend. Her last words to Faust damn him forever: "Why those bloody hands? Go, you fill me with horror!" In a joyous choiring of seraphic voices, Marguerite's soul is borne to heaven as Mephistopheles, with a gloating cry of "Condemned!" drags his victim off to perdition. Gounod rises to sublime heights in this final trio and "Apotheosis," vividly contrasting the opposing forces of good and evil, and massing great organ-like sonorities for the moment when the prison walls open and Marguerite's tormented soul is given its final repose.

Act V, Scene 2: Faust (Nicolai Gedda) and Mephistopheles (Nicolai Ghiaurov) come to free Marguerite (Mirella Freni)

Fidelio

CHARACTERS

Florestan, *a Spanish nobleman*   Tenor

Leonore, *his wife, who disguises herself*
    and takes the name of Fidelio   Soprano

Don Fernando, *Prime Minister of Spain*
    and friend of Florestan   Bass

Don Pizarro, *governor of the prison,*
    and enemy of Florestan   Bass

Rocco, *chief jailer*   Bass

Marcellina, *Rocco's daughter*   Soprano

Jacquino, *Rocco's assistant, in love*
    with Marcellina   Tenor

Prisoners, Guards, Soldiers, and People

*The action takes place in the eighteenth century at a fortress used for the
confinement of political offenders near Seville, Spain.*

OPERA IN TWO ACTS. Music by Ludwig van Beethoven. Libretto in German by Josef Sonnleithner, after a French play by Jean Nicolas Bouilly, entitled *Lêonore, ou L'Amour Conjugal* (*Lêonore, or Conjugal Love*), said to be based on a "historical fact." Sonnleithner's libretto was revised in 1806 by Stefan von Breuning and this was in turn revised in 1814 by Georg Friedrich Treitschke. It is the last version that is now used. First produced, in three acts, at the Theater an der Wien, Vienna, on November 20, 1805. On the following March 29, the work was revived in a cut version condensed to two acts. Further revision was done in the years following, and on May 23, 1814, it was produced at the Kärntnertor-Theater in Vienna, enjoying its first emphatic success. The American première occurred at the Park Theater, New York, September 9, 1839, the language being English. A German version followed in 1856 at the Broadway Theater, and the young Metropolitan Opera Company first staged it on November 19, 1884, with the phenomenal Marianne Brandt making her local debut as Leonore and Leopold Damrosch conducting.

Fidelio was Beethoven's only opera. Although the original title of the opera was *Leonore* it was found necessary to substitute *Fidelio* since there had been three operatic settings of the same play, with the same title, one by a Frenchman, Pierre Gaveaux, one by an Italian, Ferdinando Paër, who was *Kapellmeister* at Dresden, the third by a Bavarian, Simon Mayr, who was a choirmaster at Bergamo.

OVERTURE

The problem of an overture to *Fidelio* so worried Beethoven that he composed, in all, four complete specimens. The one known as "Leonore" Overture No. 1 was actually written second—for a performance in Prague in 1805 that never materialized. The manuscript was discovered in 1832 and was assumed to have been written first and then discarded, for it is simpler than No. 2, which was really the first and used at the opera's première. The following one—"Leonore" Overture No. 3—was composed for the Viennese revival four months later. The one that is now used regularly to open the opera was written for the 1814 revival. It is known simply as the Overture to *Fidelio*. Gustav Mahler introduced the practice of inserting the "Leonore" Overture No. 3 between the two scenes of Act II. All three "Leonore" Overtures differ sharply from the *Fidelio*

Overture, which, unlike them, is more in the nature of a true prelude, built around a single musical idea rather than reflecting a whole drama. The "Leonore" Overture No. 3 ranks first in popularity because of its strong musical material and highly dramatic development. It is based largely on the climactic first scene of Act II and includes music from Florestan's despairing aria and the surprising off-stage trumpet flourishes that announce the approach of Don Fernando. It was doubtless Beethoven's realization that as an overture to the opera the music anticipated too much of the drama and that a less aggressive overture would better set the mood for the lighter nature of the opening scenes which made him compose the so-called *Fidelio* Overture for the 1814 revival.

ACT I

SCENE: *The courtyard of the state prison.* The villain of the piece is Pizarro, governor of a state prison near Seville. He has imprisoned his political enemy Florestan in a secret dungeon, is slowly starving him to death, and has spread the rumor that the man is already dead. Florestan's faithful wife Leonore, however, suspects the truth and, in order to help her husband if at all possible, has disguised herself as a young man, assumed the appropriate name of Fidelio, and found herself a job as assistant to the weak but good-natured jailer Rocco.

The turnkey of the establishment is young Jacquino, who, when the curtain rises, is wooing Rocco's pretty daughter Marcellina. The girl deftly puts him off, for though she likes him, she has fallen in love, as she tells us in a sweet aria, with the new employee Fidelio. Rocco is inclined to encourage Marcellina in her new attachment, and when Leonore appears with some heavy chains she has been sent to buy, smiles as Marcellina solicitously

helps her with them. Jacquino comes back to the stage to make a foursome for the enchanting quartet (in canon form) *"Mir ist so wunderbar,"* in which each of the four uses the same generalizing words to show (a) that Marcellina thinks Fidelio is fond of her, (b) that Leonore is somewhat embarrassed by Marcellina's affection, (c) that Rocco thinks well of the match, and (d) that Jacquino is afraid he may be losing his sweetheart. Jacquino then obligingly retires from the stage—"to his lodge," as the libretto puts it. Rocco tells the remaining young couple that life isn't worth much without money; and in spoken dialogue he describes the prisoners under his care, mentioning one in the deepest of the dungeons. Leonore, in the trio that follows, shows that she feels sure the man is her husband and that Rocco's request to have her help him gives her courage.

At this point there is some martial music announcing the entrance of Pizarro. Opera houses which divide the first act into two scenes use it to make the change from Rocco's kitchen to the courtyard of the prison. Pizarro reads a letter announcing an inspection of the prison by Fernando, the King's minister, who suspects Pizarro of misusing his power. This, Pizarro decides in a florid and extremely difficult aria, is the moment to finally do away with Florestan. He orders trumpeters posted to give warning bugle calls when the minister's coach is seen approaching and then offers Rocco a purse of money to commit the murder. Rocco refuses the assignment but agrees to dig a grave for the man in his cell, and Pizarro decides to take for himself the more pleasurable job of doing away with his enemy. Leonore, who has overheard the duet between the two bassos, now has her great solo *scena* beginning *"Abscheulicher! wo eilst du hin!"* (translated in nineteenth-century operatic diction as "Accursed one! Where hasten'st thou!"). She then insists on helping Rocco dig the grave.

Paul Schoeffler as Don Pizarro, Lilli Lehmann as Leonore (Fidelio) and James McCracken as her husband, Florestan

Stuttgart: Wieland Wagner staging of Prisoners' Chorus

Now, at the request of Leonore and because it is the King's birthday, Rocco gives the dangerously unusual order that the prisoners be given a breath of air. They file out fearfully and sing a strikingly dramatic chorus, mostly soft, and interspersed with short solos, about the unaccustomed joy—"*O welche Lust*" ("O what delight!"). But Leonore fails to find Florestan among them, and Pizarro returns in anger to order them all back to their cells.

ACT II

SCENE 1: *A dark subterranean dungeon.* Florestan is revealed alone in the bleak depths of Pizarro's prison, chained and fastened to the wall. Soon he begins a poignant monologue on his grievous state. In the beautiful aria following the recitative he recalls his days of youth and spring and freedom, "*In des Lebens Frühlingstagen*" ("In the spring-time of life"). For loving liberty, for being innocent of any crime, he has been condemned to this endless torment. In his frenzy he has a vision of Leonore and cries out ecstatically to it. Rocco and Leonore now appear. In the gloom and on account of his altered appearance, she is at first unsure that the prisoner is really Florestan; but when she receives permission from Rocco to offer him some bread, she is at last certain. (The scene is carried on with softly spoken dialogue over music—literally melodrama.) When Florestan does not recognize his disguised wife, she is deeply moved by his thanking her in a gentle melody. A beautiful trio develops.

After a whistle from Rocco, Pizarro enters, gloats over Florestan, who prepares with dignity for his death, and draws a knife on the defenseless man.

Leonore rushes to shield him. "First kill his wife," she shouts defiantly. Florestan, dazed with joy, calls out, "My wife! Leonore!" In a burst of rage, Pizarro attempts to slay them both, but Leonore is ready for him. She whips out a pistol and levels it at him, crying, "One more step and you die!" At this point a trumpet sounds in the distance—then again, nearer. It is Don Fernando, the King's minister, who recognizes his old friend Florestan and orders Pizarro arrested. The scene closes with a rapturous duet between Florestan and Leonore, "*O namenlose Freude*" ("O untold joy").

(There is in the score a bit of dialogue following this duet between Don Fernando and Rocco concerning Pizarro's malice, but as it is anticlimactic and not necessary, it is almost always cut in performance.)

SCENE 2: *The courtyard of the state prison* (same as Act I). Florestan's fellow prisoners have been released by the Minister, and Leonore herself removes the chains from Florestan. Marcellina, fully recovered from her infatuation, consents to marry the turnkey Jacquino. Fernando has Pizarro led away in chains, and the chorus sings a final tribute to the devoted wife whose valor rescued her husband from certain death.

Jon Vickers as Florestan and Birgit Nilsson as Leonore

Die Fledermaus

THE BAT

CHARACTERS

Gabriel von Eisenstein, *a wealthy Austrian*	*Tenor*	Dr. Blind, *Eisenstein's lawyer*	*Tenor*
Rosalinde, *Eisenstein's wife*	*Soprano*	Frank, *jail warden*	*Baritone*
Adele, *her maid*	*Soprano*	Prince Orlofsky, *a wealthy Russian*	*Mezzo-soprano*
Dr. Falke, *his friendly enemy*	*Baritone*	Frosch, *a jailer*	*Speaking Role*
Alfred, *a tenor*	*Tenor*	Ida, *Adele's sister*	*Speaking Role*

The action takes place in an Austrian city in the late nineteenth century.

OPERETTA IN THREE ACTS. Music by Johann Strauss, Jr. Libretto in German by C. Haffner and R. Genée based on the French farce *Le Reveillon* of Meilhac and Halévy, which in turn stemmed from a German comedy by Roderich Benedix entitled *The Prison.* World première at the Theater an der Wien, in Vienna, on April 5, 1874. It next reached Berlin, July 8, 1874, and from that time on has been fantastically successful. The first New York performance, in German, was given at the New York Stadt Theater on November 21, 1874. The first performance at the Metropolitan Opera House was given on the manager's benefit night, February 16, 1905, Marcella Sembrich singing the role of Rosalinde. In the second act, a concert was interpolated, with Nordica, Homer, Caruso, and Giraldoni singing the Quartet from *Rigoletto.* The idea of an interpolated concert is sometimes used, too, on stages and discs.

No matter what the state of confusion in the last act, with its mistaken identities and unmasked disguises, the music ripples along smoothly, uncomplicatedly, winningly; and nothing seems to diminish the popularity of *Fledermaus.* It is included in this book because it is the only one of the dozens of once popular nineteenth-century Viennese operettas still given often in opera houses devoted to grand opera and performed with great star casts. It has appeared in numerous English versions—as *Night Birds, The Merry Countess, A Wonderful Night, Champagne Sec,* and *Rosalinda*—adapted and revised by many librettists. The most recent American adaptation was made by Garson Kanin (book) and Howard Dietz (lyrics) for the Metropolitan Opera production of the 1950–1951 season. The cast included Ljuba Welitsch, Risë Stevens, Patrice Munsel, Set Svanholm, and Richard Tucker, with Eugene Ormandy making his debut as a conductor at the Metropolitan.

OVERTURE

The Overture, long a popular concert favorite, is a selection of tunes from the operetta. The one that dominates, however, and that largely accounts for the gay, colorful spirit of the work, is the great Waltz from Act II.

ACT I

SCENE: *Garden and room of Eisenstein's house, evening.* Unheard by his old love inside the house, Alfred, a former suitor of Rosalinde, sings her a love

Hilde Gueden, as Rosalinde, Act III of Vienna staging

Alfred, who has been waiting for this, seizes his opportunity, enters the house, and to Rosalinde's annoyance makes himself at home in her husband's dressing gown and sits down at the table set for dinner. Drink, he tells her, and forget everything, for life is a comedy (*"Trinke, Liebchen, trinke schnell"*). Naturally, Adele receives belated permission to visit her "sick aunt."

Frank, the warden of the jail, who also plans to attend the ball, calls for his prisoner and assumes that Alfred is his man. To save her honor, Rosalinde convinces Alfred to keep up the deception. After many farewell caresses, Alfred tears himself away from his "wife" and goes off to jail with Frank.

ACT II

SCENE: *The ballroom of Prince Orlofsky's mansion.* Adele, dressed in her mistress' gown and pretending to be an actress, flirts with Prince Orlofsky, a rich dandy who believes everyone should have a good time, each in his own way (*"Chacun à son gout"*). Eisenstein is struck with Adele's resemblance to his wife's maid, but she coquettishly finds it all a laughable mistake (Adele's laughing song: *"Mein Herr Marquis"*—in the Kanin-Dietz version, "Look Me Over Once"). Frank, the jail warden, his prisoner supposedly safe in jail, arrives disguised as a nobleman and pays court to Adele. Rosalinde, disguised

Risë Stevens as Prince Orlofsky, at the Metropolitan Opera

song in the garden. (He is waiting for her husband to leave home.) Inside, Adele the maid, who has received an invitation to a ball that night, pretends to her mistress that her aunt is sick. But Rosalinde does not give her the evening off, for Adele is not so good an actress as she thinks she is. Lawyer Blind enters with his client Eisenstein, who for insulting a government official has to go to jail for eight days—three more than his original sentence, thanks to the worthy Dr. Blind's efforts. Blind advises him to go to jail and get it over with. Rosalinde assures her husband that she'll be inconsolable without him.

Falke, Eisenstein's old friend and drinking companion, comes to call, inviting him secretly to a ball to be given that night at Prince Orlofsky's (*"Komm' mit mir zum Souper"*); he can go to jail afterward. (Falke, who has been nicknamed Fledermaus, or the Bat, ever since Eisenstein had forced him home in broad daylight from a costume party dressed as a bat, plans to get even at Orlofsky's ball, for he has also secretly invited Rosalinde and her maid.) Rosalinde bids her husband a sad farewell (*"So muss allein ich bleiben"*), and he goes off with Falke, presumably to prison.

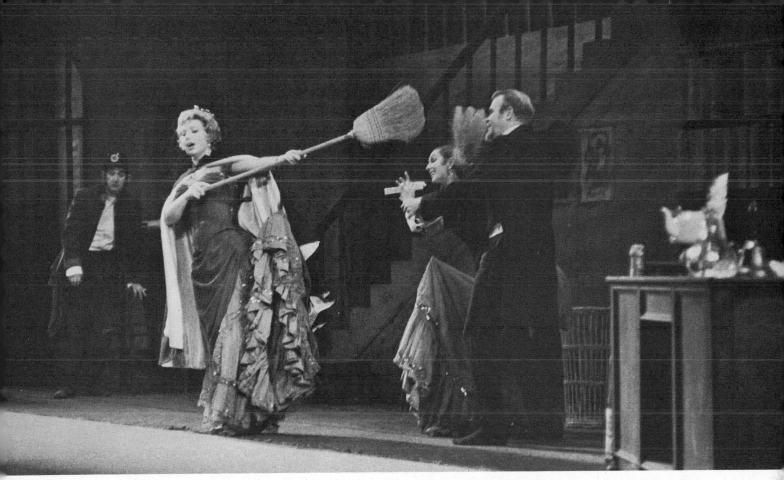

Act III: Frosch (Jack Gilford) watches Adele (Anneliese Rothenberger) audition for Frank (Roald Reitan), Ida (Nancy King)

as a Hungarian countess and masked, enters grandly, only to see her husband, whom she thought in jail, flirting with her maid and others. She decides to teach him a lesson and flirts with him herself, making certain not to remove her mask. In a game of counting their love-speeded heartbeats she makes away with his jeweled watch. In her role of Hungarian countess, she sings a czardas for the guests ("*Klänge der Heimat*") that begins with longing for home and ends with the philosophy of drink and be merry. Carried away with music and champagne, the guests decide on forming a brotherhood to last to eternity. The tipsy Eisenstein makes a last attempt to retrieve his watch from Rosalinde, but she is saved by the clock's ringing six. Eisenstein and Frank, equally drunk, become alarmed, for they should have been in jail before dawn. Not knowing each other's identity, they stagger out together.

ACT III

SCENE: *The city jail, early that morning*. Frosch, in the warden's absence, has gotten royally drunk. Alfred, who has had enough of being gallant, calls for a lawyer to get him out, and Frosch sends for Dr. Blind. Frank, still feeling the champagne, arrives at the jail, with Adele showing up soon after. He had given her his address, and she wants her gallant chevalier of the party to ask her master's forgiveness for wearing her mistress' gown. Frosch gets rid of her by locking her up in a cell. Now Eisenstein comes to give himself up, only to learn that someone else has already been arrested in his home as himself. When Dr. Blind comes to see Alfred, Eisenstein takes the lawyer's robe and wig and decides to find out what is what. Rosalinde, knowing that her husband will show up in jail, has arrived, too, wondering how to hide her indiscretion. Together with Alfred, she lays the facts before the lawyer (Eisenstein in disguise). When Eisenstein upbraids her, she flares up at him for taking the husband's side instead of hers. He removes his disguise, confronts them, and demands vengeance, whereupon Rosalinde takes out his watch, proving that she was his Hungarian countess. When all is confusion, Falke arrives with Prince Orlofsky and the party guests and explains that it was all a trick of his to even scores with Eisenstein for the bat episode. Rosalinde makes up with Eisenstein; Adele, who had offered herself to Frank, is led away by the Prince for himself; and everyone agrees that champagne was at the bottom of all their troubles.

155

Der Fliegende Holländer

THE FLYING DUTCHMAN

CHARACTERS

Daland, *a Norwegian sea captain*	Bass	Daland's Steersman	Tenor
Philip Vanderdecken, *the Flying*		Senta, *daughter of Daland*	Soprano
Dutchman	Baritone	Mary, *Senta's nurse*	Contralto
Erik, *a huntsman, in love with Senta*	Tenor		

Sailors, Maidens, Hunters, and Villagers

The action takes place in a Norwegian village in the eighteenth century.

Opera in three acts. Music by Richard Wagner. German text by the composer, founded on Heine's version of an old legend which he took from a Dutch drama. Produced at Dresden, January 2, 1843. First performed in the United States at the Philadelphia Academy of Music, in Italian, under the translated title *Il Vascello Fantasma,* November 8, 1876. Metropolitan première, in German, November 27, 1889, with Theodore Reichmann, Sophie Wiesner, Paul Kalisch, and Emil Fischer, the conductor being Anton Seidl. Seidl also conducted when the work was given at the same theater in Italian, with Jean Lassalle, Emma Albani, Sebastian Montariol, and Édouard de Reszke.

The North Sea, seldom gentle, was in one of its wildest moods when Wagner crossed it in 1839. The ship was nearly wrecked three times, and once was compelled to put up in a Norwegian harbor for safety. During the stormy voyage Wagner recalled Heine's account of the legend of the Flying Dutchman, who had been condemned to sail the seas until doomsday unless he should find a woman who would be true to him till death. Wagner was at that time exceedingly unhappy, bankrupt, and without work. The story of the unfortunate Dutchman appealed to him greatly—became a symbol of his own wretched condition. The Norwegian harbor and the song of the

Norwegian sailors enter into the opera; but, above all, it is the sea that dominates, the unceasingly restless ocean.

When Wagner finally arrived in Paris, he set to work to write a libretto for his opera; in order to relieve his strained circumstances, he sold a scenario of this libretto to Léon Pillet, manager of the Paris Opéra, the latter turning it over to a pair of librettists, Foucher and Révoil, and their libretto was set by another composer, Pierre Louis Philippe Dietsch, a conductor at the Opéra. This work, long since forgotten, was actually produced a few months before Wagner's.

With the money he received from the sale of the libretto, Wagner set himself up in a quiet apartment and began writing the music of his own opera. *Rienzi* had achieved a great success at Dresden; accordingly, the management of the opera there agreed to produce *The Dutchman*. After the dazzling, brilliant earlier work, the somber beauty of *The Dutchman*, more psychological and introspective, was a disappointment to the first audience. Dresden shelved it after four performances and did not revive it for twenty-two years. But by this time Dresden has accorded it hundreds of performances and the opera houses of the world, thousands. The opera marks a great step forward from the Meyerbeeresque *Rienzi* in the development of Wagner's musical and dramatic style; here he first uses leading motives—*Leitmotive*—to an appreciable extent, and the orchestra is treated in a truly symphonic manner.

OVERTURE

The Overture is in itself a vivid picture of the entire story: the stormy sea, portrayed as no other composer had ever succeeded in doing; the gloomy Dutchman, the curse upon him and his longing for redemption; the tranquil motive of Senta, who will bring about that redemption; for a moment of relief, the gay song of the Norwegian sailors, soon overwhelmed in the storm; and finally the crashing of the "Curse" motive, displaced by the theme of Senta, glorified and radiant, as it will be heard at the end of the opera, when across the glow of the sunset the figures of Senta and the redeemed Dutchman are seen rising from the sea heavenward.

ACT I

SCENE: *A Norwegian harbor.* The legend, as told both by Heine and by Wagner, relates to a Dutch sea captain who once swore that in spite of storms and all hell he would round the Cape of Good Hope. As a punishment for his impious vow he has condemned to sail the seas until the crack of doom. But once in seven years this "Flying Dutchman" was permitted to land; if then he could find a maiden who would be faithful unto death, she would bring release from the curse. At the opening of the opera one of these seven-year periods has elapsed, and the Dutchman, Vanderdecken, is driven by a storm to seek shelter in the same harbor where Daland, a Norwegian sea captain, has also been compelled to put up. Daland is rather impressed by this gloomy stranger, who is master of a ship with black masts and blood-red sails, and no less so by his apparent wealth. The Dutchman offers to pay well for lodgings, which Daland is quite agreeable to supply him. Suddenly, and almost bluntly, Vanderdecken asks his host-to-be whether or not he has a daughter. Daland says yes, and the Dutchman, without frill or fuss, immediately sues for her hand. This, not altogether surprisingly, delights Daland, who straightway invites the striking individual to be his guest. Presently the weather becomes more favorable, and both ships weigh anchor, headed for Daland's home.

ACT II

SCENE: *A room in Daland's house.* The second act shows Senta, Daland's daughter, at home with a crowd of girls who are spinning very busily. They

Act I: After seven years at sea, the Dutchman steps ashore to meet Daland, as staged at the Bavarian State Opera, Munich

sing, meanwhile, a most charming chorus, as the orchestra accompanies them with occasional imitation of the whirring wheels. Senta, however, has a specific aim in life, which is to be the cause of the Flying Dutchman's salvation. She sits dreamily in her armchair, gazing at the portrait of the already legendary Dutchman, in dark beard and black Spanish attire, which hangs over the entrance. Her companions quite cheerily tease Senta about her reveries, and she answers that she will sing them a much better song, a ballad about the Flying Dutchman, in which she discloses that by her love she would be the savior of this harried man.

The piece is known as "Senta's Ballad." It begins with the mariner's wild cry of "Yo-ho-ho, yo-ho-ho." And as the orchestra vividly depicts the raging ocean, she sings of the Dutchman's attempt to round the Cape, of his oath and the curse hurled upon him, and of how he is driven hopelessly across the seas in a ship with "blood-red sails." Then continuing—to the peaceful theme first heard in the Overture—she sings of his possible salvation, if anywhere on earth he can find a woman who will be faithful unto death. And in growing agitation she adds that such a woman there is and, quite oblivious of her surroundings, declares passionately that she is the one—she will save him from his unhappy fate.

With this, Erik, who loves her, enters and vainly attempts to dissuade her from her mad dream. She can give him no hope, however, and he darts out in despair. Senta's eyes are held fast by the picture and, suddenly and dramatically, she espies the Dutchman standing in the doorway, having just come in with her father. Senta and the dark mariner exchange a long, searching look, as Daland sings of their respective attributes—Vanderdecken's wealth and Senta's charms and virtues. They scarcely hear Daland, who, nettled by the lack of attention, leaves them. A long duet of mutual avowal takes place, following which Daland returns to confirm their betrothal.

ACT III

SCENE: *The bay near Daland's home.* Daland's house is seen on one side, and the ships of Vanderdecken and Daland are also partly visible. There are high cliffs rising from the sea some distance away. The villagers celebrate the sailors' return until frightened away by a ghostly chant that issues from the Dutchman's ship. Senta rushes out of her house and onto the wharf. In swift pursuit is Erik, who comes to reproach her for her faithlessness. This declaration is heard by the Dutchman, who, coming on the scene unnoticed, reflects upon the words and comes to the conclusion that if Senta is capable of being untrue to one man, she can be untrue also to another—himself. Whereupon he believes that once again he has been led almost to the point of his redemption only to be disillusioned, and now he must sail the seas for another seven years. Despite Senta's pleas, he boards his ship swiftly and orders it straight out to sea, where a storm begins to rage. But the frantic Senta, stunned only for a moment by the swift turn of circumstances, climbs speedily up one of the cliffs and, shouting after him, "Here stand I, faithful unto death!" flings herself into the ocean. And then a miracle takes place; the bleak and ghostly ship sinks at once from sight, as, rising heavenward, the figures of Senta and the Dutchman are seen clasped in an eternal embrace.

Act II: Vanderdecken (George London) is introduced to Senta (Leonie Rysanek) by Daland (Giorgio Tozzi) at the Metropolitan Opera

La Forza del Destino
THE FORCE OF DESTINY

CHARACTERS

The Marquis of Calatrava	Bass	Fra Melitone, *a friar*	Bass
Donna Leonora ⎱ *his children*	Soprano	Curra, *Leonora's maid*	Soprano
Don Carlo ⎰	Baritone	An Alcalde	Bass
Don Alvaro, *a young nobleman*	Tenor	A Surgeon	Baritone
Preziosilla, *a gypsy*	Mezzo-soprano	Trabucco, *a muleteer*	Tenor
Padre Guardiano, *an abbot*	Bass		

Spanish and Italian Peasants, Soldiers, Franciscan Friars, etc.

The action takes place in Spain and Italy about the end of the eighteenth century.

OPERA IN FOUR ACTS. Music by Giuseppe Verdi. Libretto in Italian by Francesco Maria Piave, after the Spanish play *Don Álvaro, o La Fuerza del Destino* by Ángel de Saavedra, Duke of Rivas. First performance, Imperial Italian Theater, St. Petersburg, November 10, 1862. First New York performance, Academy of Music, February 24, 1865. At its first Metropolitan Opera performance, November 15, 1918, Rosa Ponselle made her very auspicious debut. Singing with her were Enrico Caruso and Giuseppe de Luca. A revised version of the text, done by Antonio Ghislanzoni, was first heard at the Teatro alla Scala, Milan, February 20, 1869. The second version is described here, that being the one followed generally in present-day performances.

In *La Forza del Destino* we find the composer making an advance in musical style over the success that just preceded it, *Un Ballo in Maschera*. While in a general sense equally melodious, the music seems possessed of a greater seriousness and depth of purpose. The orchestral accompaniment is at once more full-bodied and colorful; the harmonics are richer and more varied. Seldom has Verdi charged a scene with a more genuine feeling of the dramatic, of tragic foreboding, than he has done in the second scene of Act II of this opera.

Richard Tucker as Alvaro

159

Act I, Scene 1: The Marquis (Luben Vichey), with Curra (Laura Castellano), bids Leonora (Zinka Milanov) good-night

OVERTURE

The Overture preceding the opera is appropriately dramatic. After a compelling blare of trumpets, a rather ominous, even sinister, melody is heard. Apparently it is meant to typify the unhappy nature of the work. This melody recurs frequently throughout the opera, at times bold and menacing, at others acting as a dark undercurrent to other themes. This is, more or less, a "Fate" motive, which, having made its point in the Overture, is replaced by other motives—notably the pathetic, desolate air of Alvaro's plea, which appears in the third act, and the very beautiful melody of Leonora's prayer, sung during the second scene of Act II. Other themes from the opera enter into the scheme, and all combine in a compelling mood picture of the tragic events to follow.

ACT I

SCENE: *Drawing room of the Marquis of Calatrava in Seville.* Don Alvaro is an aristocrat of part Inca blood, and this is so damaging in Spain that the beautiful Leonora, certain that her own family will never permit marriage, plans, instead, to elope with him. Her father, the Marquis of Calatrava, discovers them and, ignoring their protests, accuses them of shameful conduct. Assuming all the blame, Alvaro throws away his pistol and presents his bare chest to the aged noble's sword, but when the pistol strikes the floor it explodes and mortally wounds the Marquis. He dies, cursing his daughter.

ACT II

SCENE 1: *An inn at Hornachuelos.* Leonora, in male disguise, has fled from Seville to this mountain hostelry; she is alone and in despair, having lost all trace of Don Alvaro since the fatal night. Her uneasiness increases when she recognizes among the motley crowd her brother Don Carlo, who is masquerading as a student. She overhears his threats of vengeance on both his sister and her murderous lover. In the meantime, Preziosilla, a gypsy, urges all the men to go to Italy and join the fight against the Germans.

SCENE 2: *The monastery at Hornachuelos.* Leonora has come to the door of the monastery, where, kneeling in the moonlight, she prays for the Virgin's protection, in the aria *"Madre, pietosa Vergine"* ("Mother, merciful Virgin"). She knocks and, in a long duet, begs for protection from the kindly abbot, Padre Guardiano. He tells her of a deserted cave in the mountains where she may abide as a "hermit" in safety. The doors of the monastery chapel swing open, revealing in the distance the brilliantly lighted great altar. The deep tones of the organ unite with the solemn supplication of the kneeling monks and Padre Guardiano, who prays that a curse descend upon any person who should ever intrude upon or seek to learn the identity of this stranger. Then Guardiano bids Leonora depart to the mountain retreat; there none shall disturb her, for she will be under the protection of the monastery. She sings, together with the holy men, the simple and affecting prayer *"La Vergine degli angeli"* ("May the virgin of the angels guard thee").

ACT III

SCENE 1: *A wood near Velletri, Italy.* Don Alvaro, believing Leonora dead, has enlisted in the Spanish army under the name of Don Federico Herreros. He is tormented by memories of his past, and to a tender and melancholy air he soliloquizes, *"O tu che in seno"* ("O thou heavenly one").

His reveries being interrupted by a cry of distress, he goes out and rescues a wounded man—Don Carlo, his sworn enemy. Since they have never before met, and since both are going under assumed names, neither recognizes the other, and they become close friends.

Later, Don Alvaro, seemingly mortally wounded in battle, begs Carlo to swear to perform his last request. Carlo, torn with pity, swears that he will do his bidding. Alvaro begs him to search in his effects for a package of letters which he wishes burned without opening. Then, Alvaro says, he will die happy, and to a poignant melody sings farewell, while his friend replies with words of comfort—a duet of the most intense emotional fervor—*"Solenne in quest' ora"* ("Swear in this hour").

Destiny, however, cannot be thwarted, and although Carlo does not open the package, he discovers elsewhere in the wounded man's effects a picture of Leonora, and, in the aria *"Ah, egli è salvo"* ("Ah, he is saved"), he promises to deal with him.

SCENE 2: *A military camp near Velletri.* Alvaro is now restored to health, and in the early dawn strives to convince Don Carlo that he is guiltless of wrongdoing and worthy of Leonora. Intent on avenging his father's death, Don Carlo will not believe him, and insists they fight it out. Alvaro refuses until Carlo threatens to search out Leonora and take her life instead. However, a passing patrol parts the two men. The scene brightens as the camp fills with soldiers and camp-followers. A fortuneteller, Preziosilla, plies her trade; Trabucco (who had appeared briefly, along with Preziosilla, as a muleteer in Act II) tries to sell novelties; and Father Melitone, a coarse staff member of the monastery of Hornachuelos, preaches a ridiculous sermon, full of puns, and is laughed down by the soldiers. Finally Preziosilla leads the male chorus in a brilliant, unaccompanied *"Rataplan."* (The first part of this scene, being quite unnecessary for the plot, is more often omitted than not. The second part is even less germane but is usually retained, partly to afford a change of pace from the general grimness of the events, partly to give the mezzo-soprano her one opportunity to shine.)

Act II, Scene 2: Padre Guardiano (Ezio Flagello) and Leonora (Leontyne Price), in the 1967 Metropolitan Opera staging

ACT IV

SCENE 1: *Outside the monastery at Hornachuelos.* In another comic scene the crusty Father Melitone is serving soup out of an enormous caldron to a band of beggars. They so anger the old man by their complaints and wishes for the gentler ministrations of one "Father Raphael," that he kicks over the entire caldron. The Abbot Guardino reproves Melitone for his temper, who defends himself by saying that the reputedly gentle Father Raphael had himself become really angry when he called him a "wild Indian." From this we may deduce that Raphael is really Don Alvaro, who has Inca blood, and who some years before doffed his soldier's garb and enlisted as a member of Father Guardino's holy order. Yet even to the sacred calm of this retreat, Don Carlo comes seeking vengeance. While he awaits Alvaro, he sings, *"Invano, Alvaro"* ("In vain, Alvaro"), in which he remarks on the futility of Alvaro's retirement and of his "hypocrite's garb."

Don Alvaro naturally exclaims in surprise on beholding Carlo, whom he thought dead. Carlo coldly presents him with a sword: they must fight to the death. Alvaro bids him be gone: he is now a man of peace and cannot fight. To this Carlo replies, "Coward!" The friar, well schooled in ignoring his own feelings, answers, "Your menaces, wild and angry words, are cast to the winds." His lines are sung to the broken, pathetic little melody first heard in the Overture.

Alvaro tries hard to convince Don Carlo that vengeance lies with God. In return he receives the most venomous insults, including a reference to Alvaro's South American Indian blood. In the music, the pleading accents of the priest are remarkably contrasted with the sinister threats of Don Carlo. Slowly, yet inevitably, the benevolent friar becomes again the fiery man of action; he prays for self-restraint. Carlo strikes him insultingly; Alvaro seizes the weapon, and, the convent being no place to fight, the men rush away.

SCENE 2: *A wild spot near Hornachuelos.* As the curtain rises, we hear in the orchestra the agitated melody first played at the opening of the Overture. On this dark day Leonora, pale and worn, yet beautiful, has issued from her desolate cavern to pray, still tormented by memories of her ill-fated love. *"Pace, pace, mio Dio!"* ("Peace, peace, O my God!"), she implores, to a melody of haunting sadness and loveliness that rises and rises as thoughts of Alvaro come crowding. In despair, she finally exclaims that her longing for peace is vain, and turns to re-enter her cave. Suddenly one hears the sounds of clashing swords. She curses the intruders and hides.

Don Alvaro, who has mortally wounded Carlos, rushes in seeking help, and thus, for the first time since they parted after the death of the Marquis of Calatrava, the faithful lovers meet under most tragic circumstances. As soon as she understands what has happened, Leonora rushes out to help her brother, who (offstage) curses her out and, with his dying breath, drives a dagger into her. Father Guardino comes in just as Leonora staggers back, and a most moving and effective trio ends the opera as Leonora dies in her anguished lover's arms and Guardino blesses her.

Act IV, Scene 2: The Metropolitan première in 1917, with Jose Mardones (Padre Guardiano), Enrico Caruso (Don Alvaro), Rosa Ponselle (Leonora)

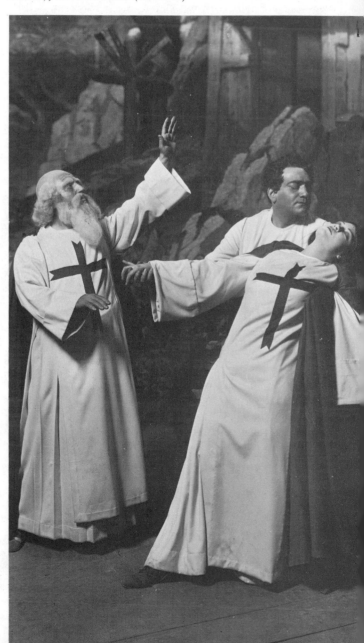

Four Saints in Three Acts

CHARACTERS

Saint Theresa I	*Soprano*	Saint Chavez	*Tenor*
Saint Theresa II	*Contralto*	Commère	*Mezzo-soprano*
Saint Ignatius Loyola	*Baritone*	Compère	*Bass*

Double Chorus of Named and Unnamed Saints and Six Dangers

OPERA IN a prelude and four acts. Music by Virgil Thomson. Libretto in "English" by Gertrude Stein ("An Opera to Be Sung"). First produced, February 7, 1934, by The Friends and Enemies of Modern Music, Inc., at the auditorium of the Avery Memorial, Hartford, Connecticut, with an all-Negro cast including Beatrice Robinson Wayne, Bruce Howard, Edward Matthews, Embry Bonner, Altonell Hines, and Abner Dorsey. Costumes and sets by Florine Stettheimer; Alexander Smallens conducted.

Four Saints in Three Acts played for one week in Hartford; six weeks at the Forty-fourth Street and Empire theaters, New York; one week at the Auditorium Theater, Chicago. These performances were all conducted either by Alexander Smallens or the composer. In the spring of 1941 two concert performances of the opera were given—one at the Museum of Modern Art, New York, under the composer's direction, and one at Town Hall, New York, Alexander Smallens conducting. In June 1942 an hour of the music was played over the Mutual Broadcasting System for the United States Treasury Department, the conductor being Alfred Wallenstein. In May 1947 the entire work was performed over the Columbia Broadcasting System. The cast in all performances remained substantially the same as that of the original production.

Although it is called *Four Saints in Three Acts,* the work actually presents some thirty or more saints in four acts. The subject matter of the opera is the religious, or saintly, life. Saint Theresa and Saint Ignatius are shown in typical scenes, each surrounded by assistants and pupils. The four saints referred to in the title are Saint Theresa; her chief helper, Saint Settlement; Saint Ignatius; and his first lieutenant, Saint Chavez. The Compère and Commère, acting as commentators, converse with each other and with the saints and announce to the audience, as masters of ceremony, the progress of the play.

Mr. Thomson suggests that listeners should "not try to understand the words of this opera literally or to seek in the music of it any direct reference to Spain." And, he continues, "If, by means of the poet's liberties with logic and the composer's constant usage of the simplest formulae in our musical vernacular, something is evoked of the gaiety and the mystical strength of lives consecrated to a nonmaterialistic end, the authors will consider their message to have been communicated."

PRELUDE

The Prelude ("A narrative of prepare for the saints") is a sort of choral overture, "To know to know to love her so. Four saints prepare for saints. It makes it well fish."

ACT I

SCENE: *The steps of the Cathedral at Ávila* ("Saint Theresa half indoors and half out of doors"). This act represents, in the form of living pictures, scenes from the religious life of Saint Theresa.

ACT II

SCENE: *A garden party or picnic in the country* ("Might it be mountains if it were not Barcelona"). The saints play games; the Compère and the Commère have a love scene, and a ballet depicts angels learning to fly. Toward evening the saints are vouchsafed a vision of the Celestial Mansions. "How many windows and doors and floors are there in it?" they reverently ask. But they are not vouchsafed an answer.

ACT III

SCENE: *Barcelona—Saint Ignatius and Jesuits mending their nets* ("Saint Ignatius and one of two literally"). Saint Ignatius and the Jesuits are at their religious and military exercises. There are a vision of the Holy Ghost ("Pigeons on the grass alas and a magpie in the sky"), a ballet of Spanish girls with sailors, a storm, which Saint Ignatius quiets, and a foretaste of Doomsday ("around is a sound"). This is followed by a choral procession and an intermezzo, which leads into a brief fourth act, or epilogue.

ACT IV

SCENE: *The saints in glory* ("The sisters and saints reassembled and re-enacting why they went away to stay"). The saints recall their earthly lives and join in a communion hymn, "When this you see remember me." The Compère announces, "Last act!" The chorus replies, "Which is a fact!"

Scene from first production of Four Saints in Three Acts, *staged by The Friends and Enemies of Modern Music, Inc.*

Die Frau ohne Schatten
THE WOMAN WITHOUT A SHADOW

CHARACTERS

The Emperor	*Tenor*	Apparition of a Youth	*Tenor*
The Empress	*Soprano*	The Voice of the Falcon	*Soprano*
The Nurse	*Mezzo-soprano*	A Voice from Above	*Contralto*
Barak the Dyer	*Bass-Baritone*	The One-Eyed	*Bass*
His Wife	*Soprano*	The One-Armed ⎬ *Barak's brothers*	*Bass*
A Spirit Messenger	*Baritone*	The Hunchback	*Tenor*
The Keeper of the Temple	*Soprano*		

Unborn Children's Voices, Watchmen's Voices, Servants, Beggar Children, Spirits

The action takes place in the imaginary empire of the Southeastern Islands in some imaginary time.

OPERA IN THREE ACTS. Music by Richard Strauss. Libretto in German by Hugo von Hofmannsthal. First performance at Vienna, October 10, 1919. First American performance at the San Francisco Opera on September 17, 1959. First heard at the Metropolitan Opera House on October 3, 1966.

From the inception of the idea for this opera to the completion of the score in 1917 took ten years, but one of the reasons for this extended pregnancy was the librettist's term of military service in World War I, chiefly as a writer of propaganda. When the war was over, composer and librettist waited almost another two years before bringing out the work in Vienna, where Strauss was director of the opera house. They did not believe the war-torn country would be ready before that to receive and understand a work so long, serious, and full of sometimes obscure symbolism. There were good grounds for such fears. The obscurity of much of the symbolism, the heavy Teutonic hand with which the fairly simple message of the opera is delivered (that childbearing is the proper end of a good and happy marriage), the very length of the opera (over three hours of playing time) have all militated against its achieving the general affection and respect that its authors and some critics believed it deserved. It took almost twenty years to reach Italy, almost half a century to reach the United States. When it finally reached the Metropolitan, the critics were divided. The *Herald Tribune* called it "a grotesque pomposity"; The New York *Times* said it "must rank with *Der Rosenkavalier*, *Elektra*, and *Salome* as a great opera." Both critics may be right. The libretto is unquestionably pompous and overliterary, while the score contains some of Strauss's finest and most eloquent pages (as, for example, the duet between Barak and his wife in the beginning of Act III) and also some of his most empty and overblown music. For Strauss, *Die Frau ohne Schatten* stood in relation to Mozart's *Die Zauberflöte*, much as his *Der Rosenkavalier* did to *Le Nozze di Figaro*.

ACT I

SCENE 1: *A flat roof overlooking the imperial gardens with an entry to the royal apartments on one side. The young Empress, married to a mortal sover-*

eign for less than a year, is the daughter of Keikobad, King of the Spirits; and her Nurse, part old family retainer and part wise woman with supernatural powers, is crouching outside the royal bedroom expecting a visit from her old master Keikobad. Instead there comes to her a man in armor, the twelfth monthly Messenger to ask whether the Empress yet casts a shadow—meaning whether she is pregnant. No, answers the Nurse; light passes through the Empress as if she were made of glass, yet the Emperor has been with her every night. The Messenger then sternly informs the Nurse that if after three more days the shadow is not cast, then the Empress must return to her father and the Emperor will be turned to stone.

The Messenger gone, the Emperor comes out ready for his daily hunt. This time, he tells the Nurse, he will go to the place where he had met his Lady to search for the Falcon that had caused them to meet.

Karin Branzell as the Nurse, Berlin State Opera

The Empress then had been in the form of a white gazelle, which the Falcon had attacked. The Lady in her present form had stepped out of the stricken body and, drunk with her beauty, he had wounded the Falcon who had done him this great service. It is to find and reward the wounded bird that he will now go, perhaps for as long as three days and nights.

When he has gone, the Empress emerges from the apartment, missing her beloved husband but also sighing for the Falcon so that she may regain the power to change her shape once more. Suddenly she sees the bird, whose voice is heard mourning not his wound but the fact that the Empress casts no

shadow and the Emperor must be turned to stone. A trio on these subjects evolves with the voice of the Falcon, the Empress, and the Nurse expressing their sorrow. Finally, with the Falcon gone, the Empress begs the Nurse to help her find a shadow; and the Nurse, from her command of wizardry, tells her she can only do it by descending among the world of common men, a place she describes with revulsion. Nevertheless, the Empress insists; and at the end of the long duet, they begin the journey together.

SCENE 2: *Inside the Dyer's house.* After an orchestral interlude descriptive of the descent of Empress and Nurse, we find the three misshapen brothers of Barak the Dyer (he being the only character in the opera with a proper name) fighting on the floor till the Dyer's Wife, a handsome wench, throws water on them. When Barak comes in carrying skins, he orders the brothers out, he calms down his wife, speaks kindly to her, and hopes that they may have children soon; but the spoiled beauty only complains and says that as he has failed to make her a mother in two and a half years, she has given up any desires —either for children or for him. The undiscouraged Dyer is satisfied to wait, and goes off with another batch of skins, carrying them himself to spare the ass some labor.

Suddenly, by magic, the Empress and the Nurse appear dressed as servants. The Empress says not a word throughout the following scene, but the Nurse flatters the Dyer's Wife for her beauty and majestic bearing, promises her the service—for three days— of her two visitors as servants, shows her visions of riches and sexual triumphs she may have if she will sell her shadow and forswear motherhood. The Dyer's Wife is almost ready to make the bargain when she hears her husband returning. Quickly, the Nurse promises service to begin the next day, summons fish that fly into a frying pan, severs the double bed in two, and disappears with the Empress. The fish, who represent the Wife's unborn children, beg for birth, but she wishes only to silence them. On Barak's entry he is delighted by the fine smell of the fish, which are now frying silently, but disgusted when his wife explains that one half of his bed will be used for a couple of poor relatives who are coming to stay with them. Yet he accepts this, for he had once been warned that his wife was a strange woman. As she goes to bed and he sits down to eat, a chorus of watchmen off stage urge husbands and wives to sleep together so that their love will bring life.

ACT II

SCENE 1: *The Dyer's house.* The Nurse, still trying to get the shadow of the Dyer's Wife, tempts her further. In the presence of the young Empress she urges the Wife to think of a handsome man she once fancied but who would pay no attention to her, and then summons the man, who is fashioned from a straw the Nurse picks up. The Wife is excited and also fearful, but just as the Nurse is urging them toward each other (with the help of supernatural voices from above), Barak returns to the house with his three brothers, some beggar children, and a huge dish of food. While the brothers and the children sing and carouse joyfully over the goodies, the Dyer's Wife refuses to have anything to do with such coarseness. She bewails her lot that she should be thrown in with people so much beneath her.

SCENE 2: *Outside the royal falcon house, deep in the woods.* On a moonlit night, the Emperor, led to this spot by the beloved Falcon which he has found again and by a letter from the Empress, is hiding behind a tree wondering what she may be doing. He feels that the house is empty even though the letter had said she would be spending three days there, alone with the Nurse, hidden from the world of men. But at the end of the soliloquy which informs us of all this, he sees her and the Nurse gliding silently through the trees and into the house, for they have promised to serve the Dyer's Wife only during the daytime. Somehow he senses that she has been among the world of men after all, and for the lie in her letter decides that he must kill her. He considers shooting her with an arrow, slaying her with his sword, or using his bare hands. But he cannot find heart to do the deed at all; and remounting his horse, he bids the Falcon lead him to a rocky ledge where he may utter his laments alone, heard by neither man nor beast. No other voice is heard in this scene.

SCENE 3: *The Dyer's house.* Once more the Nurse tries to tempt the Dyer's Wife. Barak is slow in getting ready to go out, so the Nurse puts him into a sound sleep with a drug, a trick that arouses the Wife's suspicions. She wants to leave the house, perhaps to meet the Young Man once more, but the Nurse, with her magic, causes him to appear suddenly, both frightening and attracting the Wife. The Young Man is at once attracted, but on account of the suddenness of his appearance, falls back in faint. As he does so, he reaches out to embrace the Wife, who in her fright calls on Barak for help. The Nurse throws her mantle over him, and Barak is awakened by his wife and the Empress. But he is greeted by a tirade from his Wife for shouting for help and for not being around when he was needed. She goes out with the Nurse, while Barak remains thoroughly mystified but reassured by the Empress.

SCENE 4: *Bedroom of the Empress in the falcon house.* The Empress is talking aloud while she has a

Lotte Lehmann, the original wife of Barak the dyer

nightmare. She sees a vision of the Emperor trying to enter a cave and hears the Falcon's voice predicting that he must turn to stone. The vision vanishes;

Maria Jeritza, creator of the Empress, Vienna 1919

and the Empress wakens from her nightmare, bitterly bewailing the misfortune she is bringing not only to her beloved husband but to the good Dyer as well.

SCENE 5: *The Dyer's house.* On the third day the Nurse is about to make her final attempt to secure the Wife's shadow, but she feels there are some unknown forces at work, for in the middle of the day everything is turning dark. The three brothers are terribly frightened and call on Barak for help; the Empress feels she is bringing destruction on a good man; the Nurse expresses confidence that she can get supernatural help; and Barak feels that faith in integrity is all that is needed. These reactions are expressed in a concerted number, but the Wife tries to hide her sense of guilt by calling on Barak to throw out the disgusting "dogs," meaning her brothers-in-law. Flashes of lightning create even more terror, and finally the Wife tells them all that she is selling her shadow, thus giving up any chance of ever having children. As the fire in the grate flames up, they see that she really has no shadow now, and the Nurse urges the Empress to seize it. The Empress, however, shrinks away in horror, while Barak is so shocked that he prepares to murder his wife. A sword mysteriously springs into his hand, and the Wife, thoroughly frightened now, claims that she only *said* she was selling her shadow and that it hadn't been done yet. Suddenly she understands Barak's righteousness, and she begs for a quick death. The brothers, however, restrain the Dyer, for they fear he will be punished and they remain leaderless. Yet Barak shakes them off and lifts his sword. Suddenly it flies out of his hand, Barak and his wife are swallowed up by the earth together with the hut, and the rest escape as great cascades of water plunge in.

ACT III

SCENE: *Two underground vaults divided by a thick wall.* Unaware of each other, Barak and his Wife each occupy one vault. The Wife regrets her near unfaithfulness, for she now appreciates her husband's worth, and she calls on him, exculpating herself. The Dyer berates himself for having taken this woman to love and cherish and then threatening to murder her. A shaft of light reveals a staircase first in Barak's vault, then in his wife's, and a voice calls on them to ascend.

The scene now changes to a terrace above a river, with the Messenger (from the first act) and a chorus of spirits standing before a bronze door. They hail a boat coming on the river and then disappear behind the door. The boat carries the Empress and the Nurse, and the Nurse immediately tries to get the Empress to come away. But the younger woman recognizes a trumpet blast from inside as coming from her father, Keikobad, who must pass final judgment on the Emperor. In a long argument, the Nurse insists that Keikobad now will condemn her, too, that he must return to earth, among the hated human beings, and take the shadow of the Dyer's Wife to fulfill her destiny and save her husband. However, the Empress by this time has learned that human beings may be fine, may be saved, and she refuses to do any more damage to Barak and his Wife. She is intent on rejoining her father and being judged by him, and she dismisses the Nurse, parting from her forever, to enter the gates. Meantime, the Dyer and his Wife, on different sides of the stage, are searching for each other. Each asks the Nurse for directions, and each is directed wrongly, for the Nurse hates all human beings. In desperation she calls after the one being she loves, the Empress, but the Messenger, hearing her cries, comes out, answers her rudely, and thrusts her into the boat. As it drifts away, the voices of Barak and his Wife are heard far off, each wishing only to die.

Once more the scene changes, this time to a temple-like hall. The Empress is tempted with a fountain that spurts the golden water of life, but she says she does not need it, for love is enough. Even when the Guardian of the Threshold tells her that drinking it will give her the shadow of the Dyer's Wife, she refuses, hearing the voice of the woman and of Barak still calling to each other. She calls upon her father, and there is revealed to her the Emperor, already turned to stone save for his eyes. The Guardian tells her that by drinking of the water of life, he will be restored to her. Again she refuses—and very firmly—whereupon she suddenly casts a shadow on the ground. She has now passed her final test. The Emperor rises, a fully living man once more, and the two sing a joyous duet in which they are joined by a chorus of their unborn children.

A final scenic transformation changes the shadow of the Empress into a golden bridge before a waterfall. Barak and his Wife cross the bridge toward each other, she casting a large shadow. Joyously they sing together, also joined by a chorus of unborn children, while the Emperor and Empress, standing above the waterfall, join in with their happiness over having passed the tests to which Keikobad has subjected them. The opera ends with a chorus of the unborn children of both couples, a paean to joy over dangers passed and to brotherhood.

OPPOSITE
Final scene with Emperor and Empress (James King, Leonie Rysanek, above), Barak and his wife (Walter Berry, Christa Ludwig, below), Metropolitan Opera, 1966

Der Freischütz

THE FREE-SHOOTER

CHARACTERS

Ottokar, *a Prince of Bohemia*	*Baritone*	Max, *another ranger*	*Tenor*
Kuno, *head ranger to the Prince*	*Bass*	Zamiel, *the Black Huntsman*	*Speaking Part*
Agathe, *his daughter*	*Soprano*	A Hermit	*Bass*
Ännchen, *her cousin*	*Soprano*	Kilian, *a peasant*	*Bass*
Caspar, *a ranger*	*Bass*		

Bridesmaids, Huntsmen, and Attendants on the Prince, Peasants, Musicians, Spirits, Demons, and Various Apparitions

The action takes place in Bohemia in the seventeenth century.

OPERA IN THREE ACTS. Music by Carl Maria von Weber. Libretto in German by Friedrich Kind, founded on a tale in the *Gespensterbuch,* edited by Apel and Laun. First performance, Schauspielhaus, Berlin, June 18, 1821. First performance in the United States, at Philadelphia, December 1824, in English. It entered the German repertoire of the Metropolitan Opera on November 24, 1884 and for the revival of March 22, 1924, recitatives were composed by the conductor Artur Bodanzky. Save for a concert performance at Philharmonic Hall by the Hamburg State Opera in 1967, *Der Freischütz* has been absent from New York stages for nearly forty years. A revival is planned at the Metropolitan for the 1969–70 season.

Weber, the great pioneer of nationalism in German opera, endeavored, in *Der Freischütz*, to escape Italian influence by discarding plots of intrigue, and instead sought material for his opera in the legends of his own country. Thus he opened up the dual paths of romanticism and nationalism which led, eventually, to Wagner's monumental *Ring des Nibelungen*. Originally written with spoken dialogue and based on a native subject, *Der Freischütz* forged a link between the old *Singspiel* and Wagner.

The title *Der Freischütz* means, literally, "the free-shooter," a term applied to one who used magic bullets. The story of the opera is founded on an old tradition among huntsmen in Germany, to the effect that whoever should sell his soul to Zamiel, the demon hunter, would receive seven magic bullets, which would always hit the mark. But the seventh bullet was meant for himself, and he must thus yield up his soul to Zamiel if he has not in the meantime found another victim for the demon; for every convert his life will be extended and he will receive a fresh supply of bullets.

OVERTURE

The Overture, long a concert favorite, is, in effect, a musical synopsis of the opera, presenting, as it does, the chief melodies from the score. It opens in religious calm, with a beautiful melody played by the horns. There creeps in the fearsome, sinister music of Zamiel and of the terrifying scene in the Wolf's Glen. Opposed to this baleful music is heard the triumphant outburst from Agathe's aria: "We shall meet in joy at last!" In the ensuing struggle between these forces of good and evil, thrillingly depicted in music, good is triumphant, and the Overture ends in a mood of rejoicing.

ACT 1

SCENE: *Open space before a tavern.* The first sounds heard from the stage are a shot and shouts of "Bravo!" The peasant Kilian has just defeated the professional ranger Max in a shooting match; and as the crowd marches and sings in honor of the winner, Max sits by in a deep depression. However, when Kilian starts to taunt him, he rises to attack his adversary, and only the arrival of Kuno, the head ranger, with several other rangers, prevents violence. In the dialogue that follows it becomes clear why Max feels so strongly. Recently he seems to have lost his skill at marksmanship, and unless he wins the contest scheduled for the next day before the Prince, he will lose the hand of Kuno's daughter Agathe and the probable succession to Kuno in the office of head ranger. Caspar, one of the other rangers and a rejected rival for Agathe's hand, suggests that Max

may need some supernatural assistance the next day, but Kuno shuts him up severely. Caspar, he says, is well known for his unsavory character and, besides, the shooting contests are nowadays conducted without supernatural aid. Once, apparently, there was intervention from the very devil himself. And Kilian goes on to explain that there are such things as "free" shots. By making a compact with the devil, one can get seven bullets. The first six will always hit their mark, but the seventh will be guided by the devil and hit whatever he wants to hit. After all these explanations there is an ensemble number in which everyone comments on the matter; Kilian and Max make it up between them; and the party is broken up by Kuno.

Left alone, Max sings his great aria *"Durch die Wälder, durch die Auen"* ("Through the forests, through the meadows"), in which he describes his once-carefree life. Evening is approaching as Caspar joins him, treats him to several drinks, and sings a

Scene of the Wolf's Glen from Der Freischütz, *from* The Illustrated London News, *showing 1850 Royal Opera production*

rough drinking song. During this time Zamiel (who is the devil in the person of a figure known as the Black Huntsman) twice appears silently among the trees as a reminder to Caspar what his unholy duty is. By this time Max is slightly befuddled by drink, and when Caspar thrusts his gun into his hand and suggests he shoot at a distant bird, Max takes the challenge. Much to his amazement, the bird falls at his feet, whereupon Caspar explains that he had used a "free" bullet. If only Max will meet him at night in the mysterious spot known as the Wolf's Glen, he will help him get some more bullets so that he may win the contest. Max is aware that he may be letting himself in for something really disastrous, but he is desperate now and agrees to come. After he has left, Caspar closes the act with an elaborately coloratura bass aria of triumph, *"Der Hölle Netz hat dich umgarnt"* ("The toils of hell now hold you fast").

ACT II

SCENE 1: *A room in Kuno's house.* Agathe, Kuno's daughter, speaks of her fears about the outcome of the shooting match to her cheerful young cousin Ännchen, who is tacking back up on the wall a picture of an ancestor which had fallen on Agathe and slightly hurt her. That accident also bothers Max's fiancée, for the ancestor had once been involved with "free" bullets, and this morning she had paid a visit to a good old hermit who had had an ominous dream about her and Max. The two girls have a sweet duet,

Michael Bohnen as Caspar, Metropolitan Opera

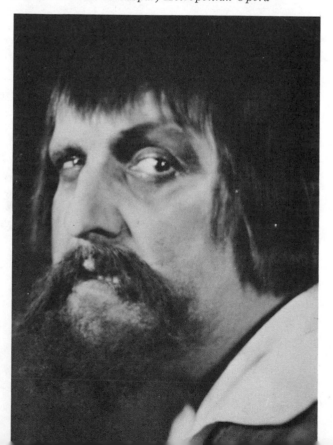

and when the subject of Max's expected visit comes up, Ännchen sings a little ditty on the subject of young love. But Agathe remains in pensive mood, and when she is left alone, sings the most famous aria of the opera, *"Leise, leise, fromme Weise"* ("Softly, softly breathe my prayer"), in which she begs the protection of heaven. At the end she sees Max coming toward her, and the aria closes with a joyous, brilliant melody which has already been heard in the Overture and will bring the opera to a close.

Max tells her he is off to the Wolf's Glen, though he gives a false reason for the visit to that spot of ill-repute. Ännchen comes in again, and the two girls, in a trio, try to dissuade him from going. He, however, remains determined, and goes off after a short and tender duet with Agathe.

SCENE 2: *The Wolf's Glen.* A tree blasted by lightning, a large dark cave, the moon shining brightly, a storm gathering, a waterfall, old trees with owls and ravens, and off stage a choir of basses singing *"Uhui! uhui!"* as evil spirits are supposed to do. This is the Wolf's Glen, where Caspar is placing a circle of black stones around a human skull, which he then strikes with his dagger, thus summoning Zamiel. In the dialogue that follows, Zamiel speaks his lines in a high, weird tenor voice while Caspar, a basso, sings his. Caspar's time, it appears, is up the next day, and he begs for three more years if he can deliver Max's soul to the devil and possibly Agathe's as well. His proposal is that Max should get the customary seven bullets and that the seventh may be directed by Zamiel at Agathe's heart. The devil admits that somehow Agathe is protected, but he will settle for only Max's soul. Caspar will have his three years of grace if he can deliver that; if not, Caspar is lost tomorrow. With that, he disappears.

In place of the skull, there has now appeared a caldron, and Caspar, after fortifying himself with a drink from his flask, proceeds to build a fire. Max, coming down the cliff, first expresses his horror of the place and the evil birds flapping their wings on the trees. He is further upset with visions of his mother ("as she looked in her coffin," he says) and of Agathe, but he agrees to do whatever Caspar tells him. Caspar then plies his magic to cast the bullets. Various ingredients go into the caldron; it hisses and boils; great birds fly about; a boar crashes through the underbrush; the off-stage basses chant; the storm breaks, with thunder and flashes of lightning. Thus the bullets are made, and the two men call on Zamiel. As Zamiel appears in the place of a tree that has been torn up, Caspar falls over in a dead faint; the Black Hunter seizes a hand of Max's; Max makes the sign of the cross with the other. Suddenly there is silence, and Zamiel disappears.

ACT III

SCENE 1: *A sunny place in the woods.* This scene is almost always omitted in performance as it is carried on entirely in spoken dialogue and serves only to explain why the single bullet Max fires in the next scene is the seventh of those cast the night before. Max was given four of them and Caspar retained three. But each now has only one left, for Max has been already making some marvelous shots before the Prince that morning and Caspar has spent two of his hunting. Max begs Caspar for his remaining one but is firmly refused; and when Max has gone off to be present at the final trial, Caspar fires his last bullet to make certain that Max's coming shot will be the seventh—the one Zamiel will be directing.

SCENE 2: *Agathe's room.* Agathe, already in her bridal dress—for she is to be married to Max at once provided he wins the contest—is still fearful about coming events, and she sings another prayer. Ännchen, also dressed for the wedding, tries to cheer her up and to explain away some of the omens that are disturbing Agathe. For one thing, Agathe dreamed the night before that she was a white dove and that Max had fired at her. But she had been changed just in time to her human form, and a horrible black bird lay at her feet. Ännchen finds a ready explanation for this, and she sings her a little story about her aunt who had also been frightened by a dream in which she was about to be attacked by a frightful beast, but on waking up, there was her watch dog. Bridesmaids now come in and sing the "*Jungfern-kranz*" ("Bridal Wreath") Chorus. Ännchen then brings in the box containing the bridal wreath and remarks that the picture of the old man had fallen down again but, she adds quickly, what could you expect on so stormy a night? But when Agathe opens the box, it is seen that the supposed bridal wreath is a silver one—the kind used for funerals. This is explained as a mistake of the servant's, and Ännchen quickly substitutes some roses that the hermit had given Agathe. (The girls do not know it, but the roses, which have stood before the small altar in the room, are now holy roses and can confer protection on their wearer.) Then, with the bridesmaids once more singing their chorus, they all leave for the festivities.

SCENE 3: *A clearing in the woods, with Prince Ottokar's tent on one side.* Everything is ready for the final trial. A rousing hunting chorus is sung by everyone present— that is, the Prince's followers as well as the local huntsmen, including Kuno, Caspar, and Max (only Caspar is hiding behind a tree and occasionally calling on Zamiel to be of help). The

Rose Bampton as Agathe at Teatro Colón, Buenos Aires

Prince compliments Kuno on the fine young man he is getting for a son-in-law, comments on his apparent nervousness, which he ascribes to its being Max's wedding day, and hopes that the bride will soon appear so that he may get to know her. Kuno requests that Max's final test be taken now lest he may be made more nervous by the presence of his bride, and the Prince graciously consents and points to a white dove on a branch as the target. Just at this moment, with Max already taking aim, Agathe and her bridesmaids appear close to the spot where the dove is. Remembering her dream, she cries, "Do not shoot! I am the dove!" The dove itself flies from the branch it sits on toward the tree where Caspar is skulking; Max seems to miss the dove, which flies off; but both Agathe and Caspar cry out and fall to the ground.

Agathe, who has been more frightened than hurt, quickly recovers consciousness, is hailed by everybody, and even has a short duet with Max. But Caspar has been hit, and as he writhes on the ground, Zamiel appears to him (though invisible to the rest) to take his soul to hell. Cursing both God and the devil, the miscreant dies, and the Prince orders his body thrown into the Wolf's Glen. Attention is then shifted to Max as the Prince demands an explanation. Max now tells about his four "free" bullets and his dealings with Caspar, and the Prince, greatly incensed, denies him Agathe's hand and gives him the choice of prison or banishment. Pleadings from Kuno, Agathe, and the whole chorus avail nothing till the Hermit makes an appearance. The Prince, who has heard of the man's reputation for holiness, asks him for a judgment, and the Hermit replies with a short sermon on the tolerance we must show to human weakness. His advice is that Max be put on probation for a year before he may marry and that the shooting contests be forever abolished. The Prince adopts this advice, and the opera closes with a grand chorus to the welcoming tune that Agathe sang when she saw Max approaching her house.

Gianni Schicchi

CHARACTERS

Gianni Schicchi, *a swindler*	*Baritone or Bass*	Gherardino, *their son*	*Child*
Lauretta, *his daughter*	*Soprano*	Betto, *a brother-in-law*	*Baritone*
Relatives of the deceased Buoso Donati:		Simone, *Buoso's cousin*	*Bass*
Zita, *his cousin*	*Contralto*	Marco, *his son*	*Baritone*
Rinuccio, *her nephew*	*Tenor*	La Ciesca, *his wife*	*Mezzo-soprano*
Gherardo, *nephew of Buoso*	*Tenor*	Spinelloccio, *a doctor*	*Bass*
Nella, *his wife*	*Soprano*	Amantio di Nicolao, *an attorney*	*Bass*

The action takes place in Florence in the year 1299 (the incident, or something like it, being historical).

Tito Gobbi as the crafty Gianni Schicchi, La Scala

OPERA IN ONE ACT. Music by Giacomo Puccini. Libretto in Italian by Gioacchino Forzano. First performance, Metropolitan Opera House, December 14, 1918, in a world première of three one-act Puccini works, the others being *Il Tabarro* and *Suor Angelica*. Together they are known as the *Trittico* (*Triptych*).

The cast at the première consisted of Florence Easton, Lauretta; Giulio Crimi, Rinuccio; Giuseppe de Luca, Gianni Schicchi, and Adamo Didur, Simone. In the Metropolitan revival of season 1935–1936, given in English, Lawrence Tibbett was the Schicchi; on January 6, 1944, Salvatore Baccaloni first appeared as Gianni at the Metropolitan, with Licia Albanese and Nino Martini as co-artists. Since then, both Italo Tajo and Fernando Corena have scored in the title role at the Metropolitan. Of the three little operas in the *Trittico*, *Gianni Schicchi* is the one most frequently revived.

SCENE: *The bedroom of the recently deceased Buoso Donati.* Gianni Schicchi is a shrewd but goodhearted Tuscan peasant of the thirteenth century. His daughter Lauretta loves Rinuccio, whose family is at present greatly disturbed because a relative, Buoso Donati, has just died, leaving his fortune to a monastery. Schicchi is consulted by the disappointed relatives in the hope that he may prove clever enough to suggest a plan for obtaining the property. As Donati's death has not yet been made public, Schicchi suggests that he himself impersonate the old man and dictate a new will, leaving the estate to Rinuccio's family. Schicchi is placed in the dead man's bed, and a notary summoned. The latter takes down the new will; after leaving a few worthless trifles to the relatives, Schicchi bequeaths the bulk of the property to himself! The relatives are highly indignant, but they dare not expose him, for in so doing they would render themselves liable to punishment. A minute after the notary and witnesses have gone, they go after Schicchi with cries of "Robber! Traitor! Scoundrel!" But Schicchi seizes a stick and drives the cursing relatives from the house. The lovers, who eventually will be Schicchi's heirs, are happily united. They sing a joyful duet, and when Schicchi returns with the stolen articles he has recaptured from the relatives, he gives them to the happy couple. He then turns to the audience and in spoken words, asks whether—though Dante* consigned him to hell—they won't render a verdict of extenuating circumstances.

* Gianni Schicchi endures his post-mortem existence among the panders and thieves in the eighth circle of hell, according to the thirtieth canto of Dante's *Inferno.*

Florence Easton, first Lauretta, Metropolitan, 1918

Metropolitan Opera: Lauretta (Roberta Peters), Gianni Schicchi (Salvatore Baccaloni), Rinuccio (Thomas Hayward), and relatives

La Gioconda

THE BALLAD SINGER

CHARACTERS

La Gioconda, *a ballad singer*	*Soprano*	Enzo Grimaldo, *a Genoese noble*	*Tenor*
La Cieca, *her blind mother*	*Contralto*	Barnaba, *a spy of the Inquisition*	*Baritone*
Duke Alvise, *an official of the State Inquisition*	*Bass*	Zuàne, *a boatman*	*Bass*
		Isèpo, *a public letter-writer*	*Tenor*
Laura, *his wife*	*Mezzo-soprano*	A Monk	*Bass*

Senators, Sailors, Ladies, Gentlemen, Populace, Masquers

The action takes place in Venice in the seventeenth century.

Act I finale showing St. Mark's Square, as designed for the Metropolitan Opera House in 1966 by Beni Montresor

Beniamino Gigli, a favorite Enzo in the U.S. and Italy

Richard Bonelli as Barnaba, spy of the Inquisition

OPERA IN FOUR ACTS. Music by Amilcare Ponchielli. Libretto in Italian by Arrigo Boito (writing under the pen name of Tobia Gorrio), based on Victor Hugo's drama *Angelo, Tyran de Padoue* (*Angelo, Tyrant of Padua*). First performance at La Scala, Milan, April 8, 1876. United States première, at the Metropolitan Opera House, New York, December 20, 1883, with Christine Nilsson in the title role.

Boito, perhaps wisely, used his anagram *nom de plume* in signing the gnarled libretto of *La Gioconda*. A fabulously gifted man, he wrote the text and composed the music for his own powerful opera *Mefistofele* (1868), besides supplying Verdi with model librettos for *Otello* and *Falstaff*. The prose play of Victor Hugo on which Ponchielli's opera is based also furnished texts for music dramas by Mercadante, César Cui, and Eugen d'Albert. Boito, not without irony, entitled the gruesome libretto, *La Gioconda* (*The Joyous Girl*). "*Che La Gioconda ci giocondi entrambi!*" he punned in a letter to Ponchielli accompanying the completed text—"That *The Joyous Girl* may bring us both joy!" The phenomenal success of the opera bore out his hope.

Few operas rival *La Gioconda* in variety of appeal. There are sumptuous spectacle and ceremony, a picturesque ballet, luscious arias and duets, and an almost unbroken pageant of violent and impassioned action. Stabbings and poisonings are frequent happenings here, while kidnaping, arson, and terrible acts of revenge form part of this high-pitched drama of Venetian intrigue. Ironically, the ever-popular ballet "The Dance of the Hours" is intended to represent a triumph of good over evil, of light over darkness. *La Gioconda* is scarcely an illustration of this victory.

Ponchielli, who taught Giacomo Puccini, helped strengthen the role of the orchestra in Italian opera. The symphonic texture is rich and ample and closely adapted to the shifting action, and of course the melodic warmth of the whole score is one of its most appealing features.

ACT I

SCENE: *Street near the Adriatic shore, Venice*. The situation before the curtain rises is as follows: La Gioconda, a ballad singer, in love with Enzo Grimaldo, a Genoese noble and captain of a ship now in the harbor of Venice, supports her blind mother, La Cieca, by singing in the streets. Barnaba, an influential police spy, has become infatuated with her and is scheming to possess her.

The grand courtyard of the Ducal palace is the scene of gay festivities. Sailors, shipwrights, townspeople, foreigners, peasants, in holiday attire, mingle freely. They raise their voices in chorus, shouting, "*Feste! Pane!*" ("Festivals and bread!"). Barnaba, who has been leaning against a pillar, moodily watching the lively scene, steps forward and announces that the regatta is about to begin. The merrymakers hasten to the shore, and Barnaba scornfully mutters after them, "Dancing over their graves," for the prisons of the Inquisition are underfoot. In a grim soliloquy we learn of his designs on La Gioconda, who now approaches, leading her sightless mother. Barnaba hides behind the column. The girl seats the helpless woman on the church steps and is about to follow the crowd when Barnaba stops her and boldly declares his passion.

Act II: Barnaba (Robert Merrill) sings a barcarolle

Shuddering with disgust, La Gioconda rebuffs him, and when he attempts to grasp her, she eludes him and rushes away. Barnaba resolves on a cruel revenge.

The crowd returns from the regatta, carrying the winner on their shoulders. Barnaba approaches the loser of the regatta and tells him that he owes his defeat to La Cieca, who is a witch. The defeated man and his friends rush to La Cieca and drag her from and church steps, crying, "Let's burn the witch!" At that moment Enzo, La Gioconda's friend, enters in disguise, as he is considered an enemy of Venice. He runs to the old woman's side and shields her from the savage mob. Against their shrill cries of "She is a witch!" he taunts them with attacking a defenseless blind woman.

The doors of the palace abruptly fly open and the Grand Duke Alvise and his wife Laura appear. Laura, formerly betrothed to Enzo, implores her husband to protect La Cieca against the mob's violence. The Duke intercedes, and La Cieca is freed. In gratitude she gives Laura her rosary, voicing her feelings in the beautiful aria *"Voce di donna."* Meanwhile, the vigilant Barnaba has observed a telltale glance pass between Laura and her former lover. As the doors of St. Mark's swing open, the crowd enters the magnificent church. Enzo remains behind, thoughtfully gazing after Laura. Barnaba, his mind already afire with a diabolical plan, approaches him. With the words of address "Enzo Grimaldo" a dramatic dialogue ensues between the two men. Barnaba immediately wins his interest by mentioning Laura. Yes, he knows about them, says the crafty spy; how they loved one another, and still do. That very night, he assures the excited nobleman, while the Duke is busy with his council, Laura will steal off and visit him on his ship. Rather

shabbily, Enzo does nothing but utter a pious hope for the girl's safety when Barnaba divulges his own passion for La Gioconda. Enzo leaves to return to his ship.

Alone, Barnaba seeks the service of a public scribe. As he dictates aloud, La Gioconda and La Cieca enter and conceal themselves. Barnaba's anonymous letter is to Duke Alvise, informing him of the meeting to take place between his wife and Enzo Grimaldo. La Gioconda overhears this with mingled emotions, shuddering at the thought of Enzo's danger and crushed by his betrayal. Filled with despair, mother and daughter enter the church.

ACT II

SCENE: *A lagoon near Venice.* Enzo's ship is shown at anchor. It is dark, and the orchestra weaves soft measures on the beauty of the Venetian night. There is even a hint of mystery in the music, of approaching tragedy. Sailors, chanting gaily, busy themselves about Enzo's ship as it rides at anchor. Down in the hold deep voices are heard singing of the terrors of the sea. They are answered cheerily by younger members of the crew perched along the rigging. Barnaba, disguised as a fisherman, appears in his boat, and hailing the Genoese sailors, he proceeds to sing a jolly ballad, full of rhythmic dash and melodic appeal—*"Ah, pescator, affonda l'esca"* ("Fisherboy, thy bait be throwing"). The friendly crew joins in at the refrain. The song ended, Barnaba commands the scribe to carry back a report on the strength of the crew, adding that he will remain and await developments.

Enzo appears and releases his men from duty with the announcement that he will keep watch himself. Stars are visible now in the beautiful Venetian sky above, and as the moon comes out from behind a cloud, the waters in the lagoon begin sparkling. Enraptured by the scene and the prospect of seeing Laura soon, Enzo begins his famous aria *"Cielo e mar!"* ("Heaven and ocean!"), in which he sings rapturously of the vision of the night and his love. A boat approaches. It is Barnaba bringing Laura. The lovers embrace ardently as the spy gives them his blessings and leaves. They resolve to sail away together when the wind rises. Enzo goes below deck to rouse the men, and Laura, already a prey to remorse, falls to her knees in prayer. At this moment La Gioconda, disguised, appears. The two women engage in a stormy quarrel over Enzo. La Gioconda is on the point of stabbing her rival, but relents as a boat quietly approaches. Laura immediately recognizes it as her husband's. Terrified, she prays to the Holy Virgin to help her, raising aloft her rosary, which La Gioconda promptly recognizes as her

Act III: Duke Alvise (Bonaldo Giaiotti), Laura (Nell Rankin)

mother's token of thanks to the woman who saved her life. Determined now to aid Laura at all costs, La Gioconda enables her to escape in a boat. Enzo appears and, calling for Laura, he is unexpectedly faced by a vengeful and taunting Gioconda. The Duke's war galleys, led by the wily Barnaba, are moving on his ship. Made desperate by the loss of Laura and the certainty of humiliating defeat, Enzo gives the order to fire the ship to prevent its being captured. To La Gioconda's further chagrin, the last word on his lips is "Laura," as the vessel sinks in flames.

ACT III

SCENE 1: *A room in Alvise's palace.* A festival is about to take place at the ducal palace as Alvise prepares a cold-blooded revenge on his faithless wife. In a fiendish aria he muses on the manner of her death. Not by a dagger thrust shall Laura die, but by poison, and, ironically, to the sounds of singing and dancing in the neighboring room. Laura enters and is promptly handed the flask of poison. This she must drink as the serenade ends in the grand ballroom of the palace, where the Duke is feting the gathered nobles of the land. With a scowl of contempt Alvise leaves Laura. But as she lifts the poison to her lips, La Gioconda, who has concealed herself in the room, rushes out and snatches the fatal flask from her. In place of the poison, she gives Laura a harmless drug that will produce a deathlike sleep. Laura now drinks and La Gioconda again hides as Alvise re-enters the chamber, notices the empty bottle, and cries, "Death has forever claimed her." As he leaves, La Gioconda reappears and remarks grimly, "I have saved her for him, for the one who loves her."

SCENE 2: *The ballroom of Alvise's palace.* For the entertainment of his noble guests Alvise has provided a sumptuous ballet, the famous "Dance of the Hours." The music begins by picturing the first faint glimmerings of dawn. Twitterings and shimmerings are heard in the violins and upper woodwinds, as the dancers enter in delicate tints. Slowly the music rises to a fierce climax. The rhythms become more energetic. It is high noon, and the brighter "Hours" of day swing into place on the stage. Evening approaches now, and the music grows serene, darker-hued, as the dancers tiptoe in, evoking the mood of twilight. There follow the somber "Hours" of night. Midnight approaches, and the music thins out to a few orchestral whispers. The harp gives out some lacy arpeggios, and in the languorous strains that follow, a solo dance is enacted. Finally, all twenty-four "Hours" gather as a unit and plunge into a rival whirl of dancing. Victory goes to the "Hours" representing Light.

This edifying spectacle no sooner ends than the guests are invited to witness a whole pageant of actual horror. The scoundrelly Barnaba rushes into the palace, dragging La Gioconda's blind old mother. At the top of his voice he charges her with practicing witchcraft. La Cieca vows that she was merely praying for the souls of the dead. Enzo is among the masquers, and when a bell begins to toll solemnly, Barnaba whispers into his ear that it is tolling for Laura. Enzo throws off his mask and reveals himself as the nobleman Alvise had proscribed. "My country and my bride you stole," he shouts at Alvise. "Now complete your crime!" The Duke, sensing the moment has come for the ghastly climax of his revenge, flings back the curtains of the death chamber, and a cry of horror comes from the crowd. Extended on a bier is Laura's body. Enzo

Dance of the Hours (Act III) at the Metropolitan Opera: Violette Verdy, Conrad Ludlow of New York City Ballet

rushes at Alvise, brandishing a poniard and shouting, "Hangman!" But before he can reach the man, guards seize him.

ACT IV

SCENE: *A ruined palace on the island of Giudecca in the Adriatic.* To this deserted island not far from Venice, La Gioconda has succeeded in bringing the unconscious Laura. Two men carry the girl into the ruined interior of an abandoned palace. La Gioconda directs the men to place her on a bed and offers to pay them for their help. They reject the money, reminding her that they are her friends. La Gioconda suddenly grows alarmed about her mother and implores the men to search every highway and piazza of Venice for her. They assure her she can depend on

Renata Tebaldi as La Gioconda contemplates suicide

them, and she clasps their hands in farewell. Left alone, she approaches the table and thoughtfully eyes the flask of poison upon it. There begins now the celebrated aria *"Suicidio,"* an aria pulsing with dramatic fervor and feverish intensity. Suicide is her sole resource, the girl reflects. Since love, mother, all hope of happiness have vanished, let her die, and jealousy will torture her no longer. As she raises the flask, a devilish thought crosses her mind. What if Laura were dead, or, if alive, what if she were to disappear beneath the silent waters of the Adriatic? The aria reaches a frenzied pitch here as eerie voices reach her from the lagoon, telling of the dead in the Orfano Canal. La Gioconda recoils from her own thought. The tempest rages on in her soul, till, crying, *"O amore! amore! Enzo! Pietà!"* she throws herself down near the table, sobbing wretchedly.

At that moment Enzo, released from prison with Gioconda's aid, enters. He looks suspiciously at the distraught girl, wondering why she has summoned him to this ruin. "What do you want of me?" he asks coldly. "To give you back the sun, life, infinite liberty, joy in the future, love, and paradise," she replies to the baffled Enzo. Would he die for Laura? she asks. Yes, he would join his beloved in her tomb. "Laura's tomb is empty," La Gioconda retorts; "I have removed her!" Enzo is appalled. Convinced that Gioconda is lying, he forces her to swear on a crucifix. As she does, he lunges at her with a dagger, when the cry "Enzo!" comes from the alcove. It is Laura. Enzo, as in a dream, watches her approach, then rushes forward and embraces her. When Laura tells him that Gioconda saved her life, both fall on their knees before the girl and bless her. With Gioconda's help, the lovers now make their escape. Only she and one other know at what price Enzo's freedom has been purchased. Barnaba had named the price—Gioconda herself.

Now, after Laura and Enzo leave, Gioconda again reaches for the poison, but before she can drink, Barnaba appears. He has come for his reward. Gioconda, terrified at first, recovers her courage and begins a grim game of pretense with the odious spy. Coquettishly she pleads for time to adorn herself properly with sparkling jewels. Barnaba assents. At length Gioconda cries, "I have kept my word. I have not lied and I have not fled. I have not betrayed you. You wanted me, you accursed demon! Take me!" As Barnaba rushes to embrace her, Gioconda stabs herself with a knife she had concealed in her dress and falls to the floor. Barnaba, in a savage access of rage, bends over the girl and shrieks into her ear, "Yesterday your mother offended me. I have strangled her!" But Gioconda can hear no longer. Furiously he rushes from the room and disappears down the dark street.

The Girl of the Golden West

LA FANCIULLA DEL WEST

CHARACTERS

Minnie, *owner of the Polka bar*	*Soprano*	Sonora	*Baritone*
Jack Rance, *sheriff*	*Baritone*	Trin	*Tenor*
Dick Johnson (Ramerrez), *a bandit*	*Tenor*	Sid	*Baritone*
Nick, *bartender at the Polka*	*Tenor*	Handsome	*Baritone*
Ashby, *Wells-Fargo agent*	*Bass*	Harry *miners*	*Tenor*
Billy Jackrabbit, *an Indian*	*Bass*	Joe	*Tenor*
Wowkle, *his squaw*	*Mezzo-soprano*	Happy	*Baritone*
Jake Wallace, *a traveling camp*		Larkens	*Baritone*
minstrel	*Bass*	José Castro, *member of Ramerrez's*	
		gang	*Bass*
		A Postilion	*Bass*

Men of the Camp

*The action takes place at the foot of Cloudy Mountain, in California
during the days of the gold fever, about 1850.*

OPERA IN THREE ACTS. Music by Giacomo Puccini. Libretto in Italian by Guelfo Civinni and Carlo Zangarini, after David Belasco's play *The Girl of the Golden West*. First performance, Metropolitan Opera House, New York, December 10, 1910, Puccini and Belasco both being present. Arturo Toscanini was the conductor, and Emmy Destinn was the Minnie, Enrico Caruso the Dick Johnson, and Pasquale Amato the Jack Rance.

The plot is concerned with rather melodramatic happenings during the days of the California gold rush of '49. While remaining true, in general, to his usual melodious style, Puccini adapted his score to a rapidly moving conversational dialogue. He also showed that he was aware of the musical progress of the times by his use of consecutive and unresolved seventh chords somewhat in the manner of Ravel, and in the employment of Debussian augmented triads. Moreover, for the sake of local color, he introduced melodies and rhythms characteristic of the South and Southwest—of plantations, Mexicans, and Indians. Yet the music, for all that, is unmistakably Italian.

ACT I

SCENE: *Interior of the Polka barroom.* Ashby, agent of the Wells-Fargo Company, enters the Polka barroom and, joining the miners, who have been drinking, singing, card-playing, and fighting, says that he is close on the track of Ramerrez, chief of the band of Mexican outlaws who have recently committed a big robbery. The sheriff, Jack Rance, in talking with the men, boasts of his love affair with the "girl" Minnie and says that he is going to marry her. One of the miners disputes his claim, and a brawl results. Minnie herself enters and stops it. She owns and runs the Polka, for she is the orphaned child of the founder of this establishment, and also acts as mother and guardian angel to the miners and cow-

181

boys who frequent the place. When Rance proposes to her in a crude fashion, she spurns him and holds him at bay with a revolver.

A stranger enters and gives his name as Dick Johnson of Sacramento. The sheriff is supicious of him, but Minnie takes his part, saying that she has met him before. Johnson is in reality none other than the hunted Ramerrez, and he has come for no better purpose than to rob the saloon. Unaware of this, Minnie recalls with Dick the time they first met and fell in love with one another. The men all go in search of Ramerrez, leaving their gold with Minnie. She declares that if anyone is to steal the gold he must do so over her dead body. Johnson has become more and more enamored of her and relinquishes his plan of robbery; now he admires her courage. She invites him to visit her in her cabin when the miners return.

ACT II

SCENE: *Minnie's dwelling.* Johnson and Minnie meet at her "shack" and idyllically sing of their love. Suddenly shots are heard outside in the darkness— the men are again searching for Ramerrez. Not wanting to be found with Johnson, Minnie conceals him, then admits the men, who are hunting, they say, for Dick Johnson, much to her dismay. Minnie declines their offered protection, and they leave. Then she turns upon Johnson with the revelations that she has just heard. Dick acknowledges their truth, but goes on to tell how he was compelled by fate to become a bandit. Since meeting her he had resolved to give up his old life, and had prayed in vain that she would never know of his past. The tense dramatic atmosphere is reflected in somber chords in the orchestra.

But Minnie cannot forgive him for having deceived her after confessing his love and sends him out into the night. A moment later shots are heard, Minnie runs to the door, opens it, and drags in Johnson, seriously wounded. She hides him in a loft under the roof. The sheriff soon enters hot on the trail. Minnie has almost overcome his suspicions when a drop of blood falls from the loft, revealing the wounded Dick's whereabouts. Knowing that the sheriff is a desperate gambler, Minnie, as a last resort, offers to play a game of poker with him, the stakes to be her own hand and Johnson's life, or else her own and the prisoner's freedom. They agree on two cold hands out of three, and each wins one of the first two. When Minnie draws a weak third hand, she asks Rance for a drink and, as he is getting it, substitutes five cards she has conveniently hidden in her stocking. Rance turns up three kings, but Minnie wins her man by flashing her full house, aces high.

ACT III

SCENE: *The Great California Forest.* Johnson, nursed back to life by Minnie, is again sought by the men and finally brought in by Sonora. Under a giant redwood, he is about to be hanged by Ashby's men. He makes one last request. Let her believe that he had gained his freedom and gone away to live the nobler life she had taught him. He touchingly apostrophizes her as the "star of his wasted life." This last request of Johnson's is sung to the most famous melody in the opera, *"Ch'ella mi creda libero"* ("Let her believe that I have gained my freedom").

Just as Jack Rance is about to carry out the execution, Minnie rushes in on horseback. She at first holds the crowd at bay with her drawn revolver, then appeals to them eloquently, reminding them of her faithful care of their needs; they should not fail her now. The "boys" relent and, in spite of Rance's protests, release the prisoner. Johnson and Minnie bid them farewell and go away together to begin life anew.

Metropolitan Opera world première of La Franciulla del West: *Enrico Caruso (Dick), Emmy Destinn (Minnie), Pasquale Amato (Rance)*

Hänsel und Gretel

CHARACTERS

Peter, *a poor broommaker*	*Baritone*	The Witch	*Mezzo-soprano* or *Tenor*
Gertrude, *his wife*	*Mezzo-soprano*	The Sandman	*Soprano*
Hänsel, *their son*	*Mezzo-soprano*	The Dewman	*Soprano*
Gretel, *their daughter*	*Soprano*		

Angels and Gingerbread Children

The action takes place "once upon a time" in a forest in Germany.

OPERA IN THREE ACTS. Music by Engelbert Humperdinck. Libretto in German by Adelheid Wette, based on Jakob and Wilhelm Grimm's fairy tale. First produced at the Hoftheater, Weimar, December 23, 1893. American première, in English, at Daly's Theater, New York, October 8, 1895. First performed at the Metropolitan Opera House, in German, November 25, 1905, with a cast including Lina Abarbanell, Bella Alten, Otto Goritz, Marion Weed, and Louise Homer; the composer supervised the production.

Humperdinck's delightful fairy opera was first destined for home performance. The composer's sister, Adelheid Wette, had written some verses based on Grimm's fairy tale which she sent to her brother to set to music for a Christmas celebration for her children. The holiday entertainment proved so successful that sister and brother elaborated it into a full-length opera. Composed in 1893, the work was warmly acclaimed at its Weimar première, and the ingratiating quality of the opera soon won a huge following the world over, the young of all ages being drawn by its childlike mood of enchantment. There is a wondrous simplicity about Humperdinck's melodies, and the charm of folk music hovers about the score. But Humperdinck was also a superb craftsman and an orchestrator of prodigious power. He had learned and absorbed much from Wagner, so much in fact that the master had engaged this worshipful disciple to supervise the epic task of preparing *Parsifal* for its world première at Bayreuth. Thus, along with a tender, homespun texture of theme, one finds in *Hänsel und Gretel* contrapuntal power and orchestral color of vast range.

PRELUDE

The musical material of the Prelude, drawn largely from the opera, is woven compactly into a deftly unified scheme. A prayer, chanted by horns and bassoons, opens the prelude in a serene mood. After some development, the tempo quickens. A trumpet calls out brilliantly over a web of woodwinds and pizzicato strings. A new melody creeps in among the strings and woodwinds, ushering us into a spooky world of sorcery and mystery. The trumpet call rings out again, and a spirit of dancelike jubilation settles on the orchestra, which finally recovers its calm with a return of the prayer motif.

ACT I

SCENE: *At Peter's home.* In a cottage by the woods dwells the family of Peter the broommaker. Both Peter and his wife Gertrude are away selling brooms, and when the curtain rises, the children, Hänsel and Gretel, are shown at work, Hänsel binding brooms and Gretel knitting. Soon they grow

William Walker and Lili Chookasian as the parents

lein steht im Walde'' ("There stands a little man in the wood"). The children now sit down together and avidly eye the basket of berries. Hänsel tries one berry, and Gretel follows suit; then they try another, and still another, and before long there are no more berries. Around them the shadows begin to gather. Night is falling, and fear seizes the children as they try in vain to find the way back to the hut. In her fright Gretel cries out for her father and mother. The woods that had been so cheerful in daylight are now overrun with unknown terrors. Mysterious, ghostly sounds seem to come from the shadows around them. But the Sandman arrives, sprinkling sleep into their eyes to a tender little lullaby, *"Der kleine Sandmann bin ich''* ("The little sandman am I"). The children say their prayers together in a simple and childlike theme of soft-spun beauty, *"Abends will ich schlafen gehen, vierzehn Engel um mich stehn''* ("When I go to sleep at night fourteen angels stand around me"). As they fall asleep, the angels they have been singing about descend in a dream and form a circle around them to protect them against the evils of the forest. The tableau is heightened by the dreamy gossamer web of the orchestra, which seems to catch all the wondrous glints of fairyland evoked by the children's sleep.

tired of their tasks, and Hänsel begins to complain of a gnawing hunger. The children begin a useless hunt about the house for food. Gretel tries to cheer her brother with singing and dancing, and Hänsel endeavors to join in the dance, but his clumsy movements only succeed in arousing Gretel's laughter. Gertrude, entering the hut, is furious at finding the children at play and goes to punish them. In her haste she breaks the pitcher of milk she had concealed for supper and then in despair sends the children out into the woods to pick strawberries. Worn and discouraged, Gertrude falls asleep. Soon Peter arrives. He is in a jolly mood, partly drunk and singing, for the day's sales have been good, and he has brought a basket of food. When he learns that the children have gone into the forest, he grows serious and fumes at his wife for sending them out. Maybe the fearful witch will seize them and turn them into gingerbread! Peter and Gertrude rush out to look for their children.

ACT II

SCENE: *In the forest.* Hänsel and Gretel are wandering through the woods, gay and carefree. While Hänsel goes picking berries, Gretel sits under a fir tree and weaves a garland of roses, meanwhile singing a sweet little folk song of long ago, *"Ein Männ-*

ACT III

SCENE: *The Witch's house.* The mist is clearing as the Dawn Fairy comes to shake dewdrops on the children, who rub their eyes and wake up. Excitedly they relate their dreams to each other, when suddenly they turn around and give a start. There before them, shining in the rays of the rising sun, stands a tempting little house made of cake. Surrounding it is a wall of gingerbread boys and girls. Forgetting all fear in their hunger, Hänsel and Gretel begin nibbling at the wall, dancing and singing the while. In the midst of their munching the Witch stalks out of the house. She tries to be friendly, but the children are frightened out of their wits. They are on the point of rushing away when a wave of the Witch's magic wand roots them to the spot. The Witch locks Hänsel in the cage and orders Gretel to do housework for her. Hänsel is now fed generously to make him more appetizing. In glee the Witch then grasps a broom, hobbles and jumps about the stage with it, and sings a weird song about the daily routine of witches (the so-called *"Hexenritt''* —the "Witches' Ride").

But while the Witch is busy fattening up her little victim, Gretel manages to steal the magic wand and, as the Witch's back is turned, frees her brother. The Witch now orders Gretel to look in the oven to see if the cakes are ready. Gretel pretends to be slow-witted and asks to be shown how it is done. As the Witch stoops in front of the open door, the children give a push together and slam the door shut. Jubilant now, Hänsel and Gretel express their joy in a delightful "Gingerbread Waltz." With a crash the oven falls apart. The spell is shattered, and all the captive children are freed from their gingerbread state. Peter and Gertrude, who have been searching the woods all night, arrive in time for the celebration. From the ruins of the oven the children extract a huge gingerbread figure—the Witch, thoroughly baked and harmless. All join in a joyous hymn of thanksgiving.

La Scala staging of Act III, with Elena Nikolai (the Witch), Renata Scotto (Gretel), Fiorenza Cossotto (Hänsel)

L'Heure Espagnole

THE SPANISH HOUR

CHARACTERS

Torquemada, *a clockmaker*	*Tenor*	Gonzalve, *a poet*	*Tenor*
Concepcion, *his young wife*	*Soprano*	Don Inigo Gomez, *a banker*	*Bass*
Ramiro, *a muleteer*	*Baritone*		

The action takes place in the shop of Torquemada, in Toledo, Spain, in the eighteenth century.

OPERA IN ONE ACT. Music by Maurice Ravel. Text in French by Franc-Nohain (pseudonym of Maurice Le Grand), after his comedy of the same title. First performance, Opéra-Comique, Paris, May 19, 1911. Initial American performance, by the Chicago Civic Opera Company, Auditorium, Chicago, January 5, 1920, with Yvonne Gall as Concepcion and Alfred Maguenet as Ramiro, Louis Hasselmans conducting. Initial performance by the Metropolitan, November 7, 1925, with Lucrezia Bori as Concepcion and Lawrence Tibbett as Ramiro, Hasselmans conducting. *L'Heure Espagnole* was also presented by the Juilliard School of Music, March 9, 1936, in an English translation by Robert A. Simon. Recently it has been staged by the New York City Opera, the Chicago Lyric Opera and the Washington Opera Society.

This is the first of two operas by Ravel, the other being *L'Enfant et les Sortilèges*. *L'Heure Espagnole* has by far been the more successful. The composer wrote for it a score that is a marvel of orchestral effects and subtle colors, easily the equal of a libretto that has long been considered perfect in every way. The opera has been given on many French stages, and outside of France—besides Chicago and New York—at London, Brussels, Rotterdam, Basel, Prague, Hamburg, Stockholm, Turin, Budapest Berlin, and other places, frequently in the local vernacular.

SCENE: *Torquemada's clock shop.* After a short introduction, based on a calm theme played by the woodwinds, the curtain rises on the little shop filled with all kinds of examples of clocks. Ramiro, a muleteer, enters. He is a tall, athletic-looking young man, who asks the clockmaker to repair his watch. While Torquemada is examining the timepiece, his young wife Concepcion comes in, reminding him that this is the day when he must regulate the municipal clocks. She further reproaches him for not bringing one of the two grandfather clocks up to her bedroom. He complains about the size and weight of these clocks, and as his wife, in an aside, remarks disparagingly about his physical powers, he picks up his tools and departs, telling Ramiro to wait for him.

Considerably nettled by the presence of Ramiro, who is interfering with a tête-à-tête she had planned to have with the poet Gonzalve, Concepcion persuades the muleteer to carry one of the grandfather clocks upstairs, in order to get him out of the way. When Ramiro departs, with the clock easily balanced on his back, Gonzalve makes his entrance, and he is effusively greeted by Concepcion. Her joy is short-lived, however, for Gonzalve's tactics are dilatory and Ramiro soon returns, proudly announcing that he has completed the job. Yet, never at a loss for ideas, Concepcion begs Ramiro's indulgence for her mistake; it was another clock she wanted moved.

Good-naturedly, the muleteer, with a remarkable

nonchalance that has already impressed Concepcion, starts to put the second clock on his shoulders, but the lady changes her mind on a sudden impulse and asks him to bring down the first. Meanwhile, she urges Gonzalve to get into the second clock, the intention being to have Ramiro carry both that and Gonzalve upstairs, an ingenious arrangement, to say the least. Gonzalve falls in with this suggestion, for the unusual transportation will provide him with a new experience. As they talk, a cheery voice is heard outside, and Concepcion, hastily closing the door to Gonzalve's temporary prison, sees that the voice is that of Don Inigo the banker, who is very amorously disposed. She tries to quiet him with the words that "clocks have ears." But this does not discourage the banker, for he continues to make advances, ceasing only when Ramiro and the first clock make their reappearance.

Willing as ever, Ramiro picks up the second clock, Gonzalve and all, and is about to go up with it, when she decides to accompany him, fearing what the uneven trip may do to her cramped poet. Don Inigo, in the meantime, thinks of playing a trick on Concepcion, and how better to do that than secrete himself in one of those grandfather clocks. This he does, after some effort, for he is a corpulent person, and presently Ramiro returns. He is now joined by Concepcion, who, in assumed dismay, declares that she just cannot bear to have in her room a clock that acts as erratically as the one now upstairs. So, Ramiro, matter-of-fact as can be, heads for the upper story to oblige the lady.

While Ramiro is out, Don Inigo playfully imitates a cuckoo from his hiding place, and Concepcion, at first nonplused, soon discovers the source of the sound. In a heated argument with Don Inigo, she is telling him off, when Ramiro comes down with the second clock, which still houses Gonzalve. The young Hercules takes it as his duty now to bring up the first clock again, and this he does, the heaviest of all the clocks thus far (with the fat and weighty banker in it) not bothering him at all. More appreciation from the lady; in fact, it begins to take on a significant edge.

Gonzalve, despite Concepcion's order to get himself off, is loath to quit his little private niche, and they are talking, he poetically, she excitedly, when Ramiro returns. Gonzalve, who has heard his footsteps, hurries to his hiding place.

Ramiro, in his simple reasoning, guesses that Concepcion is angered by the latest clock disposal, so he tells her not to fret, that he will come back directly with the first clock. And he joyfully heads for his objective. During his absence Concepcion berates the poet, who can offer no other consolation than to spout verses. And when Ramiro reappears, with clock-plus-Don Inigo, he asks if there are further

orders from her. Concepcion, now deeply interested in this simple but ever-so-powerful youth, says yes, that he must go upstairs again. "With which clock?" he asks innocently. "Without a clock," she declares significantly, and the muleteer obediently follows her up the stairs.

While the muleteer and the girl are about their affairs, Gonzalve comes out of his hideout, but, seeing Torquemada about to enter the shop, tries to go back, only to open the door of the wrong clock, the one containing Don Inigo. And when Torquemada does enter both Gonzalve and Don Inigo are in full view. Torquemada, an ingenuous soul and hardly perturbed by their presence, believes, in fact, that they have come to do business with him, and he succeeds in selling to the two men the respective clocks. The banker, however, cannot get out of his narrow cell, thanks to his obesity, and although Gonzalve and Torquemada and, lastly, Concepcion, who has now returned, all put their strength to the job, it is Ramiro, all by himself, who pulls him out— so very easily.

The opera ends with an epilogue in the form of a quintet, in which each of the characters expresses his thoughts to the audience, Concepcion remarking that Ramiro, who passes her window every morning, shall be henceforth her only dependable chronometer.

Teresa Berganza as Concepcion and Alfredo Kraus as the poet Gonzalve (Chicago Lyric Opera)

Les Huguenots

CHARACTER

Count de St. Bris \ *Catholic*	**Bass**	Raoul de Nangis, *a Huguenot*	
Count de Nevers / *noblemen*	**Baritone**	*nobleman*	*Tenor*
Marcel, *servant to Raoul*	**Bass**	Valentine, *daughter of St. Bris*	*Soprano*
Marguérite de Valois, *betrothed*		Urbain, *page to Marguérite*	*Soprano or*
to Henry IV of Navarre	*Soprano*		*Mezzo-soprano*

Ladies and Gentlemen of the Court, both Catholic and Huguenot; Pages, Citizens,
Soldiers, The Night Watch, Students, Monks, and the People

*The action of the opera takes place during 1572, the first two acts in Touraine, the
remainder at Paris.*

OPERA IN FIVE ACTS. Music by Giacomo Meyerbeer. Libretto in French by Eugène Scribe and revised by Émile Deschamps and the composer. First performance, Paris Opéra, February 29, 1836. First American performance, New Orleans, Théâtre d'Orléans, April 29, 1839. First performed at the Metropolitan Opera on March 19, 1883, during its first season, and has since been sung there in French, German, and Italian.

The most famous of Meyerbeer's operas, *Les Huguenots* has seven stellar roles, which impresarios of the past were only too eager to cast significantly. The part of the page has been done in two versions, for soprano and contralto, the latter converted especially for the contralto Marietta Alboni for the London production (in Italian) of July 20, 1848. At the Metropolitan in the 1890's prices for best seats were fixed at seven dollars to match the seven stars in the cast, who would be Jean de Reszke as Raoul, Édouard de Reszke as Marcel, Lilli Lehmann or Lillian Nordica or Félia Litvinne as Valentine, Sigrid Arnoldson or Nellie Melba or Marcella Sembrich as Marguerite, Sofia Scalchi or Eugenia Mantelli or Rosa Olitzka as the page, Jean Lassalle or Pol Plançon as St. Bris, and Victor Maurel or Mario Ancona as de Nevers. In 1905, a Metropolitan revival offered Enrico Caruso as Raoul, together with Marcel Journet, Nordica, Sembrich, Edyth Walker,

Antonio Scotti, and Plançon. And in the revival there of 1912, the seven stars were Caruso, Adamo Didur, Emmy Destinn, Frieda Hempel, Bella Alten, Léon Rothier, and Antonio Scotti. An exceptional revival took place at La Scala, Milan, in May, 1962, conducted by Gianandrea Gavezzeni and starring Franco Corelli, Nicolai Ghiaurov, Giulietta Simionato, Joan Sutherland, Fiorenza Cossotto, Giorgio Tozzi and Wladimiro Ganzaroli, with settings by Nicola Benois.

But it was standard fare in the days of our grandparents and great-grandparents. For almost a hundred years after its première *Les Huguenots* was one of the greatest vehicles for a large opera company to exhibit both its stars and its capability for putting on a magnificent production. Once, too, its score was enormously admired: arias were sung in concert, many piano transcriptions made. Even Richard Wagner, who despised the generous Meyerbeer both personally and musically, had high praise for the duet in Act IV. But it has been out of fashion for over a generation, and it is very expensive to produce. Small houses cannot do it adequately, and outside of France and, occasionally, Italy, it is very seldom mounted at all. Nevertheless, it remains a landmark in the history of opera, and one day, along with the rest of Meyerbeer's best, it may come back into fashion.

ACT I

SCENE: *The Count de Nevers' house.* A group of Catholic noblemen are dining as guests of the Count de Nevers. There is also present Raoul de Nangis, a Huguenot, who, however, is treated with respect and politeness because all present know that Marguérite de Valois, the betrothed of the King, is eager to reconcile Catholic and Protestant, and that he who furthers her purpose is likely to win royal favor. When Nevers toasts the ladies and proposes that each tell of some adventure with the fair sex, Raoul, first to be asked, willingly complies. In a romanza he tells them of an unknown beauty whom he rescued this very morning from some drunken revelers. He does not know her, but he is in love with her, he says.

The applause which greets this romantic recital is interrupted by Raoul's sturdy old Huguenot servant, Marcel, who distrusts his master's Catholic friends and sings the Lutheran choral "A Mighty Fortress Is Our God." Meyerbeer made much of this noble tune, both in the prelude and virtually every time Marcel is on the stage. The guests accept Raoul's apologies for Marcel's act and ask the old fellow to sing again. He responds with a vigorous Huguenot ditty against the "snares of Rome."

The resulting rather constrained feeling is quickly forgotten when a servant announces that a veiled lady wishes to speak to Nevers, who at once retires to meet her, amidst the banter of his friends. All are curious about the lady, and Raoul himself joins in peeping behind a curtain. It is none other than the unknown beauty he rescued that morning; at once

he believes that a liaison exists between this woman and Nevers.

Still another unexpected diversion occurs in the arrival of Urbain, who, in the very ornate but melodious "Page's Song"—"*Nobles seigneurs, salut*" ("Noble sirs, I salute you")—informs them that one of their number is addressed with the unusual request to go blindfolded in a carriage wherever his guide may take him.

Raoul, though highly puzzled when he learns that the message is addressed to him, gallantly accepts. He also wonders at the sudden respect with which he is treated, for he does not realize that the seal on the letter is that of Marguérite de Valois.

ACT II

SCENE: *Castle and gardens of Chenonçeaux.* Marguérite de Valois, surrounded by her maids of honor, rejoices, as she sings, "*O beau pays de la Touraine*" ("O lovely Touraine"), in the pleasant sunny field of Touraine after the stress of life at court. Valentine, daughter of the Count de St. Bris, enters and tells Marguérite news—she has succeeded in breaking her engagement to marry the Count de Nevers, news in which both rejoice, for Valentine does not love the man, and Marguérite has other plans for her. Valentine and some of the ladies go away as Raoul is brought before Marguérite and the bandage removed from his eyes. Though astonished to find himself before her, he gallantly offers her his sword and service. She tells him of her desire for him to marry Valentine, and as he knows of Marguérite's ambition to reconcile Catholic and Protes-

Act II as seen at La Scala, with Urbain (Fiorenza Cossotto), Raoul (Franco Corelli), Marguérite (Joan Sutherland)

tant by this union, he consents. The nobles of the court are summoned, and when they appear, they gather around the Queen and in commemoration of the union of Raoul and Valentine swear an oath of eternal truce between their parties. Valentine is brought in to be presented to her betrothed. Raoul recoils in horror and exclaims, "I her husband?" for he recognizes in Valentine the woman who called secretly on the Count de Nevers. Misunderstanding his action, all present are filled with the greatest consternation; Valentine is overcome with shame, and St. Bris, furious at the insult to his daughter, joins with Nevers in swearing vengeance. Marguérite's presence does indeed prevent immediate bloodshed, but her hopes of reconciling the warring factions are forever shattered.

ACT III

SCENE: *A square in Paris.* Near the entrance to a chapel on the banks of the Seine, a group of Catholic students has gathered about the doors of an inn; and at another inn across the way a number of Huguenot soldiers have met to drink and play dice. They sing a spirited *rataplan*. Townspeople of all sorts pass to and fro, their many-colored costumes adding glamour to the brilliant sunlight. A bridal procession passes—Valentine and Count de Nevers are to be married. While the bridal party is in the chapel, Marcel enters with a message for St. Bris, from Raoul. The wedding over, Valentine remains in the chapel to pray alone, and Marcel presents the message to St. Bris; it proves to be a challenge. The nobles re-enter the chapel.

Jean De Reszke of the Golden Age as Raoul de Nangis

Twilight falls, the curfew sounds, and the people disperse. Valentine comes from the chapel in deathly terror, for she has overheard the nobles plotting to kill Raoul. She finds Marcel waiting for his master, and warns him of the plan. It is too late for him to see Raoul before the hour of the duel, so he hastily gathers a group of Huguenot friends nearby. The two parties prove to be evenly matched, a serious fray is threatened and, in fact, is prevented only by the arrival of Marguérite, who happens to be passing. Raoul also learns that he has deeply wronged Valentine, for her visit to Nevers was made at the request of the Queen merely to break off the engagement. His remorse comes too late, for now Valentine is married to this man she never loved, and a boat, gay with lanterns and music, has come up the Seine to take her to the Count's home.

ACT IV

SCENE: *A room in Nevers' castle.* Alone at her new home, Valentine still thinks of Raoul, who suddenly and unexpectedly appears. He so longs to see Valentine that he has entered the castle at the risk of his life; she warns him, but he insists on remaining and scarcely has time to hide behind the tapestry before St. Bris, Nevers, and other leaders of the Catholic party enter. Thus, the young nobleman overhears the whole ghastly plot for the massacre of the Huguenots. Nevers alone among them refuses to swear allegiance to the plan, and he is led away under guard. While all draw their swords, three monks who have entered bless them.

The crowd having departed, Raoul comes cautiously from his hiding place; he would run to warn his friends. Valentine meets him, and fearing he may kill her father she will not let him go. They sing a surpassingly beautiful duet, which is interrupted by the sinister tolling of the great bell of St. Germain, the preliminary signal for the slaughter. Raoul makes an effort to rush to the aid of his people; Valentine clings to him but he leaps from the window into the fray.

ACT V

SCENE: *The street before Nevers' house.* After Valentine's protests that she would rather die with Raoul than return to her own faction, they go out into the night, and Raoul asks Marcel to act as priest and marry them, which he does. In their most ecstatic moment the lovers and Marcel are shot down by the soldiers of St. Bris, who, too late, discovers that they have killed his own daughter.

Idomeneo, Rè di Creta

IDOMENEUS, KING OF CRETE

CHARACTERS

Idomeneo, *King of Crete*	Tenor
Idamante, *his son*	Male Soprano
Ilia, *Trojan princess, Priam's daughter*	Soprano
Elettra, *Greek princess, Agamemnon's daughter*	Soprano
Arbace, *the King's confidant*	Tenor
High Priest of Neptune	Tenor
Voice of Neptune	Bass

The People of Crete, Trojan Prisoners, Sailors, Soldiers, Priests, Dancers

The action takes place in ancient Crete after the Trojan War.

OPERA IN THREE ACTS. Music by Wolfgang Amadeus Mozart. Libretto in Italian by Gianbattista Varesco, court chaplain to the Archbishop of Salzburg, from a French original by Danchet (set to music by Campra, 1712). First performance, in Munich, January 29, 1781. Despite its success, only one other performance—a private one—was given in Mozart's lifetime. On the one hundred and fiftieth anniversary of its first performance, it was given at the Vienna State Opera in a version drastically edited (with additional music of his own) by Richard Strauss; and at Munich in a version edited by Wolf-Ferrari. It was performed in London, in English, in 1938, and made its first United States appearance on August 4, 1947, at the Berkshire Music Festival, at Tanglewood, Massachusetts, in a version edited and conducted by Boris Goldovsky, head of the opera department of the Berkshire Music School.

Considered by some the finest *opera seria* of the eighteenth century—and said to have been Mozart's own favorite of his operas—*Idomeneo* has never gained a place in the operatic repertory. Commissioned by the Elector to write the opera for the Munich Carnival of 1781, Mozart began composing his music in October of 1780 and, as was his custom, wrote the greater part of the opera during rehearsals —adding arias to please temperamental singers (he was a mere twenty-five to his leading singer's sixty-five) and making changes to help in the staging. The last rehearsal was held on his twenty-fifth birthday, January 27, 1781, and the original cast included Anton Raaff as Idomeneo, the *castrato* Dal Prato as Idamante, Dorothea and Elisabeth Wendling as Ilia and Elettra, Domenico de' Panzacchi as Arbace, and Giovanni Valesi as the High Priest. Unlike the Italian *opera seria* of the day, *Idomeneo* utilized French (and Gluckian) techniques, with the chorus having an indispensable part in the action and the orchestra having important purely instrumental marches and interludes (such as the storm). The scenes of Act III are not clearly indicated because of cuts in the libretto and because in Mozart's day scene changes were made speedily, in full view of the audience, with musical accompaniment to bridge them, so Scene 2 should perhaps be divided into two scenes.

ACT I

SCENE 1: *Garden of the royal palace.* Ilia, Priam's daughter, who had been sent to Crete as a captive by its king, Idomeneo, has fallen in love with his son Idamante, who had once rescued her from drowning. But she fears that he is in love with Elettra (Electra), who has found refuge in Crete after taking part in the murder of her mother. Idamante then enters, waiting for his father's return from the Trojan War. He sees Ilia and tries to tell her of his love, but his language has more propriety than ardor in it. Besides, to her he is still the enemy of her people and she feels it her duty to reject his advances. News is soon brought in that Idomeneo's fleet has been sighted, and Idamante, in jubilation and perhaps because of his love for Ilia, orders the liberation of the captured Trojans.

While the Cretans and Trojans are celebrating this happy event, Elettra enters, displeased with the idea of enemy uniting with enemy—for she, too, is in love with Idamante. Arbace, the King's confidant, interrupts her angry outpourings with word that Idomeneo's ship is foundering in a storm off the coast. Everyone rushes away but Elettra, who, in a jealous rage, fears that if Idomeneo is killed, Ilia will win Idamante.

SCENE 2: *A Cretan harbor*. While the men on shore pray to the gods for mercy for those aboard ship, the tempest-tossed soldiers in Idomeneo's vessel echo their sentiments (Mozart here uses two choruses, one off stage). After a brief flareup, which sends everyone on shore scurrying to safety, the storm subsides, and Idomeneo lands with his attendants. At the height of the storm, it seems, he had vowed to Neptune that if he would quell the storm and bring him safely home, he would sacrifice to the god the first person he met on landing.

Now that the storm is over, Idamante returns to lament the death of his father. Neither recognizes the other, for Idamante was a child when Idomeneo went off to the war, and when Idamante offers the man shelter, he learns that it is his father. Horrified that Idamante is his own son, Idomeneo warns the boy never to see him again, and departs. (The story is an obvious parallel of the Jephthah tale in the Bible—Judges 11–12—where Jephthah vowed to Jehovah that, if victorious, he would sacrifice to Him the first person to come out of his house, which turned out to be his daughter.) Idamante, at a loss to discover a reason for his father's sudden anger, wonders if it has been brought about as a result for his love for Ilia. Idomeneo's soldiers then disembark and are joyously reunited with their families.

ACT II

SCENE 1: *The royal gardens*. Idomeneo confesses his vow to Neptune to his faithful counselor Arbace and

seeks advice from him on how to save his son. Arbace suggests sending the young man away, and Idomeneo hits upon the idea of sending Idamante to accompany Elettra home to Greece. Arbace leaves to make the necessary preparations, and Ilia enters. Idomeneo promises her that he will make amends for the suffering she has undergone, only to hear that she has found happiness in Crete. When she praises his son, he realizes that she must love Idamante. Neptune, he fears, may gain three victims instead of the one that is his due—himself and Ilia, too, for they cannot live without Idamante.

Elettra, pleased with the prospect of returning home with Idamante at her side, sees a happy future for herself. In the distance she hears marching music indicating that the men are on their way to provision and prepare the ship she will sail on.

SCENE 2: *The harbor*. The ship is ready, the sea is calm (the well-known *"Placido è il mar"* sung by the chorus), and Elettra and her attendants are set to sail. Idamante and Elettra bid farewell to the King, Idamante's heart being heavy over his father's unexplained antipathy toward him and also because he is leaving without having openly declared his love to Ilia. As they go toward the ship, a furious storm lashes the waters and a monster rises from the deep. Aghast, the populace recognizes at once that Neptune the sea god has put a curse upon all. Someone has been guilty of impiety to the god—but who? Idomeneo confesses—not to the people, but to the god himself—that he is the guilty one and is ready to die for his sin. The storm grows in violence, and the populace, terrified by the sea monster, run for their lives.

ACT III

SCENE 1: *The palace gardens*. Though now deeply in love with Idamante, Ilia still has not told him so. He comes to say good-by, for he has decided to slay the sea monster or die in the attempt, and Ilia can no longer hide her love. As the lovers reveal their passion, Idomeneo and the jealous Elettra interrupt them. Still not revealing his reason, the King commands his son to leave Crete forever to still Neptune's wrath and save his people. Ilia begins to believe it is she who has brought down the god's anger upon them through her love for Idamante. Elettra, burning with hatred for Ilia, realizes, now that she is faced with the lovers, that she can no longer hope to win Idamante's affections. They unite in a quartet in which Idomeneo sings of his hopelessness, and Elettra her fury, and at the end of which the lovers bid each other farewell. Ilia offers to go with Idamante, but he tells her he must go alone.

SCENE 2: *Exterior of the palace, and altar of the god Neptune.* The Cretans have been ravaged by a plague and terrified by the sea monster, and have come to Idomeneo to demand that he make the sacrifice promised the god, which will relieve their oppression. The High Priest scourges the King for his impiety and disobedience, and Idomeneo finally reveals the identity of his promised sacrifice—his own son.

As Idomeneo prays to Neptune, and the High Priest and his ministrants prepare for the sacrifice, Arbace rushes in, bearing word that Idamante has slain the monster. But the news is of no avail. Idamante makes a triumphal entry only to learn of his father's vow and that he must be sacrificed to Neptune. Stalwartly he offers himself as victim, whereupon Ilia throws herself at the altar to take the place of her lover. As she kneels, the earth rumbles, the image of the god moves as though life has been breathed into it, and the voice of an oracle proclaims the judgment of the gods to the astounded priest and populace: Idomeneo must abdicate in favor of his son, who will then rule Crete with Ilia as his queen. Everyone but Elettra is pleased; in a towering rage she calls upon the Furies to deal out to her the torments of the damned, and departs.

SCENE 3: *Front of the royal palace.* Enthroned, Idomeneo bids his people welcome their new king and queen, expressing relief at his now-unburdened conscience and peace of mind. He descends, and Idamante and Ilia take his place amid joyous celebrations in dance and song by the Cretans.

Glyndebourne Festival 1951 staging with Sena Jurinac (Ilia), Leopold Simoneau (Idamante), Birgit Nilsson (Elettra)

The Impresario

DER SCHAUSPIELDIREKTOR

CHARACTERS (*in the original*)

Frank, *the impresario* (Schikaneder in Schneider)	*Speaking part*	Herr Vogelsang	*Tenor*
Eiler, *the banker*	*Speaking part*	Madame Herz (Madame Lange in Schneider)	*Soprano*
Buff (Mozart in Schneider) } *actors*	*Bass*	Mademoiselle Silberklang (Madame Cavalieri in Schneider) } *singers*	
Herz	*Speaking part*		*Soprano*
Madame Pfeil Madame Krone Madame Vogelsang } *actresses*	*Speaking parts*		

The action takes place in Vienna in the 1780's.

COMEDY WITH MUSIC in one act. Music by Wolfgang Amadeus Mozart. Text in German by Gottlieb Stephanie. Written for and first performed at a party given by the Emperor Josef II at Schönbrunn (Vienna), February 7, 1786, and performed for the public at the Kärntnertor Theater of Vienna the same month on the 18th and 25th. The original cast included two of the most distinguished sopranos of the day, Mozart's sister-in-law Aloysia Lange and Katharina Cavalieri. In 1845 Stephanie's play was completely rewritten by Louis Schneider, and four of the characters were renamed "Mozart" (Buff of the original), "Schikaneder" (the librettist and impresario who produced *The Magic Flute*), "Madame Lange," and "Madame Cavalieri." With further adaptation, this version has held the stage for over a century and still is sometimes used. Its first American production was given in English in New York, October 16, 1916, by the Society of American Singers at the Empire Theater. Today the trend is to go back to Stephanie's original names, or something like them, and not cause the revered Mozart to appear as a minor, ludicrous character in a slight and inconsequential comedy.

Mozart, when he received the commission to compose the music for *Der Schauspieldirektor*, was already at work on the score of *The Marriage of Figaro*, which was produced the same year. There are only five musical numbers in the original score of the one-act comedy, but two of them, at least, are as treasurable as many of the thirty in *Figaro*. These are the Overture, a delightful piece for a small orchestra, and the comedy trio, in which the two sopranos try to out-coloratura each other while the tenor tries to calm them down.

SCENE: *The office of Frank, a well-respected theater-director of Vienna.* Frank has closed a season that was artistically a success and financially a disaster. He hopes to gather a troupe together for a new season in Salzburg, and promises of backing are made him by Eiler, a banker. Eiler's motives, however, turn out not to be prompted by an entirely disinterested love of theatrical art. He proposes that

Frank should engage the services, as a leading singer, of Madame Herz, a highly temperamental soprano somewhat past her prime both as a leading lady and as Eiler's mistress. She is brought in and, under protest, made to audition for Frank. She sings the aria *"Da schlägt die Abschiedsstunde"* ("The parting hour is tolling"), in which she bids farewell tragically to an imaginary lover. (In modern productions in English the aria is made to imply a warning to Eiler not to try to get rid of her.) Beginning very slowly and sadly, the short piece is designed to show off, first, the capacity for stately tragic utterance and then, before the close, her fine command of even, legato scale passages. Frank, who knows that Eiler will foot the bill, offers a generous salary, which is accepted, when another soprano, Mademoiselle Silberklang, also shows up for an audition. Her audition song, *"Bester Jüngling"* ("My good young man"), is also addressed to an imaginary lover, but one she has just met, not one with whom she has already had a history. And it soon turns out that it was Eiler who had recently met her—just a pick-up in the park—and so the two women are rivals for the biggest parts and the biggest salaries in the new company. Actually, there is room for both, as Herz is the leading-lady type and Silberklang, much less experienced and much younger, the soubrette type. (In point of fact, the two women for whom the parts were originally written, Lange and Cavalieri, were born in the same year, 1760.) A noisy argument ensues and then the great trio *"Ich bin die erste Sängerin"* ("I am the principal singer"). Here each of the two women sets forth her own claims and makes snide remarks about the other, while Vogelsang, one of the actors who has been a candidate for the new company, tries to calm them. (In modern versions, it is Eiler himself who joins the trio trying to pour oil on the troubled coloratura.) At the close, however, everything turns out all right, and there is a finale, or *vaudeville*, *"Jeder Künstler strebt nach Ehre"* ("Every artist strives for honor"). The three characters who took part in the trio are joined by Buff (the low-comedy actor of the company); each has a solo setting forth his claim to honor; and after each solo the quartet agrees that whatever contributions an individual artist may make, after all—the play's the same thing.

In modern versions, as well as in Schneider's version called *Mozart and Schikaneder*, the cast of characters is stripped down to five—the impresario, the banker, the two sopranos, and Buff, who is in these versions the stage director and general utility man of the company. Thus much of the dialogue and many complications with individual actors are stripped away, and the impresario is the only one who has no chance to sing. The action is largely

English Opera Group staging with Jennifer Eddy, Kenneth Macdonald and Margaret Price, at Covent Garden

centered around the triangle situation. The impresario, disgusted with the lack of artistic integrity of the others, resigns from the project and stalks out; Eiler takes over as the new impresario; and the two women and the stage manager happily agree to work for him.

L'Incoronazione di Poppea
THE CORONATION OF POPPEA

CHARACTERS

Poppea, *a courtesan*	*Soprano*	Damigella, *Ottavia's maid*	*Soprano*
Nero, *Emperor of Rome*	*Tenor*	Liberto, *captain of the guard*	*Baritone*
Arnalta, *Poppea's nurse*	*Contralto*	Lucano, *Nero's friend*	*Tenor*
Drusilla, *a court lady*	*Soprano*	Lictor	*Bass*
Ottone, *Poppea's former lover*	*Baritone*	Two soldiers	*Tenors*
Seneca, *an old senator*	*Bass*	Pallas Athena, *goddess of wisdom*	*Soprano*
Ottavia, *the Empress*	*Mezzo-soprano*	Amor, *god of love*	*Soprano*
Ottavia's page	*Tenor*		

Soldiers, Tribunes, Lictors, Ladies-in-Waiting, Citizens, etc.

The action takes place in Rome about A.D. *62.*

OPERA IN TWO acts, thirteen scenes. Music by Claudio Monteverdi. Text in Italian by Giovanni Francesco Busenello. Probably the first historical opera, *L'Incoronazione di Poppea* is based on an episode in the life of Nero, Emperor of Rome, A.D. 62. First performed in Venice at the Teatro SS. Giovanni e Paolo in 1642. The American première took place at Smith College, Northampton, Massachusetts, on April 27, 1926; and on February 23, 1933, it was staged by the Juilliard School of Music in New York City. More recently it has been revived throughout Europe, especially in Italy and Germany, as well as at the Glyndebourne Festival (1962), the Dallas Civic Opera (1963), and the Chicago Lyric Opera (1965) to public and critical acclaim.

The infrequency of performances of *L'Incoronazione di Poppea* can in part be attributed to the lack of a definitive version of the score. Monteverdi's complete orchestration has been lost, and all that remains is a *continuo* copy consisting of the vocal line and the single bass line. The directions and cuts, however, are written out in the composer's own hand, and on these, numerous musicologists have attempted to reconstruct the score. Thus most productions of the opera differ in orchestration and vocal casting. (Except for Seneca and the soldiers, all of the roles in Monteverdi's time were performed by women.) There are in existence several modern performing editions: Giacomo Benvenuti's consists of a prologue and three acts; G. F. Ghedini's three acts, thirteen scenes; Ernst Krenek's two acts, seven scenes; G. F. Malipiero's three acts. For the synopsis and assignment of voices given here, the Günther Rennert version produced at the Glyndebourne Festival has been utilized.

L'Incoronazione di Poppea is the fruit of Monteverdi's seventy-fifth year. In it the composer achieved a remarkable balance between music and drama, creating characters of flesh and blood. (It is ironic that his pupils soon undid their master's penetrating, human style in favor of the artificialities of florid ornamentation.) The libretto, called the least moral in all opera, finds wrong triumphing over right, lust over love. By means of expressive, dramatic recitative and arioso, which exploit every variety of musical vocabulary known in his time, Monteverdi draws sharp profiles of his characters, not all of them sympathetic.

Chicago Lyric Opera: Attilio Colonnello's production of L'Incoronazione, *originally created for the Dallas Civic Opera*

ACT I

SCENE 1: *Outside Poppea's house in Rome.* The warrior Ottone joyously returns from the front, only to find two of Nero's guards asleep on the steps of the home of his mistress, the courtesan Poppea. To his despair Ottone realizes that the Emperor Nero has taken Poppea as a lover and that he now must face an unassailable rival. When the soldiers awaken, they complain bitterly about the corruption of Rome and of Nero's obsession for Poppea, which forces them to stay on guard all night. Just then Nero steps from the house, followed by Poppea. The Emperor, having satisfied his passion, is anxious to leave, but Poppea, her eyes fixed on the throne, uses all the wiles at her command to make Nero promise that they will meet again and that his consort, the Empress Ottavia, will be set aside in her favor.

SCENE 2: *Poppea's room.* Arnalta, Poppea's nurse, warns her mistress that her game is dangerous and that Ottavia may have her murdered. Poppea laughs, saying that love is on her side.

SCENE 3: *The Imperial Palace.* Ottavia, aware of Nero's infatuation with Poppea, gives voice to her anger and humiliation, oblivious to the comforting words of her companion Drusilla. The Page an-nounces the arrival of the aged philosopher Seneca, who holds to old moral values. Knowing Ottavia's misery, Seneca gently advises her to maintain her dignity, to remember her rank and position. Ottavia asks that he and the people pray for her, but the Page, incensed by the old man's lack of action on his lady's behalf, threatens him unless he agrees to assist Ottavia in her plight. Left alone, Seneca is visited by a vision of Pallas Athena, the goddess of wisdom, who warns him of impending death. As the vision fades, Nero himself enters, informing Seneca that he intends to depose Ottavia as consort in favor of Poppea. Seneca's disapproval fans the flames of Nero's temper. Near hysteria, the Emperor swears that despite Ottavia, Seneca, and the populace of Rome he will make Poppea his wife.

SCENE 4: *Poppea's bedroom.* When Nero visits his beloved, he tells her he intends to keep his promise to rid himself of Ottavia. His only regret is that all Rome is not worthy of Poppea's beauty. The courtesan, blandishing Nero with all her charms, now suggests that the one other major obstacle between her and the throne, Seneca, be removed. At once Nero dispatches Liberto, the captain of the guard, to Seneca with a message of death.

SCENE 5: *Outside Poppea's house.* Ottone laments that he is barred from his beloved's house, while the

197

door stands open for Nero. When Poppea steps forth on a balcony, she reveals her imperial ambitions to her former lover and curtly dismisses him, saying that she now belongs to Nero. Left alone, Ottone utters his despair, until Drusilla arrives. She tries to convince him that faithfulness to Poppea in such a situation is useless. Both in gratitude and for lack of hope, Ottone pledges to forget Poppea and to love Drusilla instead, promises he knows he cannot keep.

SCENE 6: *Garden of the Imperial Palace.* Ottavia's page tells the maid Damigella of a pain in his heart that he has never felt before. Realizing that he loves her, Damigella promises to help soothe his suffering.

SCENE 7: *Seneca's house.* The philosopher is contemplating the solitude of death when Liberto enters bearing Nero's death command. With dignity and resignation, Seneca tells the messenger to inform Nero that he is already in his grave. Then, surrounded by his faithful pupils, Seneca prepares for death.

ACT II

SCENE 1: *The Imperial Palace.* Delighted by the news of Seneca's death, Nero sings love songs with his friend Lucano, and drinks himself into a stupor.

SCENE 2: *Another part of the palace.* Ottavia, no longer able to bear her disgrace, tells Ottone to murder Poppea, suggesting that he disguise himself as a woman to gain entry to the courtesan's house. He agrees to the conspiracy even though he still feels a lingering love for Poppea. Ottone then informs

Drusilla of the plot and borrows a cloak from her, which she willingly surrenders.

SCENE 3: *Poppea's bedroom.* The courtesan exults over Seneca's suicide, for this assures her that she will be Nero's wife. Arnalta lovingly sings her mistress to sleep with a lullaby. When Ottone steals into the room disguised in Drusilla's cloak, Amor, the god of love, stands guard over Poppea and prevents him from striking the sleeping figure. Poppea awakens and cries out for Arnalta, who quickly summons other help.

SCENE 4: *A street.* Drusilla, thinking only of her love for Ottone, is arrested by a group of lictors led by Arnalta, who accuses her of the attempted murder. Nero enters and orders the girl executed. Ottone, however, arrives in time to confess that it was he who tried to kill Poppea. Nero, satisfied with this declaration, banishes Ottone and Drusilla from Rome and reaffirms his purpose to repudiate Ottavia.

SCENE 5: *The Imperial Palace.* Ottavia sadly bids farewell to her family and Rome.

SCENE 6: *A street.* Arnalta anticipates her future as first lady to the Empress Poppea. She laughingly recalls past indignities as a servant; now, however, all will bow and scrape to her, seeking Poppea's favor.

SCENE 7: *The Imperial Palace.* Poppea is crowned Empress of Rome. Her resplendent coronation is attended by all the tribunes and councils of the empire, who pay homage to their new sovereign. Nero and Poppea, unscathed by the pain they have caused others, exultantly proclaim their love.

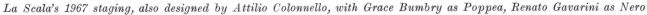

La Scala's 1967 staging, also designed by Attilio Colonnello, with Grace Bumbry as Poppea, Renato Gavarini as Nero

Jenůfa

CHARACTERS

Grandmother Buryja, *householder of the mill*	*Contralto*	Jenůfa, *stepdaughter of Kostelnicka*	*Soprano*
Laca Klemen ⎱ *half-brothers,*	*Tenor*	The Miller	*Baritone*
Steva Buryja ⎰ *her grandsons*	*Tenor*	Mayor of the Village	*Bass*
Kostelnicka (*the Sexton's widow*), *her daughter-in-law*	*Soprano*	The Mayor's Wife	*Mezzo-soprano*
		Karolka, *their daughter*	*Mezzo-soprano*

Shepherd Boy, Maid, Cowhand, Woman, Chorus of Villagers

The action takes place in southeastern Moravia in the late nineteenth century.

OPERA IN THREE ACTS. Music by Leoš Janáček. Text in Czech by the composer after Gabrielle Preissová's novel of Moravian rural life. First performed at the National Theater, Brno, Czechoslovakia (then Austrian Moravia), January 21, 1904. Première of revised version at National Theater, Prague, May 26, 1916. Successful in Vienna and Cologne 1918, Frankfurt 1923, Berlin 1924. American première at the Metropolitan Opera House, December 6, 1924, with Maria Jeritza, who had "created" the German version (text translated by Max Brod) in Vienna; lasted five performances (one season). Revivals in America by Chicago Lyric Opera (1959) and Hamburg State Opera (Lincoln Center Festival 1967). Notable repertory productions by National Theater, Munich, in the 1950's and Sadler's Wells, London, in the 1960's (translated by Norman Tucker), Covent Garden, 1968.

Leoš Janáček (1854–1928) is considered alongside Smetana and Dvořák as one of the triumvirate of great Czechoslovak composers. Born in an era when artistic nationalism was struggling under the Austrian monarchy, he was highly sensitive to folk music and the accents of regional speech, but his work also shows that he absorbed the examples of Moussorgsky, Debussy, Richard Strauss, and other international figures in what was then modern music. It was long customary to dismiss Janáček as having been born too late for romanticism and too early for the twentieth century; gradually widening acquaintance with his works, however, has changed this image to one of a highly individual and creative innovator within the musical heritage of his native Moravia.

Jenůfa, the fourth of Janáček's nine operas, was his first and most lasting success for the lyric stage. In many ways the most typical of his works, it combines the more melodic, folklike character of his earlier period with the terse, powerful style of his later years, setting a subject from his own home locality (allegedly based upon an actual court case).

Janáček began to write the opera in 1894 and is believed to have substantially finished the first version in 1897. Even after the first performance—in Brno (Brünn), the city where he lived and taught, in 1904—Janáček continued to revise the score, and in 1908, depressed by the repeated refusals of the National Theater in Prague to produce it, he destroyed the manuscript. Into the revised version he poured all his grief over the death of his son and daughter. It seems that the outspoken Janáček had offended his colleague Karel Kovařovic, the musical director at the Prague theater, but repeated entreaties by partisans of *Jenůfa* and the quality of the

Maria Jeritza, compatriot of Janáček, as his Jenůfa

score itself eventually persuaded Kovařovic to produce it, and he even suggested certain cuts and
changes in orchestration, which Janáček accepted.
After the capital had finally given this accolade to
the provincial composer, he wrote his remaining
operas within the last decade of his life and found
the doors of the theater world open to him.

Jenůfa tells a story of rural common people whom
Janáček knew deeply. He understood the strength of
their passions, struggling for expression through
limited vocabulary and a superstitious, convention-
bound way of life, rich in frustration as well as in
tradition. His love for these peasant characters, and
his belief in what is tritely called the dignity of man,
enabled Janáček at the close of *Jenůfa* to show how
suffering can transmute the narrow horizon of provincial life to reach a broad, compassionate view.

The prosperous couple who owned the mill have
died some years before the action opens, leaving the
property to their son Steva. He is charming but
irresponsible, the village drunkard and braggart.
The actual running of the mill has been entrusted to
an experienced older farmer, and the household is

run by Steva's grandmother. The grandmother's
daughter-in-law, Kostelnička (the Sexton's widow),
has a stepdaughter, Jenůfa—the cousin of Steva and
stepcousin of Laca. Jenůfa is engaged to Steva, and
at the beginning of the opera she has discovered she
is already pregnant, but the others do not know it.
Laca, resentful of his status as a poor relation, is
jealous of Jenůfa and loves her himself without
quite realizing it.

ACT I

SCENE: *Outside the mill*. It is late afternoon and
Jenůfa anxiously awaits Steva, who has been exam-
ined by the local draft board. She hopes he has been
able to get a deferment in order to marry her. Laca
makes a few spiteful remarks, which she ignores as
best she can. The Miller appears with welcome news:
Steva has been deferred. Then Steva, with a group
of recruits, villagers, and musicians, arrives in a
carousing mood. He flirts with several girls, and
Jenůfa reproaches him. At the height of the general
boisterousness Kostelnička comes out of the house,
orders Jenůfa inside, and tells Steva that he will
have to give up drinking for a year if he hopes to
marry Jenůfa. The visitors leave, and the grandmother persuades Steva to sleep it off. Jenůfa and
Laca try to resume their chores. At length Laca
picks up a bouquet that Steva had gotten from one
of the village girls. He tries mockingly to pin it on
Jenůfa, at the same time trying to kiss her. She
attempts to fend him off, and either by accident or
intent (or a mixture of both) Laca slashes her cheek
with the knife he had been using.

ACT II

SCENE: *Room in Kostelnička's house*. Kostelnička is
caring for Jenůfa, who has borne her child and
named him after Steva. To fend off the curiosity of
neighbors, Kostelnička has pretended that Jenůfa
was away in Vienna visiting relatives. Now she has
sent for Steva in order to make him face his respon-
sibilities toward Jenůfa. She sends Jenufa to bed,
aided by a sleeping potion, and anxiously awaits the
young man. He arrives and readily admits that he
has failed the two women; but, he adds, he has
always been afraid of Kostelnička, and since
Jenůfa's face has been scarred he no longer feels
able to marry her. When Kostelnička persists in her
pleading, he finally says he cannot do what she wants
because he is now engaged to Karolka, the Mayor's
daughter. He offers money if Kostelnička will keep
the secret of his fathering Jenůfa's child. She is
outraged, and he runs away. Soon afterward Laca,

too, pays a visit; he has come to inquire after Jenůfa and to beg pardon for his injury to her. He confesses his love for the girl and would like to marry her, but when Kostelnička tells him about the child, he cannot stomach the idea of accepting Steva's son as his own. Seeing the danger of losing Jenůfa's only chance, Kostelnička in desperation says the baby has died a few days before. Laca is relieved, and Kostelnička sends him away to find out when Steva is to marry Karolka. Beside herself, Kostelnička realizes she has only one course left: to get rid of the baby as if it never existed. She takes it from Jenůfa's room and rushes outdoors. During her absence Jenůfa wakes up and searches frantically for the child, then supposes her stepmother has taken it to show to Steva. She prays to the Holy Virgin. Returning highly agitated, the older woman persuades Jenůfa that she had been in a fever for two days, during which the baby died.

ACT III

SCENE: *Same as Act II.* Two months later, the room is modestly decorated for Jenůfa's wedding to Laca. The Mayor and his wife arrive, and the latter wonders why Jenůfa is not wearing the traditional elaborate gown for being married in church. Some of Jenůfa's girl friends arrive to wish her happiness, followed by Karolka and the reluctant Steva, whom Jenůfa wishes to reconcile with Laca. As the ceremony is about to begin, cries are heard outside. Someone has found an infant's body under the thawing ice in the river. It dawns on Jenůfa that the child must be hers. Steva realizes this, too, and tries to flee, but Karolka obliges him to stay and face up to what he has done. The Mayor brings the child's blanket and cap, proving its identity. Now the half-demented Kostelnička agonizingly confesses her crime and begs Jenůfa's forgiveness, which is granted; then she turns herself over to the Mayor for justice. Left alone with Laca, Jenůfa gently tells him that he cannot marry her and she will go away. He replies simply that he means to come with her. Both realize they have found maturity and a love deeper than they knew before. As the curtain falls, they go to the door and look toward a new life together.

Act III: Jenůfa (Bosabelian, center) hears Kostelnička (Kniplova, kneeling) confess her crime (Hamburg Opera)

Julius Caesar

GIULIO CESARE

CHARACTERS

Julius Caesar	*Male contralto*	Cleopatra, *Queen of Egypt*	*Soprano*
	(nowadays usually	Ptolemy, *her brother*	*Bass*
	baritone or bass)	Achillas, *his adviser*	*Bass*
Curio, *his aide-de-camp*	*Tenor*	Nirenus, *Cleopatra's adviser*	*Male contralto*
Cornelia, *widow of Pompey*	*Contralto*		*(nowadays*
Sextus, *her son*	*Soprano (nowadays*		*usually bass)*
	usually tenor)		

Citizens of Alexandria, Roman and Egyptian Soldiers, Servants

The action takes place in Alexandria in 48 B.C.

OPERA IN THREE ACTS. Music by George Frideric Handel. Libretto in Italian by Nicolò Francesco Haym. First performance, at The Haymarket, London, March 2, 1724, with a star cast that included the great male contralto Senesino as Caesar, the soprano Margherita Durastanti as Sextus, and Francesca Cuzzoni, the leading soprano of the day, as Cleopatra. First American stage performance at Northampton, Massachusetts, by Smith College in English. First American professional staging at the Lincoln Center, New York State Theater, in English, by the New York City Opera Company, 1966 with the bass Norman Treigle as Caesar and Beverly Sills as Cleopatra. In concert, New York's American Opera Society has presented three other great sopranos as Cleopatra—Leontyne Price, Elisabeth Schwarzkopf and Montserrat Caballé.

Julius Caesar and Mozart's *Idomeneo* are the only examples of the old-fashioned eighteenth-century *opera seria* included in this book, for this form of entertainment is scarcely ever mounted on modern stages, the problems being very great. Constructed largely as a series of arias for solo singers, there are very few concerted numbers, with little use made of the chorus; and although elaborate stage machinery was used, especially in Italy in the earlier part of the century, the acting was formalized, the plots often absurdly complex, the stories based on mythology or not very accurate classical history. Even in its own day, as Addison pointed out satirically in *The Spectator,* Italian *opera seria* was a ludicrous and irrational form of theatrical entertainment. But the greatest problem of all for modern presentation lies in the principal attraction these shows had for eighteenth-century Europe—the kind of singing called for. No longer do we have singers trained in the arduous ways of *bel canto* with abnormally long breath spans, who can improvise elaborate cadenzas, clearly sing two-octave scales up and down in one breath, or hold a high note over several measures, with an enormous *crescendo* and then *diminuendo,* known as the *messa di voce.* Nor, if there were one around to take the part, would a modern audience be likely to tolerate a castrated man, with a voice in the female register, in the part of Julius Caesar, even if we were willing to suspend belief long enough to accept Sextus, the juvenile hero of *Julius Caesar,* sung and acted by a female.

Yet so fine is the score of this opera, so dramatically right a number of its arias, that it has been

revived during the twentieth century for a few
nights each season in various European countries and
over here, and it is not infrequently given in concert
form. Caesar is usually sung by a baritone, Sextus
by a tenor (a simple matter of transposing the parts
an octave down); and though modern singers have
trouble with the coloratura style, the quality of the
music is so high that the experience of hearing it is
rewarding. As a matter of history, so well was this
opera received in its first year that it virtually
ended the "opera war" between Handel and his
great rival composer Giovanni Bononcini, with a
victory for the Saxon.

ACT I

SCENE 1: *Outside Alexandria near a tributary of the
Nile with a bridge over it.* The first two movements
of a typical eighteenth-century French overture
(slow-fast-slow) are played by the orchestra, and
when the curtain rises, a chorus of Egyptians sings
the third movement. It is a welcome to Caesar, who
has just conquered the country, and he crosses the
bridge followed by Curio and a part of his army.
After he sings a dignified statement of victory,
Curio (first paraphrasing his master: "Caesar came
and saw and conquered") adds the news that Pompey, Caesar's Roman rival, having failed to get the
aid of Egyptian forces, is defeated. The wife of
Pompey, Cornelia, together with their son Sextus,
enter on the scene to plead for peace, and Caesar
magnanimously speaks warmly to them, offering to be
reconciled to his rival if he will come to him. Before
this can be done, Achillas, the leader of troops for
Ptolemy, Cleopatra's brother, brings in—as a gift to
Caesar—the head of Pompey. Ptolemy has sent the
gift, says Achillas, as a token of his allegiance to
Caesar. Everyone is horrified by this exercise in
political barbarism, excepting, of course, Achillas,
who is, instead, at once smitten with the beauty of
Cornelia. Caesar vigorously denounces the crime,
and orders a noble funeral.

With Caesar gone, Cornelia, who has fainted at
the sight of her husband's head, rallies and immediately tries to commit suicide with her son's sword.
But Curio stops her and (rather tastelessly, it must
be admitted) declares his love and proposes marriage. Cornelia angrily dismisses him as her husband's enemy, and he goes off resolving to forget
her. Cornelia and Sextus, now left alone, commiser-
ate, the mother singing a very sorrowful aria and the
son vowing to avenge his father.

SCENE 2: *Cleopatra's room.* Cleopatra, who has not
yet heard of Caesar's victory, sings to her handmaidens of the prospect of being Queen of all Egypt.

Beverly Sills (Cleopatra), Norman Treigle (Caesar)

But her adviser Nirenus brings her the news of
Ptolemy's ugly gift to the victor, and Cleopatra, at
once understanding the political implications, resolves to pit her wiles against Ptolemy in securing
Caesar's good will. Ptolemy himself now enters, and
what is apparently an old argument between the
sibling rivals for the throne is resumed. Cleopatra
asserts her own superior rights to the throne, de-
nouncing Ptolemy as a womanizer, and sweeps
grandly from the room. Achillas then brings his
master the news of how Caesar was angered by the
gift of Pompey's head, and he offers to murder
Caesar (just as he had Pompey) if he may be
rewarded with possession of Cornelia. Ptolemy
agrees to the terms and closes the scene with an aria,
already gloating.

SCENE 3: *A square in Caesar's camp.* Caesar is doing
honors to the ashes of Pompey when Cleopatra,
calling herself "Lydia," one of the Queen's handmaidens, comes with Nirenus to beg justice against
Ptolemy, who, she says, has robbed her. Caesar, as
well as Curio, is at once smitten with "Lydia's"
beauty and, promising to attend to the matter, goes
off with his followers. Cleopatra and Nirenus stay
behind as Cornelia and Sextus come to mourn the
ashes of Pompey. When Cornelia takes a sword from

among the trophies beside the urn, vowing to slay Ptolemy, Sextus takes it from her and says that this is his duty. Cleopatra, still calling herself "Lydia," now steps forth and offers to have Nirenus lead the avengers to Ptolemy; and when the others have gone off on their mission, she sings a brilliant aria apostrophizing the star of her anticipated success.

SCENE 4: *A hall in Ptolemy's castle.* Caesar and Ptolemy meet with polite greetings but, in asides, express deadly enmity. When Cornelia and Sextus enter, Ptolemy, seeing her for the first time, is immediately smitten; but when Sextus rashly challenges him to a duel, Ptolemy orders him arrested and Cornelia to be sent to his own seraglio, and then stalks out. Achillas, having been reassured that Cornelia will be kept safely for him, tries in vain to get Cornelia to look on him favorably; and before Sextus can be dragged away by the guards, he and his mother have a brief, sorrowing duet—one of the few concerted numbers in the opera.

ACT II

SCENE 1: *A cedar grove with, in the background, the "Palace of Virtue" and Mount Parnassus.* With the help of Nirenus and nine handmaidens dressed as the nine muses, Cleopatra is preparing to receive Caesar in the guise of the goddess of virtue. The curtain is drawn before the palace, and Caesar comes in as seductive music is played. Nirenus reveals the posed scene; Cleopatra sings a love song; but as Caesar rushes toward her, the curtain closes, and Nirenus tells the enchanted conqueror he will lead him to her.

SCENE 2: *A garden in Ptolemy's seraglio with a zoo of wild animals on the side.* Cornelia, tending the flowers, sings a sad aria and then is once more accosted by Achillas, who is again scornfully refused. Ptolemy, coming on them, once more insincerely reassures Achillas that he shall have the woman, and when Achillas leaves, presses his own suit. Cornelia angrily leaves the scene, and Ptolemy has an aria in which he says that he will use force on her. Returning to the stage alone, Cornelia decides to commit suicide by jumping over the wall and be destroyed by the wild animals. But Sextus rushes in in time to prevent her, and Nirenus follows with orders to lead Cornelia into the seraglio itself. However, he also promises to take Sextus there, too, when Ptolemy will be unarmed. The scene ends with Sextus singing a very striking aria of vengeance with a snakelike melody that suggests the reptile he likens to his revenge.

SCENE 3: *Cleopatra's room.* Cleopatra sings of the coming Caesar, and when he comes, with soft words for his "Lydia," she proposes marriage. But Curio enters to warn him that a band of armed men is on his trail to murder him. Caesar wants to stay and fight, but Cleopatra, excitedly revealing her real identity, insists that she must go forth to dissuade them. When she returns, having failed, Caesar draws his sword, goes out with Curio to meet them, and Cleopatra prays for him in one of Handel's very finest arias with a particularly eloquent obbligato.

SCENE 4: *Ptolemy's seraglio.* Ptolemy begins to make love to the resisting Cornelia when Sextus rushes in, sword in hand. He is, however, immediately disarmed by Achillas, who rushes in after him. He reports that Caesar and Curio, outnumbered by the armed band, jumped into the sea and are dead, and that Cleopatra has gone over to the Romans and is about to lead an attack against Ptolemy. He then demands his reward in the shape of Cornelia. Ptolemy makes a bitter enemy of him by refusing, and then gets ready to lead his own forces. Left alone with his mother, Sextus proposes to commit suicide, but Cornelia persuades him instead to follow to Ptolemy's camp and at least try once more to avenge Pompey's murder.

ACT III

SCENE 1: *On the shore near Alexandria.* Achillas sings an aria expressing his deadly anger at Ptolemy and swearing vengeance by joining Cleopatra's side and killing his enemy. The battle takes place as the orchestra plays warlike music; Ptolemy's soldiers win, and Cleopatra is dragged on and ordered into chains by her brother. In her closing aria she vows that her ghost shall haunt him.

SCENE 2: *Another part of the shore.* Caesar, who had jumped into the sea but not been drowned, as Achillas reported, comes back to shore alone, wondering where his followers are and whether Cleopatra is true to him. As Sextus and Nirenus, still in search of Ptolemy, enter, they hear Achillas moaning on the ground. He has been mortally wounded in the battle, but before he dies, he gives Sextus a seal which will make him leader of a hundred men who will lead him secretly to Ptolemy so that both may be avenged and Cornelia saved. Caesar, however, takes the seal from the young man and says that he himself will lead, and save Cleopatra as well.

SCENE 3: *Cleopatra's room.* Cleopatra, under guard but in the presence of her handmaidens, is preparing for death at the hands of her brother. Caesar, however, fights his way in, and the two lovers embrace.

SCENE 4: *Ptolemy's seraglio.* Once more Ptolemy tries to force his attentions on Cornelia, who, however, reveals that she has a dagger and is about to attack him, when her son enters and challenges Ptolemy to fight. Ptolemy is slain almost at once, and Cornelia has a joyous aria.

SCENE 5: *The harbor of Alexandria.* In the presence of Caesar, Cleopatra, and the Egyptian army, Nirenus reports that Curio has been successful everywhere and that Egypt acknowledges Caesar as Emperor. Sextus and Cornelia swear allegiance to him; Caesar proclaims Cleopatra Queen of Egypt; and everyone expresses general joy in the grand finale.

New York City Opera finale, with Caesar (Norman Treigle), Cleopatra (Beverly Sills), Sextus (Beverly Wolff) and Cornelia (Maureen Forrester)

Lakmé

CHARACTERS

Gerald, *a British officer*	*Tenor*	Ellen, *daughter of the Governor*	*Soprano*
Frédéric, *his friend, also a*		Rose, *her friend*	*Soprano*
British officer	*Baritone*	Mrs. Benson, *governess of the*	
Nilakantha, *a Brahman priest*	*Bass*	*young ladies*	*Mezzo-soprano*
Lakmé, *daughter of Nilakantha*	*Soprano*	Mallika, *slave of Lakmé*	*Mezzo-soprano*
Hadji, *a Hindu slave*	*Tenor*		

Hindus, English Officers and Ladies, Sailors, Bayaderes, Chinamen, Musicians, Brahmans, etc.

The action takes place in India in the middle of the nineteenth century.

OPERA COMIQUE in three acts. Music by Léo Delibes. Libretto in French by Edmond Gondinet and Philippe Gille, distantly based on the romance, *Le Mariage de Loti* by Pierre Loti. First performance at the Paris Opéra-Comique, April 14, 1883. American première, in English, at the New York Academy of Music, with Theodore Thomas conducting, March 1, 1886. First performed at the Metropolitan Opera House, in Italian, with Adelina Patti, April 2, 1890; in French, with Marie van Zandt (the original Lakmé), February 22, 1892. Among the other great interpreters of Lakmé have been Marcella Sembrich, Luisa Tetrazzini, Maria Barrientos, Amelita Galli-Curci, Mado Robin, and Lily Pons.

The story of *Lakmé* shows many points of similarity with other repertory operas. Like *Aïda, L'Africaine,* and *Madama Butterfly,* it is more or less Oriental in setting and color. Like Aïda, Lakmé is in love with her country's enemy. Nilakantha of *Lakmé* and Nelusko of *L'Africaine* have many vengeful traits in common. Both Lakmé and Selika (*L'Africaine*) poison themselves botanically, the former using the blossoms of the stramonium weed, the latter by inhaling the deadly perfume of the manchineel tree. Its resemblance to *Madama Butterfly,* of course, lies in the tragic denouement of a romance of East and West. Delibes wrote the role of Lakmé for van Zandt, the gifted and beautiful Brooklyn girl who had so fascinated the composer Massenet.

ACT I

SCENE: *A garden before a temple.* The fanatical Brahman priest Nilakantha stands before the temple he guards, exhorting the gathered worshipers to have courage and await the day when the English invaders will be driven from the land. From the temple is heard the voice of a maiden in prayer— *"Blanche Durga, pâle Siva, puissant Ganeça!"* ("White Durga, pale Siva, mighty Ganesa!"). It is Lakmé, Nilakantha's daughter, and when she comes out, the Hindus prostrate themselves, echoing the prayer devoutly. The worshipers rise and leave, but Lakmé remains with her slave Mallika. They sing a charming barcarolle; and as they are planning to bathe, Lakmé places her jewels on a bench, and the two young women depart in a boat.

Soon a party of English sightseers approaches, drawn by the exotic beauty of the temple and the luxuriant foliage and flowers surrounding it. Though warned by the English officer Frédéric, the party breaks down the frail fence surrounding the temple. As they enter the garden, the girls stop to marvel at the beautiful white blossoms. "Don't touch them!" Frédéric cries. "They're *Datura stramonium*, harmless in England, but under this sky fatally poisonous!" As the visitors presently come upon some jewels left by Lakmé, they feel increasingly conscious of trespassing and prepare to leave. Gerald, another British officer, announces he will remain to sketch the dazzling jewelry they have found. Ellen, his fiancée, joins the others. Left alone, Gerald gazes delightedly at the gems, expressing his pleasure in a charming air, *"Prendre le dessin d'un bijou, est-ce donc aussi grave?"* ("Is it such a serious thing to make a drawing of a jewel?")

While Gerald is busy with his sketch and song, Lakmé returns and regards the stranger with wonder. Fascinated by the attractiveness of this member of a race she has been taught to hate, she fails to summon the guards who would instantly kill him. Gerald, in turn, is enchanted, and is inclined to ridicule her proffered warning of danger. Lakmé is overwhelmed, but finally persuades him to leave before her father returns. Nilakantha enters, raging over the broken fence and the profaned temple. *"Vengeance! Il faut qu'il meure!"* he cries wrathfully—"Vengeance! This man must die!" As other Hindus take up the cry, Lakmé cowers in terror.

ACT II

SCENE: *A public square.* Nilakantha and Lakmé mingle with the motley crowd of a Hindu bazaar. The priest is disguised as a beggar, Lakmé as a street singer. Still searching the city for the temple intruder, Nilikantha has planned a stratagem to lure the culprit into betraying himself. Among the crowd appears the British party, conversing gaily, looking over the teeming wares of street merchants, and watching the exotic ballet of bayaderes, the sacred dancers of the priests of Brahma. Believing the profaner of his temple will step forward at the sound of Lakmé's voice, Nilakantha now commands Lakmé to sing the legend of the pathetic pariah's daughter. At first reluctant, she consents when Nilakantha assures her Brahma does not permit his believers to forget an outrage. As the entrancing "Bell Song" begins, the crowd gathers about Lakmé. She sings, *"Où va la jeune hindoue fille des parias, quand la lune se joue dans les grands mimosas?"* ("Where goes the young Hindu girl, daughter of the pariahs, when the moon plays among the huge mimosas?"). The song is one of the glories of coloratura literature, making taxing demands on vocal agility, but rewarding in its splendor of fancy and its deft effects of pseudo-Oriental color. The bells blend charmingly with the staccato flights of the high soprano voice. And for Lakmé the song about the outcast maiden has a poignant parallel in her own predicament. As the song ends, Gerald rushes forward, his ardor reviving at the sight of the Hindu girl. But Lakmé is alarmed as Gerald rapturously greets her. In the brief love duet that follows, Lakmé urges Gerald to join her in a secret grotto, where she may hide and guard him. Nilakantha now approaches, sneaks up on the British officer, and, driving a dagger into him, escapes. With a frantic cry, Lakmé rushes to Gerald. But when she realizes that the wound is not fatal, her mood brightens and in her joy she exclaims, "You are mine forever! I shall live only for you! May God protect our love!"

The exotic marketplace in Act II, as staged during the 1930's at the Metropolitan Opera House in New York

Lily Pons as Lakmé, surrounded by deadly blossoms

ACT III

SCENE: *A forest in India.* A hut stands under a huge tree deep in a tropical forest, with brilliant flowers blooming on all sides. Here Lakmé and her slave have carried the wounded Gerald, and while he lies on a bed of leaves, Lakmé watches over him, singing soothing melodies. Gerald finally opens his eyes and greets her ecstatically in a song of dreamy beauty, *"Je me souviens, sans voix, inanimée, je te voyais sur mes lèvres penchée"* ("I remember how I saw you bent over my lips, voiceless and still"). Gerald is more enamored than ever of the lovely Hindu maiden, who is nursing him back to health. Lakmé now goes to fetch water from a sacred spring, having solemnly assured Gerald that all who drink from this spring remain forever faithful in love. During her absence Frédéric, searching anxiously for Gerald, at last finds him and greets him warmly. When he realizes how much in love his friend is with Lakmé, he reminds him of his duty to his regiment, which has been ordered away. Soon Lakmé returns, and the lovers drink the magic water. While they do so, the sound of martial music comes from the distance, and Gerald starts up eagerly at the thought of his regiment. Observing this, Lakmé now knows that her hold on the British officer is broken. Secretly she culls a blossom of the deadly *Datura stramonium* and swallows it. Nilakantha enters. Furious at the sight of Gerald near his daughter, he commands his followers to kill him, but Lakmé restrains them. "If the gods demand a victim in expiation," she cries out to her father, "let them call me!" Terrified, Nilakantha watches her reel as she exclaims to Gerald, "You have given me the sweetest dream under heaven!" Lakmé dies with a smile on her lips, as Gerald gives an anguished cry of "Dead!" Raising his head, Nilakantha declares gravely, "She is now amid the splendor of the skies."

Gerald (Giovanni Martinelli), Frédéric (Giuseppe de Luca) in Metropolitan Opera production

Lohengrin

CHARACTERS

Henry the Fowler, *King of Germany*	*Bass*	Frederick of Telramund, *Count of*	
Lohengrin, *a Knight of the Grail*	*Tenor*	Brabant	*Baritone*
Elsa of Brabant	*Soprano*	Ortrud, *his wife*	*Contralto*
		The King's Herald	*Baritone*

Saxon, Thuringian, and Brabantian Counts and Nobles, Ladies of Honor, Pages, Attendants
The action takes place at Antwerp during the first half of the tenth century.

OPERA IN THREE ACTS. Music by Richard Wagner. Libretto in German by the composer, based upon medieval legends. First produced at Weimar, Germany, August 28, 1850, under the direction of Franz Liszt. First American production, Stadt Theater, New York, April 3, 1871, in German. It was given in Italian at the New York Academy of Music, March 23, 1874, with a cast including Christine Nilsson as Elsa, Annie Louise Cary as Ortrud, Italo Campanini as Lohengrin, Giuseppe del Puente as Telramund, and Nannetti as the King. It was in Italian also that *Lohengrin* entered the Metropolitan's repertoire on November 7, 1883, the cast being Christine Nilsson, Emmy Fursch-Madi, Italo Campanini, Giuseppe Kaschmann, and Franco Novara. This opera has been a very popular one at the Metropolitan, having been given there over 350 times, more often than any other in the German repertory.

Wagner's *Rienzi* had been very successful when produced at the Dresden Opera; *The Flying Dutchman* had been something of a failure, and *Tannhäuser* had appealed even less to early audiences. Thus Wagner could not succeed in having his next opera, *Lohengrin,* produced there, even though he held the post of royal conductor at that very theater. He had completed the orchestration in March 1848, and when in 1849 the wave of social unrest that was sweeping over Europe reached Dresden, he joined the popular uprising, believing that a more democratic form of government might improve artistic conditions. This "May Revolution," apparently successful at first, was soon suppressed by the military forces, and Wagner was compelled to make his escape from the country. An exile in Switzerland, he wrote to Franz Liszt the following April and begged him to produce *Lohengrin*. It is hard to realize at the present time the moral courage necessary for a man like Liszt to sponsor a work of Wagner's—Liszt, courted by kings, greatest of pianists, universally acknowledged, yet subject to endless criticism; Wagner, a political exile and comparatively unknown. Thanks to Liszt's friendly support, *Lohengrin* was produced at Weimar though not with much success. How could it have sounded with a small orchestra boasting only five first violins? Nevertheless, the opera grew in popularity, and was performed throughout Germany, so that in the course of time Wagner, still an exile, was able to say with some ironic truth that he was the only German who had not heard *Lohengrin*. Not until 1861, when, through the intervention of the Princess Metternich, he was permitted to return to Germany, was the composer enabled to hear his own opera, thirteen years after completing it.

To us the beauty of the score is familiar enough, but in the day of its origin it must have seemed like a strange language—this music which shows Wagner making another step in advance of *Tannhäuser* in the development of his style even as in *Tannhäuser* he had progressed beyond *The Flying Dutchman*. Here Wagner also reveals his increasing ability as a dramatist, for he made of the old legend with which he dealt a much more dramatic and human story than one would have expected. The character Lohengrin is a symbol of the man who, in Wagner's own words, seeks "the woman who would not call for explanations or defense, but who should love him with an unconditioned love."

PRELUDE

The Prelude, an epitome of the entire opera and one of Wagner's great inspirations, has for its one and only theme the "Grail," the sacred vessel of the Last Supper. The "story" of the Prelude, paraphrased from Wagner's own explanation, is this: "In the wonderful blue of the sky, a vision appears: angels bearing the Grail. Gradually coming earthward, its effulgent glory is shed on the worshiper who kneels transported in ecstasy. The celestial vision then recedes and disappears into the blue of the sky." This is wonderfully expressed in the Prelude with its gradual crescendo, magnificent climax, and ethereal close.

Bayreuth, 1894: Lohengrin (Emil Gerhauser), Elsa (Lillian Nordica)

Marianne Brandt as Ortrud, 1880's

ACT I

SCENE: *The banks of the Scheldt River, near Antwerp.* Seated upon a throne beneath the Oak of Justice is Henry the Fowler, King of Germany. On one side of him are gathered the knights and nobles of Saxony and Thuringia; opposite them are the counts and nobles of Brabant, headed by Frederick of Telramund; beside him, his wife Ortrud. The King has come to gather an army together, but he finds the people of Brabant torn in dissension. The trouble is due to the disappearance of young Duke Godfrey of Brabant, who, with his sister Elsa, lived under the care of Telramund. Telramund advances to make the charge that Elsa herself has killed the boy in the hope that she would succeed to the estate left by the elder duke. So certain is he of Elsa's guilt, says he, that he has married Ortrud instead. Telramund is indeed a knight of proved courage and loyalty, for in a fight against the Danes, he saved the life of the King. Yet Henry the Fowler is loath to believe the monstrous charge of fratricide against the girl, and commands that she be brought before him. Elsa, accompanied by her women attendants, approaches, a mystic look in her deep blue eyes. Replying to Telramund's charge, the King decrees that justice shall be done through ordeal by battle. Elsa is asked to name her champion. She at first declines and, when urged, replies by telling of a wonderful, mysterious vision she had, in which a knight in shining armor came to her protection. The soft, ethereal music of the Grail accompanies her words, its shimmering colors and harmonies bring-

Helen Traubel, Elsa at the 1945 Metropolitan opening

ing a vivid impression of her dream. Elsa exclaims in her ecstasy that this glorious knight shall be her champion.

Four trumpeters blow a summons to the four points of the compass, and the Herald calls for a champion to step forward to defend Elsa. There is no answer, but Elsa confidently declares that her champion abides in a remote place. She asks the Herald to repeat the call. In the meantime, Ortrud looks upon her with an evil gleam in her eyes. The King, however, is touched by the young girl's trust. Whereupon the Herald repeats the summons, and after a few anxious moments for Elsa, who falls to her knees in prayer, there is a commotion among the nobles nearest the river edge. Excitement seizes them; they walk up and down, peering into the distance, and presently they shout that a miracle is taking place. There is a swan drawing a boat, in the prow of which is a stalwart warrior. The radiant theme of the "Deliverer," which was first heard in "Elsa's Dream," sounds in the orchestra. The people now become more and more agitated, and almost all crowd the riverbank to watch the approach of this strange knight in shining armor, as his boat is drawn shoreward by a swan.

As his strange conveyance nears the bank, the knight steps on land. He takes leave of his swan, ending his song with the words "*Leb' wohl, leb' wohl, mein lieber Schwan*" ("Farewell, farewell, my beloved swan"). A mood of awe settles over the assemblage, who sing of the wonder of the event they have just witnessed.

The knight, having made obeisance to the King, advances to Elsa and, his gaze resting upon her radiant beauty, tells her that he has come at her summons, and asks if she will accept him as her betrothed, and Elsa, in an emotional transport, readily does. Continuing, he declares in the utmost solemnity that if he should succeed as her champion and become her husband there is one promise she must make: she must never ask whence he came, his rank, or his name. She promises, demurely. Again he repeats his charge; Elsa wholeheartedly accepts.

King Henry prays that the result of the combat may be heaven's own judgment. The prayer is repeated by the King and the four other principals, and, as the chorus joins them, there is a great and exciting crescendo.

The nobles warn Telramund that he may not hope to worst such a heaven-sent champion; but Telramund, urged on by his wife, will not retire. A field of battle is measured off by six nobles who solemnly stride forward and plant their spears to form a complete circle. The King beats three times with his sword upon his shield, and the fight begins. The white knight succeeds in striking Telramund to earth, but mercifully spares his life. Her innocence proved, Elsa plights her troth to the stranger amid the cheering of the crowd, while Telramund, unobserved and in disgrace, drags himself to the feet of Ortrud, who is still uncowed.

Herbert Janssen as Count Frederick of Telramund

Telramund (Walter Berry), Lohengrin (Sándor Kónya)

ACT II

SCENE: *In the fortress of Antwerp.* It is night; the moon precipitates gloomy shadows off the battlements of the great castle that rises in the background. On the steps of the cathedral, at the right of the courtyard, Telramund and Ortrud, clad in the habiliments of disgrace, crouch dejectedly. Telramund irritably blames his wife for having deceived him. Skillfully she replies that this strange knight has won by magic; if he could be compelled to divulge his name and state, his power would cease. Elsa alone has the right to compel him to reveal this secret. Possessed of it, Telramund can freely fight him again, for the first loss of blood will weaken this stranger and reduce him to nothing. Through her magical practices she has divined all this. The last of her race, Ortrud clings to the old religion of the ancient gods, Wotan and Freia, whose wrath she now calls down upon Elsa and her champion. Telramund has listened breathlessly.

Elsa comes to her window at the left of the courtyard and confides her happiness to the nocturnal breezes, in the expressive aria *"Euch Lüften, die mein Klagen"* ("Ye wandering breezes"). Ortrud bids Telramund be gone, then imploringly calls Elsa's name. The girl is startled at hearing her name through the darkness; Ortrud feigns repentance, and begs for protection, both of which, in her new-found happiness, Elsa grants. At the same time Ortrud succeeds in implanting the seeds of doubt in the girl's heart, hinting at mystery and magic, things easily believed under the circumstances. But outwardly Elsa rejects all suspicion and takes Ortrud with her into the palace.

Trumpets answering one another from the turrets of the castle announce the dawn of Elsa's wedding day. With the growing light, the courtyard begins to bustle with preparations. Servitors pass hurriedly; then come knights glittering in their armor and nobles arrayed in festive attire, a blazing pageant in the sunlight. A herald announces that Telramund has been banished and that the mysterious champion, having refused the dukedom, has been proclaimed leader of the country's forces.

The orchestra begins a soft, graceful melody while a long procession of women, dressed in the court robes of the period, come gradually from the palace and, slowly crossing the courtyard, group themselves around the doorway of the cathedral. As Elsa approaches the cathedral, all joyfully shout, "Hail! Elsa of Brabant!" and voices and orchestra swell in a climax of radiant beauty.

Just as Elsa sets foot on the church steps, Ortrud springs before her—a very different Ortrud from the suppliant of a few hours previous. She now demands priority over the bride-elect of a nameless knight. Her stormy outburst causes considerable excitement; soon the King and Elsa's champion appear. Ortrud is silenced; the knight supports his trembling bride, and the procession is resumed. Suddenly from behind a buttress where he has been lurking, Telramund steps out before them and wildly proclaims that this unknown knight is a sorcerer; the swan-drawn boat is evidence enough, and he demands his name. But the King will not listen, and the banished pair are driven away in disgrace. Elsa, her wedding processional twice interrupted, is filled with fear and grief, yet she affirms her trust in her defender. The procession is again resumed and the music grows to a splendid climax as they enter the cathedral.

ACT III

Before the curtain rises on Act III there is an orchestral prelude which, like that to the opera itself, is a great favorite of concert audiences. In this piece Wagner sets the festive mood for the wedding, the joy of the lovers, and the purity of Elsa, and he also reintroduces the ominous theme of "Warning," which has already been heard in the previous scenes.

SCENE 1: *The bridal chamber.* As the music grows softer, the curtain rises upon the bridal chamber, and the bridal procession enters. The ladies are leading Elsa, the King and the nobles conducting the bridegroom. They sing the familiar "Bridal Chorus." The procession encircles the chamber. Then, after saluting the bridal pair, the guests depart, their song gradually dying away in the distance.

Now it is that Elsa first shows the doubt in her

heart. The strange knight gently reproves her. She scarcely hears, for the poison instilled into her mind is at work. She grows more and more insistent, her own curiosity strengthened by her lover's kind protests. She fears that he will be lost to her, that he will return to the unknown land whence he has come—even now she thinks she sees the swan returning for him. In a sudden frenzy she demands to know his name. At this very moment Telramund and four henchmen steal into the chamber, swords drawn. Elsa quickly hands her husband his sword, and with the weapon he strikes Telramund dead. His followers cringingly sink down.

Lohengrin picks up Elsa, who has fallen senseless, places her on the couch, and bids Telramund's men to take up his body and bring it to the King. He then strikes a bell, summoning two lady attendants, and he instructs them to dress Elsa in her choicest attire for her appearance before the King. There, he says, he will reveal to her who he is, the rank he bears.

SCENE 2: *The banks of the Scheldt River, near Antwerp.* At the Oak of Justice, the King and the nobles await the knight and, when he appears, the nobles hail him as their leader. Their rejoicing gives way to amazement as they see the body of Telramund being borne along, and Elsa approaching, her face pale as death. The knight explains the slaying of Telramund; now he is compelled to answer the question Elsa has asked. From the orchestra are heard the ethereal harmonies of the Grail, and the knight begins his narrative.

He says that he is one of the knights of the Grail at the distant place Monsalvat; that once each year a dove is sent down from heaven to renew the wondrous powers of the Grail. All who see it are magically cleansed of earthly sin, the knights' guardians are equipped with invincible might, before which all evil influences lose their powers. Yet the knights must remain unknown for this might to be with them; if they are recognized, as they roam about righting the wrongs of the world, they must return. Further, he reveals that he is the son of Parsifal, King of the Grail, and that his name is Lohengrin.

The people express awe at his narrative. The swan is seen approaching, and Elsa gives way to her grief. Lohengrin bids her farewell most tenderly, and leaves with her his horn, his sword, and his ring—for her brother, should he ever return.

As Lohengrin steps aboard his boat, Ortrud suddenly appears from among the crowd and with a cry of triumph exclaims that her magic is superior, for it was she who changed Elsa's brother into the swan that is now to draw Lohengrin away. Thus have Ortrud's gods rewarded Elsa's faithlessness! But she has spoken too soon. Lohengrin kneels for a moment in prayer while all eyes are instinctively turned upon him. The white dove of the Holy Grail flutters down from above, the swan sinks, and in its place, Lohengrin raises from the water a boy in shining raiment and lifts him to land. "Behold the ruler of Brabant!" cries he. The boy rushes into Elsa's arms, while the dove mysteriously draws the boat on its course to Monsalvat. Lohengrin is seen, ere he disappears in the distance, his head bent sorrowfully, leaning upon his shield. "My husband! My husband!" cries Elsa, and sinks back lifeless in her brother's arms.

Wieland Wagner staging of Act II bridal procession, with Ingrid Bjoner as Elsa, Metropolitan Opera House, 1966

Louise

CHARACTERS

Louise	*Soprano*	Irma	*Soprano*
Her Mother	*Contralto*	An Errand Girl	*Mezzo-soprano*
Her Father	*Bass*	The King of the Fools	*Tenor*
Julien	*Tenor*		

Peddlers, Working People, Grisettes, Street Boys, Bohemians
The action takes place in Paris at the end of the nineteenth century.

"MUSICAL ROMANCE" in four acts. Music and libretto in French by Gustave Charpentier. First performance at the Paris Opéra-Comique, February 2, 1900. American première at Oscar Hammerstein's Manhattan Opera House, New York, January 3, 1908, with Mary Garden making her American debut in the title role. First Metropolitan performance, January 15, 1921, with Geraldine Farrar in the name part. Other notable interpreters of the title role include Lucrezia Bori, Grace Moore, Dorothy Kirsten and Arlene Saunders.

Louise brought its indigent, socialist-minded composer fame and money. Although it stirred up a sharp controversy because of its style and content, the opera won an emphatic success with the Parisian public, in the long run becoming the most popular French opera since Massenet's *Manon*. Several factors combined to make a spectacular novelty of this so-called proletarian opera. First, there was Charpentier's musical language, protean and many-faceted in its vivid evocation of a giant metropolis in the varied moods of its teeming life. This was music pulsating with communal life, music through which wove brief, evanescent themes in a fascinating web of impressionism. And in emotional range, from gay vivacity and hearty abandon to tense drama, this music was French to the core. Then, the setting of *Louise* was something of a jolt to many reared operatically on more remote locales. Here was con-

temporary realism with a vengeance—the drab family life of Parisian tenement-house dwellers into which the devil-may-care freedom of a struggling young poet brought a disturbing note. The mansard atmosphere of working-class drudgery was a marked change from the fabled tapestries of standard opera. But the people soon came to feel the great human throb of *Louise*. The pulse of a wondrous city beat in its texture. This was Paris enshrined in warm, vibrant tone, the Paris of bright, cheery street life, the Paris of soft, sensuous nights, the Paris of Montmartre. Truly the protagonist of this opera was not the girl Louise, but the city Paris. Yet Louise is its incarnation of conflicting feelings, the symbol, perhaps, of the new freedom, the break with convention and outmoded codes. Louise's final chant of liberation is paralleled in the masterly symphonic hymn expressing the city's awakening to fresh life.

For Mary Garden, Friday, the thirteenth of April, 1900, was indeed a lucky day. She was in Paris studying. As an understudy at the Opéra-Comique she had learned and mastered the role of Louise. She was at the opera house on that fateful Friday when Marthe Rioton, who had created the part, fell suddenly ill and was unable to continue after the second act. This was Miss Garden's great chance. She was promptly summoned by the management. Her name was announced to a public that had never heard of her and was probably none too

Mary Garden as Louise, the role that brought her fame

happy over the abrupt substitution. The fair unknown sang the last two acts and the Parisians were at her feet. In the years that followed, Mary Garden sang Louise over two hundred times at the Paris Opéra-Comique. Her interpretation of the working-class heroine was one of the most absorbing portraits in the soprano wing of the opera gallery.

ACT I

SCENE: *The attic flat of Louise's family in a Paris tenement house.* Julien, a young, easygoing artist who lives across the way, is secretly conversing with Louise. Her parents frown on his attentions because of his carefree Bohemian ways, hoping for someone steadier for their daughter. It develops that Louise's parents are so bitter about Julien that they have refused to answer a letter of his. Louise now threatens that should this happen again, she will give in and elope with him. Julien has written a second letter. Louise is now eager to know when Julien, whom she has known intimately for some weeks only, first knew he was in love with her. He explains in a tender passage beginning *"Depuis longtemps j'habitais cette chambre"* (*"I occupied this room for some time"*). He had lived in a room in the house next door, never realizing that a beautiful girl lived so close to him. Then he had met Louise, and a great hope and joy awoke in him; new songs of love had come to his lips. The two are so occupied with one another that they hear and see nothing else. They are unaware that Louise's mother is standing there listening. The startled lovers separate, and the mother grasps Louise by the arm,

violently upbraiding her. Sarcastically, she quotes some of Julien's impassioned words and calls him an impudent ne'er-do-well. Leaping to her lover's defense, Louise retorts that he is none of these things; that, moreover, she is old enough to make up her own mind.

The quarreling is interrupted by the entrance of Louise's father, who is ready for food and rest after a hard day's work. But the bickering is renewed the moment the father opens Julien's second letter. The young neighbor is again asking to marry Louise, and the father now seems sympathetic. Extremely fond of Louise, he is prepared to yield to her wishes, but first they must look into the young man's character. The mother, however, puts her foot down: she will not have Julien as a son-in-law! He is a bad lot. The father, to end the matter, asks Louise to promise she will not see him again, and Louise, with an affectionate hug, gives him her word. Meanwhile, preparations for supper are being made, with Louise and her mother setting the table and bringing the food. The father tenderly asks Louise to read from the evening paper to him. When by chance she begins reading an article about Paris in the spring and the gay festivities in store, the irony of it, in her present plight, brings a sob from the unhappy girl.

ACT II

SCENE 1: *A street at the foot of the hill of Montmartre.* A light mist lies over the rooftops of Paris, which is gradually coming to life. We begin to hear its first signs of awakening in the orchestra, slowly evoking the coming of dawn and the return of bustling life. As the shadows of night disappear with the last few stragglers of the streets, men and women cross the scene on their way to work. Myriad sounds and street cries enliven the morning picture of a city going about its business. Louise and her mother appear. As they reach the workshop, the girl takes leave of her mother. Julien, who has been strolling about with his Bohemian friends, waits for the mother to depart and then brings Louise out of the shop. As Julien's written request to the parents for Louise's hand has again been turned down, he now reminds her of her promise. They must run away together! Louise listens avidly to the call of love and youth and spring, and just as she is about to yield, a stern sense of duty holds her back and she asks Julien to be patient. Perhaps someday . . . Louise rushes back into the shop, leaving Julien to nurse his grief amid the street cries of Paris.

SCENE 2: *A dressmaker's workroom.* At their sewing machines, a group of girls are singing and joking—all but Louise, who is buried in thought. Her companions begin speculating out loud on the reason for her serious mood, Irma suggesting that she is in love. This Louise denies angrily. From the courtyard below now come the soft strains of a serenade as Julien returns with carefree comrades. The girls shriek with delight and begin flirting with the serenader. Then, as the popular love song turns to an impassioned reproach of woman's faithlessness, the girls become bored, mock him, and turn their attention to a passing band. Louise, unable to pretend any longer, rushes from the shop to join Julien. The other sewing girls look out the window and laugh as they observe the couple together.

ACT III

SCENE: *A garden and house on the side of the hill of Montmartre.* The shadows of night are gathering. In the garden of their little house Louise and Julien are together, wrapped in their love. Beyond the garden the city is spread out in a great panorama, and in the distance lights are beginning to glimmer. The lovers have defied the parents' veto and are living together. Louise recalls the day she first gave herself to Julien—"*Depuis le jour où je me suis donnée.*" The memory of it still leaves her trembling, Louise sings in a passionate aria, for everything about them seems to smile on their love. "In the garden of my heart a new joy sings!" Louise exclaims. While more and more lights of the city begin to pierce the darkness, the lovers join in an ecstatic duet, and through their combined song the throbbing life of the city seems to chant. Scarcely have they reentered their villa, when a troop of Bohemian revelers arrives on the scene. They hang lanterns about the garden and call out the lovers. In an elaborate ceremony Louise is crowned Queen of Montmartre. After the King of the Fools delivers a mock heroic talk, all bow respectfully before the new queen, and the crowd resumes its merrymaking with song and dance. The festivities come to an abrupt halt as Louise's mother enters, her appearance being a signal for the crowd to disperse. With mounting grief Louise hears the bad news: her father is ill, dying from sorrow over his daughter's elopement with Julien. Bitterly her mother assures her that if she wants him to live, she must come back at once. Louise, realizing how strong her love for her father is, consents to go. Julien permits Louise to depart on the mother's promise that she will be free to come back to him.

ACT IV

SCENE: *The attic flat of Louise's family* (same as Act I). Again with her parents, Louise is beginning to sulk over the restraints of home life. Though still weak, her father is well enough now to return to work. While Louise is in her room and the mother in the kitchen, the father begins to complain of the worker's lot, how it is made doubly hard by ungrateful children. Louise suddenly flares up over the mother's broken promise to allow her to return to Julien. The father, in a conciliatory mood, draws her onto his knees and sings a tender little lullaby to her, as if she were a slumbering infant. A haunting melody passes through the orchestra as the father recalls quieter and happier days in their home life. When Louise replies there would be no quarrel if the parents did not stand in the way of her happiness, the father reminds her of all they have done for her. To this Louise retorts that she will not be cooped up, that she is starving for freedom. One word leads to another, and soon a heated quarrel develops. Excited to a pitch of delirium, Louise shouts out defiantly that she wants nothing but her Julien and the free, unfettered life of Paris. In a rage, the father opens the door and orders her out of the house. As Louise dashes out, the father runs to the door and shouts remorsefully after her, "Louise! Louise!" Then, in a fit of uncontrollable fury at the city that has lured his daughter away, he cries out, shaking his fist, "Paris! Paris!"

New York City Opera staging of Act IV, with Arlene Saunders (Louise), Norman Treigle and Claramae Turner (parents)

The Love of Three Oranges

LYUBOV K TREM APELSINAM

CHARACTERS

The King of Clubs, *ruler of an imaginary kingdom, whose costume is that of the playing card*	Bass	The Magician Tchelio, *who protects the King*	Bass
The Prince, *his son*	Tenor	Fata Morgana, *a sorceress*	Soprano
The Princess Clarissa, *the King's niece*	Contralto	Smeraldina, *her servant*	Mezzo-soprano
		Linetta ⎫ *princesses,*	Contralto
Leandro, *the King's prime minister dressed as the King of Spades*	Baritone	Nicoletta ⎬ *three oranges*	Mezzo-soprano
		Ninetta ⎭	Soprano
Truffaldino, *a jester*	Tenor	Cleonte, *the Cook (woman)*	Hoarse Bass
Pantalon, *a courtier in the confidence of the King*	Baritone	Furfarello, *a demon*	Bass
		Master of Ceremonies	Tenor
		The Herald	Bass
		The Trumpet	Bass Trombone

Joys, Glooms, Emptyheads, Jesters, Demons, Doctors, Courtiers, Monsters, Drunkards, Gluttons, Guards, Servants, Soldiers

The action takes place in an imaginary kingdom in the mythical long ago.

OPERA IN FOUR ACTS, with a prologue. Music by Serge Prokofiev. Libretto in Russian by the composer, after Carlo Gozzi's *Fiaba dell' Amore delle Tre Melarancie (The Tale of the Love of the Three Oranges)* First performance, December 30, 1921, at the Chicago Auditorium, by the Chicago Opera Company, in French, with the composer conducting, and Nina Koshetz making her American debut as the Fata Morgana. New York première, by the Chicago Opera Company, February 14, 1922, at the Manhattan Opera House, the composer again conducting. The work is now firmly established in the repertory of the New York City Opera.

Gozzi, the eighteenth-century dramatist and storyteller, had a genius for giving fresh form to old tales and legends and for devising new ones. The tales were called *fiabe,* or fables. Later dramatists found them a fertile source of suggestions for plot, and opera composers have been no less indebted to this gifted teller of tales. Puccini's *Turandot* is only one of at least six operas founded on Gozzi's masterly little *fiaba* of legendary China. The vein of satire running through Gozzi's *fiabe* has also exerted a strong appeal on subsequent writers and composers. It is not surprising that Prokofiev, no mean satirist himself, found inspiration for an opera in one of these delightful *fiabe.* Typical in this "burlesque opera" is Prokofiev's penchant for witty, sardonic writing. Moreover, in its ingenious handling of childlike fantasy and enchantment the opera belongs with Prokofiev's *Peter and the Wolf.* This cleverly evoked world of satiric sorcery is perhaps far removed from Prokofiev's main areas of artistic interest, which were Russian history and the fresh exploitation of symphonic form. The pungent note of modernism is readily heard in this music,

Clarissa (Muriel Greenspon) conspires with Leandro (Herbert Beattie) and Smeraldina (Beverly Evans). (New York City Opera)

though, compared with the more dissonant writing of Prokofiev's piano and violin concertos, it is a kind of modified modernism, diverting in its sophisticated discourse on the child's world of fairyland wonder.

PROLOGUE

SCENE: *Stage, with lowered curtain and grand proscenium, on each side of which are little balconies and balustrades.* An artistic discussion is on among four sets of personages on what kind of play should be enacted on the present occasion. The Glooms, clad in appropriately somber robes, argue for tragedy. The Joys, in costumes befitting their temperament, hold out for romantic comedy. The Emptyheads disagree with both and call for frank farce. At last, the Jesters (also called the Cynics) enter, and succeed in silencing the squabbling groups. Presently a herald enters to announce that the King of Clubs is grieving because his son never smiles. The various personages now take refuge in balconies at the sides of the stage, and from there make comments on the play that is enacted. But for their lack of poise and dignity, they would remind one of the chorus in Greek drama.

ACT I

SCENE: *The King's palace.* The King of Clubs, in despair over his son's hopeless dejection, has summoned physicians to diagnose the ailment. After elaborate consultation, the doctors inform the King that to be cured the Prince must learn to laugh. The Prince, alas, like most hypochondriacs, has no sense of humor. The King resolves to try the prescribed remedy. Truffaldino, one of the comic figures, is now assigned the task of preparing a gay festival and masquerade to bring cheer into the Prince's smileless life. All signify approval of the plan except the Prime Minister Leandro, who is plotting with the King's niece Clarissa to seize the throne after slaying the Prince. In a sudden evocation of fire and smoke, the wicked witch Fata Morgana appears, followed by a swarm of little devils. As a fiendish game of cards ensues between the witch, who is aiding Leandro's plot, and Tchelio, the court magician, attendant demons burst into a wild dance. This is graphically depicted in the deftly contrived music of an eerie waltz-scherzo. The Fata Morgana wins and, with a peal of diabolical laughter, vanishes. The jester vainly tries to make the lugubrious Prince laugh, and as festival music comes from afar, the two go off in that direction, whereupon the orchestra plays the brilliant and bizarre March, built around a swaying theme of irresistible charm.

ACT II

SCENE: *The main courtroom of the royal palace.* In the grand court of the palace, merrymakers are busy trying to make the Prince laugh, but their efforts are unavailing for two reasons: the Prince's nature is unresponsive to gaiety, and the evil Fata Morgana is among them spoiling the fun. Recognizing her, guards seize the sorceress and attempt to eject her. In the struggle that ensues she turns an awkward somersault, a sight so ridiculous that even the Prince is forced to laugh out loud. All rejoice, for the Prince, at long last, is cured! In revenge, the Fata Morgana now pronounces a dire curse on the recovered Prince: He shall again be miserable until he has won the "love of the three oranges."

ACT III

SCENE: *A desert.* In the desert the magician Tchelio meets the Prince and pronounces an incantation against the cook who guards the three oranges in the nearby castle. As the Prince and his companion, the jester Truffaldino, head for the castle, the

218

orchestra plays a scherzo, fascinating in its ingeniously woven web of fantasy. Arriving at the castle, the Prince and Truffaldino obtain the coveted oranges after overcoming many hazards. Fatigued, the Prince now goes to sleep. A few moments later Truffaldino is seized by thirst and, as he cuts open one of the oranges, a beautiful princess steps out, begging for water. Since it is decreed that the oranges must be opened at the water's edge, the helpless princess promptly dies of thirst. Startled, Truffaldino at length works up courage enough to open a second orange, and, lo! another princess steps out, only to meet the same fate. Truffaldino rushes out. The spectators in the balconies at the sides of the stage argue excitedly over the fate of the princess in the third orange. When the Prince awakens, he takes the third orange and cautiously proceeds to open it. The Princess Ninetta emerges this time, begs for water, and is about to succumb to a deadly thirst, when the Jesters rush to her rescue with a bucket of water.

ACT IV

SCENE: *The throne room of the royal palace.* The Prince and the Princess Ninetta are forced to endure many more trials through the evil power of the Fata Morgana. At one juncture the Princess is even changed into a mouse. The couple finally overcome all the hardships the witch has devised, and in the end are happily married. Thus foiled in her wicked sorcery, the Fata Morgana is captured and led away, leaving traitorous Leandro and Clarissa to face the King's ire without the aid of her magic powers.

The King of Clubs (Noel Tyl) and his melancholy son, the Prince (David Thaw), in the New York City Opera staging

Lucia di Lammermoor

CHARACTERS

Lord Enrico (Henry) Ashton,
   of Lammermoor   *Baritone*
Lucia (Lucy), *his sister*   *Soprano*
Alisa (Alice), *companion to*
   Lucia   *Mezzo-soprano*
Raimondo (Raymond) Bide-the-Bent,
   chaplain at Lammermoor   *Bass*

Edgardo (Edgar), *master of*
   Ravenswood   *Tenor*
Lord Arturo (Arthur) Bucklaw,
   Lucia's prospective husband   *Tenor*
Normando (Norman), *follower of*
   Lord Ashton   *Tenor*

Followers of Ashton, Inhabitants of Lammermoor, Wedding Guests

The action takes place in Scotland near the close of the seventeenth century.

OPERA IN THREE ACTS. Music by Gaetano Donizetti. Text in Italian by Salvatore Cammarano, after Sir Walter Scott's novel *The Bride of Lammermoor.* First performance, at the Teatro San Carlo, Naples, September 26, 1835. Initial United States production, in French, at the Théâtre d'Orléans, New Orleans, December 28, 1841. First New York performance, Niblo's Garden, in Italian, September 15, 1843. Also given at the Park Theater, in English, November 17, 1845. The opera obtained its first hearing at the Metropolitan Opera House on October 24, 1883, it being the debut of Marcella Sembrich. This was the second work to be produced at the Metropolitan, whose inaugural took place two evenings before, with *Faust.* From Adelina Patti to Joan Sutherland the opera has been the *sine qua non* of coloratura sopranos. Among the most celebrated: Melba, Tetrazzini, Galli-Curci, Pons and Callas.

This work was first produced when its composer had recently won the position of professor of composition at the Real Collegio di Musica (Royal College of Music), Naples; and it gained for him an abiding place in popular affection. Some modernists scoff at this, one of Donizetti's tragic masterpieces; it is performed too often and regarded merely as a vehicle for showing off some popular prima donna. In re-

ality its melodies are fresh and, though simple, they possess genuine beauty; even in the ornate passages they are basically expressive of the situation in which they are placed in the drama. The ensemble numbers, especially the world-renowned Sextet, rank among the finest in Italian opera.

ACT I

SCENE 1: *A wood near Lammermoor.* In the somber gardens of Lammermoor Castle the guards and their leader Norman are discussing a stranger who has been seen prowling around the place, perhaps on secret mischief. The guards leave hurriedly to search for him, but Norman remains behind to suggest to Lord Henry Ashton, who now enters, that the intruder may very likely be none other than Edgar of Ravenswood. Lord Henry is Edgar's mortal enemy and has recently acquired through treachery the Ravenswood estates. The talkative Norman further narrates, in the hearing of the kindly disposed Bide-the-Bent, that one day Lord Henry's sister Lucy was saved from the attack of an angry bull by some unknown person. She has fallen in love with him and secretly meets him every day. Lord Ashton's anger grows even more intense when the guards report that

Marcella Sembrich, first Metropolitan Lucia, in 1883

they saw the intruder and were able to recognize him as the hated Edgar. Ashton vows speedy vengeance.

SCENE 2: *A park near the castle.* Lucy, accompanied by her maid Alice, awaits Edgar at their daily trysting place. She looks with dread at a fountain nearby and tells Alice the legend about one of the Ravenswoods who stabbed his sweetheart beside it. To a wistful, pathetic melody she vows that she has seen in the dark waters an apparition of the murdered woman, in the aria *"Regnava nel silenzio"* ("The night reigned in silence").

Edgar arrives, a gloomy figure with black-plumed cavalier hat and cloak of sable. This, he tells her, must be their last meeting, for he has been ordered to France. But he proposes first to go to Henry and endeavor to end the mortal feud which exists between the two families. Lucy, knowing her brother only too well, declares that it would be useless, and entreats Edgar to keep their love secret lest they be forever parted. The information causes Edgar again to renew his vow of vengeance. Then they begin their lovely duet of parting, *"Verranno a te sull' aure"* ("My ardent sighs will come to you").

ACT II

SCENE 1: *An anteroom in Lammermoor castle.* Edgar was mistaken in his supposition that Lord Ashton's conduct is entirely a matter of personal hatred. In reality Ashton is in desperate straits and his only chance to improve his fortune is to have Lucy marry Lord Arthur Bucklaw. He intercepts all of Lucy's and Edgar's letters, and now he has forged in Ravenswood's handwriting a letter which seems to prove beyond doubt that Lucy is betrayed, her lover having deserted her for another. Ashton heaps upon her his scorn for having dared love his enemy and

asserts that he will be disgraced and ruined unless she consents to marry Lord Arthur Bucklaw, as he has arranged. The unfortunate girl, stricken nearly dumb with grief, finally consents to the sacrifice.

SCENE 2: *The great hall of the castle.* In the great armorial hall of the castle, knights and ladies are assembled to witness the wedding, and sing a gay chorus of welcome; but the pale, agitated appearance of the bride gives the lie to their joyful song. Ashton tries to explain away her condition by saying that she still mourns her mother. Wan and almost fainting, she is escorted to the table where a notary is preparing the marriage papers; then with trembling hands she signs the document that makes her Lady Arthur Bucklaw.

No sooner has she set down the pen than a stranger enters the room. All eyes are turned upon him in fear and amazement. Edgar of Ravenswood, sword in hand, pistol in belt, stalks boldly toward the table. At this most dramatic moment begins the famous Sextet *"Chi mi frena?"* (What restrains me?") It begins with Edgar and Henry; Edgar wonders why he has not rushed ahead to claim his vengeance and, on beholding the despairing Lucy, realizes that he still loves her. Henry fears for his own future and the effect that this excitement may have on his sister. The voices of Lucy and Bide-the-Bent enter, Lucy expressing her despair that death has not come to save her from this grief and shame, Bide-the-Bent kindly praying that heaven will aid and protect her. Now the voices of Alice, Arthur and the attendant knights and ladies unite in this prayer, but above the outpouring of all these conflicting feelings rise the tones of Lucy's lament, forming a climax of stirring effect.

Jan Peerce as Edgardo

The eternal enemies, Edgar and Ashton, rush at one another with drawn swords, but Bide-the-Bent restrains them, bidding them both, in heaven's name, to sheathe their weapons. Coldly asking Edgar the reason for his unwelcome visit, Ashton shows him the marriage contract. Unable to believe his eyes, Ravenswood turns to Lucy for confirmation; forlorn and in misery she tremblingly nods assent. Edgar, in furious rage, calls down the curse of heaven on Lucy and all her hated family and rushes away.

Joan Sutherland as Lucia, her first major success

ACT III

SCENE 1: *The tower of Ravenswood Castle* (often omitted). Ashton comes to the gloomy Ravenswood Castle and there challenges Edgar to a duel to take place at dawn. Amid the terrors of a terrific storm they unite in an agitated duet, praying that the vengeance-bringing morn may soon arrive.

SCENE 2: *The hall at Lammermoor Castle.* Meanwhile, at the castle, the wedding guests are still feasting and making merry. Suddenly the laughter ceases and the song dies upon their lips as Raymond enters, horror-stricken, and cries out that Lucy has gone mad and slain her husband. An instant later Lucy herself appears, pale and lovely, robed in white, her hair loose upon her shoulders. In her eyes gleams an unnatural light and her face bears the tender, questioning expression of one who strives to recall a dream. Her brain unable to endure a suffering too intense, Lucy is mad, indeed; but she is happy in her madness, for she believes herself with her lover.

This is the most familiar of the many "mad scenes" composers in the first half of the nineteenth century wrote for operatic prima donnas, and it has all the standard and popular ingredients—sweet melodies, coloratura scales, arpeggios and other decorations, passages in thirds with solo flute, flute imitations, and snatches from one or more melodies heard earlier in the opera. It is also, as was customary, divided into several sections with occasional comment from other characters on the stage, including the chorus. The Mad Scene from *Lucia*, however, is much more than coloratura fireworks; it is a legitimate and effective part of the drama. At its close, Lucy falls dying into the arms of Alice.

SCENE 3: *The tombs of the Ravenswoods.* As the night wears on, the lights still winking gaily from the castle at Lammermoor convey to the silent Edgar who stands amid the graves of the Ravenswoods no knowledge of these tragic events. In somber meditation, he soliloquizes, *"Tombe degli avi miei, l'ultimo avanzo d'una stirpe infelice. Deh! Raccogliete voi!"* ("Tombs of my ancestors, the last am I of a doomed race. Gather me unto you!"). Then, his thoughts instinctively turning to Lucy, Edgar decries Lucy's apparent treachery. Yet even as in self-pity he heaps reproaches upon the absent Lucy, he notes a train of mourners coming from the castle. He inquires whom they lament. And they tell him of Lucy's madness and of her love for him. She lies, they say, in the castle at the point of death. And as they speak, the sound of a tolling bell announces her death.

The reality of the tragedy dawning upon him, he vows that he has decided his own fate; he too, will die, hoping to join Lucy in heaven. He expresses these sentiments in the aria *"Tu che a Dio spiegasti l'ali"* ("Thou hast spread thy wings to heaven"). The others, including Raymond, try to restrain him from his suicidal purpose, but he plunges his dagger into his heart, and, as the chorus prays for his pardon, expires.

Anna Moffo in the Mad Scene at the Metropolitan Opera

Lucrezia Borgia

CHARACTERS

Don Alfonso D'Este, *Duke of Ferrara*	Bass	Astolfo ⎫ *secret agents of*	Bass
Lucrezia Borgia, *his Duchess*	Soprano	Gubetta ⎭ *Lucrezia Borgia*	Bass
Maffio Orsini, *a young nobleman*	Contralto	Rustighello, *an agent of the Duke's*	Tenor
Gennaro, *a young nobleman of unknown birth*	Tenor	Apostolo Gazella ⎫ *noblemen in*	Bass
		Jeppo Liverotto ⎪ *the service of*	Tenor
		Ascanio Petrucci ⎬ *the Republic*	Bass
		Oloferno Vitellozzo ⎭ *of Venice*	Tenor

Noblemen, Ladies in Waiting, Monks, Servants, Maskers, etc.

The action takes place in Venice and Ferrara in the early part of the sixteenth century.

OPERA IN PROLOGUE AND TWO ACTS. Music by Gaetano Donizetti. Libretto in Italian by Felice Romani, based on the tragedy of the same name by Victor Hugo. First performance, La Scala, Milan, December 26, 1833. First performance in the United States, at New Orleans, April 27, 1844. First and only performance at the Metropolitan Opera House, December 5, 1904, with Maria de Macchi (who was making her debut), Edyth Walker, Enrico Caruso, and Antonio Scotti. Revived in New York in concert to clamorous acclaim in 1965 by the American Opera Society—the occasion of the U.S. debut of Montserrat Caballé, launching one of the most brilliant careers in recent years.

Beginning at nineteen, Donizetti had composed more than forty operas by the time, at thirty-six, he produced *Lucrezia Borgia*—the fourth of his operas for the year 1833. Of all these earlier works, *Anna Bolena* is the only one ever heard these days—and that one not very often. Not that Lucrezia walks the stage today much more often than Anna, excepting in Italy. But into the early years of the twentieth century it maintained a very wide popularity, especially when it was sung—as it often was—by such vocal giants as Giulia Grisi or Therese Tietjens (as Lucrezia), Marietta Alboni, Sofia Scalchi, or Ernestine Schumann-Heink (as Orsini), and Mario or Enrico Caruso (as Gennaro).

One reason for its great success in the early nineteenth century was the horrific libretto. Donizetti asked his writer for scenes to arouse "emotions to make one shudder," scenes such as were not common in earlier opera. Romani, seizing on a sensational subject, obliged, and Donizetti composed tellingly powerful music, especially for the concerted numbers. In later operas, especially in Verdi, such effects were far surpassed, and we no longer shudder at *Lucrezia Borgia*. On the contrary, the opera is likely to be revived today only as a vehicle for an exponent of the old-fashioned art of *bel canto*, such as Montserrat Caballé, who may be far more able, with this music, to give intense pleasure through her technique and taste in *fioratura* and phrasing than through inspiring horror.

In Donizetti's time, as a matter of fact, the very name of Lucrezia Borgia could inspire horror. Beginning with the political enemies of her notable father and brother, Alexander and Caesar Borgia, rumors were spread about her penchant for poison and incest. Modern scholars have cleared her of these accusations and proved her to have been a charming, intelligent, and rather pretty blonde, with higher moral standards than her father, the Pope's. She died at thirty-nine of bearing a seventh child. Perhaps it is as well to forget these facts while listening to the opera.

Teatro dell'Opera, Rome: Banquet Hall in the Negroni Palace, where Lucrezia Borgia poisons her son, Gennaro

PROLOGUE

SCENE: *Terrace of the Grimani Palace in Venice.*
Within the palace a masked ball is going on, while a
group of six young noblemen in the diplomatic and
military service of the Republic of Venice are discussing the beauty of the Giudecca Canal (which
may be seen, with passing gondolas on it) and their
forthcoming assignment to Ferrara. The talk naturally turns to the Duchess of Ferrara, Lucrezia
Borgia, and her infamous acts. Count Orsini (a very
young man, whose role is assigned to a contralto)
insists on telling a story relating to her, but his best
friend, Gennaro, who knows the story well, goes to
sleep during the recital. Orsini's narrative, which is
punctuated by ejaculations of interest from his companions, tells how his life was saved by Gennaro
after a battle and how an aged giant of a man
dressed in black appeared to them in a wood and
solemnly warned the two young men to beware of
Lucrezia Borgia. They then leave the sleeping Gennaro to join the dancers.

Lucrezia, masked as everyone else is, enters the
terrace from a gondola, and after dismissing her
attendant spy Gubetta, is deeply moved by the sight
of Gennaro, her son by an earlier marriage, though
neither he nor anyone else knows this fact. She sings
an aria on his personal beauty (*"Com'è bello!"*),
and her husband, the Duke, passes by and recognizes
her. When she kisses Gennaro's hand, he awakens,
and immediately begins to tell her how attractive she
is. But something makes him tell her that there is
one woman to whom he is even more devoted—his
mother, whom he has never seen, but who sent him a
letter when he thought he was only a fisherman's

son, begging him never to try to find out who she
was. In the duet that follows she urges him always to
love that mother, and they pray together that the
two may meet some day. But in an intermission in
the dance Orsini returns with the others and recognizes Lucrezia at once even though she still wears
her mask. She tries to escape, but they block her
way, and each of the young men identifies himself as
a close relative of a nobleman whom Lucrezia has
had poisoned, drowned, or otherwise done away
with. The entire chorus is now in the room denounc-
ing the evil woman, but Gennaro, who has been trying to protect her, does not know who she is till Orsini
tears the mask from her face and names her. Gennaro is filled with horror; and as no one dares touch
her, Lucrezia vows vengeance on the five young men.

ACT I

SCENE 1: *A square in Ferrara.* Gennaro's house in
Ferrara is just across the square from the Duke's
palace, and the Duke, as he tells his man Rustighello
late at night, suspects his wife and the young man of
having an affair. He instructs Rustighello to kidnap
Gennaro and bring him to the palace, and they go off
when they hear sounds of carousing from the house.
Gennaro's guests—the five young noblemen we have
met in the Prologue—prepare to leave, but first twit
their host for his apparent interest in Lucrezia. To
show how he despises the very name he goes to the
palace door, where there is a brass plate with raised
letters reading BORGIA, and tears off the B, leaving
the Italian work of "orgy." As the others appreciate
the wit, Gubetta, standing on one side, remarks that
the prank may cost the young man dearly.

224

With the street empty once more, Astolfo (the Duchess' man) and Rustighello (the Duke's) meet, each intent on bringing Gennaro to his employer. As Rustighello has a band of "brigands" with him, Astolfo tactfully retires, and the Duke's men force open the door to take Gennaro prisoner.

SCENE 2: *A room in the Duke's palace.* The Duke, having heard that Gennaro is in custody, instructs Rustighello to bring in two flasks of wine, a silver and a gold one, when he gives the signal. Lucrezia now enters furiously and extracts a willing oath from her husband to avenge with death the desecration of her name the night before. But when Gennaro is brought in under guard, she is horrified, especially when he readily admits to being the author of the prank. Lucrezia begs to speak to her husband alone, and when the prisoner is removed, she first says she has changed her mind about the seriousness of the crime; but when the Duke insists that he will remain true to his oath, she implores him to be more lenient. Convinced more than ever, by her pleas, that Gennaro is Lucrezia's lover, he gives in to her so far only as to offer her the choice of how he shall die—by the sword or by poison. She chooses the latter.

Once more Gennaro is brought in, and with great flattery the Duke says that on account of Gennaro's reputation for bravery, and for having once saved the life of the Duke's father, he not only pardons him but invites him to serve in the Duke's army. This Gennaro politely refuses: he is sworn to the service of Venice. But he will be proud to accept a drink offered him, and when the two flasks are brought, he is served from the gold one, which, as Lucrezia well knows, is fatally poisoned. Confident that Borgia wine will do what it is intended to do, the Duke now leaves his wife and her supposed lover alone. Immediately she begs the young man to take an antidote she conveniently has with her in a vial, but it takes considerable persuasion to make him accept it, for he knows what the customary results are for those who accept this lady's chemical ministrations. Finally, however, he decides to take the chance, and also departs by a secret door that Lucrezia shows him, lest the Duke find him alive in the house. But even in the final notes of the long duet, he is warning her of God's vengeance if she has tricked him.

ACT II

SCENE 1: *Outside Gennaro's house.* Most of the scene is devoted to a discourse in which Count Orsini finally persuades his beloved friend Gennaro to join the five young blades from Venice in a party at the Negroni Palace to be given them that evening. Gennaro explains that his staying in Ferrara might be very dangerous for him, but Orsini laughs away his fears, and Gennaro, unable to resist, decides to risk it for one more night. Before they begin the duet, Rustighello and his brigands plan to enter Gennaro's house to avenge the Duke; and after Rustighello has overheard where the two young men are going, he calls off the brigands saying mysteriously that Gennaro is walking right into the trap set for him.

SCENE 2: *Banquet hall in the Negroni Palace.* The party for the young men is going well, with everyone slightly drunk and singing the praises of Madeira wine. Gubetta, who is also a guest, must think of a way to get rid of the ladies so that Lucrezia's plot to avenge herself for the indignities of the party in Venice may be realized. So when young Orsini says that he has written a drinking song and would like to sing it, Gubetta insults him by laughing at the very idea. Orsini offers to fight him, and the ladies, in alarm, leave. Led by Gennaro, the others all quiet Orsini down, and a servant brings in a new wine, which he calls Syracusan. Then Orsini, to this wine, finally sings his drinking song, the *Brindisi* ("*Il segreto per esser felici*"—"The secret of happiness"), which Schumann-Heink made one of the best-loved recordings over fifty years ago. Off stage some solemn singing by monks is heard, but Orsini boldly goes on with the second stanza. Suddenly the lights start going out; the young men try to leave but find all the doors locked; and Lucrezia Borgia, surrounded by armed guards, enters the room. Behind her, in the next room, are seen five coffins, and Lucrezia gravely announces that they are for the five men who treated her so scandalously in Venice. The "Syracusan" wine they have drunk is poisoned, and they have very little time left to live. But Gennaro points out that there should have been six coffins. Lucrezia, who had not counted on Gennaro's being present, is once more horrified and orders the guards to take her other victims away. Left alone with Gennaro, she again tries to persuade him to take the antidote, but he refuses. If his friends are dead, he says, he wishes to die, too. But first he intends to kill the dreadful woman; and when he attacks her with a knife, she is finally forced to reveal the dreadful secret: Gennaro himself is a Borgia, for she is the mother he has sought for so long. Now it is Gennaro's turn to be appalled—but not for long. The poison has worked too fast, and he dies in his mother's arms. At this moment Duke Alfonso, with guards and the entire chorus enter in search of Gennaro, and Lucrezia with her last words tells them who he is and how she had hoped to earn heaven's pardon through his virtues. As she falls prostrate over his body, she too dies.

Luisa Miller

CHARACTERS

Count Walter	Bass	Federica, *Duchess of Ostheim,*	
Rodolfo, *his son*	Tenor	Count Walter's niece	Contralto
Miller, *a retired soldier*	Baritone	Laura, *a peasant girl*	Mezzo-soprano
Luisa, *his daughter*	Soprano	Wurm, *a henchman of the Count's*	Bass

Villagers, Servants, Soldiers

The action takes place in the Tyrol during the first half of the eighteenth century.

OPERA IN THREE ACTS. Music by Giuseppi Verdi. Libretto in Italian by Salvatore Cammarano based on Friedrich von Schiller's play *Kabale und Liebe* (*Intrigue and Love*). First performance, Teatro San Carlo, Naples, December 8, 1849. Metropolitan première, December 21, 1929, with Rosa Ponselle as Luisa, Giacomo Lauri-Volpi as Rodolfo, Giuseppe de Luca as Miller, and Tullio Serafin conducting. Never for long a part of the standard repertoire in the twentieth century, it has had some notable revivals, especially in Vienna in 1930, in Leningrad in 1936, at the Florence Festival in 1937, and in Parma, Palermo, and Naples in 1963. In 1966 RCA Victor released a notable recording with stars from the Metropolitan Opera and in 1968 that company remounted it after thirty-seven years' rest.

Like the other three operas Verdi based on plays by the romantic eighteenth-century dramatist Schiller (*Don Carlos Giovanna d'Arco,* and *I Masnadieri,* which had been *Die Räuber*), *Luisa Miller* has strong, if naïve, revolutionary implications. Politically they were still stronger in Schiller's original play; here they are centered on the then-revolutionary idea—to quote W. S. Gilbert—"Never mind the why and wherefore, love will level ranks and therefore . . ." Rodolfo (Ferdinand in Schiller) is the son of a count; Luisa is the daughter of a retired common soldier (a musician in Schiller). The only admissible alternative to leveling these ranks in holy matri-

Rosa Ponselle, who created role of Luisa at the Metropolitan Opera

Act I, Scene 1: Luisa (Montserrat Caballé) and her father (Sherrill Milnes) joyfully greet Luisa's friends

mony is death—a wholly romantic and thoroughly revolutionary social doctrine.

In cutting down Schiller's play from five acts and thirty-seven scenes to three acts and seven scenes, Cammarano, at the expense of political intrigue, stressed the domestic relationships. This is the first of Verdi's essentially domestic operas, and it comes, in the Verdi canon, at the end of the first period, looking forward to the great trio of operas that began the second—*Rigoletto, Il Trovatore,* and *La Traviata.* One of the ways in which there are striking foreshadowings in *Luisa Miller* is the inclusion of pivotal and very moving duets between fatherly baritones and deeply-in-love sopranos (as in *Rigoletto, La Traviata,* and not long after, *Simon Boccanegra*). Another, even more striking sign of the transitional nature of the score is the fact that the first two acts represent essentially the old school of operatic structure—successive set arias and concerted numbers more or less evenly divided up among the lead singers—while the last act moves ahead to a more genuinely dramatic structure, with the recitatives less clearly marked off from the "numbers" and the progress of the musical pieces dictated by the dramatic requirements rather than by the even distribution of parts to singing stars.

OVERTURE

The overture to *Luisa Miller* deserves to be much better known to concert-goers than it actually is. Though widely varied in its dramatic colorings, it is based almost entirely on one musical theme, and its contrapuntal development is as fine as it is in some of Verdi's more mature works.

ACT I

SCENE 1: *The village square.* Before church, the villagers are celebrating the birthday of the popular Luisa, and she herself sings an aria (*"Lo vidi e'l primo palpito"*) telling of her love for a young huntsman she knows only as "Carlo." Like everyone else, she expects soon to marry him, only her father expressing any misgivings about the handsome stranger, who is also present. When the church bells call in the villagers, the ominous figure of Wurm, a retainer of the ruling Count's, stops Miller and urges him to forward his own suit for Luisa's hand. In an aria (*"Sacra la scelta"*) Miller tells Wurm that he cannot be a tyrant and force his daughter's hand in such a matter. Thereupon Wurm tells him that "Carlo" is really the son of Count Walter, implying that Miller's original misgivings are well founded: the son of a count cannot possibly have honorable intentions. Left alone, Miller voices his despair and prays that heaven may keep his daughter pure (*"Ei m' ha spezzato il cor"*).

SCENE 2: *A room in the castle of the Count.* Having been told by Wurm of Rodolfo's infatuation, the Count summons his son and, as he waits for him, sings an aria (*"Il mio sangue"*) in which he expresses his ambitions for his son and also hints mysteriously as to his own uneasy conscience and remorse for some misdeed. When Rodolfo enters, his father tells him that his old childhood friend Federica, Duchess of Ostheim, is about to arrive and that Rodolfo must propose. Horrified, the young man

Act II, Scene 2: Wurm (Ezio Flagello), Count Walter (Giorgio Tozzi), Duchess (Louise Pearl), Luisa (Montserrat Caballé)

tells his father that he cannot, but before the matter can be argued, the gracious lady comes in, with servants singing her praises.

Left alone with his intended bride, Rodolfo acknowledges their long friendship but finally admits that he cannot propose marriage as his heart is already given to another. In a long duet Rodolfo continues to beg for pardon, but Federica, with dignity but passion, insists that a woman scorned can scarcely be expected to forgive.

SCENE 3: *Outside Miller's house.* After a brief off-stage hunting chorus, Miller tells his daughter who "Carlo" really is and sternly warns her that his intentions cannot be honorable, for Rodolfo's intended bride has already arrived at the castle. He is reassured, however, when Rodolfo comes and, kneeling with Luisa before the old man, asks for a blessing, as he regards himself already married to her. He even says that he will reveal a dark secret about his father should the Count try to obstruct the nuptials. But the Count himself enters at that very moment, demands an end to the "intrigue," and calls Laura a "vile seductress." When Rodolfo threatens his father with his sword, the Count calls in soldiers to arrest Miller and Luisa, and with the soldiery, all the villagers arrive as well. In a fine, typically Verdian second-act finale, all express their conflicting emotions simultaneously, while Rodolfo alternately threatens his father's life, threatens to go to prison with Luisa, and even threatens to kill the girl. Finally, however, he gains the freedom of

Miller and his daughter by saying he will tell all how his father happened to become the Count—the secret that has been alluded to twice before.

ACT II

SCENE 1: *A room in Miller's house.* A group of villagers, led by Laura, bring Luisa the alarming news that they have seen her father being dragged to prison in chains. Wurm enters, gets rid of the villagers, and then tells Luisa that her father has insulted the Count, that he is now in prison, and that he will be executed unless she will save him. The only way to do this, he says, is to write the letter he has been told by the Count to dictate to her—and he proceeds to dictate. The letter is addressed to Wurm himself and says that Luisa knew from the first who her new lover was and merely hoped to entrap him. She really loved Wurm all along, and now, to evade Rodolfo's indignation, she invites Wurm to elope with her that very night. At first, having written, she declines to give the letter to Wurm, but when he points out that her refusal will cost her father his life, she tearfully gives up the missive and also agrees to go to the castle to show the Duchess herself that she loves Wurm. The scene ends with a powerful duet as Wurm expresses his joy and Luisa her despair.

SCENE 2: *A room in the castle.* After another remorseful but determined soliloquy by the Count

228

about his son, Wurm enters to report the success of his visit to Luisa. In the duet that follows, we finally learn the secret that Rodolfo has been threatening to reveal. Wurm and the present Count had waylaid the old Count one night, murdered him, and spread the rumor that it had been done by bandits. But now, for the first time, Wurm learns that Rodolfo had come on the scene before the old man died and had heard the truth. Wurm is horrified and fears that he may still land on the gallows. The entrance of the Duchess Federica ends their lamentations, and Count Walter tells her that Rodolfo had never won Luisa's heart and that he will prove it very shortly. Luisa is summoned and, with great difficulty and many heartbreaking asides saves her father's life by claiming that she never really loved Rodolfo but has always been in love with Wurm. Federica is generously impressed with the beauty and character of Luisa and presses her to tell the real truth; but Luisa acts her part well enough to make the Duchess believe what she really wants to believe, and the act closes with a quartet in which each of the characters voices his—or her—own feelings about the situation.

SCENE 3: *A garden in the castle.* A messenger delivers Luisa's lying letter to Rodolfo, who recognizes the handwriting and cannot doubt that she wrote it herself. In despair, he sings the best-known aria of the opera, *"Quando le sere al placido,"* recalling how the girl had sworn her love and how she was betraying him. When Wurm enters, Rodolfo gives him a choice of two pistols, for they must die together on the spot. Wurm, however, fires his into the air, thus summoning soldiers, castle servants, and Count Walter himself. With false compassion, the Count seems to relent and suggests that Rodolfo marry Luisa after all. But the young man tells his father of the betrayal in the letter (which he knew about, of course, all along), and so the Count suggests that his son drown his sorrow by marrying the Duchess Federica forthwith. Rodolfo is now indifferent to what his fate may be: "Prepare the altar or the tomb for me," he sings in the grand finale to the act.

ACT III

SCENE: *A room in Miller's house.* A group of villagers, once again led by Laura, are commiserating with Luisa, who sits at a desk, deathly pale, writing another letter. It is night, and through the window may be seen the lighted church where Rodolfo's wedding is soon to take place—a fact the villagers tell the audience but not Luisa. When they have left, Miller, who has been released from prison, asks what letter she is writing. Requesting its delivery to

Rodolfo, she shows it to her father, who reads it aloud. In veiled language, Luisa is telling her lover that she has been betrayed, that she will now take her own life, and that she hopes he will come to the house at midnight. Greatly moved, Miller tells his daughter how necessary she is to him and what a deep sin suicide is. Sadly, Luisa tears up the letter, and the two agree to leave their home the next morning to wander the rest of their lives as beggars.

When her father retires to rest, Luisa kneels down to pray, and Rodolfo steals softly into the room. He tells an attendant to ask his father to come for him when the ceremony is ready, and then places a vial of poison into a water flask. Rodolfo then asks Luisa whether she had in truth written the letter to Wurm, and when she admits she had done so, asks for a drink and presses one on her. He then indulges in some passionate self-pity which Luisa cannot really understand, but when the hour is struck by the castle clock, he finally tells her that they both have drunk poison. In a tender duet they both welcome death, though when Luisa tells him the truth—that she wrote the letter only to save her father's life, and that she never loved Wurm—his self-reproaches are loud. Miller, summoned by them to the room, has all explained to him, and a beautiful final trio is sung. As Luisa dies in her father's arms, the Count, Wurm, and the villagers enter and Rodolfo, with his last strength, seizes his sword and slays Wurm.

Act III: Miller (Sherrill Milnes) witnesses the death of Luisa (Montserrat Caballé) and her lover, Rodolfo (Richard Tucker)

Lulu

CHARACTERS

The Animal Trainer	*Bass*	The Wardrobe Mistress	*Mezzo-soprano*
Lulu	*Soprano*	The Theater Manager	*Baritone*
Dr. Ludwig Schön, *a newspaper*		The Prince, *an African explorer*	*Tenor*
publisher	*Baritone*	Rodrigo, *an acrobat*	*Baritone*
Alwa, *his son*	*Tenor*	Countess Geschwitz	*Mezzo-soprano*
The Painter	*Tenor*	The Student	*Mezzo-soprano*
Dr. Goll, *a medical specialist*	*Bass*	The Servant	*Tenor*
Schigolch, *a street musician*	*Bass*	Jack the Ripper	*Acting role*

The action takes place in Germany, France, and England, before World War I.

OPERA IN THREE ACTS. Music by Alban Berg. Text in German by Frank Wedekind, a condensation by the composer of the two plays *Erdgeist* and *Die Büchse der Pandora*. Première at the Municipal Theater, Zurich, June 2, 1937. First American performance in English by the Sante Fe Opera Company, August 7, 1963. First American performance in German by the Hamburg State Opera at the Metropolitan Opera House, New York, June 24, 1967.

Berg had been working on *Lulu* for seven years when he died in 1935. The first two acts had been completed in every respect. The two scenes of Act III (one in a gambling casino in Paris, the other in Lulu's London flat) had also been completed except for the detailed scoring, but the instrumentation was indicated in what is known as short-score form. In addition, some of the scoring for the final act was done by the composer for a "Lulu Symphony" of orchestral passages that Berg had prepared in 1934. Helene Berg, the composer's widow, has so far refused permission to various able musicians—German, French, and American—who have asked to realize Berg's indicated scoring so that the entire opera may be performed as Berg conceived it. The manuscript of Act III is in existence but inaccessible. What producers do about it currently is described in the synopsis below.

Wedekind's heroine, if heroine she is, has been variously described as a personification of the Eternal Feminine, a female Faust, and a latter-day Lilith. (Indeed, everyone seems to have a different name for the lady, even the characters in the play: Schigolch calls her "Lulu," but Dr. Schön and his son know her as "Mignon," Dr. Goll prefers "Nelly," and the Painter decides to rename her "Eva.") Further controversy centers about Lulu's character. Is she predator or victim? Is she a soulless harlot, or is she "more sinned against than sinning"?

Before the action of the opera begins, Dr. Ludwig Schön, a powerful newspaper magnate, has found Lulu, scarcely more than a child, "selling flowers in front of the Alhambra Cafe." Ignorant of her true name and origins, he calls her "Mignon," makes her his mistress, and introduces her into his household. On the death of his wife (by whom he has a son, Alwa), Schön decides he must break with his young protégée in favor of a respectable marriage, and arranges her own marriage to Dr. Goll, a rich and elderly medical specialist.

In a prologue played in front of the curtain, the Animal Trainer invites the public to preview the "menagerie" of wild beasts who are shortly to figure in the action of the opera. A serpent—the sideshow's star attraction—is carried out: it is Lulu.

ACT I

SCENE 1: *The Painter's studio.* Lulu, dressed as Pierrot, is having her portrait painted as Schön and Alwa look on. Alwa, a dilettante composer whose latest piece is soon to be produced, has come to take his father to a rehearsal at the theater. Lulu's ironic reference to Schön's young fiancée is curtly ignored. When father and son have left, the Painter makes a clumsy attempt to seduce his fascinating subject. She at first eludes him, with the nervous reminder that her husband is due at any moment, but then passively submits to his embraces. Dr. Goll, in a jealous rage, bursts through the door, suffers a heart attack and dies. While the Painter goes for help, Lulu muses laconically on her fate. The Painter returns and is shocked by her unfeeling attitude. "Have you a soul?" he asks her. But to this and all his earnest questions Lulu apathetically repeats; "I don't know." She goes into the other room to change out of her costume. Alone with the corpse, the Painter voices his fear over this sudden turn of events, saying that he would willingly change places with the dead man. Lulu re-enters. Her hands are trembling; she cannot do up the hooks of her dress. As the Painter helps her, the curtain falls.

SCENE 2: *The drawing room of the Painter's house.* Despite his earlier misgivings, the Painter has made a seemingly happy marriage with Lulu—or, as he prefers to call her, Eva. The morning mail brings news of the sale of another of his paintings and an announcement of Dr. Schön's impending marriage to a young girl of high social position. Lulu receives this latter news with a show of irritation. The doorbell rings. "A beggar," says the Painter, who has sent the man away. When the Painter has retired to his studio, Lulu stealthily admits the beggar. It is old Schigolch, an asthmatic and alcoholic street musician who pretends to be Lulu's father. She gives him money and a drink, and together they talk of the old days. The bell rings a second time, and as Schigolch makes his way out, Dr. Schön enters. His forthcoming marriage is being compromised by Lulu's repeated visits to his house, and he sternly demands that Lulu make a final break with him. He has twice arranged brilliant matches for her; she must now leave him in peace. But Lulu will not be put off so easily. "If I belong to any man on earth, it is to you," she declares passionately. As the discussion grows more heated, the Painter enters. Lulu leaves abruptly, and Schön decides to speak frankly with the Painter. "You're married to half a million marks," he repeats over and over to his mystified friend. And to the Painter's growing horror, he reveals Lulu's sordid past: her doubtful origins, her association with Schigolch, his own liaison with her, the arranged marriage with Dr. Goll, the various names men have given her. All his idealistic illusions shattered, the Painter disappears into an adjoining room—"to talk to her." But when Lulu re-enters from the studio, it becomes clear that the Painter has decided on a far more desperate course. Having locked the door behind him, he has cut his throat. As Schön tries to force the door, Alwa enters with news of a revolution in Paris. In the ensuing confusion, Schön, realizing that his marriage is now further jeopardized by fresh scandal, telephones the police. Lulu quickly dresses to go out. "I can't stay here any more," she says. Then, noticing blood on Schön's hand, she wipes it off with her own handkerchief. "Your husband's blood," he says, recoiling. Yes, she

San Francisco Opera's Act I, Scene 1: Painter (Brian Sullivan), body of Goll, and Lulu (Evelyn Lear)

Hamburg: Schön (Blankenheim) and Lulu (Anneliese Rothenberger)

answers, but now there is no trace of it, and Schön must marry her. The doorbell announces the police.

SCENE 3: *A theater dressing room.* Lulu, thanks to Schön's shrewd publicity, has made a successful debut as a dancer in a music hall. Alwa, who has provided a score for the show, is sharing champagne and conversation with Lulu in her dressing room. His father, it seems, is still intent upon a fashionable marriage, and has come to the theater with his fiancée. Alwa reminisces about the past, when Lulu lived with them, and confesses his boyish infatuation for her. Lulu tells him about her latest admirer, a prince who wants to marry her and take her with him to Africa. The entr'acte bell calls her to the stage, and Alwa, left alone, toys with the idea of composing an opera about Lulu's career. The Prince enters and talks fatuously about his admiration for Lulu and her "art"; she is to him the embodiment of *joie de vivre,* and he intends to make her his wife. To the agitated ringing of the stage bell, Lulu hurriedly re-enters, followed by her dresser and the theater manager. She has had a fainting spell and cannot go on with her dance. Schön appears and furiously orders her onto the stage. In a fit of temper, she refuses. When the others leave, Schön tries to reason with her. Artfully she admits that he was right to put her in her place by making her perform before his fiancée, and meekly agrees to go on with her number—after a moment's rest. When

she reveals the Prince's intention to marry her and take her off to Africa, Schön's defenses begin to crumble. He had not counted on losing her altogether, it seems, not even after his marriage. Seizing her opportunity, Lulu declares that she will bide her time. Sooner or later Schön's young wife will seek her out for advice and consolation. Schön now realizes that in spite of his every precaution his marriage is doomed. Lulu, fully mistress of the situation, cruelly orders him to go back to his fiancée and asks that the Prince be sent to her. Schön, powerless to act, agrees to break off his engagement. As Lulu dictates, he writes a letter to his fiancée, begging her to forget him. "I am writing to you in the presence of a woman who completely dominates me." Burying his face in his hands, he groans, "Now comes the execution." Lulu readies herself for the dance.

ACT II

SCENE 1: *The drawing room of Schön's house.* Although she has at last married Dr. Schön, Lulu does not lack for admirers. One of these, a lesbian, Countess Geschwitz, pays the Schöns a visit and urges Lulu to attend the ladies-only ball she is sponsoring that evening. Promising that she will do her best to come, Lulu accompanies the Countess to the door. Left alone, Schön expresses his revulsion at the state of his marriage. Lulu returns, and in spite of her affectionate blandishments, Schön announces that he must spend the afternoon at the stock exchange. When the two have left the room, the Countess furtively reenters and conceals herself behind a screen. An ill-assorted group of Lulu's hangers-on appear, and profiting from Schön's weekly absence, make themselves at home in the drawing room. They are Schigolch, Lulu's aged "father"; Rodrigo, a boastful circus acrobat; and a love-sick student. Lulu joins them, but when their bantering is interrupted by Alwa's unexpected arrival, the intruders hurry off to hide in different parts of the house. The servant (who is also smitten by the mistress of the house) serves Lulu and Alwa food and drink. Alwa's idealistic talk soon gives way to an impassioned declaration of love for his father's wife. Not even Lulu's casual admission that it was she who poisoned Alwa's mother can deflect the young man's ardor. Schön, who had only pretended to leave the house, is a horrified witness to the scene. Brandishing a revolver, he interrupts his son's love-making and routs some of Lulu's cronies from their hiding places. He demands that Lulu kill herself and end their intolerable marriage. In a heartfelt outburst, Lulu defends herself: "I have never pretended to be anything but what people take me for; and no one has ever taken me but for what I am." But Schön will not be placated, and forces her to turn the revolver against her own head. The student, crying for help, bolts from his hiding place beneath the table, throwing Schön off guard. Lulu fires five shots at her husband. He collapses, and Lulu, horrified by what she has done, runs to his side: "The only one I ever loved!" But Schön orders her out of his sight, and calling loudly for Alwa, dies in his son's arms, warning him that he will be the next victim. Lulu begs Alwa to keep her from being arrested, but when the police arrive, it is Alwa who lets them in.

An orchestral interlude links the two scenes of this act. It was composed by Berg as an accompaniment to a motion picture sequence which would recount to the audience highlights of the intervening action. Lulu has been sent to prison as Schön's murderess. But Countess Geschwitz has engineered a brilliant plan for her escape. Learning of a cholera epidemic in Hamburg, the Countess secures a nursing certificate, enters a hospital in that city to tend the sick, and purposely contracts the disease herself. During a visit to the prison, she manages to infect Lulu as well, and when both women are confined to the same isolation ward in the local hospital, contrives to make them resemble each other as much as possible. When discharged as cured, she returns to Schön's house to meet with her fellow conspirators— Alwa, Schigolch, and Rodrigo. At this point the curtain goes up and the stage action is resumed.

SCENE 2: *The drawing room of Schön's house.* The Countess, still weakened by her illness, lies on the sofa. With her are Alwa and Rodrigo, impatiently awaiting Schigolch, who is to accompany the Countess back to the hospital. Once there, she will claim that she has left her watch behind, enter the isolation ward, change clothes with Lulu, and thus effect Lulu's escape. Rodrigo plans to marry Lulu as soon as she is free and to take her abroad, where they will make their livelihood as an acrobatic team. When Schigolch and the Countess have left, Rodrigo reviles Alwa for his respectful treatment of the Countess, and for having forced him to pose as a servant in the household as part of the conspiracy. As Alwa answers him sharply, the Student enters. He has run away from the reformatory, determined to save Lulu at any cost. As he is totally ignorant of the plot already afoot, Alwa (out of pity) and Rodrigo (out of spite) lie to him that Lulu has died of cholera. Heartbroken and in despair, he leaves. Schigolch arrives at last with Lulu, now dressed in the Countess' clothes. Rodrigo, disgusted by the wasted appearance of his "bride," rushes off to uncover the plot to the police. Unperturbed, Lulu—who has merely affected a haggard look to rid herself of Rodrigo's unwanted attentions—reveals herself to

Alwa, her beauty unimpaired. She explains the Countess' ingenious scheme, and notes with heartless satisfaction that Geschwitz now lies in her place as "the murderess of Dr. Schön." Alwa, oblivious to everything but his passion for Lulu, rapturously describes her body in an extended metaphor of musical terms. Lulu urges him to cross the frontier with her to freedom that very night, and he readily agrees. When she tonelessly reminds him that they are lying on the very sofa where his father bled to death, he silences her with kisses.

ACT III

The third and last act of the opera, left incomplete by the composer's death, deals with Lulu's dwindling fortunes and ultimate degradation, first in Paris and later in London. Current production practice joins the two orchestral passages from this act (fully scored by Berg for inclusion in the 1934 symphonic suite) as musical background for a pantomine-pendant to the second act. Speeches from the last scene of Wedekind's play are employed at the discretion of the producer, and Geschwitz's dying apostrophe to the dead Lulu (also completed by 1934) is sung. Until the opera is finally offered to the public in its definitive form, a brief outline of the last scene will suffice for present purposes:

Lulu, now a London streetwalker, leads a client into her sordid rooms. Geschwitz, half mad with jealousy and revulsion, tries to block their way into the bedroom, but is scornfully pushed aside by Lulu, who explains that the woman is her "sister." As Geschwitz listens in horror to her screams, Lulu is brutally murdered—for her client is none other than Jack the Ripper. Rushing from the bedroom, Jack stabs Geschwitz as well. The dying woman crawls toward the open door. "Lulu, my angel," she moans. "I shall never leave you. Never . . ."

Act III: Death of Countess Geschwitz (Kerstin Meyer)

Macbeth

CHARACTERS

Macbeth, *Thane of Glamis and a general*	*Baritone*	Lady in Waiting *to Lady Macbeth*	*Soprano*
Lady Macbeth, *his wife*	*Soprano*	A Physician	*Bass*
Banquo, *a general*	*Bass*	Fleance, *son of Banquo*	*Mime*
Duncan, *King of Scotland*	*Mime*	Hecate, *chief of the witches*	*Dancer*
Malcolm, *his son*	*Tenor*	An Armed Head ⎤	*Baritone*
Macduff, *a nobleman*	*Tenor*	A Bloody Child ⎬ *apparitions*	*Soprano*
A Murderer	*Baritone*	A Crowned Child ⎦	*Soprano*

Nobles, Noblewomen, Refugees, Scottish and British Soldiers, Attendants
The action takes place in medieval Scotland.

OPERA IN FOUR ACTS. Music by Giuseppe Verdi. Libretto in Italian, after Shakespeare, by Francesco Piave, in collaboration with Andrea Maffei. First produced at the Teatro della Pergola, Florence, March 14, 1847. A new version, involving considerable revision, was produced at the Théâtre-Lyrique, Paris, on April 21, 1865, the French text being the work of Nuitter and Beaumont. The American première of *Macbeth,* in the original version, occurred at Niblo's Garden, New York, on April 24, 1850. Ninety-one years later, on October 24, 1941, the New Opera Company produced the revised version for the first time in America at the Forty-fourth Street Theater, New York. Fritz Busch conducted, and the cast was headed by Jess Walters as Macbeth and Florence Kirk as Lady Macbeth. The first Metropolitan Opera performance took place on February 5, 1959, with Leonard Warren as Macbeth and Leonie Rysanek as his lady. Since then it has returned to the repertory with increasing frequency.

Verdi was only thirty-four when he wrote the first of his three Shakespearean operas. The other two, *Otello* and *Falstaff*, belong to the very last phase of his career, the period of perhaps his greatest dramatic and expressive power. Yet in *Macbeth* this power is already foreshadowed in the broad sweep of style and the marked flair for compelling dramatic emphasis. A great devotee of Shakespeare's works, Verdi resolved to be as faithful as possible to the original play, even supplying Piave with his own prose version, besides strict instructions about the sequence of scenes and details of characterization. Still, certain sharp differences may be noted by anyone familiar with both the play and the opera— differences stemming in part from the special romantic approach of the period to Shakespeare. Macduff and Malcolm are reduced to vague semblances of the Shakespearean originals, and because of the need to tighten the earlier scenes, the nobler side of Macbeth is almost lost in the unrelieved portrait of villainy. Actually, it is Lady Macbeth who looms as the dominant figure of the opera, and to her Verdi allotted the best pages of his score. Among the most absorbing moments of the opera are her aria *"La luce langue"* ("The light fails"), in which she voices a conflict of fear and exultation, and the stupendous *scena* of the sleepwalking episode, in which a Verdi biographer averred that "the composer rises to the level of the poet and gives the full equivalent in music of the spoken word."

Leonard Warren as Macbeth, his last new role, in 1959

sung softly, she urges him to do the deed that very night. The King and his entourage enter briefly and cross the stage to their own apartments, and then, left alone, Macbeth has his great soliloquy (*"Mi si affaccia un pugnal?"*—"Is this a dagger which I see before me?"). A night bell sounds, and Macbeth fearfully steals off in the direction of the King's quarters. On his return he finds Lady Macbeth awaiting him. His hands are bloody and he still holds the bloody dagger. Scornfully, Lady Macbeth seizes the dagger and goes in to complete the work Macbeth has failed to do—that is, smear with blood the drugged grooms who sleep with the King so that it may appear that they are the murderers.

When she returns without the dagger, there is knocking at the gate, and Lady Macbeth takes her unmanned husband to their own quarters lest they be found. It is Banquo and Macduff who have been knocking, and they are coming to waken the King. Macduff quickly discovers the murder; the two men summon everyone in the castle, and the act ends with a rousing ensemble, in which Macbeth and his wife take part, expressing the horror and dismay of everyone.

ACT I

SCENE 1: *A blasted heath.* A small chorus of witches (which Verdi regarded as one of the three main characters in the opera) sings nasally and dances awkwardly before Macbeth and Banquo, returning from battle, come upon them. Macbeth is Thane of Glamis, but they greet him with the title of Thane of Cawdor, and Banquo is greeted as the progenitor of future kings. The two generals are surprised by such promises of elevation—and amazed when one of the promises is immediately fulfilled. Messengers arrive from King Duncan with the news that the Thane of Cawdor has been executed for treason and his lands and title assigned to Macbeth. Macbeth is prompted to suppress thoughts of regicide; Banquo is made uneasy; and the witches once more sing and dance.

SCENE 2: *The great hall of Macbeth's castle.* Lady Macbeth, a stronger, more direct character than her husband, in the opera as in Shakespeare, is reading a letter from him describing the meeting with the witches. She suppresses no thoughts about ambition; and when an attendant announces that the King is planning to spend the night in her castle, she invokes the powers of hell to aid in her contemplated murder (*"Or tutti sorgete"*). Immediately thereafter Macbeth arrives, and in a tense duet, which should be

ACT II

SCENE 1: *A room in Macbeth's castle.* Macbeth is now King, but he is uneasy not only with his conscience but also in the memory of the witches' prophecy that Banquo's line, not his, will become kings. Lady Macbeth urges on him the murder of Banquo, and when he has left, sings her great aria of fierce determination, *"La luce langue"* ("Light is fading").

SCENE 2: *A park near the castle.* A band of assassins hired by Macbeth is waiting to waylay Banquo and sings a typical Italian opera conspirators' chorus. They hide when Banquo enters with his little son Fleance, and he has a fine bass aria (*"Come dal ciel precipita"*) in which he likens the deepening dusk to the darkness that he sees coming over the land. He is about to resume his way when the assassins fall on him, but Fleance escapes.

SCENE 3: *The banquet hall.* The new King and Queen are entertaining the nobility at a banquet, and Lady Macbeth sings a rather stiff and ungraceful *brindisi*, or drinking song, of welcome. At the close of the first stanza one of the assassins reports softly to Macbeth that Banquo has been murdered but that the son escaped. When he returns to his seat, Macbeth finds it occupied by Banquo's ghost (though, of course, no one else can see it). His temporary loss of presence of mind and his addressing an apparently empty chair is apologized for and covered up by his wife when she sings another stanza of the drinking song, ironically proposing the health of the absent Banquo. But Macbeth again breaks down, speaking so violently and frankly to the ghost in his chair that at least one of the guests, Macduff, now suspects the truth. The act ends with a second great ensemble, the guests in confusion, Lady Macbeth repeating that the dead cannot come back to life, and Macbeth determining to wrest the truth from the witches.

ACT III

SCENE: *In the woods, with a dark cave.* The witches, hovering over a caldron, again sing in their nasal way, and then there is a dance, in the middle of which Hecate comes and, in pantomime, instructs them about the near approach of Macbeth. When he arrives, he demands that they tell him what the future holds for him. To weird woodwind music, then, which comes from below the stage, the witches summon three apparitions. The first is the head of an armed warrior, who tells Macbeth to beware of Macduff; the second, a bloody child, seems to contradict the first by assuring Macbeth he need fear no man of woman born; and the third, a crowned child, tells him he shall never be vanquished till Birnam Wood comes to Dunsinane. All this appears to Macbeth to be very encouraging until an apparition of eight kings passes over the stage, the last of whom is Banquo with a mirror in his hand. Macbeth, understanding this to portend a line of kings stemming from Banquo, as the witches had predicted, tries to attack the last figure with his sword; but the apparitions, along with the witches themselves, vanish and Macbeth falls fainting to the ground.

The supernatural note of the music changes as Lady Macbeth enters and demands to know what Macbeth has learned. He tells her of the implied prophecy about Banquo, and she furiously vows that this shall not happen; all opposed to them must be exterminated. Macbeth's courage and determination are thus once more restored by his wife, and the scene ends with a powerful duet.

ACT IV

SCENE 1: *Open country near Birnam Wood.* A band of refugees from the tyranny of Macbeth sing a chorus ("*Patria oppressa!*") expressing patriotic sorrow over the misfortunes of Scotland. Macduff, whose wife and children have been murdered on orders of the tyrant, then has a most expressive aria ("*Ah, la paterna mano*") over his personal sorrow. Malcolm, at the head of a band of soldiers from England, marches in and orders all the men to cut branches from the trees of Birnam Wood preparatory to an attack on Macbeth's forces at Dunsinane Castle. The scene ends with a rousing ensemble led by Macduff and Malcolm.

SCENE 2: *Room in Dunsinane Castle.* This is the famous sleepwalking scene. Her physician and lady in waiting comment murmurously on Lady Macbeth's apparent loss of mind through a guilty conscience, and then the Lady herself wanders in, walking and talking in her sleep, recalling the circumstances of the murder of Duncan in disjointed phrases, and trying to rub out the imaginary blood on her hand. As she wanders back, crying, "To bed, to bed," her voice rises softly to a high D flat. The whole *scena* is perhaps the most eerie and strikingly original passage in any Italian opera composed in the nineteenth century, a dramatic departure from the conventional "mad scene" one might have expected.

SCENE 3: *A battlefield outside Dunsinane Castle.* Macbeth, dismayed by the invasion of troops who seem to be bearing Birnam Wood to Dunsinane, yet feels he may conquer them because of the prophecy that he cannot be overcome by any man of woman born. On hearing that Lady Macbeth has died, he grimly girds his sword for battle. The battle itself is depicted in the orchestra by a fugue. Presently, Macduff encounters Macbeth and replies to Macbeth's taunt that he was "untimely ripped" from his mother's womb. He then mortally wounds the unresisting tyrant, who, dying, has a last short aria ("*Mal per me*") in which he curses the day in which he believed the witches' prophecies. The opera closes with a paean to victory by the insurgents.

Act II banquet: Macbeth (Leonard Warren) imagines ghost of Banquo, to the horror of his Lady (Leonie Rysanek) and guests

Madama Butterfly

CHARACTERS

Cio-Cio-San (Madama Butterfly)	*Soprano*	Goro, *a marriage broker*	Tenor
Suzuki, *her servant*	*Mezzo-soprano*	Prince Yamadori, *suitor for*	
B. F. Pinkerton, *lieutenant in the*		*Cio-Cio-San*	Baritone
United States Navy	*Tenor*	The Bonze, *Cio-Cio-San's uncle*	Bass
Kate Pinkerton, *his wife*	*Mezzo-soprano*	The Imperial Commissioner	Baritone
Sharpless, *United States Consul*	Baritone	Registrar	Tenor
		Trouble, *Cio-Cio-San's child*	Mime

Cio-Cio-San's Relations and Friends, Servants

The action takes place in the early 1900's at Nagasaki, Japan.

OPERA IN THREE ACTS (originally two). Music by Giacomo Puccini. Libretto in Italian by Luigi Illica and Giuseppe Giacosa, based on the play by David Belasco, in turn founded on a short story by John Luther Long. First performance, La Scala, Milan, February 17, 1904. American première, in English, Washington, D.C., October 15, 1906. First performance at the Metropolitan Opera House, in Italian, February 11, 1907, with Geraldine Farrar in the title role and Enrico Caruso as Lieutenant Pinkerton.

It was Frank Neilson, stage manager of Covent Garden, who induced Puccini to see Belasco's play at the Duke of York's Theatre in London. Though he knew no English, Puccini immediately grasped its operatic possibilities. Later he confessed he fell in love on the spot with the pathetic little geisha girl. The years 1902 and 1903 were occupied with writing the new opera. Intent on achieving authentic atmosphere, Puccini went so far as to consult the wife of the Japanese Ambassador on many details. Friends of hers even supplied him with actual Japanese tunes, and Victor records of native music made in Japan were also made available to Puccini. When the opera was finished, Puccini was convinced he had written his masterpiece. The Milanese public and press failed to agree with him, however. In fact, the world première of *Madama Butterfly* brought Puccini his most humiliating experience in the theater, for the occasion was a resounding fiasco. This, despite the fact that Rosina Storchio (later to become celebrated in the role) sang Cio-Cio-San, Giovanni Zenatello was the Pinkerton, and Cleofonte Campanini conducted. With the very entrance of Cio-Cio-San the crowd showed its opposition. After the first act, Puccini, limping from injuries suffered in a motor crash, appeared on the stage, only to be greeted by a volley of catcalls. For the rest of the performance he remained fuming in the wings. As the jeers of the crowd reached him, he would mutter, "Louder, louder, you beasts! Shriek at me! Yell your lungs out! You shall see who is right! This is the best opera I have ever written!" After the riotous performance Puccini, pale and shaken, expressed his thanks to Campanini and the singers, and returned home with the mistreated score under his arm.

The failure of that première has been variously explained. Some insist an anti-Puccini cabal was at

Licia Albanese as Cio-Cio-San arrives for her wedding, in the San Francisco Opera's staging of the first act

work. Others blame the fiasco on the absence of any real solo for tenor in the first version. The long second act (in the original version) has been given as another cause. In any case, Puccini was right in his angry prophecy, in the opinion of many critics. *Madama Butterfly* became a world favorite, its main aria, Cio-Cio-San's "*Un bel dì*," almost reaching the status of a "hit" song. However, Puccini did make some revisions. He broke up the second act into two parts, separating them by an intermezzo. Moreover, the tenor role was augmented by an arioso. Three months after the disastrous première at Milan, *Madama Butterfly* proved a spectacular success at the opera house of Brescia. That performance marked the beginning of its conquest of the world. Puccini's revenge on the Milanese hooters had come sooner than expected.

ACT I

SCENE: *Exterior of Pinkerton's house at Nagasaki.* It is all vastly amusing. This matchbox of a house and its sliding panels, or *shoji*, in place of walls, neat and ingenious devices—and ridiculously inexpensive! Pinkerton, Lieutenant in the United States Navy, is charmed and amused as the self-important matrimonial agent Goro shows him over the little house he is to make his home during a not-too-prolonged stay in Japan. Presently Sharpless, United States Consul, turns up. Pinkerton tells him delightedly about the beautiful Japanese girl by whom he has been captivated, and whom he is to marry Japanese fashion for nine hundred and ninety-nine years, but with the privilege of annulling the marriage any month. The Consul has a dim suspicion that the experiment may turn out more seriously than his friend anticipates, but Pinkerton will not listen to hints of tragedy. "Whisky?" proposes the naval lieutenant. Having filled their

glasses, the men drink the toast "America forever!" and then to the folks at home and to the time when Pinkerton will have a "real" wedding back in "God's country."

The two men stand looking out over the glorious scenery, so different from the homeland that to an American it is a make-believe world. From the foot of the hill girlish voices are heard, gradually drawing nearer. The music pulsates glowingly while the girls chatter about the beauty of the day and the flowers. Among them is Cio-Cio-San, "Madame Butterfly," and to Pinkerton this little creature in her kimono is a butterfly indeed. Her voice soars above the others while she sings of the ecstasy of her love.

As the music reaches its climax, the girls appear on the terrace and prostrate themselves before the "augustness" of Pinkerton. Sharpless enters into a conversation with Butterfly and learns that what he feared is true—the girl is seriously in love with Pinkerton. He also learns that since the death of her father she has had to support herself and mother by becoming a geisha.

The bride's relatives, great numbers of them, now arrive. While the guests are all busied with the refreshments, Pinkerton amusedly watches Butterfly, who draws from her capacious sleeves her possessions—such trifles as handkerchiefs, a jar of carmine, a fan, and, with great solemnity, a long sheath. The officious Goro whispers an explanation to Pinkerton: the dagger was sent to her father by the Mikado—and he was obedient, Goro adds grimly. Thus is Pinkerton reminded that he is in the land given to seppuku, or hara-kiri, a condemned gentleman's privilege to die by his own hand. Butterfly also shows her *ottoke*, images of her forefathers; but she confides to Pinkerton that she has been to the mission and adopted his religion, innocently adding that she will try to be frugal, for she knows that he has paid for her the sum of a whole hundred yen. She declares that for his sake she is willing to forget race, kindred, and ancestors; and to prove this last, she throws away their images.

Goro commands silence, and the quaint ceremony of signing the marriage contract takes place. The gaiety of congratulations is suddenly interrupted, for Cio-Cio-San's uncle rushes in, violently enraged. Being a bonze, or Japanese priest, he has learned that Butterfly has forsaken the faith of her ancestors upon marrying this foreigner. Therefore, he curses her with threats of eternal punishment; and all her relatives likewise denounce her, for in deserting her gods she has likewise deserted her people. All rush away in horror, leaving Butterfly weeping bitterly. Pinkerton consoles her, and in the thought of his love she is again happy. Night falls over the scene, and they sing of their happiness together.

ACT II

Scene: *The interior of Butterfly's house.* Beyond the room one can see the garden with cherries in bloom, bright in the spring sunshine; but the wall panels being only partly open, the room remains in semidarkness. Before an image of Buddha kneels Suzuki. Occasionally she rings a handbell while she prays that Butterfly's weeping may be ended. Butterfly, who is standing motionless near a screen, tells her that the gods of Japan are lazy—her husband's God will answer her more quickly. Although the money that Pinkerton left is almost gone, Butterfly is still so firm in her belief that her husband will return that she commands the doubting Suzuki to say that he will. Suzuki complies in spite of her tears.

Greatly touched by this, Butterfly, to reassure herself as well as Suzuki, affirms her belief, in an impassioned aria, that some fine day (*"Un bel dì"*) a great ship will appear far in the horizon . . . the boom of cannon will announce its arrival in the harbor . . . they will see him coming from a distance . . . climbing the hill. Butterfly will hide for a moment just to tease him . . . he will call for her by the old names of endearment . . . so let fears be banished, Butterfly declares, utterly carried away by the joy of her anticipation, for he will return. She knows it!

At the moment she has finished this declaration of her trust, Sharpless appears. Goro, who has conducted him here, waits outside. "Madame Butterfly," he calls. "Madame B. F. Pinkerton, beg pardon!" the wife corrects. Then turning and recognizing her visitor, she greets him cheerfully. He has a letter from Pinkerton, he tells her. She is the happiest of women, she replies; and then without wait-

ing for Sharpless to read she asks him when the robins build their nests in America . . . for, she continues, Pinkerton had said that he would come back in the happy season when the robins return . . . now, for the third time, the robins are building their nests. Sharpless, in his embarrassment, is forced to reply that he never studied ornithology. Goro laughs outright at this.

The marriage broker now presents Yamadori, a wealthy suitor, who, though he has had many consorts and divorced them all, says that he is madly in love with Butterfly and is prepared to swear eternal faithfulness to her. She repulses him and his proffered wealth, for she is married to an American, and in his country people remain faithful! Broker and suitor disposed of, Sharpless attempts to resume reading the letter; everything he reads is interpreted by Butterfly as some happy assurance that her husband will soon return. The Consul has not the heart to go on. He asks Butterfly what she would do if Pinkerton were never to come back to her. As if struck by a deathblow, Butterfly gravely replies that she might again become a geisha or she might kill herself. Horrified, Sharpless advises her to marry Yamadori. This greatly offends Butterfly. Ordering Suzuki to bring in "Trouble," the name she has bestowed on her little son, she points to the child in agitated pride, and exclaims, "And this? Can such as this be forgotten?" She asks Sharpless to write to her husband and tell him what a beautiful son he has. Thus does the Consul learn to his surprise that, unknown to Pinkerton, there is a child. In true motherly joy, her attention concentrated entirely on little Trouble, Butterfly bids her child not to believe the Consul when he says that Pinkerton will not return.

Sharpless leaves, fearful for the future. Soon after he has gone, a cannon shot is heard booming from over the harbor, announcing the arrival of an American warship. With the help of a telescope Butterfly spells out its name—*Abraham Lincoln.* Pinkerton's ship!

So, then, the agony of waiting is over! He has come with the robins—her lover, her husband, her adored one! In a moment the two women are feverishly rushing to the garden to gather cherry blossoms to deck the house. They sing the joyous "Duet of the Flowers" throbbing with the excitement and exultation of the rejoicing Butterfly, who then hastens to put on the wedding dress she wore on that day long ago, so that she may greet her lover as he first knew her. Little Trouble, too, is arrayed in his finest.

Night has been falling; the servant closes the *shoji* and brings in several Japanese lanterns, which cast a dim glow over the darkened room. But they must await Pinkerton's return. They must be ready to welcome him. In her anxious, joyful expectancy Butterfly has pierced three little holes through the wall so that they may watch for him. Trouble sits before one, supported by cushions; at another kneels Suzuki; close up against a third stands Butterfly, rigid and motionless, watching, waiting. A wonderful melody, first heard during the reading of the letter, floats across the scene, softly hummed from a distance. Trouble soon falls asleep, then Suzuki dozes off. Now Butterfly keeps her vigil alone.

ACT III

SCENE: *Same as Act II.* The gray light of dawn begins to enter the room. Butterfly still stands, motionless, watching; Suzuki and Trouble are sound asleep. The lanterns become even dimmer as the day grows brighter. Like the morning sunlight, the music now sparkles with vagrant Japanese melodies. Suzuki having awakened and begged her to lie down to rest awhile, Butterfly takes little Trouble and goes with him into an inner room. No sooner has she gone than Sharpless and Pinkerton arrive. Suzuki is overjoyed at seeing them, but they motion her to keep silent. She points out how Butterfly has decorated the house and tells how she waited all night. The servant, on opening the *shoji*, exclaims in surprise as she catches sight of a strange woman in the garden. Fearfully she asks who it is. When Sharpless explains that it is Pinkerton's wife, Suzuki cries out in grief.

Sharpless asks Suzuki to prepare Butterfly for this bitter revelation, adding that the American woman has come to adopt the child. Pinkerton, overwhelmed with remorse, leaves the house after asking Sharpless to console Butterfly the best he can. A moment later Butterfly rushes in, joyfully expecting to find Pinkerton. Instead she sees Sharpless, a foreign woman, and Suzuki in tears. Slowly she begins to suspect the dreadful truth. She asks if *he* is alive, her voice hushed with expectant fear. Only Suzuki's broken "yes" is needed, and Butterfly now knows that she has been deserted. Mrs. Pinkerton expresses her helpless sympathy and asks to take the child. Butterfly, having listened in pathetic dignity, replies that only to Pinkerton will she yield her son. She will be ready in half an hour. Sharpless and Mrs. Pinkerton take their leave; Butterfly orders Suzuki to go into another room with the child.

Then she takes from its sheath the dagger with which her father had carried out the custom of his people, and reads the inscription written upon its blade: "To die with honor when one can no longer live with honor." She raises the knife to her throat. At that instant the door opens and little Trouble runs to her with outstretched arms. Butterfly drops the knife, impetuously seizes the child and covers him with kisses. Having bade him a heart-rending farewell, she gives her son a doll and an American flag, urges him to play with them, then gently bandages his eyes. Again she takes the dagger and goes behind the screen. A moment later the blade is heard falling to the floor. Butterfly staggers forward, groping her way to her child, takes his hand, and smiles feebly as she embraces him and dies.

Pinkerton is heard calling her name. A moment later he rushes into the room, followed by Sharpless. He kneels beside Butterfly, sobbing with grief and shame. Sharpless takes the child and turns away.

The orchestra thunders out a solemn Japanese melody. Over and above the very last note of that melody there sounds a poignant, questioning chord, as though this tragedy were not yet, nor ever would be, ended.

As Suzuki (Joann Grillo) weeps, Kate and Sharpless hear Cio-Cio-San (Renata Scotto) promise to surrender her child

The Magic Flute

DIE ZAUBERFLÖTE

CHARACTERS

Sarastro, *High Priest of Isis*	Bass	First Lady	*attendants of*	Soprano
Tamino, *an Egyptian Prince*	Tenor	Second Lady	*the Queen*	Mezzo-soprano
Papageno, *a birdcatcher*	Baritone	Third Lady	*of the Night*	Contralto
The Queen of the Night	Soprano		*belonging to*	
Pamina, *her daughter*	Soprano	First Boy	*the Temple*	Soprano
Monostatos, *a Moor*	Tenor	Second Boy	*and fulfilling*	Mezzo-soprano
Papagena	Soprano	Third Boy	*the designs of*	Contralto
The High Priest of Isis			*Sarastro*	
(*the speaker*)	Bass-baritone			

Priests and Priestesses of the Temple of Isis, Male and Female Slaves, Warriors of the Temple, Attendants, etc.

The action takes place in the Temple of Isis at Memphis and its vicinity about the time of Ramses I.

OPERA IN TWO ACTS. Music by Wolfgang Amadeus Mozart. Libretto in German by Emanuel Schikaneder, based on a tale by Wieland, "Lulu, or The Magic Flute." First performance, Theater auf der Wieden, Vienna, September 30, 1791, with Mozart conducting. Paris première, as *Les Mystères d'Isis*, August 20, 1801. American première, in English, Park Theater, New York, April 17, 1833. First performance at the Metropolitan Opera House, March 30, 1900, in Italian, with a cast headed by Marcella Sembrich, Emma Eames, Milka Ternina, Andreas Dippel, and Pol Plançon.

Schikaneder, who provided Mozart with the libretto of this immortal operatic allegory, has been called everything from arrant scalawag to wayward genius. So with his libretto. Sober critics have dismissed it as a fabric of absurdities. Others, equally sober, have found it a consistent tissue of allegorical symbols, the work of a master of subtle suggestion and satire. If the latter position is correct, *The Magic Flute* is a wondrous representation of Freemasonry, of which both Mozart and his erratic collaborator were enrolled members.

A seeming wonder book of sorcery and fantasy thus becomes the illustrated manifesto of a social and political creed, perhaps even a shrewdly veiled assault on all forms of autocratic rule, including that of the Hapsburgs. With this interpretation, the "Mysteries of Isis" are nothing more than the mysteries of Freemasonry. Maria Theresa, who actually used violence in breaking up Masonic gatherings, presumably appears as the Queen of the Night. In Tamino, scholars have discerned the Emperor Josef II, who often acted in defense of the secret order. And the Austrian people themselves supposedly have a spokeswoman in Pamina. Again assuming the presence of Masonic ritual, *The Magic Flute* reveals three levels of meaning. The fantastic tale itself, with its fairyland aura of wonder and witchcraft, is one. The Masonic symbolism is another. And the third is the moral allegory involved: the struggle of humanity through adversity, self-sacrifice, and love to achieve true wisdom and nobility.

And what kind of music did the divine Mozart

give to this fairy extravaganza with a double allegory? A godlike magic breathes through this score, said Wagner. The quintessence of art, he called it. The young of all ages are drawn by this miraculous blend of mystery, romance, and comedy. *The Magic Flute* is perhaps the most original flight of Mozart's creative fancy. It owes next to nothing to his predecessors of opera and symphony. Ravishing melodies abound in every scene. *The Magic Flute* is indeed magic.

OVERTURE

The Overture, in E flat major, 4-4, opens with three massive chords for full orchestra. These later break into the brilliant allegro of the fugue section. A mysterious Masonic significance is supposed to attach to these solemn chords, which form the only part of the Overture to appear in the opera itself.

ACT I

SCENE 1: A lonely landscape. Rugged cliffs loom on all sides. To the left, in the foreground, is a cave. In the background the Temple of the Queen of the Night is visible. Alone and unarmed, Tamino, an Egyptian Prince separated from his traveling companions, is being pursued by a serpent. Overcome by fright and fatigue, he collapses at the entrance to the cave. Three veiled ladies, attendants of the Queen of the Night, fly from the Temple, armed with silver javelins, and with the cry "Die, monster!" they

Metropolitan Opera Pamina (Pilar Lorengar), Papageno (Hermann Prey)

New York City Opera Queen of the Night (Beverly Sills)

pierce the serpent with their weapons. The three ladies gaze admiringly on the unconscious youth, then hurry off to tell the Queen of the occurrence.

At the sound of a flute Tamino revives, sees the dead serpent, and hides himself. Papageno, a roguish birdcatcher and would-be ladies' man, enters. Prepared to strike a bargain with the Queen's attendants, he places his bird cage on the ground and announces his presence by blowing on his pipes. The roguishness of the man may be gathered from his merry song *"Der Vogelfänger bin ich ja"* ("The birdcatcher am I"). Though birdcatching is his occupation, he would much rather be catching pretty girls, confesses Papageno the fowler. Tamino steps from his hiding place and, assuming that Papageno killed the serpent, thanks him for saving his life. As Papageno ostentatiously accepts the honor, the three veiled ladies, who have overheard the falsehood, step forward and rebuke him. One of them places a padlock on his lips, reducing his vocabulary to "hm, hm, hm." The three ladies then turn to Prince Tamino, one of them offering him a picture of the Queen's beautiful daughter. In a suavely tender song—*"Dies Bildnis ist bezaubernd schön"* ("This picture is bewitchingly lovely")—Tamino rhapsodizes on the girl's beauty, ending with a vow to make her his forever.

On that pledge there is a loud clap of thunder, and as the scene darkens, the mountains open and show the star-bedecked throne of the Queen of the Night. In anxious tones the Queen informs Tamino of her daughter's plight, and the purpose of the picture now becomes clear. The lovely Pamina has been abducted by a scoundrel, and the Queen can still hear her helpless screams. Tamino is to recover the girl and avenge the Queen, for which he will be rewarded with Pamina's hand. There is another thunderclap as the Queen withdraws, leaving Tamino deeply moved by her plea. From the three ladies, Tamino learns that the abductor was none other than Sarastro, high priest of Isis. His interest excited by Pamina's beauty and the mother's words, Tamino promptly agrees to undertake the rescue. A magic flute is given Tamino, one capable of protecting its bearer in all dangers. Papageno is instructed to accompany him on his adventure. Before the two men leave, the ladies remove the padlock from the birdcatcher's lips, with a warning about future lying. Papageno is now given a casket containing chimes whose magic power will offer them further protection. The ladies take leave of Tamino and Papageno, who set out on their mission, guided by three boys.

SCENE 2: *A room in Sarastro's palace*. Pamina is being guarded by Monostatos, a Moor, who has been using his position to force his attentions on her. Papageno breaks into the room while the Moor is absorbed in watching the captive princess. True to form, the birdcatcher is entranced by the girl's beauty. The Moor, turning around, starts up in fright, and for his part Papageno is just as frightened by the Moor's appearance. Each takes the other for the devil, and they scurry off in opposite directions. Remembering Tamino's instructions, Papageno finally overcomes his fear and returns to Pamina's chamber. Once back, he tells her the purpose of his visit and proceeds to compare her, itemizing all details, with the portrait that he wears on a ribbon around his neck. He urges Pamina to place her trust in him. When Pamina learns that Papageno has neither wife nor sweetheart, she counsels him to have patience, and the pair join in a duet of infinite grace and rippling gaiety on the theme that "men who are in love cannot fail to be goodhearted" —"*Bei Männern, welche Liebe fühlen, fehlt auch ein gutes Herze nicht.*" The melody of this duet is from an old German folk song. After some hesitation Pamina leaves the castle in Papageno's company.

SCENE 3: *A grove and entrance to the temples*. Led by three boys carrying silver palm branches, Tamino has reached Sarastro's castle and is now in a secret grove in the middle of which stand three temples. At two of the entrances Tamino is denied admittance. At the third a priest of Isis appears, and for the first time Tamino hears of the true character of Sarastro. He is a man of lofty ideals, governing with virtue and truth. Still incredulous, Tamino sneeringly reminds the priest of Pamina's abduction. The priest refuses to explain, mysteriously promising an answer to the riddle when "the land of friendship" will lead Tamino into "the sanctuary of eternal union." The priest disappears through the same portal from which he emerged.

Alone, Tamino is a prey to conflicting thoughts. Love for the Pamina of the portrait and pity for the Queen still dominate his heart, but a yearning for true wisdom and a desire to know the real nature of Sarastro have gripped him, too. A mysterious voice assures him that Pamina still lives and that soon—or never—his eyes will find the light. As Tamino puts the magic flute to his lips and plays, its effect is truly magical! The panpipes of Papageno immediately answer, and Tamino rushes off to find his lost companion. Misled by echoes, he takes the wrong direction. He has scarcely left when Pamina and Papageno appear before the castle. Papageno silences the terrified girl when she thoughtlessly calls aloud for Tamino. He tries his panpipes, and promptly comes the response of the magic flute. But Pamina's outcry has brought Monostatos and a troop of slaves upon them. When all hope seems lost, Papageno remembers the casket of chimes. As the cover flies open and the magic bells begin to play, a spell is cast over the slaves, whose enchanted limbs move only in time with the music.

Pamina and Papageno again set out to find Tamino, but it is too late. A brilliant flourish of trumpets and drums is heard, and to the cry, "Long live Sarastro!" the high priest of Isis makes a majestic entrance, followed by a host of celebrants.

Tamino (Michele Molese) with flute and boasts at the New York City Opera

Throwing herself at Sarastro's feet, Pamina admits her guilt in trying to escape, but accuses Monostatos of designs upon her. Sarastro urges her to rise and tells her that he knows what is in her heart, but warns her that only evil can come from her mother. At that moment Monostatos and his slaves bring in the captured Prince. As they catch sight of one another, Tamino and Pamina rush into each other's arms. Sarastro orders Monostatos whipped; then, turning to two of his priests, he instructs them to bring veils for Pamina and Tamino. The lovers are then conducted into the temple of probation, to be purified by the secret rites.

ACT II

SCENE 1: *A palm grove.* In the Temple of Wisdom the priests of Isis have assembled to consider whether Tamino is ready to be initiated into the final mysteries. Sarastro pleads warmly for the youth and reveals that the gods have ordained his marriage to Pamina. All signify their approval by blowing into their horns. Sarastro now leads the priestly gathering in a solemn invocation to the gods, *"O Isis und Osiris!"* begging them to grant the worthy couple strength and courage for their impending trials. Sarastro and the priests then depart in a solemn procession.

SCENE 2: *Courtyard of the temple.* Tamino and Papageno are led out by priests, who warn them that they are to be subjected to severe tests of faith and fortitude. Tamino will see Pamina, but he must not speak to her, for the probation will have begun. Papageno is undecided, but his hesitation vanishes when a priest announces that Sarastro has reserved a beautiful bride—appropriately named Papagena—for him. But he, too, is not to speak to her till the appointed time. Before they leave, the priests caution the companions against the wiles of women. Silence must be maintained at all costs! It now grows dark. Suddenly three torches, borne by the three veiled ladies of the Queen of the Night, flash in the dark, and Tamino's trial begins. Expressing horror at finding the Prince and his companion in this den of evil, the ladies implore him to flee before it is too late. They warn them that their death is already ordained and remind Tamino of his vow to help the Queen, who has herself stolen into Sarastro's temple in search of her kidnaped daughter. Tamino listens unmoved, then rebukes Papageno for speaking out and breaking his oath of silence. The three ladies flee in terror as a burst of thunder is heard and priests rush in, wrathfully condemning the intruders to perdition for defiling the sacred threshold.

SCENE 3: *A garden.* Moonlight falls upon Pamina, who lies sleeping on a bench overhung with roses. Monostatos steals in cautiously and, smitten by the sight of Pamina, attempts to steal a kiss. As he approaches the sleeping girl, the Queen of the Night appears and cries out, "Back!" In imperious tones she bursts into a magnificent soliloquy, *"Der Hölle Rache kocht in meinem Herzen"* ("The vengeance of hell seethes in my heart"), the delivery of which demands great dramatic power and supreme vocal technique in handling the brilliant flurry of staccati in the high soprano register. The Queen addresses the sleeping girl in dire tones. Avenge your mother, she cries, or be forever disowned as her daughter! Pamina awakens, and with a cry of "Mother! Mother!" falls into the Queen's arms. Pamina recoils, however, when the Queen hands her a dagger. "You must kill Sarastro and bring me back the mighty zodiac!" demands the Queen. Before Pamina can protest, there is a roar of thunder and the Queen disappears. Monostatos again approaches the anxious girl, promising a way out for mother and daughter if she will yield to him. Pamina draws back horrified, and as the Moor comes nearer, Sarastro appears and steps between them. Angrily, the high priest orders Monostatos out. As Pamina pleads for her mother's safety, Sarastro in a noble and moving cavatina—*"In diesen heil'gen Hallen."* ("Within these sacred halls")—assures her that in this holy place vengeance is a stranger and enemies are forgiven.

SCENE 4: *A hall in the Temple of Probation.* Though Sarastro is satisfied with their behavior thus far, the ordeal has only begun for Tamino and Papageno. Led in once more by the priests, the companions are again warned about keeping their lips sealed. But Papageno, unable to restrain himself, begins chattering away with an old woman who brings him a drink of water. A menacing roar of thunder speedily frightens her away and reminds Papageno of his vow. Presently the three youths reappear, bringing with them the flute, the bells, and a table covered with food. Papageno applies himself diligently to a repast as Tamino plays on his flute. Drawn by the magic tones, Pamina appears and greets Tamino rapturously, only to be met by a stony silence. Certain now that Tamino no longer loves her, the girl expresses her sadness in a touching aria, *"Ach, ich fühl's, es ist verschwunden, ewig hin mein ganzes Glück!"* ("Ah, I feel it, love's happiness has vanished forever!")—an aria calling for infinite grace of phrasing and delicacy of style. Hoping now only for death, Pamina leaves, with Tamino gazing sorrowfully after her. At that point the priestly trumpets ring out again, and Tamino wrenches

Papagena (Patricia Welting) and Papageno (Theodor Uppman) in fine feathers of Marc Chagall's Metropolitan décor

Papageno away from his feasting, reminding him of the tests still to come.

SCENE 5: *A place near the Pyramids.* Still obliged to keep silent, Tamino is brought in, veiled by the priests, to be subjected to further trials of faith and endurance. Pamina, also wearing a veil, follows him, and is soon informed that Tamino is waiting to bid her good-by. Hopefully, Pamina rushes to him, only to be motioned away in apparent coldness. Again Pamina reproaches him for his apathy, declaring that her love is stronger than his. Sarastro assures them both of a happy outcome to the trial if they will only be patient, and as he accompanies Tamino, two priests lead the despairing Pamina away. As they all depart, Papageno enters, thirsty and bewildered. Angrily, he cries out to the Speaker that he would renounce all hope of heavenly bliss for one glass of wine. A huge wine goblet appears, and as Papageno drinks and grows gay, he plays his magic chimes and chants merrily of the tender little wife he would like to have. Suddenly his wish comes true. In comes the old woman again, announcing herself as the coveted bride and swearing eternal constancy to him. Papageno is warned that to spurn her will mean an everlasting diet of bread and water for him. With the whispered reservation of remaining true to her "as long as I see no fairer one," Papageno

accepts, and the old woman is suddenly transformed into a young beauty. With a cry of "Papagena!" the birdcatcher tries to embrace her, but the Speaker intervenes, and, taking the young woman by the hand, drags her off with the words: "He is not yet worthy of you!"

SCENE 6: *A garden with a lake in the background.* Pamina is delirious in her grief. Her mother's command to murder Sarastro and Tamino's apparent coldness are too much for her. Her mind is beginning to snap, and Pamina raises the dagger to kill herself, when the three youths stop her, warning her gravely that suicide is punished by God. They assure her that Tamino loves her dearly and would be driven insane were he to hear of this rash act of hers. Pamina rejoices over this assurance and asks to be led to Tamino.

SCENE 7: *A wild mountain spot.* A huge iron gate stands between two caves on a mountainside. On one side is a roaring stream, on the other a brightly glowing fire. It is twilight. Tamino appears with two priests. From outside comes the sound of Pamina's voice. The priests tell Tamino that he who overcomes dangers in pursuing his ideals will conquer death and become godlike. Tamino attests his fearlessness, and as a reward the priests bring out Pamina. The lovers embrace ardently. Tamino points to the deadly caverns through which they must venture as a final test. Pamina, certain that love will smooth the way, takes him by the hand and urges him to play the magic flute for protection—the flute that she now reveals was fashioned by her father from a thousand-year-old oak. The lovers emerge from probation of fire unscathed. Once more with the help of the flute's protective tones, they brave the cavern of water. As they reappear, again unharmed, the gathered priests hail them in an exultant chorus on their consecration to Isis. Pamina and Tamino now wend their way to the temple.

SCENE 8: *A small garden.* Despairing over his unrequited love for Papagena, Papageno resolves to kill himself by hanging. As he sallies out dramatically with a rope, a nearby tree beckons conveniently. Just then the three youths hurry in, chiding Papageno on his rashness and asking him why he does not use his magic chimes to help him out of his misery. Papageno jumps at the suggestion, and now the bells peal cheerily as he wishes out loud for the little maiden. The three youths vanish, and presto! they are back with Papagena. The two greet each other ecstatically and chatter gaily about the lovely little Papagenos

and Papagenas that will be theirs once they are wed. They leave arm in arm.

SCENE 9: *Rugged cliffs.* It is night. Monostatos, the Queen of the Night, and the three ladies steal silently toward Sarastro's temple, all bearing torches. These creatures of evil are making one final effort to destroy Sarastro's power. For his connivance Monostatos has been promised Pamina as bride. Thunder and the roar of rushing water reach the ears of the conspirators. There is a flash of lightning as the earth opens and wraps the villainous crew in eternal night.

SCENE 10: *The Temple of the Sun.* Sarastro is presiding over a solemn conclave of priests and priestesses. As the three youths stand by with flowers in their hands, Tamino and Pamina appear before him in priestly robes. In a majestic address, Sarastro pronounces the couple consecrated in the worship of Isis. The sun's rays have banished night and the forces of darkness. And now the celebrants raise their voices in homage to Isis and Osiris, chanting, "The strong have conquered, and may beauty and wisdom be their eternal reward!"

Finale of 1955 Metropolitan staging with Brian Sullivan (Tamino), Jerome Hines (Sarastro), Lucine Amara (Pamina)

Manon

CHARACTERS

Manon, *a girl of fifteen*	Soprano	Guillot de Morfontaine, *a roué,*	
Chevalier des Grieux	Tenor	*Minister of France*	Bass
Count des Grieux, *his father*	Bass	De Brétigny, *a nobleman*	Baritone
Lescaut, *Manon's cousin, one of the*		Pousette ⎫	Soprano
Royal Guards	Baritone	Javotte ⎬ *three*	Mezzo-soprano
		Rosetto ⎭ *actresses*	Mezzo-soprano

Students, Guards, Travelers, Gamblers

The action takes place in Amiens, Paris, and Le Havre about the year 1721.

OPERA IN FIVE ACTS, music by Jules Massenet. Libretto in French by Henri Meilhac and Philippe Gille, after the novel *Les Aventures du Chevalier des Grieux et de Manon Lescaut* by the Abbé Antoine François Prévost. First produced at the Opera-Comique, Paris, January 19, 1884. First American performance, at the Academy of Music, New York, December 23, 1885, in Italian. First performance at the Metropolitan, in French, January 16, 1895, with a cast comprising Sibyl Sanderson, who made her American debut, Jean de Reszke, Mario Ancona, and Pol Plançon.

The Prévost romance has had several operatic settings besides Massenet's, including one each by Auber and Puccini, while Halévy made it the subject of a ballet. The libretto for the present setting is rather fragmentary, although the delicately molded score does everything to disguise such shortcomings. Massenet, it is said, composed the music during the summer of 1882, at The Hague, while residing in the very quarters formerly occupied by the Abbé Prévost. It is Massenet's best-loved and most successful work.

Sibyl Sanderson, first Metropolitan Manon, in 1895

ACT I

SCENE: *The courtyard of the inn at Amiens.* Among the variegated crowd gathered at the courtyard of an inn at Amiens to meet the arrival of the coach is Lescaut, member of the Royal Guard and soldier of fortune. He has come to meet his young cousin Manon and is to escort her to a convent. He is pleasurably surprised to find her as beautiful as she is unsophisticated. He accepts her proffered lips in cousinly greeting, then hastens within to engage rooms.

No sooner has he gone than the old roué Guillot de Morfontaine trots out into the courtyard and begins to pay marked attention to the girl, who is thereby amused and a trifle flattered. Some among the crowd make game of the old libertine, who, however, is soon called back to the inn by his traveling companion de Brétigny. Among those haunting the courtyard are three girls of doubtful character, whose fine apparel is not lost on Manon. She thinks, between sighs and tears, of her own sad lot and her approaching gray life in a convent. Her musings are interrupted, for the handsome Chevalier des Grieux, son of the Count des Grieux, has entered, and, struck by Manon's beauty, addresses her. They become quickly acquainted and, almost before they know it, fall in love.

A carriage previously placed at the disposal of the girl by the infatuated Guillot unexpectedly draws near; intoxicated with her new-found love, she suggests impulsively that they fly together to Paris. Des Grieux joyfully agrees, and they sing rapturously of the life they will live together there. Suddenly Manon hears the voice of her cousin Lescaut; the lovers leap into the carriage and disappear.

Lescaut comes out wrathfully; there has been

Giuseppe di Stefano as the Chevalier des Grieux, 1947

Victoria de los Angeles as Manon at Cours-la-Reine

gambling in the inn and he has lost his money, and now he learns that he has also lost his cousin. Guillot appears, anticipating another tête-à-tête with Manon; instead he is accused by Lescaut of having abducted the girl. A crowd assembles, watching the growing argument, which is calmed by the observing innkeeper, who says that Manon departed with a young man. In the distance they hear the departing coach.

ACT II

SCENE: *The Chevalier des Grieux's apartment in Paris.* Manon and des Grieux are now happily living together in Paris. Des Grieux is writing to his father and trembles for fear the old man may read in anger what he writes from the heart. "Afraid?" says Manon, who stands looking over his shoulder. "Then we'll read together." She takes the letter and begins to read: "She is called Manon, so young and fair . . ." Some little glint of the girl's weakness is visible in her response to his glowing phrase. "In her eyes shines the tender light of love." "Is this true?" asks Manon. Des Grieux will soon ask himself the same question, but now he continues reading his poetic rhapsody. He is certain that his father will give his consent, and they embrace tenderly. As he passes to go out, he notices a bouquet of flowers mysteriously left for Manon. She returns only an evasive answer to his questions. As the perturbed des Grieux opens the door to leave, Lescaut and de Brétigny enter. Lescaut demands satisfaction for the abduction of his cousin. Des Grieux takes him aside, and shows him the letter to his father as proof of his honorable intentions. De Brétigny, left with Manon, makes the best of his time; he says that des Grieux is to be carried away by his own father that very night and urges her to fly with him. Knowing that de Brétigny can give her the pretty things for which her heart longs, Manon hesitates—and is lost. Lescaut, now seemingly appeased, departs with de Brétigny, and des Grieux goes out to mail his letter. Left alone, Manon struggles with herself and sings a charming farewell to the little table at which des Grieux and she have been so happy, *"Adieu, notre petite table"* (*"Farewell, our little table"*).

When he returns he finds her in tears which she cannot quite conceal. Seeking to comfort her, he tells her of his dream, singing a sweet, rapturous melody, while the orchestra supplies a softly murmuring accompaniment. He describes the little home he plans to share with her, in the aria *"En fermant les yeux"* (*"As I close my eyes"*), better known, perhaps, as "The Dream."

A knock on the door halts the dream; Manon starts guiltily. She tries to prevent him from opening, knowing that he is to be abducted, but he insists

—is captured and borne off. Now Manon is in despair.

ACT III

SCENE 1: *Cours-la-Reine*. It is a holiday, and crowds are making merry on the square in Paris known as Cours-la-Reine. Old Guillot is flirting with any girl who will look at him, and Lescaut obliges with a sentimental little tune, *"O Rosalinde."* De Brétigny mocks Guillot and warns him against trying to steal his latest mistress from him, who is Manon. As a matter of fact, that is precisely what Guillot hopes to do—and he goes off to engage some dancers to entertain everyone. When Manon arrives, she sings the delightful *"Gavotte."*

Presently the old Count des Grieux joins the crowd, and she overhears him telling de Brétigny that his son the Chevalier is studying at the semi-

Act III, Scene 1: Manon (Licia Albanese) fascinates a crowd at Cours-la-Reine by singing a brilliant gavotte

Act IV: Manon (Anna Moffo), Des Grieux (Nicolai Gedda) and Lescaut (Frank Guarrera) in the gambling casino

nary of St. Sulpice with the idea of entering the priesthood. And so, when Guillot returns with his little ballet company, Manon has no heart for the entertainment but steals away to where she will find her first lover.

SCENE 2: *At the Church of St. Sulpice.* In the lobby of St. Sulpice, young des Grieux has just preached his first sermon and is receiving congratulations on its excellence. Presently his father interviews him alone and tries—but without success—to persuade him to abandon his new profession. As he tells us in a beautiful soliloquy (*"Ah! fuyez, douce image"*) when his father has left, the newly made abbé hopes to forget his love for Manon in the religious life.

A religious service now begins, and as the choir within intones a *"Magnificat,"* Manon slips into the lobby and prays fervidly that God may forgive her and that she may be reunited with des Grieux. The young man, coming from the service, tries at first to resist the temptation she eloquently offers, but it is too attractive for him, and as the curtain descends, he leaves the church with his love.

ACT IV

SCENE: *Gambling salon of the Hotel de Transylvanie.* Lescaut, for a change, is winning, while old Guillot, as usual, pays as much attention to the girls present as to the cards. Manon leads in her reluctant lover des Grieux and manages to persuade him to try his hand. Guillot is his opponent, and the young man, with beginner's luck, wins some considerable

sums. Guillot thereupon accuses him of cheating, and they almost come to blows. The old roué, however, leaves the house, muttering a threat.

When he returns very shortly, he has police officers with him and demands that des Grieux and Manon be put under arrest. They are already in custody when the Count des Grieux arrives, and his son pleads with him to save Manon. The Count says he can do nothing now but will see that the Chevalier is released later. As for Manon, she knows that she cannot be saved: women of light character were dealt with severely once they came into the hands of the police.

ACT V

SCENE: *On the road to Le Havre.* Manon has been sentenced to deportation to the colony of Louisiana, and Lescaut, with des Grieux, has resolved to try to rescue her on the way to the harbor. In the distance the guards are heard singing; and then two of them come on discussing Manon, who, they say, is on the point of death. Lescaut, without too much difficulty, bribes the guards to leave their sick prisoner for a while with des Grieux. He proposes that they should go to the new country together and begin a new life. But Manon is past any such undertaking. As night descends, she becomes almost delirious and can think only of repentance and of the one time in her life when she was happy—the time with des Grieux. In her lover's arms once more, she becomes weaker and weaker, and she dies, uttering the pathetic words *"Et c'est l'histoire de Manon Lescaut."* Her story is done.

Manon Lescaut

CHARACTERS

Manon Lescaut, *a young girl*	*Soprano*	Géronte de Ravoir, *Treasurer*	
Lescaut, *her brother, a sergeant of*		*General*	*Bass*
the King's Guards	*Baritone*	Edmond, *a student, friend of*	
Chevalier des Grieux	*Tenor*	*des Grieux*	*Tenor*

An Innkeeper, a Dancing Master, a Sergeant, a Captain, Singers, Students, Citizens, Courtesans, Sailors

The action takes place in Amiens, Paris, Le Havre, and Louisiana during the early part of the eighteenth century.

OPERA IN FOUR ACTS. Music by Giacomo Puccini. Libretto in Italian by a group of writers, including Ruggiero Leoncavallo, Domenico Oliva, Marco Praga, Giuseppe Giacosa, Luigi Illica, and Giulio Ricordi, after the romance by the Abbé Prévost. First performance at the Teatro Regio, Turin, February 1, 1893. First United States performance, Grand Opera House, Philadelphia, August 29, 1894. Metropolitan première, January 18, 1907, with Lina Cavalieri as Manon and Enrico Caruso as des Grieux. Puccini's opera served to introduce two artists new to the Metropolitan, Lucrezia Bori, who made her debut as Manon, and Giorgio Polacco, who conducted, on November 11, 1912, Caruso again appearing as des Grieux.

Manon Lescaut is the earliest of Puccini's operas to hold a permanent place in the repertoire. In *Manon Lescaut* Puccini gives promise of the genius for effective operatic composition that was to flower three years later in *La Bohème,* and eventually to win him the rank of the foremost of modern Italian opera composers. In writing *Manon Lescaut* Puccini also displayed a certain boldness of spirit, for only a few years previously Massenet had written his own successful setting of Prévost's novel, while Puccini was himself still a young and relatively unknown composer. It seems inevitable to compare the two

Lina Cavalieri as Manon in 1907

251

works: Puccini's presents four relatively detached scenes that follow the novel rather closely; Massenet's departs somewhat from the novel in order to present a more unified drama, yet neither may be considered as having a better-than-average libretto. Puccini's opera makes no attempt to be anything other than Italian opera; Massenet's is thoroughly French in character. Both remain favorites.

ACT I

SCENE: *In a square of Amiens.* Students are singing and whiling away the time in front of an inn at Amiens. Des Grieux, dressed as a student, pensive and lonesome, enters but does not join heartily in the revels. Manon, with her rather irresponsible brother Lescaut and a chance acquaintance, Géronte, alight from a coach; and while the men are busied with arrangements at the inn, des Grieux speaks to her. She is, she tells him, on her way to a convent, rather against her will; just then her brother calls her from the inn. She assures des Grieux she will return later. Left alone, des Grieux meditates on the beauty of the woman he has just seen, singing an aria in which he declares that he has never before seen such a wonderful beauty, *"Donna non vidi"* ("Maiden so fair").

Géronte, an old libertine, secretly orders a swift horse and carriage with which he intends to abduct Manon, but Edmond, a student friend of des Grieux, overhears the plot. Warned by Edmond, the young

Manon (Dorothy Kirsten) at her dressing table, Act II

people elope and leave the irate Géronte to be consoled by Lescaut's suggestion that they will be found in Paris. It will be easy, he says, to lure a woman from a poor student.

ACT II

SCENE: *Géronte's apartment in Paris.* The opening of the second act reveals that Lescaut's prophecy has come true, for Manon, tiring of the humble life with des Grieux, is established in Géronte's luxurious apartment. But now, we discover, she is also tiring of that, for she asks Lescaut about des Grieux. When told that he has been gambling heavily in order to obtain enough money to win her back, she gazes at the rich hangings, the wealth about her, and sighs longingly for des Grieux and his simple little cottage (*"In quelle trine morbide"*) Musicians come to sing for her entertainment; they are followed by

Jussi Bjoerling as the Chevalier des Grieux, 1949

the old Géronte himself and a crowd of his cronies. Manon delights them all by dancing a minuet under the guidance of the dancing master. Then all but Manon leave for some brilliant party or other, she to follow presently. Suddenly des Grieux appears. He reproaches her for her faithlessness, singing, *"Ah! Manon, mi tradisce"* ("Ah! Manon betrays me"), but overcome by her nearness and earnest pleading, he soon joins her in a passionate duet of love.

They are found thus by Géronte, who returns to discover the cause of Manon's delay. He conceals his anger under the cold, polished manner of the man of the world, pretends to be forgiving, and leaves them with what seems to them to be an ironic indifference, although he does utter a threat or two. Alarmed, des Grieux urges her to come away with him, but, characteristically, she hesitates to give up all this splendor. However, she asks des Grieux's forgiveness for her apparent lack of enthusiasm, and just then Lescaut rushes in with the news that Géronte has turned her in to the police; the lovers must save themselves quickly. Again her love of pretty things is her undoing, for she stops to gather up her valuables, or as many as she can pick up under pressure, and secretes them in her cloak. She hides in an alcove, panic-stricken, and when Géronte and guards appear, they demand her surrender. Manon comes forth, and in her fear lets slip the cloak, the jewels falling to the floor. Géronte, at this, laughs sarcastically, and Manon is led away alone, charged with being an abandoned woman.

ACT III

An intermezzo is played here, expressing Manon's grief and des Grieux's despair.

SCENE: *In a square of Le Havre near the harbor.* Banished from France as an "undesirable," Manon is waiting to embark for the French province of Louisiana. Des Grieux and Lescaut bribe the guard, and are prevented from rescuing her only by the sudden arrival of the ship's captain. Des Grieux would follow when Manon is led away with a crowd of women who are also to be deported, but is restrained by the guard. In desperation he pleads with the captain, singing an intensely fervent aria, *"Guardate, come io piango."* The captain is sympathetic and finally consents to allow him aboard.

ACT IV

SCENE: *A vast plain near New Orleans.* The country is barren and uneven, and the approaching night is made gloomier by low overhanging clouds. Manon and des Grieux have fled to this desolate spot. They wander about, vainly seeking shelter, until Manon is exhausted, when des Grieux continues the search alone. Manon sings a pathetic soliloquy (*"Sola, perduta, abbandonata"*—"All is now over") and when des Grieux returns, Manon sinks, dying, into his arms.

Act IV: In the wasteland of Louisiana, Manon Lescaut (Mary Curtis-Verna) dies in the arms of Des Grieux (John Alexander)

The Marriage of Figaro

LE NOZZE DI FIGARO

CHARACTERS

Count Almaviva, *Grand Corregidor of Andalusia*	*Baritone*	Don Curzio, *counselor-at-law*	*Tenor*
Figaro, *his valet and major-domo of the château*	*Baritone*	Cherubino, *head page to the Count*	*Soprano or Mezzo-Soprano*
Dr. Bartolo, *a physician of Seville*	*Bass*	Countess Almaviva	*Soprano*
Don Basilio, *music master to the Countess*	*Tenor*	Susanna, *head waiting woman to the Countess, betrothed to Figaro*	*Soprano*
Antonio, *gardener of the château and Susanna's uncle*	*Bass*	Marcellina, *Dr. Bartolo's housekeeper*	*Contralto*
		Barbarina, *Antonio's daughter*	*Soprano*

Servants, Officers of the Court, and Peasants

The action takes place at Count Almaviva's château in the country near Seville in the eighteenth century.

OPERA BUFFA IN FOUR ACTS. Music by Wolfgang Amadeus Mozart. Libretto in Italian by Lorenzo da Ponte, after Beaumarchais' comedy, *Le Marriage de Figaro,* the second in a trilogy which opens with *The Barber of Seville,* subject of Rossini's famous operatic comedy, and closes with *The Culpable Mother.* Mozart's work was first performed at the Burgtheater, Vienna, May 1, 1786, the composer conducting. There is some dispute as to the first performance of the opera in America, since it is said to have been given in New York, under the title *The Follies of a Day,* as early as 1799, although a performance at the Park Theater, New York, in English, presented on May 10, 1824, was advertised as the "first time in America." Be this as it may, *The Marriage of Figaro* was quite popular in English versions produced during the early part of the nineteenth century. It was given in Italian at the Academy of Music, New York, on November 23, 1858, and in German at the German Opera House, also New York, on December 18, 1862. The Metropolitan première took place in Italian on January 31, 1894, with Lillian Nordica as Susanna, Emma Eames as Countess Almaviva, Sigrid Arnoldson as Cherubino, Mario Ancona as Figaro, and Édouard de Reszke as Almaviva. Enrico Bevignani conducted.

The Marriage of Figaro remains one of the greatest masterpieces of comedy in music. Mozart's melodies, with all their charm, perfection of form, utter spontaneity, and apparent naïveté, are enormously faithful to character and situation. Moreover, they sparkle with all the wit and gaiety of Beaumarchais' humorous work. Nor, for that matter, can anything but praise be said for the shrewdly contrived libretto of da Ponte, who here, as in *Don Giovanni,* is at the top of his art.

Although Beaumarchais' comedy teems with social and political implications—Figaro's witty and highhanded attitude toward his aristocratic master, Almaviva, being in those days a sign of things to come—there is really little of it in the opera.

OVERTURE

The Overture to *The Marriage of Figaro* is a bubbling, delightful piece of music more or less in sonata form, full of good humor and activity. Its themes are its own, not appearing anywhere else in the opera, yet they are entirely in the spirit of the whole work. There is no free fantasia, although the coda is longer than ordinary. This overture is a very popular one in the concert hall.

ACT I

SCENE: *The room assigned to Figaro and Susanna.* Figaro is busy measuring the size of the room given to him and his bride-to-be, Susanna. He remarks how convenient it will be for him to wait on his master, the Count, and yet equally convenient for Susanna to attend her mistress, the Countess. Susanna suddenly dampens his ardor by remarking that the Count has had a more subtle reason in giving them a room so near his own. She calls Figaro a "goose" for not observing this or realizing that the Count was moved by anything other than generosity in paying her dowry. Figaro intends to investigate these matters, feeling quite capable of handling his employer. He makes this attitude known in the aria *"Se vuol ballare, signor contino"* ("If you wish to dance, my little Count"). So soon has the gallant young Count Almaviva grown faithless to his wife, the formerly beloved Rosina! Still further troubles are to beset the erstwhile barber of Seville, for old Dr. Bartolo, whom he outwitted in former days, still bears a grudge against him. Bartolo discovers that in a weak moment Figaro promised to marry the aged Marcellina, and that the old lady would compel him to fulfill the contract. Susanna fortunately overhears the plotting of this unattractive couple. After a short encounter Susanna and Marcellina make for the center door, where, in an amusing duet, exaggerated compliments give way to abuse. When they have gone, the adolescent Cherubino enters, who is at the tender age susceptible to anything feminine, and has fallen deeply in love, if you please, with no less a personage than the Countess herself. He describes his feeling in the endearing and swift-moving aria *"Non so più cosa son"* ("I know not what I am doing").

Suddenly the Count is heard approaching, and Cherubino hastily conceals himself behind a large armchair. The Count has come to complain against Cherubino, whom he suspects of paying attention to the Countess. But even as he speaks, a knock is heard. The Count hastily hides behind the same chair as the page, who, cleverly darting around out

Cherubino (Teresa Berganza), Susanna (Mirella Freni), Figaro (Cesare Siepi) in Act I finale, Metropolitan Opera

of the Count's way, sinks into the depths of the chair. Susanna quickly covers him with a dress that happens to lie at hand. The busybody Basilio enters and taunts Susanna for flirting with the Count, then twits her about Cherubino. As soon, however, as Basilio mentions Cherubino's name in connection with that of the Countess, Almaviva, unable to stand it longer, jumps from his hiding place and demands an explanation. He goes on to tell how a short while ago he discovered the boy concealed under a table, flirting with Barbarina. In order to demonstrate how he found the youth when he lifted up the tablecloth, the Count goes over to the armchair and pulls away the dress. And lo! there again is Cherubino! The Count is beside himself with rage and a fine ensemble develops.

At this point Figaro returns with a group of peasants, who sing a complimentary song to the Count, thus changing the whole tone of the scene. When they have departed, Almaviva has a sudden inspiration. There is a commission vacant in his

Act II, the Countess's room: Rosina (Elisabeth Rethberg), Figaro (Ezio Pinza), Susanna (Bidù Sayão), Basilio (Alessio De Paolis), Almaviva (John Brownlee), Marcellina (Irra Petina), Bartolo (Salvatore Baccaloni), in the 1940 Metropolitan Opera revival

regiment; Cherubino shall have it. He must go at once. Figaro laughingly tells the page that now instead of tender love-making he will have weary marching, and he apprises him of all this in the tripping, mock-military aria *"Non più andrai"* ("Now your days of philandering are over").

ACT II

SCENE: *The Countess' apartment.* When the curtain rises, we find the Countess alone. She is meditating upon her happy past and unhappy present. Still deeply in love with her husband, she slowly realizes that she is not the only woman in his life. She then gives vent to her feelings in a touching and expressive song in which she prays that her husband's affection may be restored to her, or else to let her find escape from her grief in death. This is the aria *"Porgi amor"* ("Love, thou holy purest impulse").

Susanna then enters, and the two ladies despair because of the Count's wayward affections, although Susanna tries to hearten her mistress. The resourceful Figaro, entering, reveals a plan, already put into effect, for reawakening the Count's interest in his wife—make him jealous by letting him discover a note arranging a rendezvous between the Countess and a lover. They decide to send Susanna in the Countess' place, and Cherubino, dressed as Susanna, to meet the Count. Thus it is hoped that through ridicule the Count will be persuaded to remain faithful to his Countess.

Cherubino comes, delighted at the thought of seeing the Countess before his departure. He sings, *"Voi che sapete"* ("What is this feeling?"), a delineation of the love emotion characteristic of early youth. Continuing with their plot, the women proceed to dress him in the maid's garments. Susanna sings a fascinatingly humorous aria in which she coquettishly bids him kneel before her and tells him first to turn one way and then another while she adapts the feminine apparel to his person, *"Venite, inginocchiatevi"* ("Come, kneel down").

The Countess happens to notice Cherubino's officer's commission, and observes that the seal to it has been forgotten. Suddenly her husband is heard angrily knocking outside. Cherubino scurries into hiding in a closet. The Count enters just in time to hear him upset a chair in his blind haste, and, observing his wife's confusion, he demands admission to the closet. Susanna, concealed in an alcove, hears the Countess refuse on the ground that her maid is in the closet, dressing. The suspicious Count, however, goes out for a crowbar to break down the door and insists on taking the Countess with him. As soon as they have gone Cherubino emerges and escapes through the window, and Susanna quickly hides in the cabinet in his place. When the Count returns, prepared to batter away, the Countess finally confesses that Cherubino is there. Then follows a dramatic duet which depicts the Count's heated anger and the anxious pleading of the Countess. Thus she is quite as startled as her husband when Susanna suddenly appears! The Count then becomes penitent and asks his wife's forgiveness.

Figaro now enters to accompany Susanna to the wedding. Shortly after, as luck would have it, Antonio the gardener enters in an inebriated state. He is carrying a couple of shattered flowerpots and demands an audience with his master. He wants to lodge a complaint against someone who had jumped out of the window of the Countess' room and escaped through the garden. Figaro with great difficulty silences the Count's newly aroused suspicions by announcing himself as the culprit. The gardener spoils this by producing a paper that was dropped by the fugitive; the Count says that he will believe Figaro's story if he is able to tell what this paper contains. Through a quick whisper from the Countess passed along by Susanna, Figaro learns it is Cherubino's commission. This would make things look rather bad for the Countess, but the quick-witted Figaro, again prompted by the women, declares that he had the commission in his pocket in order to have it looked after, for it lacked a seal. The day is saved, but Figaro now has a worse problem to face. Marcellina enters with her lawyer and demands that Figaro shall keep his promise to marry her. The Count, rather eager to settle accounts with the valet, says that he will look into this!

ACT III

SCENE: *A hall in Almaviva's château.* Count Almaviva plans to force Susanna to accept his attentions by threatening to make Figaro wed the aged Marcellina; and Susanna, wishing to further the plans of her mistress, seems to surrender. As he goes away, rejoicing in his triumph, the Count overhears Susanna exclaim to Figaro, "Our cause is victorious!" Growing suspicious, the Count resolves to punish Figaro at once and deal with Susanna later.

Accordingly, Marcellina, her lawyer, the Count, and Bartolo arrive to inform Figaro that he must marry as he has promised, or pay damages. Figaro thinks he may be rich enough to pay the damages, for he has just discovered clues that suggest that he may be of noble birth. While he is explaining, Marcellina suddenly asks if he has a spatula mark upon his right arm. He has. By this she knows him to be her long-lost son by none other than Bartolo! Mother and son embrace and are so discovered by

Susanna, who is much distressed until matters are explained. At last Susanna and Figaro are free to go ahead with preparations for their wedding. The Countess then arrives. She is deeply concerned as to how her husband will take the deception that is to be practiced on him in the garden. She is still deeply in love with him and deplores the fact that she must seek the help of her servants to win back his affection. In an aria of tenderness and beauty, she regrets her lost days of happiness, *"Dove sono"* ("They are over").

Continuing with the plot, Susanna meets with the Countess and at her dictation writes a letter to the Count fixing exactly the time and place of their rendezvous. Known as the "Letter Duet," with Susanna repeatedly echoing her mistress' dictation. The letter is sealed with a pin which the Count is to return as a sign that he will keep the appointment. Rather than send Cherubino, the Countess herself has decided to go disguised as Susanna.

The wedding of Susanna and Figaro forthwith takes place. Cherubino, in female attire, Barbarina, and a group of peasant girls present a bunch of flowers to the Countess as the festivities commence. Then, during a brief dance in dignified Spanish style, Susanna contrives to slip the letter to the Count, who pricks his finger on the pin. Figaro observes this without, however, suspecting anything.

ACT IV

SCENE: *The garden of the château.* Barbarina, the gardener's daughter, is looking for a pin she has

Act III: Susanna (Judith Raskin), Countess (Lisa Della Casa)

lost, the pin with which Susanna had sealed her letter to the Count, and which Barbarina had been entrusted to return. Figaro learns of this from the unsuspecting child, and hastily decides that Susanna actually is faithless and intends to yield to the Count that very evening. He sings his aria *"Aprite un po' quegli occhi,"* in which he warns all men of the fickleness of women.

It is night in the park of the château, just such a night as is made for love and intrigue. Figaro has come to the rendezvous intending to spy on the supposed infidelity of his bride; he conceals himself just as the Countess and Susanna enter. The mistress hides, too, and the maid, awaiting the Count, and knowing that her husband is listening, sings a wonderfully beautiful soliloquy addressed to her supposed lover, *"Deh vieni, non tardar"* ("Come, do not delay"). She does this with the quaintly humorous idea of harassing her husband.

Cherubino, having an appointment with Barbarina, suddenly appears on the scene, and seeing the Countess, whom he believes to be Susanna, attempts to kiss her. The Count arrives, just in time to see this, and, stepping between them, unexpectedly receives the kiss himself. As Cherubino draws back, Figaro advances into his place. The Count then gives a box on the ear to Figaro, whom he takes for Cherubino. The page then takes flight. The Count proceeds to make ardent love to his wife, whom he believes to be Susanna, so cleverly does she imitate her maid's voice and manners.

Figaro, wild with fury at this spectacle, unexpectedly meets Susanna, who similarly is impersonating the Countess. He accordingly tries to awaken the jealousy of the supposed Countess by telling her of her husband's conduct. Susanna, however, reveals herself; and the Count, seeing Figaro apparently embracing the Countess, promptly forgets the supposed Susanna and, violently seizing Figaro, calls for help. Explanations follow, and the Count, perceiving himself outwitted, begs his wife's forgiveness. It is of course, graciously granted.

Act IV: After the masquerade in the garden, the Countess (Sena Jurinac) forgives the Count for his conduct

Martha

CHARACTERS

Lady Harriet Durham ("Martha"),		Plunkett, *a wealthy farmer*	Bass
maid of honor to Queen Anne	Soprano	Lionel, *his foster brother, afterwards*	
Nancy ("Julia"), *her maid and*		*Earl of Derby*	Tenor
friend	Mezzo-soprano	The Sheriff of Richmond	Bass
Sir Tristan Mickleford ("John"),			
Lady Harriet's cousin	Bass		

Ladies, Servants, Farmers, Hunters and Huntresses, Pages, etc.

The action takes place in England during the reign of Queen Anne (1702–1714)

OPERA IN FOUR ACTS. Music by Friedrich von Flotow. Libretto in German by Wilhelm Friedrich (pen name for Friedrich W. Riese), adapted from the original French scenario by Vernoy de Saint-Georges for the ballet "Lady Henriette." First performance at the Kärntnertor-Theater, Vienna, November 25, 1847. American première, in English, at Niblo's Garden, New York, November 1, 1852. First performance at the Metropolitan Opera on March 14, 1884, in Italian, with Marcella Sembrich and Roberto Stagno. It was during the Metropolitan performance of February 10, 1897, that the French basso Armand Castelmary suffered a heart attack and died on stage in the arms of the Polish tenor Jean de Reszke, the Lionel of the cast.

The libretto of *Martha* has an interesting linguistic history. It began in French. J. H. Vernoy de Saint-Georges, who had earlier collaborated on the text of Donizetti's *La Fille du Régiment*, was commissioned by the director of the Paris Opéra to write a sketch for a ballet. It happened that the French gentleman had two aristocratic lady friends who had been mistaken for servant girls at a carnival. They related their experience to Vernoy de Saint-Georges, who immediately saw a ballet in the episode. Flotow, one of three composers engaged to compose the music for it, liked the ballet story so much he asked Vernoy de Saint-Georges to turn it into an opera libretto.

Lionel (Beniamino Gigli) and "Martha" (Frances Alda)

259

Nancy (Rosalind Elias) hears Tristan (Lorenzo Alvary) invite Harriet (Victoria de los Angeles) to the fair

This the obliging Frenchman did, writing it, of course, in his native French. Flotow then had the libretto freely translated into his native language, German, by "W. Friedrich." Later an Italian translation was made, and after that one in English, both excellent. Soon the opera *Martha* became so familiar to English operagoers that they came to think of it as an English opera. This was understandable because the locale is the English countryside. Besides, the beautiful Irish folk tune "The Last Rose of Summer," with Thomas Moore's words, was inserted into the opera by Flotow. On the other hand, the Italians found the no less celebrated aria *"M'appari"* so Italian in language and style that many assumed both the original language and the composer were Italian. Donizetti would have proudly signed his name to that luscious melody. There was further confusion, however. Each country changed both the setting and the century of the story. In the original version, the time is the eighteenth century, the place England. The French altered it to the nineteenth century, and the Italians threw it back to the fifteenth. In whatever language or setting, *Martha* was a huge success, thanks to its gracious blend of romance and tunefulness, the brisk ensembles, the colorful fair scene, and of course the two supreme moments of Lionel's aria and Martha's delivery of "The Last Rose of Summer."

OVERTURE

There is a charming and melodious overture, which pictures the shifting moods of comedy, romance, and dramatic conflict arising in this so-called *opera semi-* *seria.* From the finale of Act III comes the lovely horn solo that follows the brief and somber opening of the Overture. This is worked up to a resounding climax, and a bright and restless little theme enters, developed into a passage of frank gaiety. A rustic tune follows, accompanied by a jangling tambourine, picturing the servant girls at the fair. The two main themes are then reviewed, varied, and combined, and the coda sets in for a merry drive to the brilliant end. It is a popular concert overture.

ACT I

SCENE 1: *Lady Harriet's boudoir.* Beautiful young Lady Harriet, maid of honor to Queen Anne, has grown weary of the monotonous ritual of court life. Admirers, social position, and court festivities have begun to bore her, and the brilliant pageant of fashion, jewels, and flowers has become an empty show. Her faithful maid Nancy enters. Finding her mistress weeping, she tries to comfort her, reminding her of her enviable position, but Lady Harriet replies that it has only brought her boredom. Nancy now boldly ventures that it is love that is missing in her life. Harriet's cousin Sir Tristan Mickleford is announced. He is an absurd old coxcomb who prides himself on a vast knowledge of women. To amuse Lady Harriet he proposes a whole new set of elegant diversions, but the proposal only brings gales of laughter. The song of servant maids on their way to Richmond Fair comes through the open window, giving Lady Harriet a sudden inspiration. The three of them will join the merrymakers! Nancy and Sir Tristan object stoutly, but Lady Harriet orders them along. Peasant costumes worn at a recent court ball are procured for the adventure. Sir Tristan, accordingly, is transformed into a farmer named "John"; Nancy becomes the servant girl "Julia"; and Lady Harriet is disguised as her friend "Martha." Hence the title of the opera.

SCENE 2: *The fair at Richmond.* The fair is in full swing. In the fashion of the time, servant girls have come here to seek employment with wealthy farmers, and they may be heard bargaining sharply with prospective masters. Two young farmers, Lionel and Plunkett, mingle with the motley crowd. From their conversation we learn that Lionel is Plunkett's adopted brother; also, that Lionel's father, a mysterious stranger in the neighborhood, had given Plunkett a ring on his deathbed. Should his son ever find himself in trouble, he had instructed, the ring should be presented to Queen Anne. So far no occasion has arisen to test the ring's power. When the three masqueraders appear, Lionel and Plunkett are immediately attracted by the beauty of the two "servant girls" and offer to hire both of them. In the spirit of the prank the girls accept, Sir Tristan remonstrating in vain. "Julia" and "Martha" take the money proffered them and by so doing unwittingly bind themselves legally to their new masters for one year. Sir Tristan tries to drag the girls off, but the crowd drives him away with jeers. The terrified impostors are now led away by the two farmers.

ACT II

SCENE: *A farmhouse.* As the curtain rises, Lionel and Plunkett enter, dragging with them their reluctant new hired help. The ladies soon recover their breath and, realizing they are not in any serious danger, resolve to plague their new employers. When the two young farmers show the girls the room that is to be theirs, the girls promptly announce they are tired and will shut themselves in indefinitely. Taken aback, the farmers remind them they have been paid to work; and when the men order supper, their command again falls on deaf ears. Lionel, the more gallant of the farmers, requests the girls to show their skill at spinning. Blandly they plead ignorance, and Lionel and Plunkett are obliged to sit down and show them. At this point the orchestra begins a merry little tune that moves at breakneck speed to the end of the ensemble. Rapid scales and darting staccato passages illustrate the hustle and bustle involved in the act of setting up the spinning wheels and fetching chairs. The men sing *brr-brr* in imitation of the humming wheels, as the girls raise

their cheerful voices in a bright outcry of wonder over the strange spectacle of men spinning.

The lesson ends abruptly as "Julia" upsets Plunkett's spinning wheel and runs out of the room, with Plunkett, obviously infatuated, dashing after her. The scene is set for Lionel's avowal to "Martha." Though she laughs at him, his good looks and manly bearing have impressed her. When Lionel assures her he will be a kind and gentle master, "Martha" smilingly replies she will not make a good servant, for she can do nothing but laugh and joke. Lionel professes not to care, since his only concern is that she should be happy. Then he asks "Martha" to sing for him, and in his elation he snatches a rose from her. This gives "Martha" a cue, and she sings "The Last Rose of Summer," the old Irish melody "The Groves of Blarney," to which the poet Moore adapted his verses. Captivated by her singing, Lionel falls to his knees and protests his love, assuring her that rank means nothing to him, that, in any case, his love will elevate her to his position. "Martha" bursts out laughing at the thought of Lady Harriet rising to a farmer's rank. Lionel is crushed by this unexpected reaction, and only the noisy return of "Julia" and Plunkett relieves the strained situation.

The orchestra now sounds a saucy little melody as the charming "Good Night Quartet" begins. Holding her tightly, Plunkett exclaims to "Julia", "Don't you try this game again, young lady!" Then turning to Lionel he asks, "Where do you suppose this little vixen was? In the kitchen, breaking glasses

Plunkett (Giorgio Tozzi) sings the Porter Song, Act III

and the dishes and spilling the wine. At last I've caught her!'' The two struggle half seriously, and Plunkett is impressed by the girl's strength and spirit. The clock suddenly strikes, and all exclaim, "Midnight!" in surprise. Lionel sings a pretty melody, bidding the others good night and pleasant dreams. "Julia" sarcastically echoes his words, "Good night!" Then, as the young men take their leave, all four unite in a final ensemble of great loveliness.

There is a pause, and the girls peep out from their room. Seeing no one, they slip out quietly and hold an excited consultation. The game has gone too far! How can they escape? What would the Queen say if she heard of it? The "servant girls" shudder at the very thought. There is a furtive tap at the window. It is Sir Tristan come to rescue them. Overjoyed, the girls make their escape through the window and leap into the waiting carriage.

ACT III

SCENE: *A hunting park in Richmond Forest*. Despondent over the loss of their fascinating servants, Lionel and Plunkett seek distraction. They have come to watch the Queen and her train at the hunt. Plunkett is at an inn with a crowd of farmer friends. In spirited style he launches into a gay apostrophe to that revered tavern staple, porter. To this famous old English beverage Plunkett grandly ascribes the vigor and valor of every Briton. As the farmers disperse, leaving Lionel alone—alone with his gloomy thoughts—he meditates on his hopeless love, and a beautiful song rises to his lips, *"M'appari"* (*"Like a Dream"*), a song telling how "Martha"

Nancy (Rosalind Elias) confesses love for Plunkett (Giorgio Tozzi)

comes to him like a vision, soothing his pain and banishing his sorrow. And abruptly the vision vanishes, leaving him joyless again.

As if to bear out the song, "Martha" suddenly appears to Lionel, garbed now in the splendid raiment of a lady of the court. Puzzled and ravished by the sight of her, Lionel at once declares his love. Lady Harriet, against the promptings of her own heart, pretends he is a stranger to her. Desperate, Lionel reminds her that she still owes him a year's service. Lady Harriet now calls the hunters, crying that this man must be mad. "May God forgive you!" Lionel exclaims as he is placed under arrest. Before being led away, he gives Plunkett the ring with instructions to present it to the Queen, whose approach is announced.

ACT IV

SCENE 1: *Plunkett's farmhouse (same as Act II)*. Lionel's true identity and the innocence of his banished father have now been established. Lady Harriet herself has presented the ring to the Queen, and she comes to inform him that the title and property of the Earl of Derby are now his. She comes, too, to confess her love for him, but Lionel, his reason almost gone, waves all aside—title, wealth, and Lady Harriet. In hopes of restoring his mind, she again sings "The Last Rose of Summer" —to no avail. She pleads for forgiveness, but Lionel, still obsessed by the cruelty of her rebuff, reviles her wildly, and rushes from the room, leaving Lady Harriet in tears. The reunion of Nancy and Plunkett, however, has ripened into a real romance, and their one thought now is to bring their unhappy friends together. They agree heartily to a plan devised by Lady Harriet.

SCENE 2: *A representation of the Richmond Fair*. A crowd of merrymakers is milling about on Lady Harriet's private grounds. A reproduction of the fair scene of Act II, complete with booths and farmers and "servant girls," has been arranged as part of the plan to reunite the lovers. Harriet, Nancy, and Plunkett are dressed in the costumes they wore at their first meeting, and farmers are again bargaining with the hired help. Into this bustling scene Plunkett gently leads his ailing friend. The remembered sights and sounds begin to work on Lionel's clouded mind, and when, suddenly, he sees Harriet, clad once more as a servant, the last mist lifts. Lionel embraces her tenderly, and as the two couples pledge their troth, they blend their voices in a final delivery of "The Last Rose of Summer," altering the words this time to "The spring has returned, fresh roses now bloom."

A Masked Ball

UN BALLO IN MASCHERA

CHARACTERS

Riccardo (*Gustavus III, King of Sweden or the Count of Warwick, Governor of Boston*) — Tenor
Renato, *his friend and secretary* — Baritone
Amelia, *Renato's wife* — Soprano
Ulrica, *a fortuneteller* — Contralto
Oscar, *a page* — Soprano
Silvano, *a sailor* — Baritone
Tom / Sam } *conspirators* — Bass / Bass

A Judge, Guards, Conspirators, Dancers, etc.

The action takes place either in and near Boston or in and near Stockholm in the eighteenth century.

OPERA IN THREE ACTS. Music by Giuseppe Verdi. Libretto in Italian by Antonio Somma, after Eugène Scribe's libretto for Daniel Auber's *Gustave III, ou Le Bal Masqué*. First produced at the Apollo Theater, Rome, February 17, 1859. American première, Academy of Music, New York, February 11, 1861, in Italian. Initial performance at the Metropolitan Opera House, December 11, 1889, in German, with Lilli Lehmann as Amelia. First time in Italian at the Metropolitan, February 23, 1903, with Johanna Gadski as Amelia, Fritzi Scheff as Oscar, Louise Homer as Ulrica, Emilio de Marchi as Riccardo and Giuseppe Campanari as Renato. Édouard de Reszke as Sam, and Marcel Journet as Tom.

The story has some historical foundation in that Gustavus III of Sweden was assassinated during a masked ball at Stockholm. As luck would have it, while negotiations for the production of Verdi's opera were in progress, an Italian revolutionist made an attempt on the life of Napoleon III. Naturally, the authorities demanded changes in the opera. The composer refused to adapt his music to a butchered libretto and refused to allow its production. As a result great excitement prevailed in Naples. Crowds of people paraded, shouting, "Viva Verdi!" using the popular composer's name as a slight disguise of the fact that they were favoring a united Italy under Victor Emmanuel, thus: Vittorio Emmanuele Rè d'Italia (Victor Emmanuel, King of Italy). An odd acrostic, the letters of a composer's name! As a way out of the difficulty, the censor at Rome suggested that the title be changed and the scene trans-

Marian Anderson as Ulrica, in her Metropolitan début, 1955

ferred to Boston. The assassination of a governor in provincial Boston would not disturb the authorities. A colonial governor singing on the Italian operatic stage is not an unamusing thing for American audiences to contemplate, and Europe having more or less recovered from its sensitiveness about royal assassinations, the scene of the opera when given there is now frequently placed in Sweden.

For the Metropolitan revival of the season 1940–1941—and ever since—the action was placed in its original locale of Sweden in the reign of Gustavus III. In the cast were Zinka Milanov, Kerstin Thorborg, Jussi Bjoerling, and Alexander Sved. For a new production in 1963 even the Swedish names were used: Gustav (Riccardo), Anckarstroem (Renato), Christiano (Silvano), De Horn (Sam) and Warting (Tom).

ACT I

SCENE 1: *The home of Riccardo.* Among the assembly gathered at the palace of Riccardo are two of his enemies, Sam and Tom. Most are friendly toward the King, however, and, when he enters, sing his praises. He greets them with assurances of his interest in their welfare. Then his page Oscar presents him with a list of the guests invited to the ball. Riccardo reads the list until he comes to one name that makes him start with delight; he exclaims, "Amelia!" Meanwhile, Oscar and the people unite in singing the praises of their King. And the conspirators, headed by Sam and Tom, agree that the hour is not propitious for the success of their plans. These varied comments are expressed in a highly melodious quartet and chorus.

Riccardo now has a private conference with his minister Renato, who is also Amelia's husband. Renato warns him about plots against his life, but Riccardo is essentially a lighthearted man and refuses to take such matters seriously. Then some judges, accompanied by the pageboy Oscar, enter, and the judges ask Riccardo to sign an order banishing the fortuneteller Ulrica. Oscar, however, in a coloratura aria, defends the old woman; and Riccardo, seeing a good chance for both fun and justice, summons the whole court and invites them to visit Ulrica's hut. As for himself, he will assume the disguise of a sailor. Everyone agrees that the party will be perfectly splendid.

SCENE 2: *Ulrica's hut.* A large crowd, including the courtiers, listen as the witch, mixing her brew in a large caldron, intones vigorous incantations over it. Silvano, a sailor, asks whether he will get the promotion and the money he deserves, and Ulrica predicts that he will. Riccardo, in his disguise, slips both money and promotion secretly into Silvano's pocket,

and everyone is delighted when they find Ulrica's prediction justified. A messenger now comes to ask for a private interview and at Ulrica's request all leave the hut—all save Riccardo, who conceals himself in a corner. A veiled woman enters. It is none other than Amelia, whom he loves and who loves him. She desires to remain a loyal wife and asks the sorceress to give her peace of mind by banishing a love which she cannot control. Ulrica tells her of an herb from which can be brewed a magic potion; to be effective it must be gathered only at night near a gallows.

Amelia departs, the people re-enter, and Riccardo, in his sailor's disguise, asks to be told his fortune. The request takes the form of a barcarolle—a favorite type of sea song. Ulrica rebukes him and, examining his palm, tells him he is soon to die by the hand of that friend who will next shake his hand. Oscar and the courtiers exclaim in horror at her pronouncement, which launches the famous Quintet *"E scherzo"* ("Your absurd prophecy"). Ulrica insists that such is the decree of relentless fate. Sam and Tom are fearful lest their plot be discovered, although Riccardo sings jestingly even when everyone present refuses to shake his hand.

Renato enters, anxious for Riccardo's safety, for he has learned of the conspiracy. Happy at finding him, he greets him with a vigorous shake of the hand. Riccardo tells the witch she is a poor fortuneteller, for this is the best friend he ever had, and throws her a fat purse. For his bravery and gallantry he wins the applause of the people.

ACT II

SCENE: *A lonely field near a gallows.* Amelia goes by night to seek the magic herb at the foot of the gallows. She sings a dramatic aria (*"Ma dall' arido"*), praying heaven to release her from her hopeless love. A clock strikes midnight, and she fancies that she sees a phantom rising before her.

The vision resolves itself into Riccardo, who now approaches. Although she confesses her love, she begs him to give up their love for the sake of Renato's honor and he nobly agrees. Just then Renato appears; he has come to warn the King that his life is in danger and urges him to flee down a side path. Renato consents, at Riccardo's request, to escort this veiled lady back to the city without speaking or otherwise trying to learn her identity and then the King leaves. But Renato and Amelia are stopped by the arrival of the conspirators, who, enraged at the escape of the King, would know the identity of the lady. Renato threatens them, whereupon she herself lifts the veil, and he recognizes his wife. Filled with rage, he arranges a secret meeting with the conspirators then leads Amelia home.

ACT III

SCENE 1: *The study of Renato's house.* Alone with Amelia, Renato assails her with the most bitter fury and is at the point of killing her. She swears she is innocent and begs for a moment's respite to bid farewell to their child. This request he grants. Then, left alone, he repents of his desperate intention, reserving his wrath and vengeance, now, for Riccardo, whose portrait is on the wall, and he remarks on this in the aria *"Eri tu"* (*"Was it thou?"*).

The conspirators now enter and are both surprised and pleased when Renato tells them that he knows they are plotting to take the King's life and wishes to join them. Each wants to strike the fatal blow, and it is agreed to draw lots. Amelia returning at that moment, Renato sardonically orders her to make the drawing from an urn. She does so, and the name on the slip is—Renato's. At the end of the quartet Oscar comes in with invitations to the masked ball to be held that night, and in a brilliant piece of part-writing the act closes as Amelia bewails

her fate and the others look forward, in different moods, to the masked ball.

SCENE 2: *Riccardo's apartment in the palace.* Convinced that he and Amelia must be separated, Riccardo is in process of signing an order sending Renato and his family abroad, although he is desolate at the thought of never again seeing Amelia. At the end of his aria he receives an unsigned warning against his attending the ball. Being Riccardo, he resolves to go nevertheless.

SCENE 3: *The ballroom in the palace.* Amid the brilliant merrymaking at the masked ball, Renato cleverly finds out Riccardo's disguise from the King's page. Riccardo has come to the ball in spite of Amelia's warnings, and though she again warns him, he refuses to leave—he is no coward. He tells Amelia of his plan for the future; he will never see her again. Just as he is saying, "Farewell," Renato rushes in and stabs him in the back. Riccardo forgives him, and assures him that Amelia is guiltless; then with his dying breath he begs that no one attempt to avenge his death.

The King of Sweden dies at a brilliant masked ball, as staged at the Metropolitan Opera in 1940–41

Medea

CHARACTERS

Medea, *a sorceress, Princess of Colchis*	*Soprano*	Neris, *Medea's attendant*	*Mezzo-soprano*
Jason, *Prince of Thessaly*	*Tenor*	Two handmaidens	*Sopranos*
Glauce, *Princess of Corinth*	*Soprano*	Captain of the Guard	*Baritone*
Creon, *King of Corinth*	*Bass*	The two young sons of Jason and Medea	*Mimes*

Soldiers, Argonauts, Attendants, Citizens of Corinth

The action takes place in Corinth in legendary Greece.

OPERA IN THREE ACTS. Music by Luigi Cherubini. Libretto by François Benoît Hoffmann (translated into Italian by Carlo Zangarini), closely based on Euripides' tragedy. Première, Théâtre Feydeau, Paris, March 13, 1797. First American performance (in concert form), November 8, 1955, Town Hall, New York, presented by the American Opera Society with Eileen Farrell in the title role. First American stage performance, September 12, 1958, at the San Francisco Opera, again with Farrell as Medea. The chief reason for the revival of interest in this long-neglected work, however, must be credited to another American-born soprano, Maria Callas, who participated in the first modern-day staging at the Florence May Festival in 1953 and later brought her searing portrayal of the vindictive Colchian princess to the stages of Milan, Rome, Dallas, London, and Epidaurus, Greece. Callas also participated in the first complete recording of *Medea*.

Luigi Cherubini was a contemporary of Mozart's who survived both Beethoven and Weber and lived on into the early days of Verdi and Wagner. A prolific composer with some fourteen operas to his credit, Cherubini was one of the Italian musicians who ruled the operatic roost in Paris. This he did with an iron fist. In later years he served as administrator of the Paris Conservatory, where he grew more and more pedantic; criticism by such writers as Berlioz characterized him as a crabbed discipli-narian who thwarted the invention of young talent. Among the sins of this Italian was his denial of entry to the Conservatory of Franz Liszt—on the grounds that Liszt was not French! Bitter memories of such personal tyrannies did their share to contribute to the eventual neglect of Cherubini's music, thought by some historians to be as dry and inflexible as the man himself.

An eclectic in the best sense of the word, Cherubini combined Germanic compositional solidity with acquired Gallic rhetoric and natural Italian passion. His music provided a bridge between the classicism of Gluck and the romanticism of Beethoven, who like Haydn greatly admired Cherubini's music. Though less gifted melodically than many, Cherubini nevertheless exerted a profound influence on the development and structure of grand opera, both French and German.

Medea, or *Medée* (the original title), Cherubini's fourth opera for Paris, won a tepid reception at its first performance, though in Germany it fared better, holding the stage for nearly half a century. It clearly surpasses all of the composer's earlier stage works for breadth of design, unity of conception, richness of orchestration, and unremitting dramatic force. In its original form *Medea* was an *opera-comique;* that is, musical numbers alternated with spoken dialogue. In 1854 Franz Lachner set this spoken text to music and it is the composed-through version that is always heard today. Though Cherubini allotted each of his major characters a solo aria, it is Medea herself who overshadows the entire work. For this reason the opera can only be produced when a sufficiently magnetic soprano is available who can survive the title role's formidable musical and dramatic demands. It is said that the opera curtailed the career of more than one soprano who attempted it, and the lack of sopranos with the proper vocal and stage ability has surely added to *Medea*'s unjust neglect. The rising number of successful contemporary productions, however, with sopranos other than Callas—Farrell, Gerda Lammers, Inge Borkh, Rita Gorr, Gwyneth Jones, Magda Olivero—augurs well for the work's future place in the repertory.

The legend of Jason and the Golden Fleece provided the background for Euripides' tragedy and the libretto Hoffmann derived from it for Cherubini. Jason, son of the Thessalian King Aeson, in order to win back his rightful throne from a usurping uncle, sets out for Colchis in his ship, the Argo, accompanied by a band of fifty heroes. Their mission is the recapture of the Golden Fleece. Before he will yield the sacred talisman, the Colchian King Aeëtes subjects the Greek Prince to a series of dangerous ordeals. But the King's daughter Medea, out of love for Jason, employs her magic arts to insure the victory of the Argonauts. Jason, winning the Fleece, and gratefully taking Medea as his wife, sets sail for Thessaly. On the return voyage, Medea, to distract her wrathful father in his pursuit of the Argo, slays her younger brother and casts his dismembered body into the sea (knowing that Aeëtes will not allow his son's remains to go unburied). She later poisons Jason's wicked uncle, and thus secures for him his rightful throne. But Jason, forgetful of Medea's crimes in his behalf, soon abandons her, and leaving his own kingdom with his two sons, travels to Corinth, where he seeks the hand of King Creon's daughter Glauce.

ACT I

SCENE: *The courtyard of Creon's palace in Corinth.* Glauce, on the eve of her wedding to Jason, is beset by fears of Medea's revenge. Her servants and the women of the court attempt to reassure her. Glauce and Jason plead with Creon to protect Jason's sons from the Medea-hating populace of Corinth, and the King willingly promises that the boys shall go unharmed. Jason's followers and comrades-in-arms, the Argonauts, march before the royal family, triumphantly displaying the Golden Fleece, which they lay at the feet of their commander's fiancée. But Glauce, troubled at the mention of Colchis, seeks reassurance in Jason's arms. Medea, he swears, shall never threaten their happiness. Creon begs for the blessing of the gods on the coming nuptials.

A guard appears to announce the arrival of a mysterious veiled woman at the palace gates. It is Medea, and to the fearful consternation of the crowd, she reveals that she has come to thwart Jason's plans for marriage. When she threatens Glauce's life, the enraged Creon orders her to leave

Jason (Jon Vickers) resists the entreaties of his wife, Medea (Maria Callas), La Scala staging, 1962

the city at once. Left alone with Jason, Medea pleads with him to return to her once more, reminding him that she has sacrificed all, family and homeland, for his sake. But Jason is unmoved, and in a duet that concludes the act, each one lays the blame for the present unhappy state of affairs on the Golden Fleece.

ACT II

SCENE: *The exterior of Creon's palace, and, to one side, the entrance to the Temple of Hera.* Medea, already weighed down by her impending banishment from Corinth, laments the loss of her children, who, she unhappily foresees, will be taught to hate their mother. Neris, her attendant, enters to announce the growing wrath of the Corinthians at Medea's presence in the city, and the arrival of Creon. In spite of the King's command that she quit his kingdom without further delay, Medea implores him to be allowed asylum among his people; there she will live out her remaining years in obscurity and forgetfulness of past wrongs. But Creon, implacable, demands her immediate departure. One more day, at least, Medea pleads. The King, at first suspicious that she will use this reprieve to work her threatened revenge, reluctantly accedes to her request. As he departs, Medea, overcome, collapses on the palace steps. Neris, approaching her prostrate mistress, gently assures her of her unwavering devotion; she

Creon (Nicolai Ghiaurov) hears out Medea (Maria Callas)

will faithfully follow Medea into exile. Stirring from her reverie, Medea turns once more to thoughts of vengeance. Jason must die, and Glauce with him, she vows; but she does recoil at the prospect of slaughtering her own and Jason's children.

Jason now appears, troubled by the news that Creon has granted Medea's wish to remain one day more in Corinth. When he refuses to yield their children to Medea's care, Medea, freshly stung by his cruelty, reverts to her earlier vengeful thoughts, artfully masking her intent with a show of maternal grief. Moved at last, Jason agrees to release the children to her for the one remaining day, and Medea, in seeming gratitude, bids him a final sad farewell. But even as the populace prepares to celebrate the marriage of Jason and Glauce, Medea sets her murderous plans in motion. Bidding Neris to fetch the diadem and mantle given her by Apollo, she orders that they be sent to Glauce as a gift on her wedding day. As the wedding cortege passes into the temple, Medea exults in her coming revenge.

ACT III

SCENE: *Before the temple's entrance, with Creon's palace at one side.* Medea, alone, invokes the infernal gods in the realization of her revenge. As Neris leads in her children, she steels herself to strike the fatal blow; but, again overcome by her natural feelings, she lets the dagger fall from her hand, and tearfully embraces her sons. Neris tells her that the diadem and mantle have been gratefully received by Glauce, and driven to a savage outburst at this news, Medea reveals that she has poisoned the gifts and that Glauce, wearing them, will die in horrible agony. At Medea's frantic urgings that the children now be shielded from her continued passion for vengeance, Neris hurriedly withdraws with them into the temple.

In an extended monologue, Medea now regrets her wavering, and once more resolves to complete her vengeance with the slaughter of Jason's children. From within the palace, she hears the anguished cries of Jason and the court, lamenting Glauce's death. As they emerge from the palace, Medea, calling on the aid of the eternal Furies, rushes into the temple. Jason and the others, calling for Medea's death, now learn from Neris that Medea plans to murder her own children. As they rush to the temple, Medea appears at the entrance, brandishing a bloody knife, announcing that her vengeance is now complete. Why has she slain the innocent, despairing Jason asks her. "Because they were your children," she replies. And now her ghost will lie in wait for him in Hades. She has set the temple on fire, and as the others express their horror at her crimes, she perishes in the flames.

The Medium

CHARACTERS

Madame Flora (Baba), *the medium*	*Contralto*	Mrs. Gobineau	*Soprano*
Monica, *her daughter*	*Soprano*	Mr. Gobineau } *Mme. Flora's clients*	*Baritone*
Toby, *a mute*	*Mime*	Mrs. Nolan	*Mezzo-soprano*

The action takes place in Madame Flora's parlor, today.

MUSICAL DRAMA IN TWO ACTS. Music and libretto in English by Gian Carlo Menotti. Commissioned by the Alice M. Ditson Fund of Columbia University, it was first produced at the Brander Matthews Theater, Columbia University, New York, on May 8, 1946, with a cast consisting of Evelyn Keller as Monica, Leo Coleman as Toby, Claramae Turner as Madame Flora, Beverly Dame as Mrs. Gobineau, Jacques La Rochelle as Mr. Gobineau, and Virginia Beeler as Mrs. Nolan, under Menotti's own stage direction and with Otto Luening conducting. It was revised and restaged for the Ballet Society and performed at the Heckscher Theater, on February 18, 1947. Its successful reception encouraged Chandler Cowles and Efrem Zimbalist, Jr., to produce it on Broadway. With Menotti's *The Telephone* as a curtain raiser, it opened on May 1, 1947, at the Ethel Barrymore Theater in New York. After running for 211 performances it toured the United States and important European cities and finally was made into a motion picture with most of the Broadway cast repeating their roles. The only cast changes from the first performance for the Broadway engagement were Marie Powers as Madame Flora and Frank Rogier as Mr. Gobineau.

In calling *The Medium* "a musical drama" rather than "an opera" Mr. Menotti at one and the same time broke new ground and went back to the principles of Gluck and even Monteverdi. That is, the implication of the phrase "a musical play" was that the play's the thing, the music only the language in which it is written. And if the play is truly the heart of the matter, then, reasoned the composer-librettist, it should be produced in America as the most successful plays are produced in America—for a run on

Mme. Flora (Marie Powers) summons dead spirits

Toby (Leo Coleman) with Monica (Evelyn Keller)

Broadway. And so it was written, cast, directed, and performed. The Broadway run was successful; so was a national tour; so have been a number of European productions. And it has, nevertheless, entered the repertoire of some repertory opera groups, notably the New York City Opera.

Mr. Menotti has said in an interview that an initial long run is the only salvation for modern opera composers. "Otherwise," he said, "we have only premières and the work dies quickly. In a long run, you get a new audience every night, and more and more people get to know your work." Mr. Menotti's career seems to illustrate the position pretty consistently. Operas like *The Island God* and *The Last Savage*, both well introduced at the Metropolitan, have not fared nearly so well as *The Medium, The Consul,* and *The Saint of Bleecker Street,* all of which had first runs of many nights to many audiences. As for *Amahl and the Night Visitors,* that is seen every Christmas by millions on television and by many thousands in the school and college productions prompted by its familiarity.

ACT I

SCENE: *A squalid room with a stairway descending to the street; the room is equipped with a large puppet theater to one side; in the center is a three-legged table with a garish Victorian lamp overhead.*

Toby, a mute picked up from the streets and raised by Madame Flora, pulls silks and beads from a trunk and makes himself a costume, while Monica, Madame Flora's daughter, mirror in hand, combs her hair. She warns Toby that her mother will beat him if she catches him with her things, but, drawn into his game, she plays queen to his king. The door below is slammed, but before they can put the things away, Madame Flora has spied them. She is angry that nothing has been made ready and the people for the séance are arriving at any minute. Asked where she has been all night, Madame Flora answers, on the doorstep of a client who had refused to pay. Monica dresses in white, with a veil on her head, as Toby opens the curtains of the puppet theater, where the controls for the séance apparatus are, and tries them out. The doorbell rings, Monica leaves, Toby hides in the theater, and Madame Flora presses the buzzer to open the door and settles down to a game of solitaire.

Mr. and Mrs. Gobineau, old clients, and Mrs. Nolan, a new one, enter. Mrs. Nolan has come to speak to the spirit of her daughter Doodly. The Gobineaus come regularly to communicate with their baby boy, who laughs for them. Mrs. Gobineau relates how he drowned in a pool while playing. Madame Flora announces that it is time to begin, and they sit down at the table and the light is turned off. Madame Flora begins to moan, simulating going into a trance, and Monica appears in a faint blue light in the puppet theater, asking, "Mother, Mother, are you there?" Mrs. Nolan, believing it is her daughter, speaks to her. Monica tells Mrs. Nolan to give away her things and burn the rest except for a gold locket. When Mrs. Nolan says there was no gold locket, Monica disappears. Then the Gobineaus speak to their son, and Monica answers in giggles. Suddenly Madame Flora jumps up from her chair, looks around the room, and, terror-stricken, asks who touched her. The Gobineaus try to soothe her, but she orders everyone out. As they leave, they ask, Why be afraid of our dead?

Monica comes into the room to find out what had happened. Madame Flora tells her that they must never hold a séance again, they must give back the money, for while she was pretending to be in a trance a cold hand clenched her throat. Then, thinking it might have been Toby, she pulls back the curtain of the puppet theater, to see him motionless inside. She drags him out and hysterically accuses him of doing it. Monica pulls her away and, sitting down, has her rest her head in Monica's lap. Monica sings the tale of the black swan, and Madame Flora grows calm, but suddenly the voice of the daughter and the sound of the giggles ring in the medium's ears. After sending Toby to see if anyone is hiding, she forces him to his knees, begins to pray, but the laughter of the Gobineau child sounds again.

ACT II

SCENE: *Same as Act I, a few days later.* Toby has been operating the puppets for Monica and comes out to take a bow. As Toby dances, Monica sings a waltz ("Monica, Monica, dance the waltz"), and Toby tries to tell her of his love. Understanding, Monica stands behind him and says his words for him, then rushes in front of him to answer as herself. When Toby cries because of his inarticulateness, Monica assures him that he has the most beautiful voice in the world.

Madame Flora comes up the stairs, and Monica rushes to her room. Distraught, she tries to wheedle Toby into admitting that he clutched at her throat in the séance—finally, promising him Monica in marriage if only he will confess. Infuriated by his lack of response, she takes out a whip and beats him until the constant ringing of the doorbell sobers her. Monica runs in to comfort Toby, and Madame Flora, exhausted, admits the Gobineaus and Mrs. Nolan, telling them there will be no more séances, returning their money, and admitting that she is a fraud. When they disbelieve her, she shows them her apparatus and tricks. She has Monica repeat her performance as Mrs. Nolan's daughter, but that woman says Monica's was not the voice she heard. And the Gobineaus are certain that Monica's laugh is not their son's. Mrs. Nolan even explains that she found the gold locket, but Madame Flora brushes that away, explaining that everyone has a locket—it's an old trick. They beg her to begin the séance, but she is intractable, finally ordering them out, crying, "Fools!"

Toby must go, too, Madame Flora decides. When Monica says that she will go with him, her mother locks her in her room. "Mother, Mother, are you there?" rings out again. Madame Flora pours herself several drinks and tries to calm her nerves by reminding herself of all the hideous things she has seen in life and not been afraid. She tries to laugh at her fear that the dead can return, but the laughter turns to hysteria. Begging God to forgive her sins, she sinks into a drunken sleep.

Toby returns stealthily and scratches on Monica's door but can't make her hear him. He opens the trunk, but the lid falls, waking up Madame Flora, and he hides in the puppet theater. She cries out, "Who's there?" takes a revolver out of a drawer, and trembling with fright demands that whoever is in the room speak. When the curtain of the theater moves, she screams and fires at it. Blood runs slowly down the white curtain, and as she thinks she has killed the ghost, Toby's lifeless body falls into the room. Monica bangs with her fists upon the door, and Madame Flora unlocks it and lets her in. When Monica sees what has happened, she runs out of the house, calling for help. Madame Flora, kneeling beside Toby's body, still asks him if it was he.

Act II: Frightened by her conscience, Mme. Flora (Marie Powers) sends away her clients

Mefistofele

CHARACTERS

Mefistofele, *the Devil*	*Bass*	Marta, *her mother*	*Contralto*
Faust, *a philosopher*	*Tenor*	Elena (*Helen of Troy*)	*Soprano*
Wagner, *his favorite student*	*Tenor*	Pantalis, *her companion*	*Contralto*
Margherita, *a peasant girl*	*Soprano*	Nereus, *an attendant*	*Tenor*

Mystic Choir, Cherubs, Soldiers, Students, Citizens of Frankfort, Witches, Sirens, Naiads, etc.

Most of the action takes place in sixteenth-century Frankfort, Germany, but there are scenes in heaven, in the Hartz Mountains, and in the Vale of Tempe in Greece.

OPERA IN prologue, four acts, and epilogue. Music by Arrigo Boito. Libretto in Italian by the composer, based on the drama *Faust* by Johann Wolfgang von Goethe. First performance at La Scala, Milan, March 5, 1868, which was a failure. Much shortened and revised, it was a success at Bologna, April 10, 1875. First American performance at Boston, in English, November 15, 1880. The same month it was performed, in Italian, at Philadelphia, New York, and Chicago. It entered the repertoire of the Metropolitan Opera during its first season, on December 5, 1883, and has had a number of notable revivals with such artists as Nilsson, Calvé (who sang both Margherita and Elena), Farrar, Alda, Caruso, Plançon, Chaliapin, and Didur. In 1920 Beniamino Gigli made a sensational Metropolitan debut in the role of Faust.

Arrigo Boito, who composed only two operas (*Nerone* was the other) and little else, was as much a patriot-politician as a composer and even more a man of letters. In his early twenties he fought under Garibaldi, and at seventy he was elected to the Italian Senate, where he was very active. All his life he wrote critical and poetical works of sufficient influence and merit to be collected and published in two separate ventures years after his death. In the history of opera his name is prominent not merely for *Mefistofele* but for many librettos he supplied other composers, including *La Gioconda* for Pon-

chielli and those two masterpieces of literary legerdemain, Verdi's *Otello* and *Falstaff*.

Being of such a literary and philosophical bent, when Boito came to write his own libretto for an operatic version of Goethe's *Faust*, he was not satisfied, as Gounod and other composers had been, to confine himself to the story of Marguerite, which ends with Part I of the drama. He also included sections of Part II, with much philosophical dialogue and very little action. This was one of the causes of the sensational failure of the première, but only one. Another was its excessive length: the performance took well over five hours. Even more important, on that occasion, was Boito's reputation, already at twenty-six, as a champion of what was then considered the avant-garde in music. The house was filled with champions of the young man (who, besides being composer-librettist, was also conductor) and his bitter opponents. The first scenes went well, but as the long work drew on, the opponents began to be heard from—catcalls, whistles, insults, finally fighting and a full-fledged riot, which spilled out into the street. The management tried, later in the week, dividing the opera in two and giving it on successive nights. But again there were riots, and the opera was withdrawn on the demand of the chief of police. No one dared mount it again for seven years.

Boito had learned from the disaster. When Bologna produced the work in 1875, it was, despite the addition of some new, attractive numbers, much trimmed down; the role of Faust was promoted from baritone to tenor; and the orchestration had been touched up. Still further revisions were made for Venice the following year, and ever since, *Mefistofele* has been virtually a staple of repertory opera in Italy, having achieved over 5,000 performances in its first century of existence there. Across the Alps it has not, of course, been nearly so popular, an ironic fact because the enmity to Boito was based on his ambition to bring into Italy a pan-European—especially a German—influence in opera. Yet, though many Faust operas have been composed (including one by a female composer-librettist named Louise Angélique Bertin), only Gounod's receives more frequent revivals.

PROLOGUE

In the realms of space, invisible angels and cherubim, accompanied by celestial trumpets, sing in praise of the Supreme Ruler. Through the clouds that cover the entire stage appears Mefistofele, expressing his contempt for "that small God of Earth who, like the grasshopper, pokes his head among the stars only to fall back trilling into the grass." The mystical choirs answer, "Is Faust known to thee." much as in the Book of Job, which Goethe followed with some faithfulness in this scene. And as God, in Job, permitted Satan to influence that upright man, so Mefistofele is permitted to wager with heaven that he can lure Faust to his destruction.

ACT I

SCENE 1: *A square in Frankfort.* It is Easter Sunday, and crowds are moving in and around the gates of the city. A stranger dressed as a gray friar seems to inspire fear in some of the people. The aging philosopher Faust, in company with his favorite disciple Wagner, observes this man and says to Wagner, "I see his footsteps marked in fire." The young man, however, can see none of this and thinks his master may be going insane. They leave the stage, with the friar following close after.

SCENE 2: *The studio of Faust.* Returning alone to his studio, Faust does not see the friar slip in behind and conceal himself in an alcove. The aged philosopher delivers his soliloquy "*Dai campi, dai prati* ("From the green fields"), a serene melody in which he speaks of his love of God and his fellow men. As Faust starts meditating over a huge tome, Mefistofele springs forth and, throwing aside his cloak of the gray friar, is revealed as a dapper

cavalier with a black cloak over his arm. As the spirit that denies all good, he offers to Faust the privilege of traveling with him all over the world in search of knowledge, which is what the old man craves. Here on earth Faust will be served; below their roles will be reversed. Faust replies, "If thou wilt bring me one hour of peace, if thou wilt unveil the world and myself before me, if I may find cause to say to one fleeting moment, 'Stay, for thou art beautiful,' then let me die and let hell's depths engulf me." The contract is signed, Mefistofele spreads his cloak, and as both step on it, they disappear.

ACT II

SCENE 1: *Margherita's garden.* Faust, now a handsome young man who has assumed the name of Henry, woos Margherita at dusk, as she wonders why so magnificent an aristocrat should notice her. Mefistofele, meanwhile, makes love to the girl's mother, Marta. A very effective quartet develops as the two couples wander about the garden. When Faust learns that Margherita sleeps with her mother, Faust gives the girl a sleeping draft for the old lady, assuring her that it is harmless. Then, as the scene closes, Margherita avows her love for Faust. "I love thee! I love thee!" she cries as she surrenders.

Fyodor Chaliapin as Mefistofele, the role in which he made his Metropolitan début, in 1907

SCENE 2: *The summit of the Brocken.* Mefistofele has taken Faust to a wild peak in the Hartz Mountains where, beneath the moonlight, he may behold the people over whom his companion holds sway. The winds shrill weirdly, and flames dart forth from the jagged rocks as they reach the place. Once at the summit, Mefistofele summons forth his infernal subjects—demons, witches, wizards, goblins, imps—who acclaim him as King. They dance with joy when he shatters a crystal globe to symbolize his power over the earth. To this saturnalia Faust pays little heed. He beholds a vision of Margherita on her way to prison for the murder of her baby and her mother. He is especially horrified by a crimson thread about her neck, symbolizing the headsman's axe. Mefistofele urges him on, but Faust takes no part in the orgy with which the act closes.

ACT III

SCENE: *Margherita's prison cell.* Margherita has been doomed to die for poisoning her mother and drowning her baby, and she has lost her mind. Here she sings her great and deeply touching aria *"L' altra notte in fondo al mare"* ("To the sea one night in sadness"). Outside the cell Faust begs Mefistofele to save the girl, and when he enters, is torn with pity. In the duet that follows, Margherita recalls their scenes of love-making and Faust urges her to fly away with him. (*"Lontano, lontano"*—"Far away, far away"). Mefistofele, who has left them together to make arrangements for the girl's escape, now returns, and Margherita is frantic with terror to behold him. She refuses to leave the prison, and she dies in Faust's arms. Mefistofele cries out, "She is judged!" but a chorus of celestial beings announces salvation. Faust and his companion leave just as the headsman and jailers come to conduct the girl to the scaffold. (This climax marks the end of Part I of Goethe's drama.)

ACT IV

SCENE: *The Vale of Tempe in Thessaly.* In the search for the "beautiful moment," Mefistofele transports Faust to the banks of the Peneus. Here the so-called "Night of the Classic Sabbath" is being celebrated by a band of Grecian maidens singing and dancing. It is a beautiful, peaceful place, where Mefistofele does not feel at home, and eventually he slinks away to return to the Brocken. Helen of Troy appears with her retinue and, absorbed by a vision, she tells the tale of the fall of Troy. Faust now enters, richly dressed as a knight, and accompanied by Helen's companions, Nereus and Pantalis.

Act III: Margherita (Renata Tebaldi) in prison

He kneels at Helen's feet and addresses her as his ideal of beauty. In a duet they pledge their love to each other as the rest of the group on the stage join in a scene of visual and oral beauty in striking contrast, with its serenity, to the earlier scenes of the opera and the last one to come.

EPILOGUE

SCENE: *The studio of Faust.* Not even Helen of Troy has afforded the bliss for which Faust had offered his soul. Once more withered and feeble, he has returned to his studio, and Mefistofele stands behind him, still hoping to win on his bargain. Faust, looking back on his memories, cries, "Reality was grief, and the Ideal but a dream!" Yet to the last he seeks the Ideal, and his swan song is a desire to be king of a peaceful land where under wise laws he may give happiness to the people. As he sings his final aria, *"Giunto sul passo"* ("Nearing the end of life"), throngs of angels gather near, and the vision of heaven becomes brighter with the approach of death. A celestial chorus sings *Aves* to the Lord as the angels bear up the soul of the departed philosopher. A shower of roses falls upon his dead body and upon Mefistofele, too, stifling him with their perfume. He disappears as the triumphant hosts cry out their Hallelujahs against the strong, clear notes of silver trumpets.

Die Meistersinger

THE MASTERSINGERS

CHARACTERS

Hans Sachs, *cobbler*	Bass-Baritone	Magdalene, *Eva's nurse*	Soprano
Pogner, *goldsmith*	Bass	Mastersingers: Vogelgesang, *furrier;* Nacht-	
Beckmesser, *town clerk*	Bass	igall, *buckle-maker;* Kothner, *baker;*	
Walther von Stolzing, *a young*		Zorn, *pewterer;* Eislinger, *grocer;* Moser,	
Franconian knight	Tenor	*tailor;* Ortel, *soap boiler;* Schwarz,	
David, *apprentice to Hans Sachs*	Tenor	*stocking weaver;* Foltz, *coppersmith*	
Eva, *Pogner's daughter*	Soprano	Night Watchman	Baritone

Burghers of all Guilds, Journeymen, Apprentices, Girls, and People

The action takes place in Nuremberg in the middle of the sixteenth century.

Magdalene (Ernestine Schumann-Heink) and Eva (Johanna Gadski), 1890's

OPERA IN THREE ACTS. Music and libretto by Richard Wagner. First performance, in the original German, at the Hof-und-National-Theater, Munich, June 21, 1868. American première, at the Metropolitan Opera House, January 4, 1886, with Emil Fischer as Sachs, Albert Stritt as Walther and Auguste Seidl-Kraus as Eva, Anton Seidl conducting.

Though completed in 1867, *Die Meistersinger* was first sketched out by Wagner in 1845 as a companion piece to *Tannhäuser*. Twenty-two stormy years intervened before the completion of a masterpiece which the celebrated Polish pianist Ignace Paderewski once hailed as "the greatest work of genius ever achieved by any artist in any field of human activity." It was with perhaps a sense of mingled relief and regret that Wagner finally scrawled on the bottom of the last score sheet: "The completion of *Die Meistersinger*, Triebschen, Thursday, October 24, 1867, 8 o'clock in the evening."

The vast contrapuntal power of the music is never there for its own sake, but as a kind of inevitable flowering of the very theme of the opera, of the poetic idea embedded in the conflict of schools. This poetic, or aesthetic, idea is represented in the struggle between the liberal-minded Walther, rebelling against the doctrinaire tenets of the guild, and Beckmesser, the scoundrelly pedant, opposed, like all hidebound custodians of the older ways, to any progress in the arts. As everyone knows, in this Beckmesser the composer pilloried forever Eduard Hanslick, the dreaded critical oracle of Vienna who had become the archenemy of Wagnerism. In the fair-minded Hans Sachs, Wagner represented enlightened public opinion, respectful of the great masters, yet willing to grant all innovators the right to be heard and, if genuine, to be accepted. The historic Sachs was, of course, somewhat different from Wagner's cobbler-poet. In a deeper sense, it is the aging Sach's hopeless and self-denying love for the young and beautiful Eva Pogner that explains why *Die Meistersinger* is sometimes called a "tragi-comedy."

Instead of legendary sources, Wagner this time depends to a large extent upon actual history for the basis of his comedy. He conceived the work at first as a sort of humorous variation on the contest theme of *Tannhäuser.* In that opera Wagner had treated of the medieval minnesingers, nobles who sang of exalted love—the German counterparts of the French *trouvères,* or troubadours. Like the chivalry of which they were an expression, the minnesingers disappeared with the coming of the Renaissance. In their place there arose, among the middle-class trade guilds, bands of singers who, patterning themselves after the minnesingers, took the name "mastersingers" (*Meistersinger*). To become an enrolled member of one of these groups of mastersingers, the ambitious youth, while learning his trade, was obliged to study the arts of singing and poetry, too. After passing various examinations, he then worked his way up through the several degrees of "Scholar," "Schoolman," "Singer," "Poet," and finally "Master." The purpose of the guild was to foster a love of the noblest ideals in art. However, in the course of time, the Mastersingers' Guild inevitably adopted a dogmatic outlook. Excessive value was now given to pedantic and traditional rules. Most famous of the mastersingers was Hans Sachs, cobbler, poet, and dramatist, who lived at Nuremberg (1494–1576) and helped combat the pedantry of his colleagues.

Wagner did a thorough historical research before he penned this vivid picture of life in Nuremberg, crowded with its wealth of amusing and picturesque details. Two of the musical motives employed, "The Banner" and "The Art Brotherhood," were gleaned from some "Prize Master Tones" included in an old book by J. C. Wagenseil, printed at Nuremberg in 1697. Yet Wagner does not thrust this history upon us, but allows it to form a diverting and realistic background for the human and romantic story he has to tell.

PRELUDE

The Prelude (or *Vorspiel*) begins at once with the theme of the mastersingers, assertive, pompous, even stolid, but nevertheless of a striking vigor and beauty.

After these characteristics of the mastersingers have been emphasized by repetition, the placid, springlike motive of "Waking Love" is heard in the woodwinds. This soon gives way to the proud "Banner" of the mastersingers, emblem-theme of the self-complacent pride of that group of tradesmen-musicians. Closely joined with it is the suave theme of the "Art Brotherhood," the melody with which the citizens of Nuremberg hymn their praise of all that is finest in their native art. This is developed to a magnificent climax; then follows a motive expressive of Walther's love, the motive of "Longing."

This leads directly into the beautifully lyric theme that will finally blossom in its fullest glory during the "Prize Song," the theme of "Love Confessed." This, in turn, grows directly into the more impassioned motive of "Love's Ardor." These melodies are then combined, and, "Love's Ardor" seemingly in the ascendancy, developed into a climax. This climax is suddenly broken off, and we hear the pompous theme of the mastersingers, parodied in a perkish manner by the woodwind. Into this the motives of "Love's Ardor," "The Art Brotherhood," and "Longing" make various attempts to enter. In the bass is heard the derisive theme of "Ridicule." "Love's Ardor" again triumphant, there is now a dazzling climax during which the motive of the "Mastersingers" sounds forth in the bass like a call to arms. As this tumult subsides we hear in broad, magnificent phrases the theme of "Love Confessed," sung by the violins, while far below is played the motive of the "Mastersingers." At the same time, woodwind instruments in the middle voices chatter along with the "Banner"—one of the most remarkable feats of thematic interweaving ever achieved; yet there were once musicians who said that Wagner knew no counterpoint! These various motives are then heard separately, in ever-growing sonority and richness, until the brilliant close of the Prelude.

ACT I

SCENE: *The Church of St. Katherine in Nuremberg.* With the very last chord of the Prelude, we behold the interior of the church. The people gathered there are singing a fine, stately chorale to Saint John, for this is the eve of that saint's day.

Only a few of the last rows of pews are visible. One of them is occupied by Eva and her nurse

Magdalene. At one side, leaning against a pillar, is Walther von Stolzing. According to a custom of the period, long pauses occur at the end of each line of the chorale that is being sung. During these pauses Walther and Eva exchange glances. The knight is plainly enamored of the girl, and she, though shy and modest, betrays considerable interest in him. Their mutual awareness is romantically expressed by the orchestra during these pauses.

When the chorale is ended and the congregation leaves, Walther, a total stranger in Nuremberg, for the first time learns that Eva's father has made a singular arrangement: he intends to give his daughter as bride to the winner of the song contest to be held on the morrow. Only masters of the guild may compete, however.

Walther promptly decides to become a master and win the contest—and Eva. Yet he has not the slightest idea of the conditions and requirements of the contest. Magdalene is now called on to assist. She in turn calls upon her suitor David, a young apprentice, to instruct Walther in the rules observed by the Mastersingers' Guild. As there is to be a test immediately, David begins his instruction at once, while his brother apprentices arrange the chairs and furniture for the guild meeting. But David, an apprentice cobbler as well as musician, so garbles the rules of art and the rules of his trade that Walther is left helpless and confused. Soon the mastersingers arrive to stately march rhythms, and the guild roll is called. Pogner addresses them, saying that he offers his daughter, Eva, in marriage to the winner of the coming contest, provided, of course, that he meets with her approval as well. Walther now asks to be given a trial for admission to the Mastersingers' Guild. The masters, though surprised at his boldness, give their consent.

As their duly appointed "Marker," Beckmesser takes his place in the enclosed stand erected for him. Besides being a formidable stickler for rules, he is also eager to wed Eva himself. The result can well be imagined. Walther's freely improvised song *"Fanget an"* ("Now begin") is punctuated by the sound of the scratching of the pencil on a slate as the Marker notes down the "errors." At the end of the first verse the masters refuse to hear any more. Hans Sachs alone is in favor of having the youth continue.

A master of genuine merit, Sachs has detected in the song a touch of true inspiration. He admits that the "rules" of the guild have been disregarded, but suggests that other rules may govern in this instance. He is shouted down, however, and the indignant young knight is dismissed amid the jeers of the apprentices. The trial has ended in confusion, and Sachs turns away in a mood of semihumorous despair.

ACT II

SCENE: *A street in Nuremberg (the houses of Pogner and Hans Sachs are seen separated from each other by a narrow alley, but both facing the same broader street, which is shown sectionally across the stage).* As night falls over the town, the apprentices are busily putting up the shutters on the quaint old Nuremberg houses. Meanwhile, they sing in joyful anticipation of the midsummer festival. They are disposed to ridicule David, who has suffered Magdalene's ire as a result of Walther's failure. Sachs drives them away, chasing David off to bed, but first he has his workman's bench so placed that he can work at his cobbling and at the same time watch the street. Soon he finds he cannot work, for the beauty of the summer's evening and recollections of Walther's song have obsessed him. The orchestra murmurs, like a merest breeze stirring in the summer night, and Sachs, putting aside his work, dreamily notes the scent of elder blossoms in the air (*"Was duftet doch der Flieder"*) and reverts to the strangely fascinating song of Walther, the song defying all rule and measure (*"Kein' Regel wollte da passen"*). Eva appears. Despairing of her chances to have Walther for a husband, she coyly hints that Sachs himself might be a welcome suitor. The captivating duet begins with her words *"Gut'n Abend, Meister!"* (*"Good evening, Master!"*). She has known and loved this kind man from childhood and is aware of his sterling qualities. Indeed, Sachs, a middle-aged widower, has had dreams of winning Eva for himself. But now he realizes that her true love is for Walther, and accepts this with manly resignation. He merely shakes his head over the turn of events as Eva leaves him and he resumes work. Soon Sachs observes Walther and Eva across the street, talking together. The lovers have decided to elope. Sachs "accidentally" places his lamp where the light will fall upon them, and they are deterred for fear of being seen. While they debate their plan, however, a stranger approaches, and they quickly draw back into the shadows. The stranger is Beckmesser. The pompous scalawag has come to serenade his lady with the song he hopes to sing on the morrow. Sachs, hearing him tinkle on his lute, breaks in with a lusty song of his own, *"Jerum! Jerum!"* (*"Cobbler's Song"*), and Beckmesser is greatly discomfited.

He pretends that he has come to inquire about a pair of shoes, and Sachs replies civilly that he is working on them. In the meantime Magdalene, in Eva's stead, has appeared at the window, and Beckmesser, thinking her to be the lady of his dreams, grows more ardent in his serenading. Then Hans Sachs proceeds to act as Marker, hammering on the shoe at every mistake. In this way, accompanied by a sharp obbligato, Beckmesser continues. In his agitation, however, his song runs wild, and Sachs's hammer blows become loud and frequent. The thumping waxes more and more vehement as the mistakes of the now irate Beckmesser increase. The disturbance naturally arouses the neighbors, who begin peering through the windows. Even David is awakened, and seeing the town clerk apparently serenading Magdalene, who is still at the window, he curses furiously and, jumping quickly from his room, proceeds to give the astonished Beckmesser a

Act II: Eva (Ingrid Bjoner) visits Sachs (Otto Wiener) on Midsummer's Eve. (Metropolitan Opera staging)

sound beating. Magdalene screams aloud at seeing her David fighting in the street, and the townspeople, still in their picturesque nightgowns, hurry down to the scene. Observing two of their members fighting, the guildsmen join in eagerly, and soon the street is in an uproar.

Walther and Eva, who have been in hiding, decide that this is a good opportunity to elope. But the observant Sachs seizes the pair and pushes Eva in the door of Pogner's house. Then with a well-placed kick he sends David scurrying into his own house, and follows him, drawing Walther after him. Meanwhile, the good women of the town, distressed at the behavior of their husbands and sweethearts, suddenly pour water upon the brawlers from the windows above. All quickly scatter to the safety of their homes. At that moment the night watchman is heard sounding his horn in the distance. When he reaches the scene of the disturbance, all is miraculously quiet again. He announces the hour, singing an antique ditty in a quavering voice. His horn is again heard in the distance as he wanders off, staff and lantern in hand, through the slumbering streets.

ACT III

The third act is preceded by a prelude of remarkably evocative beauty. It is built principally on the theme of Sachs's monologue, in which, during a moment of despair, he declares that all things human are but vanity, and on the vigorous chorale with which the people greet him in the closing scene of the opera.

SCENE 1: *Interior of Sachs's workshop.* The early-morning sun streams through the window at which Sachs sits. Engrossed in reading a large folio, he fails to notice David entering with a basket of good things to eat. David has patched it up with Magdalene and is thus in a happy frame of mind. But he is still fearful that his rowdy behavior in the previous night's disturbance will bring a thrashing from his master. Falteringly, he now begins to explain, declaring that the night before was just a *Polterabend* —a night of merrymaking on the festival of Saint John. Sachs appears to pay little heed; then suddenly he asks the amazed youth to sing the song of the day—a carol of Saint John. This tells the story of the child of a woman of Nuremberg christened in the river Jordan by Johannes, the saint, after whom Sachs was named; though on his return to Nuremberg the name "Johannes" was abbreviated to "Hans." David, struck with a sudden thought, exclaims joyfully: "Hans! Hans! Why, then, it's your name day, too, Master!" In childish glee he offers Sachs the flowers and cakes that Magdalene has just regaled him with. Sachs declines them graciously.

Act II: Sachs (Otto Wiener) marks Beckmesser (Karl Schmitt-Walter)

Though still preoccupied, he understands the apprentice's hopes and desires and dismisses him with a pleasant word. The kindly cobbler then sits in meditation—a meditation which becomes vocal in the stirring lines beginning with the words *"Wahn! Wahn! Überall Wahn!"* ("Mad! Mad! The whole world is mad!").

Having just awakened, Walther now enters from an adjoining room and joins Sachs in conversation. He is bursting with a wonderful dream he has had in which a marvelous poem and melody found their way into his heart. Sachs desires to hear it, and we now hear the first lovely stanzas of the *"Preislied"* ("Prize Song"). The older master is struck by its beauty and inspiration, and tactfully he instructs the young poet-composer in the technical devices necessary to make the song acceptable to the judges.

After the two men have written down the poem, they leave the room. Presently Beckmesser enters and, snooping about, notices the song. Believing it to be by Hans Sachs himself, he pockets it for his own use after the manner of plagiarists the world over. When Sachs returns, the town clerk scolds him for planning to enter the contest. Sachs denies this. Beckmesser accordingly produces the manuscript, and Sachs, grasping the situation, does not undeceive him. Divining Beckmesser's intentions, and knowing the town clerk incapable of making good use of the poem, Sachs gives it to him, promising not to divulge its true authorship. Greatly delighted, Beckmesser leaves.

Eva enters now, clad in festival robes. Her shoe pinches, she says, and Sachs, knowing well what is in her heart, pretends to busy himself adjusting the offending footwear. Walther enters, also festively garbed in a knightly costume. On seeing his adored Eva, he stands as in a trance and softly sings the last stanza of his song. Overwhelmed with emotion, Eva sinks weeping into Sachs's arms. Deeply moved himself, Sachs gives her into Walther's care and then bursts into a stanza of his brusque cobbler's song to steady himself. Eva vows her gratitude and love to her old friend, but Sachs sagaciously replies that he would avoid the fate of King Marke. At this the orchestra knowingly quotes a phrase from *Tristan und Isolde*. David and Magdalene now appear, also in gala attire. Sachs invites them all to a christening. But first he seeks to name Walther's song. Since a qualified witness is needed, and a mere apprentice will not do, the kindly cobbler gives David his freedom, making him a full journeyman cobbler with the customary box on the ear. David is overjoyed, for now he will be able to marry Magdalene. These five characters now give voice to their mingled emotions of happiness, love, and, for Sachs, a mellow nostalgia, in an indescribably lovely quintet, *"Selig wie die Sonne"* ("Brightly as the sun"). Then they leave together for the contest, David carefully closing the door after them.

SCENE 2: *A field on the shores of the River Pegnitz.* In an open meadow on the banks of the river, the people of Nuremberg have assembled for the song contest. The various trade guilds arrive in procession —tailors, shoemakers, bakers. The band of youthful apprentices is there also, and soon a gaily decorated boat overflowing with smartly dressed girls arrives. The apprentices hurry to help them ashore, then at once begin dancing with them, the orchestra accompanying them with a delightfully rustic, waltzlike tune. David seizes a pretty girl and starts to dance with her. The other apprentices frighten him by saying his Magdalene is watching (*"Aha! da streicht die Lene!"*).

Finally the mastersingers arrive in great pomp, their banner with the picture of their patron King David fluttering at the head of the procession. At the sight of Sachs the crowd rises briskly and breaks into an exultant chorale, the words of which were taken from an actual poem by the historical Hans Sachs, *"Wach' auf! es nahet gen den Tag"* ("Awake! the dawn of the day draws near"). Sachs, deeply moved, thanks them for their kindness, and announces the terms of the contest in an impressive address beginning *"Euch macht ihr's leicht"* ("Words light to you").

As the oldest of the contestants, Beckmesser is selected to begin. Still smarting from his beating of the previous night, grievously flustered, and with his stolen song only half learned, he now attempts to adapt the poem to his own serenade melody. The result is a hopeless jumble which at first excites the wonder, then the derision of the audience. Enraged, Beckmesser declares that the song is not his, but the work of Hans Sachs. The masters, believing this a spiteful fabrication, call upon Sachs for an explanation. Eloquently he insists that the song would be good if properly sung, and persuades the crowd and the judges to let it be interpreted by the author, Walther von Stolzing. The crowd listens in wonder-

Friedrich Schorr, the distinguished Sachs of the 1920's and 30's

ing silence as the young knight begins his rapturous song *"Morgenlich leuchtend in rosigem Schein"* ("Morning was gleaming with roseate light"). This tells of the vision of a lovely garden in which the singer found the most beautiful of all maidens, Eva. Around the melodic beauty and expressiveness of the song a glowing orchestral accompaniment seems to entwine itself tenderly.

The people listen with growing excitement, and at the close of the song the masters rise and acclaim Walther as victor. Eva confers on her lover a wreath of laurel and myrtle, then leads him to her father, before whom they both kneel. Pogner extends his hands over them in benediction and presents the emblem of the Masters' Guild to the young knight. But Walther, remembering his reception of the day before, and conscious also of his noble birth, refuses the honor. In consternation, all turn to Sachs for guidance. The cobbler-poet goes to Walther, takes him impressively by the hand, and, while the orchestra brings into review many of the motives first heard in the Prelude, urges him not to despise the old masters, *"Verachtet mir die Meister nicht."* Then, turning to the crowd, he warns that disunity among the Germans would be the death of holy German art (*"die heil'ge deutsche Kunst"*).

Thoroughly won over, Walther is now willing to accept the mastersingers' emblem. Sachs embraces the couple, who then remain standing beside him, Walther at one hand, Eva at the other. Before this group Pogner kneels as if in homage. Thus the cobbler-musician and the two lovers become symbols of Art and Life, enshrined in the incomparable splendor of the song of the people, who now repeat the final words of their beloved cobbler-poet, and shout exultantly, "Hail Sachs! Hans Sachs! Hail Nuremberg's beloved Sachs!"

Mignon

CHARACTERS

Mignon, *a girl stolen by gypsies*
                                Mezzo-soprano

Philine, *an actress*   *Soprano*

Frederic, *a young nobleman*   *Buffo tenor or Contralto*

Wilhelm Meister, *a student on his travels*   *Tenor*

Laerte, *an actor*   *Tenor*

Lothario, *a wandering minstrel*   *Bass*

Giarno, *a gypsy*   *Baritone*

Antonio, *a servant*   *Bass*

Townsfolk, Peasants, Gypsies, Actors, and Actresses

The action takes place in Germany (Acts I and II) and Italy (Act III) in the late eighteenth century.

OPERA IN THREE ACTS. Music by Ambroise Thomas. Libretto in French by Michel Carré and Jules Barbier, based on episodes in Goethe's novel *Wilhelm Meister*. First performance, Opéra-Comique, Paris, November 17, 1866. American première, in Italian, New York Academy of Music, November 22, 1871. First Metropolitan performance, in Italian, October 31, 1883.

Thomas was fifty-five and a composer of modest reputation when *Mignon* brought him fame and money. Largely because of *Mignon* and the subsequent opera *Hamlet* the grand cross of the Legion of Honor was conferred upon him in 1894, when he was eighty-three years old. A man of vast learning, he was appointed director of the Paris Conservatory in 1871, remaining in that post till his death on February 12, 1896. Thomas' instinct for the theater shows clearly in both *Mignon* and *Hamlet*. A flair for fluent, romantic melody marks his music, and his facile skill as orchestrator is evident in the ever-popular Overture to *Mignon*. Grace and elegance go hand in hand in Thomas' music, and in lyric expression he is related to Gounod. Of course, the plot of *Mignon* differs radically from the original story of Goethe's weighty philosophical novel. Little of the

Luisa Tetrazzini as the frivolous actress Philine

281

tragic poetry and cynicism of the novel survives in the libretto, and the central situation is saved by the familiar theatrical device of mistaken identity. Yet with all the liberties taken, the opera has its own dramatic and romantic appeal.

OVERTURE

The Overture to *Mignon* is typically French in its lilting grace and delicacy. Woven into an adroitly balanced fabric are the principal themes of the opera. The tranquil mood of the opening, with its harp cadenza, reminds us of the kindly minstrel Lothario. Next, the horn evokes a mood of romantic nostalgia in the melody of Mignon's *"Connais-tu le pays?"* Violins take up the strain, letting it die away in a mood of calm mystery. Philine's rippling polonaise *"Je suis Titania"* then brings in a contrasting note of vivacious coquetry, and the Overture ends on a bright note of gaiety.

ACT I

SCENE: *Courtyard of a German inn*. Mignon, daughter of noble parents, was stolen from her home by gypsies. Shortly after, her mother died of grief, and her father Lothario, driven nearly mad by the loss, is wandering as a minstrel in search of his child.

Lothario has found his way to an inn where a crowd of people is drinking and feasting. Broken with age, Lothario has lost his memory. Yet, though even his name and home are forgotten, he is still blindly seeking the lost daughter whom he vaguely believes to be alive.

Into the courtyard troops a band of gypsies. Giarno, their mercenary leader, orders Mignon to dance for the crowd, but Mignon, grown tired of her master's insolent commands, refuses to go through her performance. When Giarno threatens to beat her, Lothario, stirred with a sudden sympathy for this young girl, runs to protect her. As the feeble old man is powerless before the gypsy, a young student, Wilhelm, who is looking on, rushes to the rescue. With his pistol drawn he forces Giarno to release the girl, and in gratitude Mignon divides a bouquet between her rescuers. Wilhelm receives the applause of a troupe of traveling actors, among whom is Philine. This beautiful young actress of designing temperament attracts Wilhelm's attention, much to the jealousy of Frederic, a young nobleman.

Curious about the girl he has rescued, Wilhelm questions her regarding her childhood. But Mignon remembers nothing except that she was captured as a child by gypsies in some distant country, which she now describes in the nostalgic aria *"Connais-tu le pays?"* (*"Knowest thou the land?"*). Mignon's

song expresses the passionate longing of the orphan for the home of her infancy, and reaches a fervent climax in the hope that she may die there. Moved to pity, Wilhelm arranges to buy the girl's freedom from her master. Mignon, infatuated with her rescuer, wishes to follow him on his travels, but Wilhelm, rather embarrassed, suggests that she remain in the village with some kind-hearted people. Mignon is saddened by this, but agrees to accompany the aged Lothario, who, moved by some strange impulse, has come back to bid her good-by. Wilhelm at length yields to the girl's entreaties and allows her to accompany him disguised as a servant. Philine, meanwhile, receives an invitation to visit the castle of Baron Rosenberg for a party in honor of Prince Tieffenbach. She is to bring along the troupe of actors and any guests she may care to. She promptly invites Wilhelm, who has caught her fancy. He accepts her invitation and goes along as poet of the company.

ACT II

The second act is preceded by the very popular Intermezzo, a dainty gavotte, gay and graceful in its eighteenth-century elegance.

SCENE 1: *A boudoir in the castle*. Philine sits at her mirror, studying her charms and applying cosmetics. She is thinking of Wilhelm, for she is much infatuated with this handsome, romantic student. Soon he enters, accompanied by Mignon, who is greeted by the actress with civil yet subtly cattish remarks. The poor girl does not resent this, however, and, curling up in a great chair by the fire, apparently goes to sleep. Yet she observes, under half-closed lids, that Wilhelm is paying court to the actress, to whom he has given the bouquet of blooms presented to him by Mignon herself. Presently Philine and Wilhelm leave, and Mignon, longing to emulate the actress, goes to the adjoining room and tries on one of Philine's many gowns. Frederic leaps in through the window. "I'm here!" he exclaims. "I've broken all the rules of etiquette, but I'm here!" Then he begins to sing the charming gavotte, telling of his rapture at being in his beloved Philine's room, *"Me voici dans son boudoir"* (*"I am in her boudoir"*).

Wilhelm unexpectedly enters, in search of Mignon. Jealous accusations about Philine are exchanged by the young men, and in the heat of the quarrel they draw swords. But as Mignon rushes between them, Frederic recognizes Philine's gown and goes away laughing. Wilhelm, realizing that difficult situations may arise from having the girl constantly about, has now come to tell Mignon that they must part. The girl begins to cry, saying that it is Philine who has persuaded him to drive her away, but he calms her fears in a tender farewell.

Philine, re-entering, utters some sarcastic remarks about Mignon's borrowed raiment, words that bring a flush of anger to the girl's cheeks. Rushing from the room, Mignon dons her old gypsy costume and returns in time to see Wilhelm leading the actress away on his arm. "That woman! I detest her!" cries the gypsy girl in despair.

SCENE 2: *The gardens of the castle.* Thinking her love for Wilhelm hopeless, Mignon is about to drown herself when she hears the strains of a harp. It is the minstrel Lothario. He now enters and listens sympathetically to the girl's tale of sorrow and her desire for vengeance. The half-crazed old man starts curiously when she expresses the hope that heaven's lightning will strike and burn down the castle, and he goes away muttering her words to himself.

The performance in the theater having ended, the players and guests come out into the garden. Philine, who is still in her costume of the Fairy Queen in *A Midsummer Night's Dream,* has had a brilliant success. Glowing with triumph, she sings *"Je suis Titania"* ("I am Titania"), the rhythm of which is that of a polonaise. Lothario returns and whispers to Mignon that she need not grieve—her vengeance is now complete, for he has set fire to the castle. Noticing Mignon, Philine is suddenly seized by a cruelly jealous thought. She orders the girl to bring from the castle a bouquet she has forgotten. Since Philine knows that the flowers were given by Mignon to Wilhelm there is malice enough in her request; yet Mignon goes gladly. Immediately, word comes that the castle is on fire, and Wilhelm, realizing that Mignon is in danger, rushes off to her rescue. Soon he returns with the unconscious girl in his arms. Mignon is still clasping the withered flowers, and Wilhelm exclaims that he saved her against her will.

ACT III

SCENE: *Count Lothario's castle in Italy.* Wilhelm has brought Mignon and Lothario to an old castle in Italy, one that he is half inclined to purchase. Mignon is recovering from a dangerous illness, and Wilhelm comes to take Lothario's place outside her sickroom. Satisfied that he has quieted the restless girl, Lothario sings a suave lullaby, *"De son coeur j'ai calmé la fièvre"* ("I have calmed the fever of her heart"). Wilhelm now meditates on her guileless heart and loyalty, and as the realization dawns on him that he loves her, he sings a romance—a melody of the utmost simplicity, naive as Mignon herself— *"Elle ne croyait pas dans sa candeur naïve"* ("She did not believe in her utter frankness"). The song rises to a passionate climax as the young man exclaims, "Gentle spring! give her one soft, caressing kiss! O my heart, give her one fond sigh of love!"

Mignon comes with feeble steps to the balcony. As she looks out on the landscape, strange memories begin to stir within her. Seeing Wilhelm, she becomes greatly agitated, fearing that Philine may be with him. He soothes her with the assurance that he loves her alone, but she insists that only Lothario is faithful. Meanwhile, a strange thing has happened. Once more in familiar surroundings, Lothario has recovered his reason and memory. He has remembered finally that he is Count Lothario and that the castle is his! But a great sadness comes over him as he recalls the disappearance of his daughter, Sperata. At the sound of that name, echoes sound in Mignon's reawakened memories. When Lothario shows her the jewels and prayer book of his lost child, she recognizes them, and, unconsciously, she now begins to sing the prayers of her early childhood. Thus father and daughter are reunited, and Wilhelm being admitted to the family circle, their happiness is complete.

Act II, Scene 2, as designed for Milan's Teatro alla Scala by Lila de Nobili (Giulietta Simionato as Mignon)

Nabucco

NABUCODONOSOR — NEBUCHADNAZZAR

CHARACTERS

Nabucco (Nebuchadnezzar), *King of Babylon*	Baritone	Zaccaria, *high priest of Jerusalem*	Bass
Abigaille, *reputedly his elder daughter*	Soprano	Anna, *his sister*	Soprano
Fenena, *Nabucco's daughter*	Soprano	Abdallo, *a Babylonian officer*	Tenor
Ismaele, *nephew to the King of Jerusalem*	Tenor	High Priest of Babylon	Bass

Soldiers, Priests, Citizens of Jerusalem

The action takes place in Jerusalem and Babylon in the sixth century B.C.

OPERA IN FOUR ACTS. Music by Giuseppe Verdi. Libretto in Italian by Temistocle Solera. First performance at La Scala, Milan, March 9, 1842, with Giuseppina Strepponi (who married Verdi seventeen years later) as Abigaille. Repeated sixty-six times that year in Milan. First American performance at New York, April 4, 1848. A great success when first produced, it had productions in other countries in the 1840's and 50's, and for some decades continued as part of the regular repertoire in Italy. Later obscured by Verdi's less youthful works, but "rediscovered" in the 1920's in the big Verdi revival; then "rediscovered" in Italy in the 1930's. It achieved its first performance at the Metropolitan Opera on opening night of the 1960–61 season.

As Verdi recalled it in an autobiographical sketch published almost forty years later, 1840 was the most disastrous year he ever had. Both his dearly beloved first wife and his two small children died within a space of three months, and his second opera, *Un Giorno di Regno (King for a Day)*, was hissed off the stage at its première. The fact is that the deaths in his immediate family were spread out over a period of three years, his wife's being the last. So deep was his depression that he did not want to finish *Un Giorno,* which had been contracted for after the success of his first opera, *Oberto,* and only the insistence of the impresario of the Scala opera house made him stick to his contract. When that failed, only eleven weeks after Margherita Verdi's death, Verdi went into such a deep depression that he vowed he would never write anything more. He shut himself up in a furnished room and did nothing at all. Bartolomeo Merelli the impresario still held a contract for another opera by Verdi, still had complete faith in the twenty-six-year-old maestro, but it took him over a year to persuade Verdi even to read a libretto, and at that he had to resort to a kind of trickery. He absolutely forced on him a libretto by "the famous poet Temistocle Solera," which Otto Nicolai had refused (he wrote *The Merry Wives of Windsor* instead) and asked Verdi to read it and then give it back to him. Verdi, by his own account, took it home. "At home," he said, "I threw the manuscript with a violent gesture on the table and stood rigid before it. Falling on the table, the manuscript opened itself and, without my quite realizing it, my eyes fixed on the page before me at this particular line: *"Va, pensiero, sull' ali dorate."*

A chapter of operatic history was begun that

Tito Gobbi as Nabucco at the San Francisco Opera

night. Verdi said that, fascinated and much moved by the biblical subject and the virtual paraphrases from the Old Testament, he had the whole thing almost by heart before morning. When the opera was produced in 1842, Verdi, not yet twenty-nine, was at once recognized as a leading Italian opera composer, possibly the successor to Rossini, who had written nothing for the past dozen years, and Donizetti, who, though only forty-five, had already composed some seventy operas and, as it turned out, had only one masterpiece, *Don Pasquale*, to compose before he died in 1848. As for Bellini, the third of the triumvirate of the great ones of the generation, he had died seven years before.

A few lines should be added here about those words in the manuscript libretto which first struck the composer's eyes: "*Va, pensiero, sull' ali dorate*" ("Go, thought, on golden wings"). They constitute the first line of the chorus of the Hebrews in captivity, a noble, inspiring melody sung almost entirely in unison. Milan in 1842 was ruled by Austria, and the alert audience responded not only to the music but to the analogy they clearly perceived between their own subjection to a foreign power and the Hebrews'. Despite the strict police regulations against encores (for fear of demonstrations), the crowd became so demanding for a repetition that it had to be given. The melody became a hit tune, and it played a sentimental part on three other occasions in the personal story of the composer. A quarter of a century later, when his lifelong friend and patron, the father of Margherita, was on his deathbed, Verdi went to see the old man for the last time. Barezzi's favorite melody had been "*Va, pensiero*," and his

son-in-law went to the piano and played and sang it to him just before he passed away. When it came time for Verdi's own funeral, in 1901, there was, as his will instructed, a very simple one, attended by a very few people, and with no music planned. But spontaneously, these few, at the cemetery, began humming "*Va, pensiero*." A month later there was a state funeral, when his body along with that of his second wife (who had sung a leading role in the première of *Nabucco*), was transferred from the cemetery to the home for old musicians he had endowed. Half of Milan's population of 200,000 is said to have lined the streets. And Arturo Toscanini, standing outside the chapel, led a chorus of 800 in "*Va, pensiero*."

ACT I

SCENE: *Before the Temple of Jerusalem.* The people of Jerusalem, led by their priests, passionately cry out against their defeat in the field of battle by Nabucco, King of Babylon, but the Hebrew high priest Zaccaria bids them take heart, for Jehovah has performed miracles on their behalf before. (Historically, this was Babylon's third invasion of Judea and took place in 586 B.C.). Ismaele, a royal leader of the Jews, however, rushes in to inform the populace that Nabucco is now marching on the temple, and all cry out in agony.

But the Jews still have, as a hostage, Nabucco's daughter Fenena, whom Ismaele learned to love at a time when she had rescued him from the Babylonian prison into which he had been thrown while on a

Elena Suliotis as Abigaille at La Scala, Milan

diplomatic mission. He assures her that he will protect her, but their exchange is interrupted by the entrance of Abigaille, reputedly Fenena's elder sister and also in love with Ismaele. She has with her an advance guard of Babylonian soldiers and threatens both lovers with death. But she also tells Ismaele that if only he will love her, she can save him as well as his people. This offer the young man refuses. The situation, though not the music that develops in the ensuing trio, is fairly parallel with that in *Aida*.

But now Zaccaria returns in high excitement, saying that the Babylonian army is on its way to the temple, and a moment later it arrives with King Nabucco at its head. Zaccaria threatens to kill the hostage Fenena should the Babylonians desecrate the place, but the King merely taunts the old man with the defeat of the Jews. Enraged, Zaccaria is about to stab Fenena but is prevented from doing so by Ismaele. Thereupon, Nabucco orders that the temple be sacked and fired and the Jews led into captivity.

ACT II

SCENE 1: *A hall in the Palace of Babylon*. Nabucco is absent, supposedly campaigning with his army, and he has left Fenena to act as regent. Abigaille, who has heard a rumor that she is not really the King's daughter but was born a slave, has in her hands a document which proves the rumor true. She is deeply shocked. First she thinks of her love for Ismaele, but then she works herself up into a rage, vowing to bring down everyone—her father, her sister, herself —before her true birth can be made generally known. The first part of her *scena* over, the High Priest of Babylon enters with other priests to report that Fenena is planning to liberate the Jews and demand that Abigaille lead the forces to overthrow the unsisterly regent. Abigaille's vigorous and aggressive agreement to the proposal (the cabaletta to the aria), punctuated as it is with responses from the priests, constitutes one of the strongest features of the generally muscular score.

SCENE 2: *Another hall in the palace*. The Hebrews, though now in captivity, are permitted their own meetings. Zaccaria leads them in an impressive prayer to Jehovah for guidance. The Jews then demand punishment for Ismaele, who they feel had betrayed them by releasing the hostage Fenena. Fenena, however, has become a convert to Judaism, as Zaccaria reminds them. Abdallo, an old military adviser of Nabucco's, rushes in to inform the Jews that the King is reported dead and that Abigaille is threatening Fenena's life. A moment later Abigaille

herself enters with Babylonian officers to take the crown from Fenena. The rumor of Nabucco's death in battle, however, is proved false when the King enters this tense scene, predicting dire results from the incident. He seizes the crown himself, puts it on his head, and, in high excitement, proclaims himself God. In a tremendous ensemble scene, he demands that all worship him; the Jews refuse to do so; and Zaccaria denounces the impiety of the act. The heavens, too, are outraged; for a bolt of lightning strikes the crown from Nabucco's head, and when he recovers, it is apparent to all that he has been struck mad. Abigaille once more rises to the occasion by seizing the crown herself and announcing that the glory of Babylon is not dead.

ACT III

SCENE 1: *The throne room of the palace*. Abigaille is now regent, and she decides, with the vigorous assent of her Babylonian advisers, to have all the Jews, including Fenena, murdered.

The advisers having left, Nabucco is led in by Abdallo, and the rest of the scene is one of those many long, melodious, and usually powerful soprano-baritone duets which are the glories of many Verdi operas. (*Oberto*, the composer's first, had had one, too.) Nabucco is outraged to find someone else occupying his throne, and he tells Abigaille the truth about her birth. Abigaille, who had already discovered the facts, tears up the document proving them. She also takes advantage of his distracted mental state to get him to sign the death sentence of the Jews, and she then informs him that he is no longer King but a prisoner. Neither supplication nor anything else can now help the poor demented man.

SCENE 2: *The banks of the Euphrates*. The Jews, gathered by the river, sing the four stanzas of their great chorus of homesickness for Jerusalem—"*Va, pensiero*." Zaccaria preaches to them, trying to instill courage and predicting the downfall of Babylon. (Originally the librettist had written a love scene in here for Ismaele and Fenena, but Verdi made him substitute Zaccaria's prophecy, which turned out to be another high point in the score.)

ACT IV

SCENE 1: *A prison cell*. Nabucco awakens from a nightmare. Looking from the window, he sees Fenena being led to the place of execution, and he prays to the God of Judea for forgiveness for his pride and for the rescue of his daughter. Jehovah apparently hears him, for the faithful Abdallo enters with some guards, sees that Nabucco has become sane again, and follows him out of prison to make good the rescue Nabucco has prayed for.

SCENE 2: *The place of execution.* After a funeral march, the Jews prepare themselves for death, and Fenena sings a short but moving prayer. Nabucco, with his followers, arrives to stop the mass murder, and the statue of the god of Babylon falls mysteriously to the ground and is shattered. The King now announces his conversion to the worship of Jehovah, and the Jews rejoice. Abigaille, who has suffered a palace revolution and has taken poison, arrives with two soldiers, calls on God for forgiveness, and dies. Before the curtain comes down, Zaccaria promises Nabucco great glory as a follower of Jehovah.

Act I: Zaccaria, high priest of Jerusalem (Nicolai Ghiaurov), threatens to kill Nabucco's daughter, Fenena (Gloria Lane)

Norma

CHARACTERS

Pollione, *Roman proconsul in Gaul*   *Tenor*
Flavio, *a centurion*   *Tenor*
Oroveso, *the Archdruid, Norma's*
   father   *Bass*
Norma, *high priestess of the Druid*
   temple of Esus   *Soprano*

Adalgisa, *a virgin of the temple*
   of Esus   *Mezzo-soprano*
Clotilda, *confidante of Norma*   *Soprano*

Priests and Officers of the Temple, Gallic Warriors, Priestesses and Virgins of the
Temple, and the Two Children of Norma and Pollione

The action takes place in Gaul during the Roman occupation, about 50 B.C.

OPERA IN FOUR (ORIGINALLY TWO) ACTS. Music by Vincenzo Bellini. Libretto in Italian by Felice Romani, based on a tragedy by L. A. Soumet. First performance, Teatro alla Scala, Milan, December 26, 1831. The United States première of *Norma* took place in Philadelphia, January 11, 1841, when it was given (in English) simultaneously in two different theaters. Produced in New York in an English version, Park Theater, February 25, 1841. Also in New York, given in Italian, at Niblo's Garden, September 20, 1843. First Metropolitan performance on February 27, 1890, in German, a benefit for Lilli Lehmann, who sang the title role. Revived there again on November 16, 1927, with Rosa Ponselle in the name part, Giacomo Lauri-Volpi as Pollione, Marion Telva as Adalgisa, and Ezio Pinza as Oroveso. In the 1950's and 1960's it has served as a vehicle for Maria Callas and Joan Sutherland.

Bellini's *Norma* appeared in the same year *La Sonnambula* had won exceptional favor, and it was no less successful. The technique of the work is that of the older Italian opera school, in which airs and ensemble numbers, based on the simplest harmonic and melodic architecture, are plentiful. This does not mean, however, that emotional quality is absent, or even meager; and such numbers as "*Casta diva*"

Nicola Rossi-Lemeni as Oroveso

288

Act I as staged at Covent Garden in 1967, with Joan Sutherland as Norma invoking the moon goddess

and the great duet *"Mira, O Norma"* are remarkable for sincerity of emotional expression, notwithstanding their clear simplicity of style, and recent revivals of the opera have proved that they still are effective. Those who weary of declamatory modern opera, in which the music is constantly changing in agreement with the most swift and subtle moods that emotion throws upon the stage, at the expense of clearly defined melody, will have no quarrel with the simplicity of *Norma*. Certainly the role of Norma ranks as one of the very greatest and most difficult of soprano roles and has been a favorite with many generations of singers. Among the great sopranos of the past who have sung the role are Jenny Lind, Giulia Grisi, Lilli Lehmann, Rosa Ponselle, Gina Cigna and Zinka Milanov.

OVERTURE

The Overture introduces us to the prevailing moods of the opera. After a few introductory measures of a martial nature, the first theme is heard. This is soon followed by a melody of the opening chorus of Druid soldiers. These subjects are developed into a flowing overture whose purpose is not to present a musical synopsis of the plot, but to set the stage, so to speak, for its unfolding.

ACT I

SCENE: *Night in the sacred Druid forest.* In the dark forest Oroveso, the Archdruid, and the Druidical soldiers and priests await the rising of the moon, at which mystic hour Norma is to perform the sacred rite of cutting the prophetic bough of mistletoe. They sing a sturdy chorus, swearing vengeance upon their Roman oppressors.

The Druids having gone away, Pollione, the Roman proconsul, and his lieutenant Flavio approach. From their conversation we learn that Norma, the daughter of Oroveso and Druidical high priestess, has fallen in love with Pollione, and violating her vows of chastity has borne him two sons. Now, however, Pollione is secretly in love with Adalgisa, one of the virgins of the temple; and that he is conscience-stricken he reveals in his cavatina *"Meco all' altar di Venere."*

When his narrative is suddenly interrupted by sounds of a March signaling the approaching Druids, the two Romans conceal themselves. Norma appears before her people and, fearing for the life of her lover, addresses them, saying in a recitative that the time is not yet ripe to rise against their oppressors; then in the famous aria *"Casta diva"* ("Queen of heaven") she prays for peace, and in an aside, *"Ah! bello, a me ritorna"* ("Return to me"), gives voice to her love, while the Druids hymn the day of their vengeance.

Adalgisa, after an eloquent prayer, meets Pollione in the forest, succumbs to the persuasiveness of his aria *"Va, crudele"* ("Go, cruel one"), and they plan to seek safety and happiness in Rome.

ACT II

SCENE: *Norma's secret dwelling in the forest.* Norma and her faithful confidante Clotilda discuss the high priestess' difficulties, and Norma tells her that she both loves and hates her children. They hear footsteps, and Clotilda spirits the children away, as Adalgisa enters. The latter falls upon her knees before Norma, confessing her shameful devotion (for she has been consecrated to virginity). Under

289

prompting she points to the man involved, Pollione, who has just come in. Whereupon Norma, revealing him as her own lover, heaps imprecations on the head of the proconsul, in which she is joined by Adalgisa, all three then joining in the powerful trio, *"Oh! di qual sei tu"* ("Oh, whose are you?"). The clanging of the sacred shield is heard, and Norma hastens to her religious duties.

ACT III

SCENE: *Interior of Norma's dwelling.* Nearly crazed with anger, Norma thinks of killing her husband and her children and letting herself be burned on the funeral pyre. Only thus can she atone for her secret relationship, since death is the punishment for any priestess who dares violate her vows of chastity. She advances, in a very dramatic *scena,* with uplifted dagger toward the sleeping children, but the sight of the innocent victims overcomes her. Then she summons Adalgisa, and, urging her to go with Pollione, begs her to care for the children, who, following her death, will be motherless. Moved by her generosity, Adalgisa entreats Norma not to do this, and the two priestesses unite in singing the celebrated duet *"Mira, O Norma"* ("Hear me, Norma").

Adalgisa (Marilyn Horne) and Norma (Joan Sutherland)

Adalgisa (Marion Telva) and Norma (Rosa Ponselle)

ACT IV

SCENE: *A wooded region near the temple.* The Gallic warriors, summoned by Norma, convene in the sacred forest. Apprised by Clotilda that Pollione will not leave Adalgisa and return to her, Norma now would proclaim war and destruction on the Romans, and she looses her anger in *"Guerra, guerra!"* ("War! war!"), the passion of her outburst being echoed by the massed Druids. When Pollione is discovered in the midst of the soldiers, he is seized and brought before the high priestess for judgment. He is given the choice of death or immediate departure— without Adalgisa—from Gaul.

Norma, rising to emotional heights, sings, *"In mia mano alfin tu sei"* ("At last, you are in my hands"). But the mingled feelings of pity, duty, and love are too much for her, and she would pardon him, but Pollione rejects this generosity contemptuously, saying that he will not give up Adalgisa. Therefore, Norma confesses her guilt to the astonished people and claims purification by death on the funeral pyre. Now Pollione, overwhelmingly affected by her devotion, asks only that he may die with her. After confiding her children to her father's care, Norma is covered with a black veil. She takes the hand of her lover in her own, and together they walk toward the flames of expiation.

Orfeo

LA FAVOLA d'ORFEO

CHARACTERS

Orpheus, *a musician*	*Tenor*	Hope	*Mezzo-soprano*
Eurydice, *his bride*	*Soprano*	First Shepherd	*High tenor*
Apollo, *god of music*	*Tenor*	Second Shepherd	*Tenor*
Pluto, *god of the underworld*	*Bass*	A Nymph	*Soprano*
Proserpine, *his wife*	*Contralto*	First Spirit	*High tenor*
Charon, *ferryman of the Styx*	*Bass*	Second Spirit	*Tenor*
Sylvia, *a messenger*	*Mezzo-soprano*	Echo	*Tenor*
Music	*Mezzo-soprano*		

Nymphs, Shepherds, Spirits of the Underworld

The action takes place in Thrace and in the underworld.

OPERA IN PROLOGUE AND FIVE ACTS. Music by Claudio Monteverdi. Libretto in Italian by Alessandro Striggio. First performance at the Court Theater at Mantua, February 24, 1607 (though there had been an earlier private performance at the Accademia degli Invaghiti, perhaps on the 22nd). First known performance since the early seventeenth century, at Paris in concert form and in French, February 25, 1904. First American and first (and only) Metropolitan Opera performance, in concert form and in English, April 14, 1912. First American staged performance by Smith College (with professional guest artists) at Northampton, Massachusetts, May 12, 1929.

With so spotty a record of performance as the above—not one, so far as anyone knows, for a period of almost three hundred years—it might seem odd to include Monteverdi's *Orfeo* (or *La Favola d'Orfeo*, as it is also known) in a book dedicated primarily to the most generally popular and enduring stage works. However, the twentieth century has rediscovered a great and beautiful dramatic work; devoted efforts have been made by modern composers,

including Vincent d'Indy, Gian Francesco Malipiero, Ottorino Respighi, and Carl Orff, to adapt the score for modern instruments and performers; and many revivals, however short-lived, could be listed, along with a number of complete recordings of the opera. Most historians of opera agree that it is the first surviving stage work which may legitimately be called "an opera," even though the score published in 1609 did not use the word. It was subtitled *Favola in Musica*" (*Fable in Music*). And if the quality of an opera may be judged by the inspired justness with which the music is wedded to the words and expresses the emotions of the characters with high seriousness, this "first" opera has had few equals.

Wedding the music and the text with high seriousness was one of the principal aims of the Florentine group of intellectuals and artists who met in Florence at the close of the sixteenth century and are known as the "Camerata." Their aim was to produce a Renaissance equivalent of Athenian tragedy, which was known to have been given with music, though exactly how and just what the music was no one knew then or knows today. There were composers in the group, and two of them, Jacopo Peri and Giulio Caccini, had written music for a version of the Orpheus story by one Ottavio Rinuccini as early as 1600 and 1602 respectively. But neither had the genius, the variety, the dramatic qualities of the Monteverdi-Striggio setting.

Monteverdi and Striggio were not members of the Camerata in Florence but were in the service of the enlightened music-loving Vincenzo Gonzaga, Duke of Mantua, Monteverdi as master of the chapel music, Striggio as the humanist secretary. The composer already had a reputation, largely through his published madrigals, as a fine contrapuntist and as a forward-looking theoretician, an avant-gardist who did not hesitate to use severe dissonances and fresh combinations of sound, both in chords and in instrumentation. For the orchestra to perform Orfeo, for example, he required no fewer than thirteen chord-playing instruments, (including three organs, two clavicembali, a double harp, two chitarrones, and other instruments no longer made or played), fourteen stringed instruments, and eleven winds, all of them brass excepting one recorder. The list looks peculiarly unbalanced, and it might sound that way to modern ears if the whole band played simultaneously, which, in the score, they never do. But the list also shows why modern composers are required for extracting a transcription of some sort from the old editions before a modern performance can be given. Nor is it entirely clear what type of voice each part was intended for. The listing below, for example, contains no "baritones," for that classification had not been developed. Yet the role of Orpheus has been sung successfully, in modern performances, by baritones and, in one instance, a contralto. There may have been falsettists or castrati in the cast. We cannot be sure, and the listing given is based on the range and the clef indicated in the score.

Nor is the form of much of the music what we expect when we hear operas composed over 150 years later, which is all we hear much of nowadays. There is an approach to the aria, but much of the melodizing is a kind of emotional recitation set to appropriate pitches on different syllables, a musical projection of what the Camerata thought ancient Greek drama might be like. In addition, there are choral passages set as accompanied madrigals, frequent *ritornelli* (orchestral interludes repeated between stanzas of a set speech), and just one duet—a complete innovation at the time on the lyric stage. Thus, to us the opera on first hearing will sound very old, while to its first hearers it must have sounded excitingly new. To anyone, however, once he has taken the trouble to accept unfamiliar forms and conventions and to follow the text, it quickly becomes clear that this is a beautiful and deeply moving way to tell a thrice-familiar story.

PROLOGUE

An overture (labeled *toccata* in the score), which is brief but repeated three times and features a flourish of trumpets, precedes the appearance before the curtain of "La Musica"—Music, who introduces herself, promises to tell the story of Orpheus, and commands even the birds and the breezes to be quiet as it unfolds.

ACT I

SCENE: *A field in Thrace.* Orpheus and Eurydice are about to be married, and nymphs and shepherds, singly and in a chorus, sing rather solemnly of their happiness on this occasion. Bride and groom acknowledge and echo these appropriate sentiments, and the act ends with a fine contrapuntal chorus.

ACT II

SCENE: *A field in Thrace.* The marriage has now taken place; the nymphs and shepherds sing in praise of Eurydice, and Orpheus responds to a request for a song by contrasting his present happiness with his former sorrow. Sylvia, however, enters and brings the shocking news that Eurydice has just died in her arms of a poisonous snakebite. The nymphs and shepherds express their horror, and Orpheus, who had been struck speechless, vows to take his art to the King of Shadows (Pluto) and bring back his beloved bride. The scene closes with the chorus lamenting and Sylvia blaming herself for having been the one to bear such horrid tidings.

ACT III

SCENE: *The bank of the River Styx.* The figure known as Hope has brought Orpheus to the river he must cross to reach Pluto's underworld. She leaves him, and the grim ferryman Charon demands to know what this mortal wants in a land forbidden to all living human beings. He even suspects Orpheus of planning to abduct Cerberus, the dog who guards these realms. Orpheus eloquently pleads his cause, but Charon, though he likes the music, says it is all useless, for he has no pity in his breast. Thereupon, Orpheus waxes even more eloquent, and when the music puts Charon to sleep, jumps into his boat and begins to row. A chorus of infernal spirits sings the praise of Orpheus for his daring in successfully crossing the stormy waters in a fragile vessel.

ACT IV

SCENE 1: *Pluto's court*. Proserpine eloquently pleads the cause of Orpheus, appropriately relating how happy Pluto had made her by carrying her off from the earth into the underworld. Pluto is won over, but decrees that Orpheus may lead Eurydice back to life only if he can do so without once looking upon her while they are on the way. Two individual spirits and the court all praise Pluto's generosity.

SCENE 2: *A road in the underworld*. Orpheus, walking before the silent Eurydice, sings in praise of his lyre, which had won his way, but fears that his bride may not be following. He has almost made up his mind to risk a look backward when he hears a noise. Thinking it may be the Furies ready to snatch back Eurydice, he turns around and is about to embrace Eurydice when a spirit intervenes, tells Orpheus

there is no hope for pardon now, and orders Eurydice back to the shades of death. Orpheus tries to follow, but some invisible power prevents him, and a chorus of spirits laments the fact that a great hero who could conquer Hades still could not conquer himself.

ACT V

SCENE: *A field in Thrace*. Once more Orpheus is on earth, and he sings bitterly of his sorrow. Twice his words are repeated by Echo, a very striking effect. Finally, the god Apollo appears, addresses Orpheus as his son, tells him that he laments too much, but that he will take him to heaven, where he may once more rejoice in Eurydice's eyes. As they ascend together, they sing an elaborately figured duet. To close the opera there is a consolatory chorus of shepherds and then a dance—a *moresca*, which in English is known as a morris dance.

Eurydice (Judith Raskin) is reunited with Orpheus (Gérard Souzay) in the New York City Opera production

Orfeo ed Euridice
ORPHEUS AND EURYDICE

CHARACTERS

Orpheus, *legendary Greek singer*
  and musician   Contralto, Tenor or Baritone
Eurydice, *his wife*   *Soprano*

Amor (*Love*)   *Soprano*
A Happy Shade   *Soprano*

Happy Shades, Furies, Shepherds, Shepherdesses, Heroes and Heroines
The action takes place in legendary Thrace and Hades.

OPERA IN FOUR ACTS (sometimes three). Music by Christoph Willibald von Gluck. Book in Italian by Raniero de' Calzabigi. First produced at the Burgtheater, Vienna, October 5, 1762. American première at the Winter Garden, New York, May 25, 1863, in an English translation by Fanny Malone Raymond. The Metropolitan Opera staged it for the first time in America in the original Italian version on December 30, 1891, with a cast headed by Giulia Ravogli (Orpheus) and Sophia Ravogli (Eurydice). A magnificent revival of the opera was that of Arturo Toscanini on December 23, 1909, when Louise Homer, Johanna Gadski, and Bella Alten were in the cast. Performances recurred till 1914. Gluck's masterpiece was then shelved by the Metropolitan for twenty-two years, returning during the spring season of 1936. For that production a double cast was used, members of the American Ballet Ensemble miming the action on the stage, while the singers held forth from the orchestra pit. On November 26, 1938, Kerstin Thorborg won great acclaim in the title role. The role of Orpheus has been sung in recent times by Risë Stevens, Giulietta Simionato, Kathleen Ferrier, Shirley Verrett and Grace Bumbry.

Like many other operas, *Orfeo ed Euridice* was subjected to the trials of versions and revisions before achieving a single final status. Gluck rewrote the opera for the Paris production of August 2, 1774, using a French text by Pierre Louis Moline. Much music was added, and the part of Orpheus, originally for contralto, like so many other male roles in the operas of the time, was rewritten for tenor. The Viennese version, however, regained its primacy with the performance of November 19, 1859, at the Théâtre-Lyrique, Paris. Partly responsible for this was the sensational portrayal of the main role by the noted contralto Pauline Viardot.

Kathleen Ferrier as Orpheus

As the blessed spirits bring him the veiled Eurydice, Orpheus turns his face (Metropolitan Opera production)

In the power and pathos of its direct style, *Orfeo* was something of a revolution in opera composition. Preceding *Alceste* and its aesthetic manifesto (see p. 40), it already pronounced the challenge of truth of expression against artifice and display. There is nobility of speech here, the classic, serene beauty that one associates with Grecian art. *Orfeo* is the oldest of the repertory operas, yet in some ways the youngest, for an imperishable youth is on this music, especially the music of Orpheus' poignant outcry *"Che farò senza Euridice?"* and the "Dance of the Happy Shades," with its ethereal flute reverie. It is said that Marie Antoinette, something of a Lady Bountiful to Gluck in Paris, promptly granted him a pension of six thousand francs after the performance of *Orfeo* at the Académie Royale de Musique. For that single gesture of appreciation much could have been forgiven the tragic queen in the harsh years of revolution ahead. In ending happily, Gluck's *Orfeo* differs not only from the standard legend, but from the *Orfeo* of his great predecessor, Monteverdi (see p. 293). But neither makes use of the dreadful ending to the story provided by classical mythology. In this literature Orpheus returns to earth alone and bewails his loss so insistently that the women of Thrace cannot bear it. They accordingly tear him to pieces.

ACT I

SCENE: *The tomb of Eurydice.* Orpheus mourns his lost Eurydice at her tomb, while shepherds and shepherdesses bring flowers and join in a touching lament. Orpheus is inconsolable in his grief, Orpheus the unrivaled musician of antiquity, at whose divine music, legend tells us, trees uprooted themselves and rocks became loosened from their ledges in order to follow the wonderful sounds. For this Orpheus was the son of Apollo, god of music, and Calliope, muse of epic poetry. Amor, the god of love, is so touched by the anguish of Orpheus that he tells him he may descend to the nether world, the dark realm of Pluto, there to seek the shade of Eurydice. One condition, however, is made: if Orpheus would have Eurydice return to earth with him, he must not turn to look at her until he has recrossed the River Styx.

ACT II

SCENE: *Tartarus.* In the awesome depths of Tartarus the frightening bark of Cerberus is heard, and Furies join in a grotesque dance. Although they try to frighten him away, these dark spirits are finally moved to pity with the song of Orpheus' grief, and they allow him to continue his quest.

ACT III

SCENE: *The blessed valley.* In the happy Elysian fields beneath cheerful skies, the Spirits of the Blessed dance to the song of birds and the murmur of brooks. Gluck's music is marvelously descriptive of the chaste beauty and the tranquil felicity of these happy spirits. A flute solo of ravishing sweetness accentuates the mood of classical antiquity. Orpheus sings of the beauty of the sun and the sky (*"Che puro ciel"*), and the blessed spirits bring Eurydice to him. He begs her to follow him, and leads her off carefully averting his eyes.

ACT IV

SCENE 1: *A forest.* As they mount higher and

higher, Eurydice becomes increasingly downcast because Orpheus seems no longer to love her. Not once have their eyes met. She would rather remain below than return to earth without his love. Orpheus is bound by the agreement not to reveal the cause of his strange behavior. When they are almost in sight of the land of the living, she cries out with such heart-rending pathos that, in a moment of forgetfulness, Orpheus looks back, only to see her sink lifeless to the ground. Now his sorrow is even more profound than before. Utterly disconsolate, he expresses his grief in a melody of sublime pathos, *"Che farò senza Euridice?"* (*"I have lost my Eurydice"*). Amor, who has been watching Orpheus, is so deeply moved by this impassioned outcry that he restores Eurydice to life and permits the rejoicing lovers to proceed to the world above.

SCENE 2: *Before the Temple of Love.* In a kind of epilogue, there is a series of solos, choruses, and dances, all in praise of love.

Act IV celebration of love: Amor (Emilia Cundari), Eurydice (Hilde Gueden), Orpheus (Risë Stevens) and dancers (Michael Maule, Alicia Markova), as staged at the Metropolitan Opera during the 1954–55 season

Otello

CHARACTERS

Otello, *a Moor, general in the Venetian army*	Tenor	Lodovico, *ambassador of the Venetian Republic*	Bass
Iago, *his aide*	Baritone	Montano, *predecessor of Otello as Governor of Cyprus*	Baritone
Cassio, *lieutenant to Otello*	Tenor	A Herald	Baritone
Roderigo, *a Venetian gentleman*	Tenor	Desdemona, *Otello's wife*	Soprano
		Emilia, *Iago's wife*	Mezzo-soprano

Soldiers and Sailors of the Venetian Republic; Venetian Ladies and Gentlemen;
Cypriot Men, Women, and Children; Heralds; Greek, Dalmatian, and Albanian
Soldiers; an Innkeeper, and four Servants

The action takes place at a seaport of Cyprus toward the end of the fifteenth century.

OPERA IN FOUR ACTS. Music by Giuseppe Verdi. Libretto in Italian by Arrigo Boito, after Shakespeare. First performance, Teatro alla Scala, Milan, February 5, 1887. The cast included Francesco Tamagno, Victor Maurel and Romilda Pantaleone, Franco Faccio conducting. United States première, Academy of Music, New York, April 16, 1888, with Francesco Marconi as Otello, Antonio Galassi as Iago, Eva Tetrazzini as Desdemona, and Sofia Scalchi as Emilia, Cleofonte Campanini conducting. Tamagno made his American debut as Otello on March 24, 1890, during a spring season of opera at the Metropolitan Opera House. The first official performance at the Metropolitan took place January 11, 1892, with Jean de Reszke, Camera, Albani, and Scalchi.

Sixteen years after *Aïda* had seemed to be the crowning glory of Verdi's long musical career, the great composer astonished the musical world with *Otello*. At the age of seventy-four he showed, past all doubt, that the fierce creative spirit which burned within him was not only alive, but still glowing brightly. In that sixteen-year interval Verdi had kept close touch with the development of music. *Otello*, therefore, is essentially modern in spirit and technique. The characterization is marvelous; there are no set airs or ensembles, the scenes fusing into each other without a break. Its force and almost youthful energy, set upon a lifetime of practical musical and dramatic experience, give the work a unique place in music.

Arrigo Boito's libretto, a masterpiece of literary and theatrical power, is the greatest of his career.

ACT I

SCENE: *Exterior of Otello's castle (with a view of the harbor and the sea; in the foreground a tavern).* A storm rages and the angry sea is visible in the background. A group of Venetian citizens and soldiers watch the vessel bearing the victorious Otello as it struggles with the storm. His vessel arrives safely, and amid great rejoicing the Moor announces a complete victory over the Turkish fleet, in the difficult music of *"Esultate!"* ("Exult!").

When he has entered the castle, the soldiers begin drinking in celebration of the victory. Among them is Iago, who is secretly smarting with a desire for

Act I: Otello (James McCracken) restores peace as Desdemona (Gabriella Tucci) waits high on staircase

revenge since his comrade-in-arms Cassio has been promoted to a higher rank than himself by Otello. Iago is, moreover, greatly incensed that this Moor should have risen to be a general in the Venetian army, and now honored by being made Governor of Cyprus. He finds a willing ally in Roderigo, who loves Desdemona, and still desires her, even though she has married Otello. Iago, therefore, induces Roderigo to help in plying Cassio with wine.

Cassio at first refuses to drink, knowing his own particular weakness; but when Iago toasts Desdemona, he is obliged to respond. He is soon hopelessly befuddled, grows hilarious, finally quarrelsome. Iago now cunningly manages to have him pick a quarrel with Montano, Otello's predecessor in the government of Cyprus. Swords are drawn, Montano is wounded, and Iago fans the disturbance into a small riot.

This is put down by the appearance of Otello, who is enraged that his own soldiers should thus be fighting among themselves, and deprives Cassio of his command. Iago's crafty planning has already begun its work.

The crowd departs, leaving Otello alone with his wife, the gentle Desdemona. They sing a version in duet form of the lines in Shakespeare's play where Otello describes how Desdemona, hearing him tell of his hardships and dangers in battle, came to love him, *"Già nella notte densa"* (*"Dark is the night"*).

As Otello kisses her, the orchestra plays an impassioned phrase that will be repeated with telling effect at the end of the opera. Husband and wife now re-enter the castle. The peace of a starlight night envelops the scene.

ACT II

SCENE: *A hall on the ground floor of the Castle (with a view of the garden).* Iago plays still more subtly upon the unsuspecting Cassio; he begs him to ask Desdemona to intercede for him with Otello. Cassio goes in search of her, and, well satisfied with his work, Iago gazes after him, soliloquizing on his own philosophy of life. Like a true believer, he begins by saying that he believes in one God, but a cruel God, who has fashioned mankind in his own vile image; that life is made but to feed death, and heaven's only a lie. Verdi has matched this grim confession of faith with a remarkable musical portrayal of Iago's heartless cynicism, in the *"Credo,"* which, incidentally, was a textual invention of Boito's, since it has no counterpart in Shakespeare's work.

As soon as Iago sees Cassio in conversation with

298

ACT III

SCENE: *The great hall of the castle.* Otello seeks Desdemona, and contrives an excuse to borrow her handkerchief. She offers it, but he says this is not the one, for he would have that which he had given her. Though inwardly trembling at its loss, she says it is in her room; she will go fetch it. But Otello at once denounces her and sends her rudely away, and his wife is astonished and grief-stricken at this strange, sudden jealousy. He remains looking after her in the deepest dejection and sings a sorrowful soliloquy, declaring that nothing that fate might have done to mar his fame or fortune would have been so terrible a blow as this, *"Dio! mi potevi scagliar"* ("Lord, you could have saved me from this").

Cassio enters, and Iago, bidding Otello watch and listen from behind a pillar, goes to the demoted young officer, and with fiendish ingenuity induces him to talk of his affairs with a woman of the town, Bianca. But Otello does not hear the name, in fact is only able to grasp a part of this half-whispered, rather lewd conversation. Cassio produces the fatal handkerchief, telling Iago that he had found it in his room; he wonders who placed it there. Otello sees the handkerchief; he sees Cassio laughing; and though he does not hear all that is said, this is indeed proof enough of Desdemona's guilt. By the time Cassio has left, Otello is insane with jealousy and rage; he asks Iago to procure him poison wherewith to kill Desdemona. Iago craftily evades being involved by suggesting that she had better be

Renata Tebaldi as Desdemona, the role in which she made her Metropolitan Opera début, in 1955

Desdemona, he hurriedly calls Otello and sows in the heart of the Moor the first seed of jealousy, bidding him watch his wife carefully. Otello, much troubled, finds Desdemona and questions her. As she at once begins to plead Cassio's cause, his suspicions are more fully awakened; and when she seeks to wipe his perspiring brow with a handkerchief that was his own first gift, he tears it from her and throws it to the floor. It is picked up by Emilia, Desdemona's maid and Iago's wife. While Otello roughly berates his alarmed Desdemona, Iago forces Emilia to give him the kerchief.

Left alone with Iago, Otello gives expression to his grief, singing a fervent and heartbroken air in which he bids farewell to peace of mind, ambition, and the glory of conquest, *"Ora e per sempre addio, sante memorie"* ("And now, forever farewell").

Now Iago, the Iago whom Otello knows only as "honest Iago," pours fuel on the flame of jealousy by avowing that he has seen Desdemona's handkerchief in Cassio's room. He also declares that he has heard the sleeping Cassio speak of her in his dreams.

Otello becomes frantic with rage. Iago offers to help him to vengeance. Uniting in a most impressive duet, they call on all the heavenly bodies to witness this solemn oath in which they swear never to relent or pause until the guilty shall have been punished, *"Sì, pel ciel"* ("By heaven and earth").

Mario del Monaco (Otello) and Leonard Warren (Iago) at La Scala

strangled in the bed she has dishonored; but he will "take care" of Cassio himself. Otello agrees.

The Venetian ambassador Lodovico arrives in state, to inform Otello that he has been recalled to Venice, while Cassio is to be Governor of Cyprus in his stead. Desdemona, who has also entered, weeps for pity at seeing her lord's distress. Her every remark brings a rebuke from Otello, who believes that she weeps because of the approaching separation from Cassio. He announces his departure on the morrow, then, unable longer to contain his smoldering anger, publicly insults Desdemona and flings her to the ground. Overcome with his own feverish emotion he falls to earth in a swoon. Meanwhile, the public outside, hearing that new honors have fallen to their hero, shout, "Hail, Otello! Hail to the Lion of Venice!" But Iago points with horrible triumph to the prostrate Moor and cries, "Behold the Lion!"

ACT IV

SCENE: *Desdemona's bedroom.* Desdemona is preparing to retire, assisted by Emilia. She tells Emilia of an old song she used to hear in her childhood, a song that keeps coming back to her mind this evening. The words tell of a girl who, like herself, loved too well, and she sings this pathetic little song for Emilia, "*Salce, salce*" ("Willow, willow"), which is known in English as the "Willow Song."

When Emilia has bid her good night and gone, Desdemona kneels before the image of the Madonna, which stands over a faldstool. Here Desdemona sings her prayer, the noble "*Ave Maria*," at first in a whispered monotone, then soaring aloft in melody; the song ends with the quiet and peace of the "Amen."

Scarcely has she finished when the sinister figure of Otello is seen appearing through a secret door. He makes his way to her bed, contemplates her for a time. Then he kisses her. Otello asks her if she has said her prayers, for, he explains, he would not kill her soul. Again he accuses her of being a paramour of Cassio's. Denials are useless. He repeats charge after charge, his jealous rage mounting, and the horrified Desdemona cries for help as he takes her by the throat. Emilia knocks frenziedly on the door, and when Otello finally admits her into the room, she is stunned by the tragedy facing her and shrieks for aid. In answer others rush into the bedroom, and Otello says that he has killed his wife because of her faithlessness. Emilia explains about the handkerchief, and Montano tells Otello that Roderigo, dying, has exposed Iago's wiles. That villain makes a hurried exit, and Otello sings a lamentation, as he gazes at the lifeless form of Desdemona. He unsheathes his dagger and stabs himself and, drawing himself close to her with his remaining strength, kisses her, as the orchestra takes up again the "Kiss" motive.

Desdemona (Frances Alda) pleads with Otello (Leo Slezak), in Toscanini's 1909 Metropolitan revival

Pagliacci

CLOWNS

CHARACTERS

Canio, *master of the troupe of street players* (*"Pagliaccio"*)	*Tenor*	Tonio, *a clown* (*"Taddeo"*)	*Baritone*
		Silvio, *a villager*	*Baritone*
Nedda, *his wife* (*"Columbine"*)	*Soprano*	Beppe, *a clown* (*"Harlequin"*)	*Tenor*

Villagers and Peasants

The action takes place in the village of Montalto, in Calabria, on the feast of the Assumption (August 15) in the late 1860's.

OPERA IN TWO ACTS. Music by Ruggiero Leoncavallo, who also wrote the libretto. First performance, Teatro dal Verme, Milan, May 21, 1892. First American performance, Grand Opera House, New York, June 15, 1893. On December 11 of the same year *Pagliacci* obtained its Metropolitan première, with Nellie Melba as Nedda, Fernando de Lucia as Canio, and Mario Ancona as Tonio. Since then *Pagliacci* has remained a mainstay of the Metropolitan's repertoire, and the first-line artists who appeared in the gory lyric tragedy number in the dozens, chief of whom, of course, were Enrico Caruso, to this day the incomparable Canio, and Titta Ruffo, a celebrated Tonio.

Pagliacci was composed, one might say, in a fit of temper. Leoncavallo, who had received his musical training at the Conservatory of Naples, had, as a young musician, a hard struggle in the world. An early opera failed to be produced because the impresario ran away with the funds and left the composer nearly penniless. He managed to exist by teaching and playing the piano at café-concerts. In this latter capacity he toured the whole of Europe. During these travels he outlined a vast trilogy which

Enrico Caruso in his most famous role, Canio

was to do for Italian music what Wagner's *Ring* did for German. On his return to Italy the outline was accepted by a publisher, and Leoncavallo completed the score of the first of the three dramas in a year. No production followed, however, and the composer waited three years. Enraged at this treatment, he made overtures to a rival publisher who had conducted the competition resulting in Mascagni's sensationally successful *Cavalleria Rusticana*. Favorably received, he set to work on a short opera in a similar realistic vein. Leoncavallo wrote his libretto, drawing on his own experience for inspiration, and impetuously completed the entire work, libretto and music, in four months. It had a successful production, comparable with that of *Cavalleria* itself. This paved the way for the trilogy, but as the first of these operas failed, Leoncavallo never completed the others. Of his subsequent works, only *La Bohème* and *Zaza* have achieved any measure of success, and even these lack the fire of his earlier work.

At one time a suit was brought against the composer for having plagiarized, for *Pagliacci*, the plot of another author. Leoncavallo thereupon stated that an incident similar to the plot of the opera occurred when he was a child—a case of an actor killing his wife. Leoncavallo's father was the judge before whom the guilty man was tried. The occurrence so impressed itself upon the youthful mind of the composer-to-be that in later life he turned to it as a basis for his opera. This explanation was accepted and the suit withdrawn.

Tonio (Mario Sereni) steps before the old Metropolitan Opera curtain to sing the Prologue

At any rate, *Pagliacci* continues to remain one of the most popular operas on the modern operatic stage; a distinction shared with it only by *Cavalleria Rusticana* of all the early realist, so-called *verismo*, operas. They held this position not without cause, for both are tellingly dramatic as plays, yet contain many attractions in the power and vividness of the music.

The idea of "play within a play," which gives to *Pagliacci* its ironic quality, is of considerable antiquity, *Hamlet* being its most famous prototype in this respect. The play that occurs in *Pagliacci* is one of the Commedia dell'Arte type that has been acted for centuries by troupes of strolling players in Italy. In that antique and rather crude farce, Pagliaccio discovers his wife Columbine with Harlequin, her lover. Harlequin chases the irate husband around the room and finally kicks him out of his own house. This, in the old play, is the climax of the laugh-producing scenes.

The word *pagliaccio* is sometimes translated "Punchinello," sometimes "clown," meaning not clown in the sense of a circus performer, but the buffoon who received all the "hard knocks" in old Italian comedy; the plural, *pagliacci*, refers to the whole group of actors playing such a comedy. The final exclamation *"La commedia è finita!"* ("The comedy is ended!") is said to have been almost the last speech of the dying Beethoven.

PROLOGUE

The Prologue opens with a brief orchestral introduction that presages the drama to follow. It depicts the players themselves, as a group, in the bustle and verve of the music, then refers to Canio with a somber strain suggestive of his unhappiness and jealousy, to Nedda by way of a sinuous theme indicative of her guilty love for Silvio, and ends with the first idea of the troupe itself.

Tonio, coming through the curtain on an abrupt dissonance, asks the audience's permission with the words *"Si può?"* ("A word?"). Thereafter he launches into a lengthy explanation of the work. These players, he says, are men and women, and the author, borrowing the idea of a prologue from the "glory of old," would not repeat to his hearers that the sighs and tears of the actors are false or that they have no hearts. On the contrary, he would show them to be players in a fragment from life. So he has written the story for men, and the story is true.

Tonio knocks on the curtain, saying, "Come, let's begin," and the orchestra peals out the *"Pagliacci"* theme.

ACT I

SCENE: *The entrance to a litttle Italian village, at the junction of two roads.* A rude stage has been erected; before it Tonio stands on guard. A trumpet is heard, crude and out of tune, and the booming of a bass drum. It is a holiday, the feast of the Assumption, and gaily dressed villagers hurry to the spot, in no mood for work. Excited with the anticipation of a good time, they exclaim, "They're here, the *pagliacci!* Welcome!"

Down the road comes a characteristic procession: Beppe, dressed as Harlequin, leading a donkey, which in turn draws a brightly painted cart; in the cart lies Nedda; back of it walks Canio, in the costume of Pagliaccio, with trumpet and drumsticks. The troupe halts before the little theater, and Canio silences the noisy welcome by hammering the bass drum. With mock solemnity he announces their performance, then adds, *"Venite onorateci, signor' e signori"* ("So come then, and honor us, ladies and gentlemen"). He turns to help his wife down from the cart, but Tonio, the misshapen clown, is there before him, much to the amusement of the crowd. Canio pays him for this with a hearty box on the ear. Tonio slinks off back of the stage, muttering to himself, while the villagers rock with laughter.

One of the men suggests they go for a drink, and Canio calls to Tonio to come along. But the clown answers that he must stay to rub down the donkey, and a villager jestingly hints that Tonio might prefer staying behind with Nedda. At once on the alert, Canio exclaims, "Eh! What!—You think so?" Then, with a wry smile, he continues, *"Un tal gioco"* ("Such a game is better not played").

Nedda understands very well the cause of her husband's black looks, yet exclaims to herself, "What does he mean?" The villagers are somewhat puzzled and ask if he is serious. He rouses himself with an effort and says lightly, "Not I—I love my wife most dearly," and thereupon he kisses her on the forehead.

A troupe of bagpipe players passes, and church bells are heard ringing in the village; toward it the people now turn, slowly, in couples. As they go, they sing the famous "Chorus of the Bells," a charming melody with something of the spirit of Italian folk song.

The voices fade away in the distance, and Nedda is left alone to muse over the jealous fire she saw in Canio's eyes. "If he were to catch me!" She shudders. The bright summer sunlight soon drives away these ominous thoughts and, looking up to the sky, she sings the *ballatella "Stridono lassù"* ("Birds

Canio (Giovanni Martinelli) greets the villagers

without number"). Nedda has forgotten her tawdry world as she thinks of the freedom of the birds.

Her musing is interrupted by the unwelcome reappearance of Tonio. He tells her that he could not resist her singing; she laughs at him, saying he talks like a poet. He knows that he is ugly and deformed, yet he cannot help loving her, desiring her, violently. Nedda orders him to go or she will call Canio. "Not before I have kissed you!" he cries, rushing at her. She darts away, picks up a whip, and strikes him across the face, shouting, "You cur!" Tonio screams with pain, then cries, "By the Blessed Virgin of the Assumption I swear you'll pay me for this!"

No sooner has Tonio gone than a more welcome lover approaches. He vaults lightly over the wall and greets Nedda with a laugh. It is Silvio, one of the villagers, whom she has met on previous visits and found much to her liking. She is alarmed at the sight of him during broad daylight, but he reassures her, for he has left Canio with Beppe at the tavern, where they are drinking and are likely to remain.

Nedda tells Silvio of the clown's threats, bidding him be cautious; but the young villager laughs at her fears, and consoles her by pleading his own love with great earnestness. He begs her to run away with him to some place where they can be happy. Nedda is greatly fascinated, yet remains fearful; she is so charming when she implores him not to tempt her that he only grows more impetuous in his love-making. He reproaches her for her coldness, until at last, throwing discretion to the winds, she yields herself to the bliss of the moment and consents to go. They are so lost in the ecstasy of their passion that they do not observe Canio, who, warned by the over-observant Tonio, approaches just in time to hear Nedda's parting exclamation, "Till tonight, then! and forever I'll be yours!" Canio is unable to restrain a subdued "Ah!" Silvio disappears over the wall, and Canio, who has not seen his face, runs to follow him. Nedda bars the way. Canio thrusts her aside in fierce anger and leaps over the wall in pursuit. He is too late, for Silvio knows a path hidden by the brush, and Canio fails to discover it. Tonio, who is looking on, laughs in glee, and to Nedda's scornful "Bravo! Well done, Tonio!" replies that he will do better next time. Canio returns out of breath, exhausted, trembling with anger.

The outraged husband commands his wife to pronounce the name of her lover, but she bravely refuses. Wild with jealousy, he rushes at her with drawn dagger. Beppe, who has returned unobserved, runs forward and holds him back. People are coming from church, he says, it will soon be time for their performance; they must hurry and dress for it. Nedda, glad for an excuse, disappears into the tent-like stage; Beppe and Tonio go on about their work.

With bowed head, worn out by passion and jealousy, Canio remains alone to consider his fate. Heavy chords are played by the orchestra as he meditates, *"Recitar! mentre preso dal delirio"* ("To perform, while in this frenzy"). He continues, singing the famous arioso of heart-rending pathos *"Vesti la giubba,"* freely rendered in English as "On with the play." He moves slowly toward the theater, sobbing. Reaching the curtain that opens on the little stage, he pushes it roughly, as if not wanting to enter; then, seized by a new fit of sobbing, he again buries his face in his hands. Finally he takes several steps toward the curtain from which he had recoiled in fury, enters, and disappears.

ACT II

SCENE: *The same.* It is the hour appointed for the performance. Tonio is beating the drum to summon the villagers—it would seem rather to drown out their animated chatter as they rapidly congregate. Silvio also arrives, to feast his eyes on Nedda, greeting his friends among the spectators as he takes his seat. All are excited. Some exclaim as they enter, "Let's try to put ourselves well up in front there!" Others, true villagers impatient for the show, ask,

"What are you waiting for? Why this delaying? Everyone's here!" Then as the play begins, all shout, "Keep quiet! Be still!"

The curtains of the theater are drawn aside, revealing this scene, roughly painted: a small room with two side doors and a window at the back. A plain table and two ordinary chairs are at the right. Nedda is there alone, dressed in the costume of Columbine. She seems to be nervously awaiting someone, although she informs her audience that her husband will not be home till late this evening. From outside comes the sound of a guitar, and Columbine rushes toward the window with a little cry of joy. The voice of Harlequin (Beppe) is heard without, singing a serenade; the Italianate melody is at once dainty and sentimental; the words, a bit extravagant, are perfectly in keeping with the character and the occasion, *"O Colombina"* ("O Columbine").

Before Harlequin can enter, however, Taddeo arrives (this clownish role is justly assigned to Tonio), bearing a basket. He sings a pompous greeting, which brings a roar from the assembled villagers. He forthwith begins to make love to Columbine. Her reply is a demand for the chicken he had been sent to fetch; Taddeo kneels before her, holding up the fowl in grotesque devotion. His buffoonery is cut short by Harlequin, who enters and leads him out by the ear—to the delight of the village audience.

With Taddeo banished, the lovers can make merry. Harlequin gives his Columbine a little vial, telling her to give it to Pagliaccio. Columbine assents. Suddenly Taddeo reappears, bawling out in mock alarm, "Be careful! Pagliaccio is here!"

The "lovers" simulate the greatest alarm, while the spectators applaud lustily. Harlequin leaps from the window just as Pagliaccio enters. At that moment Columbine calls to Harlequin the very words previously spoken to the villager Silvio, "Till tonight, then! and forever I'll be yours!"

This is almost too much for Canio, who forgets for a moment his part of Pagliaccio. Then, recalling that he is supposed to be acting, he continues with his lines. "Who has been here with you? Tell me his name?" She insists that it was only Taddeo the clown, who, having rushed into hiding, now calls from the closet, "Believe her, sir, she is faithful! Ah, they could never lie, those lips." There is more laughter from the spectators.

Again Canio forgets his part; he demands, "Woman, it's your lover's name I want!" Nedda, still boldly playing Columbine, replies jokingly, "Pagliaccio! Pagliaccio!" This reminder of his part only angers the jealous actor; throwing aside his role, he answers, to music of unusually ominous force, *"No, Pagliaccio non son"* ("No! Pagliaccio no more!"). And in a long speech he tells her that he is a man seeking vengeance. Overwhelmed, he sinks on the chair by the table.

The audience, not knowing that this has no part in the play, cries, "Bravo!" Pale, but courageous, Nedda continues the role of Columbine; to a frivolous gavotte tune she remarks that the man who was with her was only the harmless Harlequin. The villagers start to laugh, but stop short on seeing the expression on Canio's face. They begin to realize that this is no mere play-acting. The faithful Beppe approaches in the background; he would interfere, but Tonio craftily holds him back. Canio, crazed with anger and jealousy, again demands her lover's name; again Nedda refuses, boldly declaring, "I will not speak! No, not even if you kill me!" In their excitement, the villagers have risen to their feet,

overturning benches; some of the women run away. Silvio draws his dagger, but the men near him, not understanding his excitement, hold him back. Nedda tries to escape toward the spectators, but Canio is too quick. With lightning speed he seizes her. There is a sudden flash, and he plunges his dagger into her heart, crying, "To you! To you!" She shrieks, then falls with a choking sound. Making a last faint effort, she calls, "Help me, Silvio!" The young villager breaks away from the men holding him and runs to his beloved. Muttering, "Ah, it's you!" Canio springs forward and strikes the dagger into him. Then, as if stupefied, he lets the knife fall and, addressing his audience for the last time, says with most bitter irony, *"La commedia è finita!"* ("The comedy is ended!").

Act II: Lucine Amara as Nedda (Columbine) onstage with Mario del Monaco as the jealous Canio (Pagliaccio)

Parsifal

CHARACTERS

Titurel, *founder and retired King of the Knights of the Grail* — **Bass**

Amfortas, *his son and present ruler* — **Baritone**

Gurnemanz, *a veteran Knight of the Grail* — **Bass**

Parsifal, *a "guileless fool"* — *Tenor*

Kundry, *an enigmatic character, serving both the Brotherhood of the Grail and their enemy, Klingsor* — *Soprano*

Klingsor, *a magician* — *Baritone*

Knights of the Grail, Klingsor's Flower Maidens, Esquires, and Boys

The action takes place during the Middle Ages in Spain, at Monsalvat, near and in the Castle of the Grail and in Klingsor's enchanted garden and castle.

CONSECRATIONAL FESTIVAL drama in three acts. Words and music by Richard Wagner. First produced at Bayreuth, July 26, 1882. First staged performance elsewhere, December 24, 1903, at the Metropolitan Opera House, New York. Because of its sacred character, the composer expressed a wish that this work should not be performed as a part of the everyday repertoire of opera houses; he hoped that it would ever remain as a "Stage-consecrating Festival Drama," played only at his own theater at Bayreuth. Accordingly, *Parsifal* was not produced elsewhere until 1903, except in concert form. Then, in spite of the legal moves of Wagner's widow, the Metropolitan Opera Company was enabled to give *Parsifal* its first performance outside of Bayreuth as Wagner's operas were not copyrighted in the U.S.A. In Europe, however, *Parsifal* was not performed outside of the composer's theater until after the expiration of the copyright in 1913 with the exception of a performance at Amsterdam in 1905.

Parsifal has long held a singular position in the world of opera, partly because of its semireligious, mystical character, partly because of its extraordinary music. Wagner first conceived the idea of an opera on the subject on Good Friday of 1858, when he was forty-five. He sketched the libretto out in 1865 but did not publish it till 1877. The following year he began composing the music, and he supervised the first production in 1882—almost a quarter

of a century from conception to production. It was his last work, for he died the following year.

The legend of the Holy Grail, which probably originated in pre-Christian Wales, first became known to the composer through a medieval poem by Wolfram von Eschenbach, the sad poet-knight who appears in *Tannhäuser* and whose literary works also supplied the source material for *Lohengrin*. Wagner used other sources as well, but it is useful to know, for the purpose of understanding Wagner's symbolism, that in the Christian versions, the Grail is identified with the chalice used at the Last Supper and also the cup that received Christ's blood from the cross. Similarly, the Holy Spear of Amfortas is identified with the spear that wounded Christ on the cross. Wagner's philosophy, which is taken very seriously by some, is based fundamentally on the doctrine of renunciation. He draws obviously on the rites of the Last Supper, the Mass of the Apostolic Church, and the ceremonies of the Christian Masonic Order of the Templars in the second scene of Act I. There is also a thinly veiled reference to the life of Christ in the baptizing of Kundry in the last act. The quasi-religious character of the book has unquestionably been partly responsible for the awe in which the work has long been held, especially in middle Europe. Because a performance is regarded by many as a religious rite rather than as entertainment, there is a tradition, often partly honored, that

Gurnemanz (Alexander Kipnis), Kundry (Margarete Matzenauer) and Amfortas (George London)

there should be no applause. Yet Wagner himself led the applause after Act II in the first season at Bayreuth.

For a long time even the most sophisticated critics regarded *Parsifal* as Wagner's masterpiece. More recent critics are generally less generous, some of them claiming that they detect the signs of waning creative powers in the overlong score. It is certainly the composer's most complex, perhaps overworked, piece, and parts of it are even more difficult to sing than *Tristan*. Nevertheless, there are passages of unequivocal grandeur, especially in those set orchestral pieces so familiar to concertgoers as the Prelude and the "Good Friday Music."

PRELUDE

The Prelude is conceived with a simplicity and dignity of form worthy of the lofty subject of the drama. Without any preliminaries, without any accompaniment, the motive of "The Last Supper" rises, calm and reverent, yet most poignant in its tone color. It is repeated with an accompaniment that induces an aspect of awesome mystery. Then is heard the tranquil motive of "The Grail." Its mood of subdued veneration is soon effaced by the motive of "Faith," which is pealed out in the most solemn majesty by the orchestral brasses. These themes are at once repeated in the loveliest of the softer orchestral voices. The theme of "The Last Supper" returns, surrounded by mysterious, ominous harmonies, and against tremulous tones low in the bass. From a fragment of it is fashioned the motive of "The Spear"—the Spear that pierced the side of the Saviour at the Crucifixion, growing into the most heart-rending, questioning lamentation—the cry of anguish of the suffering Amfortas. This resolves itself into the motive of "The Last Supper" soaring upward and dying softly away, like an unanswered question—for the thought back of the entire Prelude is, as Wagner expressed it, "Love—Faith —Hope?" The answer to the question is in the drama that follows. When played as a separate concert piece, the motive of "The Grail" is added as a final cadence, bringing the Prelude to a close in the most sublime, radiant tranquillity.

ACT I

SCENE 1: *A forest near the Castle of the Holy Grail at Monsalvat.* As dawn lights up the woods of Monsalvat, and the waking call rings out from the Castle of the Grail, Gurnemanz and his esquires awaken and kneel to offer up their morning prayer. Having so done, they would prepare for their King, who will soon approach for his morning bath in the lake, but now a weird interruption occurs. A woman hurriedly approaches—Kundry, unkempt in her apparel and fierce and dark of mien, a strange, enigmatic character who is as industrious in the service of the knights as she is in that of their archenemy Klingsor. Upon Gurnemanz she urges a vial which she has brought, and bids him give it to the King of the Grail. Perhaps it will heal the grievous wound which afflicts him. Then, utterly exhausted, she throws herself on the ground to rest just as the litter is brought in carrying Amfortas, who is the King of the Knights of the Grail. In his suffering he despairs of a cure, for balms and ointments have been tried from every land, and all have failed. Gurnemanz offers him the vial which Kundry brought. He turns to thank her, but she only bids him begone to his bath.

307

The Grail Scene at Bayreuth, with Dietrich Fischer-Dieskau as Amfortas, guardian of the sacred cup

Kundry's strange behavior has not increased the esquires' confidence in her, and as soon as Amfortas has been taken away, they accuse her of being the source of all their misfortunes. Gurnemanz rebukes them, however, recalling the help which she has frequently brought; their misfortunes happen when she is absent. Falling into a mood of reminiscence, he tells them the history of the Grail: The two treasures of Monsalvat are the cup from which Our Lord drank at the Last Supper, and the spear which pierced His side. In a vision these were given to Titurel, the father of Amfortas. He it was who built the sanctuary of Monsalvat and gathered together the band of knights for the defense of these sacred relics. Among those who wished to become a knight of the Grail was Klingsor, who was excluded by the very blackness of the passions which filled his heart. Unable to become a true guardian of the Grail, he resolved to obtain the sacred vessel by means of magic, and through sorcery he created a garden of enchanting women to lure the knights to their undoing. In time Titurel grew old and bestowed his kingdom upon his son. But Amfortas, straying too near Klingsor's realm, allowed himself to be enticed away by a woman of wonderful beauty; the magician obtained the sacred spear and with it attacked Amfortas, who, grievously wounded, escaped only

through the timely intervention of Kundry. None have since been able to win back the spear from Klingsor, who, with the aid of that weapon, will soon have gained the Grail itself. There is a single hope that the spear may be restored and Amfortas find healing for his wound: once when in the agony of his suffering the King knelt before the shrine in prayer, a heavenly vision spoke to him, saying that a chosen one, a guileless fool, would be the deliverer.

The mystical harmonies of the theme of "The Promise" are suddenly interrupted by an outcry from the shore of the lake. A wounded swan falls dying to the ground, an arrow in its breast. Since all wild life is sacred at Monsalvat, the guilty one is quickly apprehended. The author of this outrage is a youth who is quite unconscious of having done any wrong; but Gurnemanz' reproof soon humbles his pride in his archery, his eyes fill with tears, and he throws away his arrows and breaks his bow. When questioned he betrays the astonishing fact that he knows neither his own name nor that of his father. His mother he left only recently and, wandering about aimlessly, has come to this sacred domain. Kundry listens to his narrative with marked interest, displays some knowledge of his history, and startles the youth by informing him that since he left his home, his mother has died. In a sudden fury he springs at her; then, overcome by grief, he seems about to faint, and Kundry revives him with water. Then, while the weird theme of "Enchantment" is heard in the orchestra, she sinks down, unable to withstand the trancelike sleep which overcomes her. Gurnemanz, thinking that this boy may be the Promised One, turns to conduct him to the Castle of the Grail. As they walk, the scene moves, to the accompaniment of the stupendous "Transformation" music, and the shifting panorama ends when they enter the great hall of the Grail. (At many performances this moving background is omitted and the curtain merely lowered while the scenes are being changed.)

Scene 2: *The great hall of the Holy Grail.* The music assumes a stately and solemn character as the aged knight and the boy enter the sanctuary. The hall is at first empty, but is gradually filled with knights who enter in a dignified procession and take their places at the tables which are ranged around an altar beneath the great central dome. It is the hour of the sacred rite, and while the song of the liturgy echoes throughout the hall, Amfortas is carried in and assisted to a couch at the altar. From a nearby recess the voice of Titurel is heard speaking as though from a tomb. He bids his son uncover the Grail. But Amfortas cries out in agonized protest, for this sight which brings joy and peace to others only increases

308

his suffering, and, sending the blood coursing wildly through his veins, causes the wound to break out afresh. He sinks down exhausted, but presently yields to the command of his father. The shrine is uncovered, disclosing a crystal cup, and the hall is permeated by a mysterious darkness. Soon an increasingly dazzling light falls from above, and as the Grail becomes radiant with a soft glow, Amfortas lifts the sacred vessel and, slowly moving it from side to side, consecrates the bread and wine. The heavenly light gradually vanishes, the Grail is again enclosed in its shrine, and daylight returns. The knights and esquires sing a reverent hymn while the consecrated elements are distributed; but the exaltation which filled Amfortas during the ceremony passes, his wound breaks out afresh, and falling back weakly, he is carried from the hall. The knights follow, and only Gurnemanz and his companion remain. The youth has stood watching the ceremony, silent and motionless, nor does he reply when the veteran knight questions him concerning what he has seen. Irritated at his apparent stupidity, Gurnemanz opens a side door and irately turns him out.

ACT II

SCENE 1: *The inner keep of a tower atop Klingsor's castle.* The Prelude to the second act, with its sinuously winding theme of "Enchantment" and the wild crying of "Kundry," transports us to an entirely different world. At the rise of the curtain we discern vaguely the keep of Klingsor's castle so shrouded in gloom that the strange instruments of necromancy scattered about can hardly be seen. Klingsor himself is nearly invisible in the mysterious blue smoke that comes from the magic flame at which he stands, invoking some unearthly power. He summons Kundry, who rises from the shadows still in her trancelike slumber and awakens with a terrible cry. Klingsor mocks her for her devotion to the Knights of the Grail whenever he releases her from his spell; yet, he says, she was a priceless aid to him in overpowering Amfortas. She struggles against these remorse-bringing memories and curses the very thought of them. Yet Klingsor proudly tells her that a more splendid victory shall be hers today. There is but one obstacle between him and the attainment of his ambition and that is the stainless youth who even now is approaching. Let her successfully tempt him as she did Amfortas and the battle will be won. Crying out in the wildest agony, Kundry refuses to obey, but Klingsor's magic is the stronger, and at last she disappears to carry out his will. From the parapet of the tower, Klingsor watches the enemy scale the ramparts and overcome the castle's defenders.

SCENE 2: *Klingsor's magic garden.* Suddenly, the tower and magician sink into the earth, and instead there rises from the ground an enchanted garden filled with flowers of weird, exotic beauty. On the wall surrounding the garden stands the strange, little-knowing youth whom we saw ejected from Monsalvat. As he gazes about bewilderedly, there come from all sides the beautiful denizens of the place, Klingsor's flower maidens, clad in their flowing, diaphanous garments. They are in alarm, for they have discovered that some of their lovers have been slain by an unknown foe. Seeing the stranger, they accuse him. He innocently claims the victory, saying that had he not conquered, he never could have entered their lovely domain. They soon accept him as a friend; they dance about him, touching his cheeks with their soft hands. But one more lovely than they approaches. Beholding Kundry, they depart, laughing at the youth for his naïve response to their allurements—he has grown angry and turns to flee. "Tarry, Parsifal," Kundry calls, and the astonished youth remains. He remembers that once in the dim past his mother called him by that name. Kundry draws nearer through the luxuriant foliage. She tells the wondering youth that it was she who first gave him the name of Parsifal, an inversion of the Arabian *Fal parsi*—"guileless fool." She tells him of his father, the knight Gamuret, and of how he was slain in battle before the birth of his son; how Herzeleide (Heart's Sorrow), Parsifal's mother, reared him in the forest, far from the ways of men; and how, her son having departed, she pined away and died. Parsifal is naturally greatly affected and bows in grief. Kundry takes him in her arms caressingly, and while he is still shaken with emotion tells him that she comes to him as his mother's last gift. She bends over him and presses a long kiss upon his lips. Kundry's carefully thought-out plan seems to have succeeded, but only for a moment. Suddenly Parsifal starts up, crying out, *"Amfortas, die Wunde"* ("Amfortas, the wound"). He beholds as in a vision the scene in the hall of the Grail and understands for the first time its significance. Kundry's endeavors to lead his mind back to thoughts of passion only reveal to him more clearly the nature of Amfortas' temptation, and he pushes her angrily away. Now she appeals to his pity by telling him of the curse under which she lives. Ages ago she saw Him staggering under His cross and laughed. His look fell upon her and since that hour she has wandered over the earth, vainly seeking to see Him again. Now she has found Parsifal, her deliverer; if he will but embrace her, salvation shall be hers. Parsifal rebukes her, saying that she can win deliverance by leading him to Amfortas. Turning upon him with the full hatred of thwarted desire, Kundry curses him—may he never find his homeward road. She calls Klingsor to come to her aid, and the sorcerer immediately appears on the ramparts of his castle. He flings the sacred spear at the youth. And now a miracle happens. The spear, changed from its course, hovers over Parsifal. He seizes it and makes with it the sign of the cross. As with an earthquake the castle falls into ruins, the garden withers to a desert, and Kundry sinks down with a cry. In turning to depart, Parsifal exclaims to her significantly that she knows where they will meet again.

ACT III

SCENE 1: *A hermit's hut in the Grail's domain.* The Prelude to the third act at once plunges us into the gloom and desolation that have now fallen over the Knights of the Grail. The themes of "Kundry," "The Spear," "The Grail," "The Promise," and "Enchantment" all enter, but in a somber, broken form. At the rise of the curtain we are shown the rude hut where Gurnemanz now makes his solitary abode. The early light of a spring morning is breathing through the leaves of the forest as the faithful knight, now bent and hoary with age, issues from his dwelling. A strange moaning from a woodland thicket nearby has aroused him; he approaches and discovers Kundry, unconscious, yet crying out as though troubled by some frightful dream. Tending her carefully, he restores her to consciousness. She is less savage but even more wan in her appearance than when we last saw her serving the Knights of the Grail at Monsalvat. She at once resumes her humble duties and in bringing a pitcher of water from the spring observes a new arrival at the domain of the Grail. It is a knight in black armor, with visor closed; Parsifal, weary from long searching, has at last found Monsalvat. Gurnemanz asks him to remove his armor, for this is holy ground and should not be profaned, least of all on this, the most holy of days, Good Friday. Parsifal complies and, striking the spear which he carries into the ground, kneels before it in fervent prayer. Gurnemanz and Kundry, now recognizing Parsifal, are filled with mingled emotions. Parsifal, rising from his meditations, tells Gurnemanz of his joy at seeing him, of the many hardships that beset his path, of the wounds and suffering which he endured during the long search for Monsalvat, hardships all brought about because of a curse which had been placed on him. Gurnemanz is profoundly stirred on beholding again the sacred spear. He tells Parsifal of the sad estate of the knighthood: Amfortas, driven by his intense sufferings of body and soul, longs only for death and refuses to fulfill his holy office; deprived of the

heavenly sustenance of the Grail, the knights are powerless. No longer, he continues, do they journey forth in holy warfare; Titurel, deprived of the vision of the Grail, has died. Parsifal cries out in grief, accusing himself of being the cause of all these misfortunes, and sinks back, fainting. Kundry brings water, but Gurnemanz reproves her gently, saying that the sacred spring itself would be better. To it they now lead Parsifal. On reviving he asks to be conducted to Amfortas. Gurnemanz assures him that this shall be done, for this very day the obsequies of Titurel are to be celebrated, and Amfortas will again unveil the Grail. Now Kundry, eager and humble, bathes Parsifal's feet, and Gurnemanz, taking water from the spring, baptizes him, pronouncing the solemn words of invocation. Kundry takes a golden vial from her bosom and, pouring a part of its contents over Parsifal's feet, dries them with her hair, hastily unbound. Parsifal, who has been observing these ministrations in deep emotion, takes the vial from Kundry and, giving it to Gurnemanz, bids the knight anoint his head; thus it is that Gurnemanz consecrates Parsifal as King of the Grail, while in the orchestra the theme of "Parsifal" is proclaimed with great majesty.

As a first act of compassion, the new King baptizes Kundry, who falls weeping to the ground. Now the soft weaving of the theme of the "Good Friday" music rises in the orchestra, and Parsifal, looking out over the woods and meadows, remarks beatifically on the beauty of the fields and meadows on this day. Gurnemanz explains, saying, "That is Good Friday's spell, my lord!" and Parsifal speaks of the sadness of that day. Gurnemanz explains that it is not so, that this beauty of the woods and fields is caused by the spell of Good Friday, and that the flowers and trees, watered by the fears of repentant sinners, express by their luxuriance the redemption of man.

Kundry has slowly raised her head again and gazes at Parsifal with moist, beseeching eyes. A distant tolling of bells being heard, Gurnemanz says that it is midday and that the long-awaited hour has come. Gurnemanz has brought out a coat of mail and mantle of the knights, which he and Kundry put on Parsifal. As they go their way, the landscape gradually changes until finally they disappear in the rocky entrance to the castle. Processions of knights are seen in the long arched passageways; the tolling of bells constantly increases.

SCENE 2: *The great hall of the Grail.* At last the great hall becomes visible, but the tables are no longer there, and the place is dimly lighted. There enter two processions of knights, singing to one another antiphonally.

The bier of Titurel is placed at one side, and Amfortas is helped to his throne back of the altar.

He exclaims weakly at his misfortune, then breaks into an agonizing prayer. But the knights, pressing nearer to Amfortas, insist that he uncover the Grail. Amfortas, in a paroxysm of despair, cries that he will never again do so. He tears open his robe and shows them the wound, asking them, as he does so, to kill him and end his suffering. All shrink back in awe, and Amfortas stands alone in fearful ecstasy.

Parsifal, accompanied by Gurnemanz and Kundry, has entered unperceived, and now advancing stretches out the spear, touching Amfortas' side with the point. Amfortas' countenance shines with holy rapture, and trembling with emotion, he is supported by Gurnemanz. Parsifal says, "Be whole, unsullied, and absolved." And he proclaims himself King in Amfortas' place. All gaze with intense rapture on the spear, which Parsifal holds aloft.

He ascends the altar steps and, taking the Grail from the shrine already opened by the esquires, sinks before it in silent prayer. The sacred cup begins to glow with a soft light, and while the lower portion of the hall becomes plunged in darkness, the dome is filled with a heavenly radiance. As the splendor increases, the voices of the kneeling knights, esquires, and boys join in a wonderful progression, rising through marvelously changing harmonies and dying away in the distance.

A ray of dazzling light falls from above, and in it a white dove descends, hovering over Parsifal. Kundry, looking up at him, slowly falls to the ground; she is dead. Gurnemanz and Amfortas bow in homage before him. Parsifal waves the Grail over the brotherhood, blessing them, and while the orchestra plays in a final transfigured form the themes of "Faith," "The Grail," and "The Last Supper," the curtain falls.

Act III, Scene 1: Parsifal (Sándor Kónya), with Kundry (Régine Crespin) and Gurnemanz (Jerome Hines)

The Pearl Fishers

LES PÊCHEURS DE PERLES

CHARACTERS

Leila, *a priestess* — Soprano
Nadir, *a pearl fisher* — Tenor

Zurga, *chief of the fishermen* — Baritone
Nourabad, *high priest* — Bass

Priests, Priestesses, Pearl Fishers, People of Ceylon

The action takes place in legendary Ceylon.

OPERA IN THREE ACTS. Music by Georges Bizet. Libretto in French by Michel Carré and Eugène Cormon. First performance at the Théâtre-Lyrique, Paris, September 30, 1863. United States première at the Grand Opera House, Philadelphia, August 25, 1893. A version omitting the third act was staged at the Metropolitan Opera House on January 11, 1896. The cast was headed by Calvé, Cremonini, Ancona, and Vittorio Arimondi. New York waited twenty more years for the complete opera. It then opened the season on November 13, 1916, with a cast headed by Enrico Caruso, Frieda Hempel, Giuseppe de Luca, and Léon Rothier.

Preceding *Carmen* by twelve years, *The Pearl Fishers* lacks the dramatic power and emotional intensity of Bizet's masterpiece. Yet it breathes a charm of its own. Though less impassioned in speech than the maturer work, it boasts lovely melodies of a slightly Oriental tinge and an appealing mood of exotic fantasy. The beautiful prelude shows Bizet's superb grasp of orchestral color and already hints at the power to come in the firm musical web of *Carmen.*

ACT I

SCENE: *The coast of Ceylon.* Zurga, the newly elected leader of the little world of Cingalese fishermen, has scarcely been inaugurated when Nadir, a long-lost friend of his youth, appears. After greeting one another with affection, they recall the time when they were foolish enough to quarrel over a beautiful priestess in the temple of Brahma, Leila. In the duet *"Au fond du temple"* ("In the depths of the temple") they sing of the moment when they first saw her. Both had fallen in love with her as she was revealed to them for an instant in the dim, incense-clouded temple. Believing themselves cured of the old infatuation, they swear eternal friendship.

A veiled priestess approaches on her way to the temple to pray for the success of the fishermen. Every year she comes thus, mysteriously, and none has dared gaze upon her face, for she is held to be sacred to Brahma. At Zurga's behest, the priestess is about to take the oath of chastity when she recognizes Nadir and is startled. She is reminded by the high priest Nourabad that she may revoke her vow, but this she refuses to do and enters the temple. The people disperse, leaving Nadir alone. Agitated by the discovery that he still loves Leila, he sings an air, pathetic yet beautiful, in which he describes the lovely girl as he once heard her singing among the palms on a starlit tropical night. Around this haunting melody, with its faintly Oriental color, orchestral strings weave a fascinating atmosphere. Nadir is about to go to warn Zurga of all this, but overcome with weariness, he falls asleep on the temple steps.

There Leila sees him as she performs her holy rites. While appearing to pray to Brahma, she subtly reveals her love for Nadir. Completely under the sway of his former passion, Nadir forgets Zurga and, under cover of darkness, hastens to his love.

ACT II

SCENE: *A ruined temple.* Leila, about to begin her lonely watch, is reminded by Nourabad of the punishment that is certain to overtake her should she violate her solemn oath. She replies that she is in no danger, for once as a child she swore to protect a fugitive who had implored her aid, and even though his enemies threatened to kill her, she had kept her vow. The man was enabled to escape, and in gratitude he had given her a golden chain as a remembrance. Yet Leila now cowers in fear as the priest again threatens her with the doom certain to be hers if she prove unfaithful. But her fears vanish with the arrival of Nadir, and soon the two are completely lost in the ecstasy of their love. They are surprised by Nourabad, who alarms the people. But when fishermen advance with drawn swords, demanding death for the couple, Zurga, mindful of his pledge of friendship to Nadir, intervenes. Nourabad draws aside the veil from the girl's face, and, lo! it is none other than Leila, the very woman Nadir has sworn with Zurga to forget! Enraged at his friend's treachery, the chieftain condemns the pair to death.

ACT III

SCENE 1: *The camp of Zurga.* In a longish *scena*, Zurga contrasts the storm in his heart with the calm that has followed a storm at sea. Leila then enters and pleads with Zurga for the life of her lover, but Zurga only reveals his own jealousy. Too proud to sue for her own life, the condemned priestess excites the chieftain's wrath with her scorn. But before she leaves, Leila gives Zurga the golden chain of the fugitive, with the plea that he send it to her mother. He does not at once recognize it as his own.

SCENE 2: *The place of execution.* Just as the lovers are about to mount the funeral pyre, a distant glow, at first thought to be dawn, is seen. Zurga rushes in, crying out that the camp is on fire. When the people have scattered to save their children and possessions, Zurga explains to the couple that he has set fire to the camp in order to save them, for he has recognized Leila's golden chain. It was he who gave it to her years before when she had saved his life. Thus the lovers are permitted to escape. When the people return, Nourabad denounces Zurga, for he has again been eavesdropping. One of the fishermen stabs Zurga in the back; and as he lies dying, the voices of Nadir and Leila are heard off stage singing the Nadir-Zurga duet of Act I.

Zurga (Giuseppe de Luca), Leila (Frieda Hempel) and Nadir (Enrico Caruso), in 1916 Metropolitan Opera production

Pelléas et Mélisande

CHARACTERS

Arkël, *King of Allemonde*	Bass	Mélisande, *a mysterious young princess*	Soprano
Geneviève, *his daughter-in-law*	Mezzo-soprano	Yniold, *young son of Goland through a former marriage*	Soprano
Golaud, *her elder son*	Baritone	A Physician	Bass
Pelléas, *his half brother*	Tenor		

Servants, Blind Beggars

The action takes place in legendary times in the fictional kingdom of Allemonde.

OPERA—or an "impressionistic tone picture"—in five acts. Music by Claude Debussy; poem in French by Maurice Maeterlinck. First produced, April 30, 1902, at the Opéra-Comique, Paris, with Mary Garden and Jean Périer in the title roles. First performance in the United States, at the Manhattan Opera House, New York, February 19, 1908, with mostly the original cast. First Metropolitan Opera performance, March 21, 1925, with Lucrezia Bori and Edward Johnson.

Maeterlinck's drama *Pelléas et Mélisande* has for the basis of its plot such a simple form of the eternal triangle that a mere recital of it fails to convey any of the play's great poetic charm and beauty. In fact, stripping the plot of the subtle symbolism of the lines is like trying to present the wonderful impressionistic colors of a Monet painting in a black-and-white copy.

For this very subdued and appealing drama Debussy supplied music of great delicacy and subtly suggestive power. Often the orchestra furnishes a decorative background while the voices sing in a recitative style that closely follows the natural inflections of the speaking voice. At times of climax the music rises to greater prominence and attains remarkable beauty and emotional force, though still serving to underline the poetic sentiment of the text.

The collaboration of Debussy and Maeterlinck did not come to the greatest cordiality imaginable, for the poet objected, first of all, to Debussy's having altered the text for musical purposes, omitting sizable parts of it here and there. Then—and probably the important point—Maeterlinck had taken it more or less for granted that his mistress Georgette Leblanc would be assigned the name part. Ten years before that Maeterlinck had given Debussy carte blanche with the play, instructing him to do as he pleased with it. Now, when the opera was completed, the troubles began.

Maeterlinck, in the bitterness of his disappointment over the choice of another artist for the leading role, found everything wrong with Debussy's work. He wrote a letter to the publisher of the Paris *Figaro*, in which he excoriated the opera and everything connected with it. He said, among other things, "The *Pelléas* in question has become foreign, almost inimical to me; and, deprived as I am of any control over my own work, I am reduced to hoping that its failure [the opera's] will be immediate and resounding." However, Debussy's opera was anything but a failure, although there were those at the première who threw a few epithets at its "stammering phantoms," at its music for being a "succession of sound wraiths." And after the work's first American performance, one critic discovered that Debussy's tonal combinations "sting and blister and pain and outrage the ear."

All such feeling about a truly great work, however, has long since disappeared completely. The "spoken" song of the opera, the subtlety of the musical suggestion, and the fluid, captivating score have become matters of common understanding and appreciation. In a fine stage performance, this opera casts a unique spell over the audience.

ACT I

SCENE 1: *A forest.* Golaud has lost his way in the depths of the forest and, while wandering aimlessly about, finds a beautiful young woman weeping at the edge of a spring. Her answers to his questions are so vague and mysterious that he cannot learn whence she came, how she happens to be there, or why. She has dropped a golden crown in the spring, but will not permit him to recover it for her; nor will she allow him to come near her. She does, finally, tell him her name, Mélisande. Then, as it is growing dark and Golaud insists that they seek shelter, she follows him nervously at a distance.

SCENE 2: *A hall in Arkël's castle.* The change of scene is accompanied by a beautiful orchestral interlude in which is heard prominently a theme associated with the unhappy fate of the lovers. Six months are supposed to have elapsed, and the curtain rises disclosing the room in the somber castle of Arkël, King of Allemonde. Geneviève is reading to the King a letter that Pelléas has just received from his brother Golaud, telling of his marriage to Mélisande. Golaud fears that Arkël will not forgive him for having thus married without his consent when a union of political importance had been planned for him. Pelléas enters to ask the King's permission to go to visit a dying friend. But the father of Pelléas, who is in the castle, also is ill, and Arkël, reminding him of this, bids him place a signal light for Golaud and remain at the castle until his half brother's return.

SCENE 3: *A terrace in front of the castle.* Again a beautiful interlude accompanies the change of scene. Mélisande, Geneviève, and Pelléas, having come out of the gloomy castle to watch the ocean at sunset, see a ship that bravely embarks in spite of the threatening storm. Night approaches suddenly, and Geneviève, hurrying off to take care of her little grandson Yniold, asks Pelléas to conduct Mélisande back to the castle. To Pelléas' seemingly casual remark that on the morrow he must leave, Mélisande responds with the childlike cry "Why must you go?"

ACT II

SCENE 1: *A fountain in the park.* To escape the stifling summer noon's heat at the castle, Pelléas and Mélisande have come to an ancient, deserted fountain in one of the most remote and silent parts of the woods. After asking, "Do you know where I have brought you?" Pelléas tells her of this fountain. It is reputed to have had miraculous powers. Once it is said to have restored sight to the blind; but now even the old King is nearly sightless, and not a soul comes to the place. Mélisande's childlike question "Does it open the eyes of the blind no more?" is symbolic, since that very well is where the young people's eyes are opened to their love. She is fascinated by the water; she tries to reach it as she sits on the edge of the well, but only her long, loose-flowing hair is able to penetrate beneath its surface. Pelléas recalls it was beside a spring that Golaud found Mélisande. Now Mélisande begins to play with a ring—a ring that Golaud has given her. She throws it up in the air, high up so as to see it sparkle in the few rays of sunlight that manage to penetrate through the

Mary Garden, who was the first Mélisande

dense foliage. Pelléas begs her to be careful; suddenly the ring slips through her fingers into the dark waters of the well. They think they can see it glisten as it sinks. It never will be recovered, for the well is immeasurably deep. Moreover, they cannot stop longer now, for Pelléas heard twelve o'clock being struck just as the ring disappeared, and they will be sought at the castle.

SCENE 2: *Golaud's chamber in the castle*. The change of scene is accompanied by an orchestral interlude in which the bright, flowing music of the fountain sinks down and vanishes beneath the stern tread of a motive which can be called that of "Fate."

Golaud is lying on his bed in a room in the castle; Mélisande is at the bedside. All is going well now, he remarks, while telling her how he came to be injured. He cannot understand how it was that just as he finished counting the twelve strokes of noon, the horse on which he was riding at the hunt ran wildly away, for no apparent reason. His injuries were not serious, however, and he tenderly bids Mélisande go to sleep for the night. Suddenly she bursts into tears; and to Golaud's anxious questions she only replies that she is not happy there—it is no one's fault, not the King's, not Golaud's mother's. Pelléas —no, it is not Pelléas' fault, it is the darkness of the place. One never sees the blue sky. Golaud tries to console her. Tenderly he takes her hands, and then he notices that the ring he gave her is missing. Instantly he is alarmed. To his insistent questions she replies with childish and evasive answers, finally saying that she dropped the ring in a grotto by the sea. Golaud orders her to go at once to find it, even in the darkness of night. Pelléas, he says, will conduct her safely.

SCENE 3: *A grotto by the sea*. During the orchestral interlude the gentle theme associated with Mélisande is heard in poignant, sorrowful form and the rippling music of the fountain enters briefly. Then all is broken by an eerie formlessness, and the curtain rises on a dark cavern by the sea.

Pelléas and Mélisande come groping their way like children through the dense obscurity. He leads Mélisande into the grotto so that in case Golaud asks, she will be able to describe the place. The roar of the sea echoing through the grotto makes it seem even more dismal and terrifying. The moon throws a sudden flood of light into the cavern and reveals a group of paupers who have sought shelter there, for now a famine is raging in the land. Mélisande is so greatly frightened that Pelléas has to hurry back to the castle with her.

ACT III

SCENE 1: *A turret of the castle*. Mélisande is at a window, up in one of the towers of the castle. While she combs her unbound hair, arranging it for the night, she sings some ancient song that quaintly lists a number of saints. Pelléas comes up the watchman's path around the tower. He halts beneath the window, for tomorrow he must leave. Again in her childish way she tells him he must not leave—she will not let him take her hand to kiss it in farewell if he goes. Pelléas promises to delay his departure; she leans far out of the window so that he can reach her hand. In so doing her long, magnificent hair comes streaming down over Pelléas, overwhelming him with delicious excitement at the touch of her glorious tresses. In his ecstasy he exclaims that he will hold her thus forever. Some frightened doves fly out of the tower and hover around them in the darkness. Golaud comes silently around the path. He is agitated at finding Pelléas and Mélisande thus and, laughing nervously, scolds them for playing like children in the night—both children.

SCENE 2: *The vaults beneath the castle*. The "Fate" motive is heard. It grows suddenly to a climax, at which the expressive "Mélisande" theme enters. This in turn subsides, and the interlude closes with the ominous theme of "Vengeance."

Golaud has led Pelléas down into the subterranean vaults beneath the castle to see the stagnant pool that lies there. He bids Pelléas let him hold his arm, and then lean out over the chasm. Does he smell the deathlike stench that rises? Pelléas is alarmed at the way Golaud's hand holding aloft the lantern trembles; the two hurry out in silence.

SCENE 3: *A terrace at the entrance of the vaults*. The brothers come out from the vaults; Pelléas is happy again to breathe the pure air from the sea. Golaud cautions Pelléas about continuing such childish play with Mélisande as took place the night before. She may become a mother soon and must be spared any shock. Almost threateningly he warns Pelléas to avoid Mélisande as much as possible—though not too markedly, he adds.

SCENE 4: *A turret of the castle*. Golaud brings Yniold, his little son by a former wife, out before the castle, and by repeated questioning tries to learn more of the state of affairs between Pelléas and Mélisande. But the child's answers are so vague that they only tantalize Golaud's suspicions. A light appears in Mélisande's window, and Golaud holds Yniold up

Act III Tower Scene: Pelléas (*Theodor Uppman*) caresses
the hair of Mélisande (*Victoria de los Angeles*)

high so that he can look into the room. Yes, Pelléas is
there with Mélisande, but they do not speak. No,
they do not come near one another, and they do not
close their eyes. Then the child becomes frightened
and is about to cry aloud, so the unhappy Golaud
has to go, his fears only partly confirmed.

ACT IV

SCENE 1: *A corridor in the castle.* Pelléas meets Mélisande along a corridor in the castle, and certain that
he will leave on the morrow, he begs and obtains a
rendezvous with Mélisande—midnight at the well of
the blind. The two go their separate ways: Mélisande
returns, after a moment, with Arkël. The old King is
filled with sympathy and kindness for her; he hopes
that now since Pelléas' father has recovered, the
castle will seem less gloomy and that she will be
happier. Half soliloquizing, he says he believes that a
young, fair, and joyful being will create an atmosphere of joy around itself. In the utmost tenderness,
as if speaking to a grandchild, he asks to kiss her.
The aged, he says, need to be reminded of youth in
order to drive away for a time the menaces of death.
Golaud enters, searching for his sword. Blood is
noticeable on his brow. "I have been through a
hedge of thorns," he says, and, again, the symbolic
meaning of his words is not to be missed. He rebukes
Mélisande for her nervousness; he cannot endure the
gaze of her great open eyes. Arkël says he sees in
them only a great innocence. This releases the flood
of Golaud's pent-up fury. In cruelest irony he cries
that God himself might take a lesson in innocence
from her eyes—one would say that the angels were
continually baptizing themselves in that innocence.
He seizes Mélisande by her long hair and drags her
savagely to and fro across the floor. Arkël restores
quiet; if he were God, he says, he would have pity on
the hearts of men!

SCENE 2: *A fountain in the park.* An interlude of
great expressiveness accompanies the change of
scene: the "Fate" motive, played with passionate
intensity. Then appears the theme of Mélisande for a
moment as the music subsides. Another tense climax,
and finally gloom and foreboding.

In the uncanny silence and obscurity of midnight
the desolate fountain of the blind seems doubly
mysterious and supernatural. There Pelléas now
awaits Mélisande. He reflects how he has played with
the forces of destiny; perhaps it would be better if
he never again saw her. Yet it seems that a century
has passed since last they met. Soon he forgets his
fears under the thrill of his excitement at her approach. Mélisande recalls that they came here once

long ago. Tenderly she asks why he must leave. He hesitates, saying, "It is because . . ." then he kisses her suddenly, "I love you." Mélisande answers quietly, "I also love you." Pelléas is overwhelmed by the simple fact of her declaration. They hear the castle gates being closed for the night; but they assure themselves that they are not afraid. They rejoice that they are together. Mélisande believes that she hears Golaud behind them among the trees; Pelléas scoffs, saying that it is only the wind in the leaves; an instant later they are sure that it is he crouching in the darkness. They would conceal themselves among the shadows; but they realize Golaud has seen all; he carries his sword, Pelléas has not his. Filled with a sudden desperate abandon, they embrace wildly—it seems that the stars of the whole heavens are falling upon them. Golaud rushes out, stabs Pelléas, and pursues the fleeing Mélisande.

ACT V

SCENE: *Mélisande's chamber.* Mélisande is lying on a bed. Arkël, Golaud, and a physician are watching. The physician says that it is not of the very trifling wound Golaud gave her that she is dying—perhaps, indeed, she may recover. The others having left him alone with Mélisande in response to his earnest entreaties, Golaud begs her forgiveness. Anxiously he asks her if she will answer just one question and tell the exact truth. Then, on her assent, he asks excitedly, "Did you love Pelléas?" With the utmost naïveté she replies, "Yes, indeed, I loved him. Is he here?" Golaud believes she does not understand. Again she replies that their love was not guilty; the childlike simplicity of her manner racks the soul of Golaud. Impassionedly he demands to know the truth; Arkël and the physician re-enter, and the despairing Golaud remains as one blind. Though the air is cold, Mélisande wishes the window left open so that she may watch the setting sun. She scarcely seems to realize that she has become the mother of a little girl. When Arkël gently shows the child to her she quietly remarks, "She is very tiny, she is going to weep also." The servants of the castle gradually enter the room and take their places along the wall, where they remain waiting, silently. This is symbolic of the fact that death is near. They have not been sent for, why do they come? Golaud wonders. They make no reply to Golaud's excited questions. Mélisande stretches forth her arms—it is the struggle of the mother. Suddenly the servants drop to their knees. "What is it?" asks Arkël. The physician goes over to Mélisande, then replies, "They are right." Arkël speaks to the sobbing Golaud, "Come, now she needs silence. She was such a quiet, timid creature, a mysterious being, as is everyone. Come, we must not leave her child in this room; it must live on now and take her place. It's the turn of the poor little one."

Final scene as designed by Rouben Ter-Arutunian and staged by Gian Carlo Menotti at the Spoleto Festival

Peter Grimes

CHARACTERS

Peter Grimes, *a fisherman*	Tenor	Swallow, *lawyer and mayor of the*	
John, *his apprentice*	Mime	*Borough*	Bass
Ellen Orford, *a widow, the town*		Mrs. "Nabob" Sedley, *well-to-do*	
schoolmistress	Soprano	*widow of an East India Com-*	
Captain Balstrode, *retired merchant*		*pany agent*	Mezzo-soprano
skipper	Baritone	The Reverend Horace Adams, *the*	
Auntie, *landlady of The Boar*	Contralto	*rector*	Tenor
Two "Nieces," *main attractions of*		Ned Keene, *apothecary*	Baritone
The Boar	Sopranos	Dr. George Crabbe, *town doctor*	Mime
Robert Boles, *fisherman and*		Jim Hobson, *carter and constable*	Bass
Methodist	Tenor		

Townspeople and Fisherfolk

*The action takes place in the Borough, a small fishing town on the east coast of England
in the early part of the nineteenth century.*

OPERA IN prologue and three acts. Music by Benjamin Britten. Libretto in English by Montagu Slater, derived from the poem "The Borough" by George Crabbe. Commissioned by the Koussevitzky Music Foundation. Première at Sadler's Wells, London, June 7, 1945. First American performance at the Berkshire Music Center (Tanglewood), Lenox, Massachusetts, August 6, 1946. First Metropolitan Opera performance, February 12, 1948.

Benjamin Britten, a very prolific composer in virtually all forms, has composed almost a dozen operas, of which *Peter Grimes* is the second in time and the first in general acceptance, having been produced in many European countries as well as in South America and the Soviet Union. It is the only opera by an Englishman ever to be staged by the Metropolitan Opera Association, by whom it was revived in 1967, nineteen years after its first production there. With the exception of his first (*Paul Bunyan* written in and for the United States in 1941), all of Mr. Britten's operas have been more or less successful, notably *Albert Herring* (1947) and the "children's entertainment" *Let's Make an Opera!* (1949), but *Peter Grimes* is the one that appears to have made the most profound and lasting impression.

George Crabbe's long poem *The Borough,* on which the libretto is based, is cast in the form of a series of twenty-four letters, written in heroic couplets, which describe the inhabitants, the life, and the institutions of his native town, Aldeburgh, a fishing village on the east coast of England. This is the town where Benjamin Britten has settled and created something of a music center by conducting annual festivals and composing dramatic works to be produced first in the local church and then in others.

PROLOGUE

SCENE: *The Moot Hall (or Meeting Place) arranged for an inquest.* Lawyer Swallow, the mayor of the town, now acting as coroner, swears in Peter Grimes as witness and then proceeds to question him about his apprentice, whom he has brought home dead after being becalmed for three days without water

319

Grimes (Jon Vickers), Balstrode (Geraint Evans), Auntie (Lili Chookasian), in Act I, Scene 2

on a fishing trip. A surly, antagonistic loner, Grimes, it turns out, had insulted Mrs. "Nabob" Sedley on that occasion, had got no help from either the apothecary or the minister, and had been befriended only by Ellen Orford, the schoolmistress, who carried the body home for Grimes. Despite Grimes's general unpopularity, expressed mostly by the chorus of women, the death is called accidental, for there is only Grimes's own testimony and, besides, he had helped save the boy's life on another occasion. He is warned, however, not to take another apprentice unless he has a woman to care for him. When he is left alone with Ellen, it becomes clear that she is willing to be that woman, but he says he cannot marry her before his name is cleared. Their misunderstanding is projected through their singing in different keys, but at the end of the duet, they come together—in person and in the music—and walk out hand in hand.

ACT I

SCENE 1: *Street by the sea.* It is a threatening morning several days later. On the principal street we find old Captain Balstrode on the breakwater eying the coming storm, fishermen turning a capstan to haul in their boat, Auntie in front of The Boar inviting men in to drink (at which Boles hypocritically expresses horror), Ned Keene, from his apothecary shop calling to Auntie that he will visit the "nieces" tonight, and so forth. Everyone is acting in character on a typical day. Even the silent Dr. Crabbe (they physician-minister who wrote the poem on which the opera is based) is respectfully greeted as he passes into Auntie's pub. It is also typical of almost the whole town to turn away from Peter Grimes when he asks help in pulling up his boat. Only Captain Balstrode and Ned Keene are willing to haul away at the capstan; and when the boat has been pulled up, Keene tells Grimes that he has found a new apprentice for him, a boy from the workhouse who will have to be called for. Jim Hobson the carter makes lame excuses about doing the job until Ellen Orford comes in and offers to go along to bring the boy. But everyone thoroughly disapproves.

Gradually the storm gathers both on the stage and in the orchestra pit. Some put up shutters on the shops, while others go home. Finally just Grimes and Balstrode are left, and the worldly-wise old captain advises Grimes to leave this inimical town and enlist on a merchantman or privateer. But Grimes is obstinate. He says he will force the town's respect by becoming rich, and then he will marry Ellen. Why not now? asks the captain. But Grimes will not be taken out of pity. He must face them all down and compel respect. As the storm rises, the two men shout at each other, Balstrode finally calling Grimes a fool and going into the pub. Left alone, the half-mad man sings his aria "What harbor shelters peace?" in great lyrical arches, ending, significantly, on an unresolved chord, as the wind grows stronger and stronger.

SCENE 2: *Inside The Boar.* During the interlude to change scenery the orchestra goes on depicting the storm, which is still raging at ten-thirty that night. Most of the town is gathered at the tavern, Mrs. "Nabob" to pick up some laudanum from Keene, and Methodistical Boles—now quite drunk—making advances to Auntie's "nieces," who have come downstairs in their nightgowns. Grimes comes stumbling in out of the storm, and when he sings a strange song about the constellations and their significance ("Now the Great Bear and Pleiades"), they think him mad, and Boles, claiming that the devil has got Grimes's soul, attacks him with a bottle. Balstrode, however, intervenes and calls for a song. Ned Keene then begins a striking and very complex round in 7/4 time, which everyone picks up till Grimes sings his own strange and mystical version of the fishing song. Yet the others manage to finish their round, at the end of which Ellen and Hobson, with the new apprentice for Grimes, break

in. They have been delayed by the storm, and all three are soaked and muddy. Grimes, without even thanking Ellen or the carter, insists on taking the boy home at once, storm or no storm.

ACT II

SCENE 1: *Outside the church.* After a sunny, peaceful prelude, we find Ellen sitting outside the church, where a service is going on a few Sundays later. She is knitting and speaking to the silent apprentice. Presently she discovers tears in his clothes and bruises on his neck and fully understands their significance. When Grimes comes in gloomily to get the boy for work, she pleads with him to give him a holiday at least on Sunday. An argument ensues, and Grimes strikes Ellen and takes John the apprentice away.

The church now begins to empty, and as some of the congregation have heard a part of the quarrel, they know that Grimes has again been mistreating an apprentice. Working themselves up into a pitch of great excitement, a posse of men is organized to follow Grimes, despite the pleas of Ellen and Balstrode. Even the rector feels that something must be done. The scene ends with Auntie, her two girls, and Ellen singing a quartet about how childish men are.

SCENE 2: *Inside Grimes's hut.* The hut is nothing but an upturned boat, but it is very tidy. There are two doors—one to the road, the other to a cliff which has been washed away during the recent storm. Peter shoves in his sniffling apprentice and has a long aria

As his apprentice sleeps, Grimes (Jon Vickers) is haunted by a vision of his other apprentice, who died

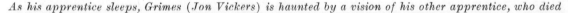

—or *scena*—during which he repeats his ambition to become rich, marry Ellen, and have children. At its close he becomes haunted by a vision of the boy who died on the boat. Then, on hearing the approaching men, he decides this new boy must have been complaining about him. Hastily he shoves the child out of the door on the cliff side and follows after him. A terrible scream is heard, and we know that the boy has fallen over the washed-away side. But when the men enter through the other door, without having heard the scream, they look around at the tidy interior and come to the conclusion that Grimes can't be quite that bad after all. All leave but Balstrode, who remains to gaze out of the other door—the one on the cliff side. Then he closes it.

ACT III

SCENE 1: *Street by the sea.* A quiet prelude, and then the curtain rises. It is a few evenings later, and there is dancing in The Boar tavern—first a polka, later a waltz. Swallow, now drunk, makes rather heavy-handed advances to the "nieces," who manage to escape him, and also Keene, who is after them. Mrs. Sedley stops Keene and tries, in vain, to impress him with her conclusion that Grimes must have murdered his apprentice, as neither has been seen for a couple of days, and yet Grimes's boat is tied up. Keene thinks it all nonsense, and when some of the town elders pass by, she goes into the shadow of the boats and mutters to herself about crime. Ellen and Balstrode come in, seriously worried by Grimes's two-day absence from his hut. Ellen shows Balstrode the apprentice's wet jersey, which she had found on the shore. Both read a sinister significance into it, but Balstrode tries to encourage Ellen by saying that they will find Peter and perhaps be able to help him yet.

When they have gone off, Mrs. Sedley comes out again from the shadows, summons Swallow, and tells him of her suspicions and the reasons for them. More of the men come out of The Boar, and Swallow, with considerable self-satisfaction, appoints Hobson, as constable of the Borough, to form another posse and find Grimes. The beach now becomes crowded, and the scene ends as the people scatter in various directions and shout, "Grimes! Peter Grimes!"

SCENE 2: *The same.* There is a strange intermezzo between the scenes suggesting, perhaps, that Peter Grimes has gone completely mad. It is now several hours later, and Grimes is by his boat, hearing the occasional shouts of the searching crowd. Weirdly, he sings of the sea, of his two dead apprentices. He imagines Ellen is with him; he curses and defies his persecutors. There Balstrode and Ellen find him, and in a calm speaking voice, Balstrode advises Peter to take his boat out to sea—and to sink with it. In a kind of trance, and with Balstrode's help, Peter pushes the boat down to the sea, and Balstrode leads the weeping Ellen away.

Dawn begins to break. Hobson and his posse meet, decide their mission has failed, and go away. Fisherwives begin bringing down nets. Dr. Crabbe nods to some acquaintances as he comes home from a case. Swallow says that the coast guard reports a boat sinking out at sea, but no one can see it through glasses. "One of these rumors," says Auntie. And an ordinary new day begins. "The cold beginning of another day," the chorus calls it in one of the very few lines quoted from Crabbe's original poem.

The borough, no longer disturbed by the presence of Grimes, resumes its routine of daily chores

Pique Dame

PIKOVAYA DAMA — QUEEN OF SPADES

CHARACTERS

Hermann, *officer of the hussars*	*Tenor*	The Countess	*Mezzo-soprano*
Count Tomsky, *his friend*	*Baritone*	Lisa, *her granddaughter*	*Soprano*
Prince Yeletsky, *betrothed to Lisa*	*Bass*	Pauline, *her friend*	*Contralto*
Czekalinsky ⎤ *Russian*	*Tenor*	The Governess	*Mezzo-soprano*
Sourin ⎥ *officers and*	*Bass*	Mascha, *a chambermaid*	*Soprano*
Tchaplitzky ⎥	*Tenor*		
Narumov ⎦ *noblemen*	*Bass*		

Guests, Soldiers, Officers, Promenaders, Masqueraders, etc.

The action takes place in St. Petersburg toward the end of the eighteenth century.

TRAGIC OPERA in three acts. Music by Peter Ilyich Tchaikovsky. Libretto in Russian by Modest Tchaikovsky, after a story by Pushkin. First performed at the Imperial Opera House, St. Petersburg, December 19, 1890. American première, in German, at the Metropolitan Opera House, March 5, 1910, and for the first time here in Russian at the New Amsterdam Theater, New York, on May 10, 1922.

Like the same composer's *Eugene Onegin*, *Pique Dame* is based on a Pushkin text, the novelette *Pikovaya Dama*, a model of narrative suspense and mounting dramatic impact. Merimée's translation of this Russian classic is virtually a French classic. As for the gambling motif which serves as psychological thread, it long remained a favorite device of Russian writers, notably Tolstoy and Dostoevsky. In preparing the libretto Tchaikovsky's brother Modest took some unavoidable liberties with the Pushkin original, but preserved the steady, unifying drive of Hermann's insensate gambling mania. Some of the music was originally written for an opera based on still another Pushkin tale, the adventure story "The Captain's Daughter." Tchaikovsky abandoned that project after almost completing it.

ACT I

SCENE 1: *A summer garden on the St. Petersburg Promenade.* The central figure of *Pique Dame* is Hermann, a lieutenant of the hussars who has fallen in love with Lisa, a granddaughter of a mysterious old Countess, once the toast of St. Petersburg. From Tomsky Hermann learns that the Countess is the reputed possessor of a secret winning-card series wrested from a titled lover. Because of her luck at the tables she has been dubbed the Queen of Spades. Should the Countess reveal the formula to another lover, however, she will forfeit her life. Hermann's hopes of amassing a fortune revive and he resolves to force the secret from the Queen of Spades. Then he will make his fortune at cards and marry Lisa.

SCENE 2: *Lisa's room.* Lisa has gathered her friends in her room, and soon Pauline joins her in a dreamy duet, after which Pauline sings a touching romanza, which suits Lisa's melancholy mood. All now take up

Pauline (Irina Archipova) and Lisa (Galina Vishnevskaya) sing for their friends. (Bolshoi Theater)

a charming dance song of the steppes, which rises in ardor till the governess enters and reminds them it is time for bed. Lisa is to marry Prince Yeletsky, yet her thoughts keep reverting to the dashing young officer Hermann. While she is alone, Hermann appears on the balcony, beckoning to her, but Lisa draws back till he vows to kill himself if she refuses to listen. In the midst of their troubled talk, the old Countess enters and scolds Lisa for staying up so late. Hermann, who has managed to hide himself in time, returns to his wooing when the Countess leaves. At length, Lisa gasps out, "I am yours!"

ACT II

SCENE 1: *A masked ball in the home of a nobleman.* Smartly clad officers mingle with brilliantly gowned ladies at this festive gathering. Prince Yeletsky is inquiring of Lisa why she appears so downcast, but Lisa remains silent. A divertissement in the pastoral style of eighteenth-century court entertainment now unfolds, relating how Chloë spurned the wealthy Plutus to marry the shy and penniless Daphnis, a parallel that is not lost on Lisa. Later when she meets Hermann, a passionate dialogue ensues at the end of which she agrees to a tryst in her room. Without suspecting Hermann's secret motive, Lisa gives him the key to the Countess' room, through which he must pass to reach hers.

SCENE 2: *The Countess' bedchamber.* Concealed behind a curtain, Hermann awaits the Countess. At length, she enters. In a wistful, nostalgic mood she recalls her youth, her brilliant conquests as a beauty,

and sings a song from Grétry's opera *Richard the Lionhearted.* Then she begins to doze off, but starts up in terror as Hermann steps from behind the curtain and implores her to divulge the wonder-working card sequence. The Countess is struck speechless with fear when Hermann, failing to get the secret by pleading, threatens her with a pistol. The Countess falls dead of fright, and the coveted formula is lost forever. At this point Lisa enters the room and rushes to the Countess' side. She is crushed when she learns of Hermann's ruse and reproaches herself for having so foolishly been his accomplice. With her cry of "Murderer!" ringing in his ears, Hermann rushes off into the night.

ACT III

SCENE 1: *Hermann's barracks.* Hermann is reading a letter from Lisa in which she expresses regret for her conduct and asks him to meet her at a place on the bank of the Neva River. Just then a funeral procession passes by and the Countess' ghost appears before Hermann. In great solemnity the ghost reveals the card formula as three, seven, and ace, in

Hermann (Jon Vickers) demands the secret of the cards from the old Countess (Regina Resnik).

Final scene as given at the Metropolitan Opera, with Jon Vickers as Hermann playing his last game

succession. Wild with joy, Hermann hurries to meet Lisa with the news.

SCENE 2: *On the canal bank near the winter palace.* A prey to conflicting emotions, Lisa awaits Hermann on the quay. We now hear one of Tchaikovsky's most imaginative passages, Lisa's *scena* and arioso, as she waits for her card-crazed officer. "It will soon be midnight," she complains, "and Hermann is not here," and the distraught girl pours all her wretchedness into a magnificent song. "Ah, how worn out with sorrow I am," she sings to the silent night. "Morning and night it crushes my heart like a heavy stone." At the stroke of twelve Hermann appears, looking wildly jubilant, bursting with his ghastly secret. Spurred by his new hopes, Hermann talks now of eloping with her. The girl joins him in an ecstatic duet, which rises to feverish passion, but Lisa is again seized by despair as Hermann, wildly mumbling the card numbers, laughs at her pleas to abandon his mad designs. Hermann dashes off, and Lisa, in a frenzy of desperation, throws herself into the river.

SCENE 3: *At a gambling house.* Officers are gathered around a faro table, Prince Yeletsky among them, as Tomsky sings a cheerful little song and the officers blend their voices in a kind of club anthem. Hermann enters, pale and shaken. Using the magic formula, he begins to play, first placing 40,000 rubles on the three. He wins, and then doubles his stakes on the seven, and again wins. Only the Prince shows courage enough to continue opposing him. Meanwhile, Hermann philosophizes on the great gamble of life, in an aria of rich melodic appeal. "What is life?" he asks, seeking to lighten the tense mood of the moment and, voicing a devil-may-care credo, he cries out, "Life is like gambling; today I lose, tomorrow you lose!" Hermann now confidently stakes all his winnings on the next card, certain it will be the promised ace. In the breathless silence of the room, he turns up the card. It is not the ace, but the queen of spades! And again the ghost of the Countess appears to Hermann, grinning vengefully now. Hermann, hopelessly mad now, takes his gun and kills himself.

Porgy and Bess

CHARACTERS

Porgy, *a cripple*	*Baritone*	Jake, *a fisherman*	*Baritone*
Crown, *a stevedore*	*Bass*	Clara, *his wife*	*Soprano*
Bess, *his girl*	*Soprano*	Sportin' Life	*Tenor*
Robbins, *a crap player*	*Baritone*	Peter, *a honeyman*	*Tenor*
Serena, *his wife*	*Soprano*	Undertaker	*Baritone*

Hucksters, Policeman, a Coroner, Detectives, Bystanders, etc.

The action takes place in and near Charleston, South Carolina, in the 1920's.

OPERA IN THREE ACTS. Music by George Gershwin. Text by Du Bose Heyward and Ira Gershwin, adapted from the play *Porgy* by Du Bose and Dorothy Heyward. Produced with an all-Negro singing cast, including Anne Brown, Ruby Elzy, Georgette Harvey, Todd Duncan, John W. Bubbles, Edward Matthews, and others, under the auspices of the Theatre Guild. First performance, Boston, September 30, 1935. First New York performance, Alvin Theater, October 10, 1935. With minor revisions and virtually the same cast the opera was revived by Cheryl Crawford, Majestic Theater, New York, January 1942, after a two-week tryout at a summer theater in Maplewood, New Jersey, September 1941. Alexander Smallens conducted all above performances, as well as the remainder of the engagements in both productions. There have been many revivals, and American *Porgy and Bess* companies have toured with great acclaim through South America and Europe, including the Soviet Union.

Porgy and Bess established overnight the standing of George Gershwin as a pioneer toward a new type of American opera. The sensationally successful play *Porgy* smelled of the soil and glowed with the rich primitive colors of American life. One of the most amazing things about George Gershwin's thoroughly amazing score is the fidelity with which it reflects and expresses and intensifies the dramatic

elements of Du Bose and Dorothy Heyward's play. What is even more important is the fact that Gershwin wrote a work which not only marked a tremendous stride in his own development, but brought opera definitely and thoroughly down to earth.

The score of *Porgy and Bess* is filled with singable melodies, which appeal so strongly to the "man in the street" that he has no trouble humming them to himself. One of the vital qualities of any artistic work is that of universality, and this quality, frequently lacking in contemporary art, is present to an astonishing degree in Gershwin's music. For once the highbrow, the middle, and low come together in agreement upon music.

ACT I

SCENE 1: *Catfish Row*. The scene is laid in Catfish Row, a section of Charleston, South Carolina, formerly occupied by the aristocracy but now a Negro tenement. As the curtain rises, an evening in this little backwater of Negro life is revealed. There is impromptu dancing, and Clara sings a lullaby to her baby, the tuneful "Summertime," while among the men a red-hot game of dice is going on. Among the crap players are Robbins and Crown, a stevedore who is the great lover of the community. Crown quarrels with Robbins and attacks the latter, killing him in the subsequent fight. Crown escapes. Sportin' Life, the neighborhood high-liver, lover, and dope peddler, attempts to induce Bess, Crown's girl, to go to New York with him, but she refuses and, when the other women shut their doors against her, she seeks sanctuary in Porgy's room. Sportin' Life puts his philosophy of life in a devil-may-care song entitled "A Woman Is a Sometime Thing."

SCENE 2: *Serena's room.* All the neighbors from Catfish Row are gathered to sing over Robbins' body and to collect money for the funeral. Porgy, a natural-born leader, comes in with Bess and leads the praying, and Serena sings a deeply felt dirge, "My Man's Gone Now." Two white detectives break in to warn Serena that the body must be buried the next day; and while they are at it, they drag off old Peter, who has done absolutely nothing. A more sympathetic white figure also calls—the undertaker, who agrees to bury Robbins and, as not enough has been collected, to wait for the balance. The act closes as Bess leads in the rousing "Oh, the Train is in the Station."

ACT II

SCENE 1: *Catfish Row in the morning.* Fishermen are working about at odd jobs, and Porgy, a cripple who gets about in a goat-cart, is contented with his life with Bess, and sings a song of his complacence entitled "I Got Plenty o' Nuttin.' " A buzzard flies over the court, and the bird of ill omen fills all the Negroes with premonitions of evil, which they express in the "Buzzard Song." Sportin' Life tries, as he has done before, to get Bess to leave Catfish Row with him, but Porgy, a powerful man even though a cripple, frightens the little dope peddler almost to death. Then Porgy and Bess have their love duet—"Bess, You Is My Woman Now"—just before a jazz band arrives, followed by a crowd, preparing to go to the big picnic on Kittiwah Island. Bess wants to stay home with her Porgy, but he persuades her to go along and have a good time.

SCENE 2: *Kittiwah Island.* The scene changes to that of the Lodge picnic held on Kittiwah Island. One of the most entertaining features of the picnic is the singing and dancing of Sportin' Life, who testifies to his skepticism about spiritual things in the highly amusing song called "It Ain't Necessarily So." Unknown to anyone, Crown, who has fled after murdering Robbins, is in hiding on the island, and at an opportune moment appears, catches Bess alone, and persuades her to stay with him there in his unsuspected retreat.

SCENE 3: *Catfish Row.* At dawn, about a week later, Jake the fisherman is preparing to go out in his boat despite some storm threats. Bess, after her stay on Kittiwah Island with Crown, has been ill and unconscious for some days, but Serena, Porgy, and others pray over her, and, as Serena tells Porgy, "All right now. Dr. Jesus done take de case." And though Porgy somehow knows where she has been, he forgives Bess. She admits she has promised to return to Crown and fears she may not be strong enough to resist. Porgy, however, promises to protect her from him.

SCENE 4: *Serena's room.* A terrible storm is raging outside, and many of the women present, whose men are out fishing, fear that Judgment Day has come. Everyone is praying when Crown forces his way into the room. He taunts Porgy for being a cripple and shocks everyone by claiming God as a friend. But when Clara sees through the window that her husband Jake's boat is overturned, it is only Crown who volunteers to go forth to help. Leaving her baby with Bess, Clara rushes out into the storm with him.

Porgy (William Warfield) and Bess (Leontyne Price)

ACT III

SCENE 1: *Catfish Row.* The women are mourning the loss of Clara, Jake, and Crown in the storm when Sportin' Life wanders in to report that Crown somehow has survived. All go out, and with the stage empty, Bess is heard from Porgy's room singing a lullaby to Clara's baby. Crown, who has been badly hurt, creeps up to the window, but Porgy's powerful hands come from the window, seize Crown by the throat, and choke him to death. Still inside his room, his voice is heard proudly saying, "Bess, you got a man now. You got Porgy."

SCENE 2: *The same.* The police cannot find out anything about the murder, but suspect Porgy and demand his presence at the inquest to identify the body. Porgy refuses to look at his victim and is dragged off to jail, and Bess sings the doleful "My Man's Gone Now." In confusion and distress, she is approached by Sportin' Life, who offers her dope and tries to persuade her to run away with him. He is at first unsuccessful, despite the Harlem joys he promises in the jazzy "There's a Boat That's Leaving Soon for New York." But he leaves a package of dope on the step to tempt her, and when he has departed, she takes the package and carries it into her room.

SCENE 3: *The same.* A week later Porgy has been freed for lack of evidence and he returns from jail in high spirits, bringing presents for all his friends. Presently he calls for Bess and she doesn't answer. He pleads for information as to her whereabouts and finally learns that, seduced by Sportin' Life, she has left for New York. Porgy asks how far it is to New York, and when he is told that it is a thousand miles away, he calls for his goat and cart and starts out undaunted on the road to find Bess. His neighbors help speed him on his way by joining him in the spiritual-like "Oh, Lawd, I'm on My Way."

Sportin' Life (Cab Calloway) shoots crap with his friends on Catfish Row

Prince Igor

KNYAZ IGOR

CHARACTERS

Prince Igor	Baritone	Kontchakovna, *his daughter*	Contralto
Yaroslavna, *his wife*	Soprano	Nurse	Soprano
Vladimir, *their son*	Tenor	Erochka, *a warrior*	Tenor
Prince Galitsky, *Igor's brother-in-law*	Bass	Skula, *a warrior*	Bass
Khan Kontchak	Bass	Ovlour, *a Polovtsian renegade*	Tenor

Courtiers, Peasants, Soldiers, Citizens, Tartars, Polovtsian Maidens and Warriors

The action takes place in medieval and semilegendary Russia.

OPERA IN a prologue and four acts. Music by Alexander Borodin. Libretto in Russian by the composer and Vladimir Stassov, based on *The Epic of the Army of Igor,* an old Russian chronicle. First produced at the Imperial Opera House, St. Petersburg, November 4, 1890. First performance in the United States, December 30, 1915, at the Metropolitan Opera House, New York City. Unfinished at the time of the composer's death, the opera was completed by Rimsky-Korsakov, Liadov, and Glazunov. Borodin had not written out the Overture, but Glazunov, who had often heard him play it on the piano, wrote the composition from memory and orchestrated it. The three men also orchestrated over half of the score and completed certain unfinished scenes. Any differences in style are virtually undetectable.

The popular theory that a musician, and, above all, a composer, is necessarily unsuited for practical affairs finds convincing rebuttal in the life and work of Borodin, for this man was one of the great scientific figures of his generation. Two of his chemical treatises have become standard texts: *Researches upon the Fluoride of Benzol,* and *The Solidification of Aldehydes.* Moreover, Borodin was a professor of medicine and an early advocate of the emancipation of women. Equally fond of science and music, he

chose the former for his career, remaining only a music lover until the age of twenty-eight, when he met Balakirev and began to devote all of his spare time to music. In that famous circle of "The Five" —Balakirev, Cui, Moussorgsky, Borodin, and Rimsky-Korsakov—Borodin was certainly one of the most richly endowed in musical originality. Because of his many professional commitments, Borodin left few compositions—among them, two symphonies, two string quartets, a number of songs and piano pieces, and his opera *Prince Igor.* All of these works, however, reveal remarkable rhythmic energy and melodic beauty. Though by no means a dramatic story, *Prince Igor* furnished Borodin splendid opportunities for effective treatment—the contrast of Russian and Oriental music, scenes of comedy, tragedy, and love, and the fiery dances of the Polovtsi. Unlike Moussorgsky, he was not highly skilled in dramatic utterance. Thus, the opera is written largely in a lyrical style, after the manner established by Glinka in *Russlan and Ludmilla.*

OVERTURE

The Overture is permeated with Borodin's characteristic energy. After an impressive introduction, an

Khan Kontchak (Boris Christoff), Yaroslavna (Frances Alda) and Prince Igor (Vjacheslav Romanovsky) in various productions

allegro movement enters, impetuous with the vigor of a Russian folk dance. A phrase of the music associated with the Oriental Polovtsi is next heard briefly, followed by the beautiful, lyrical theme of Igor's aria "No Sleep, No Rest" heard later in the second act. These themes are developed and repeated in spirited fashion, and the Overture ends in a jubilant mood.

PROLOGUE

SCENE: *The market place of Poutivle.* Prince Igor is about to start out on a campaign against the Khan of the Polovtsi. The people give him a rousing farewell. Suddenly an eclipse of the sun occurs. Frightened by the ill omen of this unnatural darkness, the people, joined by Igor's wife, the Princess Yaroslavna, beg him to postpone his departure. Undaunted, Igor entrusts the affairs of government to his brother-in-law Prince Galitsky and departs, accompanied by his son Vladimir. Two rogues, Skula and Erochka, reluctant to share the hardships of war, desert Igor's army and plan to take more agreeable service with Prince Galitsky.

ACT I

SCENE 1: *The courtyard of Prince Galitsky's house.* There is feasting and carousing at Galitsky's. The Prince himself sings a wild, reckless song, expressive of his resolve to avoid a dull, dreary life. If he were governor, he would give all a merry time, he boasts, for state and power are useless if they do not bring revelry. A group of young girls enter, bewailing the abduction of one of their friends. Their pleas for her return are so coldly mocked by the Prince, who boasts of being himself the abductor, that they leave,

greatly frightened. Galitsky's followers, aroused by the prospect of adventure, shout that they will set him up as ruler in place of Igor. The scene ends with a general carousel, and Skula and Erochka remain at the end, alone and drunk.

SCENE 2: *A room in the palace of Prince Igor.* The Princess Yaroslavna is brooding over the absence of her husband and praying for news of his safety. She sings of her loneliness and hope in an expressive aria. Her thoughts are interrupted by the entry of the group of frightened maidens, who appeal to her for protection from Galitsky. The Prince himself enters and bids them begone and they flee in terror. Yaroslavna upbraids her brother for his shameless conduct. When he taunts her for being cold and censorious, she reminds him that Igor's authority is legally invested in her. She commands him to release the abducted maiden and orders him from her sight. Scarcely has he left when the boyars enter, bringing word that Igor has met with defeat and is held captive with his son. The enemy is now approaching the city. Their loyalty aroused by this news of disaster, the boyars swear to defend their Princess and the city with their lives.

ACT II

SCENE: *The camp of the Polovtsi.* Prisoner in the camp of the enemy, Prince Vladimir has fallen in love with Kontchakovna, the daughter of the Polovtsian chief. He now comes to serenade her. He tells her that Igor disapproves of their attachment, although her father favors it. Their meeting is cut short by the entrance of Igor, who begins soliloquizing on his unhappy condition. As his thoughts turn to his wife, he sings the beautiful melody first heard

330

during the Overture, avowing, "My thoughts fly to you, oh, beloved; you alone will weep over my hapless fate!" Yet when Ovlour, a captive who is acting as guard, offers him a horse as a means of escape, Igor refuses, for he does not believe flight a fair way of treating his captor.

A moment later the chief of the Polovtsi, Khan Kontchak, approaches and greets Igor in the vigorous aria "How goes it, Prince?" in the course of which he asks why he appears so sad. When Igor pointedly refers to his loss of freedom, the Khan reproachfully reminds him he is his guest, not his prisoner, and even offers him one of his harem beauties. At length, the generous Khan promises Igor his freedom if he will agree never to fight the Polovtsi again. This Igor refuses to do, saying that if he were free he would bring a larger army and subdue them—frankness that the Khan admires. At his command, the Polovtsi slaves now enter and begin to sing and dance for Igor's entertainment. At first slow and languorous, their dance gradually develops to a climax of the most turbulent excitement. In zest, melody, and exotic color, few concert numbers rival these dances in popularity.

ACT III

SCENE: *Another part of the camp of the Polovtsi.* The Polovtsian soldiers return laden with spoils from their attack on Poutivle. Watching them, Igor is filled with pity for the misfortunes of his wife and people and now consents to flee. To aid him Ovlour plies the soldiers with great quantities of wine as they divide their spoils. After a drunken orgy the entire camp falls asleep. The chief's daughter has discovered the plot and comes to beg Vladimir not to leave. Her passionate entreaties so stir him that he is on the point of yielding when his father again arouses the sense of duty in him. However, when Igor gives the signal for the escape, Kontchakovna sounds an alarm and clings desperately to her lover until it is too late for him to flee. The Polovtsian soldiers rush in and are on the point of killing Vladimir for enabling his father to escape, when the chief enters. Sternly he forbids them to follow Igor or to slay Vladimir. He cannot help but admire Igor's bold dash for freedom, and, as he philosophically remarks, they may chain the young man to them by giving him a mate. This decision is, of course, most agreeable to both Vladimir and Kontchakovna.

ACT IV

SCENE: *Terrace of the palace.* Yaroslavna stands on the terrace of her ruined palace, gazing over the once fertile plains, now barren from the ravaging of the hostile army. Her sorrow quickly gives way to joy at the unexpected arrival of her husband. As the reunited couple enter the great church of the kremlin at Poutivle, the merry rogues Skula and Erochka quickly switch their allegiance from Galitsky back to Igor and hurriedly set the town bell ringing to summon the people. Their villainy is forgotten in the great rejoicing that greets the rightful and justly beloved Prince.

Prologue as seen at the Bolshoi Theater, Moscow: Igor prays for guidance before leaving to fight the Polovtsi

I Puritani

THE PURITANS

CHARACTERS

Puritans		Cavaliers	
Lord Walter Walton (Gualterio Valton)	*Bass*	Henrietta (Enrichetta), *widow of Charles I*	*Mezzo-soprano*
Sir George Walton (Giorgio Valton)	*Bass*	Lord Arthur Talbot (Arturo Talbo)	*Tenor*
Elvira Walton, *his niece*	*Soprano*	Sir Bruno Robertson, *an officer*	*Tenor*
Sir Richard Forth (Riccardo Forto)	*Baritone*		

Soldiers, Villagers, Servants, Attendants, etc.

The action takes place near Plymouth, England, in the 1650's.

OPERA IN THREE ACTS. Music by Vincenzo Bellini. Libretto in Italian by Count Carlo Pepoli based on the French play *Têtes Rondes et Cavaliers* (*Roundheads and Cavaliers*) by François Ancelot and Xavier Boniface Saintine which, in turn, was based (though remotely) on Sir Walter Scott's *Old Mortality,* an unhistorical historical novel. First performance at the Théâtre Italien in Paris, January 25, 1835. First American performance at Philadelphia, November 22, 1843. *I Puritani* was the fourth opera to be presented, October 29, 1883, at the Metropolitan Opera House in its opening week. Marcella Sembrich was the star, but its second performance at that house had to wait till 1917, when it was revived for Maria Barrientos. The opera was Oscar Hammerstein's choice for the opening night of his Manhattan Opera House December 3, 1907, when Enrico Caruso's rival, Alessandro Bonci, made his American debut.

The cast of the original performance in Paris (which marked a reopening of the Théâtre Italien)

The celebrated Mario, who first sang Arturo

included Giulia Grisi, Giovanni Rubini, Antonio Tamburini, and Luigi Lablache. So successful was this quartet that it became known by the name of this opera—"The Puritani Quartet." It is a work designed as a vehicle for great singers of *bel canto*, with wide ranges (the tenor, for example, must sing two high D's and even a high F) and an extraordinary command of coloratura. For many years it was seldom given outside of Italy, but with the recent renewed interest—and accomplishment—in *bel canto*, it has been revived in many countries especially for Maria Callas and Joan Sutherland, both of whom have been starred in complete recordings of the opera.

ACT I

SCENE 1: *Outside a fortress held by Lord Walton.* In the early 1650's, after the execution of Charles I but before Oliver Cromwell's becoming Lord Protector of the Realm, the Puritans and the Cavaliers are still fighting, and Lord Walter Walton is stoutly holding his castle near Plymouth. He has engaged his daughter Elvira to marry another Puritan, Sir Richard Forth, but she is in love with one of the enemy, Lord Arthur Talbot. Lord Walton is tenderhearted and romantic enough to let his daughter have her way and, when he learns of this, Sir Richard is so torn

with anger and jealousy that he refuses an invitation to become one of the Puritan leaders.

SCENE 2: *Elvira's room.* Sir George, her uncle, comes to tell Elvira of her father's decision and to say that the wedding will take place shortly. Elvira is overjoyed, especially when her noble lover formally approaches to the accompaniment of flourishes of trumpets and a chorus of pages and squires.

SCENE 3: *A large hall in the castle.* Everything is being got ready for the wedding. The gifts are brought in by pages; villagers and soldiers toast the bridal pair; Elvira, in a gay mood, sings the sprightly polacca "*Son vergin vezzosa in veste di sposa*" ("I am a charming virgin in bridal array"). In this mood she playfully leaves her veil with a mysterious guest, who turns out to be Henrietta, the widow of King Charles, who had recently been beheaded. Lord Walton has received instructions to have her sent to London, and Lord Arthur, still a gallant Cavalier though about to marry into Walton's family, is aghast, for he realizes that the woman he still regards as the Queen may suffer the fate of her husband. He persuades Henrietta to take advantage of the veil and flee from the castle with him, but at this moment Richard Forth enters, still full of anger over his rejection. He naturally thinks that it is Elvira under the veil preparing to escape

The wedding scene: Giorgio (Nicola Ghiuselev), Walton (Clifford Grant), Elvira (Joan Sutherland), Arturo (Alfredo Kraus) (San Francisco Opera production)

with Talbot. Swords are drawn, but as Henrietta starts to intervene, the veil comes off, and Richard, realizing that Arthur's escape must prevent his marriage, sends them on their way.

The escape is quickly discovered and Elvira, believing herself deserted, loses her mind. The chorus denounces Lord Arthur.

ACT II

SCENE: *The Puritan camp.* Sir George announces that Parliament has decreed the death of Lord Arthur for his part in the escape of the Queen, and he also describes the pathetic effects of madness on Elvira. Then Elvira herself enters and sings a celebrated mad scene. *"Qui la voce."* It is often compared with the more celebrated one that Lucia has in Donizetti's *Lucia di Lammermoor* (which, incidentally, had its première a few months after *I Puritani's*), although it makes no use of a flute obbligato, and Bellini's heroine is aware of what is going on about her, while Donizetti's is not. Both, of course, are replete with lovely melodies and elaborate coloratura. In the course of the scene Lord Walton and Richard, her former fiancé, try to console her, and Richard even agrees that Arthur may return provided he comes unarmed. The act closes after a stirring duet between Sir George and Sir Richard,

"Suoni la tromba," as they pledge themselves to fight against the Cavaliers.

ACT III

SCENE: *A garden near the castle.* Arthur, fleeing from the enemy, slips into the castle grounds in the hope of seeing Elvira one more time before leaving England forever. Off stage he hears his demented love singing a plaintive ballad (*"A una fonte afflito"*), and when he responds with a serenade, she appears. She recognizes Arthur and, better than this, understands his explanation that his apparent desertion was inspired by loyalty to his Queen. Her joy over this brings back, temporarily at least, her sanity. They sing the lovely but difficult duet *"Vieni fra queste braccia"* (*"Come to my arms"*).

Forgetting the present danger, they think only of their love and the consciousness that they are once more in each other's arms. But the sound of a drum reawakens Elvira's affliction. She cries out for help, believing in her madness that Arthur wishes to leave her. Soldiers rush in, Arthur is recognized, captured, and sentenced to death on the spot. Yet, just as the execution is about to take place, a messenger arrives with the news that the Cavaliers have been defeated and that Cromwell has granted pardon to all captives. With this splendid news Elvira's reason returns, and the lovers are united.

Act II: The Oath—Giorgio (Ezio Flagello) and Riccardo (Enzo Sordello) (Connecticut Opera Association production)

The Rake's Progress

CHARACTERS

Trulove, *a country squire*	Bass	Baba the Turk, *a bearded lady from*	
Anne, *his daughter*	Soprano	*a circus*	Mezzo-soprano
Tom Rakewell, *her sweetheart*	Tenor	Sellem, *an auctioneer*	Tenor
Nick Shadow	Baritone	Keeper of the Madhouse	Bass
Mother Goose, *a brothel*			
keeper	Mezzo-soprano		

Whores and Roaring Boys, Servants, Citizens, Madmen

The action takes place in the eighteenth century in England.

OPERA IN three acts and an epilogue. Music by Igor Stravinsky. Libretto by W. H. Auden and Chester Kallman inspired by William Hogarth's picture series of the same name. First performance, Venice Festival, September 11, 1951, conducted by the composer with Elisabeth Schwarzkopf, Jennie Tourel, Robert Rounseville, and Otakar Kraus in the cast. Metropolitan première, February 14, 1953, with Hilde Gueden, Blanche Thebom, Eugene Conley, and Mack Harrell, with Fritz Reiner conducting.

Despite the care with which the composer attempted to respect the prosody of the distinguished Anglo-American poet W. H. Auden and his collaborator, the words are not often easy to understand when the opera is sung, and this may be one reason for its far greater acceptance in Europe than in America. Stravinsky, in this period of his life, called his "neo-classic" period, was experimenting with old forms, and *The Rake's Progress* is a series of numbers—arias, duets, recitatives with harpsichord, and big concerted scenes as in Mozart, Rossini, Donizetti and other late eighteenth- and early nineteenth-century operas. With Stravinsky's harmonic schemes, however, one could not conceivably mistake the composer. It is almost as though one were listening to old conventions through a distorting mirror.

ACT I

SCENE 1: *The garden of Trulove's country home.* After a short fanfare prelude, we find Tom Rakewell wooing Anne in one corner of the garden while her father, in another, voices his fears that his prospective son-in-law may not make a very steady provider. With Anne gone into the house, Trulove tells Tom that a good position in business has been secured for him in London. Tom refuses the offer, and Trulove, angrily departing, tells him that though he is willing for Anne to marry a poor man, he will not tolerate a lazy one. Tom then has an aria ("Since it is not by merit we rise or we fall") vigorously announcing that he intends to rely on the goddess of good luck. At the end, however, he wishes that he had some present money. At once the Mephistophelean character of Nick Shadow, in the guise of a servant, appears at the gate and asks for Tom Rakewell. Trulove and Anne are summoned, and Nick announces that a forgotten uncle has left Tom a fortune. In the quartet that follows, only Trulove is unenthusiastic. He fears that an unearned fortune may inspire idleness. It is necessary, says Nick, that Tom should go to London to settle the

Scene 1 from the Venice première: Anne (Elisabeth Schwarzkopf), Tom (Robert Rounseville), Nick (Otakar Kraus), Trulove (Raphaël Arié)

business, and he offers himself as a servant, wages to be settled in a year and a day. (The Mephistophelean character of Nick now becomes completely clear to all readers of *Faust.*) And as Tom goes out the gate, Nick turns to the audience and announces, "The progress of a rake begins!"

SCENE 2: *The brothel of Mother Goose in London.* A vigorous chorus in praise of their respective activities is sung by whores and roaring boys (roaring boys being upper-class roisterers, also known as "Mohocks" in eighteenth-century London). Nick introduces Tom to this company and gets him to recite a sort of litany of evil he has already been taught. He stumbles, however, when it comes to defining love; but when he wishes to leave because it is getting late, Nick sets back the clock, the merriment begins anew, and Tom sings an aria recalling his vows of love to Anne. Mother Goose, however, will have none of this, and she leads the young man off to her own room. The scene ends gaily as the bawds and roaring boys sing "Lanterloo."

SCENE 3: *The garden of Trulove's country home.* Anne has not heard a word from Tom and misses

him badly. She sings a formal recitative and aria about it; her father calls from the house; and Anne, deciding her lover needs her more than her father does, decides to go to London and tells us so in a brilliant cabaletta—that is, a sort of second and more brilliant aria that in old-fashioned Italian opera was often attached to the first aria after some sort of interruption leading to a decision or a change of mind.

ACT II

SCENE 1: *Tom's quarters in London.* At breakfast by himself Tom bemoans the fact that he is not liking London and that he does not even dare think about the girl he has left. At the words "I wish I were happy," Nick Shadow appears and shows him a broadside of a circus starring Baba the Turk, a bearded lady. In a sinister aria, Nick teaches Tom to forget crippling things like a conscience and ordinary appetites. What a wonderful idea it would be for Tom to marry Baba! Tom looks at the broadside again, laughs, and agrees that with Nick's help he will marry the creature.

SCENE 2: *Outside Tom's London house.* Anne, who has come to London to persuade Tom to come back to the country, sings an aria about it, but observes servants beginning to carry all sorts of packages into the house. A sedan chair is drawn in, and from it steps Tom. He begs Anne to go home again, for he is not worthy of her. As if to corroborate that judgment, a veiled head is stuck out of the sedan chair to ask what is holding everything up. Tom has to inform Anne that this is his bride being brought to her home—Baba the Turk. A trio develops as Anne and Tom sing of their regrets over what might have been and Baba expresses her extreme impatience. Finally Anne leaves, Tom helps Baba from the chair, and a congratulatory crowd that has gathered is delighted when Baba removes her veil and shows her beard.

SCENE 3: *A room in Tom's house.* Again Tom is unhappy at breakfast as his hirsute bride jabbers away about all the peculiar odds and ends she has scattered around the once tidy quarters—stuffed birds, china, cheap jewelry from any- and everywhere. When Tom remains not only uninterested but bored, she flies into a rage, smashes all the cheaper stuff, and starts what might be called a tantrum aria. In the middle of a line Tom stuffs his own wig into her mouth, covering her face, and utterly miserable, he goes to sleep.

Nick now comes in silently, carrying a peculiar contraption into which he puts a bit of broken china and a loaf of bread, turns the handle, and has the bread alone emerge, Tom awakens and tells Nick he has dreamed that he invented a machine which could turn stone to bread and be a boon to suffering mankind. Nick, of course, has the machine right there, and Tom makes it "work." Nick suggests that there is a fortune to be made—but hadn't Tom better tell his wife? "My wife?" says Tom. "I have no wife. I've buried her." Baba is still silent behind his wig.

ACT III

SCENE 1: *A room in Tom's house.* It is months later, and a crowd is present awaiting the auctioning off of everything in the room. Baba sits there with Tom's wig still covering her face, and Anne is desperately searching for Tom and getting help from no one. Now Sellem the auctioneer enters and begins to sell off everything to a silly waltz tune—an auk, a pike, a palm—and then, sinking almost to a whisper, he puts up "an unknown object . . . a cake? an organ? an apple tree?" As the bidding rises, he snatches the wig from the "object," which turns out to be Baba. She finishes the phrase that Tom had choked off and, dominating the whole amazed crowd, advises Anne to find and reform Tom and tells the rest that she is going back to the circus and they'll have to pay to see her the next time. Off stage Tom and Nick are heard singing, and in the grand finale Anne reiterates, "I go, I go, I go, I go to him." Baba orders Sellem to fetch her carriage.

SCENE 2: *A graveyard.* A few measures of weird music for only four string instruments set the supernatural tone of the scene. Nick Shadow tells Tom that he has now served him for a year and a day and demands payment—Tom's soul. Yet, always the sporting gentleman, the Devil offers to bet the stakes on a game of cards. As, off stage, Anne sings of the power of true love, Tom wins three times running. In a rage Nick strikes Tom insane, and then sinks into the grave he had intended for Tom. The lights go down, and when they come up again, Tom is sitting on the mound of the grave, completely out of his mind. He puts grass on his head, thinking it roses, and sings a ballad, calling himself "Adonis."

SCENE 3: *Bedlam, the lunatic asylum.* Incarcerated with other madmen, Tom still thinks he is Adonis and demands that the others prepare for his wedding to Venus. They jeer at him till the jailer brings in Anne. A touching love duet follows, and at its close, Anne leads the exhausted Tom to a straw pallet and sings him a tender lullaby. Trulove comes to take Anne away, and they both bid the sleeper a farewell.

Now Tom awakens, raves wildly about Venus, who has just left him, but he cannot persuade his fellows that Venus was there at all. Hopelessly he sinks back on his pallet and dies.

EPILOGUE

Before the curtain. The quintet of principals—Tom, Nick, Baba and the two Truloves—address the audience with the moral of the tale:

> *For idle hands and hearts and minds*
> *The Devil finds a work to do.*

Bedlam at La Scala: Anne (Elisabeth Schwarzkopf) comforts Tom (Mirto Picchi), now confined to madhouse. Act III

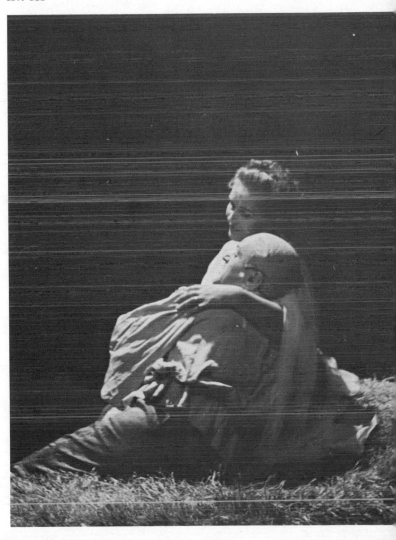

Rigoletto

CHARACTERS

Rigoletto, *a hunchback, jester to the Duke of Mantua*	*Baritone*	Count Ceprano, *a courtier*	*Bass*
Gilda, *his daughter*	*Soprano*	Countess Ceprano, *his wife*	*Mezzo-soprano*
Giovanna, *her nurse*	*Mezzo-soprano*	Monterone, *a noble of the court*	*Bass*
Duke of Mantua	*Tenor*	Borsa, *a courtier*	*Tenor*
Sparafucile, *a hired assassin*	*Bass*	Marullo, *a courtier*	*Baritone*
Maddalena, *his sister*	*Mezzo-soprano*		

Chorus of Courtiers

The action takes place at Mantua during the sixteenth century.

OPERA IN four (originally three) acts. Music by Giuseppe Verdi. Libretto in Italian by Francesco Marie Piave, founded on Victor Hugo's play *Le Roi S'amuse*. Produced, Teatro la Fenice, Venice, March 11, 1851; first performance in the United States, Academy of Music, New York, February 19, 1855. The Metropolitan mounted the opera early in its first season, November 16, 1883, with Marcella Sembrich as Gilda. In present-day performances the two scenes of what is Act I in the original score are usually presented as separate "acts," thus making of *Rigoletto* a four-act opera.

Greatly desiring a new libretto for La Fenice, Verdi requested Piave to adapt Victor Hugo's play *Le Roi S'amuse* (*The King Amuses Himself*), which, in spite of its dubious morals, was recognized by the composer as possessing operatic possibilities. A libretto was soon written, the title being changed to *La Maledizione* (*The Curse*). A new work was desperately needed by the management of La Fenice, and dismay followed the flat refusal of the police to grant permission for the performance of a work in which a king was shown at such a disadvantage. It will be remembered that Venice was then in Austrian hands, and but a short time previously, 1848–1849, there had been an Italian insurrection. At first Verdi refused to consider any other plan, and the management was in despair. Help arrived from an

Giuseppe de Luca as the court jester, Rigoletto

Monterone curses Rigoletto, seated on Duke's throne, as staged by Herbert Graf at the Metropolitan in 1951

unexpected quarter, for the Austrian police chief Martello was an ardent musical and dramatic enthusiast, and a great admirer of Verdi. He perceived that by substituting the Duke of Mantua for Francis I, and by changing the title to *Rigoletto*, the work could be presented without any material changes in the original dramatic situations. Verdi accepted this proposal. He went to Busseto, near his birthplace, and came back within six weeks with the completed musical score. The new work was a brilliant success, thus rescuing the management of the theater.

A remarkable feat of rapid composition, being written in less than forty days, *Rigoletto* still holds a firm place in the repertoire of all opera houses after more than a century. Not without reason has it held this popularity, for Victor Hugo's drama, even with Piave's numerous alterations, makes a most effective opera libretto. Moreover, it supplies three characters of interest: the hunchback Rigoletto, a vital centralizing dramatic figure who appeals to audiences and singers alike; the Duke, a brilliant tenor role and a debonair and cynical characterization; Gilda, the heroine, beloved by all coloratura sopranos. These characters have indeed been favorites with many of the greatest singers: Patti sang in the opera for the first time at New Orleans, February 6, 1861; Caruso made his North American debut singing the role of the Duke at the Metropolitan Opera House, New York, November 23, 1903; Ruffo first appeared in the United States as Rigoletto, November 4, 1912, at Hammerstein's Manhattan Opera House, Philadelphia; and on November 18, 1916, occurred the triumphant first North American appearance of Galli-Curci when she sang the role of Gilda with the Chicago Opera Company.

ACT I

SCENE: *A salon in the Ducal palace.* After a short prelude the curtain rises and we behold a fete in progress at the Ducal palace. Courtiers and ladies move gaily through the great ballroom. Through the large archway at the rear we can look into other luxurious apartments, all brilliantly lighted. Amid all the bustle and gaiety and to a frivolous, light-hearted orchestral accompaniment the Duke enters with one of the courtiers, Borsa. He confides to him that he is pursuing an unknown beauty whom he has seen in church every Sunday during the past three months. He has followed her to her house in a remote part of the city, where, he has discovered, a mysterious man visits her every evening. At this moment a group of knights and ladies happen to pass by. "What beauties!" exclaims Borsa. "Ceprano's wife is the loveliest of all!" replies the Duke. His listener warns him that the Count might hear, but the Duke shrugs his shoulders indifferently and gives vent to his philosophy in the aria *"Questa o quella"* ("'Mid the fair throng"). The melody is smooth, it seems to float through the air, yet there is irony concealed beneath its gaiety.

The courtiers dance a minuet, accompanied by music, graceful and not inappropriately reminiscent of the minuet in *Don Giovanni*. The Duke dances with the Countess, closely watched, however, by Ceprano; the fervent manner in which he kisses her hand is not lost on the jealous husband, nor does it escape the court jester, the hunchback Rigoletto. The Duke leads away the Countess, and Ceprano follows them, but not before the jester has launched a cutting taunt at the enraged Count.

Rigoletto forthwith saunters off, seeking other victims for his lord. As soon as he is out of sight, he in turn becomes the object of similar jests. The gossip Marullo enters with the news that Rigoletto keeps a mistress and visits her every night. There are shouts of delight at the thought that the pander of the Duke's romances, Rigoletto himself, is now in love. The merriment is cut short by the re-entry of the Duke, followed by Rigoletto. The Duke is saying he would like to get rid of Count Ceprano so that he might have the beautiful Countess, and Rigoletto banteringly suggests that he run off with her. Then he mentions the possibility of prison for the Count, or exile, or beheading. This sarcasm of the misshapen jester disgusts even the Duke. Ceprano is boiling with rage at such boorish jesting and bids the courtiers, who likewise have smarted under Rigoletto's ribaldry, meet him the following night, when they shall have their revenge.

The festival music of the band on the stage supplies a flippant background to the badinage of this scene; then, while the Duke and Rigoletto continue their discussion, and the courtiers and Ceprano plot their revenge, the music grows to a climax, suddenly interrupted by the voice of someone outside, struggling for admission. A moment later the aged Count Monterone bursts in. His daughter has been dishonored by the Duke; now before the entire assembly he denounces that profligate ruler. The Duke at once orders his arrest; Rigoletto mocks him. Monterone, justly incensed with this injury doubled with insult, again reviles the Duke and, turning toward Rigoletto, cries, "As for you, serpent! You who can laugh at a father's anguish; a father's curse be on your head!" Monterone is led off by guards; the

Reri Grist as Gilda at the San Francisco Opera

courtiers return to their festivities; but Rigoletto cowers, trembling with fright at Monterone's words.

ACT II

SCENE: *A deserted street*. A few somber chords are heard in the woodwinds. Then a subdued, rather suave melody in keeping with the scene—the end of a deserted street, sinister under the darkness of night. At the left, a small, humble-appearing house with a wall-enclosed courtyard; across the street, a very high wall, and beyond it a corner of Count Ceprano's palace.

Rigoletto, wrapped in his cloak, comes shambling down the street, but before he can turn in toward his house at the left, he is accosted by an ominous black-robed figure who offers his services, should they be desired, in putting rivals or enemies out of the way, charges reasonable. The hunchback does not need him now, but asks where he may be found. This assassin for hire tells his lodging, then departs, making known his name, Sparafucile.

Rigoletto stops meditatively at the doorway leading into the courtyard. Thus he soliloquizes, to music that varies with his shifting moods, in the dramatic aria *"Pari siamo"* ("We are equals"), a masterpiece of theater writing, and, understandably, a great favorite with baritones. He enters the courtyard at the moment that a young woman comes from the house. They embrace joyfully. "Gilda!" he exclaims. "Father!" she sighs in response. A cheerful orchestral melody accompanies their meeting. Knowing well the hazards of life with courtiers and Duke so near and, perhaps, the curse still ringing in his ears, he again for the thousandth time warns and solemnly enjoins her to remain strictly within the house and never to venture into the town. He even questions her to know if anybody has followed her to church; but Gilda, with some qualms of conscience, keeps silent regarding the stranger she has met there. To reassure himself further, Rigoletto calls the servant Giovanna and instructs her, too, on matters of safety for his daughter.

Suddenly thinking he hears someone knock on the street door, Rigoletto hurriedly opens the door in the courtyard and goes out to look. The Duke has been loitering outside and, while Rigoletto is in the street, he quietly glides into the courtyard and throws a purse to the servant with a sign to keep silent. He hides himself. This action takes place to an agitated orchestral accompaniment, the frightened Gilda, unaware of his presence, murmuring, meanwhile, "Heaven! if he should suspect me!" Rigoletto must leave, and returns, saying, "My daughter, farewell!" "His daughter!" exclaims the Duke to himself, surprised at this revelation. "Farewell, O my father!" (*"Addio, mio padre"*) is Gilda's reply. Father and daughter then continue in a lovely duet, Gilda saying that they need not fear, for her mother, as an angel in heaven, is watching over them, while Rigoletto continues his charge to the servant, *"Veglia, O donna"* ("Guard her, woman").

As soon as Rigoletto has departed, the Duke, who, of course, is in disguise, comes from his hiding place. Gilda, alarmed, bids him begone; but he knows well how to calm her fears. He sings a gently swaying melody, *"E il sol dell' anima"* ("Love is the sun"). Soon Gilda is heard saying, as if to herself, "Ah! This is the dear voice of my dreams!"

Gilda desires to know his name; "Gualtier Maldè," he finally admits, adding that he is only a poor, struggling student. Then as he leaves, they sing a tender farewell. Gilda remains pensive, dreaming of her lover, in the very popular florid air *"Caro nome"* ("Dear name"). This melody, with delicate accompaniment and flute passages, is one of the most exacting of coloratura arias, calling for extraordinary skill if its *fiorture* are to be performed with the grace they demand.

While she is yet singing, conspiracy is at work, for under cover of night a band of masked courtiers, led by Ceprano, has come for vengeance. Rigoletto, unexpectedly returning, runs into them, and is much alarmed to find them in his neighborhood. His fears are somewhat calmed, however, when the courtiers declare that they are bent on stealing Ceprano's wife for their friend the Duke. Rigoletto points out Ceprano's house and offers help. They insist that he must be disguised, give him a mask, and then as if to fasten it securely, tie it with a handkerchief which they pass over the holes pierced for the eyes. Confused and blinded, Rigoletto holds the ladder

against what he believes to be the wall surrounding Ceprano's house. By it the abductors climb over his own wall, enter his house, seize, gag, and carry away his daughter. Thus after a few minutes Rigoletto finds himself left entirely alone, holding the ladder. Becoming suspicious, he tears off the mask. The door to his courtyard is open. On the ground he finds a scarf of Gilda's. Frantic with fear, he rushes into the house. Gilda has disappeared. He staggers under this disaster which he has helped bring on himself. In agony, he cries out, *"Ah!—la maledizione!"* ("Ah, the curse").

ACT III

SCENE: *A salon in the Duke's palace.* The Duke is very much upset; he has returned to Rigoletto's house and found it deserted, the bird flown. He laments his loss in a very effective aria, *"Parmi veder le lagrime"* ("Each tear that falls"), so effective that we nearly feel sorry for him! Marullo and the courtiers enter with some amusing news. In a rousing chorus, they narrate their exploits of the previous night when they captured Rigoletto's "mistress."

The Duke is delighted with the details, laughing at the brilliant idea that made Rigoletto himself a party to the abduction. Knowing well that the

Act III: Rigoletto (Cornell MacNeil) berates the courtiers

woman in question is assuredly his latest inamorata, he is quite pleased when they inform him that they have brought her to the palace and left her, in fact, in the very next room. He hurries to her.

No sooner has he gone than Rigoletto enters, pitifully striving to conceal his deep distress under a laughing exterior. "Poor Rigoletto," sing the courtiers, enjoying his discomposure at the loss of one they still believe to be only his mistress. The music is remarkably descriptive of Rigoletto's anxiety, as under the disguise of cynical indifference, singing, "Tra-la-tra-la," he searches furtively about the room for some evidence of Gilda's presence. A page enters to ask for the Duke; the courtiers tell him meaningly that his lordship cannot be disturbed now. The hunchback at once grasps the situation. "She must be here, in the next room!" he cries; then making no further attempt at concealment, he pleads, "Give me my daughter." He attempts to force an entrance, but the courtiers bar his efforts. Giving way to his feelings, he rages among the Duke's followers.

The courtiers at first laugh at, then grow indifferent to, Rigoletto's plea, but their curiosity is again piqued as Gilda emerges from the Duke's apartment, runs to her father, and throws herself in his arms. Rigoletto orders the courtiers to go. Somewhat abashed, they leave the hunchback and his daughter together. Gilda tells him of the lover who followed her from church, in the plaintive aria *"Tutte le feste"* ("On every festal morning").

Rigoletto does his best to comfort the girl, clasping her to his bosom with a tenderness and love that do much to atone for his vileness. "Weep, my child," he sings, to a melody of unusual beauty and pathos. Gilda replies, and their voices unite in a duet of most touching, exquisite loveliness—music that expresses in a wonderful manner the delicate, poignant tragedy of the scene.

Gilda (Roberta Peters) confesses her love for the Duke to her father, Rigoletto (Nicolae Herlea)

By a singular chance, Count Monterone passes through the hall, being led to execution. He pauses before the Duke's portrait, exclaiming, "No thunder from heaven has yet burst down to strike you!" As he passes on, Rigoletto watches him grimly. Her father's stern demeanor frightens the girl, for he now swears a terrible vengeance on the Duke.

ACT IV

SCENE: *Sparafucile's dwelling on the deserted banks of the Mincio River*. An ancient inn, so ruined that one can see the broken staircase which leads to the loft, and even a couch within the loft itself. Near the inn is the river; beyond, the towers of Mantua reach toward the scudding clouds. Sparafucile is indoors, seated by the table, polishing his belt, unconscious that Rigoletto and his daughter are without, the latter dressed as a young cavalier, for it is her father's wish that she shall leave the city in disguise this very night.

He asks her if she still dreams of the Duke, and she confesses that she does cherish the student who came to her so full of romantic protestations. Thinking to cure her of this affection, he leads her toward the inn, so that she may peer through the dilapidated door and see the erstwhile "student" in his real character. The Duke, disguised as a soldier, enters the tavern and calls loudly for wine. While he is being served by Sparafucile, he sings one more song of the love of women. It portrays, clearly as words and music may, the indolently amorous young noble and his views of womankind, whom he charges, all and sundry, with his own worst failing, *"La donna è mobile"* ("Woman is fickle").

The murderous innkeeper Sparafucile brings the wine and then, as he goes out, knocks on the ceiling, a signal for his sister Maddalena to descend. This flirtatious gypsy girl is the bait that has been used to lure the Duke to the inn. She is wise in the ways of men, and thus, for a time, laughingly evades the Duke's caresses.

The emotions of these four characters so widely different in sentiment are expressed in the wonderful quartet *"Bella figlia dell' amore"* ("Fairest daughter of the graces"). In a most suave, ingratiating melody the Duke sings to Maddalena, and Maddalena coquettishly replies. Observing all this, the heartbroken Gilda, concealed in the darkness outside, grimly remarks how lightly they speak of love, while the stern remarks of Rigoletto are added to the others. The voices, joined in simple though effective polyphony, mount to a splendid climax, one of the finest pieces of ensemble writing in all Italian opera.

Rigoletto then bids his daughter go with all speed to Verona, where he plans to follow. He forthwith summons Sparafucile and gives him half his assassin's fee; the remainder he will pay when the Duke's body is delivered, in a sack, at midnight. Sparafucile offers to throw the body in the river, but Rigoletto wishes that grim satisfaction for himself; he will return.

While these business transactions have been taking place outside, within the flirtation has grown more intimate. A storm gathers, and the Duke decides to stay the night at the inn. On Sparafucile's re-entry he whispers to the girl that he will return to her soon, and ascends to the loft.

Even the professional coquette has fallen in love with the handsome Duke. Therefore, as soon as she is alone with her brother, she suggests that he kill the hunchback rather than her Apollo. But the honor said to exist among thieves is, apparently, found among murderers too, for Sparafucile refuses to betray his employer. His sister pleads with such urgency, however, that finally he agrees that if another guest shall arrive before midnight, he will slay him instead of the Duke, so that Rigoletto will at least have a corpse for his money.

Meanwhile the storm has been drawing nearer, adding its terrors to those of the night. In spite of the darkness, Gilda has crept back to the inn, irresistibly drawn to the haunts of the man she loves. Thus it happens that, hearing this extraordinary agreement, she sees a way to save the life of her beloved and end her own sorrow.

The storm bursts in a sudden and overwhelming fury; the moaning of the wind, the long rush of the rain, the blinding lightning and crash of thunder are but outward symbols of the emotions of Gilda. Summoning up her courage, she knocks at the door. Even the assassin seems startled that anyone should come at such a time. Sparafucile holds his dagger ready; Maddalena runs to open the door. Gilda enters. Between the lightning flashes her form is barely discernible. There is a quickly stifled outcry, then darkness and silence.

The storm's fury abates, though occasional lightning flashes illuminate the dreary scene. Rigoletto returns. He pays off the assassin and in return is given the sack with its gruesome contents. The murderer again offers to throw the body into the river; again the jester claims this privilege. Left alone he gloats over his vengeance, then starts to drag the body toward the river. At that moment he hears a sound that makes his blood run cold. The Duke has awakened, and is again singing, *"La donna è mobile."* Rigoletto trembles. Whom, then, has he in the sack? He tears it open. A sudden flash of lightning reveals the form of Gilda. The unfortunate girl, wounded unto death, begs her father's forgiveness, singing with him a touching duet of farewell, *"Lassù in cielo"* ("There in heaven"). Rigoletto implores her not to leave him thus alone on earth. A little cry of pain, and Gilda falls back dead. "Ah! The curse!" cries out Rigoletto. The music of Monterone's curse upon the Jester thunders forth in the orchestra in appalling triumph.

Act IV quartet: the Duke woos Maddalena as Gilda and Rigoletto watch with Sparafucile in background (A nineteenth-century Italian print)

Der Ring des Nibelungen

THE RING OF THE NIBELUNGS

DAS RHEINGOLD, DIE WALKÜRE, SIEGFRIED, GÖTTERDÄMMERUNG

A work without a parallel in the whole realm of music for grandeur and breadth of conception, the *Ring* occupied Wagner's ever-active mind for more than twenty-six years. While he was still a conductor at the Dresden Opera he had become greatly interested in the ancient Scandinavian, Germanic, and Icelandic sagas. There resulted a dramatic poem, *Siegfried's Death*, written by the composer in November 1848. Then, while in exile, realizing that one drama would be inadequate for the proper presentation of so vast a legend, he wrote another poem as an introduction, named *Young Siegfried* (1851). Similarly, the following year, he prefaced this with *The Valkyrie* (*Die Walküre*), and this in turn with *The Rhinegold* (*Das Rheingold*). Wagner then set to work upon the music in the proper order of the dramas, and by 1857 had completed the score through part of the second act of *Siegfried* (originally *Young Siegfried*). By this time even the undauntable Wagner had, as he termed it, grown tired of "piling one silent score upon another," and he turned to what he considered the more practicable *Meistersinger* and *Tristan*. Not until 1869, encouraged by the patronage of the King of Bavaria, did Wagner resume work on *Siegfried*. The entire *Ring* was eventually finished, with the completion of the orchestration of *Twilight of the Gods* (*Götterdämmerung*), originally *Siegfried's Death*, in 1874. Wagner termed his vast work a trilogy, considering *The Rhinegold* a preface to the story narrated in the three succeeding music-dramas, *Die Walküre, Siegfried,* and *Götterdämmerung.* Modern writers, however, regarding all four dramas as of equal importance, commonly refer to the series as a tetralogy.

No greater evidence of Wagner's ability as a dramatist can be found than the skill with which he molded the old legends into a cohesive plot. Because of the order in which the text of the *Ring* was written, redundancies naturally occur; to remove them was a labor from which even this painstaking composer shrank. Into this mighty epic Wagner crowded a wealth of philosophical ideas. He cast his dramas into an alliterative form of verse, similar to that of the sagas, and through his fusion of music and verse created an atmosphere of a remote age of myths and legends.

With the very opening of *Das Rheingold*—revolutionary as that magnificent opening must have been in its day—we realize that musically we are no longer in the world of *Lohengrin*, which preceded the *Ring* in time of composition. After long thought, Wagner had decided that if music drama was to progress beyond the classic scope of opera, it would be necessary to adapt to the theater the forceful method of thematic development perfected in the symphony by Beethoven. Only so was Wagner convinced that a fresh expressiveness could be obtained. An opera so written would no longer be opera, but "music drama," since, for Wagner, drama and music were conceived together, the melodies, harmonies, modulations, the very orchestration itself growing out of the moods and action of the drama. Wagner's music gains greatly in unity and psychological power through this use of "leading motives," which in the *Ring* are almost innumerable. A complete cataloguing and naming of all such motives was probably not contemplated by the composer. And certainly this is not necessary for the listener. Yet some knowledge of the more prominent themes does give added pleasure and understanding. For after repeated hearings and long acquaintance, the *Ring* assumes new beauties and reveals hitherto unnoticed details that often startle the attentive listener with their dramatic force and vividness.

In keeping with the magnitude of the tetralogy, Wagner made use of a gigantic orchestra, almost unprecedented in size. For special effects he introduced four of a family of instruments that he invented for the *Ring*. These instruments now known as "Bayreuth tubas" or "Wagner tubas," are really hybrids, uniting features of the French horn and trombone. Their timbre, of unusual nobility and pathos, is peculiarly suited to Wagner's purpose—that of intoning the leading motives of "Valhalla" and "The Wälsungs."

The *Ring*, as a whole, was first performed at Wagner's own theater at Bayreuth, on August 13, 14, 16, 17, 1876, as the crowning achievement of a lifetime of struggle. In the United States the complete cycle was first performed at the Metropolitan Opera House, New York, March 4–11, 1889, the in-dividual dramas having been given at earlier dates.

An undertaking of such size has naturally enlisted the services of many of the world's greatest conductors and singers. At the first Bayreuth performances, 1876, Hans Richter was the conductor and Anton Seidl and Felix Mottl, assistants; while among the singers were Lilli Lehmann, Albert Niemann, and Amalia Materna. In 1896 Ernestine Schumann-Heink sang the roles of Erda and Waltraute at Bayreuth. At the first performance of the entire *Ring* cycle at the Metropolitan Opera House, Anton Seidl was the conductor, and among the principals were Lilli Lehmann, Max Alvary, and Emil Fischer. The late Theodore Thomas was a Wagnerian pioneer in this country, in the days when it was heresy to play or like Wagner. Among the other great Wagnerian singers it is possible here to name only a few, the De Reszkes, Nordica, Ternina, Fremstad, Gadski, Eames, Homer, Matzenauer, Van Rooy, Whitehill, and, among those of more recent times, Kirsten Flagstad, Marjorie Lawrence, Elisabeth Rethberg, Lauritz Melchior, Frida Leider, Friedrich Schorr, Helen Traubel, Birgit Nilsson and Regina Crespin. Since World War II the productions at Bayreuth under the direction of Wagner's grandsons, which sacrifice realism in the interests of symbolism, have had a marked influence on many operatic productions everywhere.

Ring luminaries of the 1880's: Siegfried (Max Alvary), Brünnhilde (Amalia Materna), Wotan (Franz Betz)

Das Rheingold

CHARACTERS

Gods

Wotan, *ruler of the gods*	Bass-Baritone
Donner, *god of thunder*	Baritone
Froh, *god of sun, rain, and fruits*	Tenor
Loge, *demigod of fire*	Tenor

Goddesses

Fricka, *goddess of marriage and wife of Wotan*	Mezzo-soprano
Freia, *goddess of youth and beauty*	Soprano
Erda, *the earth goddess*	Contralto

Giants

Fasolt	*brothers*	Bass
Fafner		Bass

The Rhine-maidens

Woglinde	Soprano
Wellgunde	Mezzo-soprano
Flosshilde	Contralto

Nibelungs (Gnomes)

Alberich	*brothers*	Bass-Baritone or Bass
Mime		Tenor

MUSIC DRAMA in four scenes, prelude (*Vorabend*) to *Der Ring des Nibelungen*. Text and music by Richard Wagner. First produced, September 22, 1869, at Munich. First performance in the United States, January 4, 1889, at the Metropolitan Opera House, New York.

SCENE: *The bed of the River Rhine.*

From the depths of the orchestra is heard a long-sustained tone, calm and motionless. After a time another is added and sustained with it; these tones will continue through the entire prelude. In the midst of this stream of sound, other tones soon become audible, moving slowly upwards. This upward motion continues steadily until it is transformed into a constant and overlapping series of gentle undulations. In time these undulations are imbued with a more fluid motion and rise gradually higher. The motion now grows more rapid, surging ever upwards, in great waves of tone, until the entire orchestra is participating in this onward-flowing movement. We are hearing a semblance of what we actually behold at the rise of the curtain—the depths of the mighty river Rhine.

Here, through the greenish twilight of the waters at the bottom of the river, the three Rhine-maidens sing their nonsensical and carefree song of "*Weia! Waga!*" as they playfully swim about. Their games are interrupted, however, by the crouching dwarf Alberich, who approaches and attempts to make love to them. One by one, after urging him on with fair words, they laugh scornfully at the misshapen dwarf and swim away, eluding his grasp as he clambers over the rocks in an effort to catch one of them. Finally he remains gazing after the maidens in angry despair, thwarted in his attempt at love-making. But now the light of the sun begins to penetrate the waters and there is reflected from the pinnacle of one of the rocks a bright golden gleam. Against a shimmering accompaniment of violins we

The Rhinemaidens as seen at Bayreuth in 1876 with the young Lilli Lehmann in the center as Woglinde. Later on she became one of the greatest Brünnhildes.

hear the motive of "The Rhinegold." The maidens, rejoicing in the radiance, sing their exultant song in praise of the gold.

On questioning them, the greatly interested Alberich learns that this gleaming substance is the Rhinegold, of which the maidens are the guardians. Though valueless enough here, if forged into a ring, the gold would give the possessor unlimited wealth and power over gods and men. But in order to be able to forge such a ring, the owner must first renounce love. All this the chattering Rhine-maidens carelessly reveal. They have nothing to fear, for no being would ever renounce love, least of all this lecherous Alberich. Therefore, they swim about lightheartedly. The heedful Alberich, however, rapidly climbs up among the rocks. Thinking he is pursuing them, the maidens swim away, shouting in mock terror. Alberich renounces all love, seizes the gold, and disappears. The maidens follow in a vain attempt to catch the thief. The music rushes wildly downwards. The waters, bereft of the gold, are left in total darkness, a darkness that becomes like a dense cloud which in time dissolves into a light mist.

SCENE: *High above the Rhine valley.*

As the mist vanishes in the morning sunshine, a lofty mountaintop is revealed. On still another mountain peak in the distance, across the valley of the Rhine, is seen a mighty castle with towering pinnacles. From the orchestra is now heard the majestic "Valhalla" motive. As the day grows brighter, we behold Wotan, ruler of the gods, and his consort Fricka, who are just awakening from sleep.

The great castle Valhalla (in German, *Walhalla*) has been built for the gods by the giants, Wotan having recklessly promised in payment the beautiful goddess of love, Freia. Even while his wife upbraids him for this rash promise, Freia rushes to them for protection against the giants, who follow, claiming their reward. Freia's cries for help bring her brothers Froh and Donner to the scene. Wotan is now faced with a dilemma. For it is this same Freia who keeps the golden apples that enable the gods to live in perpetual youth. Without her they will all grow old and perish. Yet Wotan has promised her to the giants, swearing to keep his word by the sacred runes of his spear. As guardian of the law through which alone the gods remain gods, he is compelled to respect his oath. With the hope that some substitute could be found acceptable to the giants in place of Freia, he has sent Loge, the tricky god of fire, over the earth to search for one. Just as the indignant giants are about to drag away the weeping goddess, Loge appears. This subtle diplomat announces that nowhere on earth has he found anyone who did not cherish youth and love. As he sings of the universal sway of love, the orchestra sounds the theme of Freia, glowing in great beauty. The giants seem triumphant.

In a rage Wotan turns to Loge—is this his promised help? Then Loge remembers the dwarf Alberich, who did forswear love and after stealing the Rhinegold and forging of it a ring, was now amassing a vast treasure in the lower world. The giants say that this treasure will be acceptable to them in place of the goddess, but, no longer trusting Wotan, they take Freia as hostage until they shall be paid. Bereft of her presence, the gods immediately grow pallid and weak. The mountaintop is shrouded in a mist. Wotan, lost in thought, finally resolves to descend to Nibelheim and wrest the treasure from Alberich. Preceded by Loge, he enters a cavern leading to the underworld. Sulphurous vapors arising from the cavern obscure the scene, and as they mount rapidly higher the theater seems to descend into the earth. The orchestra accompanies with a vividly descriptive passage, the leading motives of "Loge," "Gold," and "Flight" being beautifully woven into the symphonic web. In time a red glow shines from a distance, and the sound of hammering on innumerable tiny anvils grows louder, then recedes. The motive that now dominates the orchestra is associated both with the idea of a "Forge" and the "Nibelungs," who are the smithies.

SCENE: *The caverns of Nibelheim.*

As the clanging of anvils dies away, we see a great subterranean cave—the abode of Alberich. Through the power of the Ring he has enslaved all the dwarfs of Nibelheim. Mercilessly he compels them to amass the treasures concealed in the bowels of the earth. Through the power of the Ring he has forced his brother dwarf Mime, a skillful craftsman, to forge for him a magic Tarnhelm that will enable the wearer to change his form or render himself invisible. Having thus made himself invisible, he now beats his slaves and the groveling Mime ferociously. Wotan and Loge approach. They flatter Alberich on his power and cunning and cleverly coax him to exhibit the magic of the Tarnhelm. At Loge's suggestion, he first transforms himself into a dragon. Loge pretends to be terrified and then says that he

Erda (Jean Madeira) in Wieland Wagner's modern Bayreuth production

Paul Kuen as Mime at a postwar Bayreuth Festival

doubts Alberich's ability to turn himself into something very small, a toad, for instance. This, too, Alberich does—and Wotan quickly puts his foot on the toad. Thus Alberich is captured, bound, and dragged back to the upper world.

SCENE: *The mountain peak above the Rhine valley.*

On the mountaintop the enfeebled gods are still waiting in gloom and silence when Wotan and Loge return with the cowering dwarf. Alberich is forced to order his slaves to bring up from the underworld all his acquired wealth. Then he is compelled to part with the Tarnhelm and the Ring, the source of his power, for these Wotan wishes to keep for himself. Alberich trembles with rage at this loss. When he is released, he pauses before going away and utters a terrific curse upon the Ring. Let it bring death and destruction to whoever possesses it. Thus will the gods who have robbed him of his power be destroyed.

While the baleful motive of the "Curse" is still ringing in our ears, the giants now return with Freia. The treasures are heaped before her, since it is agreed that not until the goddess of love is concealed by the gold will the giants give her up. Yet with all the treasure, and even the Tarnhelm added, Fasolt still sees Freia's eye shining through the pile. The Ring is needed, but this Wotan refuses to sacrifice. In a misty light, there suddenly rises from the mountain Erda, the all-knowing, all-foreseeing goddess of the earth. With the utmost solemnity she warns him to surrender the Ring before dire calamities befall them all.

Wotan would detain her to learn more, but she sinks again into the earth, with a final cry of warning. Shaken by her awesome prophecy of doom, Wotan casts the Ring on the heap. Freia is released, and the giants, starting away with their treasure, at once quarrel over the Ring. Fafner kills his brother Fasolt—the curse on the Ring, its gold, and its power, is already at work. But the mountains still remain shrouded in murky clouds. These, Donner, god of thunder, summons to himself and, swinging his mighty hammer, disappears in a storm.

And now, gleaming in the light of the setting sun, Valhalla has become visible. Like a bridge across the valley a glowing rainbow has formed, and a theme of stunning power is now heard in the orchestra. Turning to Wotan, Froh urges him to make his way across this bridge without fear.

The god, lost in contemplation of the castle, sings ecstatically of the promised safety and shelter of this new home. Bidden to join him on the trip to Valhalla, Fricka asks why he so names the castle. Enigmatically, Wotan replies that the future will explain the name.

As the gods proceed toward the bridge, Loge, remaining behind, looks after them and muses scornfully on the flaming end that awaits these proud gods glorying in their "overwhelming strength."

He follows the gods with sly unconcern. From the valley the Rhinemaidens are heard lamenting their lost gold: "Rhinegold! Rarest gold! . . . for thee now we implore. . . . O give us our glory again!" Wotan is annoyed by the sound of their plaint; at his command Loge calls down to them: "Ye in the water! Disturb us not. . . . If the gold gleams no longer upon you, then bask in the gods' augmented grandeur!" The gods laughingly turn again toward the bridge while the lamenting Rhinemaidens reply:

Rhinegold! Rarest gold!
O might but again
In the wave thy pure magic wake!
What is of worth dwells but in the waters!
Base and bad those who are throned above.

Wotan halts for a moment as if seized by a mighty thought. From the orchestra there now thunders forth, in an impressive cadence, the motive of "The Sword"—the sword which the god hopes will bring him salvation. Then, while the gods continue their journey across the bridge to Valhalla, the theme of the "Rainbow" is heard, majestic and glowing in iridescent beauty.

Salzburg Easter Festival, 1968: Wotan (Dietrich Fischer-Dieskau) invites the gods to enter Valhalla

Die Walküre

THE VALKYRIE

CHARACTERS

Wotan, *ruler of the gods*	*Bass-Baritone*	Hunding, *Sieglinde's husband*	*Bass*
Fricka, *his wife*	*Mezzo-Soprano*	The eight other Valkyries,	
Sieglinde ⎱ *his mortal children*	*Soprano*	*daughters of Woltan*	*Sopranos and*
Siegmund ⎰	*Tenor*	*and Erda*	*Mezzo-sopranos*
Brünnhilde, *a Valkyrie, Wotan's*			
daughter by Erda	*Soprano*		

MUSIC DRAMA in three acts; the "first day," of the *Ring des Nibelungen.* Text and music by Richard Wagner. First produced, June 26, 1870, at Munich. First performance in the United States, April 2, 1877, at the Academy of Music, New York. First heard at the Metropolitan Opera on January 30, 1885, with Leopold Damrosch conducting and Amalia Materna as Brünnhilde.

ACT I

SCENE: *The interior of Hunding's dwelling.* The orchestral Prelude, one of Wagner's most descriptive passages, is a vivid portrayal of a tempest: the steady beating of the rain, the crash of thunder, and the hurried tread of a solitary man in flight through the forest.

The storm subsides, the curtain rises, disclosing the interior of Hunding's dwelling—a curious abode of hides and crudely hewn timber, built around the stem of a great ash tree. A fire glows on the hearth. Suddenly the door opens, Siegmund appears, staggers weakly to the fireside, and falls exhausted before it, exclaiming, "Whoever may own this house, here must I rest!"

Sieglinde enters from another room, thinking she has heard her husband return. She is surprised to find a stranger lying at the hearth. At his request she hurries to bring him a draft of water. Siegmund revives, and they converse, finding a mysterious sympathy in one another. Siegmund would hurry away, for he has ever brought misfortune with him. Sieglinde replies that he can bring no further misfortune to this abode of unhappiness. He decides to wait for her husband Hunding, who soon arrives. During the evening meal which Sieglinde prepares, Siegmund tells of his destressful life; how, when a boy, returning with his father Wälse from the chase, he found his home burned, his mother slain, and his twin sister vanished. This crime was done by the Neidungs, who from that time relentlessly pursued father and son. Then one day the elder Wälse himself disappeared. And now, wandering alone through the forest, Siegmund attempted to rescue a girl whose family were about to give her up to a hated lover, but overwhelmed by numbers, he was forced to flee. Thus it is that Hunding recognizes in Siegmund the enemy whom he and his kinsmen have been pursuing. Now, however, though weaponless in his enemy's house, Siegmund is his guest and therefore safe, under the ancient law of hospitality. With a threat as to what dawn will bring, Hunding retires for the night, preceded by Sieglinde.

Alone in the room, now entirely dark save for the

Act I in Herbert von Karajan's 1967 Salzburg staging, with Gundula Janowitz (Sieglinde) and Jon Vickers (Siegmund)

glow on the hearth, Siegmund broods on his hapless fate. Then, as for a moment he thinks of the beautiful woman who showed him compassion, the motive of their love is heard in the orchestra. Lamenting that she should be the thrall of his enemy, he cries out, "Wälse, Wälse, where is thy sword?" for he remembers that his father had promised him a weapon whenever he should need it desperately. At this moment the fire on the hearth flickers up, and a ray of its light falls on the hilt of a sword plunged into the stem of the ash tree. Siegmund wonders what this gleam might be; then the glowing embers fade, and he lies down to sleep.

A moment later the door opens, and Sieglinde comes stealthily into the room. She whispers the information that she has put an opiate in her husband's evening draft in order that she might be able to reveal a weapon to the stranger. She now tells of her forced marriage to Hunding; how, while her kinsmen sat at the wedding feast, a stranger entered the hall—an old man with one eye hidden by his hat, and the gleam of his single eye struck terror into the hearts of all except Sieglinde. Disdaining the assembly, the old man drew a sword from his belt and with a mighty swing thrust it deep into the trunk of the ash tree. There the sword remains, for though many have tried, the stranger decreed that only one, a great hero, should withdraw it. "Oh, that I might find that man," Sieglinde exclaims, "for in him also should I find the one who shall rescue me from my woe!"

Siegmund, holding Seiglinde in an ardent embrace, replies, "The man for whom the sword and the wife were decreed holds you in his arms!" Suddenly, the great door of the house swings open; Sieglinde starts back in fright. "Who went?" she cries. Siegmund, drawing her tenderly in his arms again, tells her that no one departed, but that spring entered. The beauty of the moonlit woods now pervades the room, and Siegmund, gazing rapturously upon Sieglinde, apostrophizes the spring night, singing the lovely melody known as the "Spring Song."

In her rapture, Sieglinde answers, "Thou art the spring for which I have longed in frosty winter's spell. At thy first glance my pulses leaped. I knew that in thee all that lay hidden in my breast was awakened!" Tenderly Siegmund replies, "Oh, sweetest wonder! Woman above all! . . . What has entangled my heart now do I know! I stand and gaze upon thee in wonder!"

Sieglinde looks at Siegmund with increasing amazement as his features begin to awaken a memory of the past. She has seen herself reflected in the forest stream, and now when she looks upon Siegmund it is as if she regarded her own face. Siegmund replies that he has long had a dream image of her in his heart. In growing excitement Sieglinde asks, "Was Wälse thy father? Art thou a Wälsung!" On learning this is so, Sieglinde cries out ecstatically, "Struck then for thee was the sword! Now may I name thee, as thou hast ever been known and loved . . . Siegmund! So name I thee!"

Springing from Sieglinde's arms, Siegmund runs to the tree and places his hands upon the hilt of the sword that lies buried there, exclaiming, "Nothung! [Needful] so now I name thee, sword! come from thy

351

Hans Hotter as Wotan, the king of the gods

Gottlob Frick as Hunding, husband of Sieglinde

scabbard to me!'' With a powerful effort he draws out the sword and brandishes it before Sieglinde, who utters a cry of joy. ''Siegmund of the Wälsungs stands before thee! As bridal gift he brings this sword. Let us fly from this house, into the laughing world of spring!'' Embracing fervently, they rush forth into the forest to the accompaniment of wildly pulsating music in the orchestra.

ACT II

SCENE: *A wild and rocky pass.* There is an agitated orchestral prelude descriptive of the flight of the Wälsungs through forest and mountains. After a time a new theme, ''The Valkyries,'' enters proudly in the bass, for at the rise of the curtain Brünnhilde, the favorite of Wotan's Valkyries, is seen. She is clad in battle array and stands on a cliff over a rock-strewn mountain pass. Wotan, also fully armed, comes up the pass and, addressing her, orders her to defend Siegmund in the coming struggle. The Valkyrie dashes up the rocky height, singing the battle cry of the Valkyries: ''Ho-yo-to-ho!''

On reaching a high peak, she looks around her, then calls back to Wotan, ''Take warning, Father, prepare yourself for strife; Fricka approaches stormily . . . I leave you to her, I prefer the fighting of heroes!'' Resuming her wild cry, she disappears over the mountain.

Fricka is thoroughly enraged because of the illegal love of the Wälsung pair. *''So ist es denn aus, mit den ewigen Göttern?''* (''Have the eternal gods,

then, come to this?'') she cries. The offended Hunding has prayed to her for justice, and as goddess of marriage she must punish the guilty. In vain Wotan tells why he became the father of these Wälsungs—how, enjoined from wresting the treasure from Fafner, he had hoped to raise a hero who of his own free will would recover the Ring and prevent its falling into the hands of Alberich. But Fricka demands righteousness, taunting Wotan with trying to deceive her with deep explanations: *''Mit tiefem Sinne willst du mich täuschen?''* Siegmund must fall before Hunding, she warns, and Wotan, again compelled to uphold the law which gives him his power, reluctantly agrees.

As Fricka, proud in her triumph, departs, Brünnhilde returns to receive Wotan's further commands. She asks him the cause of his dejection. Wotan springs to his feet with an outburst of profound anguish: ''Oh, infinite shame!'' Frightened, Brünnhilde entreats him to reveal the source of his sorrow.

Wotan now dejectedly narrates to her the story of the heroes he has had gathered in Valhalla by his Valkyrie daughters. Brünnhilde asks, ''Have we ever failed?'' Wotan further divulges that the danger lies with Alberich's hosts, who in revenge for the loss of the Ring are working to overthrow the gods. In despair he exclaims, ''Fade splendor of godhood! . . . one thing only I await . . . the downfall . . . the end!'' In the utmost bitterness he cries out, ''Blessings on thee, Nibelung son! May thou inherit the empty pomp of the gods!''

''What must I do, then?'' asks Brünnhilde in alarm. ''Fight for Fricka,'' he replies. ''Ah, but you love Siegmund, and him will I shield!'' she counters. Again Wotan commands, ''Siegmund must fall!'' Brünnhilde, ever mindful of Wotan's inmost will, exclaims, ''I will shield him whom thou hast taught me to love!'' Infuriated by this show of defiance, Wotan cries, ''Dost thou scorn me? Siegmund shall fall! This be thy task!'' He storms away up the mountain, leaving Brünnhilde confused and frightened. Dejectedly she takes up her weapons and enters a cavern overlooking the mountain pass.

A tumultuous orchestral passage now calls to mind the flight of the Wälsungs, and a moment later the young couple appear, faltering and exhausted. In her growing panic Sieglinde has run ahead of Siegmund and, despite her fatigue, is anxious to go farther ahead. But Siegmund lovingly calls to her, ''Here rest awhile; Siegmund will guard thee safe.'' He overtakes her and embraces her tenderly while she gazes into his eyes. Then she starts away in sudden remorse, crying, ''Away, away! Fly from the profane one!'' Her mood suddenly changing, she confesses: ''Within your arms I found all that had awakened my love!'' Again she draws back overwhelmed with horror, pleading, ''Leave me, lest I bring dishonor upon thee!'' Siegmund exclaims, ''Fly no farther! Nothung, my sword, shall pierce the enemy's heart!'' Sieglinde does not hear him, for in her apprehension she believes Hunding and his kinsmen are approaching. In delirious terror, she cries out, then gazing vaguely about, whispers, ''Where art thou, Siegmund?'' For a moment she rests on his bosom, then starts up, exclaiming, ''Hark! Hunding's horn . . . you fall . . . the sword is in splinters!'' She sinks fainting in Siegmund's arms.

And now Brünnhilde emerges from the cavern.

The ominous ''Fate'' motive and ''Death Song'' are heard, stern and ominous. ''Siegmund,'' she calls, ''look on me . . . the messenger of death to warriors! Wotan awaits thee in Valhalla!'' Siegmund asks whom he will find in Valhalla. Brünnhilde answers, ''Wotan . . . glorious heroes . . . wish maidens . . . but Sieglinde, no, she must remain on earth.'' Siegmund bids her greet Valhalla for him; he will not go where Sieglinde is not. In her astonishment Brünnhilde asks, ''Dost thou prize Valhalla so lightly?'' Siegmund raises his eyes to Brünnhilde in scorn. ''Thou seemst fair and young, now I know thee hard and cruel. Feast on my distress!'' Deeply moved, Brünnhilde asks to guard his bride. ''None other than I shall shield her . . . may death unite us!'' cries Siegmund, drawing his sword as if to run it through Sieglinde's heart. Brünnhilde, moved by such devotion, impulsively springs forward. ''Stop! Ye both shall live, triumph shall be yours!'' And so saying, she vanishes up the mountainside.

Siegmund remains lost in thought, as storm clouds gather over the mountaintop. Hunding's horn call is heard. Siegmund kisses the sleeping Sieglinde in farewell, then, calling a challenge, rushes after the enemy and disappears among the clouds. Sieglinde restlessly dreams of her home, her father, her mother, the ominous stranger, the house in flames. She awakens in fright, calling, ''Help, Siegmund!'' She can see nothing but the dark clouds, through which are heard the voices of the combatants still seeking one another, and finally meeting on the summit of the mountain. As Sieglinde staggers toward them, there is a sudden flash of lightning, and she falls back. Brünnhilde's voice is heard urging Siegmund to attack Hunding. Yet even as Siegmund raises his sword, a ruddy glow in the clouds reveals

Olive Fremstad as Sieglinde, Wotan's mortal daughter

James King as Siegmund, her brother and lover

Wotan stretching forth his spear; on it the sword is shattered. Hunding strikes the disarmed Siegmund dead, and Sieglinde, horrified, falls fainting. Brünnhilde leaps from the rocky cliff, snatches up the pieces of the broken sword, and, lifting Sieglinde before her on the saddle, vanishes down the gorge. Wotan, in grim dejection, turns upon Hunding: "Go, slave, tell Fricka that I have avenged her!" And at the god's gesture of contempt Hunding falls dead. Then, bursting into terrible wrath, Wotan cries, "But, Brünnhilde, the disobedient—vengeance upon her!" and disappears amid a turmoil of thunder and lightning.

ACT III

SCENE: *On the summit of a rocky mountain.* One of Wagner's most stirring descriptive passages is heard at the beginning of this act—the famous "Ride of the Valkyries," picturing, with amazing vigor and realism, the wild neighing and rapid galloping of the magic steeds of the Valkyries as they dash through the storm to their retreat.

Their meeting place is the summit of a mountain, rocky and barren, with a dark cavern beneath its highest peak and a somber forest below. In the vast space beyond the precipitous edge of the mountain-top, clouds are driven before a storm. On the uppermost peak four of the nine Valkyries stand, awaiting their sisters, whom they signal with their savage war cry "Ho-yo-to-ho!" Two others answer the call as they arrive, galloping through the air on their steeds, fleet as the clouds, and wild as the lightning that plays about them. The six that have now arrived join in the war cry as they hear Rossweisse and Grimgerde approaching. They laugh wildly at their jests, then, seeing they are but eight, ask, "Where is Brünnhilde?" Suddenly Waltraute sees her coming, riding in terrifying haste and carrying not a warrior but a woman. All run forward to meet Brünnhilde. "Sister, what has happened?" they cry out in horror at her daring. Sieglinde, fully aroused now, urges Brünnhilde to escape. As for herself, she would rather be united in death with Siegmund. Brünnhilde, however, commands her to live, for she will be the mother of a child by Siegmund. Thrilled by the prophecy, Sieglinde now pleads for safety and protection. The Valkyries know of a place in the forest to the east where a dragon guards Alberich's Ring and where Wotan never goes. Sieglinde will be safe there. But no time must be lost, for the clouds grow darker and Wotan approaches. Brünnhilde urges Sieglinde, "Fly to the eastward! be brave to endure all ills . . . remember only: you bear in your womb the world's most glorious hero!" She

gives her the splinters of Siegmund's sword, saying, "I saved these from his father's death field . . . he shall wield the sword reforged . . . Siegfried let him be called!" To the ecstatic motive of "Redemption Through Love" Sieglinde, deeply moved, replies, "O radiant wonder . . . farewell . . . I go to save the loved one for him we both loved . . . be blessed in Sieglinde's woe!" Sieglinde then hurries away. A moment later Wotan, drawing near in the lowering storm clouds, calls, "Stay, Brünnhilde!" The Valkyries cry out in terror, but generously conceal the recreant daughter in their midst. Wotan strides upon the scene, fiercely demanding, "Where is Brünnhilde?" The terror-stricken Valkyries try to evade his question. Sternly he commands, "Shield her not . . . Brünnhilde, come forth!" The warrior-maid comes slowly from among her sisters, saying meekly, "Here am I . . . pronounce my punishment." Wotan answers, "I will not chastise thee. . . . Thou art no longer a child of my will . . . no longer a Valkyrie!"

Brünnhilde anxiously asks, "Dost thou cast me off?" Wotan explains sadly: "No more will I send thee from Valhalla . . . thou art forever banished from my sight. Bereft of thy godhood, thou shalt be as other women . . . to be claimed by the first passing churl." The other Valkyries are loud in their lamentation. Wotan commands them to flee the spot forever, or share a like doom, and, still grieving, they ride quickly away. Wotan and Brünnhilde remain in silence, the Valkyrie prostrate before her father. Slowly she raises her head, and timidly asks, "Was it so shameful, what I have done, that my offenses are so sternly punished?" She whispers to Wotan the secret of the Wälsungs—no craven will come from that race. "Name them not, they are outcasts with thee!" cries Wotan. He decrees that she shall be chained in sleep, a wife for the first passing stranger who wakes her. "Let horrors ward off all but a fearless hero!" pleads Brünnhilde.

"Too much thou askest!" "Then crush out my life, but let me not suffer such shame!" Seized by a sudden inspiration, Brünnhilde implores, "Oh, enkindle a fire around this rock to sear the craven who dares approach!"

Overpowered with emotion, Wotan turns eagerly toward her, raises her to her feet, and, gazing lovingly into her eyes, sings a poignant farewell to his favorite daughter. Brünnhilde sinks transfigured on Wotan's breast; then looks up into his face with deep emotion while he continues his tragic soliloquy in ever-growing anguish.

At length he places a long kiss on Brünnhilde's eyelids, and she sinks gradually into a deep slumber. Wotan lowers her onto a grassy mound overshadowed by a huge fir tree. He gazes sadly upon her, closes her war helmet, and covers her with her great shield. Then he moves slowly away, pausing to look back once again. Resolutely, he now goes to a large rock that juts from the summit of the mountain. Striking it with his spear, he summons Loge:

> *Loge, hear! Listen and heed!*
> *Appear, wavering spirit, and spread me thy*
> *Fire around this fell!*
> *Loge! Loge! Loge!*

As Wotan strikes the rock for the third time, flames pour forth and spread.

The music of Loge, god of fire and deceit, flares upward with a roar, then assumes a constantly flickering form. As the flames surround Wotan, he commandingly directs them to encircle the mountaintop. Once again holding out his spear, he utters a spell:

> *He who my spear feareth*
> *Never shall cross this fiery wall.*

He casts one sorrowful glance at the sleeping Brünnhilde and turns slowly to depart. As he reaches the fire he again looks back, then disappears through the flames.

Act III at the Metropolitan Opera, 1967: Wotan (Thomas Stewart) storms onto the Valkyries' rock in search of his disobedient daughter, Brünnhilde

Siegfried

CHARACTERS

Wotan, *disguised as the "Wanderer"* — Bass-Baritone

Siegfried, *son of Siegmund and Sieglinde* — Tenor

Mime } *brother Nibelungs* — Tenor
Alberich } — Bass-Baritone

Fafner, *giant transformed into a dragon* — Bass

Forest Bird — Soprano

Erda, *the earth goddess* — Contralto

Brünnhilde, *formerly a Valkyrie, now a mortal* — Soprano

MUSIC DRAMA in three acts; the third work in the tetralogy *Der Ring des Nibelungen*. Words and music by Richard Wagner. First performance, Bayreuth, Germany, August 16, 1876. American première, Metropolitan Opera House, New York, November 9, 1887 with Max Alvary as Siegfried and Lilli Lehmann as Brünnhilde, Anton Seidl conducting.

ACT I

SCENE: *Mime's cave in a forest.* A dark, sinister orchestral prelude, built largely from motives associated with Alberich and Mime, prepares us for the opening of the first act. In a large cavern Mime has set himself up a smithy. In this, his gloomy abode, he sits busily working at his anvil, soliloquizing meanwhile on his unhappy lot, and his musings, involve such matters as the Golden Hoard, the hammering in the Nibelung smithshops, servitude, and, finally, the Ring. No matter how strong a sword he makes, the boy Siegfried breaks it asunder. Yet he cannot succeed in welding together the fragments of Siegmund's broken sword Nothung; with that for a weapon Siegfried could quickly triumph over Fafner, who, transformed by the magic of the Tarnhelm into a dragon, still guards the Ring. With his cunning, Mime could then easily obtain the Ring from the unsophisticated Siegfried. And now that joyous youth enters from the sunlit woods, clad in his rude forest garb and leading a bear by a rope toward Mime. The dwarf runs in precipitous haste to hide himself. Siegfried laughs, and then, having driven the bear off to the woods, demands his new sword from Mime. The dwarf timorously gives it to Siegfried, who shatters the weapon with one blow and complains of this "silly switch." Mime brings food as a peace offering; Siegfried, sprawling on a mossy couch, kicks the food aside—he will prepare his own meals. Why does he continue to come here, he asks, when he feels such a loathing for this groveling dwarf. Mime attempts to persuade him that it is because he is his father, and Siegfried scornfully refuses to believe him. Now he will have the truth, and he nearly throttles the dwarf in his endeavor to gain it. Mime finally confesses that the boy is the son of an unfortunate fugitive who, overwhelmed with sorrow, sought refuge here, and died in giving birth to him. Siegfried shows great emotion, then, fearing lest the crafty dwarf be deceiving him, demands evidence. Mime produces the fragments of Nothung. Siegfried, thrilled with the thought of owning his father's weapon, orders Mime to forge the pieces into a sword and runs back into the forest.

While the dwarf is still brooding over this impossible task, Wotan appears, disguised as the Wanderer. Mime is appalled at the one-eyed warrior towering above him, especially when the Wanderer carelessly touches the earth with his long spear and a soft roll of thunder follows. The dwarf vainly suggests to the Wanderer that he go elsewhere. The visitor insists on remaining; he will answer at the price of his life any three questions Mime can propound. After successfully answering three riddles regarding the Nibelungs, the giants, and the gods, the Wanderer asks three himself at the same price. Mime successfully answers the first two regarding the birth of Siegfried and the sword, but is terrified at the third: Who will repair Nothung? This is the one thing Mime wishes to know, yet foolishly neglected to ask. Before the Wanderer departs, he generously refuses to collect his wager—Mime's head—but admonishes him to guard well his head, for it may become a prize to him who does not know fear—the forger of Nothung.

Mime remains a prey to the wildest imaginings, and when Siegfried returns, he finds the dwarf hiding behind the anvil. When he asks for the reforged sword of his father, Mime replies by asking what would a sword avail him if he know not fear? Moreover, the dwarf says, the dying Sieglinde bade him teach her son to fear ere he ventured into the world. Siegfried is impatient to learn this mysterious thing. Has he never felt a strange trembling in the depths of the forest as night falls, asks the dwarf; then Mime will take him to the great dragon Fafner; there Siegfried shall learn to fear. The youth is enthusiastic, but first he must have his sword. Mime is compelled to confess that it is impossible for him to forge the broken pieces. Siegfried then says he will himself reforge his father's broken weapon! In joyous excitement he files the pieces into powder, pours this into a crucible and places it on the forge. Then while he lustily blows the fire with the bellows, he sings for sheer youthful exuberance; the orchestra furnishes a wonderful picture of the fire as it flames up, casting off glowing sparks.

Mime realizes that the sword will now be forged— the Ring will fall into Siegfried's hands. While the youth continues with his task, singing the while the exciting "Forging Song," pouring the molten metal into a mold, plunging that into cold water, then hammering the newly formed blade on the anvil, Mime sets about to prepare a poisonous brew, for in his simple mind he has concocted an elementary plan: He will offer this brew to the boy as soon as he has slain the dragon, the thirsty youth will drink, and the Ring and its power will be Mime's! Siegfried brandishes his newly refashioned weapon and with one blow cleaves the anvil from top to bottom before the amazed and terrified Mime. The motives of "The Sword" and "Siegfried's Horn Call" rush into a jubilant prestissimo while the hero holds aloft the sword, shouting with glee.

Astrid Varnay as Brünnhilde

ACT II

SCENE: *Fafner's cave in a deep forest.* The orchestra plays another ominous prelude in which, against the shuddering of violins, is heard the theme of the giants, distorted to represent Fafner the dragon. There also enter the motives of "The Curse," "The Ring," and that of "Annihilation." In the almost inklike blackness of night we scarcely are able to discern the author of that curse, Alberich, as he sits gloomily watching before Fafner's cave in the depths of the woods, still hoping to regain the Ring. Here arrives the Wanderer, accompanied by the lightning and thunder of a sudden storm. Alberich accuses the god of coming to interfere in the course of events, which Wotan denies, saying that it is only Mime who desires the Ring, not Siegfried or himself, and in proof of this suggests to Alberich that he should call the dragon and offer to save his life in exchange for the Ring. But Fafner, aroused from his tranquil slumber and warned of the approach of his doom at the hands of a youth, refuses to give up any of his hoarded treasure. "I lie and possess," he answers. "Let me sleep." Then Alberich and the Wanderer go their separate ways, and as dawn creeps through the woodland, Mime and Siegfried approach. Now, says the dwarf, Siegfried shall learn to fear, but his prating of love and gratitude only awakens the boy's anger, and Mime slinks off muttering to himself, "Would that Siegfried and Fafner might kill each other."

Siegfried stretches himself out comfortably under a tree and, looking after the departing dwarf, exclaims that he is happy that Mime is no father of his. In the orchestra there is heard gradually rising, like a faint whisper, the wonderful music descriptive of the rustling sounds of the forest, the "Forest Murmurs." Siegfried begins his meditation, while the murmuring of the forest grows around him. He wonders about his father and his mother. Finally his attention is attracted by the song of a bird. He playfully tries to answer it on a reed. He decides he can do better on his horn, and sounds a rousing call. This awakens Fafner, who comes clumsily from his cave, and the youth, laughing at the sight, resolutely places himself in the dragon's path. In the battle that ensues, Siegfried, avoiding the lashing tail and venomous teeth, deftly plunges his sword into the monster's heart, and Fafner, though sorely wounded, admires the bravery of the young man, cautioning him, "He who led you blindly to do this deed surely plots for your death!" He sinks, dying, to the ground.

In withdrawing his sword, Siegfried receives a drop of the dragon's blood on his hand. Involuntarily he carries his hand to his lips. The result of having tasted the dragon's blood is that he can understand the song of the birds. The bird who sang for him before now tells him clearly of the Tarnhelm and the Ring. Siegfried enters the cave to search for these treasures. While he is gone, Alberich and Mime come forth from the hiding places whence they have been looking on. Their bitter quarrel as to who shall claim the Ring is ended abruptly by the reappearance of Siegfried, who has innocently taken just those two things from the dragon's hoard. Alberich vanishes with a dark threat, and Mime, with seemingly fair words, tries to induce the young hero to partake of a supposedly refreshing drink. Siegfried, however, having tasted the dragon's blood, can understand the significance of Mime's fawning deceit, and in a final burst of anger draws his sword and kills the dwarf, then drags Mime's corpse and also the body of the dead dragon into the cave. He soon emerges, and, exclaiming at the heat of the midday which sends the blood coursing through his head, throws himself down to rest under a tree. Looking up, he notices the bird twittering about with its "brothers and sisters," and is reminded that he has none.

His new-found friend tells him of a wonderful maiden who sleeps on a mountaintop girt round by protecting flames. With a shout of joy, Siegfried asks to be shown the way, and as the bird flutters off, he follows along the ground in eager pursuit.

The motive of "The Bird" dominates this scene. Mingled with it are heard the themes of "Fire," "Siegfried," his "Horn Call," and an often repeated impetuous passage expressive of Siegfried's youthful ardor. As the hero runs away, excitedly following the bird, the music swells to an exuberant climax and comes to a close with a brief passage that flutters captivatingly upward.

ACT III

SCENE 1: *A wild region.* A tempestuous orchestral prelude of unusual magnificence introduces the third act. The rhythm of "The Ride," and the motives of the "Distress of the Gods," "The Rhine," "The Fall of the Gods," "Alberich," "Sleep," "Fate," and "Wotan's Spear," all enter, with singular beauty and appropriateness. As we hear the mysterious harmonies of "Sleep," the curtain rises, revealing a savage, barren and rocky country, shrouded in obscurity. Wotan, the Wanderer, halts before a cave in the mountainside, and with great solemnity invokes the goddess of the earth.

The cavern begins to glow with a bluish light, and Erda slowly rises from the earth, her hair and garments shimmering as with hoarfrost. Dreamily she asks who wakens her. Wotan replies that he has come to her, the wisest of all beings, to learn her counsel. She wearily answers that her sleep is dreaming, dreaming that brings wisdom; but the Norns are ever awake, weaving the rope of fate from her knowledge; let him seek their counsel. Wotan, however, would not know the future; he would alter its course. Then Erda calls to mind that she once submitted to Wotan's will, bore him a daughter, the Valkyrie; why does he not seek the far-seeing Brünnhilde? The god informs her of the punishment that he has been compelled to inflict on the rebel warrior-maid; can he consult her who is no longer one of the gods? Erda is unwilling to counsel him who punishes the Valkyrie for having done his will; who, though he is a god and the upholder of truth, holds his sway through falsehood. She would return to her sleep. Wotan is resolved to accept his fate, to welcome his doom. The world, which in anger he had left to the Nibelung, he now bequeaths to the son of the Wälsungs. The splendid theme of "The Heritage of the World" is heard briefly in the orchestra. This hero, Wotan says, having gained the Ring, will awaken Brünnhilde, and she shall win the world's freedom. Gladly will Wotan yield to the eternally young. "Away, then," he says, "mother of all fear, to endless sleep, away, away!" Erda sinks into the earth.

Act III at Covent Garden: Brünnhilde (Birgit Nilsson) awakens to the kiss of Siegfried (Wolfgang Windgassen)

Wotan awaits Siegfried, who appears with the approach of dawn and demands right of way from this stranger barring his path. Wotan questions him good-humoredly and learns of the death of Fafner. He asks, too, whence comes the sword, and Siegfried answers he has forged it from a broken weapon. "Who was it first made that sword?" pursues Wotan. Siegfried answers that he cares not since a broken weapon is useless until repaired. Wotan laughs, but Siegfried becomes insistent to know the way to the fiery couch of Brünnhilde, the bird that directs him having flown. Wotan confesses that the black ravens that always accompany him have frightened the bird away, and adds that although he has always loved Siegfried's race, he was once compelled to shatter the sword of that youth's father; now he bids him beware and not arouse his ire, lest the sword be again so shattered. Siegfried cries out for joy, thinking that he has discovered his father's enemy and thus his own. Wotan angrily bars the path with his spear. Siegfried severs the weapon with a mighty blow of Nothung, and hurries excitedly up the mountainside. Wotan turns gloomily away.

The themes of "Fire," "Sleep," and "Siegfried's Horn Call" blend in a magnificent tumult while flames rise up and obscure the scene from view.

SCENE 2: *The Valkyr rock.* When the music and the flames subside, we again behold Brünnhilde still locked in her magic sleep on the desolate mountain-top. Siegfried approaches, wonderingly, and, seeing what he believes to be a sleeping knight in armor, raises the shield, removes the helmet, and cuts through with his sword the fastenings of the breast-plate. This discloses Brünnhilde in woman's dress, and Siegfried starts back in dismay. Now for the first time, the hero is shaken with what he believes to be fear. He attempts vainly to arouse her from her sleep, and at last kisses her on the lips. This breaks the spell, and Brünnhilde slowly awakens, while we hear in the orchestra the luminous chords introducing Brünnhilde's rhapsodic greeting to the world.

She greets the sun, the light, the radiant day, and asks who wakened her. The youth gazing at her, transfixed with rapture, answers that it is Siegfried who has released her from the spell. Brünnhilde continues her apostrophe; then, in music of glowing fervor, they sing joyously together.

Siegfried tries to embrace her, but Brünnhilde springs up, repulses him, and flies in the utmost terror to the opposite side of the mountaintop. She cries out in fright and shame— no god's touch has she felt! Siegfried's ardor is unabated, and already the godhood in Brünnhilde is waning. She pleads gently with the hero, calling to mind happy days that are vanished. She implores him to go his way. But soon Siegfried's ardor arouses her own, and in a duet, in which the motive of "Love's Resolution" is heard in the orchestra, the two young people fall into each other's arms, and the music swells ecstatically, while the motive of "Love's Rapture" and that of Siegfried join in a final joyous outburst.

359

Götterdämmerung

TWILIGHT OF THE GODS

CHARACTERS

Brünnhilde, *a former Valkyrie*	*Soprano*	Waltraute, *a Valkyrie*		*Mezzo-soprano*
Siegfried	*Tenor*	Woglinde		*Soprano*
Alberich, *a Nibelung*	*Bass-Baritone*	Wellgunde	*Rhine-maidens*	*Mezzo-soprano*
Gunther, *chief of the*		Flosshilde		*Mezzo-soprano*
Gibichungs	*Bass-Baritone*			*Contralto*
Gutrune, *his sister*	*Soprano*	Three Norns		*Mezzo-soprano*
Hagen, *son of Alberich and half brother*				*Soprano*
to Gunther	*Bass*			

MUSIC DRAMA in a prologue and three acts, the fourth work in the tetralogy *Der Ring des Nibelungen*. Music and text by Richard Wagner. Première, Bayreuth, August 17, 1876. First performance in the United States, Metropolitan Opera House, January 25, 1888, with Lilli Lehmann and Albert Niemann as Brünnhilde and Siegfried.

PROLOGUE

A brief though impressive orchestral prelude prepares us for the scene. In it are heard the themes of Brünnhilde's "Hail to the World," and "The Rhine" in somber hues. "Fate" sounds darkly, and the curtain rises, showing the Valkyrie's rock, now shrouded in the obscurity of night. The three Norns, the Fates of Scandinavian mythology, sit gloomily winding the rope of destiny. As they speak of the fire which Loge, at Wotan's order, maintains around the mountain, the theme of the magic flames is heard, vague, like a distant glow in the orchestra. The first Norn, unwinding a golden cord and fastening it to the fir tree, recalls that once it was a joy to perform her task, sheltered by the branches of the mighty world ash at the foot of which flowed the spring of wisdom. Wotan came to drink of the waters, she

continues, giving in payment therefore one of his eyes; he tore a branch from the world ash to make his spear. From that time the tree withered and fell in decay, and the spring became dry at its source. She then adds, "Sing, sister, for I throw you the rope . . . Know you what next befell?" The second Norn takes the rope and, having fastened it to a rock, sings as she weaves. She tells how Wotan engraved on his spear the runes of the treaties which gave him his power; how this weapon was shattered when the god opposed a young hero; how Wotan then commanded the warriors of Valhalla to destroy the world ash. "What next is decreed?" she asks, throwing the rope to the other sister. The third Norn continues the narrative: In Valhalla Wotan and his heroes sit in state; around the castle is piled the wood of the world ash. If that should be set afire, the gods will be destroyed. "Know you more?" she asks, throwing the rope back to the second Norn, who in turn throws it to the first, whose eyes are dimmed by sorrow. Wondering whether it is the dawn or the magic fire she sees, she asks what happened to Loge. The second Norn replies, telling how Wotan subdued Loge by means of his spear and bound him around Brünnhilde's rock. "Know you what then will befall?" she asks. The third Norn foresees that Wotan will plunge the broken pieces of his spear into the

Prologue as staged by Wieland Wagner, Bayreuth 1955: The Norns, Erda's daughters, wind the cord of fate

fire and then will cast the blazing spear into the heaped up boughs of the ash tree. "If you would know when this shall come to pass, give me the rope," cries the second Norn. The first Norn has it, however. "The night wanes," she sings, "I can grasp nothing more. I feel no longer the strands; the threads are broken. A dreadful sight overwhelms my senses; the Rhinegold that once Alberich stole, know you what came of that?"

The second Norn takes the rope again, fastening it to a rock. She cries in alarm, "The rope is breaking, cut by the rock! It is the curse of the Nibelung's Ring which gnaws at the strands! Know you what will hap?" The third Norn takes the rope. It is too slack, and as she stretches it, it breaks. The three sisters cry out in terror. They bind themselves together with the pieces of the broken rope. "Ended is eternal wisdom!" they lament. "The world shall hear our wisdom no more!" Then they sink into the earth to seek Erda, their mother.

Dawn begins to break, and the music swells into a fine climax developed on a theme associated with Brünnhilde, now a mortal. As the sunshine floods the mountaintop, the melody of "Siegfried's Horn Call" is heard, changed into a serious, heroic form, and Siegfried, in full armor, and Brünnhilde come out of the cave. *"Zu neuen Thaten"* ("To deeds of valor, I must send you forth!"), sings Brünnhilde. She has bestowed on him all the wisdom that she had known as one of the gods, yet thinks her gift too little. Siegfried replies passionately that though he may have been a poor scholar, he has learned well ever to remember her. She earnestly charges him not to forget the fire he crossed to win her and the love and faith they have vowed. "I must leave you here," Siegfried exclaims, "guarded by the fire. For all your runes I give you now this Ring won from a dragon." Joyfully Brünnhilde replies, "Take now my horse! Once he flew with me through the heavens, with me he lost his magic powers. Guard

him well. Speak to him oft Brünnhilde's name!" Siegfried answers rapturously, "Upon your horse I shall fight, with your shield ward me, then shall I no longer be Siegfried, Brünnhilde's arm shall I be!" Brünnhilde calls upon the gods: "Apart, who can divide us? Divided—still we are one!" They unite in their ardent duet. Siegfried then leaps on Grane's back and rides quickly down the mountain. Brünnhilde stands watching him, as he disappears. At the moment of parting the motives of "Siegfried" and "Brünnhilde" are played brilliantly by the full orchestra; then as the music grows quieter, Siegfried is heard joyfully sounding his horn call from the mountainside. Brünnhilde, standing far out on the cliff, catches sight of him again and waves delightedly before he finally vanishes from her sight. The long orchestral interlude known as "Siegfried's Rhine Journey" now is heard. The motives of "Flight" and "The Decision to Love" enter in the orchestra, and then as the curtain falls, these motives are marvelously combined together with that of "The Magic Fire." At the moment of climax there is a sudden change of key, the music associated with the Rhine enters, and in a burst of special magnificence, "The Adoration of the Gold" is combined with "Siegfried's horn call," and "Gold." The music, growing quieter and more somber, is then pervaded by the theme of "The Ring," "The Gold," and "The Renunciation of Love." And now the music makes a transition into darker, more somber sounds and, presently, we hear the motive of "Hagen."

ACT I

SCENE 1: *The hall of the Gibichungs on the Rhine.* On the banks of the Rhine is the kingdom of the Gibichungs, of whom Gunther is the chief. He is now in consultation with his sister, the fair Gutrune, and his swarthy half-brother Hagen. The latter, while extolling their prowess, laments that neither Gunther nor Gutrune is as yet married. He tells Gunther of the sleeping goddess Brünnhilde, who may be won only by a fearless hero capable of penetrating a wall of flames. Gunther would like to win Brünnhilde, yet he knows well that he cannot pass through the fire. Hagen then tells of Siegfried, the fearless hero who slew the dragon Fafner; he it is who might be persuaded to win Brünnhilde for Gunther. Moreover, Siegfried would be a worthy husband for Gutrune; should her beauty not succeed in winning his love, a magic potion will easily do so. Scarcely has this plan been devised when Siegfried arrives in his quest for adventure. He is welcomed effusively by Gunther. Then Hagen asks Siegfried if it is true that he rules the Nibelung treasure. Siegfried admits he had forgotten all about that. "Took you none of it?" asks the wondering Hagen. "Only this," replies Siegfried, pointing to the Tarnhelm, "this of which I know not the use!" Hagen explains to him the mystery of the Tarnhelm, then asks, "Was there nothing else?" "Only a Ring," Siegfried answers, "which now a glorious woman wears."

At this moment Gutrune enters the hall and advances to Siegfried, bearing a filled drinking horn. "Welcome to Gibich's house; as our guest take thou this drink!" she exclaims. Bowing to her kindly, Siegfried takes the drinking horn, which he holds before him meditatively. "If lost were all that you have taught me, one lesson I shall ne'er forget; this draft, the first my lips e'er tasted, Brünnhilde, I drink to you!" No sooner has he finished this magical draught of forgetfulness than he is fired with a sudden passion for Gutrune. When he learns that Gunther is unmarried, but desires for his wife a noble maiden who lives on a mountaintop surrounded by fire, he at once suggests that they go together to win her as a bride. They swear blood-brotherhood and set out immediately. Should they succeed, Siegfried shall be granted Gutrune's hand in marriage.

Hagen, now alone in the hall, broods over his sinister plan, while the orchestra supplies a background remarkable for its unmitigated gloom.

SCENE 2: *The Valkyr rock.* The curtain is lowered for a few moments, while the orchestra continues playing in this mood of fateful brooding. When the curtain is raised we are again at the Valkyrie's rock. Brünnhilde is sitting at the mouth of the cave, contemplating Siegfried's Ring, which she covers with kisses as though lost in happy memories. Suddenly she is startled by a distant roll of thunder, then another, nearer. A Valkyrie is approaching. A cry is heard from the distance: "Brünnhilde! Sister!" Soon the Valkyrie reaches the mountain-

top; it is Waltraute. Brünnhilde is so enrapt with her own felicity that she does not notice Waltraute's agitation, but asks her what lured her from Valhalla. Waltraute replies that serious matters bring her there. For the first time observing Waltraute's perturbed condition, Brünnhilde questions her. "Since Wotan bade you farewell," Waltraute answers, "no more has he sent the Valkyries to battle." She tells how he roamed, lonely and restlessly, over the world and returned to Valhalla, his spear shattered. How he then commanded his heroes to hew down the world ash and pile the fragments about the castle. How he now sits in state surrounded by his warriors; ever silent and gloomy, no more does he eat of Freia's apples. The other gods sit near him in silent terror. He has sent his two ravens over the earth, continues Waltraute. Should they return with good tidings, the god will smile again. The Valkyries sit trembling at his feet. Waltraute tells how once in tears she clasped herself closely against Wotan's breast, then she hesitates as she continues: "Wotan's brooding broke, and his thoughts turned, Brünnhilde, to you!" And from the orchestra there is heard the motive of "Wotan's Farewell," a whisper of ineffable pathos, like a faint echo from a vanished day. Waltraute says that, sighing deeply, he murmured as in a dream that should the Ring be given back to the Rhinemaidens, the gods and the world would be released from the curse. When Waltraute heard this, she stole secretly away through the waiting ranks of silent warriors and came here, she confides. "End the grief of the gods!" she entreats, prostrating herself before her sister. Brünnhilde replies that she understands nothing, for Valhalla knows her no longer. "The Ring," cries Waltraute, "surrender it back to the Rhine!" "The Ring?" asks Brünnhilde in amazement. "Siegfried's bridal gift? Art thou mad?"

"Oh, hear me!" pleads the unhappy Waltraute. "The woe of all the world is caused thereby! Throw the Ring into the waters, so shall you end Valhalla's grief!" "You know not what this Ring is to me," cries Brünnhilde. "More than the wonder of Valhalla, more than the immortal pleasures of the gods! Siegfried loves me! Oh, that I could teach this rapture to you! . . . Go, then!" continues Brünnhilde, "to the gods in council arrayed, and say that never shall I give up love! Nor shall they steal it from me, though proud Valhalla fall!" Crying out in anguish, Waltraute mounts her steed and rides away in a storm cloud. Brünnhilde quietly contemplates the evening landscape, and the flames that glow in the distance at the foot of the mountain.

Suddenly the fire springs up brightly, a horn call is heard. "Siegfried!" exclaims Brünnhilde excitedly, "up, up, and be clasped in the arms of my god!" The flames mount higher and higher; suddenly there springs onto the mountaintop a strange figure. Brünnhilde shrieks in terror and cowers tremblingly, murmuring, "Who dares approach?" The stranger is, of course, Siegfried, transformed by the magic of the Tarnhelm into the likeness of Gunther. He claims Brünnhilde as his bride and, though she resists him, he quickly overpowers her, takes the Ring from her finger, and orders her into the cave. He then calls Nothung to witness his faithfulness to Gunther, whose wooing he is accomplishing. He will lay the sword between himself and the woman.

ACT II

SCENE: *Riverbank before the hall of the Gibichungs.* Hagen is on watch outside of the hall of the Gibichungs. In the darkness there crouches near him the dwarf Alberich, his father. Urged on by Alberich, Hagen swears to recover the Ring before Siegfried learns of its power or is persuaded to restore it to the Rhinemaidens. Alberich goes his way as dawn approaches. Siegfried soon arrives, now in his natural form. After being greeted by Hagen and Gutrune, he tells how he penetrated the wall of flames; he adds that Gunther now follows with the bride there won for him.

Hagen mounts a rocky cliff overhanging the river near the hall, and blows a great cattle horn, which brings the vassals running. They ask, "Who is the foe?" He replies that Gunther comes bringing a wife and bids them make sacrifices unto the gods that the marriage may be blessed. He orders them to fill their drinking horns and, drinking freely, give honor due to the gods. The vassals laughingly answer that good fortune, indeed, greets the Rhine if Hagen, the grim one makes merry. But Hagen, still grave, warns them to greet Gunther's bride; to be loyal to the lady; should she be wronged, swiftly to avenge her. Gunther's boat now approaches down the Rhine, and the vassals cheer wildly, "Hail! Welcome!" Gunther leads Brünnhilde ceremoniously forward, and the vassals, bowing respectfully, sing a stately welcome. Brünnhilde, however, has remained with downcast eyes, as one in a trance, but on hearing Siegfried's voice, she is startled with sudden amazement. Noting on Siegfried's finger the Ring which she believed was taken from her by Gunther, she divines that it was Siegfried who came to her on the mountaintop and, blazing forth in terrible anger, denounces him, and declares that she is his wife. Siegfried protests this, saying that he will swear that he has not betrayed Gunther. He asks on whose weapon he shall take oath. Hagen advances, saying that the oath may be taken on his "unsullied spear point." Siegfried, placing two fingers of his right hand upon the spear point, makes his solemn declaration. Brünnhilde rushes forward and strikes Siegfried's hand from the spear. "Holy spear!" she cries, "witness my eternal oath. I pray that he may perish by your point, for here he has sworn falsely an oath." The

Act II: The betrayed Brünnhilde (Helen Traubel) sees Siegfried (Lauritz Melchior) swear the oath on Hagen's spear

vassals in their astonishment call for the help of Donner. Siegfried tells Gunther to care for his "wild mountain maid" well; she is still bewildered and angry and knows not what she is saying. Then he takes Gutrune's hand and bids the vassals and their women follow into the hall for the feasting. The procession moves away, leaving only Hagen, Brünnhilde, and Gunther, all absorbed in gloomy meditation.

"What crafty thing lies hidden here?" mutters Brünnhilde to herself, lamenting the cruelty of the man who casts her aside after having accepted her love and wisdom. And she wonders who will bring a sword to sever her bonds. Hagen, coming near, whispers that she may trust him to avenge her. Turning toward him, Brünnhilde exclaims scornfully that he is no match for Siegfried, whereupon he questions her about any weakness the hero may have. Brünnhilde, still rankling over her Siegfried's apparent deception, says, finally, that only his back is vulnerable, for although she worked all her wiles to cast a protection over him, she cast no spell over his back, knowing that he would never retreat from a foe, and thus never expose his weak point. "And there shall he be speared!" cries Hagen exultingly, and, turning toward Gunther, continues, "Up, noble Gibichung! Here stands your warrior bride! Why so sad?" But Gunther responds with an outburst of grief at his dishonor; and Brünnhilde, turning upon him, exclaims that low indeed has fallen the race that bore such faint heart as his. Gunther, overwhelmed, complains that he, the betrayer, has been betrayed. And he implores Hagen to help him. The latter realistically replies that nothing can help, save Siegfried's death. And though Gunther is appalled at the thought, remembering the oath of blood-brotherhood, Hagen insists that the oath has been broken and calls for blood. The voices of the conspirators unite briefly in a magnificent passage: Brünnhilde and Gunther call upon the gods to aid their revenge, and Hagen mutters, "Alberich, father, again shall you be true lord of the Ring!" The wedding procession of Siegfried and Gutrune comes from the hall and is joined by Gunther and Brünnhilde. The joyful music of the marriage feast sounds out brilliantly in the orchestra, but mingled with it as a strange undercurrent is the ominous motive of "Revenge."

ACT III

Scene 1: *A wild, wooded valley on the banks of the Rhine.* Again we are at the banks of the Rhine, this time at a point where it flows through a wood. In the waters swim the three Rhinemaidens, singing their fascinating song *"Frau Sonne sendet lichte*

Gunther (Herbert Janssen), Brünnhilde (Kirsten Flagstad) and Hagen (Emanuel List) pledge Siegfried's death (San Francisco Opera, 1937)

Strahlen'' (''The sun sends rays of splendor''). They pause for a moment and listen as a hunting horn is heard echoing in the distance. Then joyfully splashing about in the water, they resume their song.

Again a horn call is heard, and the Rhine-maidens dive down into the water to take counsel and await Siegfried, who, having lost his way in the hunt, soon appears on the banks of the river. The Rhine-maidens rise to the surface and call him by name. He asks where they have hidden his quarry, the bear. They say they will tell if he will give them the Ring. They taunt him, when he refuses, telling him that he should be more generous toward the pleas of young maidens. But Siegfried replies that he could not part so easily with his goods; his wife would not be pleased. Whereupon they make game of him, teasing him about being henpecked, and with a final commentary on his miserliness they dive down beneath the surface. Slightly disturbed by their words, Siegfried calls to them, offering to give them the Ring. But when the Rhinemaidens reappear they are much more solemn in both demeanor and talk. He is told to keep his Ring, to guard it until he learns the awful power it holds. Only then shall he be delivered from the curse of the Ring.

Siegfried thoughtfully replaces the Ring on his finger and asks the Rhinemaidens to reveal what they know. In the somber tones of *"Schlimmes wissen wir dir''* (''Evils await you''), they explain that the Ring is made of gold that has been stolen from the Rhine, and that its maker laid a curse upon it, dooming its possessor to death. Only the waters of the Rhine will remove this evil power it has. Siegfried's retort is that he is as unmoved by their threats as he was by their wiles. He says he was told of its curse by the dragon whom he slew, and that through the Ring he could win the riches of the world, which, he adds, he despises. In any case, he will not give it up. The Rhinemaidens, unable to make him do as they wish, remark on this self-esteeming young man who is so blind. And they add that this very day a woman shall inherit the treasure —a woman who will better do their bidding. With that they disappear.

The hunting party is heard, sounding the hunting horns and calling. Siegfried answers their call, and soon they appear—Hagen, Gunther, and a crowd of vassals. They put down their game and prepare for a repast. Siegfried says that he found no game—only ''water fowl'' who foretold his death. This gives Hagen a cue, and he asks Siegfried to tell them how he came to understand the song of birds. In the narrative *"Mime hiess ein mürrischer Zwerg''* (''Mime was a crabbed old dwarf'') Siegfried tells of his life with Mime, the forging of Nothung, the slaying of the dragon, the dragon's blood which enabled him to understand the song of birds, and the

Ring and the Tarnhelm of which a bird told him. Hagen offers a drinking horn to Siegfried, saying that the mead will help rekindle his memory. Hagen has secretly put into the mead the juice of an herb. When the hero drinks it, the effects of the earlier potion which made him forget Brünnhilde are removed. Siegfried continues his story. He tells of the forest bird's promise to lead him to Brünnhilde, of his passing through the flames. He becomes more and more enraptured as he recalls the sleeping maiden he found, his awakening kiss, and how Brünnhilde's arms enfolded him. Gunther, rising in horror, cries, ''What says he!'' At this moment two ravens circle around over Siegfried.

''What do these ravens say?'' demands Hagen. Siegfried turns to look. ''Vengeance, they say to me!'' cries Hagen. And with a fearful thrust he plunges his spear into Siegfried's back. Siegfried turns and raises his shield, intending to crush Hagen, but falls unconscious. Gunther and the vassals stand appalled, muttering, ''What deed is this?'' Hagen answers, ''Falsehood do I avenge!'' then walks gloomily away.

Gunther bends down sorrowfully at the side of the stricken man, surrounded by the sympathetic vassals. Siegfried, opening his eyes, whispers, ''Brünnhilde! holiest bride!'' The orchestra echoes the glowing music of Brünnhilde's awakening, as Siegfried addresses his last words to the absent Brünnhilde. Then he falls back lifeless. Sadly the body is lifted and carried in solemn procession to the Gibichungs' hall, while mists rising from the Rhine obscure the scene. But the music of Siegfried's death attains a height of tragic expression seldom equaled in opera. Contrasted with the ominous, relentless pulsating of the rhythm are the themes associated with the Wälsungs, Siegfried's parents, melodies of great simplicity, yet of most touching pathos. Then there gleams out the motive of ''The Sword,'' brightly, but with a new breadth and solemnity. And now we hear the rhythm of ''Death'' swelling out in tones of overwhelming power and grandeur, soon to be joined by the motives of ''Siegfried'' and of ''Siegfried's Horn Call,'' glorified in the most transcendent majesty. Then suddenly all the splendor of heroism fades, and again the music is veiled with grief. The motive of ''Brünnhilde'' is heard sorrowingly; the rhythm of ''Death'' persists, now somber-hued, and ''The Curse'' sounding darkly, the music subsides in the deepest gloom.

SCENE 2: *The hall of the Gibichungs.* When the mists clear we find that the scene has changed to the hall of the Gibichungs. In the darkness the hall and the river beyond it are barely discernible. Gutrune is anxiously awaiting the return of the huntsmen, for she has been haunted by dreams of evil foreboding.

Suddenly Hagen enters in agitation and bids her prepare lights for her lord's return; then he adds that Siegfried is dead, slain by a boar. The body is brought in; Gutrune falls fainting. Gunther would tend her, but she repulses him, and he reveals to her that it was Hagen who murdered her husband. Hagen, unashamed, approaches, claiming Siegfried's Ring. Gunther opposes him, they fight, and Gunther falls dead from a stroke of his half brother's sword. Still undeterred, Hagen reaches for the Ring, but Siegfried's arm rises threateningly; Hagen recoils in horror, and the terror-stricken women shriek. At this moment Brünnhilde enters. "Silence your wailing!" she exclaims. "Children I heard whining the loss of their milk, yet heard I not lament worthy of the highest of heroes!" Gutrune rises in a sudden burst of passion: "Ah, Brünnhilde, you it was who for envy of me set the men against Siegfried." Brünnhilde gazes sadly at her and replies, "You were never wife of his. His troth he plighted me long ere he saw your face!" The unhappy Gutrune denounces Hagen for having brought the potion which caused Siegfried's forgetfulness.

Brünnhilde remains lost in deep contemplation. Then, stirred with a sudden exaltation, she turns to the vassals and commands them to build up a mighty pile of logs by the river's edge; to kindle a fire high and bright, that in it may be consumed the body of the noblest of heroes. "Bring his steed," she continues, "that with me the horse may follow his lord." Then, gazing on Siegfried's face, she sings, "Truer than he was none! None more faithfully held promises! Yet oaths and vows has he betrayed! Ye gods, guardians of all oaths, witness now my distress; behold your eternal disgrace. Wotan, hear me! On him, the hero who wrought your will, you laid the curse which fell upon you! Yet he must betray me, that all I might comprehend! Rest, then, god!" At a sign from Brünnhilde the vassals place Siegfried's body on the pyre, which is now completed. Brünnhilde takes from Siegfried's hand the Ring, and, looking at it thoughtfully, exclaims, "Rhinemaidens who so long have lamented the gold, take from my ashes the Ring! The fire which consumes me shall cleanse away the curse! Guard well, then, the gold!" She takes a firebrand from one of the men. "Fly home, ye ravens!" she cries; "tell Wotan what ye have here seen. And bid Loge hasten to Valhalla, for at last the day of the gods reaches its twilight!" So saying, she flings the torch upon the funeral pyre, which quickly breaks into flames, and Wotan's ravens, flying up from the riverbank, disappear in the distance.

Brünnhilde's horse is now led in. "Know you whither we go?" she asks. "There lies your master; would you follow him in the flames? In my heart flames too are glowing, fast to embrace him, with

Brünnhilde (Birgit Nilsson) bids Grane follow her in death on Siegfried's funeral pyre.

him forever made one—Siegfried, Brünnhilde greets you in bliss!"

She swings herself on Grane's back, and at her urging the horse leaps forward into the burning funeral pyre. The flames, growing constantly more violent, mount upward and overrun the hall, until the very building seems ablaze. The terrified Gibichung vassals draw back, huddled together in a corner. Suddenly the flames die down, the smoke drifts away, and the river Rhine, having overflowed its banks, submerges the embers in an instant. The Rhine-maidens appear where last the pyre was seen blazing. Hagen, who has been anxiously watching, throws off his armor and plunges into the flood, shouting, "Back from the Ring!" Now for the last time, the motive of "The Curse" is briefly sounded. But the Rhinemaidens have recovered the Ring; then seizing Hagen, they drag him down into the depths. The Rhine returns to its normal course, and as the Rhinemaidens swim away rejoicing, the melody of their song is heard. Soon there enters with it the majestic theme of "Valhalla," while on the distant horizon is seen a red glow—Valhalla and its assembled gods and heroes are passing away in flames. Yet above these two themes is heard the ecstatic melody of "Redemption Through Love" swelling into a transcendent apotheosis; for though the gods be destroyed and though the gold be restored to its unsullied condition in the depths of the Rhine, there remains one power to govern the world—love.

Romeo and Juliet

ROMÉO ET JULIETTE

CHARACTERS

Juliet, *daughter of Capulet*	*Soprano*	Capulet, *a nobleman*	*Bass*
Stephano, *page to Romeo*	*Mezzo-soprano*	Tybalt, *Capulet's nephew*	*Tenor*
Gertrude, *Juliet's nurse*	*Mezzo-soprano*	Paris, *Capulet's kinsman*	*Baritone*
Romeo, *a Montague*	*Tenor*	Gregorio, *Capulet's kinsman*	*Bass*
Benvolio, *friend of Romeo*	*Tenor*	Friar Laurence	*Bass*
Mercutio, *friend of Romeo*	*Baritone*	The Duke of Verona	*Bass*

Guests, Relatives, and Retainers of the Capulets and Montagues

The action takes place in Verona in the fourteenth century.

OPERA IN prologue and five acts. Music by Charles François Gounod. Libretto in French, after Shakespeare, by Jules Barbier and Michel Carré. First produced at the Théâtre-Lyrique, Paris, April 27, 1867. American première, in Italian, at the New York Academy of Music on November 15, 1867. A performance in English occurred on January 14, 1881, at the Park Theater in Brooklyn. First performance at the Metropolitan, in French, December 14, 1891, with Jean de Reszke and Emma Eames in the title roles, and Édouard de Reszke as Friar Laurence, all making their New York debuts.

Though lacking the sustained inspiration of *Faust*, Gounod's *Roméo et Juliette* has an engaging quality of its own in its wealth of pretty tunes and graceful orchestral writing. Moreover, in its title roles it offers an irresistible appeal to tenors and sopranos of marked dramatic resource. For though the opera in no way measures up to the poetic sublimities of Shakespeare's original, it remains the most popular and practicable of the many operatic settings of Shakespeare's immortal love story. Bellini's *I Capuletti e i Montecchi* (1830) was the greatest of all the *Romeo and Juliet* operas preceding Gounod's. Comparisons between the libretto of Gounod's opera and Shakespeare's text are, of

Emma Eames, Metropolitan Opera début as Juliet, 1891

course, futile and unfair. The opera is, in any case, an adequate condensation of the action of the play. The main sequence is preserved, and if there are fewer words than in the original, there is, at any rate, the consolation of music that is sweetly sentimental and sometimes of a dazzling brilliance, as in Juliet's waltz song of the first act. Some of Shakespeare's minor characters have been eliminated, and one character has been added, the page Stephano. For those who know Shakespeare's lines, a reading of the English version of Barbier and Carré's libretto naturally yields a few surprises.

PROLOGUE

Before the action begins in Shakespeare's play, a single actor, denominated "Chorus" speaks the lines of a sonnet telling the audience about the "pair of star-cross'd lovers" they will shortly meet. In the opera the entire chorus sings a French translation of this sonnet.

ACT I

SCENE: *Ballroom in Capulet's house, Verona.* Capulet, a Veronese nobleman, is giving a masked ball in honor of his daughter Juliet's entrance into society. When the guests have gone to the banquet hall, Juliet lingers behind and gives expression to her girlish joy in the famous waltz song *"Je veux vivre dans ce rêve"* ("Is the tender dream of youth"). All the girl's excitement in the festive surroundings

throbs through the lilting arietta. She is about to leave when Romeo enters, having ventured with some of his comrades, all masked, into the house of their enemy. It is a case of love at first sight, but the meeting is cut short by the appearance of Juliet's hotheaded cousin Tybalt. Recognizing Romeo through his mask, Tybalt denounces him as a member of the hated house of Montague. A general fight is averted by the timely intercession of Capulet, who, loath to have the festivities spoiled, permits Romeo and his friends to depart in peace.

ACT II

SCENE: *Capulet's garden; Juliet's apartment above.* Romeo has again braved the wrath of the enemy for another chance to see Juliet. Gazing up at her balcony, he now sings a lovely serenade, the famous cavatina beginning *"Ah! lève-toi, soleil! fais pâlir les étoiles"* ("Rise, O sun! make the stars pale"). Juliet appears on the balcony, and the two sing a beautiful love duet. Juliet's nurse calls for her, and the girl re-enters her apartment. After a few moments she returns to bid Romeo good night. The tender scene is resumed as Romeo pleads with Juliet to linger awhile yet (*"Ah! ne fuis pas encore!"*). Taking up the melody, Juliet cautions her lover that someone may see them together (*"Ah! l'on peut nous surprendre!"*). The duet continues in this vein till Juliet bids Romeo good night and returns to her chamber. Romeo remains a few ardent moments to tell the evening breeze of his love.

Act I: Capulet (Raymond Michalski) introduces his daughter, Juliet (Mirella Freni), to his guests in the 1967 Metropolitan Opera production by Rolf Gérard

Act II: Juliet (Mirella Freni), Romeo (Franco Corelli)

restrain himself, and he in turn slays Tybalt. At this point, older and calmer men appear on the scene, including Lord Capulet and the Duke of Verona. The fighting is stopped, and the Duke banishes Romeo from Verona. This sentence appalls the just-married lover, and he leads the ensemble in an especially effective finale.

ACT IV

SCENE: *Juliet's room*. Having found a way into Capulet's house at the risk of his life, Romeo has penetrated to the room of his bride. There he bids her a tender farewell. After he has departed, Friar Laurence enters to tell the girl that it was Tybalt's dying wish that she marry Paris, and that the wedding is now being arranged. Counseling the despairing Juliet to be patient, he gives her a potion which he tells her to drink when the marriage ceremony is about to take place. It will induce a death-like trance for an extended period. After that she may escape from her tomb and fly with Romeo. The good priest leaves her. Soon Juliet sees her father and Paris approaching. Quickly draining the contents of the phial, she grows faint and appears to fall lifeless into Capulet's arms.

(The National Opéra of Paris always required a ballet to be given somewhere after Act I in any opera. For the production of 1868 at that theater Gounod obligingly supplied one, and it was performed after Juliet took the draft but before she was overcome by the effects. In modern productions the ballet is often omitted. It has pretty music, but dramatically it is utterly meaningless to perform it at this point.)

ACT III

SCENE 1: *Friar Laurence's cell*. The secret marriage of Romeo and Juliet takes place in the cell of Friar Laurence, who hopes that the union will reconcile the rival houses. At the end of the scene Juliet's nurse joins the others in a quartet suitably joyous.

SCENE 2: *A street in Verona*. Romeo's imprudent page Stephano, having come in search of his master, sings an impertinent song before the Capulet house. This brings out Gregorio, who, recognizing the lad as a companion of Romeo's at the ball, begins to attack him. Other Capulets follow behind; and when a group of Montagues arrive on the scene, the stage is set for a general brawl. Tybalt, Juliet's cousin, challenges Romeo, who refuses to fight a relative of his new bride; and thereupon Mercutio accepts the challenge instead, and is slain. Romeo cannot now

ACT V

SCENE: *Juliet's tomb*. In the silent vault of the Capulets, Juliet lies on the bier, still in a trance, as the orchestra performs a short, subdued tone poem. Having heard that Juliet has died, Romeo forces in the door to gain one last glimpse of his bride. Awed by the gloom and solemnity of the place, he bursts into an impassioned apostrophe to Juliet's tomb and hymns her beauty, still unsullied by the touch of death. He stoops to give Juliet a farewell embrace and then drinks a deadly poison. No sooner has he swallowed it than he is startled to behold signs of life in Juliet's body. But it is too late. The despairing lovers have time only to say farewell. Juliet draws a dagger concealed among her burial garments and stabs herself. Romeo and Juliet, begging God's forgiveness, enter into their eternal sleep clasped in each other's arms.

La Rondine

THE SWALLOW

CHARACTERS

Rambaldo Fernandez, *a Parisian banker*	*Baritone*	Périchaud	*friends of Rambaldo's*	*Baritone*
		Gobin		*Tenor*
Magda de Civry, *his mistress*	*Soprano*	Crébillon		*Bass*
Lisette, *her maid*	*Soprano*	Yvette	*friends of Magda's*	*Soprano*
Ruggero Lastouc, *son of a friend of Rambaldo's*	*Tenor*	Bianca		*Soprano*
		Suzy		*Mezzo-soprano*
Prunier, *a poet*	*Tenor*	A major-domo		*Bass*

Party Guests, Students, Artists, Grisettes, Dancers, Waiters, etc.

The action takes place at Paris and on the Riviera in the third quarter of the nineteenth century.

OPERA IN TWO ACTS. Music by Giacomo Puccini. Text in Italian by Giuseppe Adami based on a German libretto by Alfred Maria Willner and Heinrich Reichert. Première March 27, 1917, at Monte Carlo. First American performance at the Metropolitan Opera House, New York, March 10, 1928, with Lucrezia Bori as Magda and Beniamino Gigli as Ruggero.

When Puccini was in Vienna in 1912, he was asked to write, for a very handsome fee, the principal numbers for a Viennese operetta. Not feeling that his talents and interest lay along such lines, he refused; but two years later, on another trip to the city of waltzes, he succumbed to the blandishments of the Austrians, agreed to the subject, and signed a contract. Not long after, World War I broke out with Italy and Austria on opposite sides. Puccini soon regretted his contract and tried to get out of it. He did not like the libretto; he couldn't write an operetta anyway; and the wartime atmosphere was all wrong for it. Nevertheless, working through Switzerland, the Austrians insisted on his doing the work, but they gave up rights for certain countries, including Italy, and agreed to let Puccini compose the work as an opera with music throughout and no spoken dialogue. His young friend Giuseppe Adami, who supplied the libretto for *Il Tabarro*, co-authored the one for *Turandot*, and later wrote a biography of the composer, translated and adapted the German operetta text for Puccini's new purpose and, before the war was over, the première was given in Monte Carlo. It was only in September 1920, almost two years after the close of the war, that a performance was mounted in Vienna—in German, of course.

The story—that of a demimondaine who forswears her one true love for the sake of his family's respectability—cannot help reminding any opera lover of *La Traviata;* while the second act, in which Parisian bohemians carouse and make love in a restaurant, will remind him inevitably of the second act of *La Bohème.* Such scenes, such themes, were ideally suited to Puccini's taste and genius, and the composer was at the height of his powers when he wrote this opera. Nevertheless, despite the acclaim it received at its première, despite the fine casts that have sung it, despite the composer's own affection for the score and the pleasure which many productions in many cities have given to thousands, it has never lasted long in any company's repertoire. It has fine tunes, an exceptionally strong concerted number at the close of Act II, considerable variety, and fine orchestration. Perhaps its origin in concept as an operetta influenced Puccini to compose a less convincingly tragic score than he might otherwise have produced. But that is mere speculation. In any event, the opera has so much merit that, more than fifty years after its première, opera companies and recording companies every once in a while still mount entirely new productions.

ACT I

SCENE: *The elegant salon of Magda's house in Paris.* Rambaldo and his mistress Magda are giving a late afternoon party for their respective friends, businessmen, and gay young women; and a frivolous poet, Prunier, is maintaining as the curtain rises that, shocking though it may seem, falling in love is again becoming fashionable in Paris. Magda seems to take the subject of romantic love more seriously than the others and, ordering silence from the men (who have been discussing business on the other side of the room), asks Prunier to sing the verses he says he has been composing on the subject. Accompanying himself at the piano, Prunier begins a ballad, *"Chi il bel sogno di Doretta"* ("Who could guess Doretta's beautiful dream?"), which tells of a girl's refusal of riches from a king, "for gold cannot bring happiness." As Prunier had not thought of an ending to his story, Magda sits down at the piano and improvises one. In her version, Doretta's dream ends when she finds real love with a student. Rambaldo, customarily a cold man, says that he is so much moved by Magda's improvisation that he remembers he intended to give her a necklace before dinner but forgot. He now presents it to her, and it is admired by everyone; but Magda is not much impressed with this expression of affection.

Left to themselves on one side of the room, the four women consider the relative merits of wealth, which Magda alone among them has access to, and romantic love. Magda comes down on the side of love in an aria, *"Ore dolci e divine"* ("Sweet and wonderful hours"), in which she tells of having once encountered at the Café Bullier a strange and romantic man who ordered beer for both of them, let the waiter keep all the change, spoke to her of love, exchanged first names, and did not follow her when, much moved, she fled. Her friends are much impressed with Magda's recital of her two-hour encounter with romantic love. Prunier then joins the ladies once more and starts to read their palms. For Magda he predicts that, like a swallow, she will fly to

Lucrezia Bori (Magda), Beniamino Gigli (Ruggero), Act III

a sunnier land, to love and to who knows what ending to it.

Meantime, Magda's maid Lisette (who has apparently been annoying Prunier all evening by taking an uninvited part in some of the conversation) brings in a young man who, she tells Rambaldo, has been waiting outside for two hours to see him. This man turns out to be Ruggero Lastouc, the son of an old friend of Rambaldo's, newly arrived in Paris. There is much discussion of how a young man ought to spend his first evening in Paris, in which Lisette takes a leading part. Everyone agrees with her that by far the best thing he could do would be to go to Bullier's, and this he proceeds to do at once.

Late afternoon has now changed to evening, and all the guests leave excepting Prunier, who hides on the veranda. Lisette reminds Magda that this is her evening off, and, agreeing that she may go out, Magda goes off to her own room. For a moment the stage is empty; but then Lisette returns dressed in some of Magda's finery. Prunier steps into the room and takes the girl into his arms, making light love. He criticizes her dress, however, for everything does not go together. Lisette remedies matters by putting a black silk cape over everything and adding a good deal of make-up, and slowly they go off together, singing of love.

Barely have they left, when Magda returns to the

room so well disguised as a grisette that she can barely recognized herself in the mirror. Well pleased and murmuring a line or two from the ballad of Doretta, she is off for adventure at Bullier's.

ACT II

SCENE: *Principal room at the Cafe Bullier*. In the large salon, with an imposing stairway leading into it and a garden for dancing visible in back, flower girls, grisettes, students, men about town, and ladies of the evening are busily flirting, making pick-ups, ordering drinks, and so on. Among them are Lisette and Prunier, and sitting by himself at a table, is Ruggero, gloomily fending off the unwanted attentions of Georgette, Gabriella, and Lolette. Magda, beautiful in her disguise, appears at the head of the stairs and is at once made advances to by a group of admiring students. She gets rid of them by making believe that she has a date with that gentleman sitting by himself. This is, of course, Ruggero, who is delighted when so pretty a woman (whom he does not recognize as his hostess earlier in the evening) seats herself beside him. The initial flirting and the more serious falling in love develop much as Magda's recital of her long-ago love affair had developed in Act I, with the exchange of names (by writing them on the table), the overtipping of the waiter, and other bits being recalled in the music as well. They dance together, but this time there is a different conclusion from Magda's earlier romance: she wishes to flee, but Ruggero simply will not let her go.

Suddenly Lisette spies her mistress and speaks to her; but Magda makes believe she doesn't know what Lisette is talking about, and Prunier (who is perfectly well aware of what Magda is doing) is enough of a kindly man of the world to dissuade Lisette from the truth. A most effective ensemble number then develops, in which each of the four lovers sings of his (or her) happiness and the crowd of other guests is enchanted with such a convincing show of romantic love. At its close, the poet's head is garlanded with flowers.

With most of the guests gone into the garden to dance, Rambaldo comes slowly down the stairs. He has seen Magda and Ruggero despite Prunier's tactful efforts to distract his attention, and he demands that Magda come home with him. Stoutly, Magda refuses, saying that she loves Ruggero; and Rambaldo, with consummate dignity, takes his leave. Ruggero, who has been dragged off by Lisette, now returns with Magda's shawl on his arm. "Paulette," he says, addressing Magda by the name she had given him, "it is almost dawn and time to leave." As

if waking from a dream, Magda throws herself into his arms and, declaring their love for each other, they leave arm in arm.

ACT III

SCENE: *Outside Magda and Ruggero's villa near Nice*. Magda and Ruggero, enjoying a fine evening on the Côte d'Azur, are enjoying even more each other's company as they tell of their mutual love. Their money has run out, but they do not mind if they have to beg, so long as they have each other. But Ruggero has other plans, and he tells Magda that he has written to his wealthy and respectable family to ask for permission to marry her. Magda is shocked, for Ruggero has never learned of her past, which would disqualify her for marriage into his family. Ruggero eloquently sings of the future he foresees, with children to come, in his aria *"Dimmi che vuoi seguirmi"* ("Tell me that you will follow me"), and he leaves her, quietly sobbing and wondering how she can tell him of the impossibility of their ever marrying.

When she has followed Ruggero into the villa, Lisette and Prunier come in quarreling. It seems that Prunier had tried to carve a career for her as an actress. She made her debut in Nice on the previous night and was a total failure, being greeted with nothing but hisses. So disillusioned is Lisette that she now wishes to return as a maid to her beloved mistress, and Prunier, falling in with the idea, has brought her to Magda's villa. Magda is summoned by a major-domo, and Lisette is welcomed back to her old job. Prunier, meantime, has let Magda know that she is much missed in Paris, that no one believes she can remain away from the old life for very long, and that Rambaldo (whom he tactfully does not name) would be happy to welcome her back at any time. He then takes—ostensibly—his final leave of Lisette, but not before making a date with her for ten o'clock the same evening.

Now Ruggero emerges joyfully from the villa. He has in his hand a letter from his mother, and he insists that Magda read it aloud. Magda can scarcely go through with it, for the letter warmly welcomes the idea of Ruggero's marrying and becoming a father—"if you know that she is good, meek, pure, and that she has all the virtues." Heartbroken, Magda tells the unsuspecting Ruggero that her past has made her unfit to be anything but his mistress, that she can never ruin him by marrying him, and that they must now part. Despite Ruggero's frantic pleas, she turns toward the villa, desperately unhappy but knowing that the swallow must now fly back.

Der Rosenkavalier

THE CAVALIER OF THE ROSE

CHARACTERS

Princess von Werdenberg (the Feldmarschallin)	*Soprano*	Herr von Faninal, *a parvenu*	*Baritone*
		Sophie, *his daughter*	*Soprano*
Baron Ochs von Lerchenau, *her cousin*	*Bass*	Marianne, *Faninal's housekeeper*	*Soprano*
		Valzacchi, *an intrigant*	*Tenor*
Octavian, *a young boy, scion of a noble family*	*Mezzo-soprano*	Annina, *his accomplice*	*Contralto*

A Singer, a Flute Player, a Notary, Commissary of Police, Lackeys of Faninal, a Master of Ceremonies, an Innkeeper, a Milliner, a Noble Widow and Thee Noble Orphans, a Hairdresser and his Assistants, Waiters, Musicians, Guests, two Watchmen, Kitchen Servants, and several suspicious Apparitions

The action takes place in Vienna during 1744, the early part of the reign of Maria Theresa.

"A COMEDY for music by H. von Hofmannsthal . . . music by Richard Strauss." Thus reads the title page of the score, an indication of the poet's importance. First produced, January 26, 1911, at the Royal Opera House, Dresden. First performed in the United States, December 9, 1913, at the Metropolitan Opera House, New York, with Frieda Hempel as the Princess, Margarete Ober as Octavian, Anna Case as Sophie, Otto Goritz as Baron Ochs, Hermann Weil as Faninal, and Carl Jörn as the Singer. Alfred Hertz conducted.

Die Meistersinger, Falstaff, and *Der Rosenkavalier*—these are generally acknowledged to be the greatest masterpieces of operatic comedy of the past hundred years. The libretto of *Der Rosenkavalier,* by one of the most prominent turn-of-the-century Continental authors, is in itself a masterpiece, combining elements of the comedy of intrigue, the comedy of manners, a bit of farce, and satire, all held together by the blended humor and pathos of Hof-

Maria Olszewska as Octavian, the Count Rofrano

Act I, as staged in 1968 at the Vienna Opera: The Princess von Werdenberg (Christa Ludwig) holds her morning levée

mannsthal, the symbolist and poet. For this, Strauss supplied thoroughly captivating music. Although, from a historical point of view, it is a bit of an anachronism, he has made frequent use of the ever-delightful waltz, securing thereby an inimitable atmosphere of lightness and romance.

While making use of innumerable leading motives, Strauss revealed a wealth of beautiful straightforward melody, hitherto unsuspected of the composer of the great symphonic poems.

INTRODUCTION

Der Rosenkavalier begins with an orchestral introduction typical of Richard Strauss, yet sounding the mood of the work: impetuous, capricious, and witty. It grows to an impassioned climax ("parodied," according to Strauss's directions). The music then subsides to a mood of tranquillity mingled with tender yearning.

ACT I

Scene: *The Marschallin's boudoir.* As morning sunbeams steal into her room, the Princess von Werden-

berg embraces her young lover, Octavian, Count Rofrano. A little blackamoor, Mahomet, brings the princess her breakfast and Octavian playfully hides, but at the sound of loud voices in the ante-chamber, both he and the princess panic, for they fear it is her husband unexpectedly returning from a hunting expedition. Their mirth is aroused again when they recognize the gruff voice of Baron Ochs, the princess's bumptious cousin. To disguise himself, Octavian quickly dons the dress of a chambermaid, "Mariandel." Ochs enters and, while discussing his forthcoming marriage to Sophie von Faninal, young daughter of a wealthy Viennese, he flirts with "Mariandel," much to the princess's amusement. Ochs tells his cousin that he needs a cavalier to present a silver rose—the token of engagement—to his fiancée, at which the princess slyly suggests Octavian. Seeing the young count's picture, Ochs is amazed by its resemblance to "Mariandel."

The room now fills with retainers and others petitioning for favors from the princess. An Italian tenor sings an aria, but is cut short by Ochs's arguing with a notary over his dowry. Hiring two Italian intriguers, Annina and Valzacchi, to track down "Mariandel," he departs, leaving the princess alone to muse before the mirror on her waning youth and the realization that her affair with Octavian must soon end. When Octavian returns, now dressed in riding habit, he is confused by her changed mood and stunned when she says that one day he will tire of her. Unable to break her melancholy, he leaves. The princess calls him back, but it is too late. Then, summoning the blackamoor, she sends Octavian the silver rose.

ACT II

SCENE: *The reception hall in Faninal's mansion.* As Faninal and Sophie nervously await the cavalier of the rose, Marianne, the girl's duenna, describes the arrival of his coach. Lackeys announce Octavian, who rapturously presents Ochs's silver rose to Sophie. Chaperoned by Marianne, the two young people hold a polite conversation, rudely interrupted by the arrival of the bridegroom, whose crude manners and amorous boasting repel Sophie. When Faninal and Ochs retire to another room on business, Sophie and Octavian embrace each other, realizing their love. But Annina and Valzacchi catch them and call for Ochs, who speaks coarsely to his fiancée

Richard Mayr, famous Baron Ochs of the Vienna State Opera during the 1920's and 30's

Act II: In Faninal's ornate reception hall, Sophie (Hilde Gueden) accepts silver rose from Octavian (Risë Stevens) as Marianne (Thelma Votipka) looks on approvingly. Metropolitan Opera Production

and is wounded slightly in the arm by Octavian when he draws his sword to protect Sophie's honor. All depart except Ochs and his motley servants, who watch their master soothe his wounded vanity with a bottle of wine. Soon Annina, now in Octavian's employ, delivers a note from the mysterious "Mariandel," agreeing to a rendezvous. Ochs, waltzing around the room to the lovely Viennese waltz music, refuses to tip Annina, who, when his back is turned, shakes her fist at him.

ACT III

SCENE: *A private room at a rundown inn.* Octavian, Annina, Valzacchi and their cronies rehearse the tricks they plan to play on Ochs, who shortly arrives for supper with "Mariandel." Again in the chambermaid's gown, Octavian greets his "suitor" and sits down to eat with him. Suddenly grotesque heads pop out of trap doors and secret windows, frightening Ochs. Then Annina, surrounded by children, storms in, claiming that Ochs is her husband. The police arrive to quell the near riot that ensues, but it erupts again with the entrance of Faninal and Sophie, shocked to find Ochs in a tryst with a chambermaid. Faninal collapses and is carried to an

Lotte Lehmann as the Marschallin

adjoining room. Then, as Octavian is confessing his masquerade to the chief of police, the Princess herself enters. Realizing the situation at a glance, she forces Ochs to renounce Sophie, though he now understands her own relationship with Octavian. As waiters and lackeys demand payment, Ochs beats a hasty retreat. Octavian, with some hesitation, introduces Sophie to the Princess, who, in the beautiful trio that ensues, laments that she has lost her young lover even sooner than she expected. She then thoughtfully goes to comfort Faninal and the two young people ecstatically embrace, renewing their vows of love. They run happily from the room, but after a moment the little blackamoor appears, searches for Sophie's handkerchief, finds it and skips out.

Elisabeth Schumann as Sophie

Salome

CHARACTERS

Herod, *Tetrarch of Judea*	Tenor	Five Jews	{ Four Tenors / One Bass
Herodias, *his wife*	Mezzo-soprano	Two Nazarenes	{ Tenor / Bass
Salome, *her daughter*	Soprano		
Jokanaan (*John the Baptist*)	Baritone	Two Soldiers	Basses
Narraboth, *Captain of the guard*	Tenor	A Cappadocian	Bass
The Page of Herodias	Mezzo-soprano	A Slave	Mime

The action takes place on a terrace of the palace of Herod about A.D. 30.

OPERA IN one act. Music by Richard Strauss. Text, Oscar Wilde's French poem, as translated into German by Hedwig Lachmann. First performance, Dresden, December 9, 1905. First American production, Metropolitan Opera House, January 22, 1907, in German, with Olive Fremstad, Marion Weed, Carl Burrian, and Anton van Rooy in the leading roles, and Alfred Hertz conducting. There had been, prior to this performance, a dress rehearsal at which more than 2,000 people were present. These two showings were the only ones given at the Metropolitan until January 13, 1934, the work being banned, apparently, because of strong moralistic objections voiced in both press and pulpit. The 1934 performance, under Artur Bodanzky's direction, offered Göta Ljungberg, Dorothee Manski, Max Lorenz, and Friedrich Schorr in the cast. Although between 1907 and 1934 there were no *Salome* performances at the Metropolitan, the breach was filled by Oscar Hammerstein's company, which gave the work a triumphant production (in French) at the Manhattan Opera House with a cast including Mary Garden, Augusta Doria, Charles Dalmorès, and Hector Dufranne, Cleofonte Campanini conducting. This was the cast on January 28, 1909. Hammerstein repeatedly presented the opera, and his tradition was followed, after his retirement, by the Chicago Civic Opera Company.

Salome's dance, interpreted by Marjorie Lawrence

More than once in his extraordinary career Richard Strauss shocked the musical public. He administered the greatest shock of all, however, with the one-act opera *Salome;* but it was the text and the action, rather than the music, which in this instance offended a certain section of the operagoing fraternity. Music suggesting the ecstasies of physical love is not in itself—removed from stage presentation, that is—offensive; but the morbidity and sensual decadence of certain scenes in *Salome*, which are accompanied by voluptuous sounds in the orchestra, touched with no gentle hand the sensibilities of operagoers in a more conservative day.

SCENE: *A terrace in the palace of Herod.* The story of the opera deals with the passion of Salome for Jokanaan (John the Baptist), who has been imprisoned by Herod Antipas, Tetrarch of Judea, because he had publicly reproached Herod for marrying his brother's wife, Herodias. Jokanaan is kept imprisoned in a cistern in the courtyard of Herod's palace. On a beautiful moonlit night Salome, coming out on the terrace of the palace, hears the prisoner's voice as he foretells a great catastrophe. Infatuated with the voice, she asks the guards to let her see the prisoner. They obey unwillingly, as they have orders to let no one see Jokanaan. When he is brought from the cistern, Salome is immediately possessed of a fierce desire for him, but her brazen advances are repulsed; Jokanaan curses her, comparing her unfavorably with her wicked mother, and counsels her to seek out the Lord and ask forgiveness for her sins. She begs stubbornly for kisses but the prophet refuses to let her touch him.

Narraboth, an officer in charge of the guard over Jokanaan, is in love with Salome, and, hearing her passionate entreaty to the apostle, is suddenly filled with despair and kills himself at her feet. Jokanaan descends into the cistern. At this moment Herod and his wife, with their court, appear. Herod, already distracted by troubles with the Jews, with his wife, and with a passion for Salome, his stepdaughter, is deeply disturbed upon finding the dead body of the young soldier. He orders it removed and to soothe his tormented soul asks Salome to drink from his cup, to eat with him, to show some sign of interest in him. She refuses. Jokanaan from his cistern is heard declaiming against the evils of Herod's family, and Herodias demands that Herod silence the prisoner and hand him over to the Jews for punishment. Herod is unwilling to do this because he rather fears Jokanaan. Again the voice of the prisoner resounds, foretelling the coming of the Saviour. When Herod asks who the Saviour might be, he is told by the Nazarenes that he has already come and that he has raised the dead and performed other miracles.

With fear added to his other troubles, Herod asks Salome to dance, hoping to be distracted from his ominous forebodings. Salome refuses until Herod promises to grant anything she will ask if she will dance for him. Inspired with an evil thought, Salome performs the seductive "Dance of the Seven Veils."

When it is over, she throws herself at the feet of Herod and then demands her fee—the head of Jokanaan, brought to her on a silver charger. Herod is horrified and offers her instead all his store of jewels and riches. Stubbornly Salome insists that he keep his oath and give her what she wishes. Egged on by his wife, Herod finally acquiesces and orders Jokanaan beheaded.

The executioner, a giant Negro, descends into the well, and Salome eagerly listens for the sound of the death stroke. Presently the head is brought to her on a great silver tray. In a hideous ecstasy compounded of amorousness, vindictiveness, satisfied revenge, and unsatisfied passion, Salome fondles and kisses the lips of the dead man's head, singing wildly of his beauty and of her triumph.

Herod, suddenly revolted by the sadistic and insatiable passion of Salome, tells his wife that her daughter is a fiend. Commanding that the lights be extinguished, he turns suddenly and orders his soldiers to kill Salome. They instantly crush her to death beneath their shields.

The Princess of Judea (Birgit Nilsson) claims her prize, the head of Jokanaan, while Herodias (Irene Dalis) and Herod (Karl Liebl) sit by in horror

Samson and Delilah

SAMSON ET DALILA

CHARACTERS

Samson, *a Hebrew leader*	*Tenor*	Abimelech, *Satrap of Gaza*	*Bass*
Delilah, *a priestess of*		An Old Hebrew	*Bass*
Dagon	*Mezzo-soprano*	Messenger of the Philistines	*Tenor*
High Priest of Dagon	*Baritone*		

Chorus of Hebrews and Philistines

The action takes place in Gaza, in Palestine, about 1150 B.C.

OPERA IN THREE ACTS. Music by Camille Saint-Saëns. Libretto in French by Ferdinand Lemaire, based on the Biblical story in the Book of Judges. First produced at the Hoftheater, Weimar, December 2, 1877, in German with Lassen conducting. American première, as an opera, at the French Opera House, New Orleans, January 4, 1893. First performance at the Metropolitan, February 8, 1895, with Francesco Tamagno and Eugenia Mantelli in the title roles. In concert form the work had already reached New York's Carnegie Hall on March 25, 1892. A brilliant Metropolitan revival of *Samson et Dalila* was that of November 15, 1915, the opening night of the season. In the cast were Enrico Caruso, Margarete Matzenauer, and Pasquale Amato, with Giorgio Polacco conducting.

Though successful with his earlier operas, Saint-Saëns had trouble with his Biblical opera in his own country. Factional disturbances divided musical Paris at the time as a result of the revolutionary theories propounded by Wagner's operas. Saint-Saëns found himself grouped with the operatic left wing, although later he came to be regarded as an archconservative. Luckily, a powerful friend came to Saint-Saëns' aid, none other than Franz Liszt, who was known for his championship of ill-treated composers. Saint-Saëns was invited to Weimar, where Liszt was the ruling spirit, and *Samson et Dalila* was produced there, in German, with great success. Yet,

Paris waited thirteen years before taking cognizance of an opera that was destined to become a hardy perennial of the French repertory. The French première occurred on October 31, 1890, at the Théâtre Eden. Two years later it was produced at the Opéra.

Samson et Dalila has been frequently given in oratorio form because of the Biblical story and the profusion of choral music. As a work for the theater, it is the only one of Saint-Saëns' numerous operas to continue to hold the stage. Into this score the composer poured his best inspiration. Hebrew chants contrast vividly with the sensuous music of the pagan Philistines, and throughout the score one marvels at the facile workmanship. An Oriental at-

Risë Stevens as the seductress Delilah

Jon Vickers as Samson at the Chicago Lyric Opera

mosphere of warm moods and colors is evoked through the music of the Bacchanale, and in voluptuous appeal few operatic arias surpass Delilah's *"Mon coeur s'ouvre à ta voix"* ("My heart at thy sweet voice").

ACT I

SCENE: *A public square in the city of Gaza.* Before the rise of the curtain an invisible chorus of Israelites is heard bewailing their bondage and imploring Jehovah for release. At the rise of the curtain they are seen dimly, for it is early morning in a public square in Gaza, in the city of their conquerors. As they lament their servitude, Samson comes forward and in stirring tones urges his countrymen to arise and cast off the Philistines' yoke.

At first they continue their lamentations, but his fervent avowal of faith soon stirs them to action, and the Israelites exclaim, "It is the Lord who speaks through him! Let us follow Samson, and Jehovah be our guide!" Their ringing shouts now attract Abimelech, the Satrap of Gaza, who emerges from

his palace with his bodyguard. He taunts the Israelites with the reminder that they are helpless. Of what avail their prayers to Jehovah? Did he befriend them in the day of battle? And Abimelech warns them: Better turn to Dagon, the greatest of gods. This blasphemy moves Samson to declare himself the appointed leader of the Chosen People. The Israelites join him in singing a spirited battle hymn: "Arise, O Israel, and break asunder the chains that bind you! Let righteousness be victorious!"

Abimelech attacks Samson with drawn sword. Samson wrests the weapon from him and runs him through. The Satrap falls, calling for help. This is the signal for revolt, and the Israelites follow Samson in a sudden bid for freedom. When they have disappeared, the gates of the temple of Dagon swing open and the High Priest approaches with his attendants. Horrified at the sight of the murdered ruler, he calls down a curse on Samson, his people, and his God. The High Priest and his panic-stricken followers are forced to flee with the body of Abimelech as the victorious Hebrews return, chanting hymns of praise. It is Samson's hour of triumph.

Once more the gates of the temple of Dagon open. This time it is the seductively beautiful priestess Delilah who appears. While maidens bearing garlands of victory sing and dance, Delilah works her charm upon the hero. "I come to celebrate the victory of him who reigns in my heart," sings the priestly siren. An old Hebrew solemnly warns Samson. But, though he prays for divine power to resist the enchantress, the chosen leader is already vanquished. While the young girls continue their dance, Delilah sings to Samson her "Song of Spring," full of a sensuous appeal which is not lost on the stalwart rebel leader. Delilah returns to the temple with her dancing girls. As she goes, she casts an inviting glance at Samson, who gazes after her with longing.

ACT II

SCENE: *Delilah's house.* Night is descending upon the valley as Delilah, more sumptuously clad than ever, waits outside her dwelling for the approach of Samson. In a sensuous aria, *"Amour! viens aider ma faiblesse"* ("Love! come aid my weakness"), she calls upon love to come to aid her in gaining power over this man whom she really hates as the leader of a despised people.

The High Priest comes to Delilah, enjoining her not to fail in her purpose. After he has gone, Samson approaches to keep the rendezvous hinted at by Delilah in her "Spring Song." The powerful Israelite is still hesitant, but gradually his struggling sense of duty is overcome by temptation. For Delilah has begun to play on the man's emotions with a song of ravishing beauty, *"Mon coeur s'ouvre à ta voix"* ("My heart at thy sweet voice"), in which she pleads irresistibly that Samson remain with her. During this exquisite melody a storm has gathered, the swift pattering of the rain being suggested in the accompaniment. Delilah tries her utmost to persuade Samson to betray the secret of his miraculous strength. The growing fury of the storm seems a symbol of the increasing turmoil of his feelings. Delilah alternately threatens and pleads. If he will not share his secret with her, she complains, he does not really love her. Though weakening, Samson still refuses, praying for strength. Seemingly in despair, Delilah runs into her house, crying out that he is a coward, that his heart is without love. Trembling with conflicting emotions, Samson raises his arms hopelessly to heaven, then hurries after her. The storm breaks over the scene in all its fury. As Philistine soldiers approach stealthily, Delilah appears at the terrace for a moment and summons them in. Samson is speedily overpowered.

ACT III

SCENE 1: *The mill of Gaza.* Samson, slayer of thousands of the foe, is now helpless. Blinded, shorn of the long locks which were the secret of his great strength and weighed down with chains, he slowly turns the mill that grinds grain for the Philistines. Out of the depths of his misery he calls upon the Lord for mercy. Nearby his fellow countrymen sing,

"For love of a woman he sold his power and made us captives!" Samson is led away.

SCENE 2: *The temple of Dagon.* From the orchestra are heard soft chords and harp arpeggios, mild as the first glow of dawn which penetrates the temple of Dagon, crowded now with rejoicing Philistines. Repeating the dainty melody sung by the dancing girls in the first act, the Philistines sing the praises of the dawn which puts darkness to flight, and of love, which alone brings happiness.

As they finish singing, an oboe plays a weirdly exotic cadenza, and as the orchestra sounds a brisk dance rhythm, a group of dancers rush foward and begin a lurid bacchanal. The music, at times softly yet luxuriantly voluptuous, grows to a climax of frenzied Oriental revelry.

The dance ended, Samson is led in by a child. All mock him with the cruelest scorn. Derisively, Delilah flings at him phrases of her former love song. Then all turn their attention to the morning sacrifice to the god Dagon, whom the High Priest and Delilah invoke in broad, canonic phrases. Meanwhile, Samson has directed that he be led between the two massive pillars that support the roof of the temple. Finally his unceasing prayers are answered, for he suddenly feels his old strength returning. While all are lost in the ecstasy of pagan worship, he seizes the pillars with a mighty effort, and as they crumble, the roof crashes to the ground, burying Samson with his enemies.

Act III at the Metropolitan Opera: Delilah (Rita Gorr) and the High Priest (Gabriel Bacquier) mock the blinded Samson (Jess Thomas)

Semiramide

CHARACTERS

Semiramide, *Queen of Babylonia*	*Soprano*	
Arsace, *a Scythian captain in the Queen's*		
army (in reality, the son of Semiramide		
and the dead King Ninus)	*Mezzo-soprano*	
Assur, *an Assyrian prince*	*Bass*	
Idreno, *King of India*	*Tenor*	
Azema, *an Assyrian princess*	*Soprano*	
Oroe, *high priest of the Magi*	*Bass*	
Ghost of Ninus, *the dead King, called*		
Nino in the opera	*Bass*	

Courtiers, Attendants, Soldiers, Magi

The action takes place in the city of Babylon, 1000 B.C.

OPERA IN two acts. Music by Gioacchino Rossini. Text in Italian by Gaetano Rossi, after Voltaire's tragedy *Sémiramis* (1748). Première, February 3, 1823, Teatro La Fenice, Venice. American première, 1825, by Manuel Garcia's company, at the Park Theater, New York. Other important American productions include December 20, 1882, by the Patti-Mapleson Company, New York; and January 12, 1894, Metropolitan Opera Company, New York.

Rossini's brilliant career as a composer of Italian operas, both comic and serious, began and ended in Venice. His first opera, *La Cambiale di Matrimonio* (to a libretto by Rossi) was produced there in 1810. Thirteen years and thirty operas later, La Fenice offered his *Semiramide* (on a text by the same librettist), the last of his operas composed for the Italian stage. Rossini's most famous and most ambitious *opera seria* was the result of a double commission. In the summer of 1822 La Fenice offered him the unprecedented fee of five thousand francs to provide two works for the coming season. The first of these, *Maometto* (a hasty and unsatisfactory revision of his 1820 Neapolitan fiasco, *Maometto II*), proved a total failure with the Venetian public at its première late in 1822. But with the triumphant production of *Semiramide* in February of the following year, Rossini's fame and popularity as Italy's

foremost composer were fully vindicated. Although the opera had cost him a mere thirty-three days' labor (the composer's own admission), it took the operatic capitals of Europe and America by storm, and was long regarded as Rossini's crowning achievement. Critical opinion, however, has not always dealt kindly with Rossini's Babylonian epic. Musicologists tend to agree (with no less an authority than Beethoven) that Rossini's genius was at its happiest and most spontaneous in the buffa genre; occasional passages of inspired vocal writing notwithstanding, many critics have dismissed *Semiramide* as an artful pastiche of threadbare "formula" numbers and sure-fire musico-dramatic "effects." The opera's unremitting popularity in the nineteenth century was no doubt due to the favor it enjoyed with the reigning divas of the day. The leading roles of Semiramide and Arsace provide gratifying vehicles for the female voice. After Colbran (the first Semiramide, and Rossini's wife), Pasta, Malibran, Sontag, Grisi, Patti, and Melba won popular acclaim in the role of the hapless queen; and the no-less-rewarding mezzo role of Arsace was a favorite of Pasta and Malibran (again), as well as Viardot, Alboni, Brambilla, Trebelli and Scalchi. Indeed it is the very nature of these leading roles (which require florid singing of almost insuperable

First act of Semiramide *as staged at the Teatro alla Scala, Milan, with Joan Sutherland (center) as the Queen of Babylonia*

difficulty), and not critical disapproval of the opera *qua* opera, which has proved *Semiramide's* undoing. The scarcity of singers able to cope with the soprano and mezzo roles (not to mention tenors and basses capable of negotiating the fioritura passages Rossini wrote into their parts), led to a sharp decline in performances of *Semiramide* after the turn of the century. Besides the difficulty of casting the leading roles, Voltaire's implausible plot (a curious and none-too-successful melding of the Oedipus and Agamemnon legends) has militated against effective stage performances of the work—although notable exceptions have been provided by La Scala in 1962 the Boston Opera Group in 1965 and the 1968 Florence May Festival, all with Joan Sutherland in the title role. No doubt *Semiramide* survives most happily in concert performance, and has so been given,

with great success with Joan Sutherland and Marilyn Horne, in New York and Los Angeles in 1964.

The following events antecede the action of the opera: The Assyrian Queen Semiramide, aided by her paramour, Assur, himself a prince and a general in the royal army, has poisoned her husband Nino. The dying King discloses the conspiracy in a letter to his friend Fradate, exhorting him to save his young son Ninia, whose life is threatened by the usurper Assur. Ninia is carried off to Scythia, given the name of Arsace, and grows to manhood in total ignorance of his royal origin. Entering the Assyrian army, he soon rises to the rank of captain. Unaware that the young man is her son (and that he is in love with the Princess Azema), Semiramide resolves to marry him and make him king. But Assur has not

Semiramide (Joan Sutherland) with her son, Arsace (Giulietta Simionato)

relinquished his ambitions for the throne; and he, too, loves Azema. A third aspirant to both the Princess' hand and the vacant throne is Idreno, King of India.

ACT I

SCENE 1: *The Temple of Baal.* The high priest Oroe, attended by the other Magi, has received a cryptic message from the god, which he interprets as a warning that the day of reckoning and justice is at hand. The populace is admitted to the temple; they are hopeful that Semiramide will at last name Nino's successor to the throne. Present with them are Assur and Idreno, both eager to press their suits for Azema and the crown. The Queen, accompanied by attendants and the Princess Azema, appears and is warmly greeted by the crowd. Seeing that her secret choice, Arsace, has not yet arrived, Semiramide hesitates to make her nomination (*"Di tanti regi"*). But when she approaches the altar at the high priest's urging, there is a flash of lightning and a clap of thunder. Fearful of this evil portent, the crowd disperses. Arsace now enters the vacant temple (*"Eccomi alfine in Babilonia"*). He wonders

at his queen's unexplained summons, and dwells on his love for Azema. Oroe, returning from the sanctuary, welcomes the young captain, and half reveals to him his sacred mission as avenger of the murdered Nino. Arsace, perplexed by the priest's mysterious words, is next confronted by Assur, who scornfully upbraids him for having quit his military post. When he learns that Arsace has come to Babylon at the Queen's own bidding, and, further, that he intends to ask for Azema's hand, Assur's scorn turns to fury, and he vows that Arsace shall win neither the Princess nor the throne.

SCENE 2: *The Hanging Gardens of Babylon.* Semiramide is hopeful that Arsace will return her love for him, and that their joint reign will restore peace in the land. When word comes from the oracle of Memphis that, with the coming of the young warrior and "new nuptials," her sufferings will be at an end, the Queen joyfully sends for Arsace. Arsace, though ever obedient to his sovereign's wishes, fails to realize that she is in love with him. Together they sing of their future happiness (*"Serbami ognor"*)— the Queen thinking of Arsace, and he of Azema —little knowing that they are at cross-purposes.

SCENE 3: *The throne room of the palace.* Before her assembled subjects, Semiramide makes all swear that they will honor her choice of king and consort (*"Giuri ognuno"*). Arsace is named to the joyous approval of the populace, and the hand of Azema is promised to Idreno. The furious Assur tries to stir up his supporters against the "Scythian upstart," but the Queen silences him and bids Oroe to unite her in marriage to the astonished Arsace. But even before the horrified priest can protest the union, the ghost of Nino himself emerges from the tomb, and addressing himself to Arsace, affirms that the young man shall indeed be king—but only after his own murder shall be avenged. Arsace must first descend into the vaults of the tomb and sacrifice a victim to the ghost of Nino and the wrathful gods. The guilt-racked Queen attempts to follow her husband's ghost into the tomb, but is repulsed. "When the gods will it," the specter tells her, "I shall call you."

ACT II

SCENE 1: *A room in the palace.* Semiramide threatens to banish Assur if he persists in opposing her plans for Arsace. In a duet (*"Se la vita ancor t'e cara"*) they heap mutual reproaches on each other for the murder of Nino fifteen years before. When Semiramide seeks to mitigate her own guilt in the matter, Assur reminds her both of the horrid night of the crime and the ghost's demand for a sacrificial victim. But the Queen, confident that

Arsace will protect her from all harm, is heartened by the sound of an off-stage chorus acclaiming the young captain. She vows to punish the rebellious Assur, and he, in turn, plots vengeance on them all.

SCENE 2: *The sanctuary of the temple.* Readying him for his sacred mission of revenge, Oroe reveals to Arsace that he is, in fact, Ninia, Nino's long-lost son. He then shows the youth the letter his dying father had written, exposing the queen and Assur as his murderers. Overwhelmed with horror and grief that he is betrothed to his own mother, and required to slay her in expiation of her awful crime, Arsace momentarily falters. But Oroe, arming him with Nino's own sword, exhorts him to slay Assur.

SCENE 3: *The Queen's apartment.* Semiramide cannot understand Arsace's reluctance to marry her and assume the throne. At last putting aside evasive answers, Arsace bids her read the contents of the letter Oroe has given him. Having learned the awful truth, Semiramide urges her son to slay her on the spot ("*Ebbene, a te: ferisci*"), but Arsace, moved to compassion, pardons her, and before leaving on his fateful mission in the vaults below, bids her calm her fears. Idreno enters the deserted antechamber and sings of his love for Azema ("*La speranza più dolce*"). When the Princess herself enters, Idreno pleads with her to accept his suit. As she can no longer hope to win Arsace, the young girl passively agrees to marriage with Idreno.

SCENE 4: *A remote corner of the palace near the tomb.* Assur prepares to enter the tomb himself, where he intends to kill Arsace. He is interrupted by a group of his followers, who tell him that Oroe has revealed his hand in the King's murder and raised the populace against him. Undeterred, Assur swears once more that the "Scythian" shall never rule over them; but when he attempts to enter the tomb, he is transfixed by an unseen force. Begging for mercy ("*Deh! ti ferma*"), Assur struggles against his unseen adversary, as he imagines he is being drawn toward the edge of a bottomless pit. Released from the evil spell, he again reassures his shaken followers, and finally enters the monument.

SCENE 5: *The vaults of the tomb.* Accompanied by Oroe and the other Magi, Arsace enters the tomb, still uncertain of the chosen victim. "The gods will guide you," Oroe assures him, retiring with the priests. As Arsace searches through the impenetrable gloom, Assur enters, bent on his own vengeance. As he, too, is lost to view, Semiramide, with the intention of protecting her son against Assur's murderous assault, appears and prays for help from Nino's ghost ("*Al mio pregar*"). All three, each one unseen by the others, express their fears ("*L'usato ardir, il mio valor dov'è?*"). When Oroe, concealed behind the monument, cries out to Arsace—or Ninia, as he now correctly names him—to strike the avenging blow, the young man drives his sword into Assur. Before the villain is carried off, he hears Oroe proclaim Arsace the son and rightful heir of Nino before the assembled populace. A joyful chorus ("*Vieni, Arsace*") celebrates his triumph.

La Scala staging of the final scene in which Arsace kills not Assur, as in story above, but his own mother, Semiramide

La Serva Padrona
THE SERVANT MISTRESS

CHARACTERS

Uberto, *a prosperous bachelor*   *Bass*   Vespone, *his butler*   *Mime*

Serpina, *his maid*   *Soprano*

The action takes place in Italy in the eighteenth century.

OPERA BUFFA in two scenes (or *intermezzi*). Music by Giovanni Battista Pergolesi. Libretto in Italian by Gennaro Antonio Federico. First performance at the Bartolomeo Opera House in Naples, August 28, 1733. First American performance at Baltimore, in French, June 14, 1790. First Metropolitan Opera production, February 23, 1935, with Editha Fleischer and Louis d'Angelo. Revived there in 1942 with Bidu Sayao and Salvatore Baccaloni.

To mitigate the tragic solemnities of eighteenth-century *opera seria*, impresarios sometimes offered *intermezzi* between the acts of the tragedies—short, light comedies, usually with a soubrette and a *basso buffo*, for a change of pace. *La Serva Padrona* was written in two parts to be played in the intermissions between Pergolesi's own three-act *Il Prigionier Superbo* (*The Proud Prisoner*), which was a failure, like all six of Pergolesi's tragic operas. The intermezzo opera, however, was wildly successful throughout Italy, and sixteen years after the composer's death at the age of twenty-six, became the centerpiece in an engaging chapter of operatic history—"The War of the Buffoons." In 1752–1753 *La Serva Padrona* had a *succès fou* in Paris, being performed almost two hundred times, and intellectuals like Rousseau and Diderot seized upon it to publish pamphlets—no fewer than sixty altogether—to attack (or defend) the stately musical stage works of Lully and Rameau. Thus, in a sense, was

opera buffa born to strike an eventually mortal blow at *opera seria*, much as had happened a few years earlier in London with the production of the "ballad opera" called *The Beggar's Opera*.

But the book and score of *La Serva Padrona* have more to recommend them than a historical circumstance. The little work has so much charm and vitality that it is, even today, being constantly given by opera workshops and other small companies, and there have been numerous recordings.

INTERMEZZO I

SCENE: *A room in Uberto's house.* Uberto, alone in his morning room, complains energetically because his morning chocolate is hours late, and he cannot therefore go out. When his two servants come in (one of them a mute), he tries to discipline them, but Serpina the maid has higher spirits than her master and more courage. The chocolate isn't ready, she says, so he'll just have to do without; and when he tries to answer back, she says that, furthermore, he won't be allowed to go out at all; she'll lock the door on him. In desperation Uberto decides the house needs a mistress and instructs Vespone the butler to go out and find a wife for him. "Why not me?" says Serpina. And in the duet that closes the scene, he protests that he never will marry his

Paolo Montarsolo as Uberto and Anna Moffo as his pert maid, Serpina, in a production created for Italian television

servant, but there is enough weakness in his protests to encourage Serpina and the audience—to have little faith in them.

INTERMEZZO II

SCENE: *The same.* Some time later (that afternoon? no one knows—or cares particularly) Serpina leads into the room Vespone disguised as a uniformed soldier with frightening whiskers. When he is hidden outside the door, Serpina reports to her master that as he will not marry her, she is planning to marry instead one Capitano Tempesto, a man with unbridled temper. She then sings him a sentimental little aria about how one day he will remember her fondly. Thus softened up, he agrees to meet the happy fiancé; and while she goes to fetch the Capitano, he admits to the audience that he is really rather attracted to his attractive maid. Without actually uttering a word, Vespone manages to appear dangerous, striding all over the place, and letting Uberto know, through Serpina, that he demands a dowry of forty thousand crowns; and if it is not forthcoming, he'll see to it that Uberto marries the girl himself. To establish his ability to make his threat stick, Vespone draws his sword and makes other warlike gestures. Finally Uberto succumbs, agreeing to do that which, as we knew all along, he wanted to do anyway. Even when Vespone removes his false mustachios, Uberto sticks gladly to his bargain; and the opera closes with a duet. The affianced couple describe how their happy hearts beat now: his goes *tippiti-tippiti*, hers *tappatà-tappatà*.

Simon Boccanegra

CHARACTERS

Simon Boccanegra, *Doge of Genoa* — *Baritone*
Maria Boccanegra, *his daughter, known as Amelia Grimaldi* — *Soprano*
Jacopo Fiesco, *known as Andrea* — *Bass*

Gabriele Adorno, *Genoese nobleman* — *Tenor*
Paolo Albiani, *favorite courtier of the Doge* — *Bass-baritone*
Pietro, *another courtier* — *Baritone*
Amelia's Maidservant — *Mezzo-soprano*

Soldiers, Seamen, Commoners, Senators, Court of the Doge, etc.

The action takes place in and near Genoa around the middle of the fourteenth century.

OPERA IN a prologue and three acts. Music by Giuseppe Verdi. Text in Italian by Francesco Maria Piave (later revised by Arrigo Boito), founded on a Spanish drama by A. García Gutiérrez. First performance, Teatro la Fenice, Venice, March 12, 1857. First given in Boito's revised version, Milan, March 24, 1881. United States première, Metropolitan Opera House, January 28, 1932, with Lawrence Tibbett as Simon, Giovanni Martinelli as Adorno, Ezio Pinza as Fiesco, Claudio Frigerio as Paolo, Paul Ananian as Pietro, Maria Müller as Maria. Tullio Serafin conducted.

Verdi himself looked upon the première of his work as a fiasco. Some others thought so, too, yet there were contributing circumstances—the tenor and baritone originally chosen for the roles of Simon and Gabriele were both ill and unable to appear; in addition, there was opposition from the audience, which, as the *Gazzetta di Venezia* described the occasion, behaved rudely, and created a disturbance, "such as could not possibly have been engineered by a public so proverbially courteous as that of Venice." The press, however, was almost unanimously favorable toward the work, its decline being blamed entirely on the indifference of the public. Given at La Scala, Milan, March 24, 1881, with Boito's revision of the libretto, besides Verdi's considerably altered score, the opera was eminently successful.

Not the most consistently expressive of Verdi's scores, the music of *Simon Boccanegra* yet contains many pages of true eloquence and dramatic power. Notable among these are Fiesco's prologue aria *"Il lacerato spirito,"* which was once a standby of the recital hall; the *"Miserere,"* also in the prologue; the vivid finale of Act I; the duet between Simon and Fiesco in the last act. As for the libretto, it seems to be no better than average in quality of drama and motivation, despite Boito's shrewd revisions.

PROLOGUE

SCENE: *A square in Genoa before the Fiesco Palace.* Paolo and Pietro, together with other commoners, scheme to place the public favorite, the corsair Simon Boccanegra, on the Doge's throne. Simon arrives, his intention apparently being to enter the palace to seek news of Maria, Fiesco's daughter, with whom he has been carrying on a secret love affair. Apprized, however, of the commoners' plans, he accepts the honor, swearing fealty to the cause, having learned, too, that Maria is kept prisoner within the palace. As all depart, Fiesco, surrounded by his followers, emerges, and after a recitative in

Act 1, Scene 1: Paolo (Ezio Flagello) arrives at the Grimaldi Gardens with the Doge of Genoa, Simon Boccanegra (Leonard Warren), in the Metropolitan Opera production

which he bids farewell to the palace, "haughty mound, chill sepulcher of my beloved one," he sings the celebrated bass aria *"Il lacerato spirito"* ("My torn soul"), wherein he laments the death of his daughter Maria. The mourners leave, and Simon returns, unaware of her death, to see Maria. In an interview with Fiesco he is asked the whereabouts of the daughter born of the illicit union. Simon declares his ignorance and, after listening to the fiery vow of eternal enmity made by Fiesco, enters the palace on the latter's departure. Soon he emerges, aggrieved by the stunning discovery of Maria's

demise. And in the midst of his grief the supporters return and proclaim him Doge.

ACT I

SCENE 1: *The Grimaldi Gardens on the outskirts of Genoa.* Twenty-five years have elapsed. A young woman, Amelia Grimaldi, who is a supposed orphan, lives under the protection of one Andrea, really Fiesco. She is actually the daughter of Simon Boccanegra and Maria, although this fact is unknown to either her or the fictitious Andrea. Her true name is, like her mother's, Maria, and as she gazes at the distant horizon, she sings an aria, *"Come in quest' ora bruna"* ("As in this dark hour"). Meanwhile, we learn that Fiesco, still detesting Simon, has joined Gabriele Adorno, a young nobleman who loves Amelia, in a conspiracy against the present Doge, who is, of course, Simon Boccanegra. Paolo, however, now comfortably installed in the graces of the ruler, has himself a desire to wed Amelia, but he is rebuffed, and therefore plots to abduct her.

Simon visits the Grimaldi home, there meeting Amelia, and soon discovers that she is his daughter. He reveals his identity to her, in turn swearing her to secrecy. Later, he tells Paolo to give up all hope of winning her, much to that suppliant's dismay.

SCENE 2: *The council chamber in the Doge's palace.* In the council chamber the Doge, with his lawmakers, is attending to affairs of state, when a clamor is heard outside. As the sounds increase, Gabriele and Fiesco are brought before him, the former accused of having slain a certain Lorenzin, to whose home Amelia had been brought after her abduction. Amelia is also present now, having been freed, and Paolo, fearing that his part in the deed will be discovered, attempts to escape. Simon, however, orders the doors barred.

In the heat of a strong passion, Gabriele exclaims that someone in a high place is responsible for the murder, and he hurls himself, sword in hand, at Simon, when Amelia gets between the two men. As the situation gradually becomes calmer, thanks to Simon's impressive plea, he, suspecting Paolo, calls upon him to join all in placing a curse on the culprit. And this Paolo does, not without a visible nervousness. In the meantime, Gabriele and Fiesco, the latter not recognized by Simon, are put into temporary custody.

ACT II

SCENE: *The Doge's quarters in the Ducal palace.* The malcontent Paolo steals into the Doge's chamber, together with Pietro, and when the latter has left, pours the contents of a poison vial into Simon's drinking bowl. Under escort of Pietro, who soon departs, Gabriele and Fiesco appear, and to the latter's query about where they are, Paolo answers, "In the rooms of the Doge, where I, Paolo, would talk with you." In their conversation, which is not to Fiesco's liking, Paolo urges him to stab Boccanegra. This Fiesco is loath to do, whereupon Paolo orders him back to his dungeon, meanwhile staying

Maria Müller as Amelia Grimaldi, alias Maria Boccanegra, at the Metropolitan Opera in 1932

Gabriele. He plays on the young nobleman's jealousy, with the information that Amelia is in the palace. But not successful with those tactics, he threatens Gabriele with death unless he delivers the fatal blow.

Torn with doubts, Gabriele sings his aria *"O inferno, Amelia qui!"* ("O fury! Amelia here!") right after Paolo's departure, and the lady in question herself presently appears. Gabriele accuses her of disloyalty, with which some stormy moments ensue, though later Amelia, unwilling to disclose her relationship to the Doge, begs Gabriele to hide, for she has heard a fanfare of trumpets announcing the arrival of her father. Gabriele conceals himself, and the Doge enters reading a document. He greets his daughter lovingly, and in their talk he is informed that Gabriele is the man she loves, and she pleads for his life. The Doge, wearily falling into a chair, drinks the poisoned wine, while reluctantly agreeing to give Gabriele his freedom. The effect of the poison places the Doge in a stupor, and soon he is asleep. Gabriele rushes out, gazes at him a moment, then, unsheathing his dagger, is about to stab him, but again Amelia saves her father's life. Amelia does all she can to prove her innocence without revealing her secret, but finally when the Doge awakens he himself makes the disclosure, and Gabriele, throwing himself at the Doge's feet, asks his forgiveness, vowing to take up arms in his cause.

ACT III

SCENE: *Within the palace.* The scene overlooks the illuminated city of Genoa. Great shouts come up from the crowds below as they acclaim the victory of Boccanegra over his enemies. Paolo, instigator of the revolt, has been condemned to death, and as he is being led away, he confides to Fiesco that the Doge will die long before himself. The Doge, visibly failing from the effects of the poison, makes his appearance, preceded by a captain of the Arbalisters and a trumpeter. The captain addresses the multitude below from the balcony, telling them that it is the Doge's wish not to "offend with clamorous joy the heroes' deaths." The captain and the trumpeter depart, and Fiesco approaches the Doge, who complains of feeling a strange throbbing through his temples. In an apostrophe to the sea he exclaims, "Why was not its cradle the corsair's tomb?" and Fiesco exultingly remarks that it would have been better so, for the pall of death is upon him. When Fiesco admits his identity, the Doge contentedly informs him that their old enmity is ended, for now, as he had been once asked to do, he consigns to Fiesco's paternal care the young Amelia, the granddaughter he had long ago sought. Fiesco's happiness at the discovery is soon changed to a tragic sadness, as he bemoans Simon's imminent death. Amelia and Gabriele enter, and in difficult whispers Simon tells her that she is of noble blood, for she is Fiesco's granddaughter. His last wish is that Gabriele be named his successor, and, before the awed gathering, he dies.

Act I, Scene 2, as presented at the Teatro dell'Opera, Rome, with the Doge (Tito Gobbi) presiding over his council in his magnificent chambers

La Sonnambula

THE SLEEPWALKER

CHARACTERS

Amina, *fiancée of Elvino*	*Soprano*	Teresa, *a milleress*	*Mezzo-soprano*
Elvino, *a wealthy peasant*	*Tenor*	Count Rodolfo, *lord of the village*	*Bass*
Lisa, *an innkeeper, in love with*		Alessio, *a peasant in love with Lisa*	*Bass*
Elvino	*Soprano*	A Notary	*Tenor*

Peasants and Peasant Women

The action takes place in a Swiss village in the early nineteenth century.

Maria Callas, La Scala's Amina in 1955

OPERA IN two acts. Music by Vincenzo Bellini. Libretto in Italian by Felice Romani. First produced at the Teatro Carcano, Milan, March 6, 1831, with Giuditta Pasta and Giovanni Battista Rubini creating the roles of Amina and Elvino. The great Maria Malibran was heard as Amina in an English version of the opera in London in 1833. *La Sonnambula* was first performed in America at the Park Theater, on November 13, 1835, in English. The first American performance in the original Italian occurred at Palmo's Opera House, New York, on May 13, 1844. Four years later Bellini's sleepwalking opera underwent another change—as *The Room Scrambler,* a burlesque produced at the Olympic Theater of New York. It entered the repertoire of the Metropolitan Opera during its second month, on November 14, 1883, with Marcella Sembrich as Amina. Jenny Lind was long identified with the role of Amina, and so were Adelina Patti, Marcella Sembrich, Luisa Tetrazzini, and Amelita Galli-Curci. Among the brilliant Metropolitan revivals of *La Sonnambula* was that of 1905, when Sembrich sang Amina; Caruso, Elvino; and Plançon, Rodolfo. In 1909 the Spanish soprano Elvira de Hidalgo caused a minor stir by

Act I: Elvino (John Alexander) greets his sweetheart, Amina (Joan Sutherland), in the 1963 Metropolitan Opera production

walking barefoot during Amina's somnambulist wanderings. Lily Pons was largely responsible for keeping the opera in the repertory in the early 1930's. On February 21, 1963 Joan Sutherland starred in a new production at the Metropolitan, where Roberta Peters and Gianna d'Angelo later also sang the role.

Earlier generations doted on this unpretentious little opera. By 1850 *La Sonnambula* figured seasonally in the repertory of most major opera houses of Europe, but for later generations the rising tide of Wagnerism diminished its vogue. Recently it has been revived in several countries for Maria Callas and Joan Sutherland, both of whom have recorded it.

ACT I

SCENE 1: *A village square.* The betrothal of the charming Amina to Elvino is being merrily celebrated on the village green when a handsome stranger arrives, asking the way to the castle. As it is a considerable distance, he decides to put up at the village inn for the night. The sight of these surroundings revives memories in the stranger that find their expression in the aria *"Vi ravviso"* ("As I

view these scenes"). Night is approaching, and Amina's foster mother Teresa declares that it is time for all to go home lest the phantom that has lately been haunting the neighborhood appear. The people depart, and the stranger enters the inn. Elvino, remaining with Amina, reproaches her bitterly for her unseemly interest in the stranger. Her tears stop him, and he begs her forgiveness, saying that he is jealous even of the breeze that plays with her hair. The lovers then unite in a duet of reconciliation.

SCENE 2: *A room at the inn.* Lisa, the proprietress of the inn, stops at the stranger's door to see if he is comfortable, but when he starts to flirt with her, she coyly slips away. As she does so, she drops her scarf. The stranger is stupefied at the unexpected sight that now confronts him: Amina calmly walks in through the window, saying, "Elvino, are you still jealous? I love only you." He realizes at once that she is walking in her sleep. Not knowing what to do in this most embarrassing predicament, he slips out the window. Meanwhile, Lisa has been peeping from an adjoining room. Herself in love with Elvino, and jealous of Amina, she runs off to inform the youth of his Amina's faithlessness. When she returns with Elvino and the villagers, Amina is soundly asleep in

Nineteenth-century lithograph of the sleepwalker Amina, treading her way across a perilous bridge while her friends anxiously watch. Act II, Scene 2

the stranger's bed. The luckless girl awakens with a start and runs, bewildered, to her lover. Though she protests her innocence, he thrusts her from him and rushes away. Amina is left to despair under the cold looks that meet her from all sides.

ACT II

SCENE 1: *An open spot in the forest*. The villagers, having decided that, after all, Amina must be innocent, sing of their determination to go to the stranger (who has turned out to be Count Rodolfo, long-absent owner of the castle) and ask him to explain. When they have left, Amina, with her foster mother Teresa, comes to the same spot and sings a touching aria about her unfortunate plight. Elvino also comes here, but not seeing the two women, pours out his heart on the same subject. Yet, when Amina steps forward to plead her innocence, he denounces her and tears the betrothal ring off her finger. Even the villagers, returning from a visit to the Count, cannot convince Elvino, and in a heartbroken final aria, he bids her be happy with her new lover.

SCENE 2: *An open field near Teresa's mill*. Elvino has transferred his affections to the now triumphant Lisa, and the two start out for the church. They are met by the Count, who assures Elvino of Amina's innocence, but Elvino still refuses to believe and bids Lisa follow him. Again they are stopped, this time by Teresa, who, having heard of his proposed marriage, now shows Elvino Lisa's scarf, found in the Count's room. "Deceived again!" cries the perplexed bridegroom, wondering aloud if any woman is to be trusted. Once more the Count assures him of Amina's innocence. "But where is the proof?" asks Elvino. "There!" cries the Count suddenly, pointing to the roof of the mill. And there, to everybody's astonishment, Amina appears in her nightdress, carrying a lamp. It is plain to all that she is walking in her sleep. They watch her breathlessly for fear she will fall. She crosses the narrow, fragile bridge directly over the revolving water wheel and descends the stairs, singing to herself a tender, melancholy air in keeping with her plight. Overcome with mingled joy and chagrin, Elvino rushes to her. Amina awakens to find her lover kneeling at her feet. With a cry of delight, she raises him to his feet and falls into his arms. Amina now expresses her happiness in the brilliant but tender aria *"Ah! non giunge"* ("Ah! he does not arrive"). Nothing now remains to mar their happy union. Even the mystery of the castle "ghost" has become clear, and Bellini's pastoral opera closes with general rejoicing.

Still sleep-walking, Amina (Joan Sutherland) dreams of her beloved Elvino (Nicolai Gedda), standing nearby with Teresa (Lili Chookasian) and other villagers

Suor Angelica

SISTER ANGELICA

CHARACTERS

Sister Angelica	*Soprano*	Sister Osmina	*Soprano*
The Princess, *her aunt*	*Contralto*	Sister Dolcina	*Mezzo-soprano*
The Abbess	*Soprano*	The Infirmary Sister	*Soprano*
The Sister Monitor	*Soprano*	The Mistress of the Novices	*Mezzo-soprano*
Sister Genevieve	*Soprano*		

Questuants, Novices, and Postulants

The action takes place in a convent in the late seventeenth century.

OPERA IN one act. Music by Giacomo Puccini. Libretto in Italian by Giovacchino Forzano. World première at the Metropolitan Opera House, December 14, 1918, as one of three operas labeled *Il Trittico (The Triptych)* by the composer, the other two being *Il Tabarro* and *Gianni Schicchi*. The European première of the *Trittico*, at the Teatro Costanzi in Rome, on January 11, 1919, was the greatest triumph of Puccini's life. The cast at the world première starred Geraldine Farrar as Sister Angelica and Flora Perini as the Princess.

Despite Puccini's wish and attempts to have the three operas performed as a whole, *Il Tabarro* and *Suor Angelica,* which were not so well received as *Gianni,* soon were dropped from the repertory, and *Gianni* was coupled with a number of other operas. *Suor Angelica* was Puccini's favorite of the *Trittico* —perhaps because, like a mother who loves her weakest child, it was not the public's favorite, or possibly because of the special appeal of its theme, since his eldest and favorite sister was a nun.

SCENE: *Inside the convent, showing the small church and the cloister. Toward one side, the cemetery; toward the other, a vegetable garden. In the center is a fount.*

THE PRAYER. The sisters are in church, singing. Two postulants, late for prayers, enter the church. Sister Angelica, also late, kneels down and kisses the threshold before going into church. At the end of prayers, the sisters come from the church and pass in front of the Abbess for her blessing.

THE PENANCES. The Sister Monitor tells the two late postulants that, for omitting a duty, as penance they must say twenty prayers for all in need of absolution. One sister is sent to her spinning wheel, while Sister Osmina, for hiding roses in her sleeves and denying it, is sent to her cell.

THE RECREATION. The Sister Monitor bids the sisters relax and play. Sister Angelica waters the grass and flowers as Sister Genevieve recounts the yearly spectacle of the water fount turning gold for three evenings. The sisters recall a dead nun, and Sister Genevieve proposes that they carry some of the golden water to her tomb. When the sisters answer that the dead sister must wish for that, Sister Angelica reproves them, saying wishes are buds of the living. Sister Genevieve confesses that sometimes she wishes for things—to see a lamb, for she had been a shepherdess. The stout Sister Dolcina, before she can say anything, is told that her wish is something good to eat. When Sister Angelica is asked if she has any wishes, she haltingly answers no. The sisters say that she lies, for she longs to hear from her family (she had been a princess and had been forced to take vows). The Infirmary Sister rushes in for her help for a sister stung by wasps, and Sister Angelica picks some herbs for a lotion.

THE RETURN FROM THE QUEST. Two questuants enter with a donkey laden with gifts, one of them telling the sisters that a magnificent coach is outside the garden gate. Sister Angelica, trembling, describes the coach, but the questuant is not sure that it is the one. The visitors' bell rings, and Sister Genevieve prays that the visitor will be for Sister Angelica. The Abbess enters, calling Sister Angelica and motioning the others away. The sisters fill a watering can with the golden water and leave for the cemetery. Sister Angelica, who has waited seven years for a word from outside, asks who the visitor is. The Abbess tells her to pray, then announces the visitor.

THE PRINCESS. Sister Angelica's aunt, the Princess, enters coldly, while Sister Angelica is deeply moved. She informs the sister that, in accordance with Angelica's dead parents' wishes, she has divided the children's inheritance, for the youngest sister is to be married. The aunt remains hard and unyielding to Sister Angelica, still unforgiving for the sin Angelica committed. Sister Angelica asks about her son, the baby who had been taken from her, and the Princess tells her that he died two years ago. Sobbing, Sister Angelica falls to the ground. The document dividing the inheritance is brought out for her signature, and the Princess departs.

THE GRACE. Kneeling, Sister Angelica thinks of her baby and wishes to join him in death. It is dark when the sisters return from the cemetery, and they assure Sister Angelica that her wish will come true. Left alone, Angelica makes a fire, gathers herbs and flowers, boils them in a pot with some of the golden water, and places the poisonous brew in front of the cross. She bids farewell to the departed sisters, kisses the cross, and drinks the poison. But her look of exaltation suddenly gives way to anguish.

THE MIRACLE. She has damned herself by taking her own life. Praying to the Virgin to save her—love for her son drove her out of her mind—Sister Angelica hears the angels pleading with the Holy Mother for mercy. A mystic light bathes the church, the door opens, and from it comes the Virgin with a little boy, whom she pushes toward the dying nun.

Geraldine Farrar as Sister Angelica in the finale of 1918 world première at the Metropolitan Opera

Il Tabarro

THE CLOAK

CHARACTERS

Michele, *a barge captain*	*Baritone*	Giorgetta, *Michele's wife*	*Soprano*
Luigi, *a longshoreman*	*Tenor*	Frugola, *Talpa's wife*	*Contralto*
Tinca, *a longshoreman*	*Tenor*	Song Peddler	*Tenor*
Talpa, *a longshoreman*	*Bass*		

Longshoremen, Midinettes, Organ Grinder, Two Lovers

The action takes place in Paris, along the Seine River, early in this century.

OPERA IN one act. Music by Giacomo Puccini. Libretto in Italian by Giuseppe Adami, from Didier Gold's *La Houppelande*. World première at the Metropolitan Opera House, December 14, 1918, as one of the three operas forming the *Trittico* (*Triptych*), the other two being *Suor Angelica* and *Gianni Schicchi*. The cast at the première consisted of Claudia Muzio as Giorgetta, Luigi Montesanto as Michele, Giulio Crimi as Luigi, Angelo Bada as Tinca, Adamo Didur as Talpa, and Alice Gentle as Frugola; Roberto Moranzoni conducted.

Though *Il Tabarro* has been performed apart from its companion pieces, it has not achieved the success of *Gianni*. It is, however, a fine example of *verismo* opera, and its musical picture of life on the River Seine is a masterpiece of tone painting.

SCENE: *Michele's barge on the bank of the Seine.* Michele watches the sunset as the longshoremen go about their tasks of unloading cargo. His wife Giorgetta comes out of the cabin, takes down her wash, waters her plants, and cleans the bird cage. The men ought to have wine, she tells Michele, and when he tries to kiss her for her thoughtfulness, she turns away from him. Disappointed, he leaves for the hold

as the longshoremen Luigi, Tinca, and Talpa enter, tired and hot. Giorgetta goes for the wine and pours them drinks. An organ grinder passes on shore, and Giorgetta and Tinca dance to his music until Luigi shoves Tinca aside, holds Giorgetta tightly, and shows them how to dance. The dance ends awkwardly with Michele's return, and the men leave.

Giorgetta is anxious to know which of the men Michele plans to take with him on their next trip, but, much to her annoyance, he is noncommittal. But he does promise Luigi to hire him for the journey. A song peddler, hawking the latest ballad, passes by, and Giorgetta spots Frugola, Talpa's jealous wife, who is looking for him. While the midinettes gather to hear the peddler's spring song, Giorgetta asks Michele why he acts so strangely tonight. When he tells her he is always kind, she answers that she would rather be beaten than be subjected to his silences. Frugola, a bag over her shoulder, comes on board the barge, asking if Talpa is through work. She pulls out some of the junk she has collected in her bag to show Giorgetta and rambles on about her cat (Michele has disappeared into his cabin), and soon the longshoremen are ready to quit work for the day. Tinca is bound for a tavern, but Luigi cannot

Metropolitan Opera's 1946 production, which starred Licia Albanese (Giorgetta), Lawrence Tibbett (Michele) and Frederick Jagel (Luigi)

drink away his troubles; everything is forbidden to the poor, he complains, even love.

As Talpa and Frugola prepare to go home, she tells Giorgetta of her dream of one day having a cottage of their own to retire to. Giorgetta's dream is of getting off the barge and living in her beloved village of Belleville. Luigi, who was also born there, and Giorgetta recall the joys of former days. Unconsciously they have held hands, but suddenly realizing they are not alone, they unclasp them. After Talpa and Frugola have left, Luigi goes to embrace Giorgetta, but she stops him, telling him Michele will kill him if he finds out they are lovers.

Michele comes from the cabin, and Luigi tries to explain away his still being on board by thanking him for the promised job. When Michele goes to light the lanterns, the lovers bid each other good-by; Giorgetta tells Luigi she will leave the gangplank out for him and light a match when it is safe for him to come aboard.

Michele, returning, wonders why Giorgetta no longer loves him, but she assures him she does and tells him it is bedtime. No, she will not sleep in the cabin; it suffocates her. Michele recalls last year, when with their baby they were happy—and how he used to enfold her and the baby in his cloak as in a caress. He begs her to love him again, but she cuts him short, feigning sleepiness. When he tries to kiss her, she runs off. He watches her retreating figure, then mutters, "Strumpet!" Two lovers pass by on the shore, saying good night, taps sound from a nearby army barracks, and Michele puts his cloak over his shoulders and stares down at the river, thinking of his sorrows. He then takes out his pipe and lights it, and Luigi, believing it to be Giorgetta's signal, jumps onto the barge. Michele catches him by the throat and forces a confession from him before strangling him to death.

Giorgetta calls to Michele from the cabin, but before she comes out, he throws his cloak around the body of Luigi, who has held on to him in a death grip. Michele calms the nervous Giorgetta, and when she coquettishly tells him she only wanted to be near him, he asks, Under my cloak, as you used to be? At her yes, he flings open the cloak, and the body of her lover falls at her feet. She draws back, but Michele hurls her upon Luigi's body.

The Tales of Hoffmann

LES CONTES D'HOFFMANN

CHARACTERS

Hoffmann, *a poet*	Tenor	Luther, *an innkeeper*	Bass
Nicklausse, *his companion*	Mezzo-soprano	Andrès, *servant to Stella*	Tenor
Hoffmann's loves:		Spalanzani, *an inventor*	Tenor
Stella, *an opera singer*	Soprano	Cochenille, *his servant*	Tenor
Olympia, *a mechanical doll*	Soprano	Schlemil, *Giulietta's lover*	Bass
Giulietta, *a courtesan*	Soprano	Pitichinaccio, *Giulietta's admirer, a*	
Antonia, *Crespel's daughter*	Soprano	*dwarf*	Tenor
His evil geniuses:		Crespel, *a councilor of Munich*	Baritone
Lindorf, *a councilor of Nuremberg*	Baritone	Frantz, *his servant*	Tenor
Coppélius, *partner of Spalanzani*	Baritone	Voice of Antonia's Mother	Mezzo-soprano
Dapertutto, *an army officer*	Baritone	The Muse of Poetry	Soprano
Dr. Miracle, *a physician*	Baritone		

Students and Party Guests

The action takes place in Nuremberg, Venice, and Munich in the early nineteenth century.

FANTASTIC OPERA in three acts, with prologue and epilogue; music by Jacques Offenbach; text in French by Jules Barbier and Michel Carré, founded on a play by these authors, derived from three stories by E. T. A. Hoffmann. (Carré's name appears as co-librettist only in the first edition of the vocal score.) First produced, February 10, 1881, at the Opéra-Comique, Paris, the score revised and orchestrated, in part, by Ernest Guiraud. First performance in the United States, October 16, 1882, at the Fifth Avenue Theater, New York, by Maurice Grau's French Opera Company upon their first American appearance. Oscar Hammerstein's revival of the work—Manhattan Opera House, November 14, 1907—established it in this country. The cast, on that occasion, boasted Maurice Renaud, Charles Gilibert, and Charles Dalmorès in the principal male roles. First performance at the Metropolitan, January 11, 1913, with Umberto Macnez as Hoffmann, Adamo Didur as Coppélius, Dinh Gilly as Dapertutto, Léon Rothier as Dr. Miracle, Frieda Hempel as Olympia, Olive Fremstad as Giulietta, Lucrezia Bori as Antonia, and Jeanne Maubourg as Nicklausse; Giorgio Polacco conducted.

The historical Ernst Theodor Amadeus Hoffmann, author, lawyer, composer, literary critic, and caricaturist (1776–1822), was a figure of some importance in the early German Romantic movement. His three fantastic stories on which the opera is based (entitled "The Sandman," "New Year's Eve Adventure," and "Councilor Crespel") are far more macabre than they are in the Barbier-Carré version. Through making Hoffmann himself the central figure in each of them, and adding the framework of the prologue and epilogue, the librettists endowed their play with an effective unity further enhanced when the roles of the four evil geniuses (Lindorf, Coppélius, Dapertutto, and Dr. Miracle) are performed by the same baritone, and the four loves (Stella, Olympia, Giulietta, and Antonia) by the same soprano—feats of vocal virtuosity seldom undertaken nowadays. They also achieved a neat prepositional pun in the title, for "of" can mean either "by" or "about," and in *Tales of Hoffmann* (or *Les Contes d'Hoffmann*) it means both. The close of the epilogue reflects a tragic bit of biography: Hoffman died at the age of forty-six, a confirmed drunkard.

Although Offenbach wrote many a successful *opéra comique*, this fantastic opera is now ranked as his masterpiece. Without being pretentious as music, the score has a delicacy, grace, and poetic feeling perfectly adapted to the fanciful imagination of Hoffmann's *Tales*. Offenbach began his work in 1877, but before it was completed, he became seriously ill. Believing it to be his finest piece of work, he was anxious to witness the first performance; unfortunately, he died, October 5, 1880, some four months before the opera was first produced.

Prologue: As Nicklausse (Janis Martin) listens, Hoffmann (Nicolai Gedda) begins his tales.

his three great loves of the past. (In an aside, he notes that Stella is all three rolled in one—an artist, a courtesan, a young girl.) He begins: "The name of the first was Olympia . . ."

PROLOGUE

SCENE: *Taproom of Luther's Tavern in Nuremberg.* Next door to Luther's Tavern there is supposed to be an opera house in which a performance of Mozart's *Don Giovanni* is going on, with a woman named simply "Stella" singing one of the leading roles. Councilor Lindorf enters the almost empty tavern and bribes Stella's servant Andrès to give him a letter from the prima donna addressed to Hoffmann. In it there is a key to her room. (Note: In many performances this opening is omitted, as well as the roles of and all references to Stella and Lindorf.)

Now the intermission in the supposititious performance of Mozart is reached, and a troupe of students come in noisily demanding drinks of mine host Luther, who serves them as they sing their "Drinking Song." Presently Hoffmann, accompanied as always by Nicklausse, joins them. He is in a strange mood, but when the students demand a song from him, he obliges with the weird "Ballad of Kleinzach," during which he twice wanders away from its tripping rhythm into the praise of a beautiful woman. Then, after a few unpleasant remarks to Lindorf, he agrees to tell the students the stories of

ACT I

SCENE. *A physician's drawing room.* The famous scientist Spalanzani has what many consider a beautiful daughter, Olympia. She is, however, not really his daughter but a wonderful mechanical doll, made by the scientist and his friend Coppélius. Hoffmann has seen this automaton through the window, and now comes to Spalanzani's house, ostensibly as his pupil, but really to make love to Olympia. Coppélius has persuaded him to wear a certain pair of spectacles with which to look at the girl. At an entertainment given by Spalanzani, Olympia sings the oddly mechanical coloratura "Doll Song" with its birdlike roundelays. At two points the song seems about to stop, a servant, Cochenille, touches her shoulder, the sound of a spring is heard, and the song "Olympia's Aria" continues.

Hoffmann is so enraptured by her beauty and by her singing that he will not listen to his friend Nicklausse when he tries to enlighten him; and so carried away is he that when he tells the doll of his passion, he believes she returns his affection, although she only says, "Yes, yes," whenever he happens to touch her shoulder. This odd couple begin a dance which grows faster and faster until Hoffmann falls to the floor in a swoon, thereby breaking

Act I: In drawing room, guests hear Olympia (Roberta Peters) perform with Cochenille (Alessio De Paolis) in attendance, Spalanzani (Paul Franke) at harp.

his spectacles—and his illusion. Now Coppélius enters in a great rage, for Spalanzani has bought Olympia and paid for her with a worthless draft. In his anger, Coppélius breaks the priceless doll to pieces. Spalanzani and Coppélius have it out with fisticuffs, and the guests laugh at Hoffmann, whose first love has ended in disillusionment.

ACT II

SCENE: *Venice, the gallery of Giulietta's palace, overlooking the Grand Canal.* Nicklausse sings with Giulietta the gently swaying, famous "Barcarolle."

Hoffmann also is here, and in spite of Nicklausse's warning, he allows himself to become fascinated by Giulietta. This beautiful courtesan is really under the sway of the magician Dapertutto; for him she has stolen the shadow of her lover Schlemil, for him she now similarly sets out to ensnare Hoffmann in order to steal his reflection in a mirror. He responds to her advances with great ardor.

Surprised by the jealous Schlemil, Hoffmann fights a duel with him, using Dapertutto's proffered sword. Schlemil is killed, and Dapertutto disappears. A moment later Giulietta passes in her gondola, in the mocking company of the dwarf Pitichinaccio. Nicklausse hurries Hoffmann away lest he be arrested for the death of Schlemil.

Act II: The courtesan Giulietta (Grace Moore) accepts diamond from Dapertutto (Lawrence Tibbett), payment for Hoffmann's shadow.

ACT III

SCENE: *A room in Crespel's house, Munich.* Hoffmann is in love with Antonia, daughter of Councillor Crespel, at whose house we now see him. Antonia, like her mother before her, has a remarkably beautiful voice, and, also like her, is afflicted with consumption. Although singing gives his daughter great happiness, Crespel forbids her since he knows so taxing her strength will be fatal to her. At first Hoffmann is delighted to hear her sing when alone with her and joins her in a charming duet; but after he has overheard a conversation between Crespel and Dr. Miracle and learns of the danger, he makes Antonia promise never to sing again. When, however, Crespel and Hoffmann have gone, Dr. Miracle, the evil genius that has haunted Hoffmann as Coppélius and as Dapertutto, returns, and, summoning the spirit of Antonia's mother, whom he has likewise killed, he persuades the girl to sing. Finally she falls exhausted, and when Hoffmann and Crespel return, she sinks dying in her father's arms. So ends in tragedy Hoffmann's third love story.

EPILOGUE

SCENE: *Taproom of Luther's Tavern.* The boon companions thank Hoffmann for his tales and take their leave. The Muse of Art now comes to console Hoffmann, and for a moment he is aroused to great ecstasy and repeats the passionate aria he had sung to Giulietta. Then he falls, face forward, across the table—asleep? "Dead drunk," remarks one of the students in departing; but the girl who leans upon his arm, pauses as she goes out and throws a flower from her bouquet at Hoffmann's feet. (When the Stella episode is included, it is she who asks, "Hoffmann asleep?" and it is Nicklausse who answers, "No, just dead drunk," and thereupon wins her over to her new lover, Councilor Lindorf.) Off stage the students repeat their "Drinking Song."

Act III: Beneath a portrait of her dead mother, Antonia (Lucine Amara) sings happily with her beloved, Hoffmann (Richard Tucker), at the Metropolitan Opera.

Tannhäuser

CHARACTERS

Hermann, *Landgrave of Thuringia*	Bass		Walther von der Vogelweide, *minstrel*	
Tannhäuser, *a minstrel knight*	Tenor		knight	Tenor
Wolfram von Eschenbach, *his friend*			Biterolf, *minstrel knight*	Bass
and a minstrel knight	Baritone		Heinrich der Schreiber, *minstrel*	
Elisabeth, *niece of the Landgrave*	Soprano		knight	Tenor
Venus	Soprano		Reinmar von Zweter, *minstrel knight*	Bass
			A Young Shepherd	Soprano

Thuringian Nobles and Knights, Ladies, Elder and Younger Pilgrims, Sirens, Naiads, Nymphs, Bacchantes

The action takes place in the vicinity of Eisenach at the beginning of the thirteenth century.

OPERA IN three acts. Music and book in German by the composer. First produced, Hoftheater, Dresden, October 19, 1845. Initial American performance, Stadt Theater, New York, April 4, 1859, being the first of Wagner's operas to be given in the United States. It was *Tannhäuser* that inaugurated the German regime at the Metropolitan Opera House, when the work was presented there on November 17, 1884, with Auguste Kraus, Anna Slach, Anton Schott, Adolf Robinson, and Josef Kögel in the principal roles, with Leopold Damrosch conducting. The so-called Paris version of the opera was first heard at the Metropolitan on January 30, 1889, featuring Lilli Lehmann as Venus. Anton Seidl conducted.

The famous Paris première of *Tannhäuser* on March 13, 1861, was a failure, owing chiefly to chauvinistic intrigue and interference. Only after an imperial order from Napoleon III, obtained through the good offices of the Princess Metternich, was the way cleared for its production at the Opéra. With typical enthusiasm, Wagner now found the opportunity to make certain revisions he had had in mind. These were principally concerned with lengthening the opening scene, laid in the mountain retreat of Venus, providing it with what is now sometimes called the "Parisian Bacchanale," while augmenting the dialogue between the goddess and the minstrel knight. In 1861, with *Lohengrin, Das Rheingold, Die Walküre,* a portion of *Siegfried,* and all of *Tristan und Isolde* already composed, Wagner was at the very top of his creative powers. However, despite the dramatic and musical excellence of the material and the previously proved effectiveness of the entire opera, it was received with much sarcasm and ill feeling by the press and intelligentsia.

Further, the members of the fashionable Jockey Club had expected the ballet to take place in the second act, by which time—their leisurely dinners ended—they could repair to the opera house to absorb art in the comfortable manner. Wagner's opposition to any such suggestion, of course, was strong, and he left the dancing in the Bacchanale of the first act where it best belonged. At any rate, after three nights, the opera was withdrawn. Paris did not hear it again until thirty-four years later, May 13, 1895.

All of Wagner's works for the stage possess either a legendary or historical foundation; *Tannhäuser* rests on both. According to medieval romance, the gods and goddesses of antiquity did not die, but took

Jess Thomas as Tannhäuser, Act III, San Francisco Opera

a fearsomely voluptuous dance are seen. These are the "Venusberg's" seductive spells, that show themselves at dead of night. . . . Attracted by the tempting show, a comely human form draws nigh; 'tis Tannhäuser, love's minstrel. He sounds his jubilant "Song of Love" in joyous challenge, as though to force the wanton witchery to do his bidding. Wild cries of riot answer him; the rosy cloud grows denser round him, entrancing perfumes steal away his senses.

In the most seductive of half-lights, his wonder-seeing eye beholds an alluring female form; he hears a voice that sweetly murmurs the siren call . . . Venus herself it is. . . . Then heart and senses burn within him: . . . before the goddess' self he steps with that canticle of love triumphant, and now he sings it in ecstatic praise of her. . . . The wonders of the Venusberg unroll their brightest before him; tumultuous shouts and savage cries of joy mount up . . . in drunken glee bacchantes drive their raging dance and drag Tannhäuser to the warm caresses of love's goddess, who bears him where no step dare tread. . . . A scurry, like the sound of the Wild Hunt, and speedily the storm is laid. Only a wanton whir still pulses in the breeze, a wave of weird voluptuousness . . .

But dawn begins to break already; from afar is heard again the Pilgrims' Chant. As this chant draws closer . . . as the day drives farther back the night, that whir and soughing of the air—which had erstwhile sounded like the eerie cries of souls condemned—now rises, too, to ever gladder waves; so that when the sun ascends at last in splendor, and the Pilgrims' Chant proclaims in ecstasy to all the world, to all that lives and moves thereon, Salvation won, this wave itself swells out the tidings of sublimest joy. . . .

In the Paris version of the opera the Overture coalesces with the music of the opening scene, in the Venusberg. It is this version which nowadays is most often given.

Lilli Lehmann as the goddess of love, Venus

refuge in the underworld. Thus it was believed that the goddess of love, Venus, had established her court near the Wartburg beneath a mountain which came to be known as the Venusberg, there to prey upon the souls of men. The Landgraves who ruled in Thuringia were patrons of the arts and held contests of song. The minnesingers, a class of lyric poets and musicians, generally of noble birth, who sang of idealized love and beauty, were at their height in Germany from about 1150 to 1350 and often took part in such contests. Those appearing in the opera were actual characters. The historical Tannhäuser seems to have been too fond of the things of this world, and thus the legend arose concerning him that he had dwelt in the Venusberg. As treated by Wagner, the legend becomes symbolical of the struggle between the lower and the higher in human nature.

OVERTURE

Wagner himself wrote for the orchestra at Zurich an explanation of the meaning of the Overture. Greatly abridged, it runs as follows:

To begin with, the orchestra leads before us the Pilgrims' Chant alone; it draws near, then swells into a mighty outpour, and finally passes away. Evenfall; last echo of the chant. As night breaks, magic sights and sounds occur, a rosy mist floats up . . . the whirlings of

ACT I

SCENE 1: *The interior of the Venusberg*. The immense cavelike grotto, illuminated by mysterious multicolored lights, where Venus holds her court—the Venusberg. Here languorous youths, urged on by the enticements of nymphs, lead in a wild dance. Into their midst dash a throng of bacchantes who cause the dance to grow even more riotous. Satyrs and fauns appear from the clefts in the rock walls of the cavern and, running headlong after the nymphs, bring the dance to a tumult of frenzy. With the increasing madness of the dance, the music has grown to a climax of the wildest voluptuousness. The three graces vainly attempt to quell the riot. They awaken sleeping cupids, who fly above the tumult and shoot their arrows at the surging crowd below. Stricken with the pangs of love, the wounded take flight. The music subsides from its impassioned turbulence and, glowing with a wonderful, silvery iridescence, sinks into a profound calm. A rosy mist falls over the cave until only Tannhäuser, Venus, and the three graces are visible in the foreground. And now through the mist there appears a cloud picture of the abduction of Europa. From a remote portion of the grotto is heard the song of sirens.

Rosa Raisa as Elisabeth, the Chicago Opera

The vision fades, and another is revealed: the soft glamour of the moon, Leda and the swan at a woodland pool. This vision also disappears, the graces withdraw, and Venus and Tannhäuser remain silent and motionless. The music dies away in a final languorous sigh.

Tannhäuser, beside the reclining Venus, starts up suddenly as from a dream. He has grown weary of the soft, sensuous life of Venus' court, and although the goddess of love herself uses all the fascinations in her power, each time he begins to sing his hymn in her praise he forgets his theme and tells of his longing for earth with its mingled joys and sorrows. When she finds that the allurements of herself or her realm avail nothing, the goddess threatens him, saying that on earth he will be scorned, an outcast among men. Tannhäuser replies that he trusts in Mary. At the name of the Blessed Virgin, Venus and all her kingdom instantly disappear, and Tannhäuser finds himself standing in a valley near the castle of the Wartburg.

SCENE 2: *The valley of the Wartburg*. It is a bright spring morning; a shepherd boy plays on his pipe and sings merrily while nearby can be heard the tinkle of his flock's bells; a band of pilgrims on their way to Rome pass by, singing their chant. Tannhäuser, shaken with emotion, falls on his knees in devout thankfulness. While he is yet kneeling, the sound of hunting horns is heard gradually drawing nearer, and soon the Landgrave and a party of minnesingers come along the path. They recognize Tannhäuser and greet him joyfully. When they ask where he has stayed for so long, he vaguely replies that he wandered far, that he is unhappy and would still continue his wanderings. Nor can all their entreaties and promises cause him to return to them, until the noble-hearted Wolfram reminds him that here lives Elisabeth, and adds that she has sorrowed greatly since his departure. Deeply moved, Tannhäuser consents to remain.

ACT II

SCENE: *The hall of minstrels in the Wartburg*. All is in readiness for a song contest. Elisabeth enters, singing to the hall her joyful greeting, in the brilliant aria *"Dich, teure Hall"* ("Hail, hall of song").

Wolfram enters, conducting Tannhäuser to her. She is overjoyed, but modestly refrains from revealing her happiness too openly. When she asks where he has been so long, he again vaguely says that he wandered in a distant land; only by a miracle did he escape; and, he adds, it was she who caused him to return. They sing a duet in praise of this power which has reunited them; then Tannhäuser leaves to prepare for the contest. Elisabeth's uncle, the Landgrave, enters and informs her that he will offer her hand to the singer she crowns as victor in the contest. At this moment a trumpet fanfare announces the arrival of the time appointed; a hurrying figure, as of pleasant agitation, is played by the strings; then a broad, magnificent march theme is announced. Elisabeth and the Landgrave welcome their guests as they enter. The chorus of voices singing, "Hail, bright abode, Landgrave Hermann, hail!" swells in power and brilliance even as the number of those assembled constantly grows. Finally, when the hall is filled with the nobles, the march comes to a dazzling close.

The Landgrave addresses them in welcome— *"Blick' ich umher"* ("Gazing on this fair assembly")—states the theme of the contest, "Love," and pages collect lots to determine the beginner. The minnesingers hymn the praises of virtuous love.

Tannhäuser, growing more and more agitated, replies to each of them, singing of the delights of merely sensual passion. Finally, inspired by some unnatural force, he bursts into his hymn in praise of Venus: Those who know her not know not love! The women hurry from the hall as from a place unholy;

the men, drawing their swords, rush at Tannhäuser. Elisabeth, though heartbroken at her betrayal, throws herself before him, and pleads that they allow him to seek heaven's forgiveness. The Landgrave consents on condition that Tannhäuser will seek pardon from the Pope. A group of younger pilgrims are heard singing as they start on their journey to Rome. Stricken with remorse, Tannhäuser rushes out to join them.

The Prelude to Act III, described in the score as "Tannhäuser's Pilgrimage," combines several themes, including the theme of "Penitence," that of Elisabeth's intercession, and the one symbolizing Tannhäuser's suffering. These are the main elements of the music, although we hear also references to the themes of "Repentance," the "Pilgrims' Hymn," and others.

ACT III

SCENE: *The valley of the Wartburg.* Elisabeth, by a crucifix, kneels in prayer. From a distance is heard the song of returning pilgrims, gradually drawing nearer.

Elisabeth rises and scans them in the greatest

Act II as seen in 1966 at the San Francisco Opera: Landgrave Hermann greets his guests in the Hall of Song.

anxiety as they pass by and disappear in the distance. *He* is not among them. She sinks once more before the crucifix and in the greatest agony of soul sings the affecting plea to the Virgin Mary, "Elisabeth's Prayer."

Wolfram has been standing at a distance, sorrowfully watching, and when Elisabeth rises and starts to return to the castle, he gently asks if he may not accompany her. By her gesture she declines. Meanwhile night has fallen over the valley and the evening star glows on high. Thinking of Elisabeth, Wolfram sings a wonderfully expressive apostrophe to the star, accompanying himself on his minstrel's harp—"*O du mein holde Abendstern* ("O star of eve").

A gloomy motive is heard in the orchestra, and Tannhäuser appears, haggard and weary. In a broken voice he asks of Wolfram the way to the Venusberg. Wolfram recoils in mingled horror and pity. He urgently questions Tannhäuser, who then tells of his pilgrimage: how he suffered every privation and hardship over dangerous mountains and rocky paths; how he prostrated himself before the Pope, and in deepest contrition confessed his sin,

only to be told that pardon and salvation can never be for him, so long as the papal staff is barren of leaves.

He fled from Rome in despair. Now, without hope of salvation, he seeks forgetfulness at the Venusberg. A ruddy glow illuminates the recesses of the mountain; the song of the sirens and the voluptuous music of the Venusberg are heard; Venus appears, holding out her arms to welcome Tannhäuser. Wolfram pleads with him, but the minstrel spurns his entreaties. At this moment when Venus seems to have won her prey, Wolfram recalls to Tannhäuser the name "Elisabeth." The knight stands as if spellbound. Recognizing her defeat, Venus vanishes with all her magical companions. Bells are heard tolling, for Elisabeth has died during the night, and now the mournful music of her funeral train draws near. As the procession of mourners enters the valley carrying the bier, Tannhäuser, broken with grief and exhaustion, sinks dying beside Elisabeth. But as his soul takes its flight, the second band of pilgrims arrives. They carry the papal staff which has brought forth green leaves—a miracle revealing that Tannhäuser has been pardoned.

Bayreuth Festival staging by Wieland Wagner of Act III finale: Tannhäuser (Wolfgang Windgassen), comforted by Wolfram (Hermann Prey), dies in grace.

Thaïs

CHARACTERS

Thaïs, *a courtesan*	*Soprano*	Palemon, *an old monk*	*Bass*
Athanaël, *a monk of the Cenobite*		Albine, *an abbess*	*Mezzo-soprano*
order	*Baritone*	Crobyle, *a slave*	*Soprano*
Nicias, *a young Sybarite*	*Tenor*	Myrtale, *a slave*	*Mezzo-soprano*

Monks, Nuns, Citizens, Servants, Dancers, etc.

The action takes place in and near Alexandria in the fourth century.

OPERA IN THREE ACTS. Music by Jules Massenet. Libretto in French by Louis Gallet, after the novel by Anatole France. First performed at the Paris Opéra, March 16, 1894. American première, at Oscar Hammerstein's Manhattan Opera House, New York, on November 25, 1907, with Mary Garden and Maurice Renaud in the chief roles. First Metropolitan performance, February 16, 1917, with Geraldine Farrar as Thaïs and Pasquale Amato as Athanaël.

Massenet wrote *Thaïs* for the lovely Sibyl Sanderson, just as he had written *Esclarmonde* for her five years before. The California soprano was a sensation in the role, thanks mainly to her dazzling beauty. But for power and glow of interpretation, the singer inseparably linked with the part is Sanderson's protegée, Mary Garden, who triumphantly launched her American career with *Thaïs*.

In this opera Massenet is perhaps at his best as operatic craftsman. The patterns are clear and precise, and the moods of religious fervor and romantic ecstasy are deftly contrasted and blended. Both in the vocal and in the instrumental writing the score pulses with drama and passion. In the "Meditation," moreover, it boasts an orchestral interlude of haunting appeal.

ACT I

SCENE 1 : *Cenobite dwellings near the Nile*. At a time when Alexandria is wrapped in luxury and profligacy, Thaïs, a priestess of Venus, is recognized as the most beautiful of women. Athanaël, a Cenobite monk who has been to the city in an effort to preach the gospel, returns to his devout associates with strange stories of Alexandria's wickedness. At night his sleep is troubled by a vision of Thaïs, posing in the Alexandrian theater before a great throng noisily applauding her beauty. Awaking with a start, he is determined to save her. Against the advice of the aged monk Palemon, he sets out upon his mission. The monks pray for him.

SCENE 2 : *Nicias' house in Alexandria*. In Alexandria Athanaël finds a friend of his unregenerate days named Nicias, whose palace occupies a commanding situation. Nicias greets his old friend with courtesy, but is moved to laughter at his whimsical resolve to reform the lovely Thaïs, upon whom Nicias himself has squandered a fortune. Willing to help for old

Act I, Scene 2: A voluptuous dance entertains guests at Nicias's party in the 1939 Metropolitan Opera revival.

times' sake, however, he commands his household slaves to array Athanaël in rich robes, concealing his monkish habit. When at last Thaïs herself arrives she is at first repelled, then intrigued by this austere visitor. Athanaël tells her that he has come to bring her to the only true God, whose humble and devout servant he is. Thaïs' reply is flippantly pagan—she believes only in the joy of living. But she is none the less impressed. Athanaël leaves, horrified, as Thaïs begins to disrobe, to pose as Venus.

ACT II

SCENE 1: *Thaïs' house.* In her room lies Thaïs. The floor is carpeted with precious rugs from Byzantium. The air is laden with the exotic perfumes of flowers in vases of agate, and incense burns before a statue of Venus. Yet Thaïs is wearied of the world and her luxury. The words of the strange monk haunt her memory. She fears that beauty and happiness will quickly fade. Taking a mirror, she contemplates herself, and begs it to assure her that she shall be forever beautiful. *"Dis-moi que je suis belle"* ("Say that I am lovely"), she sings with fervid longing. At this moment Athanaël enters. He speaks to her of life everlasting, of the eternal beauty of the spirit. Thaïs tries at first to triumph over him with her allurements, then succumbs to fear. The righteous Athanaël leaves, declaring, "On thy threshold till dawn I shall await thy coming!" The curtain falls, but the orchestra continues playing with the famous "Meditation," symbolical of the conversion of Thaïs. To a harp accompaniment, a solo violin plays a melody of haunting sweetness.

SCENE 2: *Before Thaïs' house.* True to his word, Athanaël waits before Thaïs' house. From another house nearby come the sounds of revelry. Toward dawn Thaïs appears, worn and repentant after a sleepless night of torment, ready now to follow this holy man into the wilderness. She leaves everything behind, begging only for a small statue of Eros— love himself, for, she says, love has long been a rare visitor among men. She asks to take the statue along to set up in some monastery as an emblem of the love celestial. Athanaël listens patiently until she remarks that this was a gift from Nicias. He then seizes the statue and casts it to the ground, shattering it into a thousand fragments. They enter her palace to destroy the treasures, relics of pagan revels. Thaïs accepts this sacrifice without protest.

As soon as they have gone, Nicias appears. Having won heavily at gambling, he orders dancing, wine, and music. When Thaïs and the stern monk return, they are greeted by a scene of wanton revelry. This quickly changes to a near riot, for the companions of Nicias are furious at the threatened loss of Thaïs. And they are furious at Athanaël, for in his zeal he has set fire to her palace. The crowd is about to seize and kill the monk. To save him, Nicias throws gold coins among the assailants. As the people scramble for the money, Athanaël and Thaïs escape toward the desert and a life of worship and repentance. Only when they have left does Nicias discover, through rising flames, that his erstwhile friend and loving Christian monk has set fire to the house.

ACT III

SCENE 1: *An oasis in the desert.* Tortured by thirst

and weary from her long journey across the desert, Thaïs nearly faints. Yet, the journey is almost over. The monk drives her on remorselessly, bidding her "mortify the flesh," and she goes willingly. Finally she staggers from weakness, and Athanaël, moved to pity, allows her to lie down while he bathes her feet and gives her fruit and water from the oasis at which they have arrived. Thaïs now seems a new person, raised beyond the dominion of flesh to a great spiritual exaltation. She rejoices when the Abbess Albine and the White Sisters come to lead her to a cell in a nearby convent. Thaïs has found the peace for which her soul secretly craved. But now it is Athanaël whose soul is troubled.

SCENE 2: *The Cenobite dwellings near the Nile* (often omitted). Back among the brethren of the Cenobite camp, Athanaël is compelled to confess to the aged Palemon that he has saved Thaïs at the cost of his own soul. Raging passionately at himself, he struggles to cast from his mind the memories of his human weakness, of her intoxicating beauty. He longs for Thaïs. In his sleep, a vision comes to him of the courtesan, lovely, confident, mocking, as he first beheld her in Alexandria. Then the vision changes. Her face is aglow with the fervor of religious ecstasy as she lies dying in the convent. With a cry of terror he awakens and rushes out into the darkness.

SCENE 3: *The garden of the monastery.* Thaïs, worn with three months of severe repentance and self-denial, is dying, surrounded by the White Sisters, who respectfully withdraw when Athanaël enters.

Maurice Renaud as Athanaël in Act I, Scene 2

Utterly distraught, the monk implores Thaïs to return to Alexandria. There they shall live happily, for all that he has taught her is false. The ecstatic music of the "Meditation" surges again from the orchestra, and now Thaïs, heedless of the words of Athanaël, sings of the gates of heaven opening before her, the smiles of angels, the beating of celestial wings. Suddenly she falls back dead, and Athanaël, anguished by a frightful remorse, cries out in despair.

Act III, Scene 3: Thaïs (Helen Jepson) dies repentant, attended by White Sisters and Athanaël (John Charles Thomas)

Tosca

CHARACTERS

Floria Tosca, *a celebrated singer*	*Soprano*	Spoletta, *a police agent*	*Tenor*
Mario Cavaradossi, *a painter*	*Tenor*	Sciarrone, *a gendarme*	*Bass*
Baron Scarpia, *chief of police*	*Baritone*	A Jailer	*Bass*
Cesare Angelotti, *a political prisoner*	*Bass*	A Shepherd Boy	*Mezzo-soprano*
A Sacristan	*Bass*		

The action takes place in Rome in 1800.

OPERA IN three acts. Music by Giacomo Puccini. Libretto in Italian by Giuseppe Giacosa and Luigi Illica, after Victorien Sardou's play *La Tosca*. First performance, Teatro Costanzi, Rome, January 14, 1900. United States première, Metropolitan Opera House, February 4, 1901, with Milka Ternina, Guiseppe Cremonini and Antonio Scotti; Luigi Mancinelli conducted.

It is fashionable today in higher-browed musical circles to deplore the enormous and continuing success of this opera, for it is said to be nothing but melodramatic theatricalism (as if the word "melodrama" were not, etymologically, practically a definition of "opera"). The Sardou play was written as a vehicle for the greatest of melodramatic actresses, Sarah Bernhardt, and was an enormous success (three thousand performances claimed by the author) before Puccini's music endowed it with an even longer life. Other composers than Puccini thought the play might make a fine opera. Verdi toyed with the idea of setting it for some time; Alberto Franchetti actually acquired the musical rights even before Puccini (some skulduggery on the part of the publisher Ricordi got them away from him); and Mascagni thought the libretto so strong that it would overshadow the music. Obviously he was wrong; and when one has a great singing actress in the leading role, one like Maria Callas, a performance becomes as much a theatrical as a musical event. The part of Baron Scarpia demands almost as much in the way of acting, but few baritones today,

Antonio Scotti as Baron Scarpia

however well they may sing the part, are able to endow the figure with the aristocratic elegance that marked the great performances of Antonio Scotti. Cavaradossi's is a more conventional acting part, and so Puccini needed to hear only a private run-through of "*Recondita armonia*" to turn to the youngster he had been sent to fill in as a substitute and ask him, "Who sent you to me? God?" The youngster's name was Enrico Caruso, who, in the final decision, did not sing in the world première, much to his disappointment.

ACT I

SCENE: *The Church of Sant' Andrea della Valle.* As the curtain rises, three somber chords (always associated with Scarpia) are thundered out by the orchestra, and we behold the high-vaulted interior of the Church of Sant' Andrea. Angelotti enters, pale, disheveled, panic-stricken, in prison garb. He barely has time to conceal himself before the Sacristan appears, going about his duties. A moment later Cavaradossi appears, returning to work. He has been painting a fair-haired, blue-eyed Madonna, using for his model an unknown worshiper in the church whose beauty has impressed him. He is unaware that she is the sister of his friend Angelotti, and anyway his interest is purely artistic. Drawing from his bosom a miniature of his beloved, the dark-eyed Tosca, he sings of the strange manner in which the various features of her loveliness blend into a harmonious whole, "*Recondita armonia*" ("Strange harmony").

The Sacristan goes, after a covetous glance at Cavaradossi's lunch basket. A moment later the wild-eyed Angelotti appears, relieved at finding his old friend, who promises him aid in escaping. Tosca is heard calling outside for her "Mario." Cavaradossi gives the fugitive a few hurried directions, and Angelotti disappears, taking with him a woman's dress left as a disguise for him by his sister.

Tosca enters. The temperamental singer is angry at Mario's delay in admitting her and is suspicious, having heard voices. The painter quiets her jealous fancies, and they arrange to meet that evening. Tosca leaves, and Mario goes to aid Angelotti further his escape.

The members of the choir enter, hurriedly preparing for a festival to celebrate Napoleon's defeat. Their excitement is suddenly hushed at the entrance of Scarpia, the dreaded chief of police. The escaped

Act I: Tosca (Renata Tebaldi), thinking herself betrayed by her lover, Cavaradossi, is comforted by Scarpia (Leonard Warren), Metropolitan Opera.

Act II: Tosca (Maria Callas) with Cavaradossi (Renato Cioni) in Franco Zeffirelli's Covent Garden production.

prisoner has been traced to the church. A fan is discovered belonging to Angelotti's sister, and overlooked by the prisoner in his haste. Tosca, still doubting her lover, returns to church under some trivial pretext. She is greeted not by Mario, but by Scarpia, who approaches her courteously. Flatteringly saying that she comes to church devoutly, to pray, not like other women who come to distribute their favors, Scarpia arouses her jealousy by showing her the fan. Tosca becomes greatly excited and leaves the church, weeping. Scarpia orders three of his agents to follow her. The cardinal and a great procession now enter the church, advancing toward the high altar, and a *"Te Deum"* is sung. The voices of the choir mount in sacred song, and Scarpia, kneeling in mock devotion, can be heard muttering to himself while he gloats over the anticipated destruction of his rival and the moment when Tosca shall be his own. At this thought he joins with the final magnificent outburst of the choir.

ACT II

SCENE: *Scarpia's apartment in the Farnese Palace.* Scarpia restlessly awaits news of his prey—Cavaradossi and Angelotti. Hearing Tosca's voice leading the choir in a victory cantata sung in the Queen's apartment nearby, he sends a message to her, saying that he has received word of her lover. This, he knows, will be bait enough for Tosca, tormented as she is with jealousy; again Scarpia rejoices at the thought of his conquest. Yet a moment later he is angered, for Spoletta, his agent, brings word that Angelotti cannot be found. He is quickly consoled, however, on hearing that Cavaradossi has been captured. The painter, when brought in, refuses to divulge Angelotti's hiding place. Accordingly he is consigned to the torture chamber—just as Tosca appears. Scarpia greets her with an exaggerated courtesy, and bluntly tells her that her lover is in the next room being tortured; for each refusal the pain-producing instrument is tightened. Tosca trembles with anxiety, and Scarpia sadistically opens the door so that she may hear Mario's stifled cries. The artist urges her to reveal nothing. Scarpia bids her look at her lover; one glance, and Tosca cries out in horror; even the hardened Spoletta is appalled at the abominable proceedings. The ever-augmented pain brings a fearful cry from Mario, and Tosca, no longer able to endure this, tells Scarpia where Angelotti is hidden. Cavaradossi is then brought in, still racked with pain, near fainting. Suddenly word comes that the reported defeat of Napoleon was a mistake; he was really the victor. Scarpia stands abashed, but Mario, in spite of his weakness and Tosca's whispered admonition to remain silent, gives a shout of victory. The enraged official orders Cavaradossi to prison and death.

When Mario has been taken away, Scarpia begins his cruel love-making. He says he has long adored Tosca, has sworn to possess her; he will brook no refusal. Her spirit crushed, Tosca weeps for shame and sings her famous plea *"Vissi d'arte"* ("Love and music"). She has devoted her life to art and love, has gone regularly to church and been generous in bestowing charity; how can she deserve this cruel treatment?

Scarpia replies to her impassioned prayer cynically, and at last in desperation Tosca says that she will yield to his unholy demand if he will rescind the order of execution and write a passport giving Mario and herself safe-conduct to leave the country.

Scarpia is overjoyed. He informs her that a mock execution will be necessary, summons Spoletta for a moment to give him some secret instructions, then turns to his desk to write the required papers. Meanwhile, Tosca surreptitiously takes from the table a sharp knife and conceals it. Scarpia advances toward her, overpowering in his triumph. He takes her in his arms; Tosca drives the knife into his body, and he falls, crying for help with his final breath. First Tosca washes the blood from her hands; then with grim reverence, she places lighted candles at the head and a crucifix on the bosom of the corpse, crosses herself, and steals noiselessly away.

ACT III

SCENE: *The terrace of Castel' Sant' Angelo.* Mario is brought out from his cell to the terrace of the Castle of Sant' Angelo. The city is still in darkness although the sound of sheep bells on the distant hillsides, the song of a shepherd boy and then the clanging of the great bells in the church tower announce the approach of dawn. Told by the jailer that he has only one hour to live, Cavaradossi sings a touching farewell to his dreams of art and to his beloved, recalling their former meetings on starlit nights in quiet gardens, *"E lucevan le stelle"* ("The stars were shining").

He is suddenly startled by the arrival of Tosca.

She tells him of the death of Scarpia, and he commends the gentle hands that struck the blow, even though regretting that they should have had to be soiled with the blood of such a scoundrel. The soldiers come, the shots of the supposedly mock execution are fired, and Mario falls. Tosca, waiting till the firing party has gone, bids him rise—"Now, Mario, all is safe." He does not answer. She rushes to him, stunned by the knowledge that Scarpia has tricked her. Mario is dead. She throws herself on the body in an agony of grief. Spoletta and the soldiers approach to seize her as Scarpia's murderer. Before they realize her intention she evades them, quickly climbs the parapet of the castle, and leaps to freedom and death. The orchestra thunders out *"E lucevan le stelle."*

Act III: Cavaradossi (Jess Thomas) meets unexpected death atop the Castel' Sant' Angelo, Bavarian State Opera staging, Munich.

La Traviata

THE STRAYED ONE

CHARACTERS

Violetta Valery, *a courtesan*	*Soprano*	Baron Douphol, *a rival of Alfredo*	*Baritone*
Flora, *her friend*	*Mezzo-soprano*	Gastone de Letorières, *party guest*	*Tenor*
Alfredo Germont, *a young man from the*		Marquis d'Obigny, *party guest*	*Baritone*
country	*Tenor*	Dr. Grenvil	*Bass*
Giorgio Germont, *his father*	*Baritone*	Giuseppe, *Violetta's servant*	*Tenor*
		Annina, *Violetta's maid*	*Soprano*

Ladies and Gentlemen, Masquers, Servants

The action takes place in Paris and environs circa *1840.*

OPERA IN three acts. Music by Giuseppe Verdi. Libretto in Italian by Francesco Maria Piave, after Alexandre Dumas' *La Dame aux Camélias.* First performance, Teatro la Fenice, Venice, March 6, 1853. First performance in the United States, Academy of Music, New York, December 3, 1856. Initial hearing at the Metropolitan, November 5, 1883, with Marcella Sembrich as the heroine, Violetta.

After the première of *La Traviata* Verdi wrote to no fewer than three friends that it had been "a fiasco." Imaginary reasons for this "fiasco" have been described by many later writers who weren't there: the cast was inadequate and the costumes were "modern"; the prima donna was too fat to be a convincing consumptive and she sang badly. Well, the first reviewers all agreed Madame Salvini-Donatelli sang splendidly, and the fact is that the costumes and *mis en scène* were, on the evidence of the still-extant designs and the handbills, in the style "of the 1700's," i.e., about 150 years older than "modern." Furthermore, the reviews were favorable, Verdi took bows after each of the acts, and he stayed on to do the same for two more performances. There were ten given during a rather short season. This is scarcely the record of a fiasco. True, the opera was not received with the triumphant acclaim

that at once greeted Verdi's two previous masterpieces, *Rigoletto* and *Il Trovatore,* and to Verdi, anything less than hosannas might have looked comparatively like a failure. It is also true that Victorian critics in the Anglo-Saxon countries found the sympathetic treatment of a courtesan not to their taste. But the public has always known better. Today, well over a century after that misnamed fiasco, *La Traviata* is as warmly loved as ever. Only the grandest of Verdi's grand operas, *Aïda,* receives as many performances annually in major opera houses, and Violetta has been a favorite role with every great soprano (and hundreds not so great) from Patti and Sembrich to Callas and Sutherland.

PRELUDE

The Prelude begins with very soft, tranquil harmonies, high in the strings, similar to the Prelude to the scene of Violetta's death, Act III. There follows a haunting melody, passionate, yet sentimental—the melody of the heroine's parting in the second act. This melody is repeated by the violoncellos while the violins play embroidery above, symbolizing the gayer side of Violetta's character. At the close the music fades gently away, making all the more striking the contrast with the brilliant music of the opening.

Three celebrated Violettas in the 1940's: Licia Albanese, Bidù Sayão and Jarmila Novotna

ACT I

SCENE: *A salon in Violetta's house.* Violetta's elaborately furnished salon is the meeting place of the gayer element of Parisian life. Tonight an unusually lively entertainment seems to be taking place. Alfredo Germont is introduced to Violetta as another of her admirers, and at her request he sings a jovial drinking song, *"Libiamo ne' lieti calici"* ("A bumper we'll drain"), in which Violetta and the guests join.

Music is heard from the adjoining ballroom, toward which the guests proceed. Violetta is seized by a sudden faintness, an ominous forewarning of consumption, but at her request the guests continue into the ballroom; Alfredo, however, remains behind. Violetta cannot quite understand why a young man of such evidently good standing should be concerned with her—a mere butterfly. He confesses that he loves her, has loved her since the day when first he happened to see her a year ago. At first Violetta thinks his protestations mere banter; when she begins to realize their seriousness, she is profoundly moved and begs him to go—she is unworthy, he must forget her. Alfredo's tender confession of love and Violetta's nervous response are beautifully expressed in their duet *"Un dì felice"* ("Since first I saw you").

The rosy light of dawn begins to penetrate the curtained windows. The guests take their leave; Alfredo follows. Violetta is left alone in the room, which is now in disorder and tawdry under the growing daylight. She meditates on the night's happenings, saying to herself, in recitative, "How strangely those words have moved me." Then singing a hesitant but most expressive little air, *"Ah,*

fors' è lui" ("The one of whom I dreamed"), she continues to speculate on the possibilities of this new situation.

An instant later she becomes suddenly transformed, for, thinking that her dreams are hopeless, she begins a dazzling coloratura aria, singing, *"Sempre libera"* ("Ever free"), in which she rather gives the impression that she may no longer squander her days in the pursuit of pleasure, now that a new interest has entered her life. And as she hears the voice of Alfredo off stage singing his first avowal of love, her scales become ever more feverishly joyous.

ACT II

SCENE 1: *A country house near Paris.* Violetta and Alfredo have been living a life of idyllic happiness in a little country house near Paris. Poetical young man that he is, Alfredo is enraptured at having found in Violetta a true mate. Singing a very melodious aria, *"De' miei bollenti spiriti"* ("Wild my dream of youth"), he tells of his contentment in this haven of peace and love, and contrasts it with his own turbulent youth.

The practical affairs of life, however, recall him from his amorous dreams; for the maid enters, and upon questioning her, Alfredo learns that Violetta has secretly had all her jewels sold in order to keep this secluded home. He is much ashamed on thus suddenly realizing his position, and hurries to the city to obtain funds.

Violetta enters; no more is she the painted courtesan of the city, but a gracious, modest young woman. On reading an invitation to a party at the home of a former friend, Flora, she smiles in refusal; such

Act II, Scene 1: Violetta (Anna Moffo) promises Germont (Robert Merrill) to leave Alfredo.

things do not interest her now. Presently Alfredo's father appears and makes himself known. He is none too polite in his greetings, for he has been greatly distressed at what he conceives to be his son's boyish entanglement. Violetta maintains such dignity, however, that he is soon charmed and abashed, especially when he learns that, far from being dependent upon Alfredo, she has sold her property to support him. Thus abandoning his former attitude, he throws himself wholly on her mercy. Alfredo has, it seems, a younger sister, whose marriage to a nobleman will be jeopardized if this scandalous *mésalliance* continues in the Germont family. Violetta at first refuses to give up her lover; then, as the father continues to plead, she begins to realize that her continued alliance with Alfredo will ultimately react to his disadvantage. She finally yields, singing through her tears, *"Dite alla giovine"* ("Tell your daughter"), a moving song in which Violetta renounces all claim to Alfredo for the sake of his sister. Violetta continues, saying, "Now command me." Germont answers, "Say you do not love him." She replies, "He'll not believe me." Violetta thinks of a plan; but she is shaken with sobs and pleads for consolation; she will need courage in order to go through with her resolve. The father comforts her tenderly, then leaves.

As soon as Germont has gone, the unhappy Violetta writes a note of farewell to Alfredo and makes ready to leave for Paris. Alfredo returns, and is mystified by her confusion. His father has written him a stern letter demanding an interview—Alfredo expects him at any moment. Not even suspecting that Violetta and his father have ever met, he believes that the charm of her bearing and personality will cause the elder Germont to relent. Violetta begs to be excused for a time, saying that she will return and throw herself at his father's feet, he will forgive them, they will then be happy forever! But before she goes out she questions Alfredo with such extreme anxiety, "Do you love me? Do you truly love me?" and says "Farewell" with such tenderness that her lover is deeply moved.

In a very few moments a servant comes with a note for Alfredo. It is in Violetta's handwriting. He tears it open, staggers as he realizes its meaning. His father has entered unobserved, and tries to console his son by recalling their home, singing, *"Di Provenza il mar"* ("Thy home in fair Provence").

The father appeals in vain to Alfredo to return to his home. Gazing vaguely about the room, Alfredo notices Flora's letter and on reading it concludes that, having abandoned him, Violetta will make her plunge back into a life of gaiety at Flora's fête. Burning with anger and jealousy, he rushes out to seek revenge.

SCENE 2:* *A gallery in Flora's Parisian house.* The scene changes. Festivities are being held in the richly furnished and brightly lighted salon in Flora's home. The first feature of the entertainment is a masquerade. The music ripples along with the utmost frivolity; gypsies appear and contribute to the gaiety with their jangling tambourines and a little byplay at fortune-telling. They are followed by another group dressed in Spanish costume who sing a festive song of matadors.

To this party now comes Alfredo, who remarks with assumed indifference that he knows nothing of Violetta's whereabouts. The primary feature of the entertainment being gambling rather than dancing, he joins the game and is extremely lucky in his winnings. When Violetta arrives, leaning on the arm of Baron Douphol, she is shocked at seeing Alfredo. Pretending not to notice her, Alfredo remarks, "Misfortune in love brings luck at cards." The Baron is plainly disturbed by Alfredo's presence, cautions Violetta not to speak to him, then goes over and joins the game. Again Alfredo wins; angry words follow between Alfredo and the Baron that threaten to lead to a duel. The tension is relieved, fortunately, by a servant's announcement that the banquet is ready. All withdraw to the adjoining salon.

Violetta returns immediately, followed by Alfredo, whom she has asked to see privately. She begs him to leave the house at once; thus he will

* This scene, in most performances today, is called Act III. Act III becomes Act IV.

418

avoid further trouble. He will go only on one condition—that she come with him. Though her heart is breaking, she remembers her promise to the elder Germont and says she cannot—she is bound. "To whom?" questions Alfredo anxiously. "To Douphol? then you love him!" With a painful effort she replies, "Yes!" Trembling with fury, Alfredo flings wide the doors and calls back the astonished guests. Before them all he denounces Violetta, and shouting, "I call on you to witness that I have paid her back!" he flings a purse at her feet. She sinks fainting in the arms of Flora. All are shocked at Alfredo's outrageous conduct. Germont enters at this moment and remonstrates his son, and the one great ensemble number in this generally soft-voiced opera brings the act to a close. As the curtain drops, the Baron challenges Alfredo to a duel.

ACT III

SCENE: *Violetta's bedroom.* Violetta is now a mere shadow of her former self, for her unhappiness has greatly aggravated her illness. Although the doctor reassures Violetta, he whispers to the faithful maid that her mistress has not long to live. Left alone, Violetta reads a letter she has received from Germont; meanwhile the orchestra whispers touchingly a strain of the first duet of the lovers:

Amelita Galli-Curci as Violetta, Act II

You have kept your promise. The duel took place, and the Baron was wounded, but is improving. Alfredo is abroad. I myself have revealed your sacrifices to him. He will return to implore your pardon. I also shall come. Hasten to recover; you deserve a bright future.—Giorgio Germont.

Act II, Scene 2: At a party in Flora's house, Violetta (Licia Albanese) is insulted by Alfredo (Cesare Valletti).

"Too late!" is her comment in a hollow voice. Then she rises, saying, "I've trusted and waited, but alas, he comes not!" She pauses to look at herself in the mirror. "Oh, how I'm faded, and the doctor said that I would soon recover, but this faintness tells plainly all is hopeless." She continues, singing a beautiful and pathetic farewell to this "fair world of sorrow," *"Addio del passato"* ("Farewell to the past"). The melody, of a delicacy like the wasted heroine herself, rises at its close to clear high tones of poignant loveliness as she exclaims, "All is ended!"

A moment later the door bursts open, and Violetta is in Alfredo's arms. In contrition he begs for forgiveness; it is at once joyfully granted. Vio-

letta's health seems to return with her happiness; even Alfredo is for a moment deceived. They plan a bright future in the quiet country life in which they first found happiness, as they sing, *"Parigi, o cara"* ("Far from gay Paris"). The joy of the meeting has been too much; soon she collapses, and Germont enters with the physician. The father blames himself for having brought all these sorrows on his son and Violetta, and again the melody of the lovers' duet is heard, whispered by the violins in ethereal, tremulous beauty. Violetta no longer feels pain; she rouses herself with an unnatural return of strength and cries, "I live! I have again returned to life!" With this she falls back upon the couch—dead.

Act III: Violetta (Renata Tebaldi), near death with consumption, and her maid Annina (Emilia Cundari) await Alfredo's return.

Tristan und Isolde

CHARACTERS

Tristan, *nephew of King Mark*	Tenor	Kurvenal, *Tristan's servant*	Baritone
Isolde, *a princess of Ireland*	Soprano	King Mark of Cornwall	Bass
Brangäne, *Isolde's attendant*	Soprano	Melot, *one of King Mark's courtiers*	Baritone

A Shepherd, a Steersman, a Sailor Lad; Chorus of Sailors, Knights, and Men-at-Arms

The action takes place during legendary times, at sea, in Cornwall, and in Brittany.

OPERA IN three acts. Music and book in German by Richard Wagner. First performed at the Hof-und-National-Theater, Munich, Germany, June 10, 1865. American première at the Metropolitan Opera House, December 1, 1886, with Anton Seidl conducting, and Albert Niemann and Lilli Lehmann in the title roles. In Seidl's revival of November 27, 1895, Jean de Reszke, Lillian Nordica, and Édouard de Reszke appeared for the first time as Tristan, Isolde, and King Mark. When Arturo Toscanini first directed the opera at the Metropolitan, Carl Burrian was the Tristan and Johanna Gadski the Isolde. The work reached the apex of its popularity during the late 1930's when Kirsten Flagstad and Lauritz Melchior portrayed the title roles.

Tristan und Isolde is romantically supposed to enshrine Wagner's love for Mathilde von Wesendonck, the beautiful wife of a wealthy silk merchant of Zurich who helped Wagner through one of his many financial crises. Wagner was ardently in love with his friend's wife. Since circumstances prevented any real development of the romance, the theory is that *Tristan und Isolde* is the memorial of a tragically unfulfilled passion. Whether such was the sequence of events or not, it is hard to say. Certainly Wagner's feelings for the lovely Mathilde added fervor and intensity, and perhaps pain, to the process of composition. For like Tristan, he suffered the anguish of loving the hopelessly unattainable.

Among all the stories that have been told of unhappy love, a few, handed down for generations, seem well-nigh immortal. Among these is the legend of Tristan and Isolde. This story has been narrated in a variety of forms by poets from medieval times to the present. In the poetic versions of Gottfried von Strassburg, Matthew Arnold, and Swinburne the drinking of the love-potion is a purely accidental affair. Thus Tristan and Isolde are made innocent victims of their love. Omitting the love potion, Tennyson makes the passion between the two a guilty, conscious one. With Wagner, Tristan and Isolde are in love before the drinking of the potion, which serves primarily as a way of removing the ethical restraints of the lovers.

Writers on aesthetics are fond of pointing out that *Tristan und Isolde*, with little of the complexity and violent action of the *Ring*, more closely approaches the condition of a perfect music drama. Yet this minimum of outward action in *Tristan und Isolde* may prove a stumbling block. Few works for the lyric stage are so highly charged with drama, but it is an inward, psychological drama, intensely absorbing and profoundly moving. Wagner was at the summit of his powers when he brushed aside the half-finished *Ring* to write this more practical music drama. How "practical" it proved is illustrated by the fact that at Vienna, after more than fifty rehearsals, the work was abandoned as impossible! With time, however, Wagner's impassioned score

Act I: As Isolde (Birgit Nilsson) listens, Brangäne bids Tristan speak to her mistress. Setting designed by Nicola Benois for La Scala

won the recognition it deserved. This tense, feverishly glowing music is built from a wealth of leading motives, flowing together in an irresistible unity and forming a continuous commentary on the action. But since these motives are themselves so largely subjective in character and associated with emotions or states of mind, the names given them are merely convenient labels of identification. Following closely every changing mood of the drama, this fervid music grows in intensity as the tragedy unfolds, attaining an almost unbearable poignancy and beauty of passionate expression in the last act.

LEGENDARY EVENTS PRECEDING THE MUSIC DRAMA

Isolde, Princess of Ireland, was betrothed to Sir Morold, slain by Tristan in the war against Cornwall. This heartless adversary had sent the head of the slain warrior back to the Princess, who discovered in it a splinter of steel from the sword of her lover's murderer.

Tristan, however, had also been gravely wounded in the fight, and his wound would not heal. Having learned that the Princess of Ireland was skilled in magic balms and potions, he disguised himself, assumed the name of Tantris, and went to Ireland to seek her aid. Moved by his suffering, Isolde tended him without suspecting his identity. Then, one day, she was horrified to discover that she had been sheltering Sir Morold's slayer, for the splinter of steel exactly fitted a notch in the stranger's sword. Seized with a desire for revenge, she raised the weapon to kill the stricken man. At that moment

their eyes met. Powerless against the piteous appeal of his glance, she let fall the sword and, concealing the secret of his identity, continued to tend him. The knight recovered and departed with many declarations of gratitude.

Tristan soon returned, however, this time under his true name, as an emissary to seek the hand of Isolde for his uncle King Mark. Her parents assented, believing, as did Mark, that this alliance would end the long strife between Ireland and Cornwall. Grieving bitterly, for she secretly loved Tristan and believed that he loved her, Isolde was compelled to follow the knight to Cornwall.

PRELUDE

The Prelude to *Tristan und Isolde* is one of Wagner's most impassioned compositions. Built marvelously from a few brief themes which will be of prominence during the course of the action, it begins with a mere whisper, like a sigh of deepest yearning. Played by the cellos, this motive is known as "The Confession to Love." The effect of this is heightened by the poignant interrogation of the "Desire" theme which immediately follows. After a reiteration there enters the eloquent motive of "The Glance," expressive of the origin of the mutual passion of Tristan and Isolde. This is followed by the suave motive of the "Love Philter." There now begins a gradual crescendo in which the theme of "Deliverance by Death" is heard, growing to a climax of overpowering vehemence. The tumult of emotions finally subsides, and as the music ends in a mood of expectancy, the curtain rises.

ACT I

SCENE: *The deck of a ship.* On board Tristan's ship a magnificent pavilion has been erected to house Isolde. From above, in the masthead, a sailor sings of his "Irish maid, wild and amorous maid," a song that only increases Isolde's unhappiness. The ship is now nearing Cornwall, and the Princess is growing indignant at Tristan's persistent refusal to see her. She has grown desperate at the thought of the loveless marriage that awaits her. Her maid Brangäne suggests that with the aid of a magic potion she can win the love of King Mark after she is married to him. Isolde bids her bring the casket containing the potion. From it she selects, not the love philter, but a swift death-bringing poison. Isolde commands the maid to prepare a draft. Vengeance and a speedy end to her sorrows are her aim, for she will die and Tristan with her!

She summons Tristan, and at first declares to him that she has resolved to avenge her murdered lover Morold. Tristan boldly offers her his sword; he is ready to die. Isolde now relents, explaining that she ought not to deprive her husband-to-be of his most trusted knight. She suggests that as a pledge of peace, they drink a cup of reconciliation and forgetfulness. While outside the sailors shout joyfully as the ship approaches land, the trembling Brangäne

Frida Leider as Isolde

sets about preparing the drink. Isolde presents the cup to Tristan, who resolutely grasps it. He has divined her intentions and is glad thus to end the grief which oppresses his heart. He drinks, but before he has finished Isolde snatches the cup from his hands and drains it, to the dregs. Their plans go amiss, however, for Brangäne, reluctant to see her mistress die, has substituted the love potion for the poison. Overcome with emotion, the lovers gaze longingly at one another, and then sink into each other's arms, as a great shout outside announces the arrival of the ship at Cornwall.

Lauritz Melchoir as Tristan

ACT II

SCENE 4: *A garden before Isolde's chamber.* Isolde is waiting impatiently before her dwelling. The King has gone on a hunt, and through the soft air of this lovely summer night the sound of the hunting horns can be heard, growing fainter in the distance. Brangäne is fearful lest the hunt be merely a ruse, planned by Melot, who she thinks suspects the true state of affairs. Heedless of the admonition, Isolde, by extinguishing the torch burning at her doorway, gives the signal for Tristan to come. Then, excitedly, she waves her scarf to her approaching lover. While Brangäne watches from the tower, singing a song of warning at the approach of day, the lovers rapturously embrace, oblivious of all but their love. They sing of this love in ecstatic outbursts, appealing to the soft night to delay the dawn that will bring sorrow and separation. *"O sink' hernieder, Nacht der Liebe!"* ("Descend upon us, O night of love!"). They sing, too, of death, which would bring

Brangäne (Blanche Thebom) holds the love potion, Act I

freedom, and of their complete felicity. As their ecstasy reaches a fevered pitch, Brangäne utters a piercing cry of warning. Kurvenal rushes in, shouting, "Save yourself, Tristan!" It is too late! The King enters with his courtiers and Melot. Deeply grieved that he should have been betrayed by his beloved knight and nephew, the King reproaches Tristan in poignant tones. Melot rushes at Tristan with drawn sword. Tristan pretends to respond to the attack of his treacherous friend, but, letting his sword fall, receives the fatal thrust.

ACT III

SCENE: *A castle garden in Brittany.* An orchestral prelude wondrously pictures the desolation of Tristan's castle, his prolonged suffering, and the wide expanse of the ocean. The scene shows the garden of Tristan's ancestral castle in Brittany. It is situated on a rocky cliff overlooking the sea. A shepherd who is on watch looks over the wall and asks Kurvenal about Tristan. Refusing to disclose the cause of his master's distress, Kurvenal orders the shepherd back to his watch and instructs him to play a lively melody the moment he sees a ship. After scanning the sailless horizon, the shepherd begins a plaintive melody on his reed pipe as he gradually disappears down the cliff. Tristan awakens, and upon hearing the mournful tune cries out dejectedly, "Ever the sorrowful melody!" At the sound of Tristan's voice, Kurvenal is overjoyed. "Life returns to my Tristan!" he exclaims. Still only half conscious, Tristan asks, "Where am I?" Kurvenal assures him that he is in Kareol, in his own castle, surrounded by his faithful followers. But Kurvenal's reassuring words fail to awaken Tristan's memory. He knows not whence he came nor whither he goes, for he longs

now only for death. In oblivion he will be once more united to Isolde. When Kurvenal assures him that he has sent for her, Tristan becomes still more excited and delirious. He now works himself up into a frenzy of anticipation, even believing that he sees the ship bringing his beloved. Then the mournful tune of the shepherd's pipe is heard again, and Tristan, exhausted by his fevered imaginings, falls back in despair, as though lifeless. Kurvenal, fearing him dead, bends over to hear his breathing.

While Tristan slowly revives, a feverish vision of Isolde comes to him, and we hear the motives of "Desire" and "Love's Peace" in the orchestra. Again he is convinced his beloved is approaching.

Kirsten Flagstad as Isolde

This time he is not deceived, for as he exclaims, "The ship! Isolde's ship!" the shepherd begins a lively tune. Kurvenal runs to the watchtower and describes the approach of the vessel while Tristan listens in mounting agitation from his couch. For a moment, when the ship is hidden behind the cliff, Tristan is alarmed, for the rocks there are treacherous. "Who is the helmsman," he cries, "some accomplice of Melot's? Do you also betray me? Do you not yet see her? All is lost then!" A moment later the ship comes into view, Isolde is on the deck, waving to them. In a delirium of joy, Tristan sends Kurvenal to meet her.

Alone now, Tristan tosses on his couch in growing restlessness. Soon he raises himself, tears the bandage from his wound, and staggers forward to meet Isolde. He hears her voice, and his dazed mind thinks of it as the light of the torch which once summoned him to her. "Do I see the light?" he cries. Having overtaxed his vanishing strength, he sinks dying into the arms of his beloved, with a final, heart-rending gasp, crying, "Isolde!" In despair Isolde calls to him, but in vain; he cannot return even for the one hour she pleads for. Distractedly she cries out that she will heal his wounds, and then, realizing that he is forever silent, she falls unconscious.

The shepherd hurries in and calls softly to Kurvenal that another ship has come. Recognizing it as King Mark's and believing that the sovereign has come to attack Tristan's castle, Kurvenal summons his men to its defense. Brangäne is heard calling her mistress from a distance. Melot, too, approaches, and Kurvenal, rushing at him, savagely strikes him down

as he enters the gate. Having thus avenged his master, Kurvenal attacks the others of the King's retinue. Brangäne rushes in to tend Isolde, and Kurvenal, gravely wounded, totters toward his master. With his dying breath, he entreats, "Chide me not, O Tristan, if I try to follow you!"

King Mark is stunned by the death of Tristan, once his most faithful of knights. Frantically, he calls, "Awake, and hear my grief!" Brangäne, having revived Isolde, pleads for forgiveness, saying that she has told the King of the love potion. Mark muses sorrowfully: "When I understood what I had failed to grasp before, how glad I was to find my friend was blameless! So to unite you, I hurried with flying sails. . . . Yet I only added to the harvest of death; error increased our woe!" Brangäne asks pleadingly, "Do you not hear, Isolde?" And now the *"Liebestod"* ("Love Death") begins. She imagines Tristan to be living, transfigured, as the exultant avowal of a deathless love rises to her lips—*"Mild und leise wie er lächelt"* ("Mild and softly he is smiling"). At first somber, then transformed, growing ever lighter, the magnificent song continues. As Isolde becomes more and more carried away by her vision, the theme of "Ecstasy" enters, constantly growing more agitated, swelling toward a climax, only to begin anew. Isolde exclaims, "Hear you not . . . round me flowing . . . growing nearer . . . clearer . . . the wondrous melody?" The music, having reached its summit of passion, seems to burst in shattering glory, then melt away in deepest calm. As though glorified, Isolde sinks into the arms of the faithful Brangäne and dies upon Tristan's body. King Mark raises his arms in blessing over the dead.

Former Metropolitan Opera staging of Act III: In Brittany, Tristan (Lauritz Melchior) is reunited with Isolde (Helen Traubel) a moment before he dies.

Il Trovatore

THE TROUBADOUR

CHARACTERS

Leonora, *a noble lady of the court of a princess of Aragon* — Soprano
Azucena, *a wandering Biscayan gypsy* — Contralto
Manrico, *a young chieftain under the Prince of Biscay, reputed son of Azucena* — Tenor

Count di Luna, *a powerful noble of Aragon* — Baritone
Ferrando, *a captain of the guard, under di Luna* — Bass
Inez, *Leonora's attendant* — Soprano
Ruiz, *a soldier in Manrico's service* — Tenor

A Messenger, a Jailer, Soldiers, Nuns, Gypsies, Attendants, etc.
The action takes place in Biscay and Aragon in the middle of the fifteenth century.

OPERA IN four acts. Music by Giuseppe Verdi. Libretto in Italian by Salvatore Cammarano (completed after his death by Leone Emanuele Bardare), after a play by Antonio García Guitiérrez. First performance, Teatro Apollo, Rome, January 19, 1853. First American performance at New York, May 2, 1855. Metropolitan première, October 26, 1883, with Alwina Valleria as Leonora, Zelia Trebelli as Azucena, Roberto Stagno as Manrico, Giuseppe Kaschmann as Count di Luna.

Ever since its first production *Il Trovatore* has ranked as one of the most popular of operas. And it has good reason to be, for its music is melodious and its action swift. The plot, it is true, is overmelodramatic and not very easy to follow, yet the irrepressible verve of Verdi's music sweeps all else before it; even without knowing the story one can feel the forceful surge of many of the scenes. *Il Trovatore* is, indeed, a triumph of the composer's uncanny skill in expressing the dramatic; here, at times, on a mere dance rhythm, such as a waltz or mazurka, he develops melodies of passionate beauty and dramatic appropriatensss. *Il Trovatore* preaches no moral and cloaks no philosophy; it aims only at

telling an exciting story of a gypsy's vengeance, and in that it succeeds admirably.

EVENTS PRELIMINARY TO THE OPERA

The old Count di Luna, now long since dead, had two sons of almost the same age. One night, while they were still infants, asleep under a nurse's charge, a gypsy hag who had stolen unobserved into the old Count's castle, was discovered bending over the cradle of the younger child. She was instantly driven away, yet because the child grew wan and pale afterwards she was believed to have bewitched it. She was caught and after the fashion of the times burned to death at the stake.

Her daughter Azucena, then a young gypsy woman with a child of her own, witnessed the execution. She swore vengeance. The following night she crept into the castle and stole the younger child of the Count from its cradle. Then she hurried back to the scene of the execution, where the fire that had consumed her mother still raged. She intended to throw the Count's child into it, thus securing her vengeance. Blind, half crazed with the horror of the sight she had witnessed, she hurled into the flames *her own child.* Her vengeance temporarily thwarted, Azucena fled with the Count's child and rejoined her gypsy tribe. She revealed her secret to no one, brought the infant up as her own son, and though she has grown to love him, still cherished the thought that through him she might wreak vengeance upon his family. When the opera opens, this child has grown up, known by the name of Manrico the Troubadour. Azucena has become old and wrinkled but still thirsts for vengeance, and the old Count has died, leaving his elder son, the Count di Luna appearing in the opera, sole heir to his title and possessions.

ACT I ("The Duel")

SCENE 1: *Vestibule in the Palace of Aliaferia.* The retainers of Count di Luna are keeping guard in an outer chamber of Aliaferia Palace. The captain of the guard, Ferrando, passes away the time with a story of the gypsy who was burned for casting a spell on one of the children of the former Count, and of her daughter, who for vengeance stole the present Count's brother and is believed to have burned him to death at the place of her mother's execution. He relates his tale, while singing a markedly rhythmical melody expressive of the weird horror of his narrative, *"Abbietta zingara"* ("Despicable gypsy"). A clock strikes midnight, and the retainers, already frightened by the gruesome tale, rush out in terror.

SCENE 2: *The gardens of the palace.* In the gardens of the palace the fair Leonora strolls with her attendant and companion, Inez. To her she confides her interest in an unknown knight, victor at a recent tourney. She knows that her love has been requited, for the hero has since serenaded her. Thus it is that they refer to him as *"Il Trovatore"* ("The Troubadour"). She tells of his serenade and the emotions it has awakened, in an aria of unusual beauty and expressiveness, *"Tacea la notte placida"* ("Peaceful was the night"). Leonora's companion speaks of an evil presentiment and begs her lady to forget her hero, but Leonora cannot.

The ladies enter the palace just as the Count di Luna comes into the garden. He has barely appeared before the voice of the troubadour is heard from a nearby clump of bushes singing his serenade. Leonora again comes out of the palace. Mistaking the Count in the shadows of the trees for her troubadour, she hurries toward him. At that moment the moon happens to emerge from behind the dense clouds that are hurrying across it. Leonora then realizes her mistake, sees the troubadour, and rushes to him declaring her love for him. The Count is in a terrible rage and demands to know the intruder's identity. Unmasking, the troubadour reveals himself as Manrico, a follower of the Prince of Biscay, and thus proscribed in Aragon. Unable to restrain their jealousy, the two men draw their swords and rush away to fight a duel. Leonora falls fainting.

Act I, Scene 2: Leonora (Antonietta Stella) in dismay hears di Luna (Leonard Warren) challenge Manrico (Carlo Bergonzi) to a duel, Metropolitan Opera.

ACT II ("The Gypsy")

SCENE 1: *A ruined house at the foot of a mountain in Biscay.* It is dawn at a gypsy camp in the Biscay Mountains. There is a bright campfire, and groups of gypsies are scattered about. Azucena hovers near the fire while Manrico, at a distance, holds his sword, at which he looks thoughtfully.

As the daylight grows brighter, the gypsies bestir themselves about their duties; working at the forges, they swing their hammers and bring them down on the clanking metal singing the famous "Anvil Chorus."

The aged Azucena has been gazing abstractedly at the blaze of the campfire. When the gypsies pause to rest a moment from their labors, she begins to sing, as to herself, of the vision that plagues her memory as she watches the blaze. The gypsies draw near and attentively listen to her song, a melody perfectly in keeping with the character of this wild gypsy woman and of the harrowing scene she describes, "*Stride la vampa*" ("Flames soaring upward").

When she has finished, the gypsies depart, the echoes of their song becoming fainter and fainter from down the mountains. Azucena is still trembling with the horror of the memory she has revived, still seems to hear the command "Avenge thou me!" As in a trance, not realizing what she is saying, she continues her narrative, describing her attempt at revenge and her frenzy when she realized she had destroyed her own child instead of her enemy's.

The story sets Manrico thinking. "I'm not your son, then. Who am I?" The gypsy woman, with a quick instinct for prevarication, avoids the question, claiming him as her son. She changes the subject by reminding him how she had nursed him back to life after the almost fatal wound he had received in the battle between the forces of Biscay and Aragon, at Petilla. The enemy forces were led at that battle by the Count di Luna, whom a short time before Manrico had overcome in a duel. Why, asks the gypsy, had he spared the Count's life?

Manrico replies, in a melody smooth and flowing, yet with a certain martial vein, saying that the foe lay at his mercy, and his sword was raised to strike the fatal blow, when he seemed to hear a voice from heaven, crying, "Do not strike!" This is all expressed in the aria "*Mal reggendo all' aspro assalto*" ("At my mercy lay the foe").

The music grows more agitated as Azucena with the utmost vehemence urges her supposed son never to allow this enemy to escape again, but to kill him without hesitation.

Ruiz enters with a message from the Prince of Biscay, ordering Manrico to take command of the defense of the castle Castellor, also informing him that Leonora has believed reports of Manrico's death at the battle of Petilla, and is about to take vows at a convent. Manrico leaves despite Azucena's protests.

SCENE 2: *The cloister of a convent near Castellor.* Count di Luna has determined that before Leonora assumes her vows he will carry her away by force, and has come here with a body of troops. While they lurk outside the chapel, the Count thinks of the happiness that will soon be his, singing, "*Il balen del suo sorriso*" (usually known in English as "The Tempest of the Heart").

The nuns are heard singing within their convent, and when they issue from the convent, conducting Leonora to the chapel where the ceremony is to take place. Leonora pauses to bid farewell to her faithful attendant Inez, then turns to enter the chapel. The Count and his followers now rush forward, and the women draw back in terror. At this moment Manrico appears with his soldiers, and wards off the baffled Count and his troops, and rescues his beloved, though not before a striking ensemble number is performed.

ACT III ("The Gypsy's Son")

SCENE 1: *A military encampment.* The Count di Luna has laid siege to Castellor, whither Manrico has taken Leonora. The soldiers of the Count are about to attack, and they sing a rousing chorus telling of their hopes of winning fame and booty when they capture the castle. They march away singing their stirring war song, and their voices grow softer as they disappear in the distance.

Azucena, in her anxiety to see her son, has attempted to get through the besieging forces. She is captured and brought before the Count as a possible spy. Questioning brings out the story of her past and her connection with the episode of the Count's childhood. Ferrando swears she is the murderess of di Luna's long-lost brother. Azucena, in her extremity, cries out the name of Manrico, and the Count, on finding that she claims the troubadour as her son, vows a double vengeance. She is bound and dragged away.

SCENE 2: *A hall adjoining the chapel of Castellor.* Within the stronghold of Castellor, Manrico and Leonora await the hour appointed for their marriage. Their happiness is troubled, however, by the fear that the Count di Luna may soon attack the castle. Thus it is that Manrico attempts to quiet Leonora's alarm, singing an aria of his devotion to her, "*Ah! sì, ben mio*" ("Ah, yes, beloved").

As he finishes this declaration of love, the solemn music of the organ in the adjoining chapel announces the beginning of the ceremony. Manrico takes his bride's hand to lead her to the altar. At that very moment Ruiz enters with the news that Azucena has been captured by the besiegers. Already faggots are being heaped together, for she is to be burned at the stake as was her mother. Delay would be fatal. Manrico drops Leonora's hand, draws his sword, and, while his soldiers are being summoned, gives vent to his rage and horror in the famous aria "*Di quella pira*" ("Tremble, ye tyrants").

He then rushes away to the rescue.

ACT IV ("The Ordeal")

SCENE 1: *A wing of the Palace of Aliaferia; a dungeon tower, showing a barred window.* Defeated by Count di Luna and his forces, Manrico has been taken captive and cast into the dungeon tower of Aliaferia, where Azucena has already been chained. Outside of these frowning battlements Leonora lingers, for on this clouded night she has come with a despairing hope of saving her lover. She wears a poisoned ring so that if need be she can take her own life. Her thoughts turn toward Manrico, and she sings a poignantly expressive melody declaring her hope that love may even penetrate into his dungeon, "*D'amor sull'ali rosee*" ("Love, fly on rosy wings").

Within the tower voices begin a solemn chant of "*Miserere*," praying for heaven to have mercy on the soul of him about to perish. Meanwhile, a deep-toned bell tolls out the announcement of Manrico's impending doom. The mournful ecclesiastical chant and the tolling knell sounding from the tower across the blackness of the night fill Leonora with terror; while the orchestra accompanies with shuddering chords in slow but irresistibly reiterated rhythm, like the approach of doom, she sings of her fears. From his prison the troubadour sighs forth his plaint "*Sconto col sangue mio*" ("Paid with my blood"). And he closes his song with the words "Do not forget me! Leonora, farewell." While the voices resume their chant and the bell continues tolling, Leonora exclaims that she can never forget him; that she will save his life with the sacrifice of her own. Then Manrico resumes his song. To it the voices of the chanting priests supply a funereal background, and interwoven with it is the cry of Leonora —a marvelously impressive ensemble.

The Count enters, Leonora begs mercy for Manrico, but he refuses, gloating over his triumph. As a last resource she offers to marry the Count if her lover may go free. So great is di Luna's passion for Leonora that he agrees. While he is giving orders to one of the guards, Leonora swallows the poison she has concealed in her ring, muttering to herself that his prize will be a cold and lifeless bride.

Act IV, Scene 2: Manrico (Franco Corelli) comforts Azucena (Fiorenza Cossotto) in the prison, La Scala production.

SCENE 2: *A gloomy dungeon.* In the gloom of their prison Manrico and Azucena await execution. The gypsy pictures to herself the horror of the flames leaping around herself even as they did around her mother. She falls overwhelmed with terror, and Manrico reassures her, softly urging her to rest. Then thinking of the happy days that are past, Azucena meditates nostalgically, as in a dream, "*Ai nostri monti*" ("Home to our mountains"). Again Manrico tries to comfort her; then their voices are heard together, while Azucena falls asleep, still thinking of her gypsy home.

Leonora enters with news of Manrico's freedom. His joy, however, is turned to desperation as he learns the price to be paid. In a sudden frenzy he accuses Leonora of betraying his love. At this moment the poison begins to claim its victim, and Leonora sinks to the floor at Manrico's feet. The lover, who now realizes the full extent of her sacrifice, is all contrition and pleads for forgiveness. The Count suddenly appears, pausing on the threshold. Leonora confesses to the troubadour that she prefers death in his presence to life as another's bride. Then she sinks lifeless to the ground.

Perceiving that Leonora has cheated him, di Luna orders Manrico to instant execution, and drags Azucena to the window to witness the death of her son. The old gypsy is crazed with excitement, blind to the external world. "It is ended," the Count exclaims when the executioner's work is done.

"He was your brother!" she shrieks. "You are avenged, O mother!" Then she falls lifeless.

The Count, overwhelmed with horror, exclaims, "And still I live!"

Les Troyens

THE TROJANS

PART I

LA PRISE DE TROIE (The Fall of Troy)

CHARACTERS

Priam, *King of Troy*	Bass	Coroebus, *engaged to Cassandra*	Baritone
Hecuba, *his wife*	Mezzo-soprano	Panthus, *a Trojan priest*	Bass
Aeneas	Tenor	Andromache, *widow of Hector*	Mime
Helenus	Bass	Astyanax, *her son*	Mime
Cassandra } *their children*	Mezzo-soprano	Ghost of Hector	Bass
Polyxena	Soprano	A Greek Officer	Bass
Ascanius, *son of Aeneas*	Soprano		

Greek and Trojan Soldiers, People of Troy

The action takes place in and outside the city of Troy during the end of the siege as recounted by Vergil.

OPERA IN two parts and six acts. Music by Hector Berlioz. Libretto in French by the composer based on Books I, II, and IV of Vergil's *Aeneid* (and one passage on Shakespeare's *The Merchant of Venice,* Act V). First performance (Part II only) at the Théâtre-Lyrique in Paris, November 4, 1863. First complete performance in Karlsruhe, in a German translation, December 5 and 6, 1890, twenty-one years after Berlioz' death. First stage performance of the entire work in the English-speaking world (in English), Glasgow, March 18 and 19, 1935. As early as May 6, 1882, there had been a concert version in English of Part I only performed at the Seventh Regiment Armory, and this was followed up five years later at the Academy of Music, January 13, with a concert version of Part II. The first unified, uncut version in the original French to be heard in America was given by the American Opera Society at Carnegie Hall in New York, in concert form, on the nights of December 29, 1960, and January 12, 1961. Sir Thomas Beecham was supposed to have directed these performances but became ill and Robert Lawrence took his place. A very much cut version in English of both parts was mounted at the Boston Opera House, under Boris Goldovsky, on March 27, 1959, and the San Francisco Opera also mounted a cut stage production in the seasons of 1966 and 1968. The only available version on discs is in French and well performed under the direction of Georges Prêtre but consists merely of "selections."

"*Les Troyens* is the most important French opera of the nineteenth century," says Professor Donald Grout unequivocally in his *Short History of Opera,* and few critics would disagree with him, even though it is unlikely that many have had the opportunity to witness a staged performance of the entire opera. The scarcity of complete performances of this masterwork is the composer-librettist's fault. First of all, it takes, by his own computation, almost three and a half hours of playing time. Add sufficient time between curtains to change the usually very elaborate scenery (let alone a few normal intermissions between acts), and the audience must either stay for some five hours or come on two separate evenings.

Management has usually opted for the second alternative, or else given only Part II, or else condensed the whole work mercilessly. Even during the first very successful production Part I was eliminated before rehearsals began (a prologue was substituted), and by the time the twenty-second and final performance was given, ten complete numbers had been cut, including some of the finest. Yet, length is not the only hurdle to production. So expensive is it to put on the stage, with its many scenes and scenic effects, its plethora of major and minor roles, that Léon Carvalho, the original producer, had to secure a large subvention from the French government before he could mount even a truncated version.

Berlioz, who had campaigned for a performance for several years and been put off again and again by the National Opéra, was understandably bitter about the cuts and rather unfairly criticized Carvalho for the quality of the production. This, from contemporary accounts, was very good, and it certainly impressed the public, the press, and such knowledgeable musicians as Meyerbeer. Nevertheless, the aging composer prayed for death and never even started to compose another opera. It is at least good to know that proceeds from the sale of the manuscript to a publisher and royalties from these performances enabled the composer to give up the music reviewing he hated doing but did extremely well. He died, aged sixty-five, three years after the close of the first production, knowing that his work was the greatest of the French Romantic composers, and convinced *Les Troyens* would never be given in its entirety.

ACT I

Scene 1: *Abandoned camp of the Greeks outside of Troy.* The Greeks have apparently given up the siege of Troy, and the people are celebrating in their emptied camp. News comes that the enemy has left behind a huge wooden horse supposedly as an offering to the goddess Pallas Athene. Everyone but Cassandra rushes off to see this wonder. She is the beautiful daughter of the Trojan King and has been cursed by Apollo with the capacity to utter true prophecies which will never be believed. This time she has seen the ghost of her brother Hector, slain by Achilles, and she knows that their father, too, is doomed. Her lover, the warrior Coroebus, comes to persuade her to join the other celebrants, but she only continues her gloomy prophecy that the city will fall and her lover be killed. Though like everyone else he thinks her mad, Coroebus speaks tenderly to her, and she promises to marry him. But death, she adds, is even now preparing their bridal bed.

Scene 2: *Before the citadel of Troy.* King Priam

Régine Crespin as the clairvoyant Cassandra, Act II

and Queen Hecuba are presiding over the celebration of the victory, and there is an elaborate ballet. Hector's widow Andromache and their child Astyanax silently pass across the stage as everyone receives them with solemn respect, Cassandra still uttering dire predictions—this time that Hecuba has even greater disasters than her husband's death in battle awaiting her.

A slow funeral march has been sung when Aeneas rushes in with a report of the fate of Troy's high priest Laocoön. Alone in sharing Cassandra's misgivings about the horse, he had uttered his famous sentiment: "I fear the Greeks bearing gifts," and hurled a javelin at the huge figure. At once two serpents had appeared from the sea and squeezed to death both Laocoön and his two sons. Aeneas, however, interprets these events as the revenge of the goddess for the priest's act of impiety and orders the horse drawn into the city to appease her. Again Cassandra warns against this foolish action, and again she is disregarded. As night falls, an elaborate scene develops to the music of the famous "Trojan March." Some have heard that the clank of armor comes from inside the monstrous figure, yet group after group files on and off the stage, and finally, to great rejoicing, the horse is drawn in. Only Cassandra cries, "It is finished! Death has seized its prey!"

ACT II

Scene 1: *Bedroom of Aeneas.* Ascanius, the hero's

little son, who has been disturbed by noises in the street, slips into his sleeping father's room, does not dare wake him, and slips out again. Then the ghost of Aeneas' brother Hector visits the sleeper, warns him of the impending fall of the city, and—in a solemn address consisting of a slowly descending chromatic scale, one sentence per note—instructs him to set sail for Italy to found a new empire that will rule the world. Scarcely has the ghost departed when the priest Panthus, badly wounded and carrying the statuettes of their gods, reports how a well-armed band of Greeks poured out of the horse in the middle of the night, slew many, including King Priam, and are continuing their work of destruction. Aeneas promptly places himself at the head of a band of soldiers who have followed Panthus into the chamber and rushes out to do battle.

SCENE 2: *The Temple of Vesta.* Troy has now fallen to the Greeks, and a band of virgins wail a prayer to the mother of Zeus. Cassandra tells them that though Aeneas has escaped with a band of followers to found a new Troy, Coroebus has been slain, and the most dreadful doom awaits these women. She urges them all to fling themselves from the top of the temple to their death, and some of the younger ones, frightened by such heroic measures, are driven out of the temple. The leader of a band of Greeks coming to look for treasure is at first struck with awe by the sight of the remaining women wailing as they play their lyres. Many of them hurl themselves from the temple to their deaths, but Cassandra and her sister Polyxena stab themselves. With her last breath Cassandra, stretching her arms toward Mount Ida, cries, "Italy!"

PART II
LES TROYENS À CARTHAGE (The Trojans at Carthage)

CHARACTERS

Dido, *Queen of Carthage*	*Mezzo-soprano*	The Ghost of Cassandra	*Mezzo-soprano*
Anna, *her sister*	*Contralto*	The Ghost of Coroebus	*Baritone*
Narbal, *her minister*	*Bass*	The Ghost of Hector	*Bass*
Aeneas, *leader of the Trojans*	*Tenor*	The Ghost of Priam	*Bass*
Ascanius, *his son*	*Soprano*	Mercury	*Bass*
Iopas, *a poet*	*Tenor*	First Trojan Soldier	*Baritone*
Hylas, *a Trojan sailor*	*Tenor*	Second Trojan Soldier	*Bass*

Courtiers, Soldiers, Sailors, Workmen, Naiads, Fauns, Wood Nymphs, etc.

The action takes place in Carthage after the fall of Troy.

ACT I

SCENE: *The gardens of Queen Dido's palace.* Seven years before the opera begins, Dido, Princess of Tyre, had escaped after the murder of her husband and, with a band of followers, had founded the city-state of Carthage in North Africa. Now, after years of hard toil, she and her subjects are holding a festival of thanksgiving for their success. The festival over, her sister Anna tells Dido that it is time for her to marry again and provide her subjects with a king. Not to be considered is the already rejected King Iarbas of Numidis who, it is said, is threaten-

ing to invade. In the duet that ensues, Dido, though wishing to remain faithful to the memory of her husband, admits that she yearns for love.

Now Iopas, a poet, announces that a storm has forced a fleet into the harbor of Carthage and that the strangers desire an audience. The *"Trojan March"* is heard—in a minor key—and in come the Trojans, led by Ascanius, while Aeneas himself remains in disguise. Dido, who knows about the Trojans, accepts the gifts of Ascanius and welcomes the party. But Narbal, Dido's chief minister, comes with the news that the Numidian Iarbas is already invading the country and laying it waste. Aeneas now steps forth, and his offer to lead his own followers against the Numidians is at once accepted.

Act II, Scene 1: Near a grotto, Dido (Régine Crespin) is wooed by Aeneas (Jon Vickers), in the San Francisco Opera production.

ACT II

SCENE 1:* *A forest with an entrance to a grotto.* The combined forces of the Trojans and Carthaginians have presumably now thrown back the invaders. The scene that follows, done almost entirely in mime and ballet, is familiar to concertgoers as "The Royal Hunt and Storm." Deep in the forest, naiads are playing about but jump into a stream of water when they hear hunting horns. Ascanius and others engaged in a royal hunt pass across the stage; then come Dido and Aeneas, separated from the rest of the party. A terrific storm is brewing, and the two pass into the grotto where, as we are told in the *Aeneid,* their love is consummated. The storm waxes fierce; a tree is struck by lightning and bursts into flames; naiads and satyrs dance by, calling, "Italy! Italy!"; and fauns pick up burning twigs and dash off making the same call. At the height of the storm great clouds drift in, making the stage darker; but at the end the storm passes, the sky is clear, the music soft.

SCENE 2: *The gardens of Queen Dido's palace.* The Carthagians are preparing to celebrate the victory over the Numidians, and Anna and Narbal hold a discussion of state matters. The minister is uneasy because Dido is neglecting her duties in entertaining her guests. Anna points out that Dido is obviously in love with Aeneas and he would make an ideal King

* Berlioz originally placed this scene at this point in the opera. Modern scores place it at the end of the act.

of Carthage. Both, however, are uneasy because they know that Aeneas has been destined by the gods to go on to Italy.

Now Dido enters, and an elaborate ballet is staged for the celebration. Iopas, the court poet, is called on for a song in praise of Ceres, goddess of agriculture, and then, at Dido's request, Aeneas tells of the fate of Andromache. Though she had intended to be faithful to the memory of Hector, she was allotted to the Greek King Pyrrhus after the fall of Troy and married him to become Queen of Epirus. Dido understands the poignant relevance to her own situation of this narrative, and a beautiful concerted number apostrophizes the oncoming dusk. The scene closes with a love duet between Aeneas and Dido, the text being based on the Jessica-Lorenzo exchange beneath the moonlight in the last act of *The Merchant of Venice.* But by a column, in the moonlight, appears Mercury, messenger of the gods, calling, "Italy, Italy, Italy!"

ACT III

SCENE: *The harbor of Carthage at night.* The Trojan fleet is all but ready to sail, and the young sailor Hylas sings a soft, nostalgic song, longing for Troy. Two soldiers regret leaving. They have enjoyed their stay, having been especially appreciative of the hospitality of the local girls. It is the one comic passage in this tragic opera.

More seriously, Aeneas laments in a long monologue his severance from his beloved Dido. Even now

Act IV, Scene 2: Abandoned by her lover, Dido (Giulietta Simionato) prepares for her immolation, in the monumental La Scala staging, 1960.

he considers returning to her for a last visit, but the ghosts of Priam, Hector, Cassandra and Coroebus demand his immediate departure. And when Dido comes in to beg of him to remain, he is firm. The gods, he says, demand the sacrifice, and he must die in founding Rome. From pleading, then, she turns to anger, denounces him as a "monster of piety," and sweeps out. And now the sailors make their final preparations in high spirits and end the scene, as so many have ended before, with the cry "Italy, Italy, Italy!" Aeneas swiftly boards his ship.

ACT IV

SCENE 1 : *A room in Dido's palace, the next morning.* Dido pleads with her sister Anna to go to the shore and beg Aeneas to remain—if not forever, at least for a few days, and Anna tries to tell her that it is hopeless—the gods have commanded. But as this dialogue is going on, there are cries off stage about a whole fleet at sea, and Iopas rushes in with the news that the ships sailed at dawn and are now barely visible. Dido becomes wild. She not only curses Aeneas but says she should have served him Ascanius in a dish. Appalled by the wild orders she gives—to have the Carthaginian fleet pursue the Trojan ships and burn them, to bring in the priest of Pluto and burn everything that might remind her of Aeneas—they leave her. Dido now has her greatest scene. She knows she must inevitably die on the sacrificial pyre she has ordered; and she sings a moving farewell to her city, her people, her sister, and to the memories of her love.

SCENE 2 : *A terrace overlooking the sea.* The pyre has been built, and on it are a couch, the Trojan's helmet and sword, and a bust of Aeneas. The priests of Pluto intone a prayer; Narbal and Anna call upon the gods to curse Aeneas; and Dido climbs up on the pyre, throws herself, sobbing, on the couch, and predicts historic events—the coming of the Carthaginian hero Hannibal and the final destruction of the city by Rome. She has now seized the sword and plunged it into her breast. Crowds have rushed in, and Dido dies in her sister's arms as the Carthaginians swear eternal hatred of the descendants of Aeneas. Ironically, a vision of Rome is seen.

Turandot

CHARACTERS

Princess Turandot	*Soprano*	Ping, *the Grand Chancellor*	*Baritone*
The Emperor Altoum, *her father*	*Tenor*	Pang, *the General Purveyor*	*Tenor*
Timur, *dethroned Tatar King*	*Bass*	Pong, *the Lord of the Kitchen*	*Tenor*
Prince Calaf, *the Unknown Prince,*		A Mandarin	*Baritone*
Timur's son	*Tenor*	The Prince of Persia	*Mime*
Liù, *a young slave girl*	*Soprano*		

Crowds, Guards, Servants, etc.

The action takes place in Peking during legendary times.

Opera in three acts. Music by Giacomo Puccini. Libretto in Italian by Giuseppe Adami and Renato Simoni, after a *fiaba* by Carlo Gozzi. First performance, Teatro alla Scala, Milan, April 25, 1926, with Rosa Raïsa as Turandot, Maria Zamboni as Liù, Miguel Fleta as Calaf, Giacomo Rimini as Ping, and Arturo Toscanini conducting. The initial United States production took place at the Metropolitan Opera House, November 16, 1926, with Maria Jeritza, Martha Attwood, Giacomo Lauri-Volpi, and Giuseppe de Luca, Tullio Serafin conducting.

Unfortunately, Puccini died before completing this opera. The last part of Act III, beginning with the final duet between Turandot and Prince Calaf, *"Principessa di Morte,"* was completed by Franco Alfano from sketches left by Puccini. When this place was reached, at the first performance, Toscanini made an abrupt ending and, turning to the audience, remarked simply, "At this point the master laid down his pen."

In *Turandot* Puccini advanced beyond any of his previous work in harmonic subtlety, orchestral coloring, and choral writing, even introducing much more polyphony than was his wont. Yet in its wealth of melody the opera is distinctly Puccinian.

Giacomo Lauri-Volpi as Calaf, Maria Jeritza as Turandot, at the Metropolitan Opera première, 1926

ACT I

SCENE: *The walls of the great violet city of Peking.* Amid the confusion of the listening crowd that has gathered at the imperial palace, an old man makes his way, supported and guided by a young slave girl, Liù. Suddenly a youth hurries toward them from the crowd. Their whispered conversation reveals that the old man is the dethroned Timur, King of the Tatars, the youth, his son Calaf, called the "Unknown Prince." Soon there is a movement of agitation in the crowd, because the Prince of Persia, attempting to solve Turandot's riddles, and failing, as all others have done, is now being led to execution. For the Princess Turandot, as a mandarin has previously announced, has decreed that whosoever would win her hand must solve three riddles, and, failing, suffer death. The people, moved by the youthfulness of the Persian Prince, cry for mercy. But Turandot,

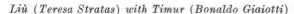

Liù (Teresa Stratas) with Timur (Bonaldo Giaiotti)

Turandot's ministers at the Metropolitan Opera: Pong (Robert Nagy), Pang (Charles Anthony), Ping (Frank Guarrera)

when she appears upon the balcony, silences them by the mere sight of her matchless beauty. The thud of the executioner's ax is heard; then the head of the Persian Prince is seen, raised on a pike over the city gates.

The Unknown Prince is greatly thrilled by the beauty of Turandot. Forgetting her cruelty and heedless of the prayers of his father and Liù, and of the warnings of the ghosts of Turandot's executed lovers, and unmindful of the counsels of the three court officials, Ping, Pang, and Pong, he determines to brave the Princess' enigmas. In token of his intention he sounds the great gong that hangs at the palace gate three times, calling out the name of the Princess.

ACT II

SCENE 1: *A pavilion in the palace.* The three ministers, Ping, Pang, and Pong, engage in a lively discussion on the nuisances and troubles brought to the kingdom by Turandot's game of riddles. They also long for the quiet of their respective homes; but as the curtains are drawn to reveal the next scene, they resignedly walk into it to observe "the next torture."

SCENE 2: *The throne room.* A multitude is already assembled, when Turandot comes before them and tells of her grandmother, the chaste Princess Lou-ling, who, ravished by the invading Tatars, died most unhappy. To avenge her ancestor's wrongs,

436

Turandot has meted out a cruel fate to all who would be her suitors. She turns to the Unknown Prince and propounds her direful enigmas. One by one the Unknown Prince answers them, boldly and correctly; he is greeted by shouts of joy from all except Turandot. The Princess, dismayed, begs to be saved from the stranger; but her father, Emperor and guardian of the law, decrees that her word must be held sacred. Turandot, therefore, pleads with the conqueror for her freedom, and he, answering, says that he will indeed release her from her vow and give up his life even as though he had failed in the trial, should she be able to learn his name ere the morrow.

ACT III

SCENE: *The palace gardens near Turandot's apartments.* Thus it comes about that during the entire night heralds search through all the city, but none they find who can rightly name the Unknown Prince. Someone then whispers that an old man and the girl Liù had been seen with him. They are brought to the palace, but Liù cries out that she alone knows the Prince's name, and then, fearing she may reveal the secret during the tortures to which she will be subjected, she quickly seizes a dagger from one of the soldiers and plunges it into her heart. Turandot is troubled—what moved the girl to such self-sacrifice? The Prince, reproaching Turandot, clasps her passionately. Thus is the Princess vanquished, and she confesses that she loves the Unknown Prince. He likewise says that such is his love that he would be happy to die for her, and reveals his name. Knowing him to be the enemy Tatar prince, Turandot again becomes proud and unattainable. Dawn now approaching, she leads him to the palace to announce her victory and his doom. At the throne of the great Emperor she cries out that she has learned the stranger's name; then looking at Calaf, she is shaken by a strange emotion, and murmurs, "His name is Love!"

Act II: Turandot (Birgit Nilsson), in Nicola Benois' La Scala setting, pronounces a riddle to Prince Calaf (Giuseppe Di Stefano).

Vanessa

CHARACTERS

Vanessa, *a beautiful baroness, about*		Anatol, *a man in his early twenties*	*Tenor*
forty	*Soprano*	The Old Doctor	*Bass*
Erika, *her niece, about twenty*	*Mezzo-soprano*	Nicholas, *the major-domo*	*Baritone*
The Old Baroness, *Vanessa's mother*		A Footman	*Tenor*
and Erika's grandmother	*Mezzo-soprano*	The Young Pastor	*Mime*

Servants, Guests, Peasants

The action takes place in Vanessa's castle in a northern country about 1905.

OPERA IN FOUR ACTS. Music by Samuel Barber. Libretto in English by Gian Carlo Menotti. Première, Metropolitan Opera House, January 15, 1958, with Eleanor Steber, Rosalind Elias, Regina Resnik, Nicolai Gedda, and Giorgio Tozzi in the leading roles. Dimitri Mitropoulos conducted. The opera won the Pulitzer Prize for musical composition in 1958 and was produced at the Salzburg Festival that summer, though with no great critical acclaim. In its original reception it fared far better. The New York critics generally praised the work for its great skill and taste, and six of the seven performances in its first season were completely sold out. Carried over to the next season, the opera was then shelved for six years and revived with part of the same cast in the season of 1964–1965. The première of Mr. Barber's only other opera, *Antony and Cleopatra*, was the opening night attraction when the Metropolitan Opera moved to Lincoln Center in the fall of 1966, but it was less well received. However, the tenure of American operas at the Metropolitan has never been very durable. Of the twenty there produced, only Deems Taylor's *Peter Ibbetson* (première February 7, 1931) lasted longer than *Vanessa* in the repertoire, being given for four successive seasons.

Librettist and composer had been close friends for many years, and Mr. Menotti, who has written the librettos for every one of his own many operas, supplied Mr. Barber with one of the finest he—or any other modern writer—had ever written. It is very unusual as an opera book, for although the dramatic emotions and motivations are always crystal clear (as they must be in a play that is sung), it is still a subtle character study, the three leading roles being convincing three-dimensional human beings, consistently differentiated in every line they utter. Thus, although the plot and values of the story are essentially late nineteenth century romanticism, the psychological projection is distinctly, although non-Freudian, of our own time. Mr. Barber, in his score, takes full advantage of both the romantic and contemporary aspects of his collaborator's work.

ACT I

SCENE: *The richly furnished drawing room of Vanessa's castle.* As Vanessa watches a snowstorm raging outside, her niece Erika is ordering from the major-domo an elaborate dinner. Vanessa impatiently interrupts with criticism, her impatience inspired by the failure of her awaited guest to arrive. Impatiently she orders the tower bell to be rung to guide the expected sleigh; impatiently she interrupts

Erika's calm reading aloud of lines from *Oedipus at Colonus* and reads them aloud herself, with exaggerated passion. Her mother the Baroness, who has refused to speak to her daughter for years, rises to go to bed, and a few moments later the tower bell rings faster and the sound of a sleigh is heard. Asking Erika to let her meet the guest alone, Vanessa paces the room in great agitation, then turns off most of the lights and seats herself before the fire in a great chair, her back to the door.

The figure of a young man appears in the doorway, and, without moving from the seat where she cannot see him or he her, Vanessa addresses him as "Anatol" in a long speech. Deep but suppressed emotion marks her words (and the music) as she tells him that she has waited over twenty years for his coming, growing older with bitterness, freezing her beauty while waiting, but always knowing that he would come. Now, unless he can say that he still loves her, he must leave the house this very night. For the first time the man speaks: "I believe I shall love you," he says.

Vanessa whirls around, sees that this is not the man she had expected, calls him "impostor" and "cheat," and cries to Erika for help. Erika rushes in and helps her aunt, faint with emotion, from the room. When she returns, the young man, who has been examining the rich furnishings, explains, with no great show of emotion, that he really is "Anatol," but the son of Vanessa's old lover, who is now dead. Erika at first repeats Vanessa's decree, made as she left the room, that Anatol must leave at once. But he pleads the difficulty of the storm, says he is sure Vanessa will let him stay the night once she knows who he is and, having found out that Erika is Vanessa's niece, seats himself at the little table that had been laid out for his father's supper, and invites Erika to join him. He opens a bottle of wine, pours himself a glass, lifts it toward her, and asks, "What is your name?" "Erika," she answers.

ACT II

SCENE: *The same as Act I*. It is a bright Sunday morning a month later, and Erika, questioned by her grandmother the Baroness, is telling of her relationship to Anatol. The night he came, she had had too much wine, and she stayed all night with him in his room. That was the only time this happened, and he has offered her marriage. She does love him—or someone like him, as she puts it—but she also hates him for his superficiality. And besides (here Vanessa's happy laughter is heard from outside) it is Vanessa who now loves him, quite blindly. The conversation is interrupted by the return of Vanessa and Anatol from skating, and they are shortly

Rosalind Elias (Erika) and Eleanor Steber (Vanessa), Metropolitan Opera world première, 1958

visited also by the Doctor, who reminisces about old garden parties, games, and dances, and even tries, with no great success, to teach a step or two to Anatol as Erika and Vanessa sing a folk song, "Under the Willow Tree."

When the Doctor takes Anatol into the sun parlor at the back of the stage (where they are joined by a young clergyman for the breakfast that is laid out), Vanessa remains behind. Her eyes aglow, she describes how she had skated with Anatol, how he suddenly let go of her hands and, looking into her eyes, said how he hated to leave . . . that he would like to stay as master of her house. But when Erika asks, "And then?" Vanessa laughs and goes off to greet the young clergyman. The Baroness, who wants Erika to marry Anatol, insists she must speak to him about this, and Erika takes the opportunity a moment later when he returns from the sun parlor. Anatol at first squirms under her very direct questioning, but then, with the Baroness as witness, offers to marry Erika. He cannot offer eternal love but he thinks, in his superficial fashion, that they may have a very good time traveling around Europe together. Who knows? The love might even last! Erika is very dubious indeed, but before she can give a definite answer, Vanessa returns. It is time for services in the chapel; the servants are lined up to follow; Anatol offers his arm to Vanessa; but Erika says she will join later.

Off stage we hear the first hymn being sung as a servant brings Erika her cape. She refuses it, and then cries out after the others, "No, Anatol, my answer is no! Let Vanessa have you, she who for so little had to wait so long." Sobbing hysterically, she throws herself on the sofa.

ACT III

SCENE: *Entrance hall to the castle with part of the ballroom visible.* It is New Year's Eve, and the Doctor is scheduled to announce the engagement of Vanessa and Anatol. However, he has misplaced his speech, as we find out from a short scene he has, somewhat tipsy, with the major-domo. Vanessa comes out to him, upset because her mother and Erika have refused, so far, to come down for the party, and the announcement should be made about now. She sends the Doctor up the stairs to see what he can do, and Anatol joins her, comforting her with assurances about Erika and with light words of love. The Doctor, returning, says it is all nothing—that Erika will be down shortly. But under his breath he tells Anatol that the girl had simply refused to speak to him.

Peasants come in prepared to do some dances; music is heard from the ballroom; and then the Doctor is heard making his announcement, at which everyone applauds and proposes toasts. As this is going on, Erika, pale and weak, starts to descend the stairs, clutches at her stomach, and faints. The major-domo rushes to her offering help, but she immediately regains consciousness, dismisses him, and continues down the stairs. As the dance music is heard from the ballroom, she mutters, "His child . . . must not be born!" and goes out of the front door. Several couples dance in and out of the entrance hall; then the Baroness appears at the top of the stairway, calls Erika, and, seeing the open door, rushes out, still calling after her granddaughter.

ACT IV

SCENE 1: *Erika's bedroom.* At dawn, a few hours later, the silent Baroness, the Doctor, and Vanessa are awaiting the searching party of peasants led by Anatol. Vanessa dominates this part of the scene, for she is deeply distressed by the possibility of their finding Erika dead; yet—characteristically—she stresses her own sorrow and the shadow cast on the happiness she was until then experiencing. Soon the party returns, Anatol bearing the unconscious Erika, still in her party dress. Under the Doctor's

Act IV, Scene 1: Erika (Rosalind Elias) with the taciturn old Baroness (Blanche Thebom)

orders he places her gently on the bed in an alcove, and the peasants are dismissed with thanks. As the Doctor examines his patient, Anatol tells the weeping Vanessa that Erika was found hidden in a small ravine, unconscious, her ball dress damp with blood. "She must have fallen," is his easy explanation, and we never learn whether he appreciated the fact that she had had a miscarriage. But Vanessa is still uneasy. "Does she love you?" she demands; and Anatol swears that she does not—Erika will tell her so if she asks. Vanessa's response is to beg him to take her away soon, and Anatol lovingly reassures her on this point, too.

When the Doctor has accompanied the engaged couple out of the room so that Erika may rest, she calls to the Baroness from the alcove. The dialogue is very brief but very significant. "Do they know?" asks Erika. "How can I tell?" says the grandmother. "They only lie to themselves and to each other. . . . And your child?" "He will not be born, thank God,'' says Erika. Whereupon the Baroness rises from her seat and leaves the room without replying to Erika's calls after her. She will never speak to her again.

SCENE 2: *The drawing room.* It is two weeks later, the wedding has just taken place, and the married couple, in traveling clothes, are supervising the loading of the luggage as they prepare for the trip to Paris. The Doctor comments sentimentally on how long he has known Vanessa, who gets rid of both him and Anatol tactfully so that she can have a last word with her niece. She wants, she says, to know the truth about "that night"—whether Erika did what she did because of Anatol. Erika swears that it was not. It was because she thought she loved someone who did not love her. Who was it? Vanessa wants to know. But Erika refuses to tell. He just wasn't the man for her. Fortunately, to save Erika from more

lies, Anatol returns at this moment and bids Vanessa to hurry, for it is getting late. The Doctor, too, returns, and there are some appropriately sentimental remarks on the occasion before the five principal characters—Vanessa, Erika, the Baroness, Anatol, and the Doctor—stand suddenly still in their places, in effect step out of the realistic psychological drama they have been acting out, and sing a quintet in canon form, commenting philosophically on what has happened and is happening at this moment. "To leave, to break, to find, to keep, to stay, to wait, to hope, to dream, to weep and remember: To love is all of this, and none of it is love."

Finally Erika is left alone in the room—alone with only the Baroness, who stonily refuses to say a word. Erika orders all the mirrors in the house draped once more and the gate to be shut to all visitors.

"Now," she says, "it is my turn to wait."

Act IV, Scene 2: Vanessa (Eleanor Steber) and Anatol (Nicolai Gedda) bid farewell to the Doctor (Giorgio Tozzi), the old Baroness (Regina Resnik), Nicholas (George Cehanovsky) and Erika (Rosalind Elias).

La Voix Humaine

THE HUMAN VOICE

CHARACTER

"The Human Voice," *an elegant young woman*   *Soprano*

The action takes place in Paris in the 1950's.

OPERA IN one act. Music by Francis Poulenc. Text in French slightly adapted by the composer from Jean Cocteau's "monodrama" of the same name. Première at the Opéra-Comique in Paris, February 6, 1959, with Denise Duval in the single role and Georges Prêtre conducting. Mademoiselle Duval also introduced the work to Italy, in French, February 18, of the same year, and on February 23, 1960, she and Monsieur Prêtre introduced the work to America in concert form with the American Opera Society at Carnegie Hall in New York City. Poulenc wrote the opera with the singular singing and acting talents of Mlle. Duval in mind, just as he had written the role of Blanche in *Dialogues des Carmélites* for her. An English version by Joseph Machlis was telecast by CBS-TV January 26, 1962, with Marjorie Madey as "the human voice" and Alfredo Antonini conducting.

.The idea of presenting a dramatic slice of life through the use of a single character and a telephone was not a new one when Poulenc composed his opera. In 1932 Cocteau's little play had entered the repertoire of the Comédie-Française; even before that Dorothy Parker had used the idea in a most effective short story; there have been many vaudeville and radio sketches based on the device; and Gian-Carlo Menotti's *The Telephone*, composed as a curtain-raiser for *The Medium* in 1947, had given operatic currency to the form, though it is true that there are two singers in his cast. Yet Poulenc's work easily transcends them all in that it is so much more than a

trick and can be considered as high and serious art. When Puccini wanted to compose an opera based on Ferenc Molnar's *Liliom*, the playwright refused permission, for then, he said, the work would be known in the future as Puccini's opera, not Molnar's play. But Cocteau readily granted permission to Poulenc and paid the finest tribute possible to the result when he wrote, after the first performance, "Thanks to Francis Poulenc and to Denise Duval, my play has acquired the mysterious power of the Greek, Chinese, Japanese theaters, where a truth greater than truth transcends life and raises realism to the height of style." He included Mlle. Duval in his generous tribute because this concentrated little masterpiece, without anything resembling an aria, requires the creative services of a singing actress who can understand, project, and persuade not merely with her appearance and acting ability but with the subtle but dramatic coloring of her voice and phrasing of the music. For, as he also did in *Dialogues des Carmélites*, Poulenc provided a musical setting which completely respects and inevitably emphasizes the rhythms and emotional phrasing of the prose text.

SCENE: *In Jean Cocteau's own words:* "The small set represents the corner of a woman's room, a gloomy, bluish chamber with, to the left, an unmade bed and to the right, a door opening on a white, well-lighted bathroom. Before the prompter's box, an easy chair and a table: telephone, low lamp. The curtain discloses a scene of murder [*Une chambre de meurtre*]. In front of the bed, on the floor, a woman stretched out in a night robe, as if assassinated.''

Cocteau's references to death in these stage directions are figurative rather than literal. The subject of the play is the death of a love affair, and it is the heart and spirit of the woman that are in their death agonies, not her body.

The woman (she is given no name) has been interrupted in a long telephone call—how long, we do not know precisely because it seems to have been going on for some time and its resumption lasts the full length of the opera—almost three quarters of an hour.

The telephone rings almost immediately, after a few agonizing chords from the orchestra, and the woman succeeds in getting off the wire some other feminine subscriber to the party line. From time to time, the call is again interrupted, for the telephone service in Paris is notoriously bad. It always occurs at inopportune moments—but then, there could not be any opportune moment for interruption in this agonizing, almost lethal farewell.

For the man at the other end of the line, who has initiated the call, has been her lover for some years and, as we slowly become aware, this is his final good-by. The next day he is to be married to someone else. The call is resumed with practical matters—such as the woman's report that she has had dinner with her friend Martha (who has been just perfect in her understanding ways), and that it will be perfectly simple for him to send for their letters whenever he wishes. Of course she understands; it isn't necessary to apologize. She has made up her mind to be brave about it all, and she will be. (It is obviously not the first time, nor will it be the last, that she expresses this determination, but one knows it is only a sincere hope, not a conviction, that she may succeed.) And so the scene goes on—at times almost incoherent, at times almost sentimental as she reminds her lover of good days they have had together, at times reassuring to the man who is obviously really worried about her, at times desperate, as when she admits to having attempted suicide. There is, thus, great variety in the kind of thing she has to say to her lover, great variety in her reactions to his unheard but apparently kindly answers. Yet over it all there lies the tragedy of her desperation, her grasping at straws of hope, her pitiful attempts at self-control. From time to time she paces the floor (it is a long telephone cord), she throws herself on the bed, she sits quietly at the table, she kneels on the floor. Yet there is a kind of desperate dignity about her. She never pleads (excepting that he should not spend his honeymoon in the same hotel they had visited together); she never upbraids; she repeatedly says

Denise Duval as the protagonist

how kind and considerate he is being. And she obviously means it.

At the end she walks to the bed and lies down and holds the telephone tightly to her. ''My darling,'' she says. ''My beautiful darling . . . I am strong. Hurry up, now. Hang up! Hang up quickly! I love you, I love you, I love you, I love you . . . love you . . .'' and the receiver clatters down on the floor.

This is no mere little melodrama, as it would have been if, say, the woman had in the end committed suicide on the stage. It is rather, as the title suggests, a projection of the human voice—the state of quiet desperation, as Thoreau put it, in which most of us live.

War and Peace

VOINA I MIR

CHARACTERS*

Andrei, Prince Bolkonsky	*Baritone*		Hélène, Princess Kuragina, *his wife*	
Nicolai, Prince Bolkonsky, *his father*	*Bass*			*Mezzo-soprano*
Princess Marie, *his sister*	*Mezzo-soprano*		Anatol, Prince Kuragin, *her brother*	*Tenor*
Ilya, Count Rostov	*Bass*		Dolokhov, *his friend*	*Baritone*
Natasha, *his daughter*	*Soprano*		Michael, Prince Kutuzov, *Field*	
Sonya, *her cousin*	*Mezzo-soprano*		*Marshal of the Russian Army*	*Bass*
Princess Akhrosimova, *a friend of*			Napoleon Bonaparte	*Baritone*
the Rostovs'	*Soprano*		Vassili Denisov, *Pierre's friend*	*Baritone*
Pierre, Count Bezukov	*Tenor*		Platon Karateyev, *a peasant soldier*	*Tenor*
			Balaga, *a coachman*	*Bass*

Members of the Russian Aristocracy, Peasants, Partisans, Soldiers, Cossacks, Napoleon's Staff

The action takes place in Russia between 1809 and 1812.

OPERA IN thirteen scenes and a prologue. Music by Serge Prokofiev. Text in Russian by the composer and his wife, Myra Mendelssohn-Prokofieva, after the novel by Leo Tolstoy. Première (first eight scenes only), June 12, 1946, Maly Theater, Leningrad. First staging of a comprehensive version of the entire work (in Italian), 1953 Maggio Musicale, in Florence, Italy, conducted by Artur Rodzinski, with Rosanna Carteri, Fedora Barbieri, Franco Corelli, Ettore Bastianini and Italo Tajo. *War and Peace* was introduced to American audiences (in English) on January 13, 1957, when the NBC Opera Theater telecast an abridged two-and-a-half-hour version. The North American stage première took place at the Salle Wilfrid Pelletier, Montreal, Canada, on August 11, 1967, a performance by the touring Bolshoi Theater of Moscow, which first staged the opera in 1959.

Prokofiev's first notions of utilizing a Tolstoy

novel for an opera centered on the writer's *Resurrection*. It was the composer's wife who persuaded him to turn instead to *War and Peace* by reading aloud passages from that work. When the two of them set about sketching out a libretto, Hitler had recently launched his invasion of the Soviet Union. The Prokofievs, drawing on books VI, VIII, X, XI, and XIII of Tolstoy's epic, and employing the author's original dialogue wherever possible, conceived a two-part condensation of the story, dealing first with the romance of Natasha and Andrei against a background of peacetime Russia and later with the events leading up to, during, and after the French invasion of 1812. The libretto was completed in short order, and by the late summer of 1941 Prokofiev had begun to compose the music. (Some of the love themes for Natasha and Andrei were originally written for an unrealized 1936 dramatic production of Pushkin's *Eugene Onegin;* likewise, some of Kutuzov's patriotic utterances were drawn from music for the Eisenstein film *Ivan the Terrible*.) Although Prokofiev had fully composed eleven scenes by early 1943, it was not until June 1945 that

---

* In the composer's final revision of *War and Peace,* the cast of singers calls for fifty-eight separate roles. The above list mentions only those who figure most prominently in the scenario.

Scene 2: Guests dance the polonaise in the magnificent ballroom where Andrei meets Natasha, in Bolshoi Theater staging, Moscow.

any of the music achieved public performance—and then only in a concert version of selected scenes by Moscow's Philharmonic Orchestra. A month earlier Prokofiev wrote that *War and Peace* (his Opus 91) had been conceived as an act of patriotic faith in the courage and endurance of the Russian people, who bravely withstood the threat of Nazi invasion. The historic parallel to the Russians' repulse of the French in 1812 is obvious. "The idea of writing an opera on the theme of *War and Peace* became an obsession with me, even though I was quite aware of the difficulties involved in such a task. . . . I am particularly happy that, while my work started during the years of bitter oppression and war, it will be heard in the happy time of our triumphant victory."

Prokofiev continued to revise his score but never lived to hear it produced in full. He died in 1953, two years before it reached the Russian stage. For this reason there is no definitive performing edition of the opera, and it has been produced in various versions. Prokofiev himself wrote two different introductions: a formal overture (which can be heard on the abridged Heliodor recording) and a musical "epigraph," the composer's own word, a choral prologue sung by the entire company, clearly stating the score's patriotic theme. The current Bolshoi Theater production uses this choral prologue, and it is the Bolshoi production that the synopsis here follows.

SCENE 1: *A garden at Otradnoye, Count Rostov's estate, May 1809.* Prince Andrei Bolkonsky, visiting the Rostov estate on a matter of business, sits by his window, gazing into the moonlit night. Thinking of his ride that afternoon through the surrounding woodland, he recalls a huge oak tree found standing among the profusion of striplings and spring flowers. Its gnarled dead branches seemed to speak to him of the total vanity of life. Friendship and love, joy and laughter—what are they but empty lies

and foolish self-deception? It would be best, he tells himself, to live out one's life devoid of hopes and feelings. His gloomy thoughts are interrupted by the voice of Natasha, Rostov's younger daughter. The loveliness of the spring night has kept her, too, from sleep. With her cousin and companion, Sonya, she appears at her bedroom window on the floor above and talks rapturously of the wonders of nature. The Prince, though he cannot see the girl, is enchanted by her voice, deeply moved by her words, and resolves to renew his own joy in living.

SCENE 2: *A palace ballroom in St. Petersburg, New Year's Eve 1810.* Natasha, accompanied by her father and Sonya, is attending her first ball. Confused by the splendor of the palace, and too timid to join in the fashionable conversation of the other guests, she fears that she will not be asked to dance. A friend of the Rostov family, Count Pierre Bezukov, sympathizes with the young girl's plight and urges Andrei to dance with her. The Prince, waltzing with Natasha, recognizes the girl who had so moved him months before, and is once more captivated by her charm and youthful exuberance. On an impulse, surprising even to himself, he decides that the girl shall be his wife—"if, when she leaves me, she goes directly to her cousin and that other lady." The dance ends, and to Andrei's joy, Natasha runs to Sonya's side.

SCENE 3: *An anteroom in the palace of Prince Bolkonsky.* Andrei has asked for Natasha's hand, and Count Rostov has willingly approved the match. But Andrei's father, the old Prince Bolkonsky, reluctant to give his consent, has sent his son abroad to reconsider the proposed marriage for a year's time. The Rostovs pay a formal visit to the old Prince, who, curtly refusing them an interview, sends his daughter Marie to receive them. Keenly feeling this social snub, Rostov withdraws, leaving the girls alone together. Natasha is hurt by Marie's cold politeness, and is further humiliated when the old Prince, in an unexpected appearance, addresses her abruptly. What right have they to judge me, she bitterly asks herself. Smarting from the Bolkonskys' disdainful attitude and her father's cowardly behavior, and in despair at Andrei's enforced absence, she makes a despondent but dignified retreat.

SCENE 4: *A salon in Pierre Bezukov's palace.* Pierre's wife, the frivolous, amoral Hélène, is giving a party for some friends of dubious character. But she has also invited the Rostovs, for, although aware of Natasha's engagement to the absent Andrei, she maliciously encourages a romantic intrigue between her brother Anatol Kuragin and Natasha. The young girl, although certain of her love for Andrei, is confused and flattered by Anatol's attentions. Alone with her, Anatol passionately declares his love, giving her a letter—to be read when he has gone—in which he begs her to elope with him. In spite of Sonya's strong misgivings, Natasha is deeply affected by the young man's ardor, and laments the facts that Andrei, so far away, is powerless to restrain her from this dangerous adventure. Count Rostov enters and, scandalized by Hélène's other guests, takes the girls away.

SCENE 5: *Dolokhov's study.* Dolokhov attempts to dissuade his friend Anatol from his mad plan of elopement with Natasha. He warns him of Pierre's undoubted wrath, and points out that, as Anatol already has a secret wife, his "marriage" to Natasha will either be bigamous or invalid. But Anatol, a thorough libertine, can think only of the pleasures of the moment, and laughs away Dolokhov's fears. The coachman Balaga, a veteran accomplice to the young men's many escapades, is enlisted in the plot. The three drink to their success, and Anatol, swearing to give up his dissolute life for Natasha, bids farewell to his gypsy mistress.

SCENE 6: *A rear ground-floor room in the house of Princess Akhrosimova.* The Rostovs, departing on a trip, have entrusted Natasha to the care of their friend the old Princess Akhrosimova. Natasha plans to run off with Anatol that very night, but learns that Sonya has revealed the entire intrigue to the Princess. When Anatol arrives, his way is barred by a footman, and he makes a cowardly withdrawal. The Princess now confronts the heartbroken and mortified Natasha. Upbraiding her for her trust in the amoral Hélène and her brother, she reminds Natasha of her duty toward her parents and her fiancé. Tearfully, Natasha tells her that she has secretly broken off her engagement to Andrei, and

insists that despite the unfavorable gossip which surrounds his name Anatol is a man of honorable intentions. Pierre, having learned of his brother-in-law's most recent peccadillo, arrives at the house and is gratefully admitted by the Princess. He gently reveals to Natasha the truth of Anatol's scandalous past and his previous marriage. Now in despair, Natasha begs Pierre to go to Andrei, explain her momentary madness, and ask his forgiveness for her faithless treatment of him. But she already realizes that she has now ruined any hope of future happiness with the Prince. Her life, she sobs, is at an end. Deeply affected by her grief, Pierre unburdens his own heart, and impulsively tells Natasha that, were he free to do so, he himself would seek her hand. Then, embarrassed by this admission of his love, he leaves in haste. Natasha, still inconsolable, rushes from the room, and moments later, cries out for Sonya's help; she has taken poison.

SCENE 7: *Pierre's study.* The incorrigible Hélène is making merry with a group of guests—among them Anatol. Pierre enters, sends off his wife and her companions, and furiously orders his brother-in-law to leave Moscow at once. The frightened Anatol agrees. Alone, Pierre voices his disgust at the state of his household and his wife's amoral behavior. His friend Vassili Denisov, a lieutenant in the imperial army, arrives with news that war with France will soon begin in earnest. Napoleon is mobilizing his forces on the Russian border. Pierre decides to leave immediately for the front.

SCENE 8: *The hills near Borodino.* Partisans and guerrilla fighters are building bastions in preparation for the French attack. Members of the regular army, Andrei and Denisov among them, are arriving. Both hope to see the army's supreme commander, Field Marshal Kutuzov. Refugees from Smolensk appear, determined to aid the local peasants in repelling Napoleon's army. Andrei is preoccupied by thoughts of Natasha's faithlessness and their shattered love; he is once again convinced of the futility of living. Pierre, still in civilian dress, has come to observe the battle, and Andrei, sensing that they may never meet again, bids his friend an emotional farewell as he leaves to take command of his regiment. Moved by Andrei's words and the selfless nobility of the Russian people as they unite to protect their land from the invaders, Pierre decides on a course of action. He will enlist in the army as a common soldier. To the cheers of the partisans and peasants, Marshal Kutuzov arrives with his escort. The troops now pass in review—the Moscow grenadiers, the Yergevsky and Izmailovsky regiments, the mounted Cossacks—and Kutuzov, admiring Bolkonsky's men, asks to see the Prince.

Andrei reports to his commander, who asks him to stay on as a member of his personal staff. But Andrei feels that his place is at the front, and Kutuzov, warmly embracing him, lets him go off with his regiment. As soldiers continue to arrive, the battle finally begins.

SCENE 9: *Napoleon's encampment at the Shevardinsky Redoubt.* The Emperor-General, surrounded by his staff, observes the progress of the battle of Borodino. Certain that his army will put the Russians to rout, he imagines his triumphant entry into the fallen city of Moscow. But messengers bring word of heavy losses among the French and of field commanders dead or wounded. Fresh divisions are called for and dispatched. These unexpected reversals are discussed in worried tones by Napoleon's staff. He, too, is deeply troubled. Why is it that he can no longer summon victory with a single, dreadful sweep of his hand? A burst of cannon fire scatters his men in terror; Napoleon alone stands firm.

SCENE 10: *A hut near Fili.* Kutuzov has called together his generals for a council of war. They must decide whether to defend Moscow from the oncoming French or, abandoning the city, to move further on in preparation for a counterattack. The generals urge him to hold the city, but overriding their apprehensions, Kutuzov orders the retreat. When his staff, still doubtful of the wisdom of his plan, has left, Kutuzov reaffirms his abiding faith in the Russian people, confident that they will withstand the occupation of Moscow and eventually drive back the foe beyond the Russian border.

SCENE 11: *A Moscow street.* The city has been evacuated before the advancing French. Pierre, among those who have stayed behind, plots the assassination of Napoleon. He learns from the Rostov servants that the entire family has fled the city, taking with them the wounded officers left in their care. (Among them, unknown to Natasha, is Andrei.) Fires are breaking out all over Moscow; its citizens would sooner burn their beloved city than yield it to the conqueror. The French round up those suspected of arson, among them Pierre and a peasant soldier, Platon Karateyev, who assures Pierre that their countrymen will win the final victory. Before they can be shot, a fresh and greater blaze breaks out. Struggling through the confusion and the smoke, Napoleon arrives with his staff. He is awed by the courage and resilience of the Russian people.

SCENE 12: *A village hut on the outskirts of Moscow.* Andrei, gravely wounded, lies in a delirium, his brain troubled by thoughts of Natasha and his country's uncertain fate. When Natasha enters, he at first imagines that she is a hallucination; but, once he is in her arms, his mind begins to clear, and he recalls the happier days when they were first in love. Assured that his feelings for her have never changed, Natasha begs forgiveness. He reaffirms his love, but once more lapsing into a delirium, he dies.

SCENE 13: *The road to Smolensk.* The retreating French are taking with them their Russian prisoners, Pierre and Platon still among them. Weakened by illness, Platon cannot keep up the march and is shot. Pierre and the others are unexpectedly freed when a band of partisans, led by Denisov, rout the French column. Pirre learns that the entire Grande Armée is retreating in confusion, and that Moscow is once more in Russian hands. The Czarist troops appear in force, and with them Marshal Kutuzov on horseback. Kutuzov thanks the people for their courage and endurance and praises them for having saved their country from the foe. In a moving chorus, all hail Kutuzov as the leader who brought them to victory, and express their boundless love for Russia.

Prologue and Epilogue: Bolshoi Theater chorus intones paean to Mother Russia, first and last music heard in the Moscow production.

Werther

CHARACTERS

Werther, *a poet*	*Tenor*	Schmidt ⎱ *his friends*	*Tenor*
The Bailiff of Wetzlar	*Bass*	Johann ⎰	*Bass*
Charlotte, *his daughter*	*Mezzo-soprano*	Sophie, *another daughter*	*Soprano*
		Albert, *Charlotte's* fiancé	*Baritone*

The Bailiff's Younger Children and Citizens of Wetzlar

The action takes place in Wetzlar, Germany, in 1772.

OPERA IN four acts. Music by Jules Massenet. Libretto in French by Édouard Blau, Paul Milliet, and Georges Hartmann, based on Goethe's short novel *Die Leiden des Jungen Werthers* (*The Sorrows of Young Werther*). First produced, in German, at the Hofoper, Vienna, February 16, 1892, with a cast headed by Ernest van Dyck and Marie Renard. First performance in Paris, in French, January 16, 1893. American première at Chicago, March 29, 1894. First production at the Metropolitan Opera House, April 19, 1894, with Jean de Reszke and Emma Eames.

Although not the most popular of Massenet's many operas, *Werther* contains some of its composer's most imaginative pages. The melodies are bright and fresh, and the orchestral writing is colorful and expressive. The romantic story appealed strongly to Massenet's susceptible nature, though it has been suggested that he wrote *Werther* to show that he could portray a virtuous woman—Charlotte—in music. Friends had complained to him that all his heroines were courtesans.

ACT I

SCENE: *Courtyard of the Bailiff's home.* The widowed Bailiff has been left with many children; and as the curtain rises—after a very romantic prelude—it is midsummer and he is beforehandedly rehearsing the youngest ones in a Christmas carol.

Two friends, Schmidt and Johann, join the group and discuss with the Bailiff a young poet named Werther, who has come to town and appears to be a very melancholy sort. They also talk about another young man, Albert, the absent fiancé of Charlotte, the Bailiff's oldest child (but still in her late teens). The two young men are great friends, and Werther comes to call, singing a brief ode to nature as the rehearsal is again taken up.

There is a ball that evening in town, and when Charlotte has prepared supper for the youngsters, she goes off to the festivities with Werther. Soon thereafter the fiancé unexpectedly returns and is cordially greeted by the second-oldest daughter (she is fifteen) as her brother-in-law to be. For a while the stage is empty as a tender intermezzo is played, suggesting what we learn later to be true—that Werther has fallen completely in love with Charlotte at the ball. Night has fallen when they return, and Werther tells her of his love; but Charlotte says she had promised to marry another, and Werther, learning who her fiancé is, goes off brokenhearted prophesying that he must die if Charlotte weds Albert.

ACT II

SCENE: *Before the church.* It is three months later; Albert and Charlotte are now married; and the

448

Charlotte (Clara Petrella) with Werther (Giuseppe Di Stefano), at La Scala, Milan

townspeople have gathered to celebrate their pastor's golden wedding anniversary. Charlotte tells Albert how happy she is as his bride, and Werther sings a heartbroken melody known as the "Desolation Aria." Albert, who is really very fond of his friend, tries to comfort him by telling him how much he himself esteems the poet; and a few moments later the very practical Charlotte suggests that Werther might try falling in love with her sister Sophie. When Werther declines the offer, she insists that he go away at least until Christmas. The despondent Werther prays to God for help; and when Sophie comes to claim him for the first minuet, which he had promised her, he turns violently on her, saying that he is leaving at once and will never return. Sophie is in tears as the act closes, and Albert is beginning to suspect that things have gone too far for comfort between his friend and his young wife.

ACT III

SCENE: *A room in the Bailiff's house.* After a rather long prelude supposed to be suggestive of Werther's aimless three months of wandering trying to forget, we find Charlotte reading over some letters he had sent her. Now for the first time do we realize that Werther has really touched her heart, and she almost gives away her secret to Sophie in her song about sorrow—the *"Air des larmes."* When Sophie leaves, Charlotte appeals to God for strength to combat this illicit love. She has her opportunity at once, for a bedraggled Werther appears. It is Christmastime, and he has not had the fortitude to remain away longer than that. He pleads with her passionately;

and then, taking up a copy of Ossian (whose poetry was practically a rallying cry for early Romantics), he sings out the strikingly appropriate passage beginning *"Pourquoi me reveiller?"* ("Why awaken me?"). This is the most familiar aria in the opera.

For a brief moment Charlotte succumbs and finds herself in her lover's arms. But recalling her duty, she directs Werther never to see her again and dashes into another room, locking the door behind her. Werther leaves the house, swearing that he is going to his grave. Albert then returns, hears that Werther is back in town, finds his wife very much troubled, and is handed a note from Werther, asking him for a loan of his pistols as he is off for a long journey. Without further thought, the weapons are sent off, and only then does Charlotte realize the possible significance of the request. Desperately hoping she may not be too late, she dashes from the house.

ACT IV

SCENE: *Werther's room.* There is no intermission; but as the scenery is being changed, the orchestra plays a little tone poem depicting Charlotte's worry on her trip to try to save her lover. Midnight is tolling when she arrives to find that Werther has already shot himself. Before he dies, he hears her confess that she has loved him, and he tells her that now he is happy; life for him is only beginning. The unhappy woman throws herself on his body, while off stage come, ironically, the merry voices of the children singing the Christmas carol they had been rehearsing in Act I.

449

William Tell

GUILLAUME TELL

CHARACTERS

William Tell		Bass
Arnold	*Swiss patriots*	Tenor
Walter Fürst		Bass
Melcthal, *Arnold's father*		Bass
Gessler, *Austrian Governor of Schwitz and Uri*		Bass
Rudolph, *captain of Gessler's bodyguard*		Tenor

Ruodi, *a fisherman*	Tenor
Leuthold, *a shepherd*	Bass
Jemmy, *William Tell's son*	Soprano
Hedwig, *Tell's wife*	Soprano
Mathilde, *Gessler's daughter and a princess of the House of Hapsburg*	Soprano

Peasants, Knights, Pages, Ladies of the Train of Mathilde, Three Brides and their
Bridegrooms, Hunters, Soldiers, and Guards

The action takes place in Switzerland during the fourteenth century.

OPERA IN FOUR ACTS. Music by Gioacchino Rossini. Libretto in French by Étienne de Jouy and Hippolyte Bis, after the play by Schiller. First performance, Paris Opéra, August 3, 1829. First American performance, New York's Park Theater, in English, September 19, 1831, preceded by the opera *Cinderella* and followed by a farce, *'Twas I*. The work was presented in French at the Théâtre d'Orléans, New Orleans, December 13, 1842. Given also in French at the Park Theater, New York, June 16, 1845. Produced in Italian, Academy of Music, New York, April 9, 1855, and at the same theater in German, April 18, 1866. Initial hearing at the Metropolitan Opera House in German, November 28, 1884. Italian has since been the language of all presentations there.

William Tell is one of the longest operas in existence. It has been customary to cut a good deal of the work for anything like a comfortable evening's presentation. The uncut version had been tried in Paris in 1856, and it is said that it ran from 7 P.M. until one in the morning. It is known that after fifty-six performances of the work in all five acts, the director of the Paris Opéra ordered it shortened to three by omitting the third and fusing together the fourth and fifth. Also, for some time, only Act II of *William Tell* was presented there, permitting it to serve some other work as a curtain raiser. In passing, Rossini was once informed that the second act of *William Tell* was to be given on a certain evening. His characteristic retort was, "What, the whole of it?"

Oddly enough, although Rossini composed the score to this opera while at the high noon of his creative powers, he did not again write a work for the lyric theater. The mystery surrounding this thirty-nine years' abstinence has never been solved, although many—and varied—have been the explanations supplied, or invented.

A strongly vivid, typically Rossinian score—though, naturally, in much more dramatic vein than that of his well-known *Barber of Seville*—*William Tell* has not been given with consistency by American opera companies. The principal roles—especially that of Arnold—are by no means easy, yet one knows of other equally difficult roles in other operas, whose popularity has not waned, in spite of taxing vocal demands.

OVERTURE

Long before it became associated in every American's mind with "The Lone Ranger" radio serial, the *William Tell* Overture had established itself as the most familiar of all opera overtures, especially on pops concert programs. It begins with a lyrical passage unconventionally but very effectively scored for a quintet of cellos. Then a soft roll on the kettledrums introduces a typically Rossinian thunderstorm, complete with raindrops spattered by a piccolo. Next comes a pastoral section that features a Swiss alphorn melody (scored for French horn), then a trumpet fanfare, and finally the exciting *galop* to which one wants to reply, "Heigh-ho, Silver!"

ACT I

SCENE: *William Tell's chalet on the shores of Lake Lucerne.* The despotic rule of Governor Gessler has increasingly inflamed the spirit of the Swiss, and in this opening scene Tell, in an aside, points a contrast between the young fisherman Ruodi, who blithely sings of love, and himself, tortured by his country's oppression. The people gather, on signal from a horn, and presently preparations get under way for the celebration of three marriages by the beloved patriarch Melcthal, Arnold's father. Arnold, aggrieved by the difficulties that surround his courtship of Gessler's daughter Mathilde, speaks with Tell, who—always furiously patriotic—recites Gessler's crimes. He, therefore, asks Arnold's aid in overthrowing the tyrant. Arnold's reluctance, natural under the circumstances, is misunderstood by Tell, but after some explanations the patriot gets Arnold's word to support the rebels' cause.

In the mountains nearby the horns of Gessler's hunting party are heard, as an ominous portent. Meanwhile, Melcthal joins the three young couples in marriage, and gaiety takes possession of the scene, until the old shepherd Leuthold rushes in, seeking protection from Gessler. It seems that one of the despot's soldiers, in a sportive mood, has attempted to abduct Leuthold's young daughter, whereupon he received, for his pains, the father's ax in the middle of his skull. Leuthold begs Ruodi to ferry him over to safety on the other side of the lake, but the latter refuses, giving as his excuses the dangers present in the jagged underwater rocks and the strong current. The soldiers in search of Leuthold are heard approaching, and Tell impulsively springs into the boat, ordering Leuthold to jump in after him, and they set out for the opposite shore.

Giuseppe Danise as William Tell at the Metropolitan Opera, 1922

When the soldiers arrive they become furious at the escape of their quarry, and Melcthal, having defied their captain Rudolph, is carried off under arrest.

ACT II

SCENE 1: *A pine forest on the heights of Rütli.* Mathilde has caught a glimpse of Arnold during the hunt and thinks that if he has spied her, he, too, will come to this spot, and he does. But, awaiting him, Mathilde sings a brilliant lyric aria, "*Sombre forêt*" ("Somber forest"), in which she tells of her strong preference for an idyllic, if simple, life with Arnold, to the manifold luxuries of the court. When Arnold arrives, the two sing a duet protesting eternal love, while deploring the evil fortune that keeps them apart. Mathilde makes a quick exit when she hears the sounds of people approaching, and the newcomers William Tell and Walter Fürst are somewhat suspicious of Arnold, at first, having recognized Gessler's daughter. In any case, they reveal to him that his father has been slain by Gessler, and from now on only vengeance can motivate the young man. The three patriots now swear allegiance to their cause, and Arnold is urged to be present that night at a gathering of all the partisans.

SCENE 2: *The gathering of the cantons in a hidden wood.* The men of Unterwald, those of Schwitz and of Uri, arrive stealthily at their forest meeting spot. Tell and Walter greet them, and the furtiveness of the occasion is emphasized by the deft music of Rossini. Tell inspirits all about him with the intensity of his speech, and in a compellingly dramatic sequence all clasp hands and swear to down the tyrant, invoking, at the same time, heaven's wrath on any traitor among them.

ACT III

SCENE 1: *A ruined chapel in the grounds of the Governor's palace at Altdorf.* Arnold and Mathilde meet in the ruined chapel. He informs her of his father's execution, ordered by her own father, and sings a song of farewell to dreams, in the aria *"Pour notre amour"* ("For our love"). Mathilde, for her part, promises ever to remember him and anxiously cautions him to escape.

SCENE 2: *The market place of Altdorf.* In the market place of Altdorf, Gessler has caused to be erected a banner with his coat of arms. Topping that is his own hat, to which, by express order, all must bow. Addressing the throng, Gessler remarks on the hundred years of Austrian rule, and he orders the people to celebrate the occasion with dancing and festivity. A number of ballets and a soldiers' march take the center of the action, which is interspersed with occasional outbursts of song by the chorus.

Giovanni Martinelli (Arnold), Rosa Ponselle (Mathilde)

All who pass the Gessler coat of arms and hat bow in obeisance. However, Captain Rudolph notices that William Tell is not one of these. He remains, in fact, boldly erect. The patriot, who is with his young son Jemmy, is arrested and brought before the Governor; Tell, however, first bids Jemmy to go home and bring the message to his mother that all the beacons are to be lighted in the mountains—the signal that the moment of liberation has come.

Gessler, believing that he may further increase his pleasure by humbling Tell, orders him, fine archer that he is, to split with one of his bows an apple placed on Jemmy's head. For only a moment Tell pleads with Gessler, but on hearing the tyrant's order that Jemmy be put to death, he says that he will do as Gessler asks. He takes two arrows, secreting one in his clothes, and after some anxious moments and a prayerful look to heaven, aims, and splits the apple in two. When Jemmy rushes up to him in tearful joy, Tell embraces him, but as he does so the second arrow drops to the ground. To Gessler, who queries him about it, he says that had he failed and injured his son, he would have sent the second missile straight to Gessler's heart, whereupon Gessler gives a furious command for Tell's arrest.

ACT IV

SCENE 1: *Before Melcthal's house.* Arnold cannot bear to enter the home of his father, whose death at Gessler's hands haunts him. Most of the scene is given to his heroic mourning aria *"Asile héréditaire"* ("Ancestral home"). At its close a group of Swiss patriots enter to tell him of Tell's arrest. Aroused to action, Arnold leads them out to an attack on the Austrian despot's stronghold.

SCENE 2: *The shores of Lake Lucerne.* Grieving over her husband and her son, Hedwig is soon comforted with the joyous cries of Jemmy, who has been brought thither by Mathilde. From her Hedwig learns that Tell has escaped and is at that moment on the lake, over which a storm is brewing. At this Jemmy rushes out to call the patriots. Against storm music in the orchestra Tell appears, safe and sound, and exceedingly thankful that he is again with his dear ones. He discovers that his son has been shrewd enough, while setting fire to the house as a signal to the patriots, to save his father's bows and arrows, and exultantly calls for them. Gessler, on the hunt for Tell, appears on the rocks above, and Tell, fitting an arrow to his bow, takes aim and kills the tyrant forthwith. All is jubilation, now, and Arnold, together with other patriots, rushes in with the news that the castle has fallen. The opera closes with a rousing invocation to freedom.

Wozzeck

CHARACTERS

Wozzeck, *a soldier*	*Baritone*	2nd Apprentice	*Baritone*
Andres, *his friend*	*Tenor*	Idiot	*Tenor*
The Drum Major	*Tenor*	Marie, *Wozzeck's mistress*	*Soprano*
The Captain	*Tenor*	Margret, *a neighbor*	*Contralto*
The Doctor	*Bass*	Marie's Child	*Boy soprano*
1st Apprentice	*Bass*		

Soldiers, Apprentices, Servant Girls, Children

The action takes place in Germany, early in the nineteenth century.

OPERA IN THREE ACTS. Music by Alban Berg. Libretto in German adapted by Berg from Georg Büchner's *Wozzeck*, the twenty-five scenes of which he cut to fifteen. The world première was held at the Berlin State Opera, on December 14, 1925, and within eleven years *Wozzeck* had been given 166 performances—unusual for such a work. In the United States *Wozzeck* was first given in Philadelphia, on March 19, 1931, by the Philadelphia Opera Company, with Leopold Stokowski conducting and Anna Roselle as Marie. It was given by the same group at the Metropolitan Opera House on November 24, 1931, and was not performed again in the United States for twenty years. At their subscription concerts of April 12, 13, and 15, 1951, the New York Philharmonic Symphony Society gave concert performances of *Wozzeck* at Carnegie Hall, Dimitri Mitropoulos conducting, and it was revived by the New York City Opera Company and performed at the New York City Center of Music and Drama on April 18, 1952, in an English translation by Eric Blackall and Vida Harford. The same translation was used at the Metropolitan Opera Association's first performance on March 5, 1959.

Georg Büchner's play, found among his papers after his death at the age of 24 in 1837, was based on a real murder committed in 1824 by an ex-soldier named Johann Christian Woyzeck, who was executed. It was not till 1913, at Munich, that this strange, psychological and impressionistic drama, so far ahead of its time, reached the stage. The score was written ten years later, and it took 137 rehearsals to mount the opera for the first time at Berlin. Berg wrote mainly atonal music for *Wozzeck* and cast each scene in a specific musical form—for example, Act I, Scene 1, in a suite, while the whole of Act II, with its five scenes, is a symphony in five movements—and the result is an opera, not only powerful, but, with all its dissonances and strangeness, emotionally eloquent. Pity is the underlying sentiment, pity for the poor man driven by forces over which he has no control.

ACT I

SCENE 1: *Captain's room, early morning.* Wozzeck is shaving the Captain, who rambles on of time and the weather. He complains that Wozzeck has no moral sense because he has an illegitimate child. Wozzeck answers that he can't afford to be virtuous—he's too poor; even in heaven the poor probably have to help make the thunder. The Captain dismisses him, telling him to do less thinking.

SCENE 2: *Field outside town, afternoon.* Wozzeck and Andres, also a soldier, are cutting sticks for firewood. Wozzeck feels that the place is accursed, and his mind grows incoherent with wild fancies. He frightens Andres with his description of fire ascending to heaven, and Andres persuades him to leave.

SCENE 3: *Marie's room, evening.* Marie stands at her window with her child, watching the regiment march by. Her neighbor below, Margret, accuses her of flirting with the Drum Major, and they hurl names at each other. Marie shuts the window and, alone with her child, sings him to sleep. There is a knock at the window, and Wozzeck, who cannot come in because he must report to his barracks, speaks distractedly to her of the glow of the heavens. She is afraid he will lose his mind.

SCENE 4: *The Doctor's study, afternoon.* The Doctor upbraids Wozzeck for misbehaving. He is using Wozzeck for scientific experiments and paying him for following orders. This time the order is a diet of only beans. Wozzeck submits to these indignities to earn money for Marie and their child. When Wozzeck speaks of his hallucinations at the woods, the doctor is delighted; Wozzeck will make him famous.

SCENE 5: *Street outside Marie's house, evening.* Marie talks with the Drum Major, whose manliness she admires. He tries to caress her, and she struggles out of his grasp. But her virtue is not strong, and she gives in to his next embrace. They enter her house.

ACT II

SCENE 1: *Marie's room, morning.* Marie is admiring herself in a hand mirror, her child in her lap, when Wozzeck comes in. Her hands go to her ears, but Wozzeck has already seen the earrings—a present from the Drum Major. When she tells him she found them, he apparently believes her. He gazes at his sleeping son, noticing the beads of sweat on his brow—even in sleep the poor sweat. After giving Marie some money, he leaves, Marie feeling remorse for her behavior.

SCENE 2: *Street, during the day.* The Captain and the Doctor meet. The Doctor is in a hurry, but the Captain, a believer in taking one's time, insists on stopping him. Almost in revenge, the Doctor scares him with tales of death and by diagnosing him offhand—he will have an apoplexy producing paralysis within four weeks. Wozzeck passes by, but the Doctor stops him and the Captain takes him to task for rushing as if every beard needed shaving. Slyly the Captain asks him if he found a hair in his breakfast, while the Doctor beats time with his cane like a drum major. Wozzeck asks if they are joking, but they avoid a direct answer, and the Doctor feels his pulse. He escapes from their torments, and as he leaves, the Captain calls him a scoundrel.

Act II, Scene 1: Marie (Eleanor Steber) admires the earrings the Drum Major gave her as her child (Thomas Cooke) sleeps, as staged at the Metropolitan Opera in 1959.

SCENE 3: *Street outside Marie's house, later that day.* Wozzeck comes up to Marie and accuses her of deceiving him. Boldly she faces him and tells him not to lay hands on her—better a knife blade in her heart. The words ring in his ears.

SCENE 4: *Tavern garden, evening.* Apprentices, soldiers, and servant girls are dancing, while two drunken apprentices babble about the dreariness of life. Wozzeck sees Marie and the Drum Major, in a passionate embrace, dance past him. Before he can rush to them, the dance is over and the apprentices and soldiers sing a hunting song, Andres joining in as leader. Andres asks the distracted Wozzeck if he's drunk, but he answers, No such luck. The drunken apprentice harangues the crowd, and when they have had enough they carry him off. An idiot sidles up to Wozzeck and tells him that the joyful celebration reeks of blood. It sends his brain reeling, and he sees a red mist before him and the bodies of the dancers writhe like snakes.

SCENE 5: *Barracks, night.* Andres and Wozzeck are sleeping on a wooden bed, the other soldiers snoring nearby. Wozzeck wakes up Andres; he cannot sleep because he still sees the twisting bodies of the dancers—and the flashing of a knife blade. The Drum Major comes in, drunkenly boasting of his woman. When Andres asks him who she is, he answers: "Ask Wozzeck." Wozzeck refuses to be drawn into it and looks away, whistling. In anger the Drum Major grabs him off the bed and wrestles with him on the floor. A stronger man than Wozzeck, he threatens to choke him to death, then leaves. Wozzeck gets up and goes to his bed, staring into nothingness, feeling the pain and humiliation of another defeat, while the rest of the soldiers go back to sleep.

ACT III

SCENE 1: *Marie's room, night.* By candlelight Marie reads to her child from the Bible. Among other passages she reads of the woman taken in adultery and is filled with shame. This is the second day Wozzeck has not visited her. She prays God for mercy.

SCENE 2: *A pond in the woods, at dusk.* Wozzeck and Marie are walking. Marie is anxious to return to town, but Wozzeck makes her sit on the ground. He recalls their first meeting and asks how long their love will go on. When she tries to leave, he keeps her there, complimenting her ironically on her faithfulness. The moon rises red, and Wozzeck draws a knife. Marie tries to escape, but he tells her she will

The Doctor (Karl Dönch) baits Wozzeck (Hermann Uhde) with hints of Marie's infidelity as the Captain (Paul Franke) listens.

have no one if not himself, stabs her in the throat, and rushes off.

SCENE 3: *Tavern, night.* Apprentices and servant girls are dancing wildly, while Wozzeck, trying to forget the murder, exhorts them to dance on. After a dance with Margret he pulls her to his lap, and she notices the blood on his hand and elbow . . . it smells of human blood. Crying that he cut himself, he rushes out.

SCENE 4: *A pond in the woods, on a moonlit night.* Wozzeck searches wildly for his knife and stumbles over Marie's body, a necklace of blood around her throat. When he finds the knife, he throws it into the pond. The moon shines red, and he feels it, too, betrays him. His world all proclaiming his blood guilt, he wades into the pond to wash the blood off himself, goes out too far, and drowns. The Doctor and Captain, nearby, hear a sound as of water groaning—of someone drowning. But frightened by the eerie place, the red moon, and the strange sounds, they go quickly away.

SCENE 5: *Street outside Marie's house, bright morning.* Children are playing, among them Marie's child riding a hobbyhorse. Other children run up to them, and one cries that there is a dead woman. All the children but Marie's boy run off to try to see the body. He keeps playing with his hobbyhorse, until, seeing himself alone, he hops along after the others.

PICTURE CREDITS

About the House (Covent Garden, London)–195
Angel Records–19, 63, 258, 288, 431
Bavarian State Opera, Munich–128, 157, 277, 415
Bayreuth Festival–210, 279, 308, 347, 348, 361, 408
Bell Telephone Hour–23
Bender–154
Bergman, Beth–55, 56, 57, 82, 87, 88, 277
Betz, Rudolf (for Bavarian State Opera)–157, 352, 415
Bolshoi Theatre, Moscow–74, 324, 330, 331, 445, 447
Chicago Lyric Opera–117, 187, 197, 274, 330, 380
Columbia Records–159, 270
Connecticut Opera Association, Hartford–334
Cook, Eugene (for *Opera News*)–52, 53, 178, 179, 261, 262, 389, 401
Culver Pictures–21, 22, 23, 24, 60, 62, 67, 83, 90, 104, 107, 146, 162, 172, 177, 200, 215, 251, 259, 307, 371, 406, 435
David (for Chicago Lyric Opera)–274, 380
Davis, Myron (for *Life*)–328
Dietrich–151
Dominic–195
Dufoto, Rome–224
Edgar Vincent Associates–74, 154, 307, 377, 379
Falk, Adolf–279
Fayer–83, 151, 154, 374
Fohl, Fred (for New York City Opera)–72, 99, 110, 203, 205, 216, 218, 242, 243, 293
Freeman, John W. (for *Opera News*)–24
Galloway, Dennis (for San Francisco Opera)–231, 333
Giacomelli–336
Glyndebourne Festival–115, 193, 258
Graphic House–249
Graveth, Guy (for Glyndebourne Festival)–115
Gravina, Peter–82
Hamburg State Opera–201, 232, 233
Harvard Theatre Collection–221, 247, 345
Holdt, Hanns–352
Holland Festival–141
Indiana University–133
Jones, Carolyn Mason (for San Francisco Opera)–144, 340, 405, 433
Lackenbach, Robert (for San Francisco Opera)–76, 111, 424
La Scala Museum–15, 16, 17, 32, 134, 141
Lauterwasser, Siegfried–308, 349, 351, 361
Le Blang, Sedge (for Metropolitan Opera)–49, 70, 86, 102, 103, 145, 160, 175, 246, 248, 263, 299, 339, 375, 402, 403, 413
Lehmann, Lotte (Courtesy of)–167

Leider, Frida (Courtesy of)–423
Lloyd, Harvey (for *Opera News*)–148, 342, 436
London Records–83, 129, 151, 154, 294, 359, 394
MacWeeney, Alen (for *Opera News*)–169, 320, 321, 322
McArthur, Edwin (Courtesy of)–114
Melançon, Louis (for Metropolitan Opera)–31, 33, 37, 39, 45, 46, 91, 105, 123, 131, 136, 138, 140, 142, 152, 179, 212, 222, 236, 250, 252, 255, 260, 296, 298, 305, 317, 341, 363, 366, 381, 393, 395, 418, 419, 420, 425, 427, 436, 439, 441
Menotti, Gian Carlo (Courtesy of)–43, 97, 98, 269, 271
Metropolitan Opera Archives–137, 175, 182, 208, 300, 397, 451
Metropolitan Opera Association–15, 29, 31, 33, 35, 37, 40, 41, 45, 46, 52, 53, 59, 70, 75, 77, 78, 82, 86, 87, 88, 91, 92, 100, 103, 105, 108, 118, 119, 123, 124, 126, 127, 129, 131, 136, 137, 138, 140, 145, 148, 152, 155, 158, 160, 161, 162, 169, 175, 176, 178, 179, 180, 182, 184, 207, 208, 212, 213, 222, 227, 228, 229, 236, 240, 242, 245, 246, 249, 250, 252, 253, 255, 256, 257, 259, 260, 261, 262, 265, 278, 295, 296, 298, 300, 302, 303, 305, 311, 313, 317, 320, 321, 322, 324, 325, 339, 341, 342, 355, 363, 366, 368, 369, 371, 375, 378, 381, 389, 393, 395, 397, 399, 401, 402, 403, 410, 411, 413, 418, 419, 420, 425, 427, 435, 436, 439, 440, 441, 451, 452, 454, 455
Metropolitan Opera National Company–69, 94
Michals, Duane–40
Mili, Gjon–97, 98, 269, 271
Morton–364
Musical America–117, 273, 281, 338, 417
National Museum, Stockholm–18
NBC-TV Opera Theater–43
New York City Opera–55, 56, 57, 72, 82, 87, 88, 99, 110, 203, 205, 216, 218, 219, 242, 243, 277, 293
New York Public Library–39
The New York Times–29, 41, 108, 126, 256, 265
Norton, Margaret (for San Francisco Opera)–407
Ofiara, Sylvian (for Connecticut Opera Association)–334
Opéra-Comique, Paris–80
Peters, Pete (for San Francisco Opera)–79
Peyer–232, 233
Photo Pic–80, 414
Piccagliani, Erio (for Teatro alla Scala, Milan)–38, 44, 84, 95, 113, 149, 174, 185, 189, 198, 267, 268, 283, 285, 287, 299, 324, 331, 337, 383, 384, 385, 392, 422, 429, 434, 437, 443, 449
Pittner, Rudolf (for Volksoper, Vienna)–327
Ponselle, Rosa (Courtesy of)–226

Picture Credits

Ray-Jones, Tony (for *Opera News*)–24
Rauh, Wilhelm (for Bayreuth Festival)–353, 408
RCA Victor–11, 17, 142, 164, 208, 211, 235, 387
Renaud, Gary (for *Opera News*)–245
Richard Wagner Gedenkstätte, Bayreuth–210
Ricordi, G.–20
Rogers, Houston (for Covent Garden, London)–289, 290
Rosenberg, Arnold (for *Opera News*)–161, 184, 240, 278, 311, 440, 454, 455
Royal Opera, London–50, 106, 122, 289, 290, 359, 414
Royal Opera, Stockholm–129
Sadler's Wells Opera Company, London–65
Salzburg Easter Festival–349, 351
Salzburg Festival–28
San Francisco Opera–39, 52, 76, 79, 111, 144, 231, 238, 285, 333, 340, 364, 405, 407, 424, 433
Schumacher, Karl (for Württemburgische Staatstheater, Stuttgart–152
Seligman, Paul (for *Opera News*)–124, 155, 257
Sher, E. Fred (for *Saturday Review*)–213, 227, 228, 229, 242, 355
Skelton Studios–238

Smith, Vernon L. (for *Opera News*)–35, 59, 75, 77, 78, 92, 118, 119, 158, 176, 180, 302, 324, 325, 368, 369, 378
Sorenson, Nancy (for Chicago Lyric Opera)–330
Southern, Donald (for Covent Garden, London)–50, 359
Speidel, Elisabeth (for Hamburg State Opera)–201
Spoleto Festival–318
Staatsoper, Vienna–374
Steichen, Edward–376
Swope, Martha–69, 94, 127, 253
Talbot–270
Teatro alla Scala, Milan–38, 44, 84, 95, 113, 149, 174, 185, 189, 198, 267, 268, 283, 285, 287, 299, 337, 383, 384, 385, 392, 422, 429, 434, 437, 443, 449
Teatro dell' Opera, Rome–135, 224, 391
Teatro la Fenice, Venice–336
Toepffer, Sabine (for Bavarian State Opera)–48, 128
Villella, Tom (Courtesy of)–290
Volksoper, Vienna–327
Wide World Studio–295, 410, 411
Wilson, Reg (for Covent Garden, London)–106, 122
Württemburgische Staatstheater, Stuttgart–152

Discography

The following is a selected list of complete recordings (except where otherwise noted) of the operas discussed in this book. It does not claim to be all-inclusive, but is confined to those recordings most readily available in the United States at the time this book goes to press. Since new recordings are constantly being issued and as older recordings are sometimes withdrawn, it is recommended that for the latest information, the reader consult the monthly *Schwann Long Playing Record Catalog*. This publication is available from any record dealer.

Our list is arranged in alphabetical order by composer.

Each listing begins with the names of the principal singers, followed, after a semicolon, by the name of the conductor. The number after the conductor's name indicate's how many records are included in the album; and following that is the name of the company issuing it.

All recordings are in the original language unless another language is indicated in parentheses after the conductor's name.

All recordings are in stereo except for certain mono recordings of unusual interest that have been included. These are indicated by an asterisk (*) at the beginning of the listing.

The symbol (#) at the end of a listing indicates that in addition to the complete recording, there is available a one-record album of "Highlights," usually containing the best known arias and other numbers.

SAMUEL BARBER

VANESSA

Steber, Elias, Resnik, Gedda, Tozzi; Mitropoulos
3 RCA Victor

BÉLA BARTÓK

BLUEBEARD'S CASTLE

*Hellwig, Koreh; Susskind   *2 Bartók*
Elias, Hines; Ormandy (in English)   *1 Columbia*
Töpper, Fischer-Dieskau; Fricsay (in German) *1 DGG†*
Ludwig, Berry; Kertész   *1 London*

LUDWIG VAN BEETHOVEN

FIDELIO

*Bampton, Steber, Peerce, Janssen, Belarsky;
Toscanini   *2 RCA Victrola*

† *DGG is an abbreviation for Deutsche Grammophon Gesellschaft.*

Ludwig, Hallstein, Vickers, Berry, Frick;
Klemperer   *3 Angel#*
Rysanek, Seefried, Häfliger, Fischer-Dieskau,
Frick; Fricsay   *2 DGG*
Nilsson, Sciutti, McCracken, Prey, Böhme;
Maazel   *2 London#*
Kuchta, Muszely, Patzak, Rehfuss, Kümmel;
Bamberger   *2 Nonesuch*
*Mödl, Jurinac, Windgassen, Edelmann, Frick;
Furtwängler   *3 Seraphim*
*Konetzni, Seefried, Ralf, Schoeffler, Alsen;
Böhm   *3 Vox#*
Jurinac, Stader, Peerce, Neidlinger, Ernster;
Knappertsbusch   *3 Westminster*

VINCENZO BELLINI

NORMA

Sutherland, Horne, Alexander, Cross;
Bonynge   *3 RCA Victor#*
Callas, Ludwig, Corelli, Zaccaria; Serafin   *3 Angel#*

Norma (*cont.*)

Cigna, Stignani, Breviario, Pasero; Gui   *3 Everest/Cetra*
Suliotis, Cossotto, del Monaco, Cava; Varviso   *2 London*

I Puritani

*Callas, di Stefano, Panerai, Rossi-Lemeni;
   Serafin   *3 Angel*
Sutherland, Duval, Capecchi, Flagello;
   Bonynge   *3 London‡*

La Sonnambula

*Pagliughi, Tagliavini, Siepi; Capuana   *3 Everest/Cetra*
Sutherland, Monti, Corena; Bonynge   *3 London‡*

ALBAN BERG

Lulu

Rothenberger, Meyer, Wohlfahrt, Unger, Blank-
   enheim; Ludwig   *3 Angel*
*Steingruber, Cerny, Kmentt, Libert, Wiener;
   Häfner   *3 Columbia*
Lear, Johnson, Driscoll, Grobe, Fischer-Dieskau;
   Böhm   *3 DGG*

Wozzeck

Strauss, Berry, Uhl; Boulez   *2 CBS*
*Farrell, Harrell, Jagel; Mitropoulos   *2 Columbia*
Lear, Fischer-Dieskau, Wunderlich; Böhm   *2 DGG*

HECTOR BERLIOZ

Les Troyens

Crespin, Chauvet; Prêtre (Selections)   *2 Angel*

GEORGES BIZET

Carmen

Price, Freni, Corelli, Merrill; Karajan   *3 RCA Victor‡*
*Stevens, Albanese, Peerce, Merrill;
   Reiner   *3 RCA Victor‡*
Callas, Guiot, Gedda, Massard; Prêtre   *3 Angel‡*
De Los Angeles, Micheau, Gedda, Blanc;
   Beecham   *3 Angel‡*
Resnik, Sutherland, del Monaco, Krause;
   Schippers   *3 London‡*
Juyol, Micheau, de Luca, Giovannetti; Wolff
    3 Richmond‡

Les Pêcheurs de Perles

Micheau, Gedda, Blanc; Dervaux   *2 Angel*
Dobbs, Seri, Borthayre; Leibowitz   *2 Everest*

ARRIGO BOITO

Mefistofele

*Moscona; Toscanini (Prologue only)   *1 RCA Victrola*
Pobbe, De Cecco, Tagliavini, Neri;
   Questa   *3 Everest/Cetra*
Tagliavini, Ghiaurov; Varviso (Selections)   *1 London*
Tebaldi, Cavalli, del Monaco, Siepi; Serafin   *3 London‡*
Noni, Dall'Argine, Poggi, Neri; Capuana   *3 Urania*

ALEXANDER BORODIN

Prince Igor

Wiener, Todorov, Chekerliiski, Christoff;
   Semkow   *3 Angel*
Bolshoi Theater; Melik-Pashayev   *3 MK*

BENJAMIN BRITTEN

Peter Grimes

Watson, Pears, Pease; Britten   *3 London‡*

GUSTAVE CHARPENTIER

Louise

*Monmart, Laroze, Michel, Musy; Fournet   *3 Epic*

LUIGI CHERUBINI

Medea

Callas, Scotto, Pirazzini, Picchi, Modesti;
   Serafin   *3 Everest*
Jones, Lorengar, Cossotto, Prevedi, Díaz;
   Gardelli   *3 London*

FRANCESCO CILÈA

Adriana Lecouvreur

Gavazzi, Prandelli, Pace; Simonetto   *3 Everest/Cetra*
Tebaldi, del Monaco, Simionato; Capuana   *3 London‡*

CLAUDE DEBUSSY

Pelléas et Mélisande

*De Los Angeles, Jansen, Souzay, Froumenty;
   Cluytens   *3 Angel*
Spoorenberg, Maurane, London, Hoekman;
   Ansermet   *3 London*

LÉO DÉLIBES

Lakmé

D'Angelo, Gedda; Prêtre (Selections)   *1 Angel*
*Robin, de Luca, Borthayre; Sébastian   *3 London*

GAETANO DONIZETTI

The Daughter of the Regiment

Pagliughi, Valletti, Bruscantini; Rossi
   (in Italian)   *2 Everest/Cetra*
Sutherland, Pavarotti, Malas; Bonynge   *2 London*

Don Pasquale

Mariotti, Benelli, Basiola, Maccianti; Gracis   *2 DGG*
Noni, Valletti, Borriello, Bruscantini;
   Rossi   *2 Everest/Cetra*
Sciutti, Oncina, Krause, Corena; Kertész   *2 London‡*
La Gatta, Lazzari, Poli, Corena; La Rosa
   Parodi   *2 Vox or 2 Urania*

L'ELISIR D'AMORE

Freni, Gedda, Sereni, Capecchi; Molinari-
   Pradelli   *2 Angel*
Noni, Valletti, Poli, Bruscantini; Gavazzeni
                              3 Everest/Cetra
Gueden, di Stefano, Capecchi, Corena;
   Molinari-Pradelli   *3 London‡*
Carteri, Alva, Panerai, Taddei; Serafin   *2 Seraphim*

LUCIA DI LAMMERMOOR

Peters, Peerce, Maero, Tozzi; Leinsdorf
                           2 RCA Victrola
Moffo, Bergonzi, Sereni, Flagello; Prêtre *3 RCA Victor*
Callas, Tagliavini, Cappuccilli, Ladysz;
   Serafin   *2 Angel‡*
Scotto, di Stefano, Bastianini, Vinco;
   Sanzogno   *2 Everest*
Sutherland, Cioni, Merrill, Siepi; Pritchard *3 London‡*
*Callas, di Stefano, Gobbi, Arié; Serafin   *2 Seraphim*
Wilson, Poggi, Colzani, Maionica; Capuana *3 Urania*

LUCREZIA BORGIA

Caballé, Verrett, Kraus, Flagello; Perlea *3 RCA Victor*

FRIEDRICH VON FLOTOW

MARTHA

Rothenberger, Plümacher, Wunderlich, Frick;
   Klobucar (Selections)   *1 Angel*
Rizzieri, Tassinari, Tagliavini, Tagliabue;
   Molinari-Pradelli (in Italian)   *3 Everest/Cetra*
Berger, Tegetthof, Anders, Greindl;
   Rother   *3 Urania*

GEORGE GERSHWIN

PORGY AND BESS

Price, Warfield; Henderson (Selections) *1 RCA Victor*
*Williams, Winters; Engel   *3 Columbia*
*Original Broadway Cast   *1 Decca*

ALBERTO GINASTERA

BOMARZO

Penagos, Simon, Turner, Navoa, Torigi; Rudel *3 CBS*

UMBERTO GIORDANO

ANDRÉA CHÉNIER

Stella, Corelli, Sereni; Santini   *3 Angel‡*
Tebaldi, Soler, Savarese; Basile   *3 Everest/Cetra*
Tebaldi, del Monaco, Bastianini; Gavazzeni *3 London‡*
*Caniglia, Gigli, Bechi; de Fabritiis   *2 Seraphim*

CHRISTOPH WILLIBALD VON GLUCK

ORFEO ED EURIDICE

Verrett, Moffo, Raskin; Fasano   *3 RCA Victor*
*Merriman, Gibson; Toscanini (Act 2 only)
                          1 RCA Victrola
Bumbry, Rothenberger, Pütz; Neumann   *2 Angel*

ORFEO ED EURIDICE (*cont.*)

*Gedda, Micheau, Berton; Froment
   (in French)   *2 Angel*
Forrester, Stich-Randall, Steffek; Mackerras *2 Bach*
Fischer-Dieskau, Janowitz, Moser; Richter *2 DGG*
Fischer-Dieskau, Stader, Streich; Fricsay
   (in German)   *2 DGG*
* Simoneau, Danco, Alarie; Rosbaud
   (in French)   *2 Epic*
Ferrier, Ayars; Stiedry (Selections)   *1 London*
Klose, Berger, Streich; Rother   *3 Urania*

CHARLES GOUNOD

FAUST

De Los Angeles, Gedda, Blanc, Christoff;
   Cluytens   *4 Angel‡*
Sutherland, Corelli, Massard, Ghiaurov;
   Bonynge   *4 London*

ROMÉO ET JULIETTE

Carteri, Gedda; Lombard (Selections)   *1 Angel*
*Micheau, Jobin; Erede   *3 London*

GEORGE FRIDERIC HANDEL

JULIUS CAESAR

Sills, Wolff, Forrester, Treigle, Cossa, Malas;
   Rudel   *3 RCA Victor*
Sutherland, Horne, Elkins, Sinclair; Bonynge
   (Selections)   *1 London*

ENGELBERT HUMPERDINCK

HÄNSEL UND GRETEL

Rothenberger, Seefried; Cluytens   *2 Angel*
*Schwarzkopf, Grümmer; Karajan   *2 Angel*
Neville, Kern; Bernardi (in English)   *2 Capitol*
*Connor, Stevens; Rudolf (in English) *2 Columbia*
Berger, Schilp; Rother   *2 Urania*

LEOŠ JANÁČEK

JENŮFA

*Cadikovicova, Blachut, Zidek; Vogel   *3 Artia*

RUGGIERO LEONCAVALLO

PAGLIACCI

Amara, Corelli, Gobbi, Zanasi; Matacic *2 Angel*
*Callas, di Stefano, Gobbi, Panerai; Serafin
   (includes "Cavalleria Rusticana")   *3 Angel‡*
Carlyle, Bergonzi, Taddei, Panerai; Karajan
   (includes "Cavalleria Rusticana")   *3 DGG‡*
Gavazzi, Bergonzi, Tagliabue, Di Tommaso;
   Simonetto   *2 Everest/Cetra*
Tucci, del Monaco, MacNeil, Capecchi;
   Molinari-Pradelli   *2 London‡*
Petrella, del Monaco, Poli, Protti; Erede *2 Richmond*
*Pacetti, Gigli, Basiola, Paci; Ghione   *2 Seraphim*

PIETRO MASCAGNI

CAVALLERIA RUSTICANA

Tebaldi, Bjoerling, Bastianini; Erede	2 *RCA Victor*
*Callas, di Stefano, Panerai; Serafin (includes "Pagliacci")	3 *Angel*‡
De Los Angeles, Corelli, Sereni; Santini	2 *Angel*
Cossotto, Bergonzi, Guelfi; Karajan (includes "Pagliacci")	3 *DGG*‡
Simionato, Braschi, Tagliabue; Basile	2 *Everest/Cetra*
Simionato, del Monaco, MacNeil; Serafin	2 *London*‡
Suliotis, del Monaco, Gobbi; Varviso	2 *London*
Nicolai, del Monaco, Protti; Ghione	2 *Richmond*
*Bruna Rasa, Gigli, Bechi; Mascagni	2 *Seraphim*

JULES MASSENET

MANON

Moffo, di Stefano, Kerns; Leibowitz (Selections)	2 *RCA Victor*
*De Los Angeles, Legay, Dens; Monteux	4 *Capitol*

THAÏS

Brumaire, Dens; Prêtre (Selections)	1 *Angel*
Doria, Massard; Etcheverry	2 *Westminster*

WERTHER

*Tassinari, Tagliavini, Neviani; Molinari-Pradelli	3 *Everest/Cetra*
Juyol, Léger, Bourdin; Sébastian	3 *Urania or Vox*

GIAN CARLO MENOTTI

AMAHL AND THE NIGHT VISITORS

King, Yaghjian, McCollum, Patterson; Grossman	1 *RCA Victor*

THE CONSUL

*Neway, Lane, Powers, MacNeil; Engel	2 *Decca*

THE MEDIUM

*Keller, Powers; Balaban (includes "The Telephone")	2 *Columbia*

GIACOMO MEYERBEER

LES HUGUENOTS

*Hempel, Destinn, Caruso (Selections)	1 *Scala*

CLAUDIO MONTEVERDI

L'INCORONAZIONE DI POPPEA

László, Bible, Dominguez, Lewis, Cava; Pritchard	2 *Angel*
Bogard, Parker, Hayes, Bressler, Beattie; Curtis	4 *Cambridge*

ORFEO

*Guilleaume, Krebs; Wenzinger	2 *DGG*

DOUGLAS MOORE

THE BALLAD OF BABY DOE

Sills, Bible, Cassel; Buckley	3 *Heliodor*

MODEST MOUSSORGSKY

BORIS GODUNOV

*Chaliapin (Selections)	1 *Angel*
Lear, Uzunov, Christoff; Cluytens	4 *Angel*‡
Archipova, Ivanovsky, London, Reshetin, Gueleva; Melik-Pashayev	4 *Columbia*
London; Schippers (Selections)	1 *Columbia*
Petrov; Melik-Pashayev (Selections)	1 *Melodiya/Angel*

WOLFGANG AMADEUS MOZART

THE ABDUCTION FROM THE SERAGLIO

Marshall, Hollweg, Simoneau, Unger, Frick; Beecham	2 *Angel*
Köth, Stolte, Wunderlich, Schreier, Böhme; Jochum	3 *DGG*‡
Rothenberger, Popp, Gedda, Unger, Frick; Krips	2 *Seraphim*

COSÌ FAN TUTTE

Price, Raskin, Troyanos, Shirley, Milnes, Flagello; Leinsdorf	4 *RCA Victor*‡
Schwarzkopf, Steffek, Ludwig, Kraus, Taddei, Berry; Böhm	4 *Angel*‡
*Steber, Thebom, Peters, Tucker, Guarrera, Alvary; Stiedry (in English)	3 *Columbia*
Seefried, Merriman, Roth, Häfliger, Fischer-Dieskau, Prey; Jochum	3 *DGG*‡
Stich-Randall, Malaniuk, Sciutti, Kmentt, Berry, Ernster; Moralt	3 *Philips*
Della Casa, Ludwig, Loose, Dermota, Kunz Schoeffler; Böhm	3 *Richmond*‡
*Souez, Helletsgruber, Eisinger, Nash, Domgraf-Fassbaender, Brownlee; Busch	3 *Turnabout*

DON GIOVANNI

Nilsson, Price, Ratti, Valletti, Siepi, Corena; Leinsdorf	4 *RCA Victor*‡
Sutherland, Schwarzkopf, Sciutti, Alva, Wächter, Taddei; Giulini	4 *Angel*‡
Watson, Ludwig, Freni, Gedda, Ghiaurov, Berry; Klemperer	4 *Angel*
Nilsson, Grist, Arroyo, Schreier, Fischer-Dieskau, Flagello; Böhm	4 *DGG*
Stader, Jurinac, Seefried, Häfliger, Fischer-Dieskau, Kohn; Fricsay	4 *DGG*
Curtis-Verna, Gavazzi, Ribetti, Valletti, Taddei, Tajo; Rudolf	3 *Everest/Cetra*
Zadek, Jurinac, Sciutti, Simoneau, London, Berry; Moralt	3 *Philips*
Danco, Della Casa, Gueden, Dermota, Siepi, Corena; Krips	4 *London*‡
*Souez, Helletsgruber, Mildmay, Pataky, Brownlee, Baccaloni; Busch	3 *Turnabout*

IDOMENEO, RÈ DI CRETA

*Jurinac, Udovick, Lewis, Simoneau;
   Pritchard   *3 Angel*

THE IMPRESARIO

Grist, Raskin, Lewis, Milnes; Previn (in
   English)   *1 RCA Victor*

THE MAGIC FLUTE

Janowitz, Popp, Gedda, Berry, Frick;
   Klemperer   *3 Angel‡*
Lear, Peters, Wunderlich, Fischer-Dieskau,
   Crass; Böhm   *3 DGG‡*
Stader, Streich, Häfliger, Fischer-Dieskau,
   Greindl; Fricsay   *3 Heliodor*
Gueden, Lipp, Simoneau, Berry, Böhme;
   Böhm   *3 Richmond*
*Lemnitz, Berger, Roswänge, Hüsch, Strienz;
   Beecham   *3 Turnabout*

THE MARRIAGE OF FIGARO

Della Casa, Peters, Elias, London, Tozzi;
   Leinsdorf   *4 RCA Victor‡*
Schwarzkopf, Moffo, Cossotto, Wächter,
   Taddei; Giulini   *4 Angel‡*
Janowitz, Mathis, Troyanos, Fischer-Dieskau,
   Prey; Böhm   *4 DGG*
Stader, Seefried, Töpper, Fischer-Dieskau,
   Capecchi; Fricsay   *3 DGG‡*
Gatti, Noni, Gardino, Bruscantini, Tajo;
   Previtali   *3 Everest/Cetra*
Della Casa, Gueden, Danco, Poell, Siepi;
   Kleiber   *4 London‡*
Gueden, Rothenberger, Mathis, Prey, Berry;
   Suitner (in German)   *3 Seraphim*
*Rautawaara, Mildmay, Helletsgruber, Henderson,
   Domgraf-Fassbänder; Busch   *3 Turnabout*

JACQUES OFFENBACH

THE TALES OF HOFFMANN

D'Angelo, Schwarzkopf, De Los Angeles,
   Gedda, London; Cluytens   *3 Angel‡*
*Bond, Grandi, Ayars, Rounseville, Dargavel;
   Beecham   *3 London*
Streich, Berger, Anders, Müller; Rother *2 Urania*

GIOVANNI BATTISTA PERGOLESI

LA SERVA PADRONA

Mazzoleni, Cortis; Leitner   *1 DGG*
Scotto, Bruscantini; Fasano   *1 Everest*
Adani, Monreale; Gracis   *1 Nonesuch*
Zeani, Rossi-Lemeni; Singer   *1 Vox*

AMILCARE PONCHIELLI

LA GIOCONDA

Milanov, Elias, Amparan, di Stefano, Warren,
   Clabassi; Previtali   *3 RCA Victrola*

---

*Callas, Barbieri, Amadini, Poggi, Silveri,
   Neri; Votto   *3 Everest/Cetra*
Cerquetti, Simionato, Sacchi, del Monaco,
   Bastianini, Siepi; Gavazzeni   *3 London‡*
Tebaldi, Horne, Dominguez, Bergonzi, Merrill,
   Ghiuselev; Gardelli   *3 London*
Callas, Cossotto, Companez, Ferraro,
   Cappuccilli, Vinco; Votto   *3 Seraphim*

FRANCIS POULENC

LES DIALOGUES DES CARMÉLITES

*Duval, Crespin, Gorr; Dervaux   *3 Angel*

LA VOIX HUMAINE

Duval; Prêtre   *1 RCA Victor*

SERGEI PROKOFIEV

THE LOVE OF THREE ORANGES

*Kalliskatova, Polyakova; Dalgat   *2 Period*

WAR AND PEACE

Vasovic-Bokaevic, Papovic, Djurpejewic; Jann-
   sen   *3 Heliodor*
Vishnevskaya, Kibkalo, Krivchenya; Melik-
   Pashayev (Excerpts)   *1 Melodiya/Angel*
Vishnevskaya, Petrov, Kibkalo, Masslenikov,
   Krivtchenia, Lisitsian; Melik-Pashayev   *4 MK*

GIACOMO PUCCINI

LA BOHÈME

*Albanese, Munsel, di Stefano, Warren; Trucco
   (Selections)   *1 RCA Victor*
Moffo, Costa, Tucker, Merrill; Leinsdorf *2 RCA Victor‡*
*Albanese, McKnight, Peerce, Valentino;
   Toscanini   *2 RCA Victrola*
*Callas, Moffo, di Stefano, Panerai; Votto *2 Angel‡*
Freni, Adani, Gedda, Sereni; Schippers *2 Angel‡*
Scotto, Meneguzzer, Poggi, Gobbi; Votto *2 DGG*
Carteri, Ramella, Tagliavini, Taddei;
   Santini   *2 Everest/Cetra*
Tebaldi, d'Angelo, Bergonzi, Bastianini;
   Serafin   *2 London‡*
Tebaldi, Gueden, Prandelli, Inghilleri; Erede
                               2 Richmond‡
*De Los Angeles, Amara, Bjoerling, Merrill;
   Beecham   *2 Seraphim*

GIANNI SCHICCHI

De Los Angeles, Gobbi; Santini   *1 Angel*
Tebaldi, Corena; Gardelli   *1 London*

THE GIRL OF THE GOLDEN WEST

Gavazzi, Campagnano, Savarese;
   Basile   *3 Everest/Cetra*
Tebaldi, del Monaco, MacNeil; Capuana *3 London‡*

MADAMA BUTTERFLY

*Albanese, Rota, Peerce, Capecchi; Bellezza (Selections)	*1 RCA Victor*
Price, Elias, Tucker, Maero; Leinsdorf	*3 RCA Victor‡*
Moffo, Elias, Valletti, Cesari; Leinsdorf	*3 RCA Victrola*
*Callas, Danieli, Gedda, Borriello; Karajan	*3 Angel*
*Dal Monte, Palombini, Gigli, Basiola; de Fabritiis	*2 Angel*
De Los Angeles, Pirazzini, Bjoerling, Sereni; Santini	*3 Angel‡*
Scotto, di Stasio, Bergonzi, Panerai; Barbirolli	*3 Angel*
Petrella, Masini, Tagliavini, Taddei; Questa	*3 Everest/Cetra*
Tebaldi, Cossotto, Bergonzi, Sordello; Serafin	*3 London‡*
Tebaldi, Rankin, Campora, Inghilleri; Erede	*3 Richmond‡*

MANON LESCAUT

Moffo, Labò, Kerns; Leibowitz (Selections)	*2 RCA Victor*
Tebaldi, del Monaco, Borriello; Molinari-Pradelli	*3 London‡*

LA RONDINE

Moffo, Sciutti, Barioni, Sereni; Molinari-Pradelli	*2 RCA Victor*

SUOR ANGELICA

*De Los Angeles, Barbieri; Serafin	*1 Angel*
Tebaldi, Simionato; Gardelli	*1 London*

IL TABARRO

Tebaldi, del Monaco, Merrill; Gardelli	*1 London*

TOSCA

Price, di Stefano, Taddei; Karajan	*2 RCA Victor‡*
Milanov, Bjoerling, Warren; Leinsdorf	*2 RCA Victrola*
Callas, Bergonzi, Gobbi; Prêtre	*2 Angel‡*
*Callas, di Stefano, Gobbi; de Sabata	*2 Angel*
Frazzoni, Tagliavini, Guelfi; Basile	*2 Everest/Cetra*
Nilsson, Corelli, Fischer-Dieskau; Maazel	*2 London*
Silja, King, Fischer-Dieskau; Maazel (Selections)	*1 London*
Tebaldi, del Monaco, London; Molinari-Pradelli	*2 London‡*
Tebaldi, Campora, Mascherini; Erede	*2 Richmond‡*
*Caniglia, Gigli, Borgioli; de Fabritiis	*2 Seraphim*

TURANDOT

Nilsson, Tebaldi, Bjoerling; Leinsdorf	*3 RCA Victor‡*
*Callas, Schwarzkopf, Fernandi; Serafin	*3 Angel‡*
Nilsson, Scotto, Corelli; Molinari-Pradelli	*3 Angel*
Cigna, Olivero, Merli; Ghione	*3 Everest/Cetra*
Borkh, Tebaldi, del Monaco; Erede	*3 London‡*

HENRY PURCELL

DIDO AND AENEAS

De Los Angeles, Harper; Barbirolli	*1 Angel*
Thomas, Sheppard; Deller	*1 Bach Guild*

DIDO AND AENEAS (*cont.*)

Troyanos, Esswood; Mackerras	*1 DGG*
Baker, Clark; Lewis	*1 L'Oiseau Lyre*

MAURICE RAVEL

L'ENFANT ET LES SORTILÈGES

Gilma, Ogéas; Maazel	*1 DGG*
Danco, Wend; Ansermet	*1 Richmond*

L'HEURE ESPAGNOLE

Berbié, Giraudeau; Maazel	*1 DGG*
Danco, Derenne; Ansermet	*1 London*

NIKOLAI RIMSKY-KORSAKOV

LE COQ D'OR

Bolshoi Theatre	*2 Bruno*

GIOACCHINO ROSSINI

THE BARBER OF SEVILLE

Peters, Valletti, Merrill, Corena, Tozzi; Leinsdorf	*3 RCA Victor*
Callas, Alva, Gobbi, Olendorff, Zaccharia; Galliera	*3 Angel‡*
De Los Angeles, Alva, Bruscantini, Wallace, Cava; Gui	*3 Angel‡*
Simionato, Infantino, Taddei, Badioli, Cassellini; Previtali	*3 Everest/Cetra*
D'Angelo, Monti, Capecchi, Taddeo, Cava; Bartoletti	*3 Heliodor*
Berganza, Benelli, Ausensi, Corena, Ghiaurov; Varviso	*3 London‡*

LA CENERENTOLA

Simionato, Valletti, Meletti; Rossi	*2 Everest/Cetra*
Simionato, Benelli, Bruscantini; de Fabritiis	*3 London‡*

SEMIRAMIDE

Sutherland, Horne, Serge, Rouleau, Malas; Bonynge	*3 London*

WILLIAM TELL

Carteri, Filippeschi, Taddei, Tozzi, Corena; Rossi	*4 Everest/Cetra*

CAMILLE SAINT-SAËNS

SAMSON ET DALILA

Stevens, del Monaco, Harvuot; Cleva (Selections)	*1 RCA Victor*
Vickers, Gorr, Blanc; Prêtre	*3 Angel‡*

BEDŘICH SMETANA

THE BARTERED BRIDE

Lorengar, Wunderlich, Frick; Kempe (in German)	*3 Angel*
Tikalova, Zidek, Kovar; Chalabala	*3 Artia*
Richter, Streich, Böhme; Lenzer (in German)	*2 Vox*

JOHANN STRAUSS, JR.

DIE FLEDERMAUS

Leigh, Rothenberger, Stevens, Konya, Wächter;
    Danon   *2 RCA Victor*
Moffo, Scovotti, Stevens, Franchi, London;
    Danon (Selections)   *1 RCA Victor*
Scheyrer, Lipp, Ludwig, Terkal, Dermota,
    Wächter; Ackermann   *2 Angel‡*
Schwarzkopf, Streich, Christ, Gedda, Krebs,
    Kunz; Karajan   *2 Angel*
Welitsch, Pons, Lipton, Kullman, Tucker, Brownlee;
    Ormandy (in English)   *3 Columbia*
Gueden, Koeth, Resnik, Kmentt, Zampieri, Berry;
    Karajan   *2 London‡ and 3 London*
Gueden, Lipp, Wagner, Patzak, Dermota, Poell;
    Krauss   *2 Richmond‡*

RICHARD STRAUSS

ARABELLA

Della Casa, Rothenberger, Fischer-Dieskau;
    Keilberth   *3 DGG‡*
Della Casa, Gueden, London; Solti   *4 London‡*

ARIADNE AUF NAXOS

Rysanek, Jurinac, Peters, Peerce, Berry;
    Leinsdorf   *3 RCA Victor*
*Schwarzkopf, Seefried, Streich, Schock, Prey;
    Karajan   *3 Angel*
*Reining, Seefried, Noni, Lorenz, Kunz; Böhm   *3 DGG*

CAPRICCIO

*Schwarzkopf, Gedda, Fischer-Dieskau;
    Sawallisch   *3 Angel*

ELEKTRA

Borkh, Schech, Madeira, Fischer-Dieskau, Uhl;
    Böhm   *2 DGG‡*
Konetzki, Ilitsch, Mödl, Braun, Klarwein;
    Mitropoulos   *2 Everest/Cetra*
Nilsson, Collier, Resnik, Krause, Stolze; Solti *2 London*

DIE FRAU OHNE SCHATTEN

Bjöner, Borkh, Mödl, Thomas, Fischer-Dieskau;
    Keilberth   *4 DGG*
*Rysanek, Goltz, Höngen, Hopf, Schoeffler;
    Böhm   *4 Richmond*

DER ROSENKAVALIER

Della Casa, Rothenberger; Neuhaus (Selections) *1 Angel*
Lehmann, Olszewska, Schumann, Mayer; Heger
    (Selections)   *2 Angel*
Schwarzkopf, Ludwig, Stich-Randall, Edelmann;
    Karajan   *4 Angel‡*
Schech, Seefried, Streich, Böhme; Böhm   *4 DGG‡*
Crespin, Gueden, Söderström; Varviso
    (Selections)   *1 London*
Reining, Jurinac, Gueden, Weber; Kleiber *4 Richmond‡*
Ursuleac, Milinkovic, Kern, Weber; Krauss   *4 Vox*

SALOME

Caballé, Resnik, Lewis, Milnes; Leinsdorf *2 RCA Victor*
Nilsson, Hoffman, Stolze, Wächter; Solti   *2 London‡*
Goltz, Kenney, Braun, Patzak; Krauss   *2 Richmond*

IGOR STRAVINSKY

THE RAKE'S PROGRESS

Raskin, Young, Reardon; Stravinsky   *3 Columbia*

PETER ILYICH TCHAIKOVSKY

EUGENE ONEGIN

Vishnevskaya, Lemeshev, Lisitsian; Melik-
    Pashayev   *3 MK*
Heybalova, Startz, Popovich; Baranovich   *3 Richmond*

PIQUE DAME

Milashkina, Archipova, Levko, Andzhaparidzye,
    Mazurok; Khaikin   *4 Melodiya/Angel‡*
Smolenskaya, Borisenko, Verbitskaya, Nelepp,
    Lisitsian; Melik-Pashayev   *4 MK*
Heybalova, Cvejic, Bugarinovich, Marinkovich,
    Popovich; Baranovich   *4 Richmond*

AMBROISE THOMAS

MIGNON

Barbié, Mesplé, Dunan; Fournet (Selections)   *1 DGG*
Moizan, Micheau, de Luca; Sebastian   *3 London*

VIRGIL THOMSON

FOUR SAINTS IN THREE ACTS

Mathews, Greene, Berthea; Thomson   *1 RCA Victor*

GIUSEPPE VERDI

AÏDA

Price, Gorr, Vickers, Merrill; Solti   *3 RCA Victor‡*
*Nelli, Gustafson, Tucker, Valdengo; Toscanini
    3 RCA Victrola
*Callas, Barbieri, Tucker, Gobbi; Serafin   *3 Angel‡*
Nilsson, Bumbry, Corelli, Sereni; Mehta   *3 Angel*
Curtis-Verna, Pirazzini, Corelli, Guelfi; Questa
    3 Everest/Cetra
Tebaldi, Simionato, Bergonzi, MacNeil; Karajan
    3 London‡
Nilsson, Hoffmann, Ottolini, Quilico; Pritchard
    (Selections)   *1 London*
Tebaldi, Stignani, del Monaco, Protti; Erede
    3 Richmond‡
*Caniglia, Stignani, Gigli, Bechi; Serafin   *3 Seraphim*

UN BALLO IN MASCHERA

Price, Grist, Verrett, Bergonzi, Merrill; Leinsdorf
    3 RCA Victor‡
*Nelli, Haskins, Turner, Peerce, Merrill; Toscanini
    3 RCA Victrola

Un Ballo in Maschera (cont.)

Callas, Ratti, Barbieri, di Stefano, Gobbi; Votto
3 Angel

Stella, Tavolaccini, Lazzarini, Poggi, Bastianini;
Gavazzeni *3 DGG♯*

Curtis-Verna, Erato, Tassinari, Tagliavini, Valdengo;
Questa *3 Everest/Cetra*

Nilsson, Stahlman, Simionato, Bergonzi, MacNeil;
Solti *3 London♯*

*Caniglia, Ribetti, Barbieri, Gigli, Bechi; Serafin
2 Seraphim

Don Carlos

Stella, Cossotto, Labò, Bastianini, Christoff; Santini
4 DGG♯

Caniglia, Stignani, Picchi, Silveri, Rossi-Lemeni;
Previtali *4 Everest/Cetra*

Tebaldi, Bumbry, Bergonzi, Fischer-Dieskau,
Ghiaurov; Solti *4 London*

*Stella, Nicolai, Filippeschi, Gobbi, Christoff; Santini
3 Seraphim

Ernani

Price, Bergonzi, Sereni, Flagello; Schippers
3 RCA Victor♯

Mancini, Penno, Taddei, Vaghi; Previtali
3 Everest/Cetra

Falstaff

Ligabue, Freni, Elias, Simionato, Kraus, Merrill,
Evans; Solti *3 RCA Victor*

*Nelli, Stich-Randall, Merriman, Elmo, Madasi,
Guarrera, Valdengo; Toscanini *3 RCA Victrola*

Schwarzkopf, Moffo, Merriman, Barbieri, Alva,
Panerai, Gobbi; Karajan *3 Angel*

Ligabue, Sciutti, Resnik, Rössl-Majdan, Oncina,
Panerai, Fischer-Dieskau; Bernstein *3 Columbia*

Carteri, Pagliughi, Canali, Pini, Renzi, Meletti,
Taddei; Rossi *3 Everest/Cetra*

Ligabue, Marimpetri, Cadoni, Resnik, Alva, Capecchi,
Corena; Downes (Selections) *1 London*

La Forza del Destino

Price, Verrett, Tucker, Merrill, Tozzi; Schippers
4 RCA Victor♯

Milanov, Elias, di Stefano, Warren, Tozzi;
Previtali *4 RCA Victrola*

*Callas, Nicolai, Tucker, Tagliabue, Rossi-Lemeni;
Serafin *3 Angel♯*

Caniglia, Stignani, Masini, Tagliabue, Pasero;
Marinuzzi *3 Everest/Cetra*

Tebaldi, Simionato, del Monaco, Bastianini, Siepi;
Molinari-Pradelli *4 London♯*

Guerrini, Pirazzini, Campora, Colzani, Modesti;
La Rosa Parodi *3 Urania♯*

Luisa Miller

Moffo, Verrett, Bergonzi, MacNeil, Tozzi, Flagello;
Cleva *3 RCA Victor*

Kelston, Pace, Lauri-Volpi, Colombo, Vaghi,
Baronti; Rossi *3 Everest/Cetra*

Macbeth

Rysanek, Bergonzi, Warren, Hines; Leinsdorf
3 RCA Victor

Nilsson, Prevedi, Taddei, Foiani; Schippers *3 London*

Nabucco

Mancini, Binci, Silveri, Cassinelli; Previtali
3 Everest/Cetra

Suliotis, Prevedi, Gobbi, Cava; Gardelli *3 London*

Otello

Rysanek, Vickers, Gobbi; Serafin *3 RCA Victor♯*

*Nelli, Vinay, Valdengo; Toscanini *3 RCA Victrola*

Broggini, Guichandut, Taddei; Capuana
3 Everest/Cetra

Tebaldi, del Monaco, Protti; Karajan *3 London♯*

Tebaldi, del Monaco, Protti; Erede *3 Richmond*

Rigoletto

Berger, Peerce, Merrill; Cellini *3 RCA Victor*

Moffo, Kraus, Merrill; Solti *2 RCA Victor♯*

*Milanov, Peerce, Warren; Toscanini (Act IV only)
1 RCA Victrola

*Callas, di Stefano, Gobbi; Serafin *2½ Angel♯*

Grist, Gedda, MacNeil; Molinari-Pradelli *3 Angel*

Scotto, Bergonzi, Fischer-Dieskau; Kubelik *3 DGG♯*

Pagliughi, Tagliavini, Taddei; Questa *3 Everest/Cetra*

Scotto, Kraus, Bastianini; Gavazzeni *2 Everest*

Sutherland, Cioni, MacNeil; Sanzogno *3 London♯*

Gueden, del Monaco, Protti; Erede *3 Richmond♯*

Simon Boccanegra

*De Los Angeles, Campora, Gobbi, Christoff; Santini
3 Angel

Stella, Bergonzi, Silveri, Petri; Molinari-Pradelli
3 Everest/Cetra

La Traviata

Caballé, Bergonzi, Milnes; Prêtre *3 RCA Victor♯*

Moffo, Tucker, Merrill; Previtali *3 RCA Victor♯*

*Albanese, Peerce, Merrill; Toscanini *2 RCA Victrola*

De Los Angeles, del Monte, Sereni; Serafin *3 Angel♯*

*Stella, di Stefano, Gobbi; Serafin *2 Angel*

Scotto, Raimondi, Bastianini; Votto *3 DGG♯*

Callas, Albanese, Savarese; Santini *3 Everest/Cetra*

Sutherland, Bergonzi, Merrill; Pritchard *3 London♯*

Tebaldi, Poggi, Protti; Molinari-Pradelli *3 London♯*

Il Trovatore

*Milanov, Barbieri, Bjoerling, Warren; Cellini
2 RCA Victor

Price, Elias, Tucker, Warren; Basile *3 RCA Victor♯*

*Callas, Barbieri, di Stefano, Panerai; Karajan
2½ Angel

Tucci, Simionato, Corelli, Merrill; Schippers *3 Angel♯*

Stella, Cossotto, Bergonzi, Bastianini; Serafin *3 DGG♯*

Mancini, Pirazzini, Lauri-Volpi, Tagliabue; Previtali
3 Everest/Cetra

Tebaldi, Simionato, del Monaco, Savarese; Erede
3 London♯

RICHARD WAGNER

DER FLIEGENDE HOLLÄNDER

Rysanek, Liebl, London, Tozzi; Dorati   *3 RCA Victor*‡

Schech, Schock, Fischer-Dieskau, Frick; Konwitschny
    3 Angel‡

Silja, Kozub, Adam, Frick; Klemperer   *3 Angel*

Lear, Stewart, Borg; Loewlein (Selections)   *1 DGG*

LOHENGRIN

Amara, Gorr, Konya, Dooley, Hines; Leinsdorf
    5 RCA Victor

Grümmer, Ludwig, Thomas, Fischer-Dieskau, Frick;
  Kempe   *5 Angel*‡

Steber, Varnay, Windgassen, Uhde, Greindl;
  Keilberth   *5 London*

DIE MEISTERSINGER

Watson, Thomas, Lenz, Wiener, Kusche;
  Keilberth   *5 RCA Victor*‡

*Grümmer, Schock, Unger, Frantz, Kusche; Kempe
    5 Angel

Schorr (Selections)   *1 Angel*

Gueden, Treptow, Dermota, Schoeffler, Dönch;
  Knappertsbusch   *5 Richmond*

*Schwarzkopf, Hopf, Unger, Edelmann, Kunz,
  Dalberg; Karajan   *5 Seraphim*

Lemnitz, Aldenhoff, Unger, Frantz, Pflanzl; Kempe
    5 Vox‡

PARSIFAL

*Flagstad, Melchior; McArthur (Act II, Herzeleide
  Scene)   *1 RCA Victor*

Dalis, Thomas, London, Hotter; Knappertsbusch
    5 Philips

*Mödl, Windgassen, London, Weber; Knappertsbusch
    5 Richmond

DER RING DES NIBELUNGEN (Complete)

Nilsson, Flagstad, Crespin, Ludwig, Höffgen, Madeira,
  Windgassen, Svanholm, King, Stolze, London,
  Fischer-Dieskau, Hotter, Neidlinger, Frick; Solti
    19 London

DAS RHEINGOLD

Veasey, Dominguez, Fischer-Dieskau, Kelemen,
  Stolze; Karajan   *3 DGG*

Flagstad, Madeira, London, Neidlinger, Svanholm;
  Solti   *3 London*‡

DIE WALKÜRE

Nilsson, Brouwenstein, Gorr, Vickers, London, Ward;
  Leinsdorf   *5 RCA Victor*‡

Lehmann, Melchior, List; Walter (Act I)   *1 Angel*

Leider, Schorr (Selections)   *1 Angel*

Crespin, Janowitz, Veasey, Vickers, Stewart, Talvela;
  Karajan   *5 DGG*

Flagstad, Svanholm, Van Mill; Knappertsbusch
  (Act I)   *2 London*

Flagstad, Svanholm, Edelmann; Solti (Act III &
  Todesverkündigung Scene [Act II])   *2 London*

Nilsson, Crespin, Ludwig, King, Hotter, Frick; Solti
    5 London

*Mödl, Rysanek, Klose, Suthaus, Frantz, Frick;
  Furtwängler   *5 Seraphim*

SIEGFRIED

Nilsson, Höffgen, Windgassen, Stolze, Neidlinger,
  Hotter; Solti   *5 London*‡

GÖTTERDÄMMERUNG

Nilsson, Watson, Ludwig, Windgassen, Fischer-Dieskau,
  Frick; Solti   *6 London*‡

TANNHÄUSER

Grümmer, Schech, Hopf, Fischer-Dieskau, Frick;
  Konwitschny   *4 Angel*‡

Silja, Bumbry, Windgassen, Wächter, Greindl;
  Sawallisch   *3 Philips*

TRISTAN UND ISOLDE

*Flagstad, Thebom, Suthaus, Fischer-Dieskau, Greindl;
  Furtwängler   *5 Angel*

Leider, Melchior (Selections)   *1 Angel*

Nilsson, Ludwig, Windgassen, Wächter, Talvela; Böhm
    5 DGG‡

Nilsson, Resnik, Uhl, Krause, Van Mill; Solti
    5 London‡

CARL MARIA VON WEBER

DER FREISCHÜTZ

Seefried, Streich, Holm, Wächter, Böhme; Jochum
    2 DGG‡

Cunitz, Loose, Hopf, Poell, Rus; Ackermann
    2 Richmond

Grümmer, Otto, Schock, Kohn, Frick; Keilberth
    2 Seraphim

Index of Names

[Page numbers in italics refer to illustrations]

Abarbanell, Lina, 183
Abbey, Henry Eugene, 144
Adami, Giuseppe, 370, 398, 435
Addison, Joseph, 22
Aiken, David, 42
Alarie, Pierrette, 27
Albanese, Licia, 174, *238, 249, 399, 417, 419*
Albani, Emma, 156, 297
Alboni, Marietta, 188, 223, 382
Alda, Frances, *259, 300, 330*
Alexander, John, *253, 393*
Alfano, Franco, 435
Allen, Chet, 42, *43*
Alten, Bella, 183, 188, 294
Althouse, Paul, 73
Alvary, Lorenzo, *260*
Alvary, Max, 345, 356
Amara, Lucine, *138, 246, 305, 403*
Amato, Pasquale, 89, 181, *182, 370,* 409
Ananian, Paul, 388
Ancelot, François, 332
Ancona, Mario, 188, 247, 254, 301, 312
Anderson, Marian, *263*
André, Johann, 27
Andreassi, Maria, 96
Anelli, Angelo, 125
Anthony, Charles, *436*
Antonini, Alfredo, 442
Arié, Raphaël, *336*
Arimondi, Vittorio, 312
Arnold, Matthew, 421
Arnoldson, Sigrid, 188, 254
Aronson, Rudolph, 89

Attwood, Martha, 435
Auber, Daniel, 247, 263
Auden, W. H., 335

Baccaloni, Salvatore, *61,* 125, 174, *175, 256,* 386
Bacquier, Gabriel, *381*
Bada, Angelo, 398
Baker, Janet, *115*
Balakirev, Mily Alexeievitch, 22, 329
Balázs, Béla, 64
Baldwin, Marcia, *148*
Balfe, Michael, 22
Bampton, Rose, *173*
Barber, Samuel, 23, 438
Barbier, Jules, 101, 143, 281, 367, 368, 400, 401
Barbieri, Fedora, 444
Bardare, Leone Emanuele, 426
Barezzi, Antonio, 285
Barioni, Daniele, *92*
Baron, Alice, 128
Barrientos, Maria, 206, 332
Bartók, Béla, 64
Bastianini, Ettore, 444
Battistini, Mario, 134
Bayard, Jean François Alfred, 107
Beattie, Herbert, *218*
Beaumarchais, Pierre Augustin Caron de, 58, 254
Beecham, Sir Thomas, 51, 430
Beeler, Virginia, 269

Beethoven, Ludwig van, 19, 20, 150, 266, 302, 382
Belasco, David, 237
Bellincioni, Gemma, *90*
Bellini, Vincenzo, 16, 285, 288, 332, 392
Benedix, Roderich, 153
Benois, Nicola, *84,* 188, *422, 437*
Berg, Alban, 20, 21, 71, 230, 453
Berg, Helene, 230
Berganza, Teresa, *187, 255*
Bergonzi, Carlo, *35,* 134, *427*
Berlioz, Hector, 143, *266,* 430, 431
Bernanos, Georges, 109
Bernhardt, Sarah, 412
Bernstein, Leonard, 139
Berry, Walter, *168, 212*
Berse, Ellen, *94*
Bertati, Giovanni, 120
Bertin, Louise Angélique, 143, 273
Betz, Franz, *345*
Bevignani, Enrico, 254
Bey, Mariette, 34
Bible, Frances, *56,* 93
Bielsky, Vladimir, 99
Bis, Hippolyte, 450
Bizet, Georges, 18, *30,* 81, 312
Bjoerling, Jussi, *252,* 264
Bjoner, Ingrid, *213, 278*
Blackall, Eric, 453
Blankenheim, Toni, *232*
Blau, Édouard, 448
Bodanzky, Artur, 114, 170, 377
Böhme, Kurt, 28

Bohnen, Michael, *172*
Boito, Arrigo, 16, 139, 143, 272, 273, 297, 388
Bokor, Margit, 47
Bonci, Alessandro, 332
Bonelli, Richard, *177*
Bonner, Embry, 163
Bori, Lucrezia, *104*, 125, 186, 214, 251, 314, 370, *371*, 400
Borkh, Inge, 128, 267
Borodin, Alexander, 22, 329
Bosabelian, Luisa, *201*
Bouilly, Jean Nicholas, 150
Brambilla, Teresa, 382
Brandt, Marianne, 150, *210*
Branzell, Karin, 128, *166*
Bretzner, Christoph Friedrich, 27
Breuning, Stefan von, 150
Britten, Benjamin, 22, *23*, 319
Brown, Anne, 326
Brownlee, John, *102, 256*
Bubbles, John W., 326
Büchner, Georg, 453
Bumbry, Grace, *88, 119, 198*, 294
Burgstaller, Ludwig, 27
Burrian, Carl, 377, 421
Busch, Fritz, 234
Busoni, Ferruccio Benvenuto, 143

Caballé, Montserrat, 202, 223, *227, 228, 229*
Caccini, Giulio, 14, 292
Callas, Maria, *44*, 220, 266, 267, *268*, 288, 333, *392*, 393, 412, *414*, 416
Calloway, Cab, *328*
Calvé, Emma, 89, *90*, 272, 312
Calzabigi, Raniero de', 40, 294
Camera, Eduardo, 297
Cammarano, Salvatore, 220, 226, 227, 426
Campanari, Giuseppe, 263
Campanini, Cleofonte, 237, 297, 377
Campanini, Italo, 143, 144, 209
Capobianco, Tito, 71
Carré, Michel, 101, 143, 281, 312, 367, 368, 400, 401
Carter, John, 27
Carteri, Rosanna, 444
Caruso, Enrico, 30, *39, 83*, 89, 130, 153, 159, *162*, 181, *182*, 188, 223, 237, 251, 272, 301, 312, *313*, 332, 339, 379, 392, 413
Carvalho, Léon, 144, 431
Cary, Annie Louise, 209
Case, Anna, 373

Cassel, Walter, *55*
Castellano, Laura, *160*
Castelmary, Armand, 259
Cavalieri, Katharina, 194
Cavalieri, Lina, 30, 251
Cehanovsky, George, 45, *441*
Chagall, Marc, 245
Chaliapin, Feodor, 73, *76, 272, 273*
Charpentier, Gustave, 18, 214
Cherubini, Luigi, 266, 267
Chookasian, Lili, *184, 320, 395*
Christoff, Boris, 73, *76, 330*
Cigna, Gina, 289
Cilèa, Francesco, 30
Cioni, Renato, *414*
Clément, Edmond, 448
Cocteau, Jean, 442, 443
Colautti, Arturo, 30
Colbran, Isabella, 382
Coleman, Leo, 269, *270*
Colette (Sidonie Gabrielle Gauthier-Villars), 132
Conley, Eugene, 335
Converse, Frederick, 23
Cooke, Thomas, *454*
Cooper, Emil, 27
Corelli, Franco, *31, 46, 82*, 134, *136*, 188, *189, 369, 429*, 444
Cormon, Eugène, 312
Cossotto, Fiorenza, *185*, 188, *189, 429*
Corena, Fernando, *59, 75*, 125, *127, 131, 141*, 174
Cowles, Chandler, 96, 269
Crabbe, George, 319, 322
Crawford, Cheryl, 326
Cremonini, Giuseppe, 312, 412
Crespin, Régine, *311*, 345, *431, 433*
Crimi, Giulio, 174, 398
Cui, Cesar Antonovitch, 22, 329
Cundari, Emilia, *296, 420*
Curtis-Verna, Mary, *253*
Cuzzoni, Francesca, 202

Dalis, Irene, *378*
Dalmorès, Charles, 377, 400
Dal Prato, 191
Dame, Beverly, 269
Damrosch, Leopold, 150, 350, 404
D'Angelo, Gianna, *52*, 393
D'Angelo, Louis, 386
Danilova, Alexandra, *33*
Danise, Giuseppe, *451*
Da Ponte, Lorenzo, 101, 120, 254
Dargomijsky, Alexander Sergeivich, 22, 120

Debussy, Claude Achille, 18, *19*, 64, 314
De Hidalgo, Elvira, 392
De Jouy, Étienne, 450
De Koven, Reginald, 23
Delibes, Léo, 206
Della Casa, Lisa, *48, 50*
Del Monaco, Mario, *39, 44*, 134, *135, 299, 305*
De Los Angeles, Victoria, *145, 248, 260, 317*
Del Puente, Giuseppe, 143, 209
De Luca, Giuseppe, 30, *60*, 116, *137*, 159, 174, *208*, 226, 312, *313, 338*, 435
De Lucia, Fernando, 301
De Macchi, Maria, 223
De Marchi, Emilio, 134, 263
De Nobili, Lila, *283*
De' Panzacchi, Domenico, 191
De Paolis, Alessio, *138, 256, 402*
De Reszke, Édouard, 134, *146*, 156, 188, 254, 263, 345, 367, 421
De Reszke, Jean, 188, *190*, 247, 259, 297, 345, 367, 421, 448
De Saint-Georges, Jules Henri Vernoy, 107, 259
Destinn, Emmy, *62*, 89, 181, *182*, 188
Dickie, Murray, *28*
Didur, Adamo, 73, 116, 174, 188, 272, 398, 400
Dietsch, Pierre Louis Philippe, 156
Dietz, Howard, 153
d'Indy, Vincent, 291
Dippel, Andreas, 241
Di Stefano, Giuseppe, *248, 437, 449*
Dönch, Karl, *455*
Donizetti, Gaetano, 16, 107, 125, 130, 220, 223, 259, 260, 265
Doria, Augusta, 377
Dorsey, Abner, 163
Duffault, Jean, 128
Dufranne, Hector, 377
Dukas, Paul, 64
Dumas, Alexandre, 416
Duncan, Todd, 326
Dunham, Katherine, *37*
Dupont, Jacques, *87*
Durastanti, Margherita, 202
Duval, Denise, 442, *443*

Eames, Emma, 89, 241, 254, 345, 367, 448
Easton, Florence, 174, *175*
Eddy, Jennifer, *195*
Eddy, Nelson, 51
Einem, Gottfried von, 21

Eisenstein, Sergei, 444
Elias, Rosalind, *92, 105, 260, 262,* 438, *439, 440, 441*
Elliott, Victoria, *65*
Elmo, Cloe, *142*
Elzy, Ruby, 326
Ernster, Dezso, 27
Eschenbach, Wolfram von, 306
Etienne, C. G., 93
Euripides, 40, 266
Evans, Beverly, *218*
Evans, Geraint, 139, *320*

Faccio, Franco, 297
Farrar, Geraldine, *83,* 214, 237, 272, 396, *397,* 409
Farrell, Eileen, *40,* 266, 267
Federico, Gennaro Antonio, 386
Ferretti, Jacopo, 93
Ferrier, Kathleen, 294
Fischer-Dieskau, Dietrich, *50, 308, 349*
Fischer, Emil, 156, 275, 345
Flagello, Ezio, *161, 228, 334, 389*
Flagstad, Kirsten, 40, 114, 345, *364,* 421, *424*
Fleischer, Editha, 386
Fleta, Miguel, 435
Flotow, Friedrich von, 259, 260
Floyd, Carlisle, 24
Fokine, Mikhail, 99
Forrester, Maureen, *205*
Forzano, Giovacchino, 396
Foucher, 156
France, Anatole, 409
Franchetti, Alberto, 412
Franke, Paul, *78, 402, 455*
Fremstad, Olive, *85,* 345, *353, 377,* 400
Freni, Mirella, *122, 149, 255, 368, 369*
Frick, Gottlob, *63, 352*
Friederich, Sylvia, *94*
Friedrich, Wilhelm, *see* Riese, Friedrich W.
Friends and Enemies of Modern Music, Inc., The, 163, *164*
Frigerio, Claudio, 388
Fuente, Henriquez de la, 128
Fursch-Madi, Emmy, 120, 209

Gadski, Johanna, 263, *275,* 294, 345, 421
Galassi, Antonio, 297
Gall, Yvonne, 186
Gallet, Louis, 409

Galli-Curci, Amelita, *61,* 206, 220, 339, 392, *419*
Ganzaroli, Wladimiro, 188
García, Manuel, 58, 382
Garcia, Maria *see* Malibran, Maria
Garden, Mary, 214, 215, 314, *315,* 377, 409
Gaveaux, Pierre, 150
Gavarini, Renato, *198*
Gay, John, 22
Gay, Maria, 89
Gazzaniga, Giuseppe, 120
Gedda, Nicolai, *40, 75, 82, 88, 149, 250, 395, 401,* 438, *441*
Genée, R., 153
Gentle, Alice, 398
Gérard, Rolf, *86, 368*
Gerhauser, Emil, *210*
Gershwin, George, 24, 326
Gershwin, Ira, 326
Gerville-Réache, Jeanne, 128
Ghiaurov, Nicolai, 73, *117, 144, 149,* 188, *268, 287*
Ghislanzoni, Antonio, 34, 116, 159
Ghiuselev, Nicola, *333*
Giacosa, Giuseppe, 66, 237, 251, 412
Giaiotti, Bonaldo, *179, 436*
Gigli, Beniamino, 44, 130, *177, 259,* 272, *371*
Gilbert, W. S., 22, 226
Gilford, Jack, *155*
Gilibert, Charles, 400
Gille, Philippe, 206, 247
Gilly, Dinh, 400
Ginastera, Alberto, *24,* 71
Giordano, Umberto, 16, 30, 44
Giraldoni, Eugenio, 153
Glazunov, Aleksandr Konstantinovich, 329
Glinka, Mikhail Ivanovich, 22, 329
Gluck, Alma, *67,* 448
Gluck, Christoph Willibald von, 15, 17, 20, 40, 79, 120, *266, 269,* 294, 295
Gobbi, Tito, *117,* 174, *285, 391*
Goethe, Johann Wolfgang von, 143, 272, 281, 448
Gold, Didier, 398
Goldovsky, Boris, 430
Gondinet, Edmond, 206
Goritz, Otto, 183, 373
Gorr, Rita, 267, *381*
Gounod, Charles François, 16, 18, 143, 144, 272, 273, 281, 367
Gozzi, Carlo, 217, 435
Graf, Herbert, *339*

Gramm, Donald, *105*
Grant, Clifford, *333*
Grau, Maurice, 400
Greenspon, Muriel, *99, 218*
Grétry, André Ernest Modeste, 17
Grillo, Joann, *240*
Grisi, Giulia, 125, 223, 289, 333, 382
Grist, Reri, *340*
Grossi, 34
Grout, Donald, 430
Guarrera, Frank, *127, 250, 436*
Gueden, Hilde, 47, *50, 154, 296,* 335, *375*
Guiraud, Ernest, 400
Gutiérrez, Antonio García, 388, 426
Gutman, John, 47

Haffner, C., 153
Halévy, Jacques François, 18, 153, 247
Halévy, Ludovic, 81
Hammerstein, Oscar, 89, 332, 339, 377, 400, 409
Handel, George Frideric, 21, 22
Hanslick, Eduard, 276
Hanson, Howard, 23
Hasse, 21
Harford, Vida, 453
Harrell, Mack, 335
Hartmann, Georges, 448
Harvey, Georgette, 326
Haydn, Joseph, *266*
Hayward, Thomas, *175*
Heine, Heinrich, 156
Hempel, Frieda, 107, 188, 312, *313,* 373, 400
Henderson, William J., 143
Henze, Hans Werner, 21
Herbeck, Johann Franz von, *62*
Herlea, Nicolae, *342*
Hertz, Alfred, 373, 377
Heyward, Dorothy, 326
Heyward, Du Bose, 326
Hindemith, Paul, 21
Hines, Altonell, 163
Hines, Jerome, *118, 136, 246, 311*
Hoffmann, Ernst Theodor Amadeus, 400, 401
Hoffmann, François Benoît, 266
Hofmannsthal, Hugo von, 47, 51, 128, 165, 373, 374
Holst, Gustave, 22
Homer, Louise, *38,* 73, 153, 183, 263, 294, 345
Horne, Marilyn, *290,* 383
Hotter, Hans, *352*

Howard, Bruce, 163
Huberdeau, Gustave, 128
Hugo, Victor, 134, 135, 223, 338, 339
Humperdinck, Engelbert, 20

Illica, Luigi, 44, 66, 237, 251, 412
Indy, Vincent d', 291
Ismail Pasha, 34

Janowitz, Gundula, *351*
Jagel, Frederick, *399*
Janssen, Herbert, *211, 364*
Jepson, Helen, *411*
Jerger, Alfred, 47
Jeritza, Maria, 51 *167*, 199, *200*, 435
Johnson, Edward, *146, 314*
Jones, Gwyneth, 267
Jongeyans, George, 96
Jörn, Carl, 373
Journet, Marcel, *85*, 188, 263
Jurinac, Sena, *52, 193, 258*

Kabaivanska, Raina, *118, 119*
Kalbeck, Max, 62
Kalisch, Paul, 156
Kallman, Chester, 335
Kanin, Garson, 153
Kappel, Gertrude, 128
Karajan, Herbert von, *351*
Karamzin, 73
Kaschmann, Giuseppe, 120, 209, 426
Keller, Evelyn, 269, *270*
Kind, Friedrich, 170
King, James, *168, 353*
King, Nancy, *155*
Kipnis, Alexander, 73, *307*
Kirk, Florence, 234
Kirsten, Dorothy, *111*, 214, *252*
Kniplova, Nadezda, *201*
Kodály, Zoltán, 64
Kögel, Josef, 404
Kónya, Sándor, *212, 311*
Koshetz, Nina, 217
Kraus, Alfredo, *187, 333*
Kraus, Auguste, 275, 404
Kraus, Otakar, 335, *336*
Krauss, Clemens, 47, 79
Kriese, Gladys, *148*
Krull, Anna, 128
Kuen, Paul, *348*
Kuhlmann, Rosemary, 42, *43*
Kullman, Charles, 27

Lablache, Luigi, 125, 333
Lachmann, Hedwig, 377
Lachner, Franz, 266
Láinez, Manuel Mujica, 71
Lammers, Gerda, 267
Lane, Gloria, 96, *287*
Lange, Aloysia, 194
La Rochelle, Jacques, 269
Lasselle, Jean, 156, 188
Lasseu, 379
Latouche, John, 54
Laubenthal, Rudolf, 128
Lauri-Volpi, Giacomo, 226, 288, 435
Lawrence, Marjorie, 40, *41*, 345, *377*
Lawrence, Robert, 430
Lear, Evelyn, *231*
Leblanc, Georgette, 314
Lee, Ming Cho, 71
Le Fort, Gertrude von, 109
Legouvé, Ernest, 30
Lehmann, Lilli, *151*, 188, 263, 288, 289, 345, *347*, 356, 360, 404, *405*, 421
Lehmann, Lotte, 51, *167, 376*
Leider, Frida, 345, *423*
Lemaire, Ferdinand, 379
Leoncavallo, Ruggiero, *16,* 17, 251, 301, 302
Liadov, Anatol Constantinovich, 329
Liebl, Karl, *378*
Ligabue, Ilva, *141*
Lind, Jenny, 107, 289, 392
Lishner, Leon, 42, 96
List, Emanuel, *364*
Liszt, Franz, 81, 209, 266, 379, 422
Litvinne, Félia, 188
Ljunberg, Göta, 128, 377
Locle, Camille du, 34, 116
London, George, 47, *49*, 73, *74, 78, 158, 307*
Long, John Luther, 237
Lorengar, Pilar, *63, 242*
Lorenz, Max, 377
Loti, Pierre, 206
Ludikar, Pavel, *122*
Ludwig, Christa, *168, 374*
Luening, Otto, 269
Lully, Jean Baptiste, 17

McCormack, John, *67*
McCracken, James, *151, 298*
Macdonald, Kenneth, *195*
McKinley, Andrew, 42, 96
MacNeil, Cornell, 96, *341*
Macnez, Umberto, 125, 400
Madeira, Jean, *128, 348*
Madey, Marjorie, 442

Maeterlinck, Maurice, 64, 314
Maffei, Andrea, 234
Maguenet, Alfred, 186
Mahler, Gustav, 62, 150
Maison, René, 41
Malibran, Maria, 93, 382, 392
Malipiero, Gian Francesco, 291
Mancinelli, Luigi, 412
Manski, Dorothee, 377
Mantelli, Eugenia, 188, 379
Mapleson, Helen, 382
Marconi, Francesco, 297
Mardones, Jose, *162*
Marie Antoinette, 40, 295
Mario (Giovanni de Candia), 125, *147*, 223, *332*
Marlo, Maria, 96
Markova, Alicia, *296*
Martin, Janis, *401*
Martin, Ruth, 27, 101
Martin, Thomas P., 27, 101
Martinelli, Giovanni, 116, *117,* 134, *208, 303*, 388, *452*
Martini, Nino, 125, 174
Mascagni, Pietro, *16*, 17, 30, 89, 302, 412
Massenet, Jules, 18, 206, 214, 247, 251, 252, 409, 448
Materna, Amalia, 345, 350
Matthews, Edward, 163, 326
Mattfield, Marie, 89
Matzenauer, Margarete, 116, *307*, 345, 379
Maubourg, Jeanne, 400
Maule, Michael, *296*
Maurel, Victor, 139, *141*, 188, 297
Mayr, Richard, *375*
Mayr, Simon, 150
Mazarin, Mariette, 128
Medini, 34
Meilhac, Henri, 81, 153, 247
Melba, Nellie, *146*, 188, 220, 301, 382
Melchior, Lauritz, 345, *363*, 421, *423, 425*
Menasci, Guido, 89
Mendelssohn-Prokofieva, Myra, 444
Menotti, Gian Carlo, 23, 42, 96, 269, 270, *318*, 438
Mercer, Mabel, 96
Merelli, Bartolomeo, 284
Merimée, Prosper, 81, 323
Merrill, Robert, *39, 70, 148, 178, 418*
Méry, François Joseph, 116
Meyerbeer, Giacomo, 18, 431
Meyer, Kerstin, *233*
Michalski, Raymond, *368*

Milanov, Zinka, *91*, 134, *160*, 264, 289
Milliet, Paul, 448
Milnes, Sherrill, *227*, *229*
Mirabella, Giovanni, 120
Mitropoulos, Dimitri, 438, 453
Moffo, Anna, 107, *222*, *250*, *387*, *418*
Molese, Michele, *243*
Molière, 51, 120
Molina, Tirso de (Gabriel Téllez), 120
Moline, Pierre Louis, 294
Molnar, Ferenc, 442
Monachino, Francis, 42, 96
Mongini, 34
Montariol, Sebastian, 156
Montarsolo, Paolo, *387*
Montemezzi, Italo, 16
Montesanto, Luigi, 398
Monteverdi, Claudio, 14, *15*, 269, 291, 292, 295
Moore, Douglas, 24, 54
Moore, Grace, 214, *402*
Moore, Thomas, 260
Moranzoni, Roberto, 398
Mottl, Felix, 345
Moussorgsky, Modest, 22, 73, 329
Mozart, Wolfgang Amadeus, 16, 18, 20, 27, *28*, 101, 120, 121, 241, 242, 254, 266
Müller, Maria, 388, *390*
Munsel, Patrice, *103*, 153
Murger, Henri, 66
Muzio, Claudia, 44, *137*, 398

Nagy, Robert, *436*
Nannetti, 209
Neilson, Frank, 237
Neway, Patricia, 96, *97*, *98*
Nicolai, Otto, 284
Niemann, Albert, 345, 360, 421
Nikolai, Elena, *185*
Nilsson, Birgit, *35*, 128, *129*, *152*, *193*, 345, *359*, *366*, *378*, *422*, *437*
Nilsson, Christine, 120, 143, 144, *177*, 209, 272
Nordica, Lillian, 153, 188, *210*, 254, 345, 421
Novara, Franco, 143, 209
Novoa, Salvador, 71, *72*
Novotna, Jarmila, *417*

Ober, Margarete, 373
Offenbach, Jacques, 400, 401
O'Hearn, Robert, *131*

Olitzka, Rosa, 188
Oliva, Domenico, 251
Olivero, Magda, 267
Olszewska, Maria, *373*
Orff, Carl, 21, 291
Ormandy, Eugene, 153

Paderewski, Ignace, 275
Paër, Ferdinando, 150
Pagliughi, Lina, 107
Paisiello, Giovanni, 58
Pandolfini, Angelica, 30
Pantaleone, Romilda, 297
Parker, Dorothy, 442
Pasta, Giuditta, 382, 392
Patti, Adelina, 107, *147*, 206, 220, 339, 382, 392, 416
Pauly, Rosa, 128
Pavesi, Stefano, 125
Pearl, Louise, *228*
Peerce, Jan, *221*
Penagos, Isabel, 71
Pepoli, Count Carlo, 332
Pepusch, Johann, 22
Peralta, Frances, *104*
Pergolesi, Giovanni Battista, 386
Peri, Jacopo, 14, 292
Perini, Flora, 396
Périer, Jean, 314
Perrault, Charles, 64, 93
Perron, Karl, 128
Peters, Roberta, *105*, *175*, *342*, 393, *402*
Petina, Irra, *108*, *256*
Petrella, Clara, *449*
Piave, Francesco Maria, 134, 159, 234, 338, 339, 388, 416
Picchi, Mirto, *337*
Piccinni, Niccolò, 17, 40
Piel, Mary Beth, *94*
Pillet, Léon, 156
Pilou, Jeannette, *82*
Pini-Corsi, Antonio, 125
Pinza, Ezio, 73, 99, *100*, *120*, *256*, 288, 388
Pizzi, Pierluigi, *95*
Plançon, Pol, 188, 241, *247*, 272, 392
Polacco, Giorgio, 251, 379, 400
Ponchielli, Amilcare, 16, *17*, 272
Pons, Lily, 99, *100*, 107, *108*, 206, *208*, 220, 393
Ponselle, Rosa, 116, 134, 159, *162*, 226, 288, 289, *290*, *452*
Porpora, 21
Poulenc, François, 19, 109, 442
Powers, Marie, 96, *97*, 269, *271*

Pozzoni, 34
Praga, Marco, 251
Prêtre, Georges, 430, 442
Prevedi, Bruno, *118*
Prévost, Abbé Antoine François, 247, 251
Prey, Hermann, *242*, *408*
Price, Leontyne, *38*, *105*, *111*, 134, *136*, *161*, 202, *327*
Price, Margaret, *195*
Priest, Josiah, 114
Prokofiev, Serge, 22, 23, 217, 444, 445
Provenzale, Francesco, 15
Puccini, Giacomo, 17, 30, 31, 66, 217, 237, 238, 247, 251, 252, 370, 371, 396, 398, 412, 435
Purcell, Henry, 21, 114
Pushkin, Aleksander Sergeyevich, 73, 99, 120, 137, 323, 444

Raaff, Anton, 191
Raïsa, Rosa, *406*, 435
Rameau, Jean Philippe, 17
Rankin, Nell, *179*
Raskin, Judith, *257*, *293*
Ravel, Maurice, 18, 19, 132
Ravogli, Giulia, 294
Ravogli, Sophia, 294
Raymond, Fanny Malone, 294
Reichert, Heinrich, 370
Reichmann, Theodore, 156
Reiner, Fritz, 335
Reinhardt, Max, 51
Reitan, Roald, *155*
Renard, Marie, 448
Renaud, Maurice, 400, 409, *411*
Resnik, Regina, *83*, *324*, 438, *441*
Respighi, Ottorino, 291
Rethberg, Elisabeth, *122*, *256*, 345
Révoil, 156
Richter, Hans, 345
Ricordi, 412
Ricordi, Giulio, 251
Riese, Friedrich W. (Wilhelm Friedrich), 259, 260
Rimini, Giacomo, 435
Rimsky-Korsakov, Nicolai Andreievich, 22, 23, 99, 329
Rinuccini, Ottavio, 14, 292
Rioton, Marthe, 214
Rivas, Angel de Saavedra, Duke of, 159
Robin, Mado, 206
Robinson, Adolf, 404
Rodzinski, Artur, 444

Rogers, Bernard, 23
Rogier, Frank, 269
Romani, Felice, 130, 223, 288, 392
Romanovsky, Vjacheslav, *330*
Roselle, Anna, 453
Rossi, Gaetano, 382
Rossi-Lemeni, Nicola, *288*
Rossini, Gioacchino Antonio, 16, 58, 93, 94, 254, 285, 382, 450
Rothenberger, Anneliese, *155, 232*
Rothier, Léon, 188, 312, 400
Rounseville, Robert, 335, *336*
Rubini, Giovanni Battista, 333, 392
Rudel, Julius, 71
Ruffini, Giacomo ("Michele Accursi"), 125
Ruffo, Titta, 301, 339
Rysanek, Leonie, *53, 158, 168,* 234, *236*

Saavedra, Angel de, Duke of Rivas, 159
Sabina, Karel, 62
Saintine, Xavier Boniface, 332
Saint-Saëns, Camille, 379
Salignac, Thomas, 125
Salvini-Donatelli, Fanny, 416
Sanderson, Sibyl, 247, *247,* 409
Santley, Sir Charles, 144
Sardou, Victorien, 412
Saunders, Arlene, 214, *216*
Sayão, Bidù, 125, *126, 256,* 386, *417*
Scalchi, Sofia, 143, 188, 223, 297, 382
Scarlatti, Alessandro, 15
Scheff, Fritzi, 263
Schikaneder, Emanuel, 241
Schiller, Friedrich van, 116, 226, 227, 450
Schipa, Tito, *60,* 130
Schmitt-Walter, Karl, *279*
Schoeffler, Paul, *151*
Schoenberg, Arnold, 21
Schorr, Friedrich, 128, *280,* 345, 377
Schott, Anton, 404
Schuch, Ernest von, 128
Schumann, Elisabeth, *376*
Schumann-Heink, Ernestine, 128, 223, *275,* 345
Schwarzkopf, Elisabeth, *79, 80,* 202, 335, *336, 337*
Scott, Sir Walter, 220, 332
Scotti, Antonio, 30, 125, 134, 139, 188, 223, 412
Scotto, Renata, *185, 240*
Scribe, Eugène, 30, 130, 263

Seidl, Anton, 34, 156, 275, 345, 356, 404, 421
Sembrich, Marcella, 107, 120, 125, 134, 153, 188, 206, 220, *221,* 241, 259, 332, 338, 392, 416
Senesino, 202
Serafin, Tullio, 226, 388, 435
Sereni, Mario, *302*
Shadwell, Thomas, 120
Shakespeare, William, 101, 139, 234, 297, 367, 368, 430
Shilovsky, Konstantin, 137
Shostakovich, Dmitri, 22, 23
Siems, Margarete, 128
Siepi, Cesare, *59, 122, 124, 255*
Sills, Beverly, *57,* 202, *203, 205*
Simionato, Giulietta, 93, *95,* 188, *283, 294, 384, 434*
Simoneau, Leopold, *193*
Simoni, Renato, 435
Simon, Joanna, 71, *72*
Slach, Anna, 404
Slater, Montagu, 319
Slezak, Leo, *300*
Smallens, Alexander, 163, 326
Smetana, Bedrich, 22, 62
Solera, Temistocle, 284
Somma, Antonio, 263
Sonnleithner, Josef, 150
Sontag, Henriette, 107, 382
Sophocles, 128
Sordello, Enzo, *334*
Soumet, L. A., 288
Souzay, Gérard, *293*
Spohr, Ludwig, 143
Spontini, Gasparo, 17
Stagno, Roberto, 90, 120, 259, 426
Stahlmann, Sylvia, *111*
Stassov, Vladimir, 329
Steber, Eleanor, 27, *29,* 47, *103,* 438, *439, 441, 454*
Stein, Gertrude, 163
Stella, Antonietta, *135, 427*
Steller, 34
Stephanie, Gottlieb, 27
Sterbini, Cesare, 58
Stettheimer, Florine, 163
Stevens, Risë, *86,* 153, *154,* 294, *296, 375, 379*
Stewart, Thomas, *355*
Stokowski, Leopold, 453
Storchio, Rosina, 237
Strassburg, Gottfried von, 421
Stratas, Teresa, *436*
Strauss, Johann, Jr., 153

Strauss, Richard, 15, *20,* 21, 47, 51, 79, 80, 128, 165, 373, 374, 377
Stravinsky, Igor, 335
Strepponi, Giuseppina, 284
Striggio, Alessandro, 291, 292
Stritt, Albert, 275
Suliotis, Elena, *285*
Sullivan, Sir Arthur, 22
Sullivan, Brian, *231, 246*
Summers, Lydia, 96
Sundelius, Marie, 116
Supervía, Conchita, 93
Sutherland, Joan, *106,* 107, 188, *189,* 220, *222,* 288, *289, 290,* 333, 383, *384, 393, 395,* 416
Svanholm, Set, 153
Sved, Alexander, 264
Swinburne, Algernon Charles, 421

Tajo, Italo, 174, 444
Tamagno, Francesco, 297, 379
Tamburini, Antonio, 125, 333
Targioni-Tozzetti, Giovanni, 89
Tate, Nahum, 114
Taylor, Deems, 438
Tchaikovsky, Modest, 323
Tchaikovsky, Peter Ilyich, 22, *23,* 137, 323
Tebaldi, Renata, 30, *31, 180, 274, 299, 413, 420*
Telva, Marion, 288, *290*
Tennyson, Alfred, 421
Ter-Arutunian, Rouben, *318*
Ternina, Milka, 241, 345, 412
Tetrazzini, Eva, 297
Tetrazzini, Luisa, 107, 206, 220, *281,* 392
Thaw, David, *219*
Thebom, Blanche, *103,* 335, *424, 440*
Thomas, Ambroise, 281
Thomas, Jess, *53, 277, 381, 405, 415*
Thomas, John Charles, *411*
Thomas, Theodore, 206, 345
Thompson, Hugh, 27, *29*
Thomson, Virgil, 24, 163
Thorborg, Kerstin, *76,* 264, 294
Tibbett, Lawrence, 139, *142,* 174, 186, 388, *399, 402*
Tietjens, Therese, 223
Tolstoy, Leo, 444
Torigi, Richard, 71
Toscanini, Arturo, 66, 73, 89, 125, 139, *142,* 285, 294, *300,* 421, 435
Tourel, Jennie, 335

Tozzi, Giorgio, *124, 158,* 188, *228, 261, 262,* 438, *441*
Traubel, Helen, *211,* 345, *363, 425*
Trebelli, Zelia, 81, 382, 426
Treigle, Norman, *99,* 202, *203, 205, 216*
Treitschke, Georg Friedrich, 150
Tucci, Gabriella, *298*
Tucker, Richard, *70, 105,* 153, *159, 229, 403*
Turner, Claramae, 71, *72, 110, 216,* 269
Tyl, Noel, *219*

Ugalde, 144
Uhde, Hermann, *455*
Uppman, Theodor, *52, 105, 245, 317*
Urban, Joseph, *129*
Ursuleac, Viorica, 47

Valero, Fernando, 89
Valentino, Frank, *126*
Valesi, Giovanni, 191
Valleria, Alwina, 426
Valletti, Cesare, *127, 419*
Van Dyck, Ernest, 448
Van Rooy, Anton, 345, 377
Van Zandt, Marie, 206
Varnay, Astrid, 128, *357*
Varona, José, 71
Verdi, Giuseppe, 16, *17,* 18, 34, 116, 134, 135, 139, 159, 223, 226, 227, 234, 263, 266, 272, 284, 285, 297, 338, 339, 388, 412, 416, 426

Verdi, Margherita, 284
Verga, Giovanni, 89
Verrett, Shirley, 294
Viardot, Pauline, 40, 294, 382
Vichey, Luben, *160*
Vickers Jon, *152, 267, 320, 321, 324, 325, 351, 380, 433*
Victoria, Queen, 143
Villars, Henri Gauthier, 128
Virgil, 119, 430
Vishnevskaya, Galina, *324*
Voketaitis, Arnold, *94*
Voltaire, 383
Votipka, Thelma, *375*

Wagenseil, J. C., 276
Wagner, Richard, 16, 18, 20, 21, 31, 81, 156, 157, 209, 242, 266, 274, 276, 302, 306, 307, 344, 345, 346, 350, 356, 360, 379, 404, 405, 421, 422
Wagner, Wieland, *152, 213, 348, 361, 408*
Walker, Edyth, 188, 223
Walker, William, *184*
Wallace, Vincent, 22
Wallenstein, Alfred, 163
Wallmann, Margherita, *113*
Walters, Jess, 234
Walton, Sir William, 22
Ward, David, *65*
Warfield, William, *327*

Warren, Leonard, 234, *235, 236, 299, 389, 413, 427*
Wayne, Beatrice Robinson, 163
Weber Mozart, Constanze, 27
Weber, Carl Maria Friedrich Ernst von, 20, 170, 266
Wedekind, Frank, 230
Weed, Marion, 183, 377
Weil, Hermann, 373
Welitsch, Ljuba, *121,* 153
Welting, Patricia, *245*
Wendling, Dorothea, 191
Wendling, Elisabeth, 191
Wesendonck, Mathilde von, 421
Whitehill, Clarence, 345
Wieland, Christoph Martin, 241
Wiener, Otto, *278, 279*
Wiesner, Sophie, 156
Wilde, Oscar, 377
Williams, Ralph Vaughan, 22
Willner, Alfred Maria, 370
Windgassen, Wolfgang, *359, 408*
Wolf Ferrari, Ermanno, 16
Wolff, Beverly, *205*
Wunderlich, Fritz, *63*

Zamboni, Maria, 435
Zangarini, Carlo, 266
Zeffirelli, Franco, 139, *140, 414*
Zenatello, Giovanni, 237
Zimbalist, Jr., Efrem, 96, 269